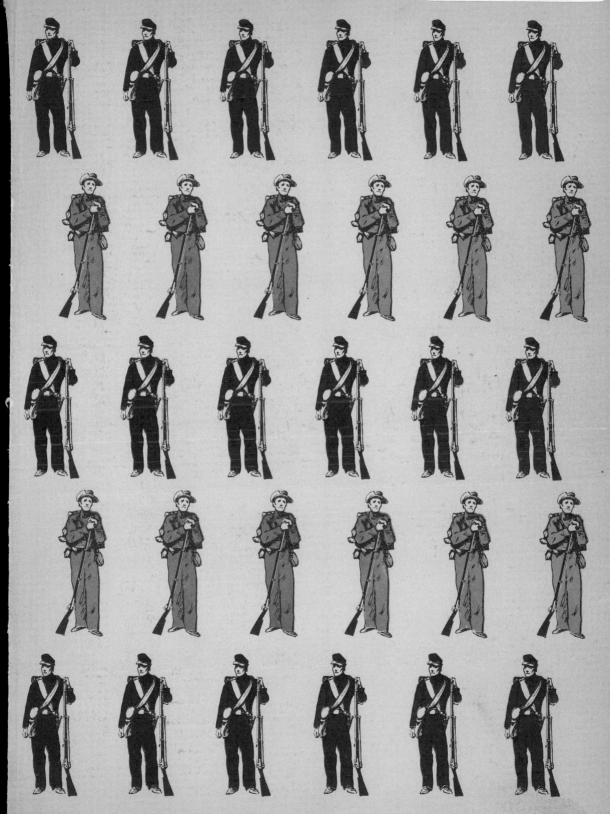

To
Bow
from
Ronny, Jacque + Kevin

Christmas 1960

A
CIVIL WAR TREASURY
of Tales, Legends and Folklore

A
CIVIL WAR TREASURY
OF TALES, LEGENDS
AND FOLKLORE

Edited, with an Introduction, by

B. A. BOTKIN

Illustrated by Warren Chappell

*

*

RANDOM HOUSE

NEW YORK

THE EDITOR AND PUBLISHERS wish to thank the following publishers and societies for permission to reprint material as indicated:

The Commercial Appeal, Memphis, Tenn., for a story by Robert Talley.

Dodd, Mead & Co., Inc., for selections from *Lincoln and the Civil War in the Diaries and Letters of John Hay,* ed. Tyler Dennett. Copyright, 1939, by Dodd, Mead & Co., Inc.

Doubleday & Co., Inc., for a selection from *That Reminds Me—,* by Alben W. Barkley. Copyright, 1954, by Alben W. Barkley.

Duke University Press, for selections from *The Frank C. Brown Collection of North Carolina Folklore,* gen. ed. Newman Ivey White. Copyright, 1952, by The Duke University Press.

E. P. Dutton & Co., Inc., for a selection from *They Knew Lincoln,* by Dr. John E. Washington. Copyright, 1942, by E. P. Dutton & Co., Inc.

Harper & Brothers, for selections from *The True Story of Mary, Wife of Lincoln,* by Katherine Helm. Copyright, 1928, by Katherine Helm.

Hastings House, Publishers, Inc., for selections from *The Negro in Virginia,* compiled by Workers of the Writers' Program of the Work Projects Administration in the State of Virginia. Copyright, 1940, by The Hampton Institute.

Houghton Mifflin Co., for selections from *A Diary from Dixie,* by Mary Boykin Chesnut, ed. Ben Ames Williams. Copyright, 1949, by Houghton Mifflin Co.

The Jewish Publication Society of America, for a selection from *American Jewry and the Civil War,* by Bertram Wallace Korn. Copyright, 1951, by The Jewish Publication Society of America.

Alfred A. Knopf, Inc., for a selection from *Three Years with Grant,* by Sylvanus Cadwallader, ed. Benjamin P. Thomas. Copyright, 1955, by Benjamin P. Thomas.

Louisiana State University Press, for selections from *Southern Legacy,* by Hodding Carter. Copyright, 1950, by Louisiana State University Press; and *Brokenburn; The Journal of Kate Stone, 1861-1868,* ed. John Q. Anderson. Copyright, 1955, by Louisiana State University Press.

G. P. Putnam's Sons, for a selection from *General Philip Kearny, Battle Soldier of Five Wars,* by Thomas Kearny. Copyright, 1937, by G. P. Putnam's Sons.

Charles Scribner's Sons, for selections from *Letters from Lee's Army,* by Charles Minor Blackford III, ed. Susan Leigh Blackford and Charles Minor Blackford III. Copyright, 1947, by Charles Scribner's Sons; *War Years with Jeb Stuart,* by W. W. Blackford. Copyright, 1945, by Charles Scribner's Sons; *R. E. Lee, A Biography,* by Douglas Southall Freeman. Copyright, 1935, by Charles Scribner's Sons; *The South to Posterity,* by Douglas Southall Freeman. Copy-

THE HISTORIES . . . are all written by "big bugs," generals and renowned historians, and like the fellow who called a turtle a "cooter," being told that no such word as cooter was in Webster's dictionary, remarked that he had as much right to make a dictionary as Mr. Webster or any other man; so have I to write a history.

—SAM R. WATKINS

Contents

CONTENTS

12. DANGER WAS THEIR BUSINESS

13. HIGH COMMAND

14. "FIRST GENTLEMAN OF VIRGINIA"

15. STONEWALL WAS "A POWERFUL FIGHTIN' AND PRAYIN' MAN"

16. JEB STUART "JINES" THE CAVALRY

17. FATHER ABRAHAM

THREE: 1863

18. "FREE AT LAST"

CONTENTS

CONTENTS

CONTENTS

xiv

CONTENTS

40. DEATH OF LINCOLN

The Shadow of Coming Events · The Prophetic Dreams · The Last Laugh · Walt Whitman on the Death of Lincoln · Elizabeth Keckley Shares Mrs. Lincoln's Grief · "Half News" of Lincoln's Death · Chittenden and the Angry Mob · The Capture of John Wilkes Booth

41. THE FLIGHT OF JEFFERSON DAVIS

Aunt Abby Says Good-by to Mr. Davis · A Raglan and a Shawl: I. Mr. Davis' Account of His Capture, II. James H. Jones's Narrative · The Shackling of Jefferson Davis

42. "I WON'T BE RECONSTRUCTED"

John S. Wise's Will · Hell at Chickamauga · "Whatever General Lee Says" · The "Button Trouble" · Lovers and War Lords: The "Marriage Oath"

43. RETURN OF THE SOLDIER

Going Home to Stay · Johnny Wickersham Comes Marching Home · Veteran's First Lie · When the Privates Ranked the Generals · Working His Passage · Salvage · "Dear Unknown"

SIX: AFTERMATH

44. A GOOD WAR DIES HARD

Letter from a Freedman to His Old Master (Written Just as He Dictated It) · "Whip Them with Pop-Guns" · He Might Have Slept with God · The Vanquished Saluting the Victor · Sleeping with Jackson · The Widow from Maine · They Met at the Panorama of the Battle of Shiloh · Point of View · "It Was Best" · "That Wasn't the Way It Happened"

Introduction

Such a tale as may be told by a soldier who is no writer to a reader who is no soldier.

—AMBROSE BIERCE

BEFORE THE CIVIL WAR became our writingest and story-tellingest war, it was our talkingest war. Walt Whitman, the wound-dresser, talking with soldiers in Washington, believed that "the real war will never get in the books," but was in the "hard meat and sinew" of soldiers' talk of campaigns, fights, and marches, with their "minutiae of deeds and passions."[1]

Swapping gossip and anecdotes based on the day's incidents and memories of similar occurrences was the favorite campfire pastime. One evening a Yankee displayed the picture of a pretty girl, taken from the body of an enemy. "Well," said a comrade, "at least I'd let the poor chap been buried with his picture!" "Stealin' that picture," said another, "was about as mean a trick as Jack Ruggles did the other day. Why, he came across a dead Johnny, lyin' flat on his face, and he turned him over and took a plug of navy out of his pocket and took a chaw, and smacked his lips and said it was mighty good. I've been hungry for tobacco, but —— me if I want any out of a dead man's pocket."

"Say, Stunchy," said another, "don't you remember the Johnny we buried in front of our lines at Shiloh, with a cartridge between his teeth? A bullet hit him in the head and killed him. He never fell over nor moved a muscle, and there he was, dead on his knees behind a stump, his gun in one hand, his hand up close to his mouth, with the big part of the cartridge in his fingers, and the paper he had bit off the end still 'tween his teeth. We couldn't straighten him, and we buried him just so."

Grim tales of pity and terror like these and sardonic jests at the expense of raw recruits or bumptious officers alike enabled the soldier to accept reality and confront destiny. Thus campfire talkfests and storytelling sessions were more than a pastime; they were a folk ritual in which all could take part and which united the "I" of the narrator with the "we" of the group. The soldier's stories were his folk literature, leveling individual differences, codifying his beliefs and attitudes, and giving him a sense of belonging.

From camp, bivouac, battlefield, and hospital, stories passed into the letters of soldiers, doctors, nurses, chaplains, and the reports of war correspondents, becoming living lore and legend for the folks back home. Told and retold, campfire tales ultimately became folk history.

This was especially true in the South, where storytelling, good talk, and long remembrance were part of the way of life for which the South was fighting. And because the war was fought on Southern soil, war stories were as close as the war itself, which was no farther than one's own yard, street, or house.

Other American wars, writes Virginia Terrell Lathrop, "have been fought far away. Silver hasn't been buried in our own yards, and sabres haven't clashed and rung up and down our own staircases. Mothers haven't shot the enemy on our own doorsteps. Wounded men have not hidden in our closets or under our beds."[2]

Mothers, nurses, scouts, spies, boy soldiers, high privates, gallant officers were folk heroes of the war. Hero tales also immortalized leaders and patron saints as comforting father images and symbols of the ideal warrior and savior; and a new mythology sprang up about such figures as Lee, Jackson, and Lincoln.

During the war its folk saga was given wide circulation in newspapers and periodicals. After the war, the growth of veterans' organizations revived storytelling sessions at social meetings (called "campfires" by the Grand Army of the Republic) and gave the writing and publication of war stories a new impetus in veterans' organs like the *Confederate Veteran* and the *National Tribune;* in veterans' columns and Memorial Day issues of local newspapers; in newspaper collections of prize stories; in patriotic regional journals like *The Land We Love, Our Living and the Dead, Southern Bivouac,* and the *Bivouac* (Boston); and in the collected papers of historical societies like the Southern Historical Society, the various state commanderies of the Military Order of the Loyal Legion of the United States, and the Rhode Island Soldiers and Sailors Historical Society.

Most popular of the Civil War storybooks were the anecdote compilations, based largely on newspaper sources, such as Frank Moore's *Anecdotes, Poetry and Incidents of the War: North and South, 1860-1865* and Frazar Kirkland's *Pictorial Book of Anecdotes of the Rebellion.* In encyclopedic collections of "laughable incidents" and brave deeds, the stories began to lose their freshness, naturalness, and authenticity as a result of considerable repetition and rewriting in the sentimental, moralizing, sensational, and heavy-handedly humorous vein of popular literature of the time. In books of veterans' and women's reminiscences collected by organizations like the United Daughters of the Confederacy an attempt was made to get back to the sources; but as the old people's memories began to wear thin, the accounts became fragmentary and confused. The military record was kept straight in collections of articles like the *Annals of the War* of the *Philadelphia Weekly Times* and the *Century Magazine's* monumental *Battles and Leaders of the Civil War.* Somewhere between the popular and the historical fell such works as Ben LaBree's *The Confederate Soldier in the Civil War* and Rossiter Johnson's *Campfire and Battlefield.*

Meanwhile veterans began publishing their reminiscences and drawing upon them in personal narratives and unit histories. The best of the privates' narratives, like Carlton McCarthy's *Detailed Minutiae of Soldier Life in the Army of Northern Virginia,* Warren Goss's *Recollections of a Private,* and John Billings' *Hardtack and Coffee,* are rich in folklore and folk humor. So, too, are frankly comic works like Wilbur F. Hinman's *Corporal Si Klegg and His "Pard"* and George W. Peck's *How Private Peck Put Down the Rebellion.* And the best of the officers' writings, such as the reminiscences of Basil W. Duke and John B. Gordon, and David D. Porter's *Incidents and Anecdotes of the Civil War,* are likewise full of nuggets of talk and incident.

In spite of occasional self-consciousness and unreliability, the regimental histories are invaluable for their circumstantial detail and anecdotal material. Along with reminiscences and personal narratives these histories have been used to good advantage by Lloyd Lewis, Carl Sandburg, Bruce Catton, Douglas Freeman, Clifford Dowdey, Burke Davis and others to make Civil War history and biography come alive and to make us contemporary with the war.

Reminiscences, personal narratives, and unit histories, somewhat mellowed by time and seasoned with humor, are the main sources of the present collection. But I have not neglected the raw material of letters, diaries, scrapbooks, miscellanies, newspapers, periodicals, pamphlets, and other ephemera.

There have been excellent documentary histories of the war, like Henry Steele Commager's *The Blue and the Gray, The Story of the Civil War as Told by Participants* (1950), and Otto Eisenschiml and Ralph Newman's *The Civil War: The American Iliad, as Told by Those Who Lived It* (1947), as well as folksy social histories like Bell I. Wiley's *The Life of Johnny Reb* (1943) and *The Life of Billy Yank* (1951). But this book represents the first attempt at a Civil War folk history and story history based on a wide variety of contemporary sources.

To supply the historical framework the selections have been arranged in six parts, corresponding to the years of the war and the aftermath. These parts are in turn divided into forty-four sections, representing main aspects of the war. Within these sections the selections are arranged by date, when known. The whole constitutes a collective saga of the human side of the Civil War, its typical experiences, heroes, traditions, myths, legends, fables, foibles, images, and symbols reflecting the American imagination at work (in a mingling of fact and fantasy) on the stuff of our most American war.

In choosing among different versions of a story I have as a rule given preference to first-hand accounts, especially when well told. I have not hesitated, however, to use a later version when it is obviously more effective. Occasionally I have taken a story out of its chronological order and placed it with closely related material. The original spelling and punctuation have not been changed, except when they interfere with clarity. Paragraphing and place names have been modernized.

The book is selective rather than comprehensive. Throughout I have sought to maintain a balance between the specific and the general, the individual and the typical, the small and the large, as well as between North and South, soldiers and civilians, combatants and noncombatants, privates and generals, men and women. The battleground of this book is the common ground of human experience and human fantasy, where both sides meet in the war in which all men are brothers under the uniform.

B. A. BOTKIN

Croton-on-Hudson, New York
June 1, 1960

January						
S	M	T	W	T	F	S
..	..	1	2	3	4	5
6	7	8	9	10	11	12
13	14	15	16	17	18	19
20	21	22	23	24	25	26
27	28	29	30	31	..	..

February						
S	M	T	W	T	F	S
..	..	..	..	..	1	2
3	4	5	6	7	8	9
10	11	12	13	14	15	16
17	18	19	20	21	22	23
24	25	26	27	28	..	..

March						
S	M	T	W	T	F	S
..	..	..	..	..	1	2
3	4	5	6	7	8	9
10	11	12	13	14	15	16
17	18	19	20	21	22	23
24	25	26	27	28	29	30
31						

ONE

In EIGHTEEN HUNDRED AND SIXTY-ONE
The cruel war had just begun.
We'll all drink stone blind;
Johnny, come fill up the bowl.

April						
S	M	T	W	T	F	S
..	1	2	3	4	5	6
7	8	9	10	11	12	13
14	15	16	17	18	19	20
21	22	23	24	25	26	27
28	29	30	..	..	..	..
..	..	..	..	..	..	..

May						
S	M	T	W	T	F	S
..	..	..	1	2	3	4
5	6	7	8	9	10	11
12	13	14	15	16	17	18
19	20	21	22	23	24	25
26	27	28	29	30	31	..

June						
S	M	T	W	T	F	S
..	..	..	..	..	..	1
2	3	4	5	6	7	8
9	10	11	12	13	14	15
16	17	18	19	20	21	22
23	24	25	26	27	28	29
30	..	..	..	..	..	..

July						
S	M	T	W	T	F	S
..	1	2	3	4	5	6
7	8	9	10	11	12	13
14	15	16	17	18	19	20
21	22	23	24	25	26	27
28	29	30	31	..	..	..

August						
S	M	T	W	T	F	S
..	..	..	..	..	1	2	3
4	5	6	7	8	9	10
11	12	13	14	15	16	17
18	19	20	21	22	23	24
25	26	27	28	29	30	31

September						
S	M	T	W	T	F	S
1	2	3	4	5	6	7
8	9	10	11	12	13	14
15	16	17	18	19	20	21
22	23	24	25	26	27	28
29	30	..	..	..	..	..

October						
S	M	T	W	T	F	S
..	..	1	2	3	4	5
6	7	8	9	10	11	12
13	14	15	16	17	18	19
20	21	22	23	24	25	26
27	28	29	30	31	..	..

November						
S	M	T	W	T	F	S
..	..	..	..	..	1	2
3	4	5	6	7	8	9
10	11	12	13	14	15	16
17	18	19	20	21	22	23
24	25	26	27	28	29	30

December						
S	M	T	W	T	F	S
1	2	3	4	5	6	7
8	9	10	11	12	13	14
15	16	17	18	19	20	21
22	23	24	25	26	27	28
29	30	31	..	..	..	..

Old Abe Lincoln came out of the wilderness,
Out of the wilderness, out of the wilderness,
Old Abe Lincoln came out of the wilderness,
Down in Illinois.
—LINCOLN CAMPAIGN SONG OF 1860

1. MR. LINCOLN
COMES TO WASHINGTON

A Scotch Cap and a Military Cloak

*

I · Joseph Howard's Dispatch

Special Dispatch to the New-York Times.
Harrisburg, Saturday, February 23, 1861—8 A.M.

ABRAHAM LINCOLN, the President-elect of the United States, is safe in the capital of the nation. By the admirable arrangement of General Scott, the country has been spared the lasting disgrace which would have been fastened indelibly upon it had Mr. Lincoln been murdered upon his journey thither, as he would have been had he followed the programme as announced in the papers and gone by the Northern Central Railroad to Baltimore.

On Thursday night after he had retired, Mr. Lincoln was aroused and informed that a stranger desired to see him on a matter of life and death. He declined to admit him unless he gave his name, which he at once did, and such prestige did the name carry that while Mr. Lincoln was yet disrobed he granted an interview to the caller.

A prolonged conversation elicited the fact that an organized body of men had determined that Mr. Lincoln should not be inaugurated; and that he should never leave the city of Baltimore alive, if, indeed, he ever entered it.

The list of the names of the conspirators presented a most astonishing array of persons high in Southern confidence, and some whose fame is not confined to this country alone.

Statesmen laid the plan, bankers indorsed it, and adventurers were to carry it into effect. As they understood, Mr. Lincoln was to leave Harrisburg at nine o'clock this morning by special train, the idea was, if possible, to throw the cars from the road at some point where they would rush down a steep embankment and destroy in a moment the lives of all on board. In case of the failure of this project, their plan was to surround the carriage on the way from dépôt to dépôt in Baltimore, and to assassinate him with dagger or pistol shot.

So authentic was the source from which the information was obtained that Mr. Lincoln, after counselling with his friends, was compelled to make arrangements which would enable him to subvert the plans of his enemies.

Greatly to the annoyance of the thousands who desired to call on him last night, he declined giving a reception. The final council was held at eight o'clock.

Mr. Lincoln did not want to yield, and Colonel Sumner actually cried with indignation; but Mrs. Lincoln, seconded by Mr. Judd and Mr. Lincoln's original informant, insisted upon it, and *at nine o'clock Mr. Lincoln left on a special train*. He wore a Scotch plaid cap and a very long military cloak, so that he was entirely unrecognizable. Accompanied by Superintendent Lewis and one friend, he started, while all the town, with the exception of Mrs. Lincoln, Colonel Sumner, Mr. Judd, and two reporters who were sworn to secrecy, supposed him to be asleep.

The telegraph wires were put beyond reach of any one who might desire to use them.

4

At one o'clock the fact was whispered from one to another, and it soon became the theme of most excited conversation. Many thought it a very injudicious move, while others regarded it as a stroke of great merit.

The special train leaves with the original party, including the *Times* correspondent, at nine o'clock.

II · A Belated Explanation

I HAD BEEN DELEGATED by the paper I represented to accompany Mr. Lincoln and his family from Springfield, Illinois, to Washington, and, of course, I did so. I stood within a yard of him, when, in Trenton, he made the memorable assertion that it was time the government put its foot down firmly, and I was with him in Philadelphia when he was comfortably housed in the Continental Hotel, where the best people in the city vied with each other to do him honor and pay him the respect so honestly his due. And, by the way, this is about as good a time as any for me to explain the Scotch cap and military cloak story, which long since passed into history, and can be found in all the cyclopedias of the day.

There isn't a word of truth in it. The intention was, after the reception and parade in Philadelphia, Mr. Lincoln and his party reviewing the torchlight Wide Awakes, and bands of music, and attended by thousands, from his rooms on Chestnut Street, to go by the early train to Harrisburg, where, as in big places, a reception was to be given and a procession had in his honor, and thence direct to Washington. This plan, however was thwarted by information brought to the Continental, and communicated, I think, first to Mr. Kingsley and subsequently intrusted to Mr. Lincoln, although the wisdom of that step was then and has ever since been doubted. The information was to the effect that the train from Harrisburg was to be thrown from the track in the hope of killing the President-elect, without regard to the lives or safety of his wife and children and a large number of notables who were accompanying them. Mrs. Kingsley and Lincoln and gentlemen in charge of the party, who were Colonel Wood, subsequently superintendent of buildings in Washington; Ward Lamon, subsequently marshal of the District of Columbia; and a detective in the secret service by the name of Burns, brother of the Burns who used to keep the Pierrepont house in Brooklyn, kept the secret well. It was an anxious night with those people and with Mr. Seward, Jr., who accompanied the detective from Washington and brought the information to the parties interested. The next morning the presidential group started, and a continuous ovation greeted them all the way to Harrisburg, where a very creditable turnout was made with speech, band and fireworks accompaniment. I went to my room in the hotel at night, and was preparing my dispatch to wire to this city when Detective Burns entered the room and locked the door.

I looked at him in amazement, and asked him what he meant. He told me I couldn't leave the room until the following morning. I asked why, and to make a long story short, in spite of my threats and representations of serious embarrassment to me personally and professionally, the conclusion was that I was not to leave until the following morning, as it was for the public good, which he, upon my promise not to use, explained, saying that Mr. Lincoln had already left by a special engine and car, and had gone back over his track in time to catch the evening train from New York, while his family and the rest of the party would continue their journey in accordance with the prearranged programme. He also informed me that the wires had been cut, and that communication with New York was a physical impossibility, but that nevertheless his orders were that none of the newspaper men should leave their rooms that night. I at once wrote a dispatch beginning as follows: "Abraham Lincoln, President-elect of the United States, is safe in the city of Washington," and then proceeded to narrate the circumstances, as unfolded to me by the detective who, with considerable mystery, said that no one would recognize Mr. Lincoln at sight, and that the plans of the conspirators were fortunately foiled.

I asked myself what possible disguise would Lincoln get in Harrisburg, and, as I wrote on, I imagined him in a Scotch cap, which would be about as marked and opposite to his high silk hat as one could conceive, and a military cloak, which I borrowed, in my imagination, from the shapely shoulders of Colonel Sumner, who was traveling with the President-elect. My dispatch was sent very early in the morning, and, by good luck, reached *The Times* office just as the day editor entered his room. His first thought was: "Well, this is a pretty time of day for Howard's dispatch to arrive," and, taking it up, mechanically glanced at it. The first sentence attracted his attention. Hurriedly reading it, and seeing its importance, he ordered it put up and an extra gotten out at once. The first thing known in this city by our esteemed contemporaries in especial and the public in general was when 1,000 newsboys electrified the town with the extra *Times* and its astounding revelation of the diabolical plot against the chosen head of the nation. Immediately the illustrated papers took the matter up, and one and all printed pictures of Mr. Lincoln fleeing from Harrisburg, arrayed in this chimerical garb, a Scotch cap and long military cloak. The story was absolutely correct, the trimmings were pure imagination.

—JOSEPH HOWARD, JR.

*

A Wager

*

DURING THE BITTER slavery debate in Congress, just before the War between the States, it was feared by many that the Southern members would be attacked in the halls of Congress or in the streets of Washington. The fear spread to such an extent that there was located in that city an organization of one hundred Southern men, known as "Minute Men," for the sole purpose of protecting the Southern members. In this organization were two young men, close friends, both tall and commanding in appearance—John Hatcher of Virginia, six feet and six inches in height, weighing two hundred and twenty pounds, and another from North Carolina also above the usual height and weight.

It so happened that on the day of the inauguration of Mr. Lincoln as President, March 4, 1861, these two friends and several other members of the "Minute Men" were near the White House while the great throng of people formed in line to shake hands with the President. The one from North Carolina suggested that they fall in line and pay their respects to the new Magistrate, to which all agreed except John Hatcher, who declared that he would never shake hands with Mr. Lincoln, as he was unfriendly to the South. Mr. Hatcher was urged to go with them. He finally consented to join the line, but declared that he "would not shake the hand of old Abe Lincoln."

The other one replied: "We are going to shake hands with Mr. Lincoln; and I will wager you the finest suit of clothes to be purchased in this city that you cannot pass by Mr. Lincoln and carry out your purpose."

"Agreed," said the tall and handsome John Hatcher.

With this compact, they fell in line, John Hatcher in the lead, his head erect, and determination shown in every line of his face. As he approached Mr. Lincoln, the retiring President, Mr. Buchanan, took him by the hand, shook it cordially, and, after receiving his name, turned to introduce him to Mr. Lincoln; but, to the surprise of Mr. Buchanan and Mr. Lincoln, John Hatcher suddenly withdrew his hand, and, letting it drop to his side, began to move on without greeting Mr. Lincoln or even looking upon his face. Mr. Lincoln grasped the situation instantly, and, moving a little to the right, extended his arm in front of John Hatcher, and, with a smile, said: "No man who is taller and handsomer than I am can pass by me to-day without shaking hands with me."

It had been reported, and was thought by many to be true, that an attempt would be made to do the President bodily harm and possibly this caused Mr. Lincoln to think that Hatcher's act was only the beginning of some trouble that was to follow.

After the young friends had left the White House, the North Carolinian said, "John, I have won the suit of clothes."

"Yes," replied John; "but who could refuse to shake hands with a man who would leave his position and put his hand in front of you and use such complimentary language as Mr. Lincoln did?"

"I have won the suit of clothes fairly," replied his friend; "but I will not take the wager, because you surrendered like a courteous Southern gentleman and shook the hand of our new President, as all Americans should do."

—C. B. Edwards

*

The War Comet

---

*

WHILE FEAR OF AN ATTACK . . . held the city [of Washington] in its grasp [in April, 1861] the Negroes cowered under the great war comet blazing in the sky. The Woodwards had an old slave named Oola, said to be a native African. She was tall and large of frame, with gray-black skin wrinkled yet drawn tight over forehead and cheek bones, and eyes whose sudden glance made us wince as though actually pricked, with tufts of white wool springing from her skull. The other servants were afraid of her evil eye and "conjure spells."

To have our fortunes told by her was a terrifying yet fascinating experience. "You see dat great fire sword, blazin' in de sky," she said. "Dat's a great war comin' and de handle's to'rd de Norf and de point to'rd de Souf and de Norf's gwine take dat sword and cut de Souf's heart out. But dat Linkum man, chilluns, if he takes de sword, he's gwine perish by it."

* * * * *

We told the Lincoln boys about Oola's prophecy of war, carefully omitting, however, the dire prediction regarding their father. Tad was greatly impressed and carried the story, as tidings of import, to his father. Mrs. Lincoln laughed, but the President seemed strangely interested.

"What was that, Tad, that she said about the comet?" asked Mr. Lincoln.

"She said," answered Tad, gratified that at least one member of his family appreciated the gravity of the omen, "that the handle was toward the north and the point toward the south and that meant the North was going to take that sword and cut the South's heart out. Do you think that's what it means, Pa?"

"I hope not, Tad," answered his father gravely. "I hope it won't come to that." But I noticed him, a few evenings later, looking out of the window intently at the comet and I wondered if he was thinking of the old Negro woman's prophecy.

—JULIA TAFT BAYNE

*
_____

Lincoln Raises a New Flag

_____
*

I WENT WITH MY MOTHER to see [the] new flag raised by President Lincoln [over the White House], the date, according to my diary, being June 29, 1861. Arriving at our destination, we went to the south portico to pay our respects to the "first lady" and were invited to join the group by Mrs. Lincoln.

There comes before my vision the brilliant group of generals and their aides, some members of the Cabinet, the cluster of ladies in hoopskirts and blossoming bonnets, and in the center the tall spare form of the President, so little known and valued then.

When the moment came for the flag to be raised, the Marine Band began the national anthem and all arose, officers at salute, civilians uncovered. When the President pulled the cord, it stuck. He pulled harder, and suddenly the upper corner of the Union tore off and hung down. A gasp of surprise and horror at the sinister omen went around, but a young staff officer, with great presence of mind, stepped quickly to the group of ladies and extending his hand, hissed imploringly, "Pins! Pins!"

They were supplied at once. Women had more pins in their clothes in those days. Mother took two out of her lace collar and some out of her dress. Mrs. Lincoln and the other ladies did the same, and the officer swiftly and efficiently pinned the corner and the flag was raised.

The band had continued to play and the people on the grounds below, standing at attention, did not notice anything untoward except a slight delay in raising the flag. When we reached home and my father heard of the incident, he warned us not to mention the tearing of the stars out of the flag to any one.

"It will be suppressed," he said. "Some people are so superstitious. It might affect enlistments and we must have troops."

In my father's diary is this comment: "Flag raised on the White House. General B. much disturbed by an unfortunate accident. I trust he will keep his discomposure to himself."

But what do you suppose Lincoln thought when he saw nine stars torn from the flag by his hand, who was its chief defender? I think he felt a sharper pang than any of us, but with his mystic nature there was a strange combination of hard common sense. I suppose he just forgot it.

—JULIA TAFT BAYNE

Sherman Tells of Lincoln's Visit

*

A SLOW, MIZZLING RAIN had set in, and probably a more gloomy day never presented itself. All organization seemed to be at an end; but I and my staff labored hard to collect our men into their proper companies and into their former camps, and, on the 23d of July [two days after the rout at Bull Run] I moved the Second Wisconsin and Seventy-ninth New York closer in to Fort Corcoran [Virginia], and got things in better order than I had expected. Of course, we took it for granted that the rebels would be on our heels, and we accordingly prepared to defend our posts. By the 25th I had collected all the materials, made my report, and had my brigade about as well governed as any in that army; although [by late July] most of the ninety-day men, especially the Sixty-ninth, had become extremely tired of the war, and wanted to go home. Some of them were so mutinous, at one time, that I had the battery to unlimber, threatening, if they dared to leave camp without orders, I would open fire on them. Drills and the daily exercises were resumed, and I ordered that at the three principal roll-calls the men should form ranks with belts and muskets, and that they should keep their ranks until I in person had received the reports and had dismissed them.

The Sixty-ninth still occupied Fort Corcoran, and one morning, after reveille, when I had just received the report, had dismissed the regiment, and was leaving, I found myself in a crowd of men crossing the drawbridge on their way to a barn close by, where they had their sinks; among them was an officer, who said: "Colonel, I am going to New York today. What can I do for you?"

I answered: "How can you go to New York? I do not remember to have signed a leave for you."

He said, "No"; he did not want a leave. He had engaged to serve three months, and had already served more than that time. If the Government did not intend to pay him, he could afford to lose the money;

11

that he was a lawyer, and had neglected his business long enough, and was then going home.

I noticed that a good many of the soldiers had paused about us to listen, and knew that, if this officer could defy me, they also would. So I turned on him sharp, and said: "Captain, this question of your term of service has been submitted to the rightful authority, and the decision has been published in orders. You are a soldier, and must submit to orders till you are properly discharged. If you attempt to leave without orders, it will be mutiny, and I will shoot you like a dog! Go back into the fort *now,* instantly, and don't dare to leave without my consent." I had on an overcoat, and may have had my hand about the breast, for he looked at me hard, paused a moment, and then turned back into the fort. The men scattered, and I returned to the house where I was quartered, close by.

That same day, which must have been about July 26th, I was near the river-bank, looking at a block-house which had been built for the defense of the aqueduct, when I saw a carriage coming by the road that crossed the Potomac River at Georgetown by a ferry. I thought I recognized in the carriage the person of President Lincoln. I hurried across a bend, so as to stand by the road-side as the carriage passed. I was in uniform, with a sword on, and was recognized by Mr. Lincoln and Mr. Seward, who rode side by side in an open hack. I inquired if they were going to my camps, and Mr. Lincoln said: "Yes; we heard that you had got over the big scare, and we thought we would come over and see the 'boys.' "

The roads had been much changed and were rough. I asked if I might give directions to his coachman; he promptly invited me to jump in and to tell the coachman which way to drive. Intending to begin on the right and follow round to the left, I turned the driver into a side-road which led up a very steep hill, and, seeing a soldier, called to him and sent him up hurriedly to announce to the colonel (Bennett, I think) that the President was coming. As we slowly ascended the hill, I discovered that Mr. Lincoln was full of feeling, and wanted to encourage our men. I asked if he intended to speak to them, and he said he would like to. I asked him then to please discourage all cheering, noise, or any sort of confusion; that we had had enough of it before Bull Run to ruin any set of men, and that what we needed were cool, thoughtful, hard-fighting soldiers—no more hurrahing, no more humbug. He took my remarks in the most perfect good-nature. Before we had reached the first camp, I heard the drum beating the "assembly," saw the men running for their tents, and in a few minutes the regiment was in line, arms presented, and then brought to an order and "parade rest!"

Mr. Lincoln stood up in the carriage, and made one of the neatest, best, and most feeling addresses I ever listened to, referring to our late disaster at Bull Run, the high duties that still devolved on us, and the brighter days yet to come. At one or two points the soldiers began to cheer, but he promptly checked them, saying: "Don't cheer, boys; I confess I rather like it myself, but Colonel Sherman here says it is not military; and I guess we had better defer to his opinion." In winding up, he explained that, as President, he was Commander-in-Chief; that he was resolved that the soldiers should have everything that the law allowed; and he called on one and all to appeal to him personally in case they were wronged. The effect of this speech was excellent.

We passed along in the same manner to all the camps of my brigade; and Mr. Lincoln complimented me highly for the order, cleanliness, and discipline, that he observed. Indeed, he and Mr. Seward both assured me that it was the first bright moment they had experienced since the battle.

At last we reached Fort Corcoran. The carriage could not enter, so I ordered the regiment, without arms, to come outside, and gather about Mr. Lincoln, who would speak to them. He made to them the same feeling address, with more personal allusions, because of their special gallantry in the battle under Corcoran, who was still a prisoner in the hands of the enemy; and he concluded with the same general offer of redress in case of grievance. In the crowd I saw the officer with whom I had had the passage at reveille that morning. His face was pale, and lips compressed. I foresaw a scene, but sat on the front seat of the carriage as quiet as a lamb. This officer forced his way through the crowd to the carriage, and said: "Mr. President, I have a cause of grievance. This morning I went to speak to Colonel Sherman, and he threatened to shoot me." Mr. Lincoln, who was still standing, said, "Threatened to shoot you?" "Yes, sir, he threatened to shoot me." Mr. Lincoln looked at him, then at me, and stooping his tall, spare form toward the officer, said to him in a loud stage-whisper, easily heard for some yards around: "Well, if I were you, and he threatened to shoot, I would not trust him, for I believe he would do it." The officer turned about and disappeared, and the men laughed at him. Soon the carriage drove on, and, as we descended the hill, I explained the facts to the President, who answered, "Of course I didn't know any thing about it, but I thought you knew your own business best." I thanked him for his confidence, and assured him that what he had done would go far to enable me to maintain good discipline, and it did.

—GENERAL W. T. SHERMAN

*

Chittenden's Story of
Lincoln and the Sleeping Sentinel

---

*

ON A DARK September morning, in 1861, when I reached my office, I found waiting there a party of soldiers, none of whom I personally knew. They were greatly excited, all speaking at the same time, and consequently unintelligible. One of them wore the bars of a captain. I said to them, pleasantly, "Boys, I cannot understand you. Pray, let your captain say what you want, and what I can do for you." They complied, and the captain put me in possession of the following facts:

They belonged to the Third Vermont Regiment, raised, with the exception of one company, on the eastern slope of the Green Mountains, and mustered into service while the battle of Bull Run was progressing. They were immediately sent to Washington, and since their arrival, during the last days of July, had been stationed at the Chain Bridge, some three miles above Georgetown. Company K, to which most of them belonged, was largely made up of farmer-boys, many of them still in their minority.

*   *   *   *   *

The story which I extracted from the "boys" was, in substance, this:

William Scott, one of these mountain-boys, just of age, had enlisted in Company K. Accustomed to his regular sound and healthy sleep, not yet inured to the life of the camp, he had volunteered to take the place of a sick comrade who had been detailed for picket duty, and had passed the night as a sentinel on guard. The next day he was himself detailed for the same duty, and undertook its performance. But he found it im-

14

possible to keep awake for two nights in succession, and had been found by the relief sound asleep on his post. For this offence he had been tried by a court-martial, found guilty, and sentenced to be shot within twenty-four hours after his trial, and on the second morning after his offence was committed.

Scott's comrades had set about saving him in a characteristic way. They had called a meeting, appointed a committee, with power to use all the resources of the regiment in his behalf. Strangers in Washington, the committee had resolved to call on me for advice, because I was a Vermonter, and they had already marched from the camp to my office since daylight that morning.

* * * * *

The more I reflected upon what I was to do, the more hopeless the case appeared. Thought was useless. I must act upon impulse, or I should not act at all.

"Come," I said, "there is only one man on earth who can save your comrade. Fortunately, he is the best man on the continent. We will go to President Lincoln."

I went swiftly out of the Treasury over to the White House, and up the stairway to the little office where the President was writing. The boys followed in a procession. I did not give the thought time to get any hold on me that I, an officer of the government, was committing an impropriety in thus rushing a matter upon the President's attention. . . .

* * * * *

[In response to the President's questioning, and at my insistence, the captain] gave a graphic account of the whole story, and ended by saying, "He is as brave a boy as there is in your army, sir. Scott is no coward. Our mountains breed no cowards. They are the homes of thirty thousand men who voted for Abraham Lincoln. They will not be able to see that the best thing to be done with William Scott will be to shoot him like a traitor and bury him like a dog! Oh, Mr. Lincoln, can you?"

"No, I can't!" exclaimed the President.

It was one of the moments when his countenance became such a remarkable study. It had become very earnest as the captain rose with his subject; then it took on that melancholy expression which, later in his life, became so infinitely touching. I thought I could detect a mist in the deep cavities of his eyes. Then, in a flash, there was a total change.

He smiled, and finally broke into a hearty laugh, as he asked me:

15

"Do your Green Mountain boys fight as well as they talk? If they do, I don't wonder at the legends about Ethan Allen." Then his face softened as he said, "But what can I do? What do you expect me to do? As you know, I have not much influence with the departments."

"I have not thought the matter out," I said. "I feel a deep interest in saving young Scott's life. I think I knew the boy's father. It is useless to apply to General [W. F. (Baldy)] Smith. An application to Secretary Stanton would only be referred to General Smith. The only thing to be done was to apply to you. It seems to me that, if you would sign an order suspending Scott's execution until his friends can have his case examined, I might carry it to the War Department, and so insure the delivery of the order to General Smith to-day, through the regular channels of the War Office."

"No! [replied the President] I do not think that course would be safe. You do not know these officers of the regular army. They are a law unto themselves. They sincerely think that it is good policy occasionally to shoot a soldier. I can see it, where a soldier deserts or commits a crime, but I cannot in such a case as Scott's. They say that I am always interfering with the discipline of the army and being cruel to the soldiers. Well, I can't help it, so I shall have to go right on doing wrong. I do not think an honest, brave soldier, conscious of no crime but sleeping when he was weary, ought to be shot or hung. The country has better uses for him.

"Captain," continued the President, "your boy shall not be shot—that is, not to-morrow, nor until I know more about this case." To me he said, "I will have to attend to this matter myself. I have for some time intended to go up to the Chain Bridge. I will do so to-day. I shall then know that there is no mistake in suspending the execution."

* * * * *

Within a day or two the newspapers reported that a soldier, sentenced to be shot for sleeping on his post, had been pardoned by the President and returned to his regiment. . . .

* * * * *

Scott said [later]: "The President was the kindest man I had ever seen; I knew him at once, by a Lincoln medal I had long worn. I was scared at first, for I had never before talked with a great man. But Mr. Lincoln was so easy with me, so gentle, that I soon forgot my fright. He asked me all about the people at home, the neighbors, the farm, and

16

where I went to school, and who my schoolmates were. Then he asked me about Mother, and how she looked, and I was glad I could take her photograph from my bosom and show it to him. He said how thankful I ought to be that my mother still lived, and how, if he was in my place, he would try to make her a proud mother, and never cause her a sorrow or a tear. I cannot remember it all, but every word was so kind.

"He had said nothing yet about that dreadful next morning; I thought it must be that he was so kind-hearted that he didn't like to speak of it. But why did he say so much about my mother, and my not causing her a sorrow or a tear, when I knew that I must die the next morning? But I supposed that was something that would have to go unexplained; and so I determined to brace up and tell him that I did not feel a bit guilty, and ask him wouldn't he fix it so that the firing party would not be from our regiment! That was going to be the hardest of all—to die by the hands of my comrades.

"Just as I was going to ask him this favor, he stood up, and he says to me: 'My boy, stand up here and look me in the face.'

"I did as he bade me.

"'My boy,' he said, 'you are not going to be shot to-morrow. I believe you when you tell me that you could not keep awake. I am going to trust you, and send you back to your regiment. But I have been put to a good deal of trouble on your account. I have had to come up here from Washington when I have got a great deal to do; and what I want to know is, how are you going to pay my bill?'

"There was a big lump in my throat; I could scarcely speak. I had expected to die, you see, and had kind of got used to thinking that way. To have it all changed in a minute! But I got it crowded down, and managed to say: 'I am grateful, Mr. Lincoln! I hope I am as grateful as ever a man can be to you for saving my life. But it comes upon me sudden and unexpected like. I didn't lay out for it at all. But there is some way to pay you, and I will find it after a little. There is the bounty in the savings bank. I guess we could borrow some money on the mortgage of the farm.' There was my pay was something, and if he would wait until pay-day I was sure the boys would help, so I thought we could make it up if it wasn't more than five or six hundred dollars.

"'But it is a great deal more than that,' he said. Then I said I didn't just see how, but I was sure I would find some way—if I lived.

"Then Mr. Lincoln put his hands on my shoulders and looked into my face as if he was sorry, and said: 'My boy, my bill is a very large one. Your friends cannot pay it, nor your bounty, nor the farm, nor all your

17

comrades! There is only one man in all the world who can pay it, and his name is William Scott! If from this day William Scott does his duty, so that, if I was there when he comes to die, he can look me in the face as he does now, and say, I have kept my promise, and I have done my duty as a soldier, then my debt will be paid. Will you make that promise and try to keep it?'

"I said I would make the promise, and, with God's help, I would keep it. I could not say any more. I wanted to tell him how hard I would try to do all he wanted; but the words would not come, so I had to let it all go unsaid. He went away, out of my sight forever. I know I shall never see him again; but may God forget me if I ever forget his kind words or my promise."

* * * * *

The next scene in this drama opens on the Peninsula, between the York and the James rivers, in March, 1862. The sluggish Warwick River runs from its source, near Yorktown, across the Peninsula to its discharge. It formed at that time a line of defence, which had been fortified by General Magruder, and was held by him with a force of some twelve thousand Confederates. Yorktown was an important position to the Confederates.

On the 15th of April, the division of General Smith was ordered to stop the enemy's work on the entrenchments at Lee's Mills, the strongest position on the Warwick River. His force consisted of the Vermont brigade of five regiments, and three batteries of artillery. After a lively skirmish, which occupied the greater part of the forenoon, this order was executed, and should have ended the movement.

But about noon General McClellan with his staff, including the French princes, came upon the scene, and ordered General Smith to assault and capture the rebel works on the opposite bank. Some discretion was given to General Smith, who was directed not to bring on a general engagement, but to withdraw his men if he found the defence too strong to be overcome. This discretion cost many lives when the moment came for its exercise.

General Smith disposed his forces for the assault, which was made by Companies D, E, F, and K of the Third Vermont Regiment, covered by the artillery, with the Vermont brigade in reserve. About four o'clock in the afternoon the charge was ordered. Unclasping their belts, and holding their guns and cartridge boxes above their heads, the Vermonters dashed into and across the stream at Dam Number One, the strongest

18

position in the Confederate line, and cleared out the rifle-pits. But the earthworks were held by an overwhelming force of rebels, and proved impregnable. After a dashing attack upon them the Vermonters were repulsed, and were ordered to retire across the river. They retreated under a heavy fire, leaving nearly half their number dead or wounded in the river and on the opposite shore.

Every member of these four companies was a brave man. But all the eye-witnesses agreed that among those who in this, their first hard battle, faced death without blenching, there was none braver or more efficient than William Scott, of Company K, debtor for his own life to President Lincoln. He was almost the first to reach the south bank of the river, the first in the rifle-pits, and the last to retreat. He recrossed the river with a wounded officer on his back—he carried him to a place of safety, and returned to assist his comrades, who did not agree on the number of wounded men saved by him from drowning or capture, but all agreed that he had carried the last wounded man from the south bank, and was nearly across the stream, when the fire of the rebels was concentrated upon him; he staggered with his living burden to the shore and fell.

An account of the closing scene in the life of William Scott was given me by a wounded comrade, as he lay upon his cot in a hospital tent, near Columbia College, in Washington, after the retreat of the army from the Peninsula. "He was shot all to pieces," said Private H——. "We carried him back, out of the line of fire, and laid him on the grass to die. His body was shot through and through, and the blood was pouring from his many wounds. But his strength was great, and such a powerful man was hard to kill. The surgeons checked the flow of blood —they said he had rallied from the shock; we laid him on a cot in a hospital tent, and the boys crowded around him, until the doctors said they must leave if he was to have any chance at all. We all knew he must die. We dropped on to the ground wherever we could, and fell into a broken slumber—wounded and well side by side. Just at daylight the word was passed that Scott wanted to see us all. We went into his tent and stood around his cot. His face was bright and his voice cheerful. 'Boys,' he said, 'I shall never see another battle. I supposed this would be my last. I haven't much to say. You all know what you can tell them at home about me. I have *tried* to do the right thing! I am almost certain you will all say *that*.' Then while his strength was failing, his life ebbing away, and we looked to see his voice sink into a whisper, his face lighted up and his voice came out natural and clear as he said: 'If any of you ever have the chance, I wish you would tell President Lincoln that

19

I have never forgotten the kind words he said to me at the Chain Bridge
—that I have tried to be a good soldier and true to the flag—that I
should have paid my whole debt to him if I had lived; and that now,
when I know that I am dying, I think of his kind face and thank him
again, because he gave me the chance to fall like a soldier in battle, and
not like a coward by the hands of my comrades.' "

—L. E. Chittenden

Secession is our watchword; our rights we all demand;
And to defend our firesides we pledge our hearts and hand.
Jeff Davis is our President, with Stephens by his side;
Brave Beauregard, our General, will join us in the ride.

   Oh, wait for the wagon,
    The dissolution wagon;
   The South is our wagon,
    And we'll all take a ride.
      —"THE SOUTHERN WAGON"

2. "SECESSION IS OUR WATCHWORD"

The War Comes to Richmond Children

*

ONE SPRING DAY in April, 1861, all Richmond was astir. Schools were broken up, and knots of excited men gathered at every street corner. Sumter had been fired upon, and Lincoln had ordered the men of Virginia to rush upon their brethren of the South and put the rebellion down. Now "the die was cast," our lot was with theirs, and come weal or woe, we would fight for independence. How merrily the sunbeams danced that day! how proud we children were of the great preparation for the illumination that night!—how few recked of

21

the great underthrob of misery, grief and want! Every patriotic citizen had his house ablaze with a thousand lights, and the dark ones were *marked*. I remember distinctly my father taking us to see the Exchange Hotel and Ballard House with the glass balcony, stretching over the street and connecting the two houses, all glittering and reflecting the crystal lights. To us it was a grand spectacle, and our hearts swelled with pride to think we could say to our tyrants: "Thus far shalt thou come, and no further."

The excitement permeated the schools, and those of our number who lived in the dark houses, or the non-illuminators, were dubbed "Yankees," "Abolitionists" and "Black Republicans," and virtually ostracized. Saturdays we would spend in the lecture-rooms of the different churches we attended, where our mothers and grown-up sisters were busy plying the needle, and cutting out clothes for the soldier boys, and indulging in such talk about the vile usurpers as would fire our young hearts with indignation. Snatches of song improvised for the emergency —"Maryland, My Maryland," "John Brown's Body," "There's Life in the Old Land Yet," &c.—grew as familiar as "I Want To Be an Angel." In fact, we had a parody which ran thus:

> *I want to be a soldier,*
> *And with the soldiers stand,*
> *A knapsack on my shoulder,*
> *And musket in my hand;*
> *And there beside Jeff Davis,*
> *So glorious and so brave,*
> *I'll whip the cussed Yankee*
> *And drive him to his grave.*

But what were our boys doing while the girls were sewing up sandbags to fortify Drewry's Bluff? It seemed the "Demon of Destruction" was possessing the whole land. The boys were keeping their patriotism warm by *playing* "Yank" and "Reb" in mock battles, and so sorely did these young archers wound each other that steps had to be taken by the city authorities toward the suppression of these hostilities. I remember being on Church Hill on one occasion, when the rowdies from Rocketts, calling themselves Yankees, came upon our boys who were unarmed. Immediately our party of little girls flew to a coal-house near, which happened to be open for replenishing, and filling our little aprons with the dusky diamonds ran into the midst of a hot battle, screaming with

22

all the enthusiasm of our young natures, "Kill them! kill them!" We bound up heads and filled pockets with "ammunition" till our nurses, noticing our escapade, came to carry us to our mamas to be punished for soiling our dresses.

—SALLIE HUNT

*

The *Pawnee* Sunday

*

ON THE DAY SUCCEEDING the night of the [April 19th, 1861] illumination [and torchlight procession, celebrating secession], the city [of Richmond] relapsed into comparative quiet; but steady watch was kept up for any hostile demonstration. Military organizations were begun, and volunteers fast filled the ranks. The Richmond Light Infantry Blues possessed some enviable historic fame. It was an organization which dated its origin prior to the Revolution of 1776, and had numbered among its ranks some of the most gallant and chivalrous of the descendants of the old cavaliers of Virginia. At this time, it was under the command of Captain O. Jennings Wise, a son of Ex-Governor Wise, and then associate editor of the *Richmond Enquirer,* which had been, since the days of the elder Ritchie, the principal organ of the Democracy of Virginia. Company F and the Richmond Greys had their ranks filled by young men generally of wealth, education and refinement, enthusiastic, brave and generous. All these companies of infantry were well drilled in military exercises, and ready to use their skill in defence of the cause which had divided the North from the South, even to the death. These companies, with the Battalion of the Richmond Howitzers, and the Fayette Artillery, composed at that time the whole military force of the city under regular organization.

It had been announced that at the slightest premonition of danger, the bell on the Capitol Square should be rung, when the military companies were to repair to their respective armories and prepare to meet any emergency. On Sunday, the 21st of April, occurred the first of a wonderful succession of Sabbath day excitements. Indeed, so common did such excitements finally become, that with few exceptions, we declared all Sunday rumors false. On this warm and balmy April day, the attendance at the different churches was more than usually large. Carefully refraining from making their pulpit discourses themes of political discussion, our clergymen nevertheless offered up the most fervent and devout prayers continually, that God, in his wisdom, might quell the surging billows of angry discord, dispose the hearts of men to peace, and stay the scourge of war; and it was noted as a singular coincidence on that day, that the peculiar lesson in the Episcopal Churches was regarded, by many, as prophetic of success to the South: "Yea, will the Lord be jealous for His land, and pity His people. Yea, the Lord will answer, and say unto His people, 'Behold, I will send you corn, and wine, and oil, and ye shall be satisfied therewith; and I will no more make you a reproach among the heathen, but will remove far off from you the Northern Army, and will drive him into a land barren and desolate, with his face toward the east sea, and his hinder part toward the uttermost sea, and his stink shall come up, and his ill savor shall come up, because he hath done great things."

The services had proceeded until just at their close in some of the churches, and in others during the last prayer, the premonitory sound of the bell on the Square disturbed the solemnity of the hour, and awoke the people to a dread sense of danger—from what source, they could not tell.

In an instant all was confusion. The men, in the excitement, rushed pell-mell from the churches; and the women, pale and trembling with affright, clung to their sons and husbands, wherever they could—but getting no response to their tearful question: "What *is* the matter? What *is* the matter?"

Hasty embraces, sudden wrenchings of the hand, tearful glances of affection, and our men rushed to their armories, to prepare they knew not for what. On every female face was the pale hue of dismay; but mingled with it, the stern, unmistakable impress of heroic resolution to yield up their hearts' most cherished idols upon the altar of their country, if need be. Silently, tearfully, our women wended their way to their homes, and from every closet, the outpourings of supplicating souls, for protection to the loved ones, went up to the ear of the Eternal.

The alarm, however, was groundless. It originated in a report that the Federal sloop of war *Pawnee,* which had been operating in Norfolk Harbor, was making her way up James River, bent upon the destruction of Richmond. In a situation entirely defenceless, with no obstacles to prevent an easy and rapid communication with the city, either by land or water, it was by no means foolish to suppose such a plan possible, and even feasible.

On passing down Main Street, a novel sight met our gaze. The different companies of infantry were all mustered, numerous pieces of artillery of light calibre, belonging to the Howitzer Battalion and the Fayette Artillery, were drawn out into the street; almost every man carried a gun of some description, and boys, who had learned to shoot, appeared with light fowling-pieces. The ridiculous was singularly blended with the solemn and impressive. Only at the slowest pace could a carriage make its way through the crowded street, and then with much risk to the lives of the occupants, from a prospect of frightened horses.

After much deliberation it was decided to send down to a convenient position on the river, a few miles below the city, several pieces of artillery to greet the coming of the intruder. This was the first movement of the Virginia military in the late war.

As twilight gathered over the city, the faint booming of distant cannon was distinctly heard, and apprehension of an engagement with the *Pawnee* was entertained; but the reports were afterwards ascertained to be only the result of a trial of the pieces. The next morning, by order of the Governor, the artillery were recalled to the city, to be sent, in a very few days, to meet an emergency of greater importance.

This day has since been familiarly known to the people of Richmond as the *Pawnee* Sunday.

—SALLIE A. PUTNAM

*

Eggleston's Ride With Stuart
Within the Union Lines

---

*

[J. E. B. STUART'S] restless activity was one, at least, of the qualities which enabled him to win the reputation he achieved so rapidly. He could never be still. He was rarely ever in camp at all, and he never showed a sign of fatigue. He led almost everything. Even after he became a general officer, with well-nigh an army of horsemen under his command, I frequently followed him as my leader in a little party of half a dozen troopers, who might as well have gone with a sergeant on duty assigned them; and once I was his only follower on a scouting expedition, of which he, a brigadier-general at the time, was the commander. [In June, 1861] I had been detailed to do some clerical work at his headquarters [at Bunker Hill] and, having finished the task assigned me, was waiting in the piazza of the house he occupied for somebody to give me further orders, when Stuart came out.

"Is that your horse?" he asked, going up to the animal and examining him minutely.

I replied that he was, and upon being questioned further informed him that I did not wish to sell my steed.

Turning to me suddenly, he said—"Let's slip off on a scout, then; I'll ride your horse and you can ride mine. I want to try your beast's paces"; and mounting, we galloped away. Where or how far he intended to go I did not know. He was enamored of my horse, and rode, I suppose, for the pleasure of riding an animal which pleased him. We passed outside our picket line, and then, keeping in the woods, rode within that of the Union army. Wandering about in a purposeless way, we got a near view of some of the Federal camps, and finally finding ourselves objects of attention on the part of some well-mounted cavalry in blue uniforms, we rode rapidly down a road toward our lines, our pursuers riding quite as rapidly immediately behind us.

"General," I cried presently, "there is a Federal picket post on the road just ahead of us. Had we not better oblique into the woods?"

"Oh no. They won't expect us from this direction, and we can ride over them before they make up their minds who we are."

Three minutes later we rode at full speed through the corporal's guard on picket, and were a hundred yards or more away before they could level a gun at us. Then half a dozen bullets whistled about our ears, but the cavalier paid no attention to them.

"Did you ever time this horse for a half-mile?" was all he had to say.

—GEORGE CARY EGGLESTON

Magruder and Sharpe: Promotion by Potion

*

JUST AFTER the battle of [Big] Bethel [Virginia, June 10, 1861], while the 1st North Carolina (Bethel) regiment was encamped in the vicinity of Yorktown, General [John B.] Magruder, then commanding that Department, issued very strict orders prohibiting soldiers from bringing liquor into camp. The General himself, it is said, was not averse to taking "a smile" occasionally, and a short while after issuing the order noticed a private in the 1st North Carolina named Sharpe, we believe, drinking something out of a canteen, which, from the manner in which his eyes sparkled, he, the General, believed was filled with an article somewhat stronger than water. The following conversation is said to have taken place between the General and the private:

"What is your name and rank, sir?" asked the General.

"My name is Sharpe, and I am a private in the 1st North Carolina!" replied the soldier.

"What is that in your canteen, sir?" sternly said the General.

"Water, sir!" promptly answered Private Sharpe.

"Give me a drink of that water, *Private* Sharpe," said Magruder.

The soldier was very much frightened, but was compelled to hand his canteen to the gallant General, who immediately proceeded to take a long and steady "pull" therefrom, and instead of punishing Sharpe, very much to the astonishment of that individual, thus addressed him:

"You are no longer Private Sharpe, sir; you are *Corporal* Sharpe."

Sharpe continued to hang around the General's headquarters, and in a short time that officer called out to him: "Corporal Sharpe, you will please hand me another drink of that water of yours!"

The canteen was promptly handed forth by the new-made corporal, and the General took another smile and remarked: "You are no longer Corporal Sharpe, sir; you are *Sergeant* Sharpe!"

Sharpe was *sharp* enough to see that if his canteen only held out he was very apt to attain the highest rank the General could confer upon him, and while there was a drop left he was determined to remain in calling distance of the General. In about a quarter of an hour General Magruder again called out lustily: "Sergeant Sharpe, you will please give me another drink of that water of yours."

The canteen was eagerly extended, and the General said: "You are no longer Sergeant Sharpe, sir; you are *Lieutenant* Sharpe!"

Sharpe, upon examining the canteen, found its contents about "played out." He immediately proceeded to trot around camp for the purpose of hunting up more *water;* but very much to his disappointment he could not find any. While passing near Magruder's tent in search of the much desired article, that officer seeing him, exclaimed: "Lieutenant Sharpe, you will please give me another drink of that water of yours."

Poor Sharpe, finding that he could do nothing towards replenishing his canteen, and that his chance for further promotion was thus "blocked," exclaimed in despairing tones: "General, it is 'played out,' and I am sorry for it; for if it had held out *I'll be d——d if I would not have been a brigadier-general before night!"*

—*Our Living and Our Dead*

*

Congressional "Bull Runners":
A Confederate View

*

WE SOON LEARNED all the particulars of that memorable battle [of Bull Run, July 21, 1861]; how the festive congressmen had come with their wives, daughters and sweethearts, on the outskirts of the army, seated in luxurious carriages, with hampers packed with champagne and all good things, to regale themselves withal, as from a safe place they would view the triumphant career of their Invincibles as they made the rebels bite the dust, and then to march over their traitorous corpses to Richmond. There, there was to be a grand ball; ladies had provided themselves with magnificent dresses, certainly expecting, after the battle was over, and the rebels were wiped out, to proceed serenely on their way to the Confederate Capital without meeting an obstacle.

When the "rebels" had been reinforced by the arch-rebels, Johnston and Jackson, with their wornout but gallant men, and when the Federals with their splendid army had turned and were frantically flying before those same "rebels," they cared for nothing but to get away. The flight of that panic-stricken mob has often been described, and by many pens, none however so graphic as that which after treating of their disgraceful race, styled them the "Bull Runners"; the *London Punch* was, I believe, the author of that appropriate name.

The battle was called the battle of Bull Run, because it took place near that stream, a poor little mountain brook, that I remember playing in when a child, as my sister's home was near it. Near there was the great battle fought that might have decided the issue if God had not willed that it should be decided not then or there. And now the homely name has become a classic, as much as any in ancient story, for as goodly men, and as glorious heroes dyed its waters that day with their blood, as any that ever fell on the hard-fought battle-fields of the world.

All along the line of pursuit of the fleeing army, our men beheld the shattered trunks of the ladies with their ball dresses; gossamer robes trampled under feet of men and horses, and which our men picked up and laughingly carried on the points of their bayonets. Huge baskets of wine and all kinds of delicacies strewed the way. We heard many laughable accounts of how the luxurious non-combatants made good their escape; of the prayers for a mule or a wagon horse, anything to bear them out of the reach of danger. The daughter of Thurlow Weed was seen on a mule that had been cut from a wagon, making her way through the crowd and din, without saddle or bridle other than a rope around the neck of her steed.

Henry Wilson, a senator, and afterwards Vice President of the United States, begged in vain of a teamster the privilege of a seat on his wagon. After repeated and emphatic refusals, he revealed his name and position. "I am Henry Wilson," said he, "United States Senator"; but the teamster, perfectly unmoved by the announcement of the dignity and importance of his petitioner, cried out, "I don't care a —— who you are," and lashing his mules, sped on his way.

—CORNELIA McDONALD

*

Jackson Stands Like a Stone Wall

---

*

THE NAME [of Brigadier General Barnard E. Bee] deserves a place in the highest niche of fame. He displayed a gallantry that scarcely has a parallel in history. The brunt of the morning's battle [at Bull Run, July 21, 1861] was sustained by his command until past two o'clock. Overwhelmed by superior numbers, and compelled to yield before a fire that swept everything before it, General Bee rode up and down his lines, encouraging his troops, by everything that was dear to them, to stand up and repel the tide that threatened them with destruction. At last his own brigade dwindled to a mere handful, with every field officer killed or disabled. He rode up to General Jackson and said: "General, they are beating us back."

The reply was: "Sir, we'll give them the bayonet."

General Bee immediately rallied the remnant of his brigade, and his last words to them were: "There is Jackson standing like a stone wall. Let us determine to die here and we will conquer. Follow me!"

His men obeyed the call; and at the head of his column, the very moment when the battle was turning in our favor, he fell mortally wounded. General Beauregard was heard to say he had never seen such gallantry. He [General Bee] never murmured at his suffering, but seemed to be consoled by the reflection that he was doing his duty.

—*Charleston Mercury*

Beauregard and the Confederate Battle-Flag

*

IT WAS AT THE BATTLE of Manassas, about four o'clock of the afternoon of the 21st of July, 1861, when the fate of the Confederacy seemed trembling in the balance, that General [Pierre G. T.] Beauregard, looking across the Warrenton turnpike, which passed through the valley between the position of the Confederates and the elevations beyond occupied by the Federal line, saw a body of troops moving towards his left and the Federal right. He was greatly concerned to know, but could not decide, what troops they were, whether Federal or Confederate. The similarity of uniform and of the colors carried by the opposing armies, and the clouds of dust, made it almost impossible to decide.

Shortly before this time General Beauregard had received from the signal officer, Captain [Edward P.] Alexander, a dispatch, saying that from the signal station in the rear he had sighted the colors of this column, drooping and covered with the dust of journeyings, but could not tell whether they were the Stars and Stripes or the Stars and Bars. He thought, however, that they were probably Patterson's troops arriving on the field and re-enforcing the enemy.

General Beauregard was momentarily expecting help from the right, and the uncertainty and anxiety of this hour amounted to anguish. Still the column pressed on. Calling a staff officer, General Beauregard instructed him to go at once to General [Joseph E.] Johnston, at the Lewis House, and say that the enemy were receiving heavy re-enforcements, that the troops on the plateau were very much scattered, and that he would be compelled to retire to the Lewis House, and there re-form, hoping that the troops ordered up from the right would arrive in time to enable him to establish and hold the new line.

Meanwhile, the unknown troops were pressing on. The day was sultry, and only at long intervals was there the slightest breeze. The colors of the mysterious column hung drooping on the staff. General Beauregard tried again and again to decide what colors they carried. He

31

used his glass repeatedly, and handing it to others begged them to look, hoping that their eyes might be keener than his.

General Beauregard was in a state of great anxiety, but finally determined to hold his ground, relying on the promised help from the right; knowing that if it arrived in time victory might be secured, but feeling also that if the mysterious column should be Federal troops the day was lost.

Suddenly a puff of wind spread the colors to the breeze. It was the Confederate flag—the Stars and Bars! It was [Jubal A.] Early with the Twenty-Fourth Virginia, the Seventh Louisiana, and the Thirteenth Mississippi. The column had by this time reached the extreme right of the Federal lines. The moment the flag was recognized, Beauregard turned to his staff, right and left, saying, "See that the day is ours!" and ordered an immediate advance. In the meantime Early's brigade deployed into line and charged the enemy's right; [Arnold] Elzey, also, dashed upon the field, and in one hour not an enemy was to be seen south of Bull Run.

While on this field and suffering this terrible anxiety, General Beauregard determined that the Confederate soldier must have a flag so distinct from that of the enemy that no doubt should ever again endanger his cause on the field of battle.

Soon after the battle he entered into correspondence with Colonel William Porcher Miles, who had served on his staff during the day, with a view to securing his aid in the matter, and proposing a blue field, red bars crossed, and gold stars.

They discussed the matter at length. Colonel Miles thought it was contrary to the law of heraldry that the ground should be blue, the bars red, and the stars gold. He proposed that the ground should be red, the bars blue, and the stars white. General Beauregard approved the change, and discussed the matter freely with General Johnston. Meanwhile it became known that designs for a flag were under discussion, and many were sent in. One came from Mississippi; one from J. B. Walton and E. C. Hancock, which coincided with the design of Colonel Miles. The matter was freely discussed at headquarters, till, finally, when he arrived at Fairfax Court House, General Beauregard caused his draughtsman (a German) to make drawings of all the various designs which had been submitted. With these designs before them the officers at headquarters agreed on the famous old banner—the red field, the blue cross, and the white stars. The flag was then submitted to the War Department, and was approved.

32

The first flags sent to the army were presented to the troops by General Beauregard in person, he then expressing the hope and confidence that they would become the emblem of honor and of victory.

The first three flags received were made from "*ladies' dresses*" by the Misses [Hetty and Jennie] Cary, of Baltimore and [their cousin Constance, of] Alexandria.

—PRIVATE CARLTON MCCARTHY

*

Stuart and Griffin Were Chums

*

GENERAL CHARLES GRIFFIN, afterward the gallant commander of the Fifth corps, and the famous Confederate chieftain, General J. E. B. Stuart . . . had been great chums at West Point, at which place Stuart had been named "Beauty."

Soon after the first battle of Bull Run [July 21, 1861], Stuart, with a small force of Confederates, advanced on Lewinsville and drove back a Federal force, a part of which was Griffin's battery. The latter left the following note with a citizen for General Stuart.

DEAR BEAUTY:

I have called to see you, and regret very much that you were not in. *Can't you dine with me at Willard's tomorrow? Keep your "black horse" off me!*

From your old friend,
GRIFFIN

To which Stuart immediately replied, as follows, sending the reply to Griffin:

DEAR GRIFFIN:

I heard that you called, and hastened to see you, but as soon as you saw me coming you were guilty of the discourtesy of turning your back upon me. However, you probably hurried on to Washington to get

33

the dinner ready. I hope to dine at Willard's, if not to-morrow, certainly before long.

Yours to count on,
Beauty

—Rev. Theodore Gerrish and Rev. John S. Hutchinson

*

Confederate Overcoats
of Oil-Cloth Table-Covers

---

*

New Orleans
September 25, 1861

WHEN I OPENED THE DOOR of Mrs. F.'s room . . . the rattle of two sewing-machines and a blaze of color met me.

"Ah, G., you are just in time to help us; these are coats for Jeff Thompson's men. All the cloth in the city is exhausted; these flannel-lined oil-cloth table-covers are all we could obtain to make overcoats for Thompson's poor boys. They will be very warm and serviceable."

"Serviceable—yes! The Federal army will fly when they see those coats! I only wish I could be with the regiment when these are shared around." Yet I helped make them.

Seriously, I wonder if any soldiers will ever wear these remarkable coats—the most bewildering combination of brilliant, intense reds, greens, yellows, and blues in big flowers meandering over as vivid grounds; and as no table-cover was large enough to make a coat, the sleeves of each were of a different color and pattern. However, the coats were duly finished. Then we set to work on gray pantaloons, and I have just carried a bundle to an ardent young lady who wishes to assist. A slight gloom is settling down, and the inmates here are not quite so cheerfully confident as in July.

—War Diary of a Union Woman in the South

34

*

Jackson Keeps the Sabbath

*

IN THE WINTER of '61-'62, while Jackson's forces were at Winchester, he sent a brigade to destroy the canal leading to Washington. The expedition proved a failure; and he attributed it, in some measure, to the fact that Sunday had been needlessly trespassed upon. So when a second expedition was planned he determined there should be no Sabbath-breaking connected with it, that he could prevent. The advance was to be made early on Monday morning. On Saturday he ordered my husband (Colonel Preston, at that time on his staff) to see that the necessary powder was in readiness. The quartermaster could not find a sufficient quantity in Winchester on Saturday, but during Sunday it was procured. On Sunday evening the fact in some way got to Jackson's ears. At a very early hour on Monday, he dispatched an officer to Shepherdstown for other powder, which was brought. Then summoning Colonel Preston, he said very decisively: "Colonel, I desire that you will see that the powder which is used for this expedition is *not the powder that was procured on Sunday*."

—MARGARET J. PRESTON

*

The Mysterious Stranger

*

DURING THE WINTER of 1861-62 [Lee] was living quietly at a little place called Coosawhatchie, on the Charleston and Savannah Railroad. He had hardly any staff with him, and was surrounded with

35

none of the pomp and circumstance of war. His dress bore no marks of his rank, and hardly indicated even that he was a military man. He was much given to solitary afternoon rambles, and came almost every day to the camp of our battery, where he wandered alone and in total silence around the stables and through the gun park, much as a farmer curious as to cannon might have done. Hardly any of the men knew who he was, and one evening a sergeant, riding in company with a partially deaf teamster, met him in the road and saluted.

The teamster called out to his companion, in a loud voice, after the manner of deaf people: "I say, Sergeant, who *is* that durned old fool? He's always a-pokin' round my hosses just as if he meant to steal one of 'em."

—George Cary Eggleston

I want to be a soldier, and go to Dixie's Land,
A knapsack on my shoulder, and a gun in my hand;
Then I will shoot Jeff Davis and Beauregard I will hang,
And make all Rebels tremble throughout our glorious land.
                    —"I WANT TO BE A SOLDIER"

3. "RALLY ROUND THE FLAG"

Mrs. Anderson Brings Reinforcement
to Fort Sumter

*

January, 1861

MAJOR [ROBERT] ANDERSON'S conduct in evacuating Fort
Moultrie and concentrating the available loyal forces of the United
States troops, then in Charleston Harbor, within the stronger walls of
Sumter, was looked upon as a breach of an implied agreement made
between the secessionists and the Government; but the new Secretary
of War, Joseph Holt, assured Major Anderson of the approval of the
Government and that his action was in every way admirable, alike for
its humanity and patriotism, as for its soldiership.

37

Before these words of approval reached Major Anderson, the Legislature of Nebraska sent greetings two thousand miles by telegraph. Indeed, every patriotic heart in the land beat responsive to the spontaneous praise of a grateful people for a deed which seemed a promise of safety to the republic.

The position of Major Anderson and his little band, composed of ten officers, fifteen musicians, and fifty-five artillerists—eighty in all— was an extremely perilous one. His friends were uneasy; his wife, a daughter of the gallant soldier, General Clinch of Georgia, was in New York City. She knew her husband was exposed to ferocious foes without, and possible traitors within, the fort.

In the emergency she remembered a faithful sergeant who had been with her husband in Mexico, but she had not seen him in seven years. His name was Peter Hart. She knew him to be a tried and trusty friend, on whom she could rely in any emergency, and she resolved to find him and place him by the side of her husband within the walls of Fort Sumter.

For a day and a half she sought a clew by visiting the residences of the various Harts named in the City Directory. She was an invalid. Her physician protested against her project, as he believed its execution would imperil her life. She would listen to no protests, but found Hart and the two started the next day for Charleston. They traveled without intermission and reached Charleston at the end of forty-eight hours.

The cars were crowded with recruits hastening to join in the attack on Fort Sumter. She neither ate, drank, nor slept, and heard her husband threatened with instant death should he fall into their hands. Their language was very violent especially respecting the destruction of the old flag-staff at Moultrie, which was considered such an insult to the South Carolinians as might not be forgiven. At the Mills House, Mrs. Anderson met her brother. She found no difficulty in procuring a permit from Governor [Francis] Pickens, who was her father's old friend, to go to Fort Sumter.

The Governor refused one for Hart, saying he could not allow a man to be added to the Sumter garrison. She scornfully asked if South Carolina, claiming to be a sovereign power among the nations of the earth, would be endangered by the addition of one man to a garrison of seventy or eighty, while thousands of armed hands were ready and willing to strike them.

The Governor, seeing the absurdity of his refusal, gave a pass for Hart, requiring from Major Anderson a pledge that he should not

38

be enrolled as a soldier. A small boat carried them to Sumter. On every hand she saw strange banners and warlike preparations. Nearing Sumter, she turned and saw the national ensign floating over the fort, the only one in the whole bay. "The dear old flag!" she exclaimed, and burst into tears.

Reaching the fort, her husband caught her in his arms, whispering, "My glorious wife!"

"I have brought you Peter Hart," she said. "The children are well. I return to-night."

In two hours, Mrs. Anderson was placed in the boat by her husband, and rowed back to the city. The same evening she started for the national capital. Her mission ended, she was utterly prostrate. A bed was placed in the car for her comfort. She was insensible when she arrived at Willard's Hotel, Washington, and after forty-eight hours of suffering from exhaustion, she proceeded to New York and rejoined her children.

This brave woman had done what the Government failed to do —she had not sent, but had taken, reinforcement to Fort Sumter.

—PAUL F. MOTTELAY, ed.
The Soldier in Our Civil War

*

Francis Brownell
Avenges the Death of Ellsworth

---

*

[ON MAY 24, 1861, the 11th New York Volunteer Infantry (New York Fire Zouaves) was forming on the wharf at Alexandria, Virginia] when [Elmer E.] Ellsworth came by the right of the line, starting up-town. With him were Mr. [H. J.] Winser of the New York *Tribune* and Chaplain [E. W.] Dodge. As they passed, one of them suggested that a guard be taken, when Ellsworth turned quickly and said: "First squad, follow me!"

The squad, consisting of Sergeant Marshall, two corporals, of whom I was one, and two privates, fell in behind, and in that order we went up Cameron Street on the double-quick.

I believed then, and still think, that Ellsworth was on the way to the telegraph office to send word that he had landed. Three blocks up Cameron, and, turning south on Royal Street, one square brought us to King, when, on turning the corner to go west, we came in sight of the Marshall House, one square ahead, with the Confederate flag flying.

Ellsworth turned abruptly to the sergeant, and said: "Marshall, go back and tell Captain Coyle to bring his company up here as soon as possible."

This was all Ellsworth said to show that he had observed the flag. He continued on up King Street, and did not turn on arriving opposite the hotel, therefore I supposed he was going to let Captain Coyle take care of the flag.

Some distance above the hotel he leaped over the gutter to cross the street, when he suddenly halted, and looked back at the flag. Perhaps it occurred to him that a glimpse of that banner might enrage the men and lead to the very thing he had promised to prevent.

Standing a moment as if revolving the matter in his mind, he then crossed the street, and entered the office of the hotel [Marshall House]. We followed in silence. A man was behind the counter, and Ellsworth asked him if he was the proprietor. He replied in the negative, and the Colonel went upstairs without making any remark.

We followed him to the attic. Each of the three flights of stairs had a landing or broad step about midway. On the upper floor, leading in from the roof, were the halyards, and Ellsworth at once pulled down the flag.

The only remark made at the time was by the Colonel, when some one attempted to cut off a piece of the bunting as a trophy, and he prevented it by saying: "Stop! Don't do that! This goes to New York!"

At this point, I must say, I firmly believe Ellsworth went up to get the flag only in the interest of peace and good order. He was actuated, I think, by the thought that if it was seen by his men it might provoke them to lawless acts. It was not bravado which inspired him, but an earnest desire to avoid unnecessary trouble. That he sent back for Captain Coyle and Company A is to me convincing proof that he did not leave the regiment simply for the purpose of taking the flag, as has been asserted, otherwise why did he, immediately on seeing it, send for aid? Why did he not go in the most direct line to the house, instead of doing as he did?

40

We started to descend the stairs, and I led the way. Ellsworth was just behind, in the act of rolling the flag into a small bundle. As I reached the first landing and turned, with half a dozen steps between me and the floor, there stood a man with a double-barreled gun resting on the banisters, the muzzle pointing at my breast.

Until this moment everything had been so quiet that we were not anticipating trouble.

Prompted by the instincts of self-preservation rather than anything else, I jumped, throwing the barrel of my gun on his, and both weapons slid along the banisters until the turn was reached, when they fell apart. In my leap I had cleared the steps from the landing to the floor, but before I could recover my equilibrium the man brought his gun to position once more.

At this instant Ellsworth came into view on the landing, and [proprietor James W.] Jackson fired. Then, whirling suddenly, he [Jackson] leveled the weapon at me. As he did so I discharged my musket and sprang forward with the bayonet. That movement saved my life, for the heavy charge of buckshot passed over my head, penetrating a door directly behind me.

The muzzle of the gun was within three or four feet of Ellsworth's breast, and the charge struck him just above the heart. With the exclamation, "My God!" he fell forward from the landing to the floor.

Jackson was shot in the corner of his left eye, through the brain, and the bayonet pierced his heart. He fell backward to the landing without having spoken a word from the first time I saw him.

I can only account for my escape by the supposition that, when I came into view on the landing, Jackson wavered for an instant, thus giving me a chance to leap to the floor. Jackson was not a brave man, and I do not believe he knew who had taken down the flag; he had been celebrating the passage of the ordinance of secession, and had gone to bed drunk at two o'clock on that morning. Some of the citizens had threatened to haul down the flag, and he swore he would defend it. He had been awakened hurriedly by some one, and told that we had gone after the flag. Without waiting to dress, clad only in his shirt and trousers, he seized his gun, and stationed himself on the stairs.

I reloaded my weapon, and the squad stood on the landing back to back in anticipation of an attack. People came out of the rooms near by, and we obliged them to stand in a row against the wall until we had full control of the situation.

41

The body was wrapped in a blanket, and I accompanied it back to the navy yard.

*   *   *   *   *

I can never forget a scene which took place in the engine house, where the body had been carried that it might be embalmed. Having a severe pain in my head, I had lain down in the quarters of the 71st New York, when a messenger came to say that the President wished to see me.

Following him to the engine house I found there the undertaker; Mr. Fox, the Assistant Secretary of the Navy; and the President, who, when I entered, was pacing to and fro, the picture of grief. Frequently, on passing the body, he would raise the sheet from the pallid face, and, with the tears rolling down his cheeks, exclaim: "My boy! My boy, was it necessary this sacrifice should be made?"

—FRANCIS E. BROWNELL

*

The Havelock and
the "Cake and Pie Brigade"

*

ENTIRELY UNACQUAINTED with the requirements of war and the needs of soldiers, it was inevitable that the first movements of women for army relief should be misdirected. They could not manifest more ignorance, however, nor blunder more absurdly, than did the government in its early attempts to build up an effective and disciplined army. Both learned by blundering.

It was summer; and the army was to move southward, to be exposed to the torrid heats of the season and climate. A newspaper reminiscence of the good service rendered British troops in India by General Havelock set the ball in motion. He had devised a white linen headdress to be worn over the caps of his men, which defended them from sunstroke, and in his honor it was named the "Havelock." Our

42

men must, of course, be equipped with this protection, and forthwith inexperienced women, and equally inexperienced men in the army, gave orders for the manufacture of Havelocks. What a furor there was over them! Women who could not attend the "sewing-meeting" where the Havelocks were being manufactured, ordered the work sent to their homes, and ran sewing-machines day and night till the nondescript headgear was completed. Havelocks were turned out by thousands, of all patterns and sizes, and of every conceivable material.

In the early inexperience of that time, whenever regiments were in camp awaiting marching orders, it was the custom of many women to pay them visits, laden with indigestible dainties. These they furnished in such profusion, that the "boys" were rarely without the means of obtaining a "permit" to the hospital until they broke up camp. While the Havelock fever was at its height, the Nineteenth Illinois, commanded by Colonel [John Basil] Turchin, was mustered in, and was ordered to rendezvous at Camp Douglas. A detachment of the "cake and pie brigade," as the rollicking fellows called them, paid the regiment an early visit, and were received by the men who were not under drill, *en Havelock.* As the sturdy fellows emerged from their tents, all wearing "the white nightcaps," as they had irreverently christened the ugly headdress, their appearance was so ludicrous that a shout went up from officers, soldiers, and lady visitors. They were worn in every imaginable fashion,—as nightcaps, turbans, sunbonnets, bandages, sunshades,— and the fate of the Havelock was sealed. No more time nor money was wasted in their useless manufacture.

—MARY A. LIVERMORE

*

Toby Tests the Maynard Rifle

---

*

TOBY IS A HIGH PRIVATE in the First Regiment of the Mississippi army. His company is armed with the breech-loading Maynard rifle, "warranted to shoot twelve times a minute, and carry a ball effectually 1,600 yards." Men who fought at Monterey and Buena

Vista call the new-fangled thing a "pop-gun." To test its efficacy, Toby's captain told the men they must "try their guns." In obedience to command, Toby procured the necessary munitions of war, and started with his "pop-gun" for the woods. Saw a squirrel up a very high tree—took aim—fired. Effects of shot immediate and wonderful. Tree effectually stripped, and nothing of the squirrel to be found, except three broken hairs. "Pop-gun" rose in value—equal to a four-pounder. But Toby wouldn't shoot toward any more trees—afraid of being arrested for cutting down other people's timber. Walked a mile and a quarter to get sight of a hill. By aid of a small telescope, saw hill in distance; saw large rock on hill; put in big load; shut both eyes—fired. As soon as breath returned, opened both eyes; could see, just could, but couldn't hear—at least, couldn't distinguish any sounds; thought Niagara had broke loose, or all out-doors gone to drum-beating. Determined to see if shot hit. Borrowed horse, and started toward hill. After travelling two days and nights, reached place; saw setting sun shining through hill. Knew right away that was where his shot hit. Went closer—stumbled over rocky fragments scattered for a half mile in line of bullet. Come to hole—knew the bullet hit there, because saw lead on the edges; walked in, and walked through; saw teamster on the other side, "indulging in profane language"—in fact, "cussin' considerable," because lightning had killed his team. Looked as finger directed—saw six dead oxen in line with hole through mountain; knew that was the bullet's work, but didn't say so to angry teamster. Thought best to be leaving; in consequence, didn't explore path of bullet any further; therefore, don't know where it stopped; don't know whether it stopped at all; in fact, rather think it didn't. Mounted horse; rode back through the hole made by the bullet, but never told Captain a word about it; to tell the truth, was rather afraid he'd think it a hoax.

"It's a right big story, boys," said Toby, in conclusion; "but it's true, sure as shooting. Nothing to do with Maynard rifle but load her up, turn her North, and pull trigger. If twenty of them don't clean out all Yankeedom, then I'm a liar, that's all."

—*The* (Oxford, Mississippi) *Intelligencer*

*

Fighting Preacher

*

IN ONE OF THE Indiana regiments [at Carrick's Ford, West Virginia, July 13, 1861], was a Methodist preacher, said to be one of the very best shots in his regiment. During the battle, he was particularly conspicuous for the zeal with which he kept up a constant fire. The 14th Ohio Regiment, in the thick of the fight, fired an average of eleven rounds to every man, but this parson managed to get in a great deal more than that average. He fired carefully, with perfect coolness, and always after a steady aim, and the boys declare that every time, as he took down his gun, after firing he added, "And may the Lord have mercy on your soul."

—HENRY HOWE

*

The Mutiny of the Highlanders

*

AT THE BEGINNING of the war it took patience and some stern military discipline to mold the civilian army into the compact, obedient machine which brought victory to the Union arms. These showy regiments of State militia had been the idols of their cities and always met with admiration when they paraded. When invited to attend a function in full-dress uniform, they met in their armories and decided whether they would go or not.

When the Highlanders [the 79th New York], in the reorganization which followed Bull Run, received orders to turn in their plaids and kilts and sporrans and dress in the regulation uniform of the army they were greatly angered, and simply exercising the well-known prerogative

45

of American citizens, the inalienable right to knock the government and their temporary superiors, they held an indignation meeting and voted not to obey the order.

Things came to a head on August 14, 1861. That day my older brother, Surgeon Charles S. Taft, U.S. Signal Corps, burst into the house while we were at lunch, saying "They're having a bad time with the Highlanders and two companies of regulars and a battery loaded with grape and canister are ordered out there. You'll see something you may never see again. Come quick!"

My father rose at once, and I slapped my big flat on my head and sped after him. "Oh, Charlie," I gasped, as I hurried to keep pace, "they will not use grape and canister! That scatters so and hits so many at once."

"If the artillerymen are ordered to fire, they will fire and so will the infantry. They are regulars, you know."

I knew, and as we hurried along I pictured those tall, proud High-landers in their tartans, kilts and sporrans and bare knees, and re-membered the splendid appearance they made in the "On to Richmond" advance of the month before, the bagpipes sounding a weird pibroch. As I remember, the camp of the Highlanders was not far from Kalorama, a beautiful place in the suburbs of Washington, afterwards taken by the government for a smallpox hospital.

We arrived just as two companies of regulars took up position on two sides of a square, the barracks being the third side, while on the fourth, in an open space, the rebellious soldiers were gathered, silent and sullen, their arms thrown in disorderly heaps upon the ground. Two companies of the Highlanders which did not join the mutiny were drawn up a little to one side at parade rest. They had the fine regimental colors with them.

A gun of the battery clanked up, wheeled and jangled into position in the center of the line facing the open space, the artillerymen standing by, ready to serve.

We were standing a little distance back of the line of regulars near a group of officers, the colonel of the Highlanders and his staff. A mounted adjutant rode into the middle of the square. He took out his watch and holding it in his hand said, "You have five minutes, men, to take your arms and fall in. If you are not in line at the expiration of five minutes, the order will be given to fire."

As long as I live I shall see that young officer on his horse, mo-tionless as a graven statue, his gold watch glittering in his hand and the lines of blue-coated regulars with still, set faces.

A long silence without stir or motion. I clutched my brother's arm and prayed, "O Lord, make them give way. Make them give way." I did not pray to close the grinning mouth of that gun or that the line of regulars be held from firing. I knew better. If that quiet captain gave the order, I knew they would fire. My mind refused to think beyond that possibility.

"Steady, Sis, steady," whispered my brother. He told me afterwards that I pinched his arm black and blue. The colonel wiped the tears from his face with a handkerchief. The adjutant spoke again and his voice made us jump.

"You have two minutes to take up your arms and fall in before the order to fire is given."

A low order ran down the line of regulars, the muskets fell as one to the "aim" and we heard the click as they were cocked. But the recalcitrants began to pick up their arms and fall into line. Faster and faster the sergeants herded them into line. Thank God, it was over. The adjutant put up his watch and rode out, saluting the colonel as he passed. But a color guard from the regulars bore off the regimental colors, the beautiful flag. I cried a little then; it seemed cruel. But I was glad when, in a few months, I heard they had been given their colors back for gallantry in action.

This incident was kept out of the newspapers at the time. It would have hurt enlistments up North, but it remains in my memory as one of the vivid and heart-rending experiences of the war.

—JULIA TAFT BAYNE

*

Corporal Casey's Scrimmage

---

*

In camp, W. Va.
August 15, 1861

[CORPORAL CASEY] is the best-known man in the [3rd Ohio Volunteer Infantry] regiment. He prides himself greatly on the Middle Fork "skrimage." A day or two after that affair, and at a time when whisky was so scarce that it was worth its weight in gold, some officers called the corporal up and asked him to give them an account of the "skrimage." Before he entered upon the subject, it was suggested that Captain Dubois, who had the little whisky there was in the party, should give him a taste to loosen his tongue. The corporal, nothing loath, took the flask, and, raising it to his mouth, emptied it, to the utter dismay of the captain and his friends. The *dhrap* had the effect desired. The corporal described, with great particularity, his manner of going into action, dwelt with much emphasis on the hand-to-hand encounters, the thrusts, the parries, the final clubbing of the musket, and the utter discomfiture and mortal wounding of his antagonist. In fact by this time there were two of them; and finally, as the fight progressed, a dozen or more bounced down on him. It was lively! There was no time for the loading of guns. Whack, thump, crack! The head of one was broken, another lay dying of a bayonet thrust, and still another had perished under the sledge-hammer blow of his fist. The ground was covered now with the slain. He stood knee-deep in secesh blood; but a bugle sounded away off on the hills, and the d——n scoundrels who were able to get away ran off as fast as their legs could carry them. Had they stood up like men he would have destroyed the whole regiment; for, you see, he was just getting his hand in. "But, Corporal," enquired Captain Hunter, "what were the other soldiers of your company doing all this time?"

"Bless your sowl, Captain, and do you think I had nothing to do but to watch the boys? Be jabers, it was a day when every man had to look after himself."

—LIEUTENANT COLONEL JOHN BEATTY

*

Grant Is Paid in His Own Coin

---

*

SHORTLY AFTER GRANT had received his commision as brigadier-general [August 7, 1861], and was placed in command of the military district of Missouri, with headquarters at Cairo [where he arrived September 4], John Steere, then a boy a little over sixteen years of age, enlisted and was ordered, with others, to report at Cairo, which they did. Five days after enlisting they were drilled in marching and manoeuvring without uniform or arms. This was continued for a few days, when the new recruits got a uniform and an old Harper's Ferry musket, one of those old affairs that every time the gun was discharged, the shooter had to go hunting for the hammer of his gun.

The morning after young Steere got his gun he was stationed at General Grant's headquarters as guard. The headquarters was located on the levee fronting the Ohio River, near the junction of the Mississippi River. It was in November, and the day was a cold and boisterous one. Steere's military experience was very limited indeed, and the inclement weather did not exactly suit him. His orders were to let no one except an officer, or one on official business, enter the building.

He stood at his post of duty until chilled through and through, when he set his musket up in one corner of the door, leaning against the sill, and himself close up against the building, with the cape of his overcoat pulled up over his ears to keep warm.

As every person who came near the place seemed to be an officer, he molested no one, devoting all his time and attention to keeping himself warm and comfortable. Morpheus courted him, and he was on the verge of taking a pleasant snooze when some one coming down the stairway aroused him. Looking up he saw an officer buckling on an elegant sword. After passing through the door the officer came to a halt, and, looking at the guard indignantly, asked: "What are you doing there?"

"I'm the guard," replied Steere.

"An excellent guard indeed. Do you know whose headquarters this is?

"Yes, sir; General Grant's."

The officer looked at the guard a moment in silence, and then thundered: "Stand up there, sir, and bring your gun to a shoulder."

Young Steere did as requested, bringing his gun to a shoulder like a squirrel hunter. The officer took the gun from him and went through the manual of arms for him. He remained with him for fifteen or twenty minutes until he taught him how to handle his gun, when he asked: "How long have you been in the service?"

"Several days."

"Do you know who I am?"

"No, sir; never saw you before."

"I am General Grant. You have deserted your post of duty, sir, which is a very serious breach of discipline. I will not punish you this time, but, young man, be very careful it does not occur again. Orders must be strictly and promptly obeyed always."

Several days after this, young Steere was put on guard on a steamboat which was being loaded with provisions and ammunition, with orders to allow no one with a lighted pipe or cigar to come within a given distance—about fifty feet. He had not been at his post of duty more than an hour when General Grant approached with a lighted cigar between his teeth. He seemed to be deep in thought, but the moment he came near the gangplank his musings were interrupted.

"Halt!" cried the young guard, bringing his gun to his shoulder.

The General was taken completely by surprise. He looked at the young guard, who had him covered with his gun, amazed, and then his countenance showed traces of rising anger. But he did not budge an inch.

"I have been taught to obey orders strictly and promptly," explained Steere, quoting the General, "and as my orders are to allow no one to approach this boat with a lighted cigar, you will please throw yours away."

Grant smiled, threw his cigar into the river, and crossed the gangplank onto the boat.

—*Cincinnati Enquirer*

*

It Had His Name on It

---

*

AMONG [the dead we left in the Cheat Mountain country in western Virginia, September 11-17, 1861] was a chap belonging to my company named Abbott; it is not odd that I recollect it, for there was something unusual in the manner of Abbott's taking off. He was lying flat upon his stomach and was killed by being struck in the side by a nearly spent cannon-shot that came rolling in among us. The shot remained in him until removed. It was a solid round-shot, evidently cast in some private foundry, whose proprietor, setting the laws of thrift above those of ballistics, had put his "imprint" upon it: it bore, in slightly sunken letters, the name "Abbott." That is what I was told—I was not present.

—AMBROSE BIERCE

*"Good-by, ole man, good-by. That's right. Skedaddle as fas'
as you kin," said the Negroes as the white man disappeared.
"When you cotch we ag'in, I 'specs you'll know it. We's gwine
to run sure enough; but we knows the Yankees, an' we runs that
way."*

—ELIZABETH HYDE BOTUME

4. RUN, SLAVE, RUN

Butler Declares Runaway Slaves
"Contraband of War"

*

ON THE DAY after my arrival at [Fortress Monroe], May 23,
three Negroes were reported coming in a boat from Sewall's Point,
where the enemy was building a battery. Thinking that some information as to that work might be got from them, I had them before me. I
learned that they were employed on the battery on the Point, which as
yet was a trifling affair. There were only two guns there, though the
work was laid out to be much larger and to be heavily mounted with
guns captured from the navy-yard. The Negroes said they belonged to
Colonel Mallory, who commanded the Virginia troops around Hampton,

52

and that he was now making preparation to take all his Negroes to Florida soon, and that not wanting to go away from home they had escaped to the fort. I directed that they should be fed and set at work.

On the next day [the twenty-fourth] I was notified by an officer in charge of the picket line next [to] Hampton that an officer bearing a flag of truce desired to be admitted to the fort to see me. As I did not wish to allow officers of the enemy to come inside the fort just then and see us piling up sand-bags to protect the weak points there, I directed the bearer of the flag to be informed that I would be at the picket line in the course of an hour. Accompanied by two gentlemen of my staff, Major Fay and Captain Haggerty . . . , I rode out to the picket line and met the flag of truce there. It was under charge of Major Carey, who introduced himself, at the same time pleasantly calling to mind that we last met at the Charleston convention. . . .

* * * * *

"I am informed," said Major Carey, "that three Negroes belonging to Colonel Mallory have escaped within your lines. I am Colonel Mallory's agent and have charge of his property. What do you mean to do with those Negroes?"

"I intend to hold them," said I.

"Do you mean, then, to set aside your constitutional obligation to return them?"

"I mean to take Virginia at her word, as declared in the ordinance of secession passed yesterday. I am under no constitutional obligations to a foreign country, which Virginia now claims to be."

"But you say we cannot secede," he answered, "and so you cannot consistently detain the Negroes."

"But you say you have seceded, so you cannot consistently claim them. I shall hold these Negroes as contraband of war, since they are engaged in the construction of your battery and are claimed as your property. The question is simply whether they shall be used for or against the Government of the United States. Yet, though I greatly need the labor which has providentially come to my hands, if Colonel Mallory will come into the fort and take the oath of allegiance to the United States, he shall have his Negroes, and I will endeavor to hire them from him."

"Colonel Mallory is absent," was Major Carey's answer.

We courteously parted.

—Major General Benjamin F. Butler

*

How William Tillman Recaptured
the *S. J. Waring*

*

[IN THE MONTH OF JUNE, 1861, the schooner *S. J. Waring,* from New York, bound to South America, was captured on the passage by the rebel privateer *Jeff Davis,* a prize-crew put on board, consisting of a captain, mate, and four seamen; and the vessel set sail for the port of Charleston, South Carolina. Three of the original crew were retained on board, a German as steersman, a Yankee who was put in irons, and a black man named William Tillman, the steward and cook of the schooner. The latter was put to work at his usual business, and told that he was henceforth the property of the Confederate States, and would be sold, on his arrival at Charleston, as a slave. Night comes on. Darkness covers the sea. The vessel is gliding swiftly towards the South. The rebels, one after another, retire to their berths. The hour of midnight approaches. All is silent in the cabin. The captain is asleep. The mate, who has charge of the watch, takes his brandy toddy, and reclines upon the quarter-deck. The Negro thinks of home and all its endearments: he sees in the dim future chains and slavery.—W.W.B.]

Tillman conferred with two of the seamen about taking possession of the schooner; but they declined adopting any plan, saying that none of them knew how to navigate her back should they succeed in getting control. Tillman thought the matter over for three days, and then made an appeal to the German, and said, "If you are a man to stick to your word, we can take this vessel easy." [He continues his story as follows:]

Then we made a plan that I was to go to my berth, and when most of the men were asleep he was to give me some sign, or awake me. We tried this for two nights, but no good chance offered. But last Tuesday night we caught them asleep, and we went to work.

The mate comes to my berth, and he touches me. He says, "Now is your time."

I went into my room and got my hatchet. The first man I struck was the [rebel] captain. He was lying in a stateroom on the starboard side. I aimed for his temple as near as I could, and hit him just below the ear with the edge of the hatchet. With that he made a very loud shriek.

The passenger jumped up very much in a fright. I told him to be still; I shall not hurt a hair of your head. The passenger knew what I was up to; he never said a word more. I walks across the cabin to the second mate's room, and I gave him one severe blow in the mole of the head—that is, right across the middle of his head. I didn't stop to see whether he was dead or no; but I jumped on deck, and as I did so, the mate, who had been sleeping on the companion-way, started from the noise he had heard in the cabin.

Just as he arose upon his feet, I struck him on the back of the head. Then the German chap jumped over, and we "mittened" onto him, and flung him over the starboard quarter.

Then we went down stairs into the cabin. The second mate was not quite dead. He was sitting leaning against his berth. I "catched" him by the hair of the head with my left hand, and struck him with the hatchet I had in my right hand. I told this young German, "Well, let's get him overboard as soon as we can." So we hauled him over on to the cabin.

He was not quite dead, but he would not have lived long. We flung him over the starboard quarter. Then I told this German to go and call that man Jim, the southern chap (one of the pirates), here. He called him aft.

Says I, "Jim, come down here in the cabin. Do you know that I have taken charge of this vessel to-night? I am going to put you in irons."

"Well," says he, "I am willing."

He gave right up. I kept him in irons till 8 o'clock the next morning. I then sent the German for him, and I said—

"Smith (the name Milnor went by on board), I want you to join us and help take this vessel back. But mind, the least crook or the least turn, and overboard you go with the rest."

"Well," said he, "I will do the best I can." And he worked well all the way back. He couldn't do otherwise. It was pump or sink.

They didn't have any chance to beg. It was all done in five minutes. In seven minutes and a half after I struck the first blow, the vessel was

55

squared away before the wind and all sail set. We were fifty miles south of Charleston, and one hundred to the eastward.

Tillman said that at first he had thought of securing all the men, and bringing them all to New York alive, in irons; but he found this was impracticable.

. . . "There were too many for that [he said]—there were five of them, and only three of us."

Tillman says he went away as a steward, but came back as a captain.

[The Federal Government awarded to Tillman the sum of six thousand dollars as prize-money for the capture of the schooner.]

—LIEUTENANT COLONEL CHARLES S. GREENE

✳

These Times Just Suit *Me!*

✳

AT CANNELTON [Western Virginia, July, 1861], a hundred slaves were employed in the coal-oil works—two long, begrimed, dilapidated buildings, with a few wretched houses hard by. Nobody was visible, except the Negroes. When I asked one of them: "Where are all the white people?" he replied with a broad grin—"Done gone, mass'r."

A black woman, whom we encountered on the road, was asked: "Have you run away from your master?"

"Golly, no!" was the prompt answer, "mass'r run away from *me!*"

The slaves, who always heard the term "runaway" applied only to their own race, were not aware that it could have any other significance. After the war opened, its larger meaning suddenly dawned upon them. The idea of the master running away and the Negroes staying was always to them ludicrous beyond description. The extravagant lines of "Kingdom Coming" exactly depicted their feelings:

Say, darkies, hab you seen de mass'r,
Wid de muffstach on his face,
Go 'long de road some time dis mornin',
Like he's gwine to leave de place?
He seen de smoke way up de ribber
Where de Linkum gunboats lay;
He took his hat and left berry sudden,
And I s'pose he runned away.

De mass'r run, ha! ha!
De darkey stay, ho! ho!
It must be now de kingdom comin',
An' de year ob Jubilo!

"Dey tole us," said a group of blacks, "dat if your army cotched us, you would cut off our right feet. But, Lor! we knowed you wouldn't hurt *us!*"

At a house where we dined, the planter assuming to be loyal, one of our officers grew confidential with him, when a Negro woman managed to beckon me into a back room, and seizing my arm, very earnestly said: "I tell you, mass'r's only just putting on. He hates you all, and wants to see you killed. Soon as you have passed, he will send right to Wise's army, and tell him what you mean to do; if any of you'uns remain here behind the troops, you will be in danger. He's in a heap of trouble," she added, "but Lord, dese times just suits *me!*"

—ALBERT D. RICHARDSON

*

Reward for a Runaway Master

*

ONE OF THE BEAUFORT (South Carolina) Negroes advertises his runaway master in the following clever travesty:

$500 REWARD.—Rund away from me on de 7th ob dis month, my massa Julian Rhett. Massa Rhett am five feet 'leven inches high, big shoulders, brack har, curly shaggy whiskers, low forehed, an' dark face. He make big fuss when he go 'mong de gemmen, he talk ver big, and use de name ob de Lord all de time. Calls heself "Suddern gemmen," but I s'pose will try now to parse heself off as a brack man or mulatter. Massa Rhett has a deep scar on his shoulder from a fight, scratch 'cross de left eye, made by my Dinah when he tried to whip her. He neber look people in de face. I mor dan spec he will make track for Bergen kounty, in de furrin land ob Jarsey, whar I 'magin he hab a few friends.

I will gib four hundred dollars for him if alive, an' five hundred if anybody will show him dead. If he cum back to his kind niggers widout much truble, dis chile will receive him lubingly.

SAMBO RHETT

BEAUFORT, S.C., November 9, 1861.

—*The Camp Kettle*

January

S	M	T	W	T	F	S
.	.	.	.	1	2	3	4
5	6	7	8	9	10	11
12	13	14	15	16	17	18
19	20	21	22	23	24	25
26	27	28	29	30	31	..
.	.	.	.	.	.	.

February

S	M	T	W	T	F	S
.	.	.	.	.	.	1
2	3	4	5	6	7	8
9	10	11	12	13	14	15
16	17	18	19	20	21	22
23	24	25	26	27	28	..

March

S	M	T	W	T	F	S
.	.	.	.	.	.	1
2	3	4	5	6	7	8
9	10	11	12	13	14	15
16	17	18	19	20	21	22
23	24	25	26	27	28	29
30	31	.	.	.	.	.

TWO

In EIGHTEEN HUNDRED AND SIXTY-TWO
That's the year we put 'em through.
We'll all drink stone blind;
Johnny, come fill up the bowl.

April

S	M	T	W	T	F	S
.	.	1	2	3	4	5
6	7	8	9	10	11	12
13	14	15	16	17	18	19
20	21	22	23	24	25	26
27	28	29	30	.	.	.

May

S	M	T	W	T	F	S
.	.	.	.	1	2	3
4	5	6	7	8	9	10
11	12	13	14	15	16	17
18	19	20	21	22	23	24
25	26	27	28	29	30	31

June

S	M	T	W	T	F	S
1	2	3	4	5	6	7
8	9	10	11	12	13	14
15	16	17	18	19	20	21
22	23	24	25	26	27	28
29	30	.	.	.	.	..

July

S	M	T	W	T	F	S
.	.	1	2	3	4	5
6	7	8	9	10	11	12
13	14	15	16	17	18	19
20	21	22	23	24	25	26
27	28	29	30	31	.	.
.	.	.	.	.	.	.

August

S	M	T	W	T	F	S
.	.	.	.	.	1	2
3	4	5	6	7	8	9
10	11	12	13	14	15	16
17	18	19	20	21	22	23
24	25	26	27	28	29	30
31						

September

S	M	T	W	T	F	S
.	1	2	3	4	5	6
7	8	9	10	11	12	13
14	15	16	17	18	19	20
21	22	23	24	25	26	27
28	29	30	.	.	.	..

October

S	M	T	W	T	F	S
.	.	.	.	1	2	3	4
5	6	7	8	9	10	11
12	13	14	15	16	17	18
19	20	21	22	23	24	25
26	27	28	29	30	31	..
.	.	.	.	.	.	.

November

S	M	T	W	T	F	S
.	.	.	.	.	.	1
2	3	4	5	6	7	8
9	10	11	12	13	14	15
16	17	18	19	20	21	22
23	24	25	26	27	28	29
30						

December

S	M	T	W	T	F	S
.	1	2	3	4	5	6
7	8	9	10	11	12	13
14	15	16	17	18	19	20
21	22	23	24	25	26	27
28	29	30	31	.	.	..

Our Jimmy has gone for to live in a tent,
They have grafted him into the army;
He finally pucker'd up courage and went
When they grafted him into the army.
                              —HENRY C. WORK

5. GONE TO LIVE IN A TENT

The Insanity Dodge

*

YOU ALL KNOW how the boys tried the insanity dodge. Well, there was one fellow in my regiment who played it most successfully. We were at Fort Grebel in February, 1862. Fort Grebel was on the branch of the Potomac, opposite Arlington Heights.

One night there was a very heavy rain, and in the morning, before the other soldiers began to stir about the camp, this fellow—I have forgotten his name—tied a string to his bayonet, took a position on the parapet, began fishing in a shallow pool, and to all appearances became entirely unmindful of his surroundings.

An hour passed. No one interrupted him, and still he could be seen quietly but regularly lifting his gun with the string from the pool, as though the gun were a fishing pole, and that he had a bite. By and by the sun came up, and while the other boys were going about camp preparing for breakfast, the fisherman still kept up his weary stroke, lifting his supposed fishing-tackle from the water almost as regularly as though it were done by a clock.

The surroundings and occasion were such that it was only necessary for a sane man to look once in order to be convinced that something was lacking about the "head-work" of the machine which was fishing in the pool.

The boys all began to talk about the matter, many of them jesting in a manner wholly amusing. But no cessation in the regular stroke of the fisherman. Finally the matter came to the notice of the captain, who at once proceeded to the interesting scene of operations.

"What are you doing there?" he demanded.

No response. The gun and string were lifted with the same regularity as ever.

"Halt!" commanded the captain.

Not a single movement of the fisherman. Up went the pretended fishing-tackle again.

"Shoulder arms!" again commanded the captain, thinking that hearing an accustomed order might bring the soldier to his senses.

But the warrior's countenance was as rigid as ever, and the fixed stare seemed riveted on the string which hung from the point of his bayonet and dropped carelessly down into the small pool before him.

The captain now concluded to report the matter to the colonel, and started off on the errand at once. He suddenly met the colonel who had also beheld the fisherman, and was coming to investigate. The captain then returned to the scene with the colonel, when the same experience was repeated.

The colonel concluded to call the surgeon, who came and examined the fisherman,—as well as possible while the incessant raising and lowering of his gun was being carried on,—and recommended that the insane fisherman be given a discharge, which was accordingly written out and handed to the captain; but before it was given to the soldier, the colonel asked: "What are you fishing for?"

No reply.

"Well, I guess you can give him the document," continued the colonel, and the captain handed it over to the fisherman, saying loudly: "Here! Take this!"

"That's what I was fishing for," replied the fisherman as he threw down his gun, pocketed the discharge, and immediately left camp, much to the amazement of the colonel, the captain and the surgeon, and *very* much to the *amusement* of all others who had heard the conversation.

—COLONEL THOMAS B. VAN BUREN

*

The Colonel Did the Thinking—

and Washing

*

WHILE WE WERE in camp at Washington in February, 1862, we were drilled to an extent which to the raw "thinking soldier" seemed unnecessary. Our colonel was a strict disciplinarian. His efforts to drill out of us the methods of action and thought common to citizens, and to substitute in place thereof blind, unquestioning obedience to military rules, were not always appreciated at their true value. In my company there was an old drill-sergeant (let us call him Sergeant Hackett) who was in sympathetic accord with the colonel. He had occasion to reprove me often, and, finally, to inflict a blast of profanity at which my self-respect rebelled. Knowing that swearing was a breach of discipline, I waited confidently upon the colonel, with the manner of one gentleman calling upon another. After the usual salute, I opened complaint by saying: "Colonel, Mr. Hackett has——"

The colonel interrupted me angrily, and, with fire in his eye, exclaimed: *"Mister?* There *are* no misters in the army."

"I thought, sir——" I began apologetically.

"Think? Think?" he cried. "What right have *you* to think? *I* do the thinking for this regiment! Go to your quarters!"

I did not tarry. There seemed to be no common ground on which he and I could argue questions of personal etiquette. But I should do injustice to his character as a commander if I failed to illustrate another manner of reproof which he sometimes applied.

One day, noticing a corporal in soiled gloves, he said: "Corporal, you set a bad example to the men with your soiled gloves. Why do you?"

"I've had no pay, sir, since entering the service, and can't afford to hire washing."

The colonel drew from his pocket a pair of gloves spotlessly white, and, handing them to the corporal, said: "Put on those; I washed them myself!"

This was an unforgotten lesson to the whole regiment that it was a soldier's duty to attend himself to his personal neatness.

—PRIVATE WARREN LEE GOSS

*

The Bugler

---

*

Camp Griffin, Va.
February 5, 1862

I LIKE CAMP LIFE very well & why shouldnt I it is so muddy that I dont have to drill but very little   I have not been on guard duty for a number of weeks. a great many days we have nothing to do but eat read write play chequers practice on my Bugle & have a good time generally. . . . A little more than 2 weeks since our Col sent to Washington for a new Bugle. the next question was who should play it. one of our tent boys from Brownington happened to be Cols orderly (as he is called) & heard the conversation   he told the Col that he knew a fellow in Co D that had played on the Alt Horn considerable in a Band. the Col said he thought the one mentioned was the one he wanted. I happened to be the chap. I got Lieut Dwinell to intercede for me & I got the Bugle with orders to go to my tent & practice the calls for skirmishing. I practice on it every day. it has been so muddy for several weeks that we have had no drill to amount to much. some afternoons the Regt is taken out on the Parade ground to fire 10 or 15 rounds of blank cartridges or perhaps to fire ball cartridges at target aside from this we have but little drill   I expect to be Regimental Bugler. I dont know how much pay I shall get. some say I shall get more than I now do &

some say I get the same. Lieut Dwinell thinks I shall get $27.00 per month if so well & good. if I get no more I shall get clear of all guard duty both Picket & Home which is the most tedious duty that we have to perform. I shall also be exempt from all drill. When the mud drys up which is very deep we shall drill in skirmishing & then I shall find out how much pay a Bugler gets. at all events it is considered quite an honor to be Bugler for a regt. When an army is advancing through an enemies country it is frequently necessary to send out a portion or a whole Reg to search the woods a little in advance of the main army so as not to meet with a sudden surprise from the enemy. in skirmishing the Capts & Lieut stand several paces behind their Cos the Col stands or rather sits on his horse on an eminence where he has a fair view of the men perhaps 50 or 100 rods behind them. the Bugler stands near him he gives orders to the Bugler & the Bugler sounds the call used to represent the command. the Capts have to be familiar enough with the calls so they can tell one from an other. they give the command to their Cos. some of the calls are short & some are quite tunes I have learned to play nearly all of them.

—CORPORAL DAN OWEN MASON

*

Passover in Camp

*

IN 1862, J. A. Joel and twenty of his Jewish comrades in the 23rd Ohio Volunteer Regiment found themselves in winter headquarters at Fayette, West Virginia, with Passover near at hand. After talking the matter over among themselves, they presented a request to their commanding officer for permission to absent themselves from duty for several days in order to observe the holiday. Their request granted, they set about organizing a *Seder* (Passover ritual dinner). The camp sutler, a Jew who was going back home to celebrate the festival with his family in Cincinnati, readily agreed to send some *Matzot*[h] to them as soon as he reached his destination. The day before Passover, therefore, a supply train unloaded seven barrels of *Matzot*[h] at the camp. Although they had not thought of asking for Passover prayer-books, the sutler had sent some of those along, too.

We were now able to keep the Seder *nights [wrote Joel in his lively narrative of the experience] if we could only obtain the other requisites for that occasion. We held a consultation and decided to send parties to forage in the country while a party stayed to build a log hut for the services. About the middle of the afternoon the foragers arrived, having been quite successful. We obtained two kegs of cider, a lamb, several chickens and some eggs. Horseradish or parsley we could not obtain, but in lieu we found a weed, whose bitterness, I apprehend, exceeded anything our forefathers "enjoyed." We were still in a great quandary; we were like the men who drew the elephant lottery. We had the lamb, but did not know what part was to represent it at the table; but Yankee ingenuity prevailed, and it was decided to cook the whole and put it on the table, then we could dine off it, and be sure we had the right part. The necessaries for the* choroutzes [charoses] *we could not obtain, so we got a brick which, rather hard to digest, reminded us, by looking at it, for what purpose it was intended.*

So the makeshift *Seder* was prepared, with the assistance of "Yankee ingenuity"! Substitutes and symbols-upon-symbols were contrived to fulfill the elaborate Passover prescriptions. It was as though the Passover tradition were being recast in a new mould. Cider served as the symbol of rejoicing, instead of wine; a whole lamb replaced a lamb-bone as the representation of the Paschal sacrifice; the agony of the servitude in Egypt was recalled by bitter weeds instead of the usual horseradish; in lieu of the delicious *haroset* [*charoses*] (an edible "mortar" concocted of chopped apple, nuts, and wine) a brick symbolized the brick-building of the Hebrew in Egypt. *Matzot*[h], eggs, and chicken were the only conventional items. But still it was a *Seder,* and the very originality of the religious symbols was an index to the devotion and piety with which these soldiers, far away from home, were determined to commemorate the exodus from Egypt.

Joel himself took the role of the leader of the service, and chanted the blessings ordained by centuries-old practice. It must have been quite a sight: these twenty men gathered together in a crude and hastily built log hut, their weapons at their side, prepared as in Egypt-land for all manner of danger, singing the words of praise and faith in the ancient language of Israel.

Everything was solemn and decorous (Passover dinners always are at the outset, until the wine stimulates some fun). But let Mr. Joel continue with his version of an unexpected development:

The ceremonies were passing off very nicely, until we arrived at the part where the bitter herb was to be taken. We all had a large portion of the herb ready to eat at the moment I said the blessing; each [ate] his portion, when horrors! what a scene ensued in our little congregation, it is impossible for my pen to describe. The herb was very bitter and very fiery like Cayenne pepper, and excited our thirst to such a degree, that we forgot the law authorizing us to drink only four cups, and the consequence was we drank up all the cider. Those that drank the more freely became excited and one thought he was Moses, another Aaron, and one had the audacity to call himself a Pharaoh. The consequence was a skirmish, with nobody hurt, only Moses, Aaron, and Pharaoh had to be carried to the camp, and there left in the arms of Morpheus.

After this debacle, the survivors nonchalantly continued with the prayers, then partook of their dinner, and completed the service with the traditional blessings and hymns.

There [wrote Joel] in the wild woods of West Virginia, away from home and friends, we consecrated and offered up to the ever-loving God of Israel our prayers and sacrifice . . . there is no occasion in my life that gives me more pleasure and satisfaction than when I remember the celebration of Passover of 1862.

—BERTRAM WALLACE KORN

*

Forfeits

---

*

Santa Rosa Island, Fla., April 17, 1862

WE HAVE A CUSTOM in camp here which will amuse you. It is intended as a sort of joke on our privations here. If one accidentally mentions some luxury which, easily obtainable at home, is inaccessible here, he is instantly tried, convicted, and fined a "muggins," or a "big

muggins," in proportion to the enormity of the offense. A "muggins" is a bottle of whisky, and a "big muggins" is a gallon jug full of the same. For instance one tantalizingly says, "Now how would you like to drop into the Astor House for a superb dinner and a glass of iced champagne?" or "How would you like to 'drop around' this lovely moonlight night and spend the evening with 'her'?" or "How would you like a lodge in some vast widow's nest?" I was fined day before yesterday for looking down by my side as I started to rise from the table and saying in my most feminine tones, *"Won't you please to get off from my frock?"*
—BREVET BRIGADIER GENERAL WILLOUGHBY BABCOCK

*

One of Our Camp Songs:
"The Girls at Home"

---

*

Camp in field 2 miles above Falmouth, Va.
May 7, 1862

THIS IS ONE of our Camp songs I have not the music to send you I like the sentiment very much

> *When the daylight fades on the tented field*
> *And the camp fire cheerfully burns*
> *Then the soldiers thoughts like a carrier dove*
> *To his own loved home returns*
> *Like a carrier dove a carrier dove*
> *And gleams beyond the foam*
> *So a light springs up in the soldiers heart*
> *As he thinks of the girls at home*
>
> *When the shadows dance on the canvass walls*
> *And the camp with melody rings*
> *Tis the good old song of the stripes & stars*
> *That the fireside circle sings*

Of the stripes & stars the stripes & stars
  For love of which we roam
But the final song & the sweeetest one
  Is the song of the girls at home

Now the silver rays of the setting Sun
  Through the lofty sycamores creep
And the fires burn low and the Sentries watch
  Or [O'er] the armed Host asleep
The Sentries watch the Sentries watch
  Till morning gilds the dome
And the rattling drums shall the sleepers rouse
  From their dreams of the girls at home
                                    —CORPORAL DAN OWEN MASON

*

"The Boys Had Home-Sickness Bad"

---

*

DURING THE OPERATIONS against Corinth [Mississippi], the 61st [Illinois Infantry] made some short marches, and was shifted around, from time to time, to different places. About the middle of May [1862] we were sent to a point on Owl Creek, in the right rear of the main army. Our duty there was to guard against any possible attack from that direction, and our main employment was throwing up breastworks and standing picket. And all this time the sick list was frightfully large. The chief trouble was our old enemy, camp diarrhea, but there were also other types of diseases—malaria and the like. As before stated, the boys had not learned how to cook, nor to take proper care of themselves, and to this ignorance can be attributed much of the sickness. And the weather was rainy, the camps were muddy and gloomy, and about this time many of the boys had home-sickness bad. A genuine case of downright home-sickness is most depressing. I had some touches of it myself, so I can speak from experience. The poor fellows would sit around in their tents, and whine, and talk about home, and what good things they would have there to eat, and kindred subjects, until apparently they lost every spark of energy. I kept away from such cases all I could, for their talk was demoralizing.

But one rainy day while in camp at Owl Creek I was in our big Sibley tent when some of the boys got well started on their pet topics. It was a dismal day, the rain was pattering down on the tent and dripping from the leaves of the big oak trees in the camp, while inside the tent everything was damp and mouldy and didn't smell good either. "Jim," says one, "I wish I could jest be down on Coon crick today, and take dinner with old Bill Williams; I'll tell you what I'd have: first, a great big slice of fried ham, with plenty of rich brown gravy, with them light, fluffy hot biscuits that Bill's wife could cook so well, and then I'd want some big baked Irish 'taters, red hot, and all mealy, and then—" "Yes, Jack," interrupted Jim, "I've et at old Bill's lots of times, and wouldn't I like to be with you? You know, old Bill always mast-fed the hogs he put up for his own eatin', they jest fattened on hickory nuts and big white- and bur-oak acorns, and he'd smoke his meat with hickory wood smoke, and oh, that meat was jest so sweet and nutty-like! —why, the meat of corn-fed hogs was nowhere in comparison." "Yes, Jim," continued Jack, "and then I'd want with the biscuits and 'taters plenty of that rich yaller butter that Bill's wife made herself, with her own hands, and then you know Bill always had lots of honey, and I'd spread honey and butter on one of them biscuits, and—" "And don't you remember, Jack," chimed in Jim, "the mince pies Bill's wife would make? They were jest stuffed with reezons, and all manner of goodies, and—"

But here I left the tent in disgust. I wanted to say, "Oh, hell!" as I went out, but refrained. The poor fellows were feeling bad enough, anyhow, and it wouldn't have helped matters to make sarcastic remarks. But I preferred the shelter of a big tree, and enduring the rain that filtered through the leaves, rather than listen to this distracting talk of Jack and Jim about the flesh-pots of old Bill Williams.

—LEANDER STILLWELL

＊

"Fool Lieutenant"

＊

Camp Parapet, above Carrollton, La.
May 23, 1862

NOT THAT OUR MEN are mutinous or disorderly; on the contrary they are as obedient and quiet as sheep. But they don't touch their caps when they meet an officer; they don't salute promptly and stylishly when on guard; in short, they are deficient in soldierly etiquette. For such sins as these the brigadier comes down upon offenders in a style which scares them half out of their wits. Two days ago he fell afoul of a gawky lieutenant who was lately promoted from a sergeantcy. The lieutenant, dressed in trousers and a red shirt, and barefoot, was seated on the head of a barrel, eating an apple and gossiping with a sentry. The general, who was taking a stroll, halted in front of him and glared at him. The lieutenant, without rising, and still munching his apple, saluted.

"Who are *you?*" snarled the general.

The lieutenant gave his name, title, company and regiment.

"What business had you talking to a guard? What are you dressed in that style for? Don't you know any better?"

The lieutenant dismounted from his barrel and tremulously entered upon a defence of his costume and behavior.

The general interrupted him: "What's your business at home?"

"General, I was a carpenter."

"I should think as much! You'd better go home and get to carpentering again. You may be a good carpenter, but you're a damn poor officer. Be off now, and don't let me catch you talking to a guard again, except when it's your duty to give him instructions."

And with an expression of disgusted despair the general stalked away to blow up a sentry whom he found sitting down on post. "I wouldn't have been so mad with that fool lieutenant," he afterwards explained, "if he hadn't saluted me with his apple core."

—CAPTAIN JOHN WILLIAM DE FOREST

71

*

Two Kinds of "Damned Fool"

*

SHORTLY AFTER the call for three hundred thousand volunteers in the summer of 1862, a whole division of troops, principally New Yorkers, were encamped about Baltimore. They were all fresh, as yet, soldiers in embryo, training for the work; and having seen only the sunny side of soldiering, were prepossessed toward the life. Just at this time a very injudicious order was put forth by the War Department, looking to the recruitment of the regular army to the full standard. It permitted the volunteers, to the number of ten in a single company, to enlist in the regulars, and held out new inducements in the way of bounty for them to do so. Of course such an order could not fail to excite strong feelings among both officers and men, many of the latter feeling inclined to take the benefit of the order, and the former being naturally indignant and anxious lest their commands should be depleted and general dissatisfaction created. The excitement raged high for a week and then subsided, without serious consequences. Very few of the men enlisted, and the department finally withdrew the offensive order. In my own regiment the opinions of the rank and file were settled against it after the first few days following its promulgation; and I really believe that the argument which influenced them more than all others was the quaint remark of one of the men, who, upon being asked if he intended to enlist in the regulars, replied with emphasis:

"No, sir! I've been a volunteer d——d fool once, and you can't make a regular d——d fool of me now."

The odd joke went through the camp like wildfire, and little more was heard of a desire to leave the regiment for the regulars.

—JAMES FRANKLIN FITTS

72

Louse Race

WE WENT INTO SUMMER quarters at Tupelo [Mississippi]. Our principal occupation at this place was playing poker, chucka-luck and cracking graybacks (lice). Every soldier had a brigade of lice on him, and I have seen fellows so busily engaged in cracking them that it reminded me of an old woman knitting. At first the boys would go off in the woods and hide to louse themselves, but that was unnecessary, the ground fairly crawled with lice. Pharaoh's people, when they were resisting old Moses, never enjoyed the curse of lice more than we did. The boys would frequently have a louse race. There was one fellow who was winning all the money; his lice would run quicker and crawl faster than anybody's lice. We could not understand it. If some fellow happened to catch a fierce-looking louse, he would call on Dornin for a race. Dornin would come and always win the stake. The lice were placed in plates—this was the race course—and the first that crawled off was the winner. At last we found out D.'s trick; he always heated his plate.

—SAM R. WATKINS

The Joint-Stock Frying-Pan Company

Cedar Mt., Va., Saturday, August 9, 1862

THE LAST PLACE to look for a stock company would be among a regiment of soldiers. After being deprived of camp kettles, mess pans, etc., each man was obliged to do his own cooking . . . in his tin dipper, which held about a pint. Whether it was coffee, beans, pork, or anything depending on the services of a fire to make it palatable, it was accomplished by aid of the dipper only. Therefore any utensil like a frying-pan was of incalculable service in preparing a meal. There were so few of these in the regiment, that only men of large means, men who could raise a dollar thirty days after a paymaster's visit, could afford such a luxury. In one instance the difficulty was overcome by the formation of a joint-stock company, composed of five stockholders, each paying the sum of twenty cents toward the purchase of a frying-pan, which cost the sum of one dollar. The par value of each share was therefore twenty cents. It was understood that each stockholder should take his turn at carrying the frying-pan when on a march, which responsibility entitled him to its first use in halting for the night. While in camp, it passed from one to the other each day in order of turn. It was frequently loaned for a consideration, thereby affording means for an occasional dividend among the stockholders. The stock advanced in value until it reached as high as forty cents per share, so that a stockholder in the "Joint-Stock Frying-Pan Company" was looked upon as a man of consequence. Being treated with kindness and civility by his comrades, life assumed a roseate hue to the shareholders in this great company, in spite of their deprivations. It was flattering to hear one's self mentioned in terms of praise by some impecunious comrade who wished to occupy one side of it while you were cooking. On this particular morning, when we started out, expecting shortly to be in a fight, the stock went rapidly down, until it could be bought for almost nothing. As the day progressed, however, there was a slight rise, though the market was not strong. When the order was given to leave knapsacks, it necessarily included this utensil, and so the "Joint-Stock Frying-Pan Company" was wiped out.

—CHARLES E. DAVIS, JR.

*

Colonel Coulter Orders a Baptizing

*

SATURDAY [September 20, 1862] our regiment crossed the battle-field and went into camp near Sharpsburg, there rejoining the brigade, which was now commanded by Colonel [Richard] Coulter of the 11th Pennsylvania; General [George L.] Hartsuff, its former commander, had been severely wounded in the battle. Coulter was a big, quick man, vigorous, impatient, and often violent in speech and action. We felt an immediate liking for him.

We changed camp several times, finally settling down near the river and about three miles west of the town. An incident occurring there gave rise to a story that grew to fabulous proportions, multiplying converts to Christianity and the Baptist persuasion, until it bore to our Northern homes the glad tidings that entire regiments had enlisted in the army of the Lord. The way it began was this. Our chaplain, the Reverend George Bullen, baptized in the chill autumnal waters of the Potomac two men of our regiment, who had confessed their faith before they had left home. A few days later, Chaplain Bullen paid his respects to Colonel Coulter at brigade headquarters; and, declining as superfluous the customary social appetizer of old Bourbon, he told the Colonel all about the baptisms. He dwelt upon the probable good effects, both godly and military; the men, he felt sure, would be the more amenable to orders and discipline; he had not omitted, he said, to remind them that they should render unto Caesar. Now it happened that Colonel Coulter, though commanding the brigade, was jealously attentive to the growing reputation of his regiment. He interrupted suddenly: "How many men did you say you dipped, Chaplain?"

"I baptized two, Colonel."

"Orderly!" The Colonel's tone was peremptory. "Tell my adjutant to detail a sergeant to take a man from each company down to the river and baptize them in the Methodist persuasion. I can't allow any damned Baptist to supplant my authority, either spiritual or temporal."

—MAJOR ABNER R. SMALL

*

Comrades in Controversy

---

*

JEREMIAH B. JONES and William R. Mitchell were two comrades belonging to Company G, of the Eighth [Pennsylvania R.V.C.], who were over six feet in height each. They were both naturally waggish and witty and overflowing with good humor. "Jerry" was long and rather thin of build, while "Bill" was both long and broad. As a number of us were lounging about the camp-fire one evening [in the fall of 1862, between Antietam and Fredericksburg], Bill said, "Jerry, where was you raised?"

Jerry answered, "Up in the mountains near the Virginia line."

"Oh, yes," said Bill, "I have heard of the place; the whole township stands on edge and the boulders stick out the side like warts on a toad's back."

"Where was you raised, Bill?" asked Jerry.

"On Barren Run, near West Newton," replied Bill.

"Oh, yes," says Jerry, "the killdeers go running over that district with a knapsack on their backs containing eight days' rations and tears of grief and despair falling from their eyes."

"I hear," said Bill, "that stock raisers in your township have to tie the sheep together by the tails and hang them over the rocks to pick the grass out of the crevices."

"There is no stock on Barren Run," replied Jerry, "as they can't raise fodder enough there to feed a sick grasshopper through the winter."

"The farmers of your township," said Bill, "have to shoot the wheat under the stones with shot-guns."

"Well," replied Jerry, "the farmers of Barren Run have to mow with a razor and rake with a fine-tooth comb."

"It would no doubt be a healthy place to live in the mountains," said Bill, "if so many of your people were not injured in scraping their shins and killed by breaking their necks falling over the rocks."

"Barren Run would also be a healthy place if so many of your people did not die of starvation while searching the barren fields with microscopes and field-glasses to find dock and dandelion enough to make a mess of greens."

"In your township," said Bill, "they always take dynamite along with the funerals to blast a hole big enough to hide the corpse in."

"And in Barren Run all funerals are accompanied by a cart load of manure to throw in the grave to rot the corpse," answered Jerry.

The controversy now ended amid the laughter of the hearers, with the honors about equal and the principals retired to their tents. The genial Mitchell bravely and nobly met his death on the bloody battle-field at Fredericksburg, and the cheerful Jones perished in the prison hell at Salisbury. Peace to their ashes.

—GEORGE W. DARBY

*

Cato, the Slave-Comedian

*

Camp Saxton, near Beaufort, S. C.
November 27, 1862

STROLLING in the cool moonlight, I was attracted by a brilliant light beneath the trees, and cautiously approached it. A circle of thirty or forty soldiers sat around a roaring fire, while one old uncle, Cato by name, was narrating an interminable tale, to the insatiable delight of his audience. I came up into the dusky background, perceived only by a few, and he still continued. It was a narrative, dramatized to the last degree, of his adventures in escaping from his master to the Union vessels; and even I, who have heard the stories of Harriet Tubman, and such wonderful slave-comedians, never witnessed such a piece of acting. When I came upon the scene he had just come unexpectedly upon a plantation-house, and, putting a bold face upon it, had walked up to the door.

"Den I go up to de white man, berry humble, and say, would he please gib ole man a mouthful for eat?

"He say he must hab de valeration ob half a dollar.

"Den I look berry sorry, and turn for go away.

"Den he say I might gib him dat hatchet I had.

"Den I say" (this in a tragic vein) "dat I must hab dat hatchet for defend myself *from de dogs!*"

[Immense applause, and one appreciating auditor says, chuckling, "Dat was your *arms*, ole man" which brings down the house again.]

"Den he say de Yankee pickets was near by, and I must be very keerful.

"Den I say, 'Good Lord, Mas'r, am dey?' "

Words cannot express the complete dissimulation with which these accents of terror were uttered,—this being precisely the piece of information he wished to obtain.

Then he narrated his devices to get into the house at night and obtain some food,—how a dog flew at him,—how the whole household, black and white, rose in pursuit,—how he scrambled under a hedge and over a high fence, etc.,—all in a style of which Gough alone among orators can give the faintest impression, so thoroughly dramatized was every syllable.

Then he described his reaching the river-side at last, and trying to decide whether certain vessels held friends or foes.

"Den I see guns on board and sure sartin he Union boat, and I pop my head up. Den I been-a-tink [think] Seceshkey hab guns too, and my head go down again. Den I hide in de bush till morning. Den I open my bundle, and take ole white shirt and tie him on ole pole and wave him, and ebry time de wind blow, I been-a-tremble, and drap down in de bushes,"—because, being between two fires he doubted whether friend or foe would see his signal first. And so on, with a succession of tricks beyond Molière, of acts of caution, foresight, patient cunning, which were listened to with infinite gusto and perfect comprehension by every listener.

And all this to a bivouac of Negro soldiers, with the brilliant fire lighting up their red trousers and gleaming from their shining black faces,—eyes and teeth all white with tumultuous glee. Overhead, the mighty limbs of a great live-oak, with the weird moss swaying in the smoke, and the high moon gleaming faintly through.

Yet to-morrow strangers will remark on the hopeless, impenetrable stupidity in the daylight faces of many of these very men, the solid mask under which Nature has concealed all this wealth of mother-wit.

—COLONEL THOMAS WENTWORTH HIGGINSON

*

The Revival at Fredericksburg

*

THE REVIVAL at Fredericksburg in the winter of '62-'63 concerned especially the infantry brigade with which I was longest and most closely associated. . . . [It] was probably the most marked religious movement in our war and, as I believe, rarely paralleled anywhere or at any time. . . . A great, broad-shouldered, double-jointed son of Anak, with a head like the Farnese Jove and a face and frame indicative of tremendous power, alike of character and of muscle, delivered himself of his "experience" in one of the most graphic and moving talks I ever listened to. He said in substance. . . .

"Brethren, I want you to know what a merciful, forgiving being the Lord is, and to do that I've got to tell you what a mean-spirited liar I am. You remember that tight place the brigade got into, down yonder at——, and you know the life I lived up to that day. Well, as soon as ever the Minies began a-singing and the shell a-bursting around me, I up and told the Lord that I was sorry and ashamed of myself, and if He'd cover my head this time we'd settle the thing as soon as I got out. Then I got to fighting and forgot all about it, and never thought of my promise no more at all till we got into that other place, up yonder at——; you remember it, tighter than the first one. Then, when the bullets begun a-hissing like rain and the shell was fairly tearing the woods to pieces, my broken promise come back to me. Brethren, my coward heart stopped beating and I pretty nigh fainted. I tried to pray and at first I couldn't; but I just said, 'Look here, Lord, if You will look, I feel I have lied to You and that You won't believe me again, and may be You oughtn't to; but I don't want to go to hell, and I'm serious and honest this time, and if You do hear me now, we'll meet just as soon as I get out safe, and we certainly will settle things.'

"Well, brethren, He did all I asked of Him, the Lord did; and what did I do? Brethren, I'm ashamed to say it, but I lied again, and never thought one thing about it at all till one day we was shoved into the very worst place any of us ever was in. Hell gaped for me, and here come the two lies I had told and sat right down upon my heart and my tongue. Of course I couldn't pray, but at last I managed to say, 'Lord! Lord! I deserve it all if I do go there, right now, and I can't pray and I won't lie any more. You can do as You please, Lord; but if You do——. But, no, I won't lie any more, and I won't promise, for fear I should lie. It's all in your hands, Lord—hell or mercy. I've got no time to talk any more about it. I've got to go to killing Yankees. But, O Lord! O Lord!—no, I daresn't, I daresn't; for I won't lie any more; I won't go down there with a fresh lie on my lips; but, O Lord! O Lord!'

"And so it was, brethren, all through that dreadful day; fighting, fighting, and not daring to pray.

"But brethren, He did it, He did it; and the moment the thing was over I wouldn't give myself time to lie again, so I just took out and ran

as hard as ever I could into the deep, dark woods, where God and me
was alone together, and I threw my musket down on the ground and
I went right down myself, too, on my knees, and cried out, 'Thank
You, Lord; thank You, Lord! but I'm not going to get up off my knees
until everything's settled between us'; and neither I didn't, brethren.
The Lord never held it over me at all, and we settled it right there."

—Major Robert Stiles

I thought a boy who shot me had a familiar face,
But in the battle's fury, 'twas difficult to trace. . . .
Oh, I quickly ran unto him and heard his story o'er;
It was my long lost brother who lay weltering in his gore.
　　　　　　　—"THE BATTLE OF ANTIETAM CREEK"

6. BROTHERS' WAR

McClellan Protects a Landmark

*

THE WHITE HOUSE on the Pamunkey River, formerly the property and home of George Washington . . . had come into the possession of General Lee when he married Miss Custis. Since the war it had been designated by General Lee as his family seat. [Mrs. Lee was here with her daughter-in-law, Charlotte Wickham Lee, when Johnston fell back toward Richmond before the advance of McClellan early in May, 1862]. When Mrs. Lee departed from the house [on the eleventh] on the approach of the Federal army, she left a note on a table which read: "Northern soldiers who profess to reverence Washington, forbear to desecrate the home of his first married life, the property of his wife, now owned by her descendants." It happened that almost the first officer who entered the house was a cousin of the Lee family, who had continued to serve in the United States Army, and commanded a regiment of cavalry. General McClellan strictly complied with the request of the owners of the house, and not only forbade any of his troops to enter the premises, but even abstained from doing so himself, preferring to encamp in the adjoining field. Upon the wall of the room where Mrs. Lee's note had been found, one of the guard wrote an answer: "A Northern officer has protected your property, in sight of the enemy, and at the request of your [overseer]."

—EDWARD A. POLLARD

*

Flowers for the Yankees

*

WHEN THE YANKEE ARMY came up [to "Powhite," Hanover County, Virginia] from the White House, we were in a great state of excitement. The morning after they came up, the officer of the day came to the house and put a guard of thirty men around it for precaution. It was not safe for Father to ride about. The officers were very considerate and very nice to us. The schoolhouse was taken for the surgeons, they stayed there. The carriage house was taken for the Yankee hospital and the sick and wounded were carried there.

* * * * *

We had beautiful roses, and the Yankees were perfectly devoted to flowers and when we would throw the old, withered ones out into the yard, the guards that were around the house would go and pick them up and carry them to camp. One morning General [Philip] Kearny rode up and asked Mother if she would sell him some of the roses. Mother told him "No," she wouldn't sell them to him, but that he could go into the garden and cut as many as he wanted. He said he wanted to send them home to his wife. After that, Mother told Uncle Anthony, the man who worked the flower garden, that he might have the flowers if he chose to take them to camp and sell them and he could have the money for them. So every morning Uncle Anthony would get a great big waiter and go into the garden and cut all the flowers and make them up into bouquets—you may know what they looked like—and carry them to camp and sell them to the soldiers, and they would be perfectly delighted to get them.

—FANNIE GAINES TINSLEY

*

Two Brave Fellows

*

"I HAD A Sergeant Driscoll, a brave man, and one of the best shots in the Brigade. When charging at Malvern Hill [July 1, 1862], a company was posted in a clump of trees, who kept up a fierce fire on us, and actually charged out on our advance. Their officer seemed to be a daring, reckless boy, and I said to Driscoll, 'If that officer is not taken down, many of us will fall before we pass that clump.'

" 'Leave that to me,' said Driscoll; so he raised his rifle, and the moment the officer exposed himself again bang went Driscoll, and over went the officer, his company at once breaking away.

"As we passed the place I said, 'Driscoll, see if that officer is dead—he was a brave fellow.'

"I stood looking on. Driscoll turned him over on his back. He opened his eyes for a moment, and faintly murmured 'Father,' and closed them forever.

"I will forever recollect the frantic grief of Driscoll; it was harrowing to witness. He was his son, who had gone South before the war."

"And what became of Driscoll afterwards?"

"Well, we were ordered to charge, and I left him there; but, as we were closing in on the enemy, he rushed up, with his coat off, and, clutching his musket, charged right up at the enemy, calling on the men to follow. He soon fell, but jumped up again. We knew he was wounded. On he dashed, but he soon rolled over like a top. When we came up he was dead, riddled with bullets."

—CAPTAIN D. P. CONYNGHAM

*

Flirtations in Warrenton

*

AFTER THE CONFEDERATES retired from Manassas Junction [during the second battle there, August 29-30, 1862] the vicinity of Warrenton was a sort of neutral ground. At one time the Southern cavalry would ride through the main street, and the next day a body of mounted Federals would pounce upon the town, the inhabitants, meanwhile, being apprehensive of a sabre combat in the heart of the place. . . .

There was some female society in Warrenton, but the blue-coats engrossed it all. The young women were ardent partisans, but also very pretty; and treason somehow heightened their beauty. Disloyalty is always pardonable in a woman, and these ladies appreciated the fact. They refused to walk under Federal flags, and stopped their ears when the bands played national music; but every evening they walked through the main street, arm-in-arm with dashing lieutenants and captains. Many flirtations ensued, and a great deal of gossip was elicited. In the end, some of the misses fell out among themselves, and hated each other more than the common enemy. I overheard a young lady talking in a low tone one evening to a captain in the Ninth New York regiment.

"If you knew my brother," she said, "I am sure you would not fire upon *him*."

—GEORGE ALFRED TOWNSEND

How Colonel Wilder Sought
General Buckner's Advice on Surrender

*

WHEN [GENERAL BRAXTON] BRAGG invaded Kentucky in 1862, [Brigadier General James R.] Chalmers [on September 14], commanding the advance, attacked [but was repulsed by] a Federal force strongly intrenched on the hills on the south side of Green River at Munfordville, where the Louisville and Nashville Railway and the turnpike both cross that river. Bragg was greatly incensed at this repulse, and ordered a large force to march at once and take the position by assault. General [Simon Bolivar] Buckner advised against this as a needless sacrifice of life, stating that he had an intimate knowledge of the surroundings, having hunted over the ground when a boy, and that a force could cross at another ferry, and by placing artillery on hills on the north side of the river could command the works in a manner to force a surrender. His advice was taken, plans were put into execution, and order given to open fire on the following morning at daylight.

About midnight Colonel (afterward General) John T. Wilder, commanding the Union forces, came under a flag of truce to General Buckner's bivouac in front of Wilder's position, and the following conversation, unique in the history of war, took place. Colonel Wilder informed General Buckner that, as he was a volunteer officer, he didn't know much about the usages, regulations, and proprieties of war; and knowing General Buckner to be an educated soldier, an old army officer who understood such matters, and esteeming him as a high-minded gentleman who would deal honestly and frankly with him, he had come to ask his advice. "Now," said he, "I know that I have a strong position, and can put up a good fight. I want to do my whole duty to my country, but I don't want to sacrifice my men unless there is a chance of making a successful resistance. Those men back there are my neighbors and friends, and I don't want to do anything that will bring disgrace upon them. You know what is right and proper under such conditions. You know my force and the strength of my position, and you know what force you have to bring against it. Now, I ask you, as a soldier and a gentleman, to tell me whether you think, under the circumstances, I should surrender or fight." His voice trembled with emotion when he spoke of his men being his neighbors and friends.

General Buckner, realizing the helplessness of Colonel Wilder's situation, was deeply impressed by his earnestness, his sincerity, and his patriotic spirit, and especially by the confidence Wilder had reposed in him; and he felt that he must treat him with perfect frankness and fairness. He told him that he could not advise him as to whether he should surrender or fight, but would give him accurate information respecting his force and its disposition, and that he must then decide for himself. He told him that he had a force amply sufficient to take the place by assault, but gave him to understand that it was not at present his intention to assault the works. He told the position and number of guns on the north of the river, with orders to open fire at daylight, and that he was satisfied these guns would render his position untenable; that, as an evidence of his good faith, he would send Colonel Wilder with a staff officer to visit the batteries.

After some further conversation, Colonel Wilder said that he accepted General Buckner's statement without visiting the batteries; but he yet hesitated, and was evidently suffering from conflicting emotions, whereupon General Buckner said: "Colonel Wilder, I think it but right to say to you that if you have any information that would induce you to believe that a prolonged resistance would materially aid the movements of the Federal forces elsewhere, I think it is your duty to hold your position as long as possible, even if necessary, to the sacrifice of your command." Colonel Wilder finally said that he had no such information, and that he would surrender his command early the following morning. A staff officer then presented to Colonel Wilder, as his vindication for surrendering, a map on which was shown the position of the guns commanding his position.

Early the next morning General Buckner visited Colonel Wilder's camp, and the arrangements for the surrender were completed. The Union forces, about four thousand strong, marched out and grounded arms, as we used to see in the pictures of the Cornwallis surrender in the old-time school histories. Colonel Wilder handed his sword to General Buckner, who returned it with a complimentary speech. Colonel Wilder served with distinction through the war.

—JOHN R. PROCTER

*

Henry Kyd Douglas Drops in on His Folks

---

*

September 17, 1862

SEVERAL WEEKS AFTER the battle of Antietam when our headquarters were at Bunker Hill, I went to Shepherdstown [West Virginia], to hear something, if possible, from home. My father lived on the Maryland side of the Potomac, on the crest of a hill, which overlooked the river, the town, and the country beyond. The Potomac was the dividing line between the two states and the two armies, and the bridge that once spanned it there had been burned early in the war.

It was a bright and quiet day, and from the Virginia cliffs I saw the enemy's pickets lying lazily along the canal towpath or wandering over the fields. Up against the hill I saw rifle-pits in a field in front of my home, and blue-coats evidently in possession of it; and then I saw my father come out of the house and walk off toward the barn. I saw no one else except soldiers. It was not a cheerful sight, and I turned away and down to the river to water my horse. As I rode into the stream several cavalrymen rode in on the other side; they saluted me by lifting their hats and I returned their salute. They invited me, laughingly, to come over, and I, being intensely anxious to hear something from home, replied that I would meet them in the middle of the river. They at once drew out of the water and dismounted, and so did I and the courier who was with me. Half a dozen of them got into the ferry-boat, which was on their side, and we embarked in a leaky skiff, my courier using a paddle which he found at hand. We met the enemy's man-of-war in the middle of the stream and grappled it, while it was held in place with poles by its boatmen. After the first greetings the captain of the gun-boat (he was only a sergeant, by the way) said to me: "I see you are a staff officer." My blunt courier broke in gruffly: "Yes, and don't you think it devilish hard for a man to be this near home and not be able to speak to his father or mother?"

This exposure of my identity was the very thing I did not wish.

87

The sergeant looked a little astonished and replied: "So you are Captain Douglas, of General Jackson's staff, are you? We knew that the old gentleman on the hill has two sons in the Confederate army, one on the General's staff." When I acknowledged his correctness, he said, with much earnestness, that I must get into their boat and go over to see my family. I began to protest that it would not do, when one of the others broke in: "Say, get in, Captain; get in. If this Government can be *busted* up by a rebel soldier going to see his mother, why, damn it, let it *bust!*"

There was a laughing chorus of assent to this that shook my doubts. I told my blue-coated friends that there was no officer among them, and that any officer who caught me on the other side might not recognize their safeguard and I might be detained. The sergeant replied that all their officers were in Sharpsburg at a dinner, and, at any rate, this party would pledge themselves to return me safely. It was an occasion for some risk and I took it. I got into the large boat and my courier came along in his skiff "to see fair play," as he grimly said.

When we reached the Maryland shore, the soldiers on the bank crowded down to the boats, and soon, Yankee-like, were in a full tide of questions, especially about Stonewall Jackson. As I had declined to leave our ships for the purpose of going up to my home, a cavalryman had gone to the house, under spur, to notify my family of my arrival. My mother soon made her appearance, very much frightened, for she believed I could only be there as a prisoner. My father, not being allowed to leave his premises without permission, could not come. As my mother approached, the soldiers, at a signal from the sergeant, drew away and sat down on the towpath, where they and my courier interviewed each other.

As this strange meeting gave my mother more anxiety than comfort, it was a brief one. Nothing passed between us, however, that could "Bust the Government" or bring trouble on the sergeant and his men. When my mother left and took her stand upon the canal bank to see us safely off, the soldiers gathered about me to have a little talk, but I did not tarry. I gave the sergeant and his crew of the man-of-war my autograph upon sundry slips of paper, and told them that if the fortune of war should make them prisoners, the little papers might be of service to them if sent to General Jackson's headquarters.

As we took our leave and got into our skiff, the chivalric, manly sergeant said to me: "We belong to"—I think—"the 1st New York Cavalry. My parents live on the banks of the Hudson, and what I have done for you, I'd like some one to do for me if in the same fix. While I'm here I'll keep an eye on your home and people and do what I can for them" (and he did). And as the skiff moved over the water and took me from home again, I raised my hat to my "good friend, the enemy," and they stood along the shore, in response, with uncovered heads; and then I waved it to my father, who stood on the stone wall which crowns the hill and gazed, but made no sign; and then to my mother on the bank, who, seeing me safely off, waved her handkerchief with a tremulous flutter, and then hid her face in it as she turned and hurried away.

I was glad to learn afterwards that no harm came to the sergeant for his rash kindness to me. I have forgotten his name, if he ever told me, but I hope he lived to return safely to his folks on the banks of the Hudson.

It is such touches as this that lighten up the inhumanities of war.

—MAJOR HENRY KYD DOUGLAS

✳

The Bargain

✳

ALL ABOUT the peach orchard [In the field of Prairie Grove, Arkansas, December 7, 1862], around the recaptured battery, behind logs, stumps and trees, the dead and wounded lay in great heaps, and soon agonized cries and piteous appeals arose upon the air from the poor sufferers, as the cold, freezing winds penetrated their wounds with rugged ice daggers. One gigantic Illinois man had his thigh shattered by a Minie bullet clear up into the body. Suffering a thousand deaths, he called to one of Shelby's brigade, and said calmly, though his features were terribly distorted: "For the love of God, friend, kill me and put me beyond such intolerable misery."

"Are you in yearnest?" replied the rough Missourian, "and may I have your overcoat and canteen?"

"Yes, yes—everything," murmured the dying man.

"Well, here goes—shut yer eyes and hold yer breath—'twill be over in a minnit."

The [dying] soldier did as desired; the Missourian placed his musket to [the other's] head and, blowing his life out like a puff of smoke, he coolly took the promised articles and rejoined his command. The canteen was filled with excellent liquor, which gave Corporal Miles and Sergeant Parnell, of Company H, Shelby's regiment, an idea, and soon they returned from the skirmish line loaded with canteens filled with the generous fluid.

—JOHN N. EDWARDS

＊

Brothers Divided

＊

"HI, YANK! is that the Sixth Corps picket-line over there?" inquired a Confederate on the Rappahannock, one day, after we had fallen back from in front of the city [of Fredericksburg] after the battle in December, 1862.

"Yes," answered the boy in blue, grumblingly, for he hadn't forgotten the thrashing yet. "Yes, of course it is; what of it?"

"Why, nothing particular, only I know somebody in it. What regiment is that on picket?"

"The ——st Pennsylvania."

"You don't say so; is Company H on post?"

"Yes, I belong to Company H."

"Well, won't you tell Harry B——, if he is alive, to come down to the edge of the river, his brother wants to see him?"

"Certainly; what regiment?"

"Eighth Alabama."

So Harry went down and through, contrary to orders, to the rebel side of the river and had a talk with his brother. Returning, after a while, to his own side, he went "on post" opposite to him and watched him as closely as if he were some stranger rebel. Truly, queer events grew out of this war.

—*The Soldiers' and Sailors' Half-Dime Tales of the Late Rebellion*

*A Minie ball goes "Zip!" with the same sound as you make
on a fiddle by giving the E string a pick and running your finger
up on it; and the sound of a shell is as if it said: "WHERE ARE
YOU? Where are you? Where are you? Where are you? FOUND
YOU!" That last is when it bursts.*
—AS TOLD BY ELI BILLINGS TO CLIFTON JOHNSON

7. THE BULLETS WHISTLE PRETTY

Nearly Buried Alive

*

THE BATTLE-FIELD of Gaines's Mill [on June 27, 1862] was
rich in spoils for the enemy. Cannon, brass and bronzed field pieces,
caissons, horses, camps, clothing, small-arms, banners, and other insignia of war fell into their hands. The woods and plains were covered
with rebel and Union dead and wounded.

The rebel accounts confess that they stripped our dead and
wounded for the clothing. The [anonymous] writer of the *Battle-fields
of the South* apologizes for it by saying: "I could not blame the poor
fellows for securing clothing of some kind; the greater number of them

were ragged and dirty, and wearing-apparel could not be obtained at any price in Richmond."

The rebel army bivouacked upon the battle-field. Generals, colonels, officers, and men were scattered through the timber, cooking their suppers or sleeping on piles of branches, while ambulances and carriages were busy all night carrying off the wounded. In the darkness, these rolled over the inanimate bodies of some and bumped against the writhing forms of others.

The rebels had removed the dead bodies to clear a space for their camp-fires, and in many cases the living were piled with the dead, or flung with them into a common grave. I heard the following story from a soldier who was shot through the head, and lay for dead:

"Though I was suffering fearfully from my wounds, for one bullet had gone through my shoulder and another passed in through my jaw, coming out through my neck, still I was fully conscious, but could not speak.

"There were plenty of dead around me, both Union and rebel, and one stalwart rebel rolled right across me in his death-agonies. I was powerless to throw him off. Soon the rebel line advanced over us and formed just in front. This revived my spirits, for now, I thought, some humane person will see me. Strange, how strong the desire of life, even in such moments! Darkness soon set in, the men stacked their arms, and commenced to light fires and cook their suppers. In removing the dead bodies out of their way, they piled a number of them on top of us. I thought to cry out; but no, I couldn't, my tongue was swollen and my mouth was full of blood. I heard ambulances moving around, and the sound of spades as they interred their dead. Now, thought I, they will come to bury those around, and will assuredly see me.

"I lay there, I don't know how long, and must have fainted, for the next thing I recollect was, feeling myself being dragged out of an ambulance, and the subject of the following conversation:

" 'By ——, Simon, this fellow has a splendid pair of boots. I guess he won't grudge them to a fellow: he'll be warm enough without them.'

"So off go my boots. Simon then took a fancy to my coat, which was a new one, and fell at tugging it off.

"I was all this time like a man in a nightmare, striving to waken from some fearful danger, but couldn't. The writhing pain, caused by twisting my shattered arm, broke the spell, and I groaned.

" 'By ——l, the fellow is not dead yet; what will we do with him?' exclaimed the ruffian who had taken off my boots.

" 'Well, you see,' said the other rebel, who had finished with my coat, and let me fall back heavily, 'if he ain't dead, he soon will [be]; so shove him in.'

"I turned around, tried to rise up, and held out my good hand towards them.

" 'No, Simon, no; I'm d——d if I bury any poor devil alive; let him have his chance; we'll leave him here.'

" 'Wal, as you choose; it would be only putting him out of pain to cover him in, or give him a crack in the sconce.'

"They soon covered up the pit and left me, forgetting to return the boots or coat.

"I lay there in the most fearful agony under the scorching sun all the following day; towards evening, fortunately, a kind doctor, going over the field, stood to examine my wounds, and then sent me to the hospital. It took me some time to come around, but you see I did; and with the exception of this hollow in my jaw and the loss of some teeth, I am not much the worse for being twice shot and nearly buried alive."

—CAPTAIN D. P. CONYNGHAM

*

Helping a Surgeon to His Senses

*

AT THE BATTLE of Savage's Station [Virginia, June 29, 1862], a corporal named Kelly, known as the "tall corporal," was badly wounded in his leg. I was hit in the arm—not a serious wound but a painful one. The next morning, as I was lying on my blanket under a tree, waiting for transportation to White House Landing, one of the men remarked: "They're going to take off Kelly's leg, sir!" I sprang to my feet, and, with my arm in its sling still giving me excruciating pain, made my way to the field hospital.

Nor was I too soon. Poor Kelly was lying in the line of promotion to the operating table. I found him greatly depressed, and wholly unreconciled to the operation. "There's no call to tack off me lig, Lootinant," said he, "and I'd rather die furst. I'll git well tidy enough af they'll lit me alone. They've nothing but a lot av conthract spalpeens awnyhow, and, be the powers, af oi had me gun they wouldn't do it! Can't ye save me, Lootinant, and may the saints bliss ye?"

I could only say, "I'll try."

I waited until Kelly was near the knife, when I earnestly expostulated with the young surgeon. He looked at me patronizingly, and said, with the politeness of an under-done "medico": "Perhaps you know this business better than I do."

The hot blood leaped in my veins, and with more emphasis than discretion, I replied: "Perhaps I do. I've got a commission for my business, and you haven't got even a diploma for yours. All that man's leg wants is proper probing and dressing, and that is all it will have. He owns the leg and wants to keep it. I am his commanding officer and your superior in rank. Do as I ask, and we will take the responsibility."

For my answer I got a sneer and: "Put him on the table."

Out came my revolver and before I realized the rashness of the proceeding I had said: "You boy-butcher! As his commander and your superior officer I order that you only probe and dress the wound. I've got one arm, as you see, but put a knife to that leg, and I'll send a bullet through your hand."

Of course I was wrong. Of course I had no command over him; but I had put my hand to the plow, and was too foolhardy to turn back. I should have come to disastrous grief if the matter had ever gone to higher authorities, but, luckily, it did not. We looked at each other for perhaps three seconds (it seemed half an hour); and whether from a prick to his diminutive conscience or because he didn't know his rights, I can't say, but he did simply probe and dress the wound.

—Captain Musgrove Davis

*

The Embalmer

---

*

[SUNDAY, JUNE 29, two days after the battle of Gaines's Mill], I set off for White Oak, but repented at Burnt Chimneys, and turned back [to Savage's Station]. In the misty dawn I saw the maimed still lying on the ground, wrapped in relics of blankets, and in one of the outhouses a grim embalmer stood amid a family of nude corpses. He dealt with the bodies of high officers only; for, said he: "I used to be glad to prepare private soldiers. They were wuth a five-dollar bill apiece. But, Lord bless you, a colonel pays a hundred, and a brigadier-general two hundred. There's lots of them now, and I have cut the acquaintance of everything below a major. I might," he added, "as a great favor, do a captain, but he must pay a major's price. I insist upon that! Such windfalls don't come every day. There won't be another such killing for a century."

—GEORGE ALFRED TOWNSEND

∗

"Go It, Molly Cottontail!"

∗

I · *Rebel Refrain*

[AT MALVERN HILL, July 1, 1862] through one of the wide gaps made in the Confederate lines by McClellan's big guns as they sent their death-dealing missiles from hill and river, there ran a panic-stricken rabbit, flying in terror to the rear. A stalwart mountaineer noticed the speed and the direction which the rabbit took to escape from his disagreeable surroundings. He was impressed by the rabbit's prudence, and shouted, so that his voice was heard above the din of the battle: "Go it, Molly Cottontail! I wish I could go with you!"

One of his comrades near by caught up the refrain, and answered: "Yes, and 'y golly, Jim, I'd go with Molly, too, if it wasn't for my character."

—GENERAL JOHN B. GORDON

II · *Vance's Version*

WHILE [ZEBULON] VANCE'S brigade of North Carolinians was lying down in line before the final advance [at Malvern Hill] a rabbit sprang from the bushes and, running along the ground in their front, caused yells and laughter, so light was the spirit of these men facing death. They called out, "Run, run, run!" A staff officer asked if he should shoot it.

Vance said [in recalling the incident], "I shook my head and called out myself: 'Run, little cottontail! I'd run too if I wasn't Governor of North Carolina!' "

—Major General A. W. Greeley

*

A Crack Shot

*

DURING THE BATTLE of the South Mountain [Maryland, September 14, 1862], the rebels held a very strong position. They were posted in the mountain pass, and had infantry on the heights on every side. Our men were compelled to carry the place by storm. The position seemed impregnable; large craggy rocks protected the enemy on every side, while our men were exposed to a galling fire.

A band of rebels occupied a ledge on the extreme right, as the Colonel approached with a few of his men. The unseen force poured upon them a volley. [Colonel Hugh] McNeil, on the instant, gave the command: "Pour your fire upon those rocks!"

The Bucktails hesitated; it was not an order that they had been accustomed to receive; they had always picked their men.

"Fire!" thundered the Colonel; "I tell you to fire at those rocks!"

The men obeyed. For some time an irregular fire was kept up, the Bucktails sheltering themselves, as best they could, behind trees and rocks. On a sudden McNeil caught sight of two rebels peering through an opening in the works to get an aim. The eyes of the men followed their commander, and half a dozen rifles were levelled in that direction.

"Wait a minute," said the Colonel; "I will try my hand. There is nothing like killing two birds with one stone."

The two rebels were not in line, but one stood a little distance back

96

of the other, while just in front of the foremost was a slanting rock. Colonel McNeil seized a rifle, raised it, glanced a moment along the polished barrel; a report followed, and both the rebels disappeared. At that moment a loud cheer a little distance beyond rent the air.

"All is right now," cried the Colonel; "charge the rascals."

The men sprang up among the rocks in an instant. The affrighted rebels turned to run, but encountered another body of the Bucktails, and were obliged to surrender. Not a man of them escaped. Every one saw the object of the Colonel's order to fire at random among the rocks. He had sent the party around to the rear, and meant thus to attract their attention. It was a perfect success.

The two rebels by the opening in the ledge were found lying there stiff and cold. Colonel McNeil's bullet had struck the slanting rock in front of them, glanced, and passed through both their heads. There it lay beside them, flattened. The Colonel picked it up, and put it in his pocket.

—FRANK MOORE, ed.
Anecdotes, Poetry and Incidents of the War:
North and South, 1860-1865

*

Crocker's Errand of Mercy

---

*

THE SENSIBILITIES of Lieutenant Lemuel L. Crocker had been aroused by the necessary abandonment of the dead and wounded, left uncared for and unattended in the precipitate withdrawal [at the battle of Shepherdstown, West Virginia, October 1, 1862]. He entreated Colonel Barnes so earnestly for permission to go and care for the forsaken ones, that the Colonel, fully comprehending the impropriety of the request, at last reluctantly consented to present it to General Fitz-John Porter, the corps commander. It met with a flat, emphatic refusal. There was no communication with the enemy, and it was not proposed to open any. War was war, and this was neither the time nor the occasion for sentiment or sympathy. But Crocker was not to be deterred in his errand of mercy, and, in positive disregard of instructions, proceeded deliberately, fully accoutred with sword, belt and pistol, to cross the river at the breast of the dam. It was a novel spectacle for an officer, armed with all he was entitled to carry, to thus commence a lonesome advance against a whole army corps. Bound upon an unauthorized mission of peace and humanity, a little experience might have taught him his reception would have been more cordial if he had left his weapons at home. Still, it was Crocker's heart at work, and its honest, manly beats bade him face the danger.

He found the bodies of Saunders, Ricketts and Moss, and Private Mishaw badly wounded, but still alive. He was bearing them, one by one, upon his shoulders to the river-bank, when he was suddenly interrupted by an orderly from General Porter, who informed him that he was instructed to direct him to return at once or he would order a battery to shell him out. His reply was: "Shell and be damned!" He didn't propose to return until the full purpose of his undertaking had been accomplished.

The orderly thus abruptly disposed of, he continued his operations, when he was again interrupted by an authority which, if it failed to command respect, could enforce obedience. He had carried all the bodies to the bank, and was returning for the wounded Mishaw, when a Confederate general—whom Crocker always thought was Lee, but in this he was evidently mistaken—accompanied by a numerous staff, came upon the ground. An aide-de-camp rode up, inquiring, with some asperity—explaining that no flag of truce was in operation—as to who and what he was, his purpose in being there, and by whose authority.

Crocker's work, which he had conducted wholly himself, had put him in a sorry plight. He was of large frame, muscular, and finely proportioned. He had carried the bodies over his left shoulder and was absolutely covered with blood and dirt, almost unrecognizable as a soldier, and his voice and form alone indicated his manhood. His reply was prompt and ingenuous: he had been refused permission to cross by his corps commander, to whom he had made his purpose known; the dead and wounded of the regiment that fought on that ground yesterday were of the blood of Philadelphia's best citizens, and, regardless of the laws of war and the commands of his superiors, he was of opinion that humanity and decency demanded that they be properly cared for, which, no one else attempting, he had determined to risk the consequences and discharge the duty himself. The simplicity and earnestness of this reply prompted the further interrogation as to how long he had been in the service. "Twenty days," responded Crocker. The gentle "I thought so" from the lips of the veteran general showed that the ingenuousness and sincerity had wholly captured him. He bade him continue his labors until they were fully completed, pointed out a boat on the shore that he could utilize to ferry his precious freight across the stream, and surrounded the field with a cordon of cavalry patrols to protect him from further molestation or interruption.

But Crocker had a host of troubles to face upon his return. He had openly violated the positive commands of his superior; he had been shamefully insulting to the messenger who bore his superior's instructions, and had acted in utter disregard of well-known laws governing armies confronting each other. Still, there was something about the whole affair so honest, so earnest, and so true, that there was a disposition to temporize with the stern demands of discipline. And he had fully accomplished his purpose—all the bodies and the wounded man were safely landed on the Maryland side. However, he was promptly arrested.

Colonel Barnes, who had watched him through all his operations, was the first of his superiors who was prompted to leniency, and he accompanied him to corps headquarters to intercede in his behalf. They were ushered into the presence of General Porter, who, shocked at such a wholesale accumulation of improprieties, and angered to a high tension by such positive disobediences, proceeded, in short and telling phrases, to explain the law and regulations—all of which, if Crocker didn't know before he started, he had had full opportunity to gather in during his experiences.

Then followed moments of painful silence, and the General inquired whether he had seen a gun which the regulars had left upon the other side the day before, and if so, what was the likelihood of its recovery. Crocker replied that he had not, but had noticed a caisson, and that he did not consider it likely it would ever come back. Returning to the subject, the General continued his reproof; but, considering his inexperience, unquestioned courage, and evident good intentions, he finally yielded, concluding that the reprimand was sufficient punishment, and released him from arrest and restored him to duty.

—*History of the Corn Exchange Regiment,*
118th Pennsylvania Volunteers

*

He Kept His Promise

---

*

[AT THE BATTLE of Prairie Grove, December 7, 1862] were two Irishmen from St. Louis—splendid, strapping fellows, full of fun and devilment. They had the very day of enlistment made a solemn agreement between each other to go into every fight, side by side, succor one another in distress, and in the event of a wound that was not mortal, the one unhurt should bear the other from the field. Charging furiously down the hill after the retreating Federals, the older, Jerry, received an ugly bullet through his right thigh, falling heavily. True to his promise, the younger, Larry, gathered him up immediately, threw him across his back and started to the rear. Meeting Dr. Spencer Brown, engaged busily among the wounded, the doctor said to him: "Ah! Larry, and why are you taking a dead man from the field?"

"Dead!—and faith he's not so aisy kilt."

"But look up and see for yourself."

The faithful comrade turned slowly around to get a glance at his companion's face, and, sure enough, during the retreat a cannon ball had taken his head smoothly and evenly off, without Larry knowing the slightest thing about it. A wondering, half-curious expression came over his countenance, as if he did not half understand matters, then, gently laying down the multilated burden, he said with great gravity, "Begorrah, but he tould me he was wounded in the *leg!*"

—JOHN N. EDWARDS

100

Buck's Baby

*

BUCK DENMAN . . . a Mississippi bear hunter and a superb specimen of manhood, was color sergeant of the Twenty-first and a member of [Lane] Brandon's company. He was tall and straight, broad-shouldered and deep-chested, had an eye like an eagle and a voice like a bull of Bashan, and was full of pluck and power as a panther. He was rough as a bear in manner, but withal a noble, tender-hearted fellow, and a splendid soldier.

[At Marye's Heights, December 13, 1862] the enemy, finding the way now clear, were coming up the street, full company front, with flags flying and bands playing, while the great shells from the siege guns were bursting over their heads and dashing their hurtling fragments after our retreating skirmishers.

Buck was behind the corner of a house taking sight for a last shot. Just as his fingers trembled on the trigger a little three-year-old, fair-haired, baby girl toddled out of an alley, accompanied by a Newfoundland dog, and gave chase to a big shell that was rolling lazily along the pavement, she clapping her little hands and the dog snapping and barking furiously at the shell.

Buck's hand dropped from the trigger. He dashed it across his eyes to dispel the mist and make sure he hadn't passed over the river and wasn't seeing his own baby girl in a vision. No, there is the baby, amid the hell of shot and shell, and here come the enemy. A moment and he has ground his gun, dashed out into the storm, swept his great right arm around the baby, gained cover again, and, baby clasped to his breast and musket trailed in his left hand, is trotting after the boys up to Marye's Heights.

And there behind that historic stone wall and in the lines hard by all those hours and days of terror was that baby kept, her fierce nurses taking turns patting her while the storm of battle raged and shrieked, and at night wrestling with each other for the boon and benediction of her quiet breathing under their blankets. Never was baby so cared for. They scoured the countryside for milk, and conjured up their best skill to prepare dainty viands for her little ladyship.

When the struggle was over and the enemy had withdrawn to his strongholds across the river, and [Brigadier General William] Barksdale was ordered to reoccupy the town, the Twenty-first Mississippi, having held the post of danger in the rear, was given the place of honor in the van and led the column. There was a long halt, the brigade and regimental staff hurrying to and fro. The regimental colors could not be found.

Denman stood about the middle of the regiment, baby in arms. Suddenly he sprang to the front. Swinging her aloft above his head, her little garments fluttering like the folds of a banner, he shouted, "Forward, Twenty-first, here are your colors!" and without further order off started the brigade toward the town, yelling as only Barksdale's men could yell. They were passing through a street fearfully shattered by the enemy's fire and were shouting their very souls out—but let Buck himself describe the last scene in the drama:

"I was holding the baby high, Adjutant, with both arms, when above all the racket I heard a woman's scream. The next thing I knew I was covered with calico and she fainted on my breast. I caught her before she fell, and laying her down gently, put her baby on her bosom. She was most the prettiest thing I ever looked at, and her eyes were shut; —and—I hope God'll forgive me, but I kissed her just once."

—MAJOR ROBERT STILES

*

How Bill Tucker Got Hurt

*

IT WAS THE CUSTOM during the war for all the gentlemen who from age or other disabilities were not in the army, to visit any soldiers who came to their neighborhood wounded or in distress of any kind, and to minister to their wants as far as possible.

Old Colonel L., of one of our eastern counties, was one of the most

102

attentive men in his county to calls of this nature. We can see the venerable old gentleman now driving his old gray horse, Dan, with one hand, and thoughtfully stroking his long white beard with the other, with a basket filled with something good, a small bundle of sugar and a little "real coffee," or something of the sort, for some poor fellow who was at home sick or wounded, or maybe to comfort some soldier's wife who was in trouble and her husband away. Mr. Bill Tucker lived in the piney woods not far from Colonel L.'s plantation. He was wounded in the arm at Fredericksburg, Virginia [December 13, 1862] and came home on furlough; as usual Colonel L. no sooner heard that Bill was at home and wounded than old Dan was hitched to the buggy and a basket of "something good" prepared by Mrs. L. Bill was not much hurt, and was intensely flattered at Colonel L.'s visit. It happened to be Sunday, and several of the neighbors had dropped in, so Mr. Bill Tucker laid himself out to entertain his company.

For some time the conversation consisted of inquiries after the absent boys. Finally, during a lull in the conversation, Colonel L. said, "Well, William, tell us how you got hurt."

"We-ell, Colonel, I'll tell you," said Bill. "You see our brigade [those who have never heard the North Carolina muffin pronounce the word 'brigade' can form no idea of the accent, and those who have must supply it for themselves, ink and paper won't do it] was on them big rollin' hills I was tellin' you about, and just before day in the mornin' Gineral Lee he came up, he did, and he said 'Whar is Gineral Hoke?' he says. 'Here I is, Gineral,' says he, and Gineral Lee he says, 'Gineral Hoke, who is the bravest man you have got in your brigade?' and Gineral Hoke he says, says he, 'Mr. Bill Tucker is the bravest man I ever see,' and he says, 'Call him here'; and Gineral Hoke says, 'Come here, Mr. Tucker, if you please,' and I come, I did, and I tuck off my cap polite-like and said, 'Good mornin', Gineral Hoke'; and they both say, 'Good mornin', Mr. Tucker,' and Gineral Lee, he says, says he, 'Mr. Tucker, them Yankees is comin' after me again,' and I said, 'Gineral, I am powerful sorry for somebody's bound to git hurt,' and he says, 'Me, too, Mr. Tucker.' Then he says, says he, 'Mr. Tucker, they tell me you is a brave man; here is a brand-new Belgium rifle and box of exploshum balls, and I want you to get out yonder beyond that thar wall and don't you let 'em come on me, Mr. Tucker.' I said, 'Gineral, it is a hard task, but I will do my best; but Gineral, don't you let 'em flank me.' The Gineral, he says, 'Mr. Tucker, I will do my best, and I'll tell Stonewall Jackson to look out for you.'

"Well, I went out and laid down behind that thar stone wall, and I tuck my exploshum balls and I laid 'em handy in the cracks of the wall, and bimeby, about sunrise, Gineral Hoke, he hollowed out, and he says, 'Look out, Bill, they's a-comin'! and here they come, and I laid thar all day and I shot 'em with that Belgium rifle and them sploshum balls a-goin' an' a-comin', I tell you; and bimeby, way long yonder jest after night, one great long high Yankee got up and he tuck up his hat and he said, 'Great Goddlemighty, Mr. Tucker, is you gwine to kill us all?' and while I was a-foolin' talkin' with him, they crope up on me and shot me in the arm, and then I was bore from the field and somebody's regiment tuck my place."

—*Raleigh* (North Carolina) *Register*

*

Lieutenant Brady Insisted on His Rights

*

ON THE MORNING of December 13, 1862, when Hancock's Division was drawn up in the streets of Fredericksburg, running parallel to the Rappahannock River, the left of the Sixty-third [New York Infantry] rested on the dock. The commissioned officers of Company B were absent, sick and wounded. Captain Joseph O'Neill was in command of the Sixty-third. He made an order detailing Lieutenant John Dwyer, of Company K, temporarily, to command Company B.

Just before the brigade moved off to charge the enemy's works, Lieutenant J. D. Brady, formerly adjutant, came to the front of Company B and remarked: "Lieutenant Dwyer, are you aware of the fact that my commission as first lieutenant antedates yours?"

"I am not aware of that fact, Lieutenant Brady. What if it does?"

"Then I should be in command of this company as your senior. I just came from Captain O'Neill, and convinced him what I say is true, and he desired me to see you and ascertain your wishes, as he had assigned you to this company. Do you wish to see the captain?"

The officer addressed said it was immaterial to him whether he was in command or not; he had been assigned without his knowledge;

104

he would see the commanding officer. Brady and Dwyer waited on the latter, when the correctness of Brady's statement was apparent. O'Neill then directed Dwyer to go back to his company, and Brady took command.

An hour later, when the brigade was charging up the heights, exposed to a withering fire from cannon and musketry, the wounded were streaming to the rear. While getting his men up into the battle line Dwyer met his friend Brady staggering and making his way as best he could to the shelter of the town. A crimson streak of blood ran down his face from a wound in the forehead, a bullet having struck him a glancing blow between the eyes. A word of recognition passed between them.

Dwyer supposed that was the end of Brady, but it was not. The latter was sent to a hospital at Washington, and was back again within a few weeks, ready for duty, after his close call from instant death.

"Lieutenant Dwyer!" was Brady's salutation the day he arrived in camp, "why did you not insist on commanding Company B that day in the streets of Fredericksburg? Had you done so, and stayed with the company you would have stopped that Rebel bullet instead of me."

"Oh, you insisted on your 'rights,'" was the reply, "and you got them."

—Major John Dwyer

There's a hungry, thirsty soldier, who wears his life away,
With torn clothes, whose better days are o'er;
He is sighing now for whiskey, and with throat as dry as hay,
Sings, "Hard crackers, come again no more!"

—"HARD CRACKERS"

---

8. HARD MARCHES, HARDTACK, SHORT FARE, AND SHORT WEAR

The High Price of Chickens

---

*

DURING THE FIGHTING at Fort Donelson [Tennessee, February 12-16, 1862], a young man came strolling down to a transport, with one arm amputated, and in the well hand holding three chickens which he had captured. A steward of one of the boats stepped up to him, and asked him if he wanted to sell the chickens. He looked at the chickens for a little while and replied, "Well, no; I had so much trouble in catching the d——d things, I believe I'll eat 'em myself"; and off he went with his *fowl* prisoners.

—LIEUTENANT COLONEL CHARLES S. GREENE

"I Mourn Your Untimely Demise"

[IN THE TEXAS BRIGADE'S "Ragged First"] a tall, powerfully built and red-faced corporal . . . was on the picket-line one day down at Yorktown [during the siege of April 5-May 4, 1862], and, being both hungry and ragged, decided to venture beyond the line in search of something he might eat or wear. He had not gone fifty yards to the front when he discovered the body of a well-dressed and splendidly equipped Yankee lying behind a little thicket of sassafras which concealed it from the view of anybody in the trenches. That he might the more exhaustively and leisurely administer on the dead man's estate, the corporal carried the body and all its attachments and belongings to the shelter of the breastworks. The inventory justified the rash venture of the self-appointed administrator, the corpse yielding a pair of extra good shoes, a suit of first-class clothing, a well-filled haversack, sixty dollars in gold, and, best of all, a canteen two-thirds full of excellent whisky. Having swallowed a good four fingers of the whisky, the corporal wiped his lips with the sleeve of his coat, put on a long, solemn face, and, looking down at the corpse, said in mournful accents:

"Poor fellow, poor fellow! Like the many of your tribe that have gone before, their departure from this vale of tears hastened by well-aimed Confederate bullets, you have gone to your eternal home in the lowest depths of that other world whose fires are never less than red hot. But, though I mourn your untimely demise, it is not with a grief that is without consolation. That you were a gentleman and not a vagabond is evident—your boots and your coat, your pants and your liberal supply of filthy lucre, in short, your whole *tout ensemble,* stamping you as that beyond any controversy. But, had I a shadow of a doubt of your being a gentleman in every sense of the word, the quality of the liquor in your canteen would resolve it in your favor by an overwhelming majority. So here's to you, Yank! Living, though an enemy of my country and therefore deserving of death, you must have been a jolly

107

good fellow—dead, you'll soon return to the dust whence you sprang. and that you may the sooner do the returning act, my comrades and I will lay you under the sod of old Virginia just as soon as we have emptied your canteen."

The corporal was as good as his word, and, assisted by his comrades, dug a grave in the sand and buried the body.

—J. B. POLLEY

*

Magruder and the Hungry Soldier

*

WITH A FAVORITE GENERAL the men took many liberties, and this very popularity seemed to destroy the deference usually paid to such high officers. . . .

Just after the battle of Williamsburg [May 5, 1862], General [John B.] Magruder and his staff stopped at the house of a widow lady on the road, and engaged dinner. Soon after their arrival a Louisiana soldier came up, and accosted the landlady with: "Madam, can I get dinner?"

"Yes, sir," was the reply; "but as I am preparing dinner for General Magruder and staff, and have not room at my table for more, you will have to wait for a second table."

"Very well, ma'am. Thank you," said the soldier, taking his seat in a position to command a view of the dining-room. Watching the movements of the servants, he waited until the feast was on the table, and while his hostess proceeded to the parlor to announce dinner to her distinguished guests, he entered the dining-room, and, seating himself at the table, waited further developments, trusting to his impudence to get him out of the scrape.

Upon the entrance of the party of officers, there was found to be seats for all but one, and one politely returned to the parlor to wait. The General took a seat next to the soldier, and, after the first course was finished, turned to him, and asked:

"Sir, have you any idea with whom you are dining?"

"No," coolly replied the soldier; "I used to be very particular on that score; but since I turned soldier, I don't care whom I eat with, so that the victuals are clean."

. . . Magruder laughed heartily . . . and even paid for the soldier's dinner, and sent him on his way.

—FRANK MOORE, ed.
Anecdotes, Poetry and Incidents of the War:
North and South, 1860-1865

*

Captain Jack and the Sutler

*

"MY GREATEST ADVENTURE there [at Malvern Hill, July 1, 1862] was with one of our worthy sutlers. I don't mean our generous, portly friend here, O'Donoghue, but Claffan. I heard he had a load of wines, and brandies, and Bourbon, and other delightful luxuries, so agreeable to the tastes of soldiers in general, and mine in particular, and that he was selling them at exorbitant prices in the rear. I went to the General and told him, 'It's too bad, General; he won't have a drop when he comes here.'

" 'Go, Captain, and order the villain up.'

"Off I rode, and sure enough, there he was with a crowd about him, selling his vile rot-gut whisky at five dollars a bottle.

" 'Claffan,' I exclaimed, 'bring up that wagon, and don't sell another drop here: the General has sent me for you.'

" 'O Lord! Captain Jack, sure you would not ask me: the shells are flying about there like hail.'

" 'Why, you rascal, I have nothing to do with that; I'm only delivering the General's orders, and you know he will have you discharged if you don't go at once.'

" 'Oh, dear! Oh, dear! Captain, if you take the wagon yourself, you can drink what you please.'

" 'Come on, you ruffian; wouldn't it be very becoming for me in my regimentals to mount your old wagon and a battle going on!'

" 'Oh, dear! Oh, dear! Captain, stay near me, any way.'

"He lashed his team for the hill, where the troops were drawn up; and as we went along, shells came whistling about. When one would burst near he'd exclaim, 'Oh, Captain darling, look at that fellow: for certain, we'll be killed.'

" 'Drive on, man; don't be frightened: you are not the first man killed to-day.'

" 'O Lord! O Lord! If I were out of this—'

"We had got just to the rear of the brigade, when a round-shot tears through the top of the wagon. Off falls Claffan like an acrobat, and rolls in under the wagon, stretched all-fours, with his face to the ground. Every shot and shell that would come round he'd kick spasmodically, hug the ground, and cry out: 'O Lord! I'm killed, I'm killed! Oh, Captain Jack! my death be on your hands. Oh, there is another. Oh, dear! Oh, dear! Good Lord, deliver me!'

"I at once sent word to the officers, and all that could took a run down and a run back with a bottle, while those that had more time drank and feasted on cakes, canned fruits, cheese, and other delicacies.

"All this time our friend was keeping up the kicking under the wagon, as if he were galvanized, and in order to keep him in proper ecstasies, after every volley, if any shot or shell was not obliging enough to come near, we were sure to supply the deficiency by rolling a round-shot against the wagon, or near, which sent him off into another fit. I became quite generous; invited all the officers, not only of our brigade, but of the whole division; gave out that I had got up the whole thing myself, and I declare to you, there is scarcely an officer's tent I go into but he will thank me for the manner in which I stood to him that day. Why, I have been tight ever since, on the strength of the sutler's store."

—"What became of Claffan?"

"We moved off and left him there. The rascal afterwards had the impudence to come to me to know what had become of his load of stuff."

—"What did you tell him?"

"Why, I told him, the villain, that I was no sutler's clerk to take care of them, and to get out with himself, or else I'd run my sword through him. This payment seemed to satisfy him, for he never troubled me since."

—Captain D. P. Conyngham

How Jim Ferris Got Himself a Pair of Leggin's

*

JIM FERRIS, of the Fifth Texas, found himself at Second Manassas in a dilapidated condition externally. The legs of his pants lacked several inches of the proper length, and in the absence of a pair of socks his ankles had been sadly lacerated by the briars and brambles through which he had been compelled to scramble in skirmishing. While running wild with his regiment when it slipped the bridle on the 30th [August, 1862], it occurred to his mind that he might supply deficiencies in his raiment by administering on the estate of some dead Yankee. A pair of leggin's to button around the calves of his legs would answer his purposes admirably, he thought, and he resolved to have them. It was midnight, though, before he began operations. Being a very large man himself, only the body of a large man could be depended upon to supply Jim's need; and in the search for such a one he wandered to and fro over the silent field of the dead until, awed by the solemnity of his surroundings, cold chills began to run down his back at the least noise; and he expected every minute to encounter a ghost. Finally he found a corpse of apparently suitable size, and, hastily turning back from its legs the oilcloth which covered it from head to foot, began with no gentle hand to unbutton a leggin'. At the first jerk the supposed deadest of all the many dead flung the oilcloth from his head, and, rising to a sitting posture, exclaimed, "Great God alive, man! Don't rob me before I am dead, if you please!" In horrified amazement, Jim sprang twenty feet at one bound, but knowing no ghost would speak so sensibly, natural politeness prompted instant apology. "Indeed, Mr. Yankee," said he, in the most gentle and winning tone he could assume, "I hadn't the least idea you were alive, or I never would have been guilty of the discourtesy of disturbing you. Please pardon me, and let me know what I can do to make amends for my rudeness." "I would like a drink of water," said the revived corpse. "Take my canteen, sir," rejoined Jim, instantly offering it, "and please oblige me by keeping it; I can easily get another."

After this experience Jim decided that, rather than risk waking another corpse, he would do without leggin's; but on his way to camp he came across a stalwart form lying at full length on the ground, and at the very first glance saw that here could be obtained the needed articles. No mistake must be made, though; and so, laying his hand on the shoulder of the Yankee, he gave him a shake, and asked, "Say, Mister, are you dead or alive?" There was no response, and next morning Jim Ferris strutted about the camp in a magnificent pair of linen leggin's.

—J. B. POLLEY

*

Unpatriotic Feet

*

AS THE CIVIL WAR dragged on, the Confederate army became skilled in making swift marches and long, hard fights on empty stomachs. But sometimes, the most valorous would drop out of the ranks from sheer hunger and exhaustion. General Lee's invasion of Maryland was especially notable for the number of worn soldiers who fell by the wayside when nature could endure no more. Some of the stragglers were returned to their regiments by the strong arm of military law; others voluntarily returned. In the latter class was a tall, gaunt farmer from the mountains north of Georgia. When asked by his commanding officer to explain his absence from the battle of Antietam [September 17, 1862], he dryly said:

"I had no shoes. I tried it barefoot, but somehow my feet wouldn't callous. They just kept bleeding. I found it so hard to keep up that though I had the heart of a patriot, I began to feel I didn't have patriotic feet. Of course, I could have crawled on my hands and knees, but then my hands would have got so sore I couldn't have fired my rifle."

—HELEN DORTCH LONGSTREET

*

The Mud March

*

AFTER THE FRIGHTFUL DISASTER to, and defeat of, the Army of the Potomac at Fredericksburg on the south bank of the Rappahannock river in December, 1862, the men of that army returned to their camps on the north side, tired, discouraged, and disheartened; not so much by their defeat (for they were used to defeats), as sorrowful and mournful for the loss of so many good, true and faithful men, without any return whatever.

The army had lost confidence in its commander, General Ambrose E. Burnside, a thoroughly loyal, brave, and good man in every way, but notably unfit to command and fight an army of the size and disposition of the Army of the Potomac.

Every one supposed, and had a right to suppose, that we would and should go into winter quarters. But that was not to be, for on the 17th of January, 1863, orders were received from army headquarters to be ready to march at once, with three days rations of hard bread, salt pork, coffee and sugar in our haversacks and sixty rounds of ball cartridges, perhaps to equalize each man's load. The roads were not even in fair condition, being in many places wet and muddy.

*   *   *   *   *

The Army of the Potomac were all ready to march, the next day, but the necessary orders were not received till the 20th, early in the afternoon, when our temporary camps were broken, and we started in a westerly direction through the town of Falmouth, that was located opposite Fredericksburg.

The grand division of General Joseph Hooker started to march on the same road, with the grand division of General William B. Franklin; but General Daniel E. Sickles of our local division called a halt to allow General Franklin's division to pass, and after remaining near the old camp of the headquarters of the army till about midnight, we returned to our own camp, wet, cold, ugly, and hungry.

113

The Rebels knew all about the proposed march; asked our pickets how long we intended to be away; if it was just a pleasure excursion, or did we mean business this time. I used to think that the rank and file of the Rebel army knew of our proposed movements long before our men did, for they often asked us to come over soon, as they wanted supplies very badly, as the food and clothing captured at Fredericksburg had long ago been used and they were anxiously looking forward to the time when we would furnish them with what they so badly needed.

We had reveille early the next morning, and in the midst of a nasty, cold, and penetrating rain storm started again on the same road we had marched over the previous day. The men were in mighty ill humor, cold, wet and dirty; but moved according to orders, all thoroughly of the opinion that the march, and the battle, in prospective, must prove disastrous.

The roads were in frightful shape, after practically receiving rain for twenty-four hours; brooks swollen to double their normal capacity and in many places hardly fordable. The axles of the wagons in some places were dragged along on top of the mass of mud. Many wagons had to be abandoned, as the teams of army mules and horses had to be doubled, and in many cases tripled, in order to keep moving. I had on a pair of long-legged boots, sent from home: while crossing over a well-traveled road one of them stuck in the mud. I went along with one boot—the other may be there yet. I tried to find it, but failed. One captain of a battery put seventy-two horses on one piece, but could not start it until he placed chains and ropes some twenty feet long on the prolonge of the gun, took a flying start, and yanked it along to the drier and firmer ground. The infantry helped the wagons and artillery all they could, by putting rails and branches of trees under the wheels; many horses and mules had their legs broken, or became exhausted, and had to be killed.

Imagine, if it be possible, the condition of the army moving on the parallel dirt roads (the same kind we have in by-ways in country towns) wet, cold, dirty, muddy, and nearly exhausted, and to cap the climax, on arriving at the fords of the upper Rappahannock, to see on the south bank signs placed in the trees by the Rebels, reading: "General Burnside Stuck in the Mud."

If the weather had been fine, our division might have crossed at United States Ford on the Rappahannock. Although the Rebels were on the south bank in force, they kindly volunteered to come over on our side of the river and help us lay pontoons, stating as the reason that "they were in great need of provisions and other necessary articles which we would bring along."

None of us can ever forget that night in bivouac. Our pioneers had been busy felling large trees (mostly black walnut) and had built an immense fire, some thirty feet in length, six or eight feet in width, and at least five feet high. The rain still continued, and while we would try to dry ourselves on one side and roast, the other side would be wet and cold.

On that never-to-be-forgotten dirty, miserable trip, we did not lose any men killed or wounded; but the army returned to camp, after being away some four days, disaffected and dissatisfied, with mighty poor opinion of their commanding officer, who a very short time after was succeeded in command by General Joseph Hooker.

—LEVERETT D. HOLDEN

*

The Spotted Cow's Hide

*

AFTER GRANT had been compelled to take the back track in consequence of [General Earl] Van Dorn's destructive raid on Holly Springs [Mississippi, December 20, 1862], where the accumulated stores of his army were destroyed, Logan's division fell back to La Grange. As is well known the loss of the stores at Holly Springs brought Grant's army to short rations, and in fact for a time to *no* rations. Under such circumstances of course every one was on the look-out for something to satisfy the demands of an empty stomach, and as it often happened, the boys did not wait to be detailed before they went on a forage. When near La Grange a Dutchman in battery L— a boy of sixteen, in years, but a man in sharpness and grit—spied a handsome spotted cow in the bush near the place where the battery went into camp. Of course he went for her forthwith. With the ready aid of his comrades the cow was captured, slaughtered, skinned and dressed, and in due time also cooked and eaten, all *secundum artem*. Having claimed the hide as his perquisite by right of discovery, and the claim being conceded, he took it to a tannery near by. Now leather was a great want in the South, and hides brought ready money on sight, and Hans found the tanner eager to buy.

Entering the shop, Hans says: "You puys hides here?"

"Yes."

"How much you give?"

"Three dollars, for good ones."

"Vel, here pe's a good one."

"Throw it down and let me see it."

Hans threw down the hide and the man proceeded to spread it out on the floor. Suddenly he jumps up and breaks out in a towering rage:

"Thunder and lightning! You d——d Yankee thief! You have killed my old spotted cow, the last cow I had, and now you come and ask me to buy the hide! D——n you, get out of my shop, the hide's mine."

The man was proceeding to appropriate the hide without further parley, but to this Hans was not at all prepared to assent, and he says: "Halt! halt! hans off! hans off! May pe the cow vas yours, I don't know, it make no difference, *that hide pe's mine,* and you can't have him mitout you pay me tree dollar, and you must let him pe, or I shoots."

As Hans suited his motions to his words, and as the man thought of the fact that a division of Yankees was near to back him up, he saw that it would be both useless and dangerous to insist upon his view of the equity of the case. So he paid Hans three dollars for the hide of his last cow, the old spotted cow that less than an hour before was quietly browsing in the brush.

—GEORGE H. WOODRUFF

Brave sentry on your lonely beat,
May these blue stockings warm your feet;
And when from wars and camp you part
May some fair knitter warm your heart.
　　　　　　　—A COMFORT NOTE

9. HOME FRONT

Mr. Davis Is Inaugurated

*

THE INAUGURATION of Mr. Davis as President of the "Permanent Government" of the Confederate States . . . we viewed, by courtesy of Mr. John R. Thompson, the State Librarian, from one of the windows of the Capitol, where, while waiting for the exercises to begin, we read *Harper's Weekly* and other Northern papers, the latest per underground express. That 22nd of February [1862] was a day of pouring rain, and the concourse of umbrellas in the square beneath us had the effect of an immense mushroom-bed. As the bishop and the President-elect came upon the stand, there was an almost painful hush in the crowd. All seemed to feel the gravity of the trust our chosen leader was assuming. When he kissed the Book a shout went up; but there was no elation visible as the people slowly dispersed. And it was thought ominous afterwards, when the story was repeated, that, as Mrs. Davis, who had a Virginia Negro for coachman, was driven to the inauguration, she observed the carriage went at a snail's pace and was escorted by four Negro men in black clothes, wearing white cotton gloves and walking solemnly, two on either side of the equipage; she asked the coachman what such a spectacle could mean, and was answered, "Well, ma'am, you tole me to arrange everything as it should be; and this is the way we do in Richmon' at funerals and sich-like." Mrs. Davis promptly ordered the outwalkers away, and with them departed all the pomp and circumstance the occasion admitted of. In the mind of a Negro, everything of dignified ceremonial is always associated with a funeral!

—CONSTANCE CARY HARRISON

*

A Heroine in Homespun

---

*

March 7, 1862

[I] MET with a very plain-looking woman in a [Richmond] store the other day. She was buying Confederate gray cloth, at what seemed a high price.

I asked her why she did not apply to the quartermaster, and get it cheaper.

"Well," she replied, "I *knows* all about that, for my three sons is in the army; they gets their clothes *thar;* but you see this is for my old man, and I don't think it would be fair to get his clothes from *thar,* because he ain't never done nothing for the country as yet—he's just *gwine* in the army."

"Is he not very old to go into the army?"

"Well, he's fifty-four years old, but he's well and hearty like, and ought to do something for his country. So he says to me, says he, 'The country wants men; I wonder if I could stand marching; I've a great mind to try.' Says I, 'Old man, I don't think you could, you would break down; but I tell you what you can do—you can drive a wagon in the place of a young man that's driving, and the young man can fight.' Says he, 'So I will'—and he's gwine just as soon as I gits these clothes ready and that won't be long."

"But won't you be very uneasy about him?" said I.

"Yes, indeed; but you know he ought to go—them wretches must be drove away."

"Did you want your sons to go?"

"Want 'em to go!" she exclaimed. "Yes, if they hadn't agone, they shouldn't a-staid whar I was. But they wanted to go, *my* sons did."

Two days ago, I met her again in a baker's shop; she was filling her basket with cakes and pies.

"Well," said I, "has your husband gone?"

"No, but he's agwine to-morrow, and I'm getting something for him now."

"Don't you feel sorry as the time approaches for him to go?"

"Oh, yes, I shall miss him mightily; but I ain't never cried about it; I never shed a tear for the old man, nor for the boys neither, and I ain't agwine to. Them Yankees must not come a-nigh to Richmond; if they does I will fight them myself. The women must fight, for they *shan't* cross Mayo's Bridge; they *shan't* git to Richmond."

I said to her, "You are a patriot."

"Yes, honey—ain't you? Ain't everybody?"

—JUDITH W. McGUIRE

*

The Contraband's Prayer

*

Santa Rosa Island, Fla.
March 13, 1862

MANY OF THE POOR FELLOWS run the greatest risk and endure the greatest hardships in escaping, and from the frequent shots and alarms on the rebel lines nearest us, I presume some are shot in the attempt and some are frightened back. Bony, who is quite a character and a great favorite with us, says that as he paddled by the sentry, just as he was nearly out of sight he heard "Who goes dar?" And then, "I get down in de boat on my knees and I say noffin. Den I hear 'em call, 'Sargent de guard! Sargent de guard!' and *I prayed to God* (solemnly) *dat if I get shot I fall in de bay and de sharks eat me up, so dey think I get away!"*

—Brevet Brigadier General Willoughby M. Babcock

✳

"The Southerners Are a Noble Race"

✳

Brokenburn, La., May 22, 1862

ALL THE BOYS are out on the river and we expect them to bring Anna Dobbs back with them to stay a few days. It seems odd to be expecting company and no flour or any "boughten" delicacy to regale them on, but we have been on a strict "war footing" for some time— cornbread and home-raised meal, milk and butter, tea once a day, and coffee never. A year ago we would have considered it impossible to get on for a day without the things that we have been doing without for months. Fortunately we have sugar and molasses, and after all it is not such hard living. Common cornbread admits of many variations in the hands of a good cook—eggbread (we have lots of eggs), muffins, cakes, and so on. Fat meat will be unmitigated fat meat, but one need not eat it. And there are chickens, occasional partridges, and other birds, and often venison, vegetables of all kinds minus potatoes; and last but not least, knowing there is no help for it makes one content. There is hardly a family in the parish using flour constantly. All kept some for a while for company and for the sick, but it is about exhausted now.

Clothes have become a secondary consideration. Fashion is an obsolete word and just to be decently clad is all we expect. The change in dress, habits, and customs is nowhere more striking than in the towns. A year ago a gentleman never thought of carrying a bundle, even a small one, through the streets. Broadcloth was *de rigueur*. Ceremony and fashion ruled in the land. Presto—change. Now the highest in rank may be seen doing any kind of work that their hands find to do. The men have become "hewers of wood and drawers of water" and pack bundles

120

of all sorts and sizes. It may be a pile of blankets, a stack of buckets, or a dozen bundles. One gentleman I saw walking down the street in Jackson, and a splendid-looking fellow he was, had a piece of fish in one hand, a cavalry saddle on his back, bridle, blankets, newspapers, and a small parcel in the other hand; and over his shoulder swung an immense pair of cavalry boots. And nobody thought he looked odd. Their willingness to fetch and carry is only limited by their strength. All the soldiers one sees when traveling are loaded down with canteen, knapsack, haversack, and blankets. Broadcloth is worn only by the drones and fireside braves. Dyed linsey is now the fashionable material for coats and pants. Vests are done away with, colored flannel, merino, or silk overshirts taking the place. A gentleman thinks nothing of calling on half a dozen young ladies dressed in home-dyed Negro cloth and blue-checked shirt. If there is a button or stripe to show that he is one of his country's defenders, he is sure of warmest welcome. Another stops to talk to a bevy of ladies. He is laden down with a package of socks and tin plates that he is carrying out to camp, and he shifts the bundles from side to side as he grows interested and his arms get tired. In proportion as we have been a race of haughty, indolent, and waited-on people, so now are we ready to do away with all forms and work and wait on ourselves.

The Southerners are a noble race, let them be reviled as they may, and I thank God that He has given my birthplace in this fair land among these gallant people and in a time when I can show my devotion to my Country.

—KATE STONE

*

A Refugee Story for Young Confederates

*

MY DEAR CHILDREN, you wish to know why I am here so far from my dear old home. I will tell you.

All of you have heard Pa and Ma talk of [Robert H.] Milroy, the Yankee General. He is a very bad man. No one where I lived had a good word for him. He took away all the horses, cows, pigs, and chickens of poor people as well as rich people. He was a brute to women, old men, like me; and did not care what became of little boys and girls. If he did not like their fathers, he would seize them, and burn their houses and fences. Ruin and this Milroy were great friends.

Well, I lived in the Valley of Virginia. My home was a sweet place not far from a fine, clear stream of water.

Pretty fish swam in the clear, silver stream. On bright days Mary and Willie got in a safe little boat which I kept in a green nook, and I took them to a shady spot where they caught fish. Many a little perch was caught and fried for dinner. Then there were beehives where the busy bees made much sweet honey; and a fine orchard with apples, pears, peaches, plums and cherries. There were cows to give milk, and horses to ride, and pigs and geese, chickens and turkeys. It was a sweet home where Uncle William and Mary and Willie lived.

Milroy with a long line of bad men, each with a gun, came to my house and took my horse, my cow, and in fact all he could lay his hands on. I told him it was wrong to take all I had, and that God would see that it did him no good. One of his men struck me, and then set fire to my house. Mary and Willie were born in that house, and when they saw the fire they ran out and cried as if their hearts would break.

So the house was soon burnt, and my little family had no good bed to lie on at night, nor a morsel to eat. But after a while a good friend took us to his house, yet it did not seem like the old home.

Now, my children, you have heard your Ma and Pa talk of Stonewall Jackson. He was a brave, good and great man.

When he went to fight the Yankees, he always prayed that he might have help from God. I knew that God would punish the bad men who burnt my house and drove us out into the woods. Sure enough it was so, for Jackson with his brave, good men came along and fought Milroy and his bad men. Our friend Jackson met Milroy just where my house was burnt. The smoke was still rising from the black ruins. Milroy ran as hard as he could out of the Valley, and Jackson after him.

Every thing looked drear and lonely. My good friend did his best to make us happy, but I could not sleep for I saw but the fire and ruins, and the bad Yankees. Mary and Willie wept themselves to sleep.

While I was at the house of this good friend, a little while after the fight with Milroy, I saw the bad Yankees under General [James] Shields and [John Charles] Frémont, and [Nathaniel P.] Banks, run away from

Jackson. The great "Stonewall" had whipped them, and their dead and wounded lay on the field of battle ghastly to see.

This Yankee, Banks, ran away to Winchester, where Uncle William, when he was a boy, went to school. Our good "Stonewall" came to that town and made Banks run across the Potomac river. When "Stonewall" got to Winchester [May 25, 1862], all the men shouted for him, and the good ladies rushed into the street and gave our soldiers all sorts of sweet and good things to eat. Even the little boys and girls clapped their hands and cried, "Huzza, for our friend, Jackson!" Tears of joy stole down the cheeks of old men like myself, when they heard the cry in every part of town, "Huzza, for glorious 'Stonewall!' " Even the little Negro boys, Tom, Jerry, Pink and Reub, joined in the cry against the hated Yankees.

And now, my little friends, stop just here, for Uncle William wants to shout too. Raise your little hands and swing them around your head every time I do, and cry, "Huzza, for 'Stonewall!' " One more, "Huzza!" one more, "Huzza!" That was well done.

Take your map and get Pa or Ma to tell you where the Valley is. It was a dear, sweet place before the Yankees came to burn and rob. God will punish them for their bad deeds, for they have made many a widow and orphan.

Here I am, my dear children, without a home, but the war will end some day, and then I will try to build a new house, and raise more horses, cows and chickens. If you ever come that way on Christmas, step in and see Uncle William.

—EDWARD M. BOYKIN

✳

A Rebel Lady's Stratagem

✳

[IN CONNECTION WITH the battle of the Cross Keys, Virginia, June 8-9, 1862, one of the most luxuriously reared women of Virginia] says: "Mr. K., you know, was compelled to evacuate his premises when the Federals took possession, and succeeding in making good his escape, left me there, with my three little children, to encounter the consequences of their intrusion upon my premises. Not wishing to appear quite so youthful as I really am, and desiring to destroy, if possible, any remains of my former beauty, I took from my mouth the set of false teeth (which I was compelled to have put in before I was twenty years old), tied a handkerchief around my head, donned my most slovenly apparel, and in every way made myself as hideous as possible. The disguise was perfect. I was sullen, morose, sententious. You could not have believed I could so long have kept up a manner so disagreeable; but it had the desired effect. The Yankees called me 'old woman.' They little thought I was not thirty years of age. They took my house for a hospital for their sick and wounded, and allowed me only the use of a single room, and required of me many acts of assistance in nursing their men, which under any other circumstances my own heart-promptings would have made a pleasure to me. But I did not feel disposed to be compelled to prepare food for those who had driven from me my husband, and afterwards robbed me of all my food and bed-furniture, with the exception of what they allowed me to have in my own room. But they were not insulting in their language to the 'old woman,' and I endured all the inconveniences and unhappiness of my situation with as much fortitude as I could bring into operation, feeling that my dear husband, at least, was safe from harm. After they left . . . I was forced to go out into the woods, near by, and with my two little boys pick up fagots to cook the scanty food left to me."

—SALLIE A. PUTNAM

*

A Wartime Marriage

---

*

Columbia, S.C., June 13, 1862

I HAVE BEEN REMEMBERING Decca's wedding, which happened last year in September. We were all lying on the bed or on sofas near it, taking it coolly as to undress. [Her mother] Mrs. Singleton had the floor. "They were engaged before they went up to Charlottes-ville," she said. "Alexander [Cheves Haskell] was on Gregg's staff, and Gregg was not hard on him. Decca was the worst in love girl I ever saw.

"Letters came from Alex, urging her to let him marry her at once, since in war times human events, and even life, were very uncertain. For several days consecutively, Decca cried without ceasing. Then she consented. We were at the hospital. The rooms were all crowded, so Decca and I slept together in the same room. It was arranged by letter that the marriage should take place. Then after a luncheon at her grand-father Minor's, she was to depart with Alex for a few days at Richmond. That was to be their brief slice of honeymoon.

"The day came, the wedding breakfast was ready and so was the bride in all her bridal array. No Alex! No bridegroom! Alas, such is the uncertainty of a soldier's life. The bride said nothing, but she wept like a water nymph. At dinnertime she plucked up heart and at my earnest request she was about to join us. Then we heard the cry: The bridegroom cometh! He brought his best man, and other friends. We had a jolly dinner. Circumstances over which he had no control had kept him away.

"His father sat next to Decca, and talked to her all the time as if she were already married. It was a piece of absentmindedness on his part, pure and simple; but it was very trying, and the girl had had a good deal to stand that morning. You can well understand."

Chorus: "Of course! To be ready to be married, and the man not to come! That's the most awful thing of all we can imagine!"

"Immediately after dinner, the belated bridegroom proposed a walk; so they strolled up the mountain for a very short walk indeed. Decca, upon her return, said to me: 'Send for Robert Barnwell. I mean to be married today!' 'Impossible,' I cried. 'There is no spare room in the house, and no getting away from here, the trains are all gone. You know this hospital is crammed to the ceiling.' But she insisted. 'Alex says I promised to marry him today. It is not his fault he could not come before.' I shook my head. 'I don't care,' said the positive little thing. 'I promised Alex to marry him today and I will. Send for the Reverend Robert Barnwell.' So I yielded. We found Robert after a world of trouble, and the bride, lovely in Swiss muslin, was married.

"Then I proposed they should take another walk, and then I went to one of my sister nurses and begged her to take me in for the night, as I wished to resign my room to Mr. and Mrs. Haskell. When

125

the bride came from her walk, she asked: 'Where are they going to put me?' That was all. At daylight next day, they took the train for Richmond, and the small allowance of honeymoon permitted in wartime."

* * * * *

June 27

Decca Haskell is dead. Poor little darling! Immediately after her baby was born, she took it into her head that Alex was killed. He was wounded, but they had not told her of it. She surprised them by asking: "Does anyone know how the battle has gone since Alex was killed?" She could not read for a day or so before she died—her head was so bewildered—but she would not let anyone else touch his letters, so she died with several unopened ones in her bosom. When Decca died, Mrs. Singleton fainted dead away, but she shed no tears.

We went there. We saw Alex's mother, who is a daughter of Landon Cheves. Annie was with us. She said: "This is the saddest thing for Alex."

"No," said his mother. "Death is never the saddest thing. If he were not a good man, that would be a far worse thing."

Annie in utter amazement whimpered: "But Alex is so good already."

"Yes. Seven years ago, the death of one of his sisters, whom he dearly loved, made him a Christian. That death in our family was worth a thousand lives."

One needs a hard heart now. Even old Mr. Shand shed tears. Mary Barnwell sat as still as a statue, as white and stony. "Grief which can relieve itself by tears is a thing to pray for," said Reverend Mr. Shand.

Came a telegram from Hampton: "All well. So far we are successful." Robert Barnwell had been telegraphed for. His answer came: "Can't leave here. Gregg is fighting across the Chickahominy." Then said Mrs. Haskell: "My son Alex may never hear this sad news," and her lips settled rigidly.

* * * * *

June 28

In a pouring rain we went to poor Decca's funeral. They buried her in the little white frock she wore when she engaged herself to Alex Haskell, and which she again put on to marry him about a year ago. She lies now in the churchyard, in sight of my window. Is she to be pitied? She said she had had months of perfect happiness. How many people can say that? So many of us live long dreary lives, and happiness never comes at all.

—MARY BOYKIN CHESNUT

✳

The Last Silk Dress

✳

THE FEDERALS had been using balloons in examining our positions, and we watched with envious eyes their beautiful observations as they floated high up in the air, well out of range of our guns. While we were longing for the balloons that poverty denied us, a genius arose for the occasion and suggested that we send out and gather silk dresses in the Confederacy and make a balloon. It was done, and we soon had a great patchwork ship of many varied hues which was ready for use in the Seven Days' campaign [June 25-July 1, 1862].

We had no gas except in Richmond, and it was the custom to inflate the balloon there, tie it securely to an engine, and run it down the York River Railroad to any point at which we desired to send it up. One day it was on a steamer down on the James River, when the tide went out and left the vessel and balloon high and dry on a bar. The Federals gathered it in, and with it the last silk dress in the Confederacy. This capture was the meanest trick of the war and one that I have never yet forgiven.

—GENERAL JAMES LONGSTREET

*

A War Correspondent
Among the Cotton-Brokers

*

THE AUTUMN and winter of 1862-63 was the golden era of card-playing and cotton-stealing. Cotton-thieves and cardsharps were to be met in every possible direction. On the boats, on the march, at the landings, every man not in uniform was likely to be a gambler in search of prey or a broker in search of cotton. As a matter of fact, all the civilians who followed the army were mainly card-players and cotton-thieves in one.

. . . The brother-in-law of Frank Blair approached me one day, and said, "I have some cotton out about ten miles in the country, and I want to get it on the levee. I don't wish to ship it or do anything more than bring it down to the landing, where it will remain till I can arrange matters with the Government. You know Grant; ask him to let me have the permit."

Alexander was a good sort of a fellow, and I saw no reason why I should not oblige him. I stepped on the *Magnolia* and stated the case to the General, who at once, without a word, wrote and handed me the permit. I went out and gave the paper to Alexander, who, in return, dropped a bill in my hands which I saw to be a hundred-dollar greenback.

"See here," I began in a remonstrative tone.

"Oh, now, don't make a damned fool of yourself!" he said with considerable impatience, as he hurried away. I gazed at the bill and looked it over. It was very nice, brand-new, glistening, with three figures in the corner that were full of attraction. I examined it carefully, and then looked for Alexander. He had disappeared. I could not throw away the artistic product, and finally I put it in my pocket.

Within five minutes another cotton-broker, named Dewees, a little fellow, who will be well remembered by all who frequented the "Thomas E. Tutt," at Milliken's Bend, came up and halted for a chat.

"I just made a hundred," I remarked as he stopped.

"How?"

"I got a permit from the old man for a fellow to haul fifty bales of cotton down to the levee."

"Who was it?" he asked.

I was on the point of mentioning Alexander's name when I was struck by the eagerness displayed by Dewees. More to annoy than for any other purpose I said, "Oh, that's a secret!"

"Here! You made a hundred getting the permit. Here's two hundred for the name of the man that's got it!"

Alexander had said nothing as to keeping his name a secret. Recalling the beauty of the single one-hundred-dollar bill in my pocket, I thought how greatly it would be enhanced by two others—a trinity of beauty. "Hand over!" was my response. In another moment the contingent in my wallet was reinforced by two others of the same green, peculiar attraction, and then into Dewees' expectant ear I whispered, "Alexander!" He was off like a rifle-bullet. What he and the other did with their piece of paper I never had even the curiosity to inquire.

—FRANC B. WILKIE (POLIUTO)

Who with the soldiers was staunch danger-sharer—
Marched in the ranks through the shriek of the shell?
Who was their comrade, their brave color-bearer?
Who but the resolute Kady Brownell!
— CLINTON SCOLLARD

10. WOMEN AT THE FRONT

How Emma Edmonds Tamed a Rebel Vixen

*

[IN 1862] I was often sent out to procure supplies for the hospitals, butter, eggs, milk, chickens, etc., and in my rambles I used to meet with many interesting adventures. In some instances I met with narrow escapes with my life, which were not quite so interesting; and the timely appearance of my revolver often rescued me from the hands of the female rebels of the Peninsula. Persons dwelling in regions which slavery has not debased can hardly imagine the malice and ferocity manifested by the rebel vixens of the slave states. . . .

. . . One morning I started, all alone, for a five-mile ride to an isolated farm-house about three miles back from the Hampton road, and which report said was well supplied with all the articles of which I was in search. I cantered along briskly until I came to a gate which opened into a lane leading directly to the house. It was a large old-fashioned two-story house, with immense chimneys built outside, Virginia-style. The farm appeared to be in good condition, fences all up, a rare thing on the Peninsula, and corn-fields flourishing as if there were no such thing as war in the land.

I rode up to the house and dismounted, hitched my horse to a post at the door, and proceeded to ring the bell. A tall, stately lady made her appearance, and invited me in with much apparent courtesy. She was dressed in deep mourning, which was very becoming to her pale, sad face. She seemed to be about thirty years of age, very prepossessing in appearance, and evidently belonged to one of the "F.F.V.'s." As soon as I was seated she inquired: "To what fortunate circumstances am I to attribute the pleasure of this unexpected call?" I told her in a few words the nature of my business. The intelligence seemed to cast a deep shadow over her pale features, which all her efforts could not control. She seemed nervous and excited, and something in her appearance aroused my suspicion, notwithstanding her blandness of manner and lady-like deportment.

She invited me into another room, while she prepared the articles which she proposed to let me have, but I declined, giving as an excuse that I preferred to sit where I could see whether my horse remained quiet. I watched all her movements narrowly, not daring to turn my eyes aside for a single moment. She walked round in her stately way for some time, without accomplishing much in the way of facilitating my departure, and she was evidently trying to detain me for some purpose or other. Could it be that she was meditating the best mode of attack, or was she expecting some one to come, and trying to detain me until their arrival? Thoughts like these passed through my mind in quick succession.

At last I rose up abruptly, and asked her if the things were ready. She answered me with an assumed smile of surprise, and said: "Oh, I did not know that you were in a hurry; I was waiting for the boys to come and catch some chickens for you."

"And pray, madam, where are the boys?" I asked.

"Oh, not far from here," was her reply.

"Well, I have decided not to wait; you will please not detain me longer," said I, as I moved toward the door.

She began to pack some butter and eggs both together in a small basket which I had brought with me, while another stood beside her without anything in it. I looked at her; she was trembling violently, and was as pale as death. In a moment more she handed me the basket, and I held out a greenback for her acceptance.

"Oh, it was no consequence about the pay"—she did not wish anything for it.

So I thanked her and went out.

In a few moments she came to the door, but did not offer to assist me, or to hold the basket, or anything, but stood looking at me most maliciously, I thought. I placed the basket on the top of the post to which my horse had been hitched, took my seat in the saddle, and then rode up and took my basket. Turning to her I bade her good morning, and thanking her again for her kindness, I turned to ride away.

I had scarcely gone a rod when she discharged a pistol at me; by some intuitive movement I threw myself forward on my horse's neck and the ball passed over my head. I turned my horse in a twinkling, and grasped my revolver. She was in the act of firing the second time, but was so excited that the bullet went wide of its mark. I held my seven-shooter in my hand, considering where to aim. I did not wish to kill the wretch, but did intend to wound her. When she saw that two could play at this game, she dropped her pistol and threw up her hands imploringly. I took deliberate aim at one of her hands, and sent the ball through the palm of her left hand. She fell to the ground in an instant with a loud shriek. I dismounted, and took the pistol which lay beside her, and placing it in my belt, proceeded to take care of her ladyship after the following manner: I unfastened the end of my halter-strap and tied it painfully tight around her right wrist, and re-mounting my horse, I started, and brought the lady to consciousness by dragging her by the wrist two or three rods along the ground. I stopped, and she rose to her feet, and with wild entreaties she begged me to release her, but, instead of doing so, I presented a pistol, and told her that if she uttered another word or scream she was a dead woman. In that way I succeeded in keeping her from alarming any one who might be within calling distance, and so made my way toward McClellan's headquarters.

After we had gone in that way about a mile and a half, I told her that she might ride if she wished to do so, for I saw she was becoming weak from loss of blood. She was glad to accept the offer, and I bound up her hand with my handkerchief, gave her my scarf to throw over her head, and assisted her to the saddle. I marched along beside her, holding tight to the bridle rein all the while. When we were about a mile from McClellan's headquarters she fainted, and I caught her as

132

she was falling from the horse. I laid her by the roadside while I went for some water, which I brought in my hat, and after bathing her face for some time she recovered.

For the first time since we started I entered into conversation with her, and found that within the last three weeks she had lost her father, husband, and two brothers in the rebel army. They had all belonged to a company of sharpshooters, and were the first to fall. She had been almost insane since the intelligence reached her. She said I was the first Yankee that she had seen since the death of her relatives, the evil one seemed to urge her on to the step she had taken, and if I would not deliver her up to the military powers, she would go with me and take care of the wounded. She even proposed to take the oath of allegiance, and seemed deeply penitent. "If thy brother (or sister) sin against thee, and repent, forgive him," are the words of the Saviour. I tried to follow their sacred teachings there and then, and told her that I forgave her fully if she was only truly penitent. Her answer was sobs and tears.

Soon after this conversation we started for camp, she weak and humbled, and I strong and rejoicing. None ever knew from that day to this the secret of that secesh woman becoming a nurse. Instead of being taken to General McClellan's headquarters, she went direct to the hospital, where Dr. P. dressed her hand, which was causing extreme pain. The good old surgeon never could solve the mystery connected with her hand, for we both refused to answer any questions relating to the wound, except that she was shot by a "Yankee," which placed the surgeon under obligations to take care of the patient until she recovered —that is to say as long as it was convenient for him to do so.

The next day she returned to her house in an ambulance, accompanied by a hospital steward, and brought away everything which could be made use of in the hospitals, and so took up her abode with us. Her name was Alice M., but we called her Nellie J. She soon proved the genuineness of her conversion to the Federal faith by her zeal for the cause which she had so recently espoused. As soon as she was well enough to act in the capacity of nurse she commenced in good earnest, and became one of the most faithful and efficient nurses in the Army of the Potomac. But that was the first and the only instance of a female rebel changing her sentiments, or abating one iota in her cruelty or hatred toward the "Yankees"; and also the only real lady in personal appearance, education and refinement that I ever met among the females of the Peninsula.

—S. Emma E. Edmonds

Kady Brownell Serves
with the Fifth Rhode Island

*

IN JANUARY [1862] Roanoke Island was taken, and the first blow struck at the rebel power. Early in March [Brigadier General Burnside] was in Neuse River, and advancing on New Bern [North Carolina]. In the organization of the [Fifth Rhode Island] regiment Kady [Brownell] was not now a regular color-bearer, but acting in the double capacity of nurse and daughter of the regiment. When the force debarked, on the thirteenth, she marched with the regiment fourteen miles, through the mud of Neuse River bottom, and early the next morning attired herself in the coast uniform, as it was called, and was in readiness, and was earnest in the wish and the hope that she might carry the regimental colors at the head of the stormers when they should charge upon the enemy's field-works.

She begged the privilege, and it was finally granted her, to go with them up to the time when the charge should be ordered. Here, by her promptness and courage, she performed an act which saved the lives of perhaps a score of brave fellows, who were on the point of being sacrificed by one of those blunders which cannot always be avoided when so large a proportion of the officers of any force are civilians, whose coolness is not equal to their courage.

As the various regiments were getting their positions, the Fifth Rhode Island was seen advancing from a belt of wood, from a direction that was unexpected. They were mistaken for a force of the rebels, and preparations instantly made to open on it with both musketry and artillery, when Kady ran out to the front, her colors in hand, advanced to clear ground, and waved them till it was apparent that the advancing force were friends. The battle now opened in good earnest. Shot and shell were flying thick, and many a brave man was clinching his musket with nervous fingers, and looking at the bristling line of bayonets and

134

gun-barrels which they were about to charge with anything but cheerful faces, when Kady again begged to carry her colors into the charge. But the officers did not see fit to grant her request, and she walked slowly to the rear, and immediately devoted herself to the equally sacred and no less important duty of caring for the wounded.

In a few moments word was brought that [her husband] Robert had fallen, and lay bleeding in the brick-yard. That was the part of the line where the Fifth Rhode Island had just charged and carried the enemy's works. She ran immediately to the spot, and found her husband lying there, his thigh bone fearfully shattered with a Minie ball; but, fortunately, the main femoral artery had not been cut, so that his life was not immediately in danger from bleeding.

She went out where the dead and wounded were lying thick along the breastwork, to get blankets that would no longer do them any good, in order to make her husband and others more comfortable.

Here she saw several lying helpless in the mud and shallow water of the yard. Two or three of them she helped up, and they dragged themselves to dryer ground. Among them was a rebel engineer, whose foot had been crushed by the fragment of a shell. She showed him the same kindness that she did the rest. . . .

The rebel engineer had fallen in a pool of dirty water, and was rapidly losing blood, and growing cold in consequence of this and the water in which he lay.

She took him under his arms and dragged him back to dry ground, arranged a blanket for him to lie on, and another to cover him, and fixed a cartridge box, or something similar, to support his head.

As soon as he had grown a little comfortable, and rallied from the extreme pain, he rose up, and shaking his fist at her, with a volley of horrible and obscene oaths, exclaimed, "Ah, you d—— Yankee ——, if ever I get on my feet again, if I don't blow the head off your shoulders, then God d—— me!" For an instant the blood of an insulted woman, the daughter of a soldier, and the daughter of a regiment, was in mutiny. She snatched a musket with bayonet fixed, that lay close by, and an instant more his profane and indecent tongue would have been hushed forever. But, as she was plunging the bayonet at his breast, a wounded Union soldier, who lay near, caught the point of it in his hand; remonstrated against killing a wounded enemy, no matter what he said; and in her heart the woman triumphed, and she spared him, ingrate that he was.

She returned to the house where Robert had been carried, and spreading blankets under him, made him as comfortable as he could be at a temporary hospital. The nature of his wound was such that his critical time would come two or three weeks later, when the shattered pieces of bone must come out before the healing process could commence. All she could do now was simply to keep the limb cool by regular and constant applications of cold water.

From the middle of March to the last of April she remained in New Bern, nursing her husband, who for some time grew worse, and needed constant and skillful nursing to save his life. When not [watching] over him, she was doing all she could for other sufferers. Notwithstanding her experience with the inhuman engineer, the wounded rebels found her the best friend they had. Every day she contrived to save a bucket of coffee and a pail of delicate soup, and would take it over and give it out with her own hands to the wounded in the rebel hospital. While she was thus waiting on these helpless and almost deserted sufferers, she one day saw two of the New Bern ladies, who had come in silks to look at their wounded countrymen. One of them was standing between two beds, in such a position as to obstruct the narrow passage. Our heroine politely requested her to let her pass, when she remarked to the other female who came with her, "That's one of our women— isn't it?" "No," was the sneering response, "she's a Yankee ——," using a term which never defiles the lips of a *lady*. The rebel surgeon very properly ordered her out of the house.

It is but justice, however, to say that in some of her rebel acquaintances at New Bern human nature was not so scandalized.

Colonel Avery, a rebel officer, soon after he was captured, said something to her about carrying the wrong flag, and that "the stars and bars" was *the* flag. "It won't be *the* flag till after your head is cold," was her quick reply. The Colonel said something not so complimentary to her judgment, when General Burnside, who was standing near, told him to cease that language, as he was talking to a woman. Immediately the Colonel made the most ample apologies, and expressed his admiration of her spirit and courage, and afterwards insisted on her receiving from him sundry Confederate notes in payment of her kindness to the wounded among his men. There was one poor rebel, who died of lockjaw from an amputated leg, whom she really pitied. He said he "allus was agin the war—never believed Jeff Davis and them would *succeed* nohow," and talked about his poor wife and his seven children (who would be left in poverty, and whom he would never see again) in a way so natural and kindly that she forgot all about the brutal engineer and the insulting woman in silk, and did all she could to make the poor old man comfortable. He was fond of smoking, and in the terrible pain he suffered, the narcotic effect of the tobacco was very soothing. Kady used to light his pipe for him at the hospital fire, and go and give it to him.

In April, Robert could bear removal, and was made as comfortable as possible on a cot on the steamship. Arriving in New York, he lay a long time at the New England Rooms; and his faithful wife, as tender as she was brave, thought only of his life and his recovery. But it was eighteen months before he touched ground, and then the surgeons pronounced him unfit for active service; and as his soldier days were over, Kady had no thought of anything more but the plain duties of the loving wife and the kind friend.

—FRANK MOORE

*

Belle Boyd Aids Stonewall Jackson

*

1 · Henry Kyd Douglas Tells How Belle Boyd Pinned a Rose on Him

IN THE EARLY AFTERNOON [of May 22, 1862], Ewell struck the pickets of the enemy within sight of and negligently near to Front Royal. They were driven in and the small body of infantry supporting them easily routed. We stopped to form on a hill overlooking the small town of Front Royal and the hurried movement of blue-coats and the galloping of horsemen here and there told of the confusion in the enemy's camp. General Jackson, not knowing the force of the enemy there was so small or so unprepared by reinforcements for his approach, was endeavoring to take in the situation before ordering an advance.

I observed, almost immediately, the figure of a woman in white glide swiftly out of town on our right and, after making a little circuit, run rapidly up a ravine in our direction and then disappear from sight.

She seemed, when I saw her, to heed neither weeds nor fences, but waved a bonnet as she came on, trying, it was evident, to keep the hill between herself and the village. I called General Jackson's attention to the singular movement just as a dip in the land hid her, and at General Ewell's suggestion, he sent me to meet her and ascertain what she wanted. That was just to my taste and it took only a few minutes for my horse to carry me to meet the romantic maiden whose tall, supple, and graceful figure struck me as soon as I came in sight of her. As I drew near, her speed slackened, and I was startled, momentarily, at hearing her call my name. But I was not much astonished when I saw that the visitor was the well-known Belle Boyd whom I had known from her earliest girlhood. She was just the girl to dare to do this thing.

Nearly exhausted, and with her hand pressed against her heart, she said in gasps, "I knew it must be Stonewall, when I heard the first gun. Go back quick and tell him that the Yankee force is very small— one regiment of Maryland infantry, several pieces of artillery and several companies of cavalry. Tell him I know, for I went through the camps and got it out of an officer. Tell him to charge right down and he will catch them all. I must hurry back. Good-by. My love to all the dear boys—and remember if you meet me in town you haven't seen me today."

I raised my cap, she kissed her hand and was gone. I delivered her message speedily, and while Jackson was asking me questions about her—for until then he had never heard of her—I saw the wave of her white bonnet as she entered the village and disappeared among its houses.

Very soon the First Maryland Infantry and Major Roberdeau Wheat's Louisiana battalion were rushing down the hill and into the town. General Jackson with a semi-smile suggested that I had better go with them and see if I could get any more information from that young lady. It took very little time to get into Front Royal and clean it out. The pursuit of the retreating Federals was kept up, with cavalry, the infantry following as quickly as possible. While this was being done I looked for Belle Boyd and found her standing on the pavement in front of a hotel, talking with some few Federal officers (prisoners) and some of her acquaintances in our army. Her cheeks were rosy with excitement and recent exercise and her eyes all aflame. When I rode up to speak to her she received me with much surprised cordiality, and as I stooped from my saddle she pinned a crimson rose to my uniform,

138

bidding me remember that it was *blood-red* and that it was her "colors."
I left her to join the General.

—MAJOR HENRY KYD DOUGLAS

II · Belle Boyd Recalls Her Wild Ride on Fleeta

"IT WAS at the time of [Nathaniel P.] Banks's retreat [from
Strasburg to the Potomac, May 25-26] that I took a midnight ride of
fifty-four miles over the mountains to find Jackson. He was at Luray.
The Federals were round Front Royal. I had all their dispositions from
Harper's Ferry down.

"There was a young Federal officer at our house who I knew
had the countersign. He fell in love with me, and I was engaged to him
to be married, but I had always refused to kiss him good-night.

"I wanted his papers, and so this night when he pressed me for
a kiss I saw these papers sticking from his pocket. Here was the opportunity, and have them I must. I kissed him and at the same time deftly
removed the packet of letters. He never missed them until long after I
had gone.

"So you see it was the kiss of Judas after all.

"Fortune favored me. Those papers were more valuable than I
had imagined.

"In the garb of a boy I mounted my horse that evening and
started on my journey. It was not a moonlight night, though the stars
were out at the commencement of my weird journey, but soon became
obscured.

"Ah, that was a wild ride that we took—Fleeta and I. I will never
forget it. With only a general conception of the way, oftentimes I got
off my course. At the best, there was only a bridle path. For much of
the route not even that, and here and there rough, hard climbs up
the stony beds of the brooks, with stiffish ledges and rocky barriers to
leap in the gloomy and precipitous ravines and gorges.

"I found Jackson and delivered my dispatches. Coming back in
the gray of the morning I was overtaken by a thunder storm. I dared
not stop, so kept straight on, wet to the skin, 'mid the gloom of the
storm and the blinding glare of the lightning.

"In one vivid flash there stood revealed the Federal guard with
rifle poised.

" 'Who comes there?' rang out his challenge.

"For the moment I forgot the countersign, when luckily kind fate produced the corporal standing close beside the sentry. The friendly lightning gave him a glimpse of me.

"Said he, 'Let the boy pass; I know him.'

"I was awfully glad he thought he did, and dashed by the picket with a lightened heart. Fleeta soon bore me to my father's door."

—As told by BELLE BOYD to CHARLES F. W. ARCHER

*

Mother Bickerdyke Cuts Red Tape

*

I · The "Tin Cup Brigade"

OCCUPIED all the time of the Corinth [Mississippi] campaign with the wounded in the rear of General [Henry W.] Halleck's army [Mrs. Mary A. Bickerdyke] was put in charge of the Main Hospital at Corinth, when our force entered that place [May 30, 1862]. While there, her indomitable force and determination to serve the soldiers had another trial and another victory. Learning that a brigade was to march through the hospital grounds, and knowing that the soldiers would be nearly exhausted from their long march under a burning sun, she got out her barrels of water which had been brought for the men in hospital, had a corps of her assistants ready with pails and dippers, and gave the soldiers water as they passed through. When the commanding officer came up, Mrs. Bickerdyke asked that the men be halted; but he refused, and, going ahead, ordered his men to march along. At the same time a voice in the rear—that of Mrs. Bickerdyke—was heard giving the reverse order, "Halt!" in very clear tones. The woman's order was obeyed, and the "Tin Cup Brigade" worked energetically for a few minutes, rejoicing in the triumph of *their* commander.

—FRANK MOORE

140

II · The Delinquent Surgeon

[IN JUNE, 1863, Mrs. Bickerdyke] was put in charge of Gayoso Hospital, in what was formerly the Gayoso Hotel, one of the largest hotels in Memphis. Here she was in all her glory. It was her ambition to make her hospital the best regulated, neatest, and most comfortable in Memphis or its vicinity, and this, in such a building, was not easy. She accomplished it, however. . . . Nothing displeased her so much as any neglect of the men on the part of the surgeon or assistant surgeons. On one occasion, visiting one of the wards at nearly eleven o'clock A.M., where the men were very badly wounded, she found that the assistant surgeon-in-charge, who had been out "on a spree" the night before and had slept very late, had not yet made out the special diet list for the ward, and the men, faint and hungry, had had no breakfast. She at once denounced him in the strongest terms.

He came in meanwhile, and on his inquiry, "Hoity toity, what's the matter?" she turned upon him with, "Matter enough, you miserable scoundrel! Here these men, any one of them worth a thousand of you, are suffered to starve and die, because you want to be off upon a drunk! Pull off your shoulder-straps," she continued, as he tried feebly to laugh off her reproaches, "pull off your shoulder-straps, for you shall not stay in the army a week longer." The surgeon still laughed, but he turned pale, for he knew her power. She was as good as her word. Within three days, she had caused his discharge. He went to head-quarters, and asked to be reinstated. General Sherman, who was then in command, listened patiently, and then inquired who had caused his discharge. "I was discharged in consequence of misrepresentations," answered the surgeon. "But who caused your discharge?" persisted the General. "Why," said the surgeon, hesitatingly, "I suppose it was that woman, that Mrs. Bickerdyke." "Oh," said Sherman. "Well, if it was her, I can do nothing for you. She ranks me."

—Dr. L. P. Brockett

III · "Loyal Cows and Hens"

IT WAS MORE DIFFICULT to supply the hospitals with milk and eggs than with any other necessaries. With the supplies furnished by government, the tea, coffee, sugar, flour, meat, and other like articles, which were usually of good quality, Mother Bickerdyke could work miracles in the culinary line, even when there was a lack of sanitary stores, if she could only have an abundant supply of milk and eggs. But these were very difficult to obtain. They could not be sent from the North, and they could not be purchased in sufficiently large quantities to supply the enormous demand. In the enemy's country, where the hospitals were located, their prices were exorbitant beyond belief. Mother Bickerdyke hit upon a plan to remedy these difficulties. When the medical director came into her hospital one morning, on a tour of inspection, she accosted him thus: "Dr. ——, do you know we are paying these Memphis secesh fifty cents for every quart of milk we use? And do you know it's such poor stuff,—two thirds chalk and water,— that if you should pour it into the trough of a respectable pig at home, he would turn up his nose, and run off, squealing in disgust?"

"Well, what can we do about it?" asked the doctor, between whom and herself there was now an excellent understanding.

"If you'll give me thirty days' furlough and transportation, I'll go home, and get all the milk and eggs that the Memphis hospitals can use."

"Get milk and eggs! Why, you could not bring them down here, if the North would give you all it has. A barrel of eggs would spoil, this warm weather, before it could reach us; and how on earth could you bring milk?"

"But I'll bring down the milk and egg producers. I'll get cows and hens, and we'll have milk and eggs of our own. The folks at home, doctor, will give us all the hens and cows we need for the use of these hospitals, and jump at the chance to do it. You needn't laugh, nor shake your head!" as he turned away, amused and incredulous. "I tell you, the people at the North ache to do something for the boys down here, and I can get fifty cows in Illinois alone for just the asking."

"Pshaw! pshaw!" said the doctor, "you would be laughed at from one end of the country to the other, if you should go on so wild an errand."

"Fiddlesticks! Who cares for that? Give me a furlough and transportation, and let me try it!"

So she came North again, and did not stop until she reached St. Louis. She was escorted as far as that city by several hundred cripples, "every one of whom had lost either a leg or an arm." These she saw placed in hospitals, and then came on to Chicago. She secured the cows with little difficulty. Jacob Strawn, of Jacksonville, one of the wealthy farmers of Illinois, with a few of his neighbors, gave the hundred cows without delay. They were sent to Springfield, Illinois,—whence Governor Yates had promised they should be shipped to Memphis,—in herds of fifteen or twenty, with some one in charge of each detachment, to take care of the animals.

The hens were sent to the rooms of the Commission in Chicago. In a week after the call, our building was transformed into a huge hennery, and all the workers therein were completely driven out. The din of crowing, cackling, and quarrelling was unbearable; and, as the weather was warm, the odor was yet more insupportable. The fowls were despatched to Memphis in four shipments, in coops containing about two dozen each.

Before her thirty days' leave of absence was ended, Mother Bickerdyke was on the return route to her hospital, forming a part of a bizarre procession of over one hundred cows and one thousand hens, strung all along the road from Chicago to Memphis. She entered the city in triumph, amid immense lowing and crowing and cackling. She informed the astonished Memphians that, "These are *loyal* cows and hens; none of your miserable trash that give chalk and water for milk, and lay loud-smelling eggs."

—MARY A. LIVERMORE

*

Phoebe Yates Pember Lends a Helping Hand

---

*

I · *"You Wait!"*

"KIN YOU WRIT ME a letter?" drawled a whining voice from a bed in one of the wards, a cold day in '62.

The speaker was an up-country Georgian, one of the kind called "Goubers" by the soldiers generally; lean, yellow, attenuated, with wispy strands of hair hanging over his high, thin cheek-bones. He put out a hand to detain me and the nails were like claws.

"Why do you not let the nurse cut your nails?"

"Because I aren't got any spoon, and I use them instead."

"Will you let me have your hair cut then? You can't get well with all that dirty hair hanging about your eyes and ears."

"No, I can't git my hair cut, kase as how I promised my mammy that I would let it grow till the war be over. Oh, it's onlucky to cut it!"

"Then I can't write any letter for you. Do what I wish you to do, and then I will oblige you."

This was plain talking. The hair was cut (I left the nails for another day), my portfolio brought, and sitting by the side of his bed I waited for further orders. They came with a formal introduction— "for Mrs. Marthy Brown."

"My dear Mammy: I hope this finds you well, as it leaves me well, and I hope that I shall git a furlough Christmas, and come and see you, and I hope that you will keep well, and all the folks be well by that time, as I hopes to be well myself. This leaves me in good health, as I hope it finds you and I—"

But here I paused, as his mind seemed to be going round in a circle, and asked him a few questions about his home, his position during the last summer's campaign, how he got sick, and where his brigade was at that time. Thus furnished with some material to work upon, the letter proceeded rapidly. Four sides were conscientiously filled, for no soldier would think a letter worth sending home that showed any blank paper. Transcribing his name, the number of his ward and proper address, so that an answer might reach him—the composition was read to him. Gradually his pale face brightened, a sitting posture was assumed with difficulty (for, in spite of his determined effort in his letter "to be well," he was far from convalescence). As I folded and directed it, contributed the expected five-cent stamp, and handed it to him, he gazed cautiously around to be sure there were no listeners.

"Did you writ all that?" he asked, whispering, but with great emphasis.

"Yes."

"Did *I* say all that?"

"I think you did."

A long pause of undoubted admiration—astonishment ensued. What was working in that poor mind? Could it be that Psyche had stirred one of the delicate plumes of her wing and touched that dormant soul?

"Are you married?" The harsh voice dropped very low.

"I am not. At least, I am a widow."

He rose still higher in bed. He pushed away desperately the tangled hay on his brow. A faint color fluttered over the hollow cheek, and stretching out a long piece of bone with a talon attached, he gently touched my arm and with constrained voice whispered mysteriously: "You wait!"

And readers, I *am* waiting still; and I here caution the male portion of creation who may adore through their mental powers, to respect my confidence, and not seek to shake my constancy.

II · A Compliment

AT INTERVALS the lower wards, unused except in times of great need, for they were unfurnished with any comforts, would be filled with rough soldiers from camp, sent to recuperate after field service, who may not have seen a female face for months; and though generally too much occupied to notice them much, their partly concealed but determined regard would become embarrassing. One day, while directing arrangements with a ward-master, my attention was attracted by the pertinacious staring of a rough-looking Texan. He walked round and round me in rapidly narrowing circles, examining every detail of my dress, face, and figure; his eye never fixing upon any particular part for a moment but traveling incessantly all over me. It seemed the wonder of the mind at the sight of a new creation. I moved my position; he shifted his to suit the new arrangement—again a change was made, so obviously to get out of his range of vision that with a delicacy of feeling that the roughest men always treated me with, he desisted from his inspection so far that though his person made no movement, his neck twisted round to accommodate his eyes, till I supposed some progenitor of his family had been an owl. The men began to titter, and my patience became exhausted.

"What is the matter, my man? Did you never see a woman before?"

"Jerusalem!" he ejaculated, not making the slightest motion towards withdrawing his determined notice, "I never did see such a nice one. Why, you's as pretty as a pair of red shoes with green strings."

145

III · *"You Can Let Go"*

FEMININE SYMPATHY being much more demonstrative than masculine, particularly when compared with a surgeon's unresponsiveness, who inured to the aspects of suffering, has more control over his professional feelings, the nurses often summoned me when only the surgeon was needed. One very cold night . . . when sleeping at my hospital rooms, an answer was made to my demand as to who was knocking and what was wanted. The nurse from the nearest ward said something was wrong with Fisher. Instructing him to find the doctor immediately and hastily getting on some clothing, I hurried to the scene, for Fisher was an especial favorite. He was quite a young man, of about twenty years of age, who had been wounded ten months previously, very severely, high up on the leg near the hip and who by dint of hard nursing, good food and plenty of stimulant had been given a fair chance for recovery. The bones of the broken leg had slipped together, then lapped, and nature anxious as she always is to help herself had thrown a ligature across, uniting the severed parts; but after some time the side curved out, and the wounded leg was many inches shorter than its fellow. He had been the object of sedulous care on the part of all—surgeons, ward-master, nurse and matron—and the last effort made to assist him was by the construction of an open cylinder of pasteboard, made in my kitchen, of many sheets of coarse brown paper, cemented together with very stiff paste and baked around the stovepipe. This was to clasp by its own prepared curve the deformed hip, and be a support for it when he was able to use his crutches.

He had remained through all his trials, neat, fresh and hearty, interesting in appearance, and so gentle-mannered and uncomplaining that we all loved him. Supported on his crutches he had walked up and down his ward for the first time since he was wounded, and seemed almost restored. That same night he turned over and uttered an exclamation of pain.

Following the nurse to his bed, and turning down the covering, a small jet of blood spurted up. The sharp edge of the splintered bone must have severed an artery. I instantly put my finger on the little orifice and awaited the surgeon. He soon came—took a long look and shook his head. The explanation was easy; the artery was imbedded in the fleshy part of the thigh and could not be taken up. No earthly power could save him.

146

There was no object in detaining Dr. ——. He required his time and strength, and long I sat by the boy, unconscious himself that any serious trouble was apprehended. The hardest trial of my duty was laid upon me; the necessity of telling a man in the prime of life, and fullness of strength that there was no hope for him.

It was done at last, and the verdict received patiently and courageously, some directions given by which his mother would be informed of his death, and then he turned his questioning eyes upon my face.

"How long can I live?"

"Only as long as I keep my finger upon this artery." A pause ensued. God alone knew what thoughts hurried through that heart and brain, called so unexpectedly from all earthly hopes and ties. He broke the silence at last.

"You can let go—"

But I could not. Not if my own life had trembled in the balance. Hot tears rushed to my eyes, a surging sound to my ears, and a deathly coldness to my lips. The pang of obeying him was spared me, and for the first and last time during the trials that surrounded me for four years, I fainted away.

IV · Rats

THE RATS . . . felt the times, and waxed strong and cunning, defying all attempts to entrap them, and skillfully levying blackmail upon us day by day, and night after night. Hunger had educated their minds and sharpened their reasoning faculties. Other vermin, the change of seasons would rid us of, but the coldest day in winter, and the hottest in summer, made no apparent difference in their vivacious strategy. They examined traps with the air of connoisseurs, sometimes sprung them from a safe position, and kicked over the bread spread with butter and strychnine to show their contempt for such underhanded warfare. The men related wonderful rat-stories not well enough authenticated to put on record, but their gourmands ate all the poultices applied during the night to the sick, and dragged away the pads stuffed with bran from under the arms and legs of the wounded.

They even performed a surgical operation which would have entitled any of them to pass the board. A Virginian had been wounded in the very center of the instep of his left foot. The hole made was large, and the wound sloughed fearfully around a great lump of proud flesh which had formed in the center like an island. The surgeons feared to remove this mass, as it might be connected with the nerves of the foot, and lockjaw might ensue. Poor Patterson would sit on his bed all day gazing at his lame foot and bathing it with a rueful face, which had brightened amazingly one morning when I paid him a visit. He exhibited it with great glee, the little island gone, and a deep hollow left, but the wound washed clean and looking healthy. Some skillful rat surgeon had done him this good service while in the search for luxuries, and he only knew that on awakening in the morning he had found the operation performed.

I never had but one personal interview with any of them. An ancient gray gentleman, who looked a hundred years old, both in years and depravity, would eat nothing but butter, when that article was twenty dollars a pound; so finding all means of getting rid of him fail through his superior intelligence, I caught him with a fish-hook, well baited with a lump of his favorite butter, dropped into his domicile under the kitchen floor. Epicures sometimes managed to entrap them and secure a nice broil for supper, declaring that their flesh was superior to squirrel meat; but never having tasted it, I cannot add my testimony to its merits. They stayed with us to the last, nor did I ever observe any signs of a desire to change their politics. Perhaps some curious gourmet may wish a recipe for the best mode of cooking them. The rat must be skinned, cleaned, his head cut off and his body laid upon a square board, the legs stretched to their full extent and secured upon it with small tacks, then baste with bacon fat and roast before a good fire quickly like canvas-back ducks.

—PHOEBE YATES PEMBER

Old Jeff says he'll hang us if we dare to meet him armed:
A very big thing, but we are not at all alarmed; . . .
For God is for the right, and we have no need to fear:
The Union must be saved by the colored volunteer.
—SONG BY A NEGRO SOLDIER

11. "A FIGHTING RACE"

Harriet Tubman Accompanies
the Union Gun-Boats

*

WHEN OUR ARMIES and gun-boats first appeared in any part of the South, many of the poor Negroes were as much afraid of "de Yankee Buckra" as of their own masters. It was almost impossible to win their confidence, or to get information from them. But to Harriet [Tubman, the Negro "Moses"] they would tell anything; and so it became quite important that she should accompany expeditions going up the rivers, or into unexplored parts of the country, to control and get information from those whom they took with them as guides.

General [David] Hunter asked her at one time if she would go with several gun-boats up the Combahee River, the object of the expedition being to take up the torpedoes placed by the rebels in the river, to destroy railroads and bridges, and to cut off supplies from the rebel troops. She said she would go if Colonel [James] Montgomery was to be appointed commander of the expedition. Colonel Montgomery was one of John Brown's men, and was well known to Harriet. Accordingly, Colonel Montgomery was appointed to command, and Harriet, with several men under her, the principal of whom was J. Plowden, . . . accompanied the expedition. Harriet describes in the most graphic manner the appearance of the plantations as they passed up the river; the frightened Negroes leaving their work and taking to the woods, at sight of the gun-boats; then coming to peer out like startled deer, and scudding away like the wind at the sound of the steam-whistle. "Well," said one old Negro, "Mas'r said de Yankees had horns and tails, but I nebber beliebed it till now." But the word was passed along by the mysterious telegraphic communication existing among these simple people, that these were "Lincoln's gun-boats come to set them free." In vain, then, the drivers used their whips, in their efforts to hurry the poor creatures back to their quarters; they all turned and ran for the gun-boats. They came down every road, across every field, just as they had left their work and their cabins; women with children clinging around their necks, hanging to their dresses, running behind, all making at full speed for "Lincoln's gun-boats." Eight hundred poor wretches at one time crowded the banks, with their hands extended towards their deliverers, and they were all taken off upon the gun-boats, and carried down to Beaufort.

"I nebber see such a sight," said Harriet; "we laughed, an' laughed, an' laughed. Here you'd see a woman wid a pail on her head, rice a-smokin' in it jus' as she'd taken it from de fire, young one hangin' on behind, one han' roun' her forehead to hold on, 'tother han' diggin' into de rice-pot, eatin' wid all its might; hold of her dress two or three more; down her back a bag wid a pig in it. One woman brought two pigs, a white one, an' a black one; we took 'em all on board; named de white pig Beauregard, an' de black pig Jeff Davis. Sometimes de women would come wid twins hangin' roun' der necks; 'pears like I nebber see so many twins in my life; bags on der shoulders, baskets on der heads, and young ones taggin' behin', all loaded; pigs squealin', chickens screamin', young ones squealin'." And so they came pouring down to the gun-boats. When they stood on the shore, and the small boats put out to take them off, they all wanted to get in at once. After the boats were crowded, they would hold on to them so that they could not leave the shore. The oarsmen would beat them on their hands, but they would not let go; they were afraid the gun-boats would go off and leave them, and all wanted to make sure of one of these arks of refuge. At length, Colonel Montgomery shouted from the upper deck, above the clamor of appealing tones, "Moses, you'll have to give 'em a song." Then Harriet lifted up her voice and sang:

> *Of all the whole creation in the east or in the west,*
> *The glorious Yankee nation is the greatest and the best.*
> *Come along! Come along! don't be alarmed,*
> *Uncle Sam is rich enough to give you all a farm.*

At the end of every verse, the Negroes in their enthusiasm would throw up their hands and shout "Glory," and the row-boats would take that opportunity to push off; and so at last they were all brought on board. The masters fled; houses and barns and railroad bridges were burned, tracks torn up, torpedoes destroyed, and the expedition was in all respects successful.

—SARAH H. BRADFORD

∗

The Captain of the *Planter*

∗

ON MAY 13, 1862, the Confederate steamboat *Planter,* the special dispatch boat of General [Roswell S.] Ripley, the Confederate post commander at Charleston, South Carolina, was taken by Robert Smalls under the following circumstances from the wharf at which she was lying, carried safely out of Charleston Harbor, and delivered to one of the vessels of the Federal fleet then blockading that port.

On the day previous, May 12, the *Planter,* which had for two weeks been engaged in removing guns from Coles Island to James Island, returned to Charleston. That night all the officers went ashore and slept in the city, leaving on board a crew of eight men, all colored.

151

Among them was Robert Smalls, who was virtually the pilot of the boat, although he was only called a wheelman, because at that time no colored man could have, in fact, been made a pilot. For some time previous he had been watching for an opportunity to carry into execution a plan he had conceived to take the *Planter* to the Federal fleet. This, he saw, was about as good a chance as he would ever have to do so, and therefore, he determined not to lose it. Consulting with the balance of the crew, Smalls found that they were willing to cooperate with him, although two of them afterwards concluded to remain behind. The design was hazardous in the extreme. The boat would have to pass beneath the guns of the forts in the harbor. Failure and detection would have been certain death. Fearful was the venture, but it was made. The daring resolution had been formed, and under the command of Robert Smalls wood was taken aboard, steam was put on, and with her valuable cargo of guns and ammunition, intended for Fort Ripley, a new fortification just constructed in the harbor, about two o'clock in the morning the *Planter* silently moved off from her dock, steamed up to North Atlantic Wharf, where Smalls's wife and two children, together with four other women and one other child, and also three men, were waiting to embark. All these were taken on board, and then, at 3:25 A.M., May 13, the *Planter* started on her perilous adventure, carrying nine men, five women, and three children. Passing Fort Johnson, the *Planter's* steam whistle blew the usual salute and she proceeded down the bay. Approaching Fort Sumter, Smalls stood in the pilot-house leaning out of the window, with his arms folded across his breast, after the manner of Captain Relay, the commander of the boat, and his head covered with the huge straw hat which Captain Relay commonly wore on such occasions.

The signal required to be given by all steamers passing out was blown as coolly as if General Ripley was on board, going out on a tour of inspection. Sumter answered by signal, "All right," and the *Planter* headed toward Morris Island, then occupied by Hatch's light artillery, and passed beyond the range of Sumter's guns before anybody suspected anything was wrong. When at last the *Planter* was obviously going toward the Federal fleet off the bar, Sumter signaled toward Morris Island to stop her. But it was too late. As the *Planter* approached the Federal fleet, a white flag was displayed, but this was not at first discovered, and the Federal steamers, supposing the Confederate rams were coming to attack them, stood out to deep water. But the ship *Onward,* Captain Nichols, which was not a steamer, remained, opened

her ports, and was about to fire into the *Planter,* when she noticed the flag of truce. As soon as the vessels came within hailing distance of each other, the *Planter's* errand was explained. Captain Nichols then boarded her, and Smalls delivered the *Planter* to him. From the *Planter,* Smalls was transferred to the *Augusta,* the flag-ship off the bar, under the command of Captain Parrott, by whom the *Planter,* with Smalls and her crew, were sent to Port Royal to Rear Admiral [Samuel F.] Du Pont, then in command of the Southern Squadron.
—*House Report No. 3505, Forty-Ninth Congress, Second Session*

*

"We Are Willing to Fight"

*

I DESIRED TO ORGANIZE a special brigade to capture and occupy all the western part of Louisiana and other places east of the Red River, and to control the mines of salt deposit in New Iberia. These mines could be approached by water, an advantage which Jefferson put forth as one of the reasons for the purchase of Louisiana.

I could get no reply from Washington that I could have any rein-forcements whatever. I had gone as far as I could get in enlisting the former soldiers of the rebel army to strengthen the regiments I then had. Accordingly I sent a confidential message to Washington saying that if they could not do anything for me by sending troops, I would call on Africa for assistance,—i.e., I would enlist all the colored troops I could from the free Negroes.

While I was waiting at Ship Island [August, 1862], the rebel authorities in New Orleans had organized two regiments from the free Negroes, called "Native Guards, Colored." When [Major General Mansfield] Lovell ran away with his troops these men stayed at home. The rebels had allowed the company officers to be commissioned from colored men; but for the field officers,—colonels, lieutenant colonels, and majors, and the staff officers,—they were white men.

I found out the names and residences of some twenty of these colored officers, and sent for them to call on me. They came, and a very intelligent-looking set of men they were. I asked them if they would like to be organized as part of the United States troops. They unanimously said they would. In all bodies of men there is always a spokesman, and while many of my guests were of a very light shade, that spokesman was a Negro nearly as dark as the ace of spades.

"General," he asked, "shall we be officers as we were before?"

"Yes; every one of you who is fit to be an officer shall be, and all the line officers shall be colored men."

"How soon do you want us to be ready?"

"How soon can you give me two regiments of a thousand men each?"

"In ten days."

"But," I said, "I want you to answer me one question. My officers, most of them, believe that Negroes won't fight."

"Oh, but we will," came from the whole of them.

"You seem to be an intelligent man," said I, to their spokesman; "answer me this question: I have found out that you know just as well what this war is about as I do, and if the United States succeed in it, it will put an end to slavery." They all looked assent. "Then tell me why some Negroes have not in this war struck a good blow somewhere for their freedom? All over the South the men have been conscripted and driven away to the armies, leaving ten Negroes in some districts to one white man, and the colored men have simply gone on raising crops and taking care of their women and children."

The man's countenance lighted up. He said: "You are General here, and I don't like to answer that question."

"Answer it exactly according as the matter lies in your mind, and I pledge you my honor, whatever the answer may be it shall harm no one of you."

"General, will you permit a question?"

"Yes."

"If we colored men had risen to make war on our masters, would not it have been our duty to ourselves, they being our enemies, to kill the enemy wherever we could find them? and all the white men would have been our enemies to be killed?"

"I don't know but what you are right," said I. "I think that would be a logical necessity of insurrection."

"If the colored men had begun such a war as that, General, which general of the United States army should we have called on to help us fight our battles?"

That was unanswerable.

"Well," I said, "why do you think your men will fight?"

"General, we come of a fighting race. Our fathers were brought here slaves because they were captured in war, and in hand-to-hand fights, too. We are willing to fight. Pardon me, General, but the only cowardly blood we have got in our veins is the white blood."

"Very well," I said, "recruit your men and let them be mustered into the service at"—I mentioned a large public building—"in a fortnight from to-day, at ten o'clock in the morning. Report, and I will meet you there. I will give orders that the building be prepared."

On that morning I went there and saw such a sight as I never saw before: two thousand men ready to enlist as recruits, and not a man of them who had not a white "biled shirt" on.

—MAJOR GENERAL BENJAMIN F. BUTLER

*

A Veteran Explains
Why the Union Army Let Negroes Fight

*

NINETY-ONE-YEAR-OLD Richard Slaughter, who enlisted in the Union army, has his own version of how Negroes came to have the privilege of fighting:

Douglass went to Abe Lincoln an' tole him to give de black man guns an' let him fight. Abe Lincoln say, "If I give him gun, when de battle start he run."

Frederick Douglass say: "Try him an' you'll win de war." Abe say: "All right, Frederick, I'll try him once." Congress didn't like it, but he made 'em like it. Den dey was more trouble. Wouldn't no General but one take de colored boys. General Peg-leg Butler, he say, "I'll take 'em." An' you know why? 'Cause his cavalry didn't have nothin' but black horses, an' dem white men didn't look right on black horses. Put dem Negroes on black horses, an' dey look jus' right. Look like I can see dem boys now. Arter dey fight de fust battle, den ev'y general in Lincoln's army wanted 'em. Dey was de braves' soldiers de Yanks ever had.

—*The Negro in Virginia*

My captain went a-scoutin'
And took my brother Jim;
He went to catch the Yankees,
But the Yankees they catched him.
—"I'LL LAY TEN DOLLARS DOWN"

---

12. DANGER WAS THEIR BUSINESS

The Andrews Raid

---

*

ON THE 8th of April, 1862—the day after the battle of Pittsburg Landing [Shiloh], of which, however, [General Ormsby M.] Mitchel had received no intelligence—he marched swiftly southward from Shelbyville and seized Huntsville, in Alabama, on the 11th of April, and then sent a detachment westward over the Memphis and Charleston railroad to open railway communication with the Union army at Pittsburg Landing.

Another detachment, commanded by Mitchel in person, advanced on the same day 70 miles by rail directly into the enemy's territory, arriving unchecked within 30 miles of Chattanooga. In two hours' time he would have reached that point, the most important position in the

West, with 2,000 men. Why did he not go? The story of the railroad raid is the answer.

The night before breaking camp at Shelbyville, Mitchel sent an expedition secretly into the heart of Georgia to cut the railroad communications of Chattanooga to the south and east. . . .

In the employ of General [Don Carlos] Buell was a spy, named James J. Andrews, who had rendered valuable services in the first year of the war, and had secured the confidence of the Union commanders. In March, 1862, Buell had sent him secretly with eight men to burn the bridges west of Chattanooga; but the failure of expected co-operation defeated the plan, and Andrews, after visiting Atlanta, and inspecting the whole of the enemy's lines in that vicinity and northward, had returned, ambitious to make another attempt. His plans for the second raid were submitted to Mitchel, and on the eve of the movement from Shelbyville to Huntsville, the latter authorized him to take twenty-four men, secretly enter the enemy's territory, and, by means of capturing a train, burn the bridges on the northern part of the Georgia State railroad, and also one on the East Tennessee railroad where it approaches the Georgia State line, thus completely isolating Chattanooga, which was then virtually ungarrisoned.

The soldiers for this expedition, of whom the writer was one, were selected from the three Ohio regiments belonging to General J. W. Sill's brigade, being simply told that they were wanted for secret and very dangerous service. So far as known, not a man chosen declined the perilous honor. Our uniforms were exchanged for ordinary Southern dress, and all arms, except revolvers, were left in camp. On the 7th of April, by the roadside about a mile east of Shelbyville, in the late twilight, we met our leader. Taking us a little way from the road, he quietly placed before us the outlines of the romantic and adventurous plan, which was: to break into small detachments of three or four, journey eastward into the mountains, and then work southward, traveling by rail after we were well within the Confederate lines, and finally meet Andrews at Marietta, Georgia, more than 200 miles away, the evening of the third day after the start. When questioned, we were to profess ourselves Kentuckians going to join the Southern army.

On the journey we were a good deal annoyed by the swollen streams and the muddy roads consequent on three days of almost ceaseless rain. Andrews was led to believe that Mitchel's column would be inevitably delayed; and as we were expected to destroy the bridges the very day that Huntsville was entered, he took the responsibility of sending word to our different groups that our attempt would be postponed one day—from Friday to Saturday, April 12th. This was a natural but a most lamentable error of judgment.

One of the men was belated and did not join us at all. Two others were very soon captured by the enemy; and though their true character was not detected, they were forced into the Southern army, and two, who reached Marietta, failed to report at the rendezvous. Thus, when we assembled, very early in the morning, in Andrews' room at the Marietta Hotel for final consultation before the blow was struck, we were but twenty, including our leader. All preliminary difficulties had been easily overcome, and we were in good spirits. But some serious obstacles had been revealed on our ride from Chattanooga to Marietta the previous evening. The railroad was found to be crowded with trains, and many soldiers were among the passengers. Then the station— Big Shanty—at which the capture was to be effected had recently been made a Confederate camp. [But it still had no telegraph connections!] To succeed in our enterprise it would be necessary first to capture the engine in a guarded camp, with soldiers standing around as spectators, and then to run it from 100 to 200 miles through the enemy's country, and to deceive or overpower all trains that should be met—a large contract for twenty men! Some of our party thought the chances of success so slight, under existing circumstances, that they urged the abandonment of the whole enterprise. But Andrews declared his purpose to succeed or die, offering to each man, however, the privilege of withdrawing from the attempt—an offer no one was in the least disposed to accept. Final instructions were then given, and we hurried to the ticket office in time for the northward-bound mail train, and purchased tickets for different stations along the line in the direction of Chattanooga.

Our ride as passengers was but eight miles. We swept swiftly around the base of Kenesaw Mountain, and soon saw the tents of the forces camped at Big Shanty (now Kenesaw Station) gleam white in the morning mist. Here we were to stop for breakfast and attempt the seizure of the train. The morning was raw and gloomy, and a rain, which fell all day, had already begun. It was a painfully thrilling moment! We were but twenty, with an army about us and a long and difficult road before us crowded with enemies. In an instant we were to throw off the disguise which had been our only protection, and trust our leader's genius and our own efforts for safety and success. . . .

When we stopped, the conductor, engineer, and many of the passengers hurried to breakfast, leaving the train unguarded. Now was the moment of action! Ascertaining that there was nothing to prevent a rapid start, Andrews, our two engineers, Brown and Knight, and the fireman hurried forward, uncoupling a section of the train consisting of three empty baggage or box cars, the locomotive and tender. The engineer and fireman sprang into the cab of the engine, while Andrews, with hand on the rail and foot on the step, waited to see that the remainder of the band had gained entrance into the rear box car. This seemed difficult and slow, though it really consumed but a few seconds, for the car stood on a considerable bank, and the first who came were pitched in by their comrades, while these, in turn, dragged in the others, and the door was instantly closed. A sentinel, with musket in hand, stood not a dozen feet from the engine watching the whole proceeding, but before he or any of the soldiers and guards around could make up their minds to interfere, all was done, and Andrews, with a nod to his engineer, stepped on board. The valve was pulled wide open, and for a moment the wheels of the "General" slipped around ineffectively; then, with a bound that jerked the soldiers in the box car from their feet, the little train darted away, leaving the camp and station in the wildest uproar of confusion. The first step of the enterprise was triumphantly accomplished.

According to the time-table, of which Andrews had secured a copy, there were two trains to be met. These presented no serious hindrance to our attaining high speed, for we could tell just where to expect them. There was also a local freight not down on the time-table, but which could not be far distant. Any danger of collision with it could be avoided by running according to the schedule of the captured train until it was passed; then, at the highest possible speed, we would run to the Oostenaula and Chickamauga bridges, lay them in ashes, and pass on through Chattanooga to Mitchel, at Huntsville, or wherever eastward of that point he might be found, arriving long before the close of the day. It was a brilliant prospect, and, so far as human estimates can determine, it would have been realized had the day been Friday instead of Saturday. On Friday every train had been on time, the day dry, and the road in perfect order. Now the road was in disorder, every train far behind time, and two "extras" were approaching us. But of these unfavorable conditions we knew nothing, and pressed confidently forward.

We stopped frequently, at one point tore up the track, cut telegraph wires, and loaded on cross-ties to be used in bridge burning. Wood and water were taken without difficulty, Andrews telling, very coolly, the story to which he adhered throughout the run, namely, that he was an agent of General Beauregard's running an impressed powder train through to that officer at Corinth. We had no good instruments for track-raising, as we had intended rather to depend upon fire; but the amount of time spent in taking up a rail was not material at this stage of our journey, as we easily kept on the time of our captured train. There was a wonderful exhilaration in passing swiftly by towns and stations through the heart of an enemy's country in this manner. It possessed just enough of the spice of danger—in this part of the run— to render it thoroughly enjoyable. The slightest accident to our engine, however, or a miscarriage in any part of our program, would have completely changed the conditions.

At Etowah Station we found the "Yonah," an old locomotive owned by an iron company, standing with steam up; but not wishing to alarm the enemy till the local freight had been safely met, we left it unharmed. Kingston, 30 miles from the starting-point, was safely reached. A train from Rome, Georgia, on a branch road, had just arrived and was waiting for the morning mail—our train. We learned that the local freight would soon come also, and taking the side track, waited for it. When it arrived, however, Andrews saw to his surprise and chagrin that it bore a red flag, indicating another train not far behind. Stepping to the conductor, he boldly asked, "What does it mean that the road is blocked in this manner when I have orders to take this powder to Beauregard without a minute's delay?" The answer was interesting but not reassuring: "Mitchel has captured Huntsville and is said to be coming to Chattanooga, and we are getting everything out of there." He was asked by Andrews to pull his train a long way down the track out of the way, and promptly obeyed.

It seemed an exceedingly long time before the expected "extra" arrived; and when it did come it bore another red flag! The reason given was that the "local," being too great for one engine, had been made up in two sections, and the second section would doubtless be along in a short time. This was terribly vexatious; yet there seemed nothing to do but wait. To start out between the sections of an extra train would be to court destruction. There were already three trains around us, and their many passengers, and others, were growing very curious about the mysterious train which had arrived on the time of the morning mail, manned by strangers. For an hour and five minutes from the time of arrival at Kingston, we remained in the most critical position. The sixteen of us who were shut up tightly in a box car, personating Beauregard's ammunition—hearing sounds outside, but unable to distinguish words—had perhaps the most trying position. Andrews sent us, by one of the engineers, a cautious warning to be ready to fight in case the uneasiness of the crowd around led them to make any investigations, while he himself kept near the station to prevent the sending off of any alarming telegram. So intolerable was our suspense that the order for a deadly conflict would have been felt as a relief. But the assurance of Andrews quieted the crowd until the whistle of the expected train from the north was heard; then, as it glided up to the depot, past the end of our side-track, we were off without more words.

But unexpected danger had arisen behind us. Out of the panic at Big Shanty two men emerged, determined, if possible, to foil the unknown captors of their train. There was no telegraph station, and no locomotive at hand with which to follow; but the conductor of the train, W. A. Fuller, and Anthony Murphy, foreman of the Atlanta railway machine shops, who happened to be on board of Fuller's train, started on foot after us as hard as they could run! Finding a hand-car they mounted it and pushed forward till they neared Etowah, where they ran on the break we had made in the road and were precipitated down the embankment into the ditch. Continuing with more caution, they reached Etowah and found the "Yonah," which was at once pressed into service, loaded with soldiers who were at hand, and hurried with flying wheels towards Kingston. Fuller prepared to fight at that point, for he knew of the tangle of extra trains, and of the lateness of the regular trains, and did not think we would be able to pass. We had been gone only four minutes when he arrived and found himself stopped by three long, heavy trains of cars headed in the wrong direction. To move them out of the way so as to pass would cause a delay he was little inclined to afford—would indeed have almost certainly given us the victory. So, abandoning his engine, he, with Murphy, ran across to the Rome train, and, uncoupling the engine and one car, pushed forward with about forty armed men. As the Rome branch connected with the main road above the depot, he encountered no hindrance, and it was now a fair race. We were not many minutes ahead.

Four miles from Kingston we again stopped and cut the telegraph. While trying to take up a rail at this point, we were greatly startled. One end of it was loosened and eight of us were pulling at it, when distant, but distinct, we heard the whistle of a pursuing engine! With a frantic pull we broke the rail and all tumbled over the embankment with the effort. We moved on, and at Adairsville we found a mixed train (freight and passenger) waiting, but there was an express on the road that had not yet arrived. We could afford no more delay, and set out for the next station, Calhoun, at terrible speed, hoping to reach that point before the express, which was behind time, should arrive. The nine miles which we had to travel were left behind in less than the same number of minutes! The express was just pulling out, but, hearing our whistle, backed before us until we were able to take the side track; it stopped, however, in such a manner as completely to close up the other end of the switch. The two trains, side by side, almost touched each other, and our precipitate arrival caused natural suspicion. Many searching questions were asked which had to be answered before we could get the opportunity of proceeding. We, in the box car, could hear the altercation and were almost sure that a fight would be necessary before the conductor would consent to "pull up" in order to let us out. Here, again, our position was most critical, for the pursuers were rapidly approaching.

Fuller and Murphy saw the obstruction of the broken rail, in time to prevent [a] wreck, by reversing their engine; but the hindrance was for the present insuperable. Leaving all their men behind, they started for a second foot-race. Before they had gone far they met the train we had passed at Adairsville and turned it back after us. At Adairsville they dropped the cars, and, with locomotive and tender loaded with armed men, they drove forward at the highest speed possible. They knew that we were not many minutes ahead, and trusted to overhaul us before the express train could be safely passed.

But Andrews had told the powder story again, with all his skill, and had added a direct request in peremptory form to have the way opened before him, which the Confederate conductor did not see fit to resist; and just before the pursuers arrived at Calhoun we were again under way. Stopping once more to cut wires and tear up the track, we felt a thrill of exhilaration to which we had long been strangers. The track was now clear before us to Chattanooga; and even west of that city we had good reason to believe that we would find no other train in the way till we had reached Mitchel's lines. If one rail could now be lifted we would be in a few minutes at Oostenaula bridge, and, that burned, the rest of the task would be little more than simple manual labor, with the enemy absolutely powerless. We worked with a will.

But in a moment the tables were turned! Not far behind we heard the scream of a locomotive bearing down upon us at lightning speed! The men on board were in plain sight and well armed! Two minutes —perhaps one—would have removed the rail at which we were toiling; then the game would have been in our own hands, for there was no other locomotive beyond that could be turned back after us. But the most desperate efforts were in vain. The rail was simply bent, and we hurried to our engine and darted away, while remorselessly after us thundered the enemy.

Now the contestants were in clear view, and a most exciting race followed. Wishing to gain a little time for the burning of the Oostenaula bridge, we dropped one car, and shortly after, another; but they were "picked up" and pushed ahead to Resaca station. We were obliged to run over the high trestles and covered bridge at that point without a pause. This was the first failure in the work assigned us.

The Confederates could not overtake and stop us on the road, but their aim was to keep close behind so that we might not be able to damage the road or take in wood or water. In the former they succeeded, but not the latter. Both engines were put at the highest rate of speed. We were obliged to cut the wire after every station passed, in order that an alarm might not be sent ahead, and we constantly strove to throw our pursuer off the track or to obstruct the road permanently in some way so that we might be able to burn the Chickamauga bridges, still ahead. The chances seemed good that Fuller and Murphy would be wrecked. We broke out the end of our last box car and dropped cross-ties on the track as we ran, thus checking their progress and getting far enough ahead to take in wood and water at two separate stations. Several times we almost lifted a rail, but each time the coming of the Confederates, within rifle range, compelled us to desist and speed on. Our worst hindrance was the rain. The previous day (Friday) had been clear, with a high wind, and on such a day fire would have been easily and tremendously effective. But today a bridge could be burned only with abundance of fuel and careful nursing.

Thus we sped on, mile after mile, in this fearful chase, around curves and past stations in seemingly endless perspective. Whenever we lost sight of the enemy beyond a curve, we hoped that some of our obstructions had been effective in throwing him from the track and that we would see him no more; but at each long reach backward the smoke was again seen, and the shrill whistle was like the scream of a bird of prey. The time could not have been so very long, for the terrible speed was rapidly devouring the distance, but with our nerves strained

164

to the highest tension each minute seemed an hour. On several occasions the escape of the enemy from wreck seemed little less than miraculous. At one point a rail was placed across the track so skillfully on a curve that it was not seen till the train ran upon it at full speed. Fuller says that they were terribly jolted, and seemed to bounce altogether from the track, but lighted on the rails in safety. Some of the Confederates wished to leave a train which was driven at such a reckless rate, but their wishes were not gratified.

Before reaching Dalton we urged Andrews to turn and attack the enemy, laying an ambush so as to get into close quarters that our revolvers might be on equal terms with their guns. I have little doubt that if this had been carried out it would have succeeded. But Andrews —whether because he thought the chance of wrecking or obstructing the enemy still good, or feared that the country ahead had been alarmed by a telegram around the Confederacy by the way of Richmond— merely gave the plan his sanction without making any attempt to carry it into execution.

Dalton was passed without difficulty, and beyond we stopped again to cut wires and obstruct the track. It happened that a regiment was encamped not a hundred yards away, but they did not molest us. Fuller had written a dispatch to Chattanooga and dropped a man with orders to have it forwarded instantly while he pushed on to save the bridges. Part of the message got through and created a wild panic in Chattanooga, although it did not materially influence our fortunes. Our supply of fuel was now very short, and without getting rid of our pursuer long enough to take in more, it was evident that we could not run as far as Chattanooga.

While cutting the wire we made an attempt to get up another rail, but the enemy, as usual, were too quick for us. We had no tool for this purpose except a wedge-pointed iron bar. Two or three bent iron claws for pulling out spikes would have given us such superiority that, down to almost the last of our run, we would have been able to escape and to burn all the Chickamauga bridges. But it had not been our intention to rely on this mode of obstruction—an emergency only rendered necessary by our unexpected delay and the pouring rain.

We made no attempt to damage the long tunnel north of Dalton, as our enemies had greatly dreaded. The last hope of the raid was now staked upon an effort of a different kind. A few more obstructions were dropped on the track and our speed was increased so that we soon forged a considerable distance ahead. The side and end boards of the last car were torn into shreds, all available fuel was piled upon it, and blazing brands were brought back from the engine. By the time we approached a long covered bridge the fire in the car was fairly started. We uncoupled it in the middle of the bridge, and with painful suspense awaited the issue. Oh, for a few minutes till the work of conflagration was fairly begun! There was still steam-pressure enough in our boiler to carry us to the next wood-yard, where we could have replenished our fuel, by force if necessary, so as to run us as near to Chattanooga as was deemed prudent. We did not know of the telegraph message which the pursuers had sent ahead. But, alas! the minutes were not given. Before the bridge was extensively fired the enemy was upon us. They pushed right into the smoke and drove the burning car before them to the next side-track.

With no car left, and no fuel, the last scrap having been thrown into the engine or upon the burning car, and with no obstruction to drop on the track, our situation was indeed desperate.

But it might still be possible to save ourselves if we left the train in a body and took a direct course toward the Union lines. Confederate pursuers with whom I have since conversed have agreed on two points—that we could have escaped in the manner here pointed out; and that an attack on the pursuing train would likely have been successful. But Andrews thought otherwise, at least in relation to the former plan, and ordered us to jump from the locomotive, and, dispersing in the woods, each endeavored to save himself.

The question is often asked, "Why did you not reverse your engine and thus wreck the one following?" Wanton injury was no part of our plan, and we could not afford to throw away our engine till the last extremity. When the raiders were jumping off, however, the engine was reversed and driven back, but by that time the steam was so nearly exhausted that the Confederate engine had no difficulty in reversing and receiving the shock without injury. Both were soon at a stand-still, and the Confederates, reinforced by a party from a train which soon arrived on the scene—the express passenger, which had been turned back at Calhoun—continued the chase on foot.

It is easy now to understand why Mitchel paused thirty miles west of Chattanooga. The Andrews raiders had been forced to stop eighteen miles south of the same town, and no flying train met Mitchel with tidings that all the railroad communications of Chattanooga were destroyed, and that the town was in a panic and undefended.

A few words will give the sequel to this remarkable enterprise.

166

The hunt for the fugitive raiders was prompt, energetic, and successful. Several were captured the same day, and all but two within a week. Even these two were overtaken and brought back, when they supposed that they were virtually out of danger. Two who had reached Marietta but had failed to board the train . . . were identified and added to the band of prisoners.

Now follows the saddest part of the story. Being in citizens' dress within an enemy's lines, the whole party were held as spies. A court-martial was convened, and the leader and seven out of the remaining twenty-one were condemned and executed. The others were never brought to trial, probably because of the advance of Union forces and the consequent confusion into which the affairs of the Departments of East Tennessee and Georgia were thrown. Of the remaining fourteen, eight succeeded, by a bold effort—attacking their guard in broad daylight —in making their escape from Atlanta, Georgia, and ultimately in reaching the North. The other six, who shared in this effort, but were recaptured, remained prisoners until the latter part of March, 1863, when they were exchanged through a special arrangement made by Secretary Stanton. All the survivors of this expedition received medals and promotion. The pursuers also received expressions of gratitude from their fellow Confederates, notably from the Governor and Legislature of Georgia.

—REV. WILLIAM PITTENGER

*

Chickasaw the Scout Goes after Salt

---

*

GENERAL [BRAXTON] BRAGG'S ARMY was in Tennessee [in the summer of 1862], after General [Don Carlos] Buell, while General [Sterling] Price had fallen back twelve miles south of Holly Springs, and was very active in collecting forces and organizing. General [William S.] Rosecrans sent for me and told me that it was necessary for him to know what Price and Bragg were doing, and asked me if I could ascertain. I told him I would try. So I resolved that myself and my best scout, L. Bennett, of Mississippi, would each make a trip, one to visit Price's and the other Bragg's army. I gave Bennett his choice, and he chose Bragg. We both started about the same time. I left my scouts in charge of Captain Cameron, Provost Marshal. I started on an old horse, with no arms, and . . . avoiding public roads as much as possible, made my way to Water Valley, north of Grenada, and south of Price's army. I there learned that Price was not able to act on the offensive, but was busy collecting conscripts, &c.

I now started back for Corinth, and found it very difficult to travel north. I procured a homespun sack, in which I carried sufficient corn to feed my horse two days. On reaching the vicinity of Rocky Ford, on the Tallahatchie River, I was arrested by a squad of the Fourth Mississippi Cavalry, commanded by Colonel Gordon, in the following manner: upon riding up to them they stopped me, and asked me where I was going. I told them I was going to Corinth, and asked if there was not a place by that name somewhere about there. They said there was, and wanted to know what I was going there for. I replied that I was going to have some salt in that sack before I came back. They said they would put me in the army. I told them I did not care for that, but I must have some salt—that I wouldn't fight without it. They told me if I went to Corinth the Yankees would get me and kill me. I told them I didn't care, I must have some salt, that my family could not live without salt, and that some of my old neighbors had been and got salt, and I knew I could, and if they would wait until I returned with my salt I would then fight as well as any of them. It was quite amusing to hear the remarks made respecting me. Some of them allowed I was a d——d old fool, and they did not think it would pay to keep me, for I would leave the first chance I got and go after my salt—that I was of no account. They laughed at me considerable, and thought I was soft in the upper story. Finally they concluded to send me to Holly Springs, along with two other prisoners, guarded by four men. We went about twelve miles and camped. I had brought my sack full of sweet potatoes, which was all we had to eat. It was now night, and I sat up roasting sweet potatoes and talking about my salt. At last one of them wanted to know why in h—l I did not stop talking about that salt. At last they all lay down and went to sleep. I then got up and saddled my old horse, emptied my sack of potatoes on the ground, tied it on the saddle, mounted and started. Upon missing me in the morning my friends no doubt allowed I had gone after that salt.

About noon of the second day after this I reached Corinth, safe and sound, and in four days afterwards I was rejoiced to see my old friend Bennett, who had been conscripted, just south of Nashville, by Colonel Biffle, and carried to Mifflin, Tennessee. After remaining a prisoner four days he succeeded in making his escape, and reached our lines with the necessary information.

—CHICKASAW THE SCOUT [L. H. NARON]

*

The Man in Blue

*

HILTON HEAD [South Carolina] was the headquarters of "the department of the South." It was garrisoned by ten thousand choice troops from seven different states, besides the First South Carolina Infantry, which was the first colored regiment organized in the Union army from among slaves of the South. Hilton Head proper was strongly fortified. It contained vast stores of provisions and immense quantities of ammunition and implements of war for the army, and also for the South Atlantic Blockading Squadron. The Confederates looked on with eager eyes, naturally desiring to obtain possession of so valuable a prize, for it was the key to the whole department of the South.

They sent swarms of spies and pretended deserters to observe its strength and take note of its weak points, and laid various plans for its capture both by land and sea, apparently never giving up the hope that it would some day fall into their hands; but so great was the vigilance exercised that it was very difficult to get through the lines with any information.

One dark and stormy night [in the winter of 1862-63] a picket on a solitary post in a lonesome place was suddenly approached by what in the dark shadows he thought was a human form. A nearer approach of the object revealed indistinctly to the picket a powerful and well-built man wearing a blue overcoat, which, together with the fact that the intruder appeared to approach from the inside of the lines, made the picket doubtful whether he was friend or foe. He evidently did not observe the picket guard, but kept slowly and cautiously advancing under cover of the darkness. The loud command to halt not being promptly obeyed, the sharp report of a rifle broke the midnight silence, for the sentinel's orders were very strict. There was a deep groan and the flash of the gun enabled the picket to see the form in the blue overcoat fall heavily to the ground as though pierced in a vital part.

The sentinel now supposing that a force of the enemy was in his immediate presence, did not leave his post to examine more closely the effects of his shot, but, like a good soldier, stood his ground until the alarm brought speedy reinforcements. The new guards found all quiet along the line. After answering their eager questions as to the cause of the firing, the picket indicated the spot where this supposed dead man had fallen, and they lost no time in examining the bushes, but, strange to relate, nothing could be found. After a thorough search, and upon talking the matter all over, the new guards concluded that the picket had allowed his vivid imagination to mistake a stationary tree for a moving man, and were disposed to ridicule his story, but he stoutly persisted that he knew his business, and wasn't fool enough not to know the difference between a tree and a man. To be on the safe side, however, the officer of the guard doubled the picket for the remainder of the night, but all remained quiet until morning. At daybreak a fresh and careful examination of the suspicious spot was made, and the soldiers were startled to find the footprints of a man. They all suddenly believed the picket's story, but they were entirely at a loss to account for the sudden disappearance of "the man in blue."

The next night a different detachment was on duty and the same scenes were enacted over again, with the exception that "the man in blue" appeared on a different post. Each night for a whole week the picket line was kept in a constant commotion by the strange visitor, and fresh detachments were sent out from time to time until there was almost a continual line of battle across that part of the island. Bodies of troops and the most daring scouts scoured the woods by day and volunteers were lying in the swamps by night. In the meantime the footprints which "the man in blue" invariably left behind in the soft sand were measured and found in every case to be identical in shape and size.

The mystery now became the absorbing topic of conversation among all the soldiers on the island.

The newly arrived One Hundred and Fifteenth New York [from the Saratoga district], hearing of the affair, and the wonder and great excitement it had produced, also became deeply interested, and being accustomed to such duty, requested permission to be placed on picket

170

in the dangerous locality for one night, feeling sure that they should be able to solve the riddle whether man or devil faced them. To their joy they were accepted. After reaching the line, the officers took the precaution to place at least two men on each post, and in the more remote and exposed places three or four. Every man had an intense desire to be the one to kill or capture the intruder, and all made haste to adjust themselves.

All was quiet until midnight, but shortly after that hour Andrew Smith, of Company H, heard a stick crack in some dense bushes a few yards distant. He instantly dropped down into the tall grass and peered out into the thick darkness. All was as still as death for a moment, when another stick cracked and there was a rustling in the leaves. Laboring under the intense excitement, as he realized that the critical time had arrived, he clutched his trusty rifle firmly, put his finger on the trigger, and pointed it in the threatened direction, ready to blaze away at the first sight of any object. Nothing appearing, Smith concluded that after all it must have been some denizen of the forest that was prowling around. He was speedily undeceived, however, for he had scarcely reached that conclusion when the terrible form in blue stood before him. At first Smith was startled and almost thunderstruck, but, being naturally a brave man, he quickly recovered his self-possession and fired his gun, aiming for the breast of the form in front. The object fell with a deep groan to the ground, there was a tumbling in the bushes for a moment, as though a death-struggle was going on, and then all was still. A dozen soldiers bounded to the spot, but "the man in blue" was gone.

Great perplexity and some degree of mortification took possession of all the picket guards, and the mystery appeared deeper than ever. When the midnight adventure was reported in the morning there was a great sensation among the troops on the island. Some of the soldiers who were inclined to be superstitious declared that the object was supernatural and that they would rather face the grape and canister of a rebel battery at short range than to be on picket when "the man in blue" appeared, while others expressed astonishment that the "old blue devil," as they called him, always managed to get away. After that night no more was ever seen or heard of "the man in blue" on the picket line, although the utmost vigilance was exercised for a long time.

One Sunday night the African church was crowded with colored people. The melody of a thousand voices united in the strange songs of the freedmen, and when the leader of the meeting with great earnestness

exhorted his people to pray for "Massa Lincum and the Union sogers"
a loud amen broke forth, and when he further exhorted them to "look out
for de spies dat was prowlin' around among de colored people," a wild
shout of approval was heard mingled with exclamations of "Bress de
Lord!"—"Massa Lincum will hang all de spies!"—"We will never be
slaves on old massa's plantation any moah."

A Negro left the church in the midst of the services, and impelled
partly by fear and partly by love of country, and with that peculiar
instinct of liberty and unfaltering loyalty to the Union common to all
the slaves of the South, he made his way to the captain of the Provost
Guard in great haste, and with trembling lips declared that "his ole
massa" was in the African church disguised as a black man. With the
determination to test the truth of the colored man's startling statement, a
squad of soldiers were sent to the African church accompanied by the
colored individual who brought the information, and in order to be
reasonably sure of reaching the spot before "ole massa" should take
a notion that he had enjoyed the services long enough and quietly slip
out, the guards made double-quick time. On reaching the church the
colored man, trembling with fear as he came in sight of his former
owner, pointed him out to the guards. He was comfortably seated among
the freedmen, apparently enjoying the services as much as any of them.
Two of the guards quietly glided down the aisle and surprised "ole
massa" by suddenly seizing him from behind and escorting him through
the long rows of astonished worshippers to the door, where he was
placed between a file of bayonets and promptly marched to the guard-
house.

A vigorous application of water soon made his black face tolerably
white. He was stoical and refused to answer any questions, and appeared
to be entirely unconcerned until preparations were made to search his
person, when his whole manner underwent a sudden change and he
visibly weakened. He trembled and appeared greatly agitated and
alarmed. A careful search of his person disclosed the fact that he was
a Confederate spy of the most dangerous character, and that a most
important capture had been made, and that had he succeeded in reaching the Confederate lines the most disastrous consequences might have
resulted to the cause of the Union. He carried drawings of the Union
forts and full plans of all our fortifications, specifying the weak and
the strong points, also giving statements of the strength of the garrison,
and, in short, the most complete information that the enemy could
possibly desire. His body was enveloped in a strong coat of mail, which

was found to be bullet-proof. His mission as a spy was so apparent that his conviction as a spy was only a matter of form. Before the sentence of death was executed upon him he made a clean breast of the whole matter, and created a great sensation by announcing that he was the man who appeared on the picket-line wearing a blue overcoat.

His history was that, having entered the Union lines as a spy and come in possession of the desired information, he became very anxious to escape, which, on account of his previous full knowledge of the country, he thought would be a matter of little difficulty. But he found that it was a matter not so easily accomplished as he had supposed owing to the vigilance and strength of the pickets. Night after night he attempted to pass the picket-line, always choosing a dark and usually a stormy night and wearing his blue overcoat and trusting to his coat of mail for protection. But he was always detected by the vigilant sentinels. He was aware of the commotion he was the means of creating, and viewed with no little concern the placing of the double picket-lines and the unusual efforts made to effect his capture, and resolved, in sheer desperation, to get away with his information at all hazards. He was frequently struck on his coat of mail, but the bullets invariably glanced off, and he escaped unharmed. When a sentinel fired at him and he knew that he was discovered, he would pretend to be shot and fall to the ground with a groan, and then, under cover of the darkness and dense foliage, would always manage to crawl away before the pickets reached him.

—Lieutenant J. H. Clark

13. HIGH COMMAND

Grant Reads the Signs

*

THE ATTACK on Fort Donelson, which established Grant's fame, is said to have been decided upon by a simple circumstance. The day before the attack [on February 15, 1862], most of the troops had marched a long distance, part of it in a bitter cold night. A council of war was called to determine whether an immediate attack should be made, or whether the troops should have a day of rest. The officers were in favor of rest. Grant said nothing, but appeared absorbed in thought. Presently, when every one had expressed an opinion, he said: "There was a deserter came in this morning. Let us see him and hear what he has to say." The man was sent for and came in. Grant looked in his haversack and then asked: "Where are you from?"

"Fort Donelson."

"Got six days' rations in your haversack, have you not?"

"Yes, sir."

"When were they served out?"

"Yesterday morning."

"The same to all the troops?"

"Yes, sir."

The soldier was sent out and Grant said: "Gentlemen, troops do not have six days' rations served out to them in a fort if they mean to stay there. These men mean to retreat—not to fight. We will attack at once."

—*New York Daily Tribune*

*

General Fitz-John Porter
and the Runaway Balloon

---

*

A PROMINENT OBJECT of interest to all the soldiers, since landing on the peninsula, has been Professor Lowe's captive balloon, which is attached to headquarters, and in which some of the officers make an ascent nearly every day, for the purpose of inspecting the rebel lines and watching their movements. Occasionally the rebels train a gun on it, and try to reach it with a shell. They do not succeed, however; but one of these shells, the other morning, came over our lines, and dropped down into the cook-house at General [Henry W.] Slocum's headquarters, scattering the camp kettles and demoralizing the cooks,— who were just then preparing breakfast.

Sometimes these ascents are quite perilous—at least the one made by General Fitz-John Porter, in front of Yorktown, early in April, proved to be. The following account of it is taken partly from the *New York Herald*:

Yorktown, Va., April 11, 1862

The exciting event of the day has been a balloon reconnaissance, by General Fitz-John Porter, on a scale of rather larger magnitude than was intended. At five o'clock in the morning General Porter took his place in Professor Lowe's balloon. He supposed the usual number of ropes were attached to it, whereas there was only one; and a place in this, as was afterwards ascertained, had been burned by vitriol used in generating gas. Taking his seat in the car, unaccompanied by any one, the rope was let out to nearly its full length—the length is about 900 yards—when, suddenly, snap went the cord! and up went the balloon! This was an unexpected part of the programme. The men below looked up with astonishment, and the general looked down with equal bewilderment.

"Open the valve!" shouted one of the men below. "I'll manage it," responded the General. Up went the balloon! higher!! higher!!! It rose with great rapidity, and the wind was taking it directly over the enemy's lines. By this time every staff officer and hundreds of others were looking at the runaway monster. It was impossible to describe the anxiety felt and expressed for the fate of him, the brave General, who was thus, apparently, being taken directly into the enemy's hands. In the meantime the General, having no wish to drop in among the rebels, thought it best to let the valve take care of itself; and, throwing out a little ballast, soon rose out of the reach of the rebel bullets, and employed his time in taking notes of the rebel objects below. Crowds of soldiers rushed from their tents, and he could hear their shouts distinctly. The map of the country was clearly discernible. He saw Yorktown and its works; York River and its windings.

Fortunately a counter-current of air struck the balloon, and its course was reversed. Its retreat from rebeldom was rapid, and when safely over our lines, he opened the valve, the gas escaped, and down he came. The car struck the top of a shelter tent, knocked the tent into "pi," and left him enveloped in a mass of collapsed oil silk. He crawled out, and found himself in the middle of a camp, not a hundred rods from General McClellan's headquarters; and was soon surrounded by the members of his staff and a squad of cavalry, who had ridden out in the direction of the descending balloon.

"You are a suspicious character!" remarked one of the officers.

"How so?" asked the General.

"In the space of half an hour, you have been *taken up* by a balloon, and *arrested* by a shelter tent."

General Porter made over one hundred ascents in the balloon while on the peninsula.

—*History of the 27th Regiment, N.Y. Volunteers*

Johnson Prays with Moody

COLONEL [GRANVILLE] MOODY, the "fighting Methodist parson," as he was called in Tennessee . . . happened to be in Nashville the day it was reported that Buell had decided to evacuate the city. The Rebels, strongly re-enforced, were said to be within two days' march of the capital. Of course, the city was greatly excited. Moody said he went in search of [Andrew] Johnson, at the edge of the evening, and found him at his office, closeted with two gentlemen, who were walking the floor with him, one on each side. As he entered, they retired, leaving him alone with Johnson, who came up to him, manifesting intense feeling, and said, "Moody, we are sold out! Buell is a traitor! He is going to evacuate the city, and in forty-eight hours we shall all be in the hands of the Rebels!" Then he commenced pacing the floor again, twisting his hands and chafing like a caged tiger, utterly insensible to his friend's entreaties to become calm. Suddenly he turned and said, "Moody, can you pray?"

"That is my business, sir, as a minister of the Gospel," returned the Colonel.

"Well, Moody, I wish you would pray," said Johnson; and instantly both went down upon their knees, at opposite sides of the room. As the prayer waxed fervent, Johnson began to respond in true Methodist style. Presently he crawled over on his hands and knees to Moody's side, and put his arm over him, manifesting the deepest emotion. Closing the prayer with a hearty "Amen" from each, they arose. Johnson took a long breath, and said, with emphasis, "Moody, I feel better!" Shortly afterwards he asked, "Will you stand by me?"

"Certainly I will," was the answer.

"Well, Moody, I can depend upon you; you are one in a hundred thousand!" He then commenced pacing the floor again. Suddenly he wheeled, the current of his thought having changed, and said, "Oh! Moody, I don't want you to think I have become a religious man because

177

I asked you to pray. I am sorry to say it, but I am not, and have never pretended to be, religious. No one knows this better than you; but, Moody, there is one thing about it—I DO believe in ALMIGHTY GOD! And I believe also in the BIBLE, and I say 'd—n' me, if Nashville shall be surrendered!"

And Nashville was not surrendered.

> —As told by ABRAHAM LINCOLN to F. B. CARPENTER

---

*

Beauty and the "Beast":
Butler's "Woman Order"

---

*

FROM THE SECOND DAY after we landed [on May 1, 1862], we had the men of New Orleans so completely under our control that our officers and soldiers could go anywhere in the city without being interfered with. I may say here, and challenge contradiction, in behalf of my gallant comrades, that from the time we landed until the time I left New Orleans, no officer or soldier did any act to interfere with life, limb, or property of any person in New Orleans, unless acting under perfectly explicit orders so to do.

One result of our conduct was that any of us, from the highest to the lowest, went where he pleased without insult or hostile act by any man in New Orleans. Insomuch was this true that for myself, I walked or rode by day or night through the streets of New Orleans anywhere I chose between Chalmette and Carrollton without any attendant or guard, or pretence of one, save a single orderly in attendance.

But not so with the women of New Orleans.

* * * * *

There were five or six women leaning over a balcony on one occasion when I was riding along quite near it, with one officer only between me and the balcony. I was face to the front, and of course people turned out to see me more or less as I went through the streets. Just as we were

178

passing the balcony, with something between a shriek and a sneer, the women all whirled around back to with a flirt which threw out their skirts in a regular circle like the pirouette of a dancer. I turned around to my aide, saying in full voice: "Those women evidently know which end of them looks the best." That closed that exhibition.

The question pressed upon me: How is this course of conduct to be changed? How is this to be stopped? We have a very few troops in the midst of a hostile population of many thousands, including more than twice our number of paroled Confederate soldiers. Many of these women who do this are young, and many are pretty and interesting, and some have a lady-like appearance. Now, I know that a police officer in Boston can hardly arrest a drunken woman in the street without causing a very considerable excitement and commotion, which very quickly expands into something like a riot if she appeals for help and has a prepossessing appearance. Some of these women desire to exhibit what they call their patriotism, and there are many of them who would be very happy to be arrested for any insult put upon a Yankee officer or soldier and have it so published. Much more will be the danger of riot if Yankee soldiers arrest the women of New Orleans on the streets for the acts which these women think proper to do as their part in carrying on the war. An order for arrests in these cases—simple arrests and transportation of "these ladies"—would be a source of perpetual turmoil at least, and possibly ripen into insurrection.

I waited sometime in the hope that this epidemic among the women would die out. But it did not; it increased. At last, on one Saturday, Flag-Officer [David G.] Farragut had been invited ashore by Colonel Deming, who was in command of the troops in the city, to take dinner with him and his friends, in compliment of Farragut's great achievements. Colonel Deming went to the levee to meet the flag-officer when he landed, and they walked up arm in arm in full uniform. While going along one of the principal streets, there fell upon them what at first they took to be a sudden and heavy shower; but it proved to be the emptying of a vessel of water upon them from the balcony above, and not very clean water at that. Of course the vessel was proof that this was done by one of "the ladies of New Orleans."

A city could hardly be said to be under good government where such things were permitted or attempted by any class of its inhabitants.

On the next day, the Sabbath, one of my officers dressed himself in full uniform, took his prayer-book in his hand, and was on the way to the church to attend divine service. As he was walking quietly along he met two very well-dressed and respectable-looking women, and, as a gentleman should, he withdrew to the outer side of the sidewalk to let them pass by. As he did so, one deliberately stepped across in front of the other and spit in his face.

Now, what could he do? Anything but take his kerchief and clean his face? I never heard but one other suggestion, and this was made by one of his fellow staff, who said: "Why didn't you do something?"

"What could I do, Davis, to two women?"

"Well," said Davis, "you ought to have taken your revolver and shot the first *he* rebel you met."

But, to be serious, the Colonel said to me: "General, I can't stand this. This isn't the first time this thing has been attempted towards me, but this is the first time it has been accomplished. I want to go home. I came here to fight enemies of the country, not to be insulted and disgusted."

"Oh," I said, "you can't resign. I'll put a stop to this."

"I don't think you can do it, General," was the reply.

I took it into very serious consideration. After careful thought and deliberation as to the best method of meeting this unique but dangerous entanglement, and running over in my mind a form for the order, I remembered that for the purpose of revision of city ordinances, I had once read an old English ordinance, which I thought, with a few changes, *mutatis mutandis,* might accomplish the purpose. There was one thing certain about it; it must be an order that would execute itself, otherwise it would stir up more strife in its execution by the police than it would quell. Therefore, after full consideration, I handed to my chief of staff, to be put upon the order books, the following order:

HEADQUARTERS DEPARTMENT OF THE GULF
New Orleans, May 15, 1862

General Order No. 28.

As the officers and soldiers of the United States have been subject to repeated insults from the women (calling themselves ladies) of New Orleans, in return for the most scrupulous noninterference and courtesy on our part, it is ordered that hereafter when any female shall, by word, gesture, or movement, insult or show contempt for any officer or soldier of the United States, she shall be regarded and held liable to be treated as a woman of the town plying her avocation.

By command of
MAJOR GENERAL BUTLER

GEO. C. STRONG, *A.A.G., Chief of Staff.*

Strong said, after he read it: "This order may be misunderstood, General. It would be a great scandal if only one man should act upon it in the wrong way."

"Let us, then," was the reply, "have one case of aggression on our side. I shall know how to deal with that case, so that it will never be repeated. So far, all the aggression has been against us. Here we are, conquerors in a conquered city; we have respected every right, tried every means of conciliation, complied with every reasonable desire; and yet we cannot walk the streets without being outraged and spit upon by green girls. I do not fear the troops, but if aggression must be, let it not be all against *us*."

My troops were New England soldiers, and consequently men well-bred in every courtesy toward women, for a well-behaved woman can safely travel alone all through New England. I did not fear that any one of them would conduct himself in such a way that he could not look me in the face and tell me of it if I asked him. I was not afraid on that score. I was only afraid the order would not be understood by the women.

There was no case of aggression after that order was issued, no case of insult by word or look against our officers or soldiers while in New Orleans.

The order executed itself.

No arrests were ever made under it or because of it. All the ladies in New Orleans forbore to insult our troops because they didn't want to be deemed common women, and all the common women forbore to insult our troops because they wanted to be deemed ladies, and of those two classes were all the women secessionists of the city.

—MAJOR GENERAL BENJAMIN F. BUTLER

*

How "Fighting Joe" Hooker
Won His Sobriquet

---

*

IT WAS THREE O'CLOCK in the morning [May 5, 1862]. . . . McClellan had come to grips with the Confederate forces [at Williamsburg], and was pressing them back upon Richmond. Every two or three hours through the night had come from the Associated Press Reporters' Agency sheets of manifold, that is tissue paper upon which a dozen sheets (by the use of carbon sheets interleaved) could be written at once—one for each newspaper. These sheets told of desperate fighting all along McClellan's line. Among his Corps Commanders was General [Joseph] Hooker, whose command had been perhaps too gravely engaged.

Just as the forms—indeed the last form, was being locked, that is, the type firmly held together in a great frame that the impression might be taken for printing, came another dispatch from the reporters with the Union army. It was a continuation of the report of the fighting in which General Hooker's Corps had been so gravely involved. At the top was written "Fighting—Joe Hooker." I knew that this was so written to indicate that it should be added to what we had had before. The compositor (typesetter) who had set it up (put it in type) had known nothing about the previous matter, however, and had set it up as a heading "Fighting Joe Hooker."

I rapidly considered what to do; as if it were yesterday I can remember the responsibility I felt and how the thing struck me. Well, I said to myself, it makes a good heading—let it go. I fully realized that if a few other proof-readers beside myself acted as I did it would mean that Hooker would thenceforth live and die as "Fighting Joe Hooker." Some did and some did not, but enough did as I did to do the business.

—SIDNEY V. LOWELL

*

The First Duty of a Soldier

---

*

IMMEDIATELY AFTER the battle of Williamsburg [May 5, 1862], as the Confederates under [General Joseph E.] Johnston were moving back toward Richmond, neither by land nor water, but by a half-and-half mixture of both, General Johnston ordered me to go at once to General [John B.] Hood. "Tell him," he said, "that a force of the enemy, estimated at from three to five thousand have landed on York River, and are ravaging the country. His brigade must immediately check the advance of this force. He is to feel the enemy gently and fall back, avoiding an engagement and drawing them from under the protection of their gun-boats, as an ample force will be sent in their rear, and if he can draw them a few miles from the river, their capture is certain."

The order was given. General Hood repeated it to the colonel of his brigade; and the Texas boys, who were "sp'iling for a fight," charged upon the enemy, who outnumbered them greatly, drove them back to the shelter of their gun-boats, killing and capturing several hundred. Returning to headquarters, I had to report a result not at all in accordance with the orders or expectations of the general in command. General Johnston seemed greatly annoyed, and sternly ordered me to repeat the exact verbal orders given Hood. Just as I did so, General Hood rode up. He was asked by General Johnston to repeat the orders received from me. When he did so, "Old Joe," with the soldierly and game-cock air which characterized him, said: "General Hood, have you given an illustration of the Texas idea of feeling an enemy gently and falling back? What would your Texans have done, sir, if I had ordered them to charge and drive back the enemy?"

Hood replied: "I suppose, General, they would have driven them into the river, and tried to swim out and capture the gun-boats."

With a smile, General Johnston replied: "Teach your Texans that the first duty of a soldier is literally to obey orders."

—J. H. L.

*

The Rivals

*

THERE WAS A REPORT in the Army of the Potomac— whether true or not matters not in this connection—that General [George B.] McClellan and General A. P. Hill were both in love with the beautiful Miss Nellie Marcy, daughter of General [Randolph B.]

Marcy, when they were at West Point, that she smiled on both these gallant gentlemen, for they were equally attractive, but that in the end she married McClellan. It so happened that in all McClellan's campaigns around Richmond [in May, 1862] (as well as at Sharpsburg [September 17]), Hill was always to the fore, and it seemed that whether struck in the front, flank, or rear, especially early in the morning, it was by A. P. Hill. McClellan's soldiers began to get tired of this sort of thing, and attributed it to spite and vengeance on the part of Hill.

Early one gloomy morning, before the sun had appeared, there were shots of artillery and rattle of musketry which told of a spirited attack. Hill was at it again. The long roll was beaten, there was commotion and confusion and a rush to arms, in the midst of which one hardened old veteran unrolled himself from his blanket and in an inimitable tone of weariness and disgust, cried out, "My God, Nellie, why didn't you marry him!"

—MAJOR HENRY KYD DOUGLAS

*

"First with the Most" Forrest

---

*

I WAS PRESENT at an interview between [General Nathan B. Forrest] and [General John H.] Morgan, when they were comparing notes of their respective expeditions made about the same date in the summer of 1862, the one into middle Tennessee and the other into Kentucky. Each seemed far more concerned to learn what the other had done and how he did it, than to relate his own performances; and it was interesting to note the brevity with which they answered each other's questions and the eagerness with which they asked their own. It was upon this occasion that Forrest used an expression which has been very often quoted. . . .

*　*　*　*　*

Morgan wanted particularly to know about his fight at Murfreesboro, where Forrest had accomplished a marked success, capturing garrison and stores and carrying off every thing, although the surrounding country was filled with Federal forces. Morgan asked how it was done.

"Oh," said Forrest, "I just took the short cut and got there first with the most men."

—GENERAL BASIL W. DUKE

*

Hindman's Letter-Writing Ruse

*

AFTER HIS ARRIVAL at Little Rock [in June, 1862], and before he had a brigade assembled to meet [General Samuel R.] Curtis, [General Thomas C. Hindman] dispatched messengers to General [Braxton] Bragg and to the Secretary of War, with communications detailing exactly the condition of the department, the scarcity of arms, the dearth of soldiers, the panic of the people, and the threatening attitude of the Federals, expressing great fears in conclusion that, should Curtis advance, Little Rock would be without a garrison and powerless for defense. The documents fell into Curtis' hands, and the urgency of their appeals convinced him of their truthfulness and the utter weakness of Hindman. The Federal general squared himself around threateningly and pushed along slowly southward, gathering up, however, as he went, all the cotton within his lengthy reach.

Meanwhile, Hindman's great brain was stimulated by the imminence of the danger, and as a last resort he opposed finesse to force— chicanery to firm lines and massive battalions. He and his chief of staff, Colonel R. C. Newton, an officer of distinguished courage, devotion, and ability, formed plans suddenly thus: a mail was fixed up ostensibly to cross the Mississippi river with letters to the Arkansas soldiers beyond, and dispatches for the Richmond authorities. Newton went to a hundred or more ladies and gentlemen whom he knew well, and who had fathers, husbands, lovers, children and brothers over there under Lee and Beauregard, and unfolded to them privately Hindman's wishes and plans. The old patriarchs wrote to their sons and bade them be of good cheer, for five thousand splendidly armed Texans had just arrived, and Little Rock was safe. Brothers wrote to brothers describing some imaginary brigade to which they were attached, and went into ecstasies over the elegant new Enfields arriving from Mexico. The young girls, true to the witchery and coquetry of their sex, informed their lovers under Cleburne and Gates, in delicate epistles, of the great balls given to the Louisianians, and how Mary Jane lost her heart here, Annabel Lee there, and Minnie Myrtle somewhere else, importuning the absent ones to make haste speedily with the war and come home, for the Louisiana and Texas gallants would take no denial and were *so nice* and fascinating.

Everybody wrote that could write, and under the sense of great peril, wrote naturally and well. Every letter was submitted to the ordeal of Hindman's acute diplomacy and Newton's legal acumen. Then Hindman wrote concisely and plainly that his efforts for the defense of the department were bearing healthy fruit. The people, alive to their danger, were volunteering by thousands. The scarcity of arms, looked upon as being an almost insurmountable obstacle, had been in a measure overcome, so that with a large number just arriving, and with several thousand more a Mexican firm at Matamoras were willing to exchange for cotton, he had great hopes of soon attacking Curtis. Then followed a list of his new organizations and the names of many officers appointed by himself for whom he asked commissions.

To get this mail now into Curtis' hands with all its heterogeneous contents—its paternal lectures, its school-boy scrawls, its labored love-letters, its impassioned poetry, its calm, succinct statements of military facts, was the uppermost question in Hindman's mind. Fate, which always favors the brave and the beautiful, favored Hindman. A young Missourian—a daring, handsome, intelligent athletic soldier from St. Joseph—Lieutenant Colonel Walter Scott, volunteered for the perilous mission, asking only a swift, strong horse and greenbacks enough for the journey. He had himself the rest—the nerve, the arms, the knightly valor.

Toiling through swamps, swimming bayous, keeping lonely vigils about lonesome, guarded roads, he reached at last the vicinity of Curtis' army. Up to this time his beautiful sorrel mare—his petted "Princess" —had been led tenderly along, watched and nursed as a man waits upon a fickle beauty. Upon her fleet limbs depended the fate of a state—upon her strong sinews the life of a rider. Bold and determined, and resolved to win all or lose all, Scott rode calmly up to the nearest pickets, and, alone as he was, and ignorant of the country as he was, fired upon them.

It was returned without damage, and he retreated back a little to bivouac hungry in a swamp by the road side.

The next morning, with the dew on the grass and the song of "half-awakened birds" thrilling on the air, he rode out broad and good into the pathway, and fired closely upon the head of thirty Federal Illinois cavalry coming out to pillage and to burn. They dashed after him fiercely. Princess, quivering with suppressed speed, pulled hard upon the bit and flecked her spotless coat with great foam splashes. Round and round wheeled Scott, firing now at the enemy almost upon him, and then dashing off followed by a handful of bullets. The saddle-bags were safe yet, and he must win. At last, feigning great exhaustion for his mare, he held her in with an iron hand, though using his spurs mercilessly, every stroke going into his own flesh. First his overcoat went, then one pistol, then another—he had two left yet, though—then his heavy leggin's, then the large cavalry roll, then as a last resort the *precious mail* went down in the road before the rushing Federals. Potent as the golden apples of Atlanta, the Illinois men stooped to gather it up and were distanced. Scott, after turning a bend in the road, caressed his poor, tried beauty and gave her the reins with a soft, sweet word. The sensitive creature dashed away superbly, and carried her rider far beyond all danger, and Scott soon returned to Little Rock to receive thanks for services well and faithfully done.

This ruse had the desired effect upon Curtis, and he halted and wavered. His own dispatches captured afterward revealed the fact, for in them were pleading supplications for reinforcements. Hindman only wanted time, and the time he gained enabled him to save the department and drive back Blunt and Curtis.

—JOHN N. EDWARDS

*

Jefferson Davis Takes Orders from Lee

---

*

[IN THE FIRST YEAR of the war] President Davis was a familiar and picturesque figure on the streets [of Richmond] walking through the Capitol square from his residence to the executive office in the morning, not to return until late in the afternoon, or riding just before nightfall to visit one or another of the encampments near the city. He was tall, erect, slender, and of a dignified and soldierly bearing, with clear-cut and high-bred features, and of a demeanor of stately courtesy to all. He was clad always in Confederate gray cloth, and wore a soft felt hat with wide brim. Afoot, his step was brisk and firm; in the saddle he rode admirably and with a martial aspect. His early life had been spent in the Military Academy at West Point and upon the then north-western frontier in the Black Hawk War, and he afterwards greatly distinguished himself at Monterey and Buena Vista in Mexico; at the time when we knew him, everything in his appearance and manner was suggestive of such a training. He was reported to feel quite out of place in the office of President, with executive and administrative duties, in the midst of such a war; General Lee always spoke of him as the best of miltary advisers; his own inclination was to be with the army, and at the first tidings of sound of a gun, anywhere within reach of Richmond, he was in the saddle and off for the spot—to the dismay of his staff officers, who were expected to act as an escort on such occasions, and who never knew at what hour of the night or of the next day they should get back to a bed or a meal. . . .

[On June 26, 1862], when General Lee had crossed the Chicka-hominy, to commence the Seven Days' battles, President Davis, with several staff officers, overtook the column, and, accompanied by the Secretary of War and a few other non-combatants, forded the river just as the battle in the peach orchard at Mechanicsville began.

General Lee, surrounded by members of his own staff and other officers, was found a few hundred yards north of the bridge, in the middle of the broad road, mounted and busily engaged in directing the attack then about to be made by a brigade sweeping in line over the fields, to the east of the road and toward Ellerson's Mill, where in a few minutes a hot engagement commenced. Shot, from the enemy's guns out of sight, went whizzing overhead in quick succession, striking every moment nearer the group of horsemen in the road as the gunners improved their range. General Lee observed the President's approach, and was evidently annoyed at what he considered a foolhardy expedition of needless exposure of the head of the government, whose duties were elsewhere. He turned his back for a moment, until Colonel [Robert H.] Chilton had been dispatched at a gallop with the last direction to the commander of the attacking brigade; then, facing the cavalcade and looking like the god of war indignant, he exchanged with the President a salute, with the most frigid reserve of anything like welcome or cordiality. In an instant and without allowance of opportunity for a word from the President, the General, looking not at him but at the assemblage at large, asked in a tone of irritation:

"Who are all this army of people, and what are they doing here?"

No one moved or spoke, but all eyes were upon the President—everybody perfectly understanding that this was only an order for him to retire to a place of safety; and the roar of the guns, the rattling fire of musketry, and the bustle of a battle in progress, with troops continually arriving across the bridge to go into action, went on. The President twisted in his saddle, quite taken aback at such a greeting—the General regarding him now with glances of growing severity. After a painful pause the President said, with a voice of deprecation: "It is not my army, General."

"It certainly is not *my* army, Mr. President," was the prompt reply, "and this is no place for it"—in an accent of unmistakable command.

Such a rebuff was a stunner to the recipient of it, who soon regained his serenity, however, and answered: "Well, General, if I withdraw, perhaps they will follow," and, raising his hat in another cold salute, he turned his horse's head to ride slowly toward the bridge—seeing, as he turned, a man killed immediately before him by a shot from a gun which at that moment got the range of the road. The President's own staff officers followed him, as did various others; but he presently drew rein in the stream, where the high bank and the bushes concealed him from General Lee's repelling observation, and there remained while the battle raged. The Secretary of War had also made a show of withdrawing, but improved the opportunity afforded by rather a deep ditch on the roadside to conceal himself and his horse for a time from General Lee, who at that moment was more to be dreaded than the enemy's guns.

—Constance Cary Harrison

Jackson's Bridge-Builder

*

GENERAL JACKSON was delayed [in his pursuit of the retreating McClellan] by the necessity of rebuilding the Grapevine bridge over the Chickahominy, and did not put his column in motion until "early dawn," of the 29th [of June, 1862]. It was on this occasion that the incident occurred in which figured Captain C. R. Mason—widely known in Virginia as "the Napoleon of railroad contractors"—whom Jackson had attached to his staff as chief of pioneers. Anxious to build the bridge and join in the pursuit of the enemy, Jackson sent for Mason, told him his wishes, and ordered him to be ready to begin the bridge, "so soon as the engineers could prepare the plan and specifications." The veteran bridge-builder at once replied: "Never mind *the pictures,* General! If you will just send me men enough *who will wade in the water and tote poles,* I will have the bridge ready by the time the engineers can prepare the pictures." Jackson cordially seconded his efforts, the bridge was ready in a marvelously short time, and the "foot cavalry" were again on the road.

—REV. J. WILLIAM JONES

*

A Special Providence

*

A FEW DAYS BEFORE the battles around Richmond [Reverend] Dr. [R. L.] Dabney [Jackson's chief of staff] preached a sermon in which he took strong Calvinistic grounds on special Providence, and told

190

the men that they need not dodge in the battle, since every shot and shell, and bullet sped on its way under the guidance of a special Providence, and hit just where and just whom the loving Father, who watches the fall of the sparrow, and numbers the hairs on the heads of the saints, should direct.

A distinguished officer told me that during the battle of Malvern Hill [July 1, 1862] he had occasion to report to General Jackson, and after hunting for some time found him and his staff under one of the heaviest fires he had ever experienced. Soon Jackson directed those about him to dismount and shelter themselves, and Dr. Dabney found a place behind a large and very thick oak gate-post, where he sat bolt upright with his back against the post. Just then there came up Major Hugh Nelson, of Ewell's staff—a gallant gentleman and a devout churchman, who had heard Dr. Dabney's sermon, and whose theological view did not fully indorse its doctrine—and, taking in the situation at a glance, rode direct for the gate-post of "Stonewall's" Chief of Staff, and giving him the military salute coolly said: "Dr. Dabney, every shot, and shell, and bullet is directed by the God of battles, and you must pardon me for expressing my surprise that you should want to put a gate-post between you and special Providence."

The good doctor at once retorted: "No! Major, you misunderstand the doctrine I teach. And the truth is, that I regard this gate-post as a *special Providence,* under present circumstances."

—Rev. J. William Jones

Sherman and the Memphis Minister

AFTER SHERMAN OCCUPIED Memphis [July 21, 1862], the people kept the churches, schools, and places of business closed, so that, save for the movements of the soldiers, the place looked like a city of the dead. He issued an order directing that the stores and shops should be opened during business hours, the schools resume their courses, and the churches hold their customary services. Among the people who called at his headquarters to protest against this order, or to ask for explanations, was the clergyman of an Episcopal church, who said that the ritual of his denomination contained a prayer for the President which, under the circumstances, embarrassed him.

"Whom do you regard as your President?" asked Sherman, bluntly.

"We look upon Mr. Davis as our President," replied the minister.

"Very well; pray for Jeff Davis if you wish. He needs your prayers badly. It will take a great deal of praying to save him."

"Then I will not be compelled to pray for Mr. Lincoln?"

"Oh, no. He's a good man, and don't need your prayers. You may pray for him if you feel like it, but there's no compulsion," answered Sherman, instantly divining that the worthy clergyman wanted to pose as a martyr before his parishioners, and had hoped that he would be ordered to use the prayer for the President of the United States. The next Sunday the prescribed prayer was so modified by the preacher as to leave out all mention of the President, and to refer only to "all in authority."

—E. V. SMALLEY

∗

Kearny Mistakes the Confederates
for His Own Men

∗

[AT CHANTILLY] just before sunset on the 1st [of September, 1862], the enemy attacked but was met by Hooker's, Reno's and Kearny's Divisions of Heintzelman Corps. The enemy was driven back entirely from our front but during that engagement we lost two of the best and one of the most distinguished of our general officers—Major General [Isaac I.] Stevens and Major General [Philip] Kearny.

∗ ∗ ∗ ∗ ∗

In the driving storm, Phil drove his blinded horse forward against it. Suddenly Phil finds himself in the presence of troops—his own troops

192

of course—that's where they should have been. Riding up to the side of an officer in blue, Phil inquired: "Captain, what troops are these? I am looking for my command." The soldier in blue Kearny addressed was Major Hawks, brother of Major General P. Hawks, who had also mistakenly entered the enemy's lines just a moment before Kearny rode up; was taken prisoner, was paroled and wrote his brother about it later.

Swift as lightning and in a whisper, the major replied: "General Kearny, this is a Confederate line and we are both securely in their power. It is sure death to attempt to escape; please, sir, do not attempt it both for your own and the country's sake!"

Kearny looking around him said gayly: "Sir, I have a good horse here; and can depend on him every time; he'll carry me through!"

As Phil turned his horse, a Confederate officer called out: "You are crazy, man; you can't get ten feet. Don't be foolish!"

General Kearny muttered something about they couldn't hit a barn.

Kearny's black colt wheeled, Kearny threw himself forward and close upon the animal's back! Twenty shots rang out! Kearny falls! Then springs towards Kearny a Confederate officer, with many others, to the point where he lay; not supposing that his wound was a mortal one. Just as the officer reached Kearny's body, however, his limbs gave a convulsive quiver and then all was over! Seeing that he was a major general, word was sent to Headquarters; and General Jackson coming to the spot immediately gave one glance at the dead officer's features and exclaimed: "My God, boys, you know who you have killed? You have shot the most gallant officer in the United States Army. This is Phil Kearny, who lost his arm in the Mexican War." He then involuntarily lifted his hat; every officer in the group followed his example; and for a moment reverential silence was observed by all. Subsequently, the body of the dead soldier was placed upon two boards; and when removed to Headquarters was followed by General Jackson and other officers while a regimental band preceded it playing a dead march.

Lee sent an aide to safeguard his friend's body; a guard was ordered; the body taken to the Stuart House "Chantilly" at Ox Hill. The aide returns to General Lee after taking from Phil's pockets all the papers, Lee looks them over; remarks that they are "private papers," burns them without inspection; and directs his aide to see that no harm is done to Kearny's person; and dictates a memorandum "to General Hooker" that the body will be sent through the lines under escort.

The Stuart House had been converted into a hospital and most of the rebel troops viewed Phil's remains; and several of them tell the story: General Kearny was a large handsome man and as he lay there, buttoned in his uniform, presented a splendid specimen of manly strength. The rebels crowded around to view the Yankee general. One poor ragged bare-footed fellow cast a longing look at the fine cavalry boots Kearny had on, remarking as he did so, "No. 9's—just fit for me," and turned over in his bed, no doubt thinking [it], as he did so, a great hardship that he was not permitted to appropriate them to his own use.

—THOMAS KEARNY

*

Magruder and His Old E Company

*

ONE OF THE MOST GALLANT and meritorious defences ever made was that of Kirby's Battery on the second day of the great battle of Antietam [September 17, 1862]. It was in an excellent position and effected terrible destruction to the enemy. The Confederates finally became exasperated, and as the story was told by a number of the rebel wounded and prisoners, General [John B.] Magruder, who commanded this battery before the war, as he sat on his horse, drew up his glass and took a long look at the battery.

Suddenly he dropped his glass and cried out: "By ——! I thought it was! I thought it was!" he repeated with intense animation. "That's my old battery, E Company, First Artillery!" (Magruder referred to ante-war times when he was in the Federal service.) "Take it, boys! take it!" he called out with extreme vehemence.

The Confederates then charged on the battery in three columns; but Kirby's fire was so rapid and deadly that they could not advance. He played on them with grape and canister, raking them down with such fearful slaughter that they did not gain but a few yards before they were compelled to fall back. Finally, after the ground was covered with dead and wounded, the enemy began to give ground, when Kirby limbered up his battery, and succeeded in getting away in safety with all his guns, and the enemy then fell back to their original position. After the last attempt to take the battery failed, Magruder, with a

194

mingled feeling of pride and chagrin, exclaimed: "Oh, by ——, boys! I knew you couldn't take old E Company! I know their metal too well!"

—FRANC B. WILKIE (POLIUTO)

*

The "Bishop" Brazens It Out

*

WHEN THE ACCOUNTS of the hard battles fought during the war are rendered by the true historian, it will be found that the battle of Perryville [October 8, 1862] was one of the hardest contested and one of the most sanguinary during the war. It was like two huge monsters together in one death-grasp, and each trying to drink the last drop of the other's blood. It was the only battle in which bayonets and butts of guns were used with death-dealing effect.

The battle of Perryville was fought in the afternoon, raging until far in the night, both sides holding their grounds and fighting like demons in the very pit of hell. It was a battle in which even generals were "seen at the front," even where the fighting was going on, as the following adventure of General Leonidas ["Bishop"] Polk will show, and as told by himself:

"Well, sir, it was at the battle of Perryville, late in the evening, in fact, it was almost dark, when [St. John R.] Liddell's brigade came into action. Shortly after its arrival I observed a body of men, whom I believed to be Confederates, standing at an angle to this brigade and firing obliquely at the newly arrived troops. I said, 'Dear me, this is very sad, and must be stopped.' So I turned around, but could find none of my young men, who were absent on different messages; so I determined to ride myself and settle the matter. Having cantered up to the colonel of the regiment which was firing, I asked, in angry tones, what he meant by shooting his own friends, and I desired him to cease firing at once. He said, with surprise, 'I don't think there can be any mistake about it, for I am d——d certain that they are the enemy.' 'Enemy!' I said, 'why I have just left them myself. Cease firing, sir. What is your name, sir?' 'My name is Colonel ——, of the ——

Indiana; and pray, sir, who are you?' Then, for the first time, I saw, to my astonishment, that he was a Yankee, and that I was in rear of a regiment of Yankees. Well, I saw that there was no hope but to brazen it out. My dark blouse and the increasing obscurity befriended me; so I approached quite close to him and shook my fist in his face, saying, 'I'll soon show you who I am, sir. Cease firing, sir, at once!' I then turned my horse and cantered slowly down the line, shouting in an authoritative manner to the Yankees to 'cease firing.' At the same time I experienced a disagreeable sensation like screwing up my back, and calculating how many bullets would be between my shoulders every moment. I was afraid to increase my pace until I got to a small copse, when I put the spurs in and galloped back to my men. I immediately went to the nearest colonel and said to him, 'Colonel, I have reconnoitered those fellows pretty closely, and I find there is no mistaking who they are. You may get up and go at them.' So I ordered Liddell's brigade to cease firing and to promptly load their guns, and for no man to pull a trigger or fire a gun unless he had a dead aim on a Yankee. After every one was loaded I ordered the firing obliquely to the left, and, when they did fire, nearly three thousand muskets blazed as one gun, and as with the deafening crash of a platoon of artillery. And I assure you, sir, that the slaughter of that Indiana regiment was the greatest I had ever seen in the war."

—"CO. AYTCH" [SAM R. WATKINS]

*

Sherman and the Coldwater Bridge

---

*

IN THE LATTER PART of November, 1862, General Sherman left Memphis with 16,000 men to join General Grant at Oxford, Mississippi. On reaching Coldwater River, about half-way between Memphis and Oxford, we found the bridge destroyed, and, as the waters were very high and the current very swift, it was necessary to build a bridge before we could cross. Lieutenant Colonel Malmburg, of the 55th Illinois, was given charge of the construction. There was quite a village on our side of the stream (its name I do not remember), composed principally of log-houses, and most of them deserted. Colonel Malmburg went to work with his men, using the logs of the houses for cribbing and the stone chimneys for anchorage, and in an incredibly short time he had two piers, composed of logs and stone, anchored in the stream midway between banks. Using more logs and the available lumber from the houses, he had by daylight a splendid military bridge, and our troops rapidly crossing. Just as the General was preparing to leave the house in which we had spent the night, two or three old gentlemen, citizens of the place, asked the General to sign a statement setting forth the value of the property taken by him for the construction of the bridge, in order, as they said, that they could recover from the United States after a ratification of a treaty of peace between the Confederate States and the aforesaid United States.

The General asked them who destroyed the bridge that spanned the stream just before we reached it. They admitted that the Confederate soldiers had.

"Well," said the General, "my men have built a very good bridge, have they not?"

"Oh, yes," said the gentlemen, "that is a powerful good bridge to be built so quickly, and in the night-time at that."

"Well, then, I will tell you what to do," said the General: "Just as soon as the last man of my command has crossed that bridge, you can have it; and if you will place a man in charge of it and require him to collect $1 toll from everybody that crosses it, you will get pay for your property a great deal sooner than you will if you wait until I sign that paper." And, bidding the gentlemen good-morning, he mounted his horse and we were away.

On the 5th of December our army arrived at College Hill, Mississippi. Leaving the army there, the General and staff passed on to Oxford, where we met General Grant. The next day we returned to College Hill, and the next morning began the return march to Memphis, to prepare for the Vicksburg campaign. As we crossed our bridge at Coldwater, I remarked to the General that it was fortunate for him that the old gentlemen had not followed his advice about collecting toll, and a very unfortunate thing for them, because "they lose $16,000 which you would have been obliged to pay."

"That is a fact," said the General; "but then, I did not expect to return so soon."

—CAPTAIN JOHN J. TAYLOR

14. "FIRST GENTLEMAN
OF VIRGINIA"

The Origin of the Lee Tomatoes

*

ONE DAY IN JUNE, 1862, General Lee rode over to General Charles W. Field's headquarters at Meadow Bridge and asked for me. I would say here that on leaving home to enter the army I carried a family letter of introduction to General Lee; and on account of that, and also my relationship to Colonel Charles Marshall, an aide on his staff, my visits at army headquarters were exceptionally pleasant.

When General Lee approached me on this occasion, he said: "Captain, can General Field spare you a little while?"

I replied, "Certainly, General; what can I do for you?"

"I have some property," he answered, "in the hands of the enemy, and General McClellan has informed me that he would deliver it to me at any time I asked for it."

Then, putting aside his jesting manner, he told me that his wife and Miss Mary Lee, his daughter, had been caught within the Federal lines at the White House, the residence of General W. H. F. Lee, his son, and he desired me to take a courier and proceed with a flag of truce to Meadow Bridge and carry a sealed dispatch to General McClellan. At the Federal headquarters I would meet the ladies, and escort them to Mrs. Gooch's farm, inside our lines.

I passed beyond the pickets to the second bridge, where I waved my flag of truce, and was asked by the Union officer of the guard to enter. When I reached the picket, the officer said he had been ordered not to permit any flag of truce to pass through his lines until he had communicated with the headquarters of General McClellan. I waited on the bridge, and when the courier returned he had orders to bring me before the General. The officer insisted on blindfolding me, and positively forbade my courier accompanying me. I was then led through the camps, where I could hear the voices of thousands laughing, talking, or hallooing. After riding an hour, a distance, as I supposed, of three or four miles, I reached the headquarters and was relieved of my bandage. The General came out and gave me a hearty welcome; and when he heard that I had been blindfolded, he was so indignant that he placed the officer, my guide, under arrest. I had never seen him so excited. He asked me into the house, produced his liquors, and gave me a dinner of the best, after which we discussed the situation at length. He asked me no questions which it would compromise our cause to answer, but we calmly reviewed the position of things from our separate points of view, and he inquired anxiously after all his old friends. (General McClellan and my brother-in-law, General Dabney H. Maury, C.S.A., formerly captain, U.S.A., had been classmates and devoted friends, and the General had visited my father's house and my own at Fredericksburg.)

About three o'clock in the afternoon, looking down the road, we saw a carriage approaching. The curtains were cut off, and it was drawn by a mule and a dilapidated old horse, driven by a Negro of about ten or twelve years, and followed by a cavalry escort. General McClellan, jumping up hastily, said: "There are Mrs. Lee and Miss Mary, now." As the carriage stopped before the door, General McClellan, greeting the ladies with marked cordiality, at once introduced me, and remarked to Mrs. Lee that the General (her husband) had chosen

199

me as her escort through the lines, and that by a strange coincidence, he (McClellan) had found in me a personal friend. He offered to accompany us in person to the river, but this was declined by Mrs. Lee as entirely unnecessary.

When we reached Mrs. Gooch's farm and our own pickets, cheer after cheer went down the long line of soldiers. Near the house we were met by General Lee and a large number of officers assembled to honor the wife and daughter of their chief.

Before leaving for Richmond, Mrs. Lee handed me from a basket, under the carriage-seat, two fine tomatoes, the finest I had ever seen, remarking that she supposed such things were scarce in the Confederacy. The seeds of these tomatoes I preserved, and, some years after the war, General Lee ate some tomatoes at my table, and praised them; whereupon we told him, to his astonishment, that those were the Lee tomatoes, and that they had been distributed all over the state under that name, from the seed of those given me by his wife.

—MAJOR W. ROY MASON

*

Father and Son

---

*

GENERAL LEE had nothing of nepotism about him, but meted out the evenest justice to all, except that he did not promote his relatives as rapidly as he did others.

His son Robert served as a private in the ranks of the Rockbridge Artillery, sharing with his comrades of that crack corps all their dangers, hardships, drudgery, and privations, when a hint from his father would have secured him promotion to some place of honor. The General told, with evident relish, that during the battle of Sharpsburg [September 17, 1862] he became very uneasy about Robert—knowing that his battery had suffered severely, and not hearing anything from him. At last he made it convenient to ride up to the battery, which had just been relieved from a very perilous position, where it had suffered fearful loss, and had his fears increased by not recognizing his son among the men. To the hearty greeting of the brave fellows, he replied, "Well! you have done nobly to-day, but I shall be compelled to send you in again."

"Will you, General," said a powder-begrimed youth whom he did not recognize, until he spoke, as his son Robert. "Well, boys, come on; the General says we must go in again, and you know he is in the habit of having his own way about such matters."

Thus, the anxiety of the Commander-in-Chief was relieved, and his son went gayly to work at his gun and contributed his full share toward "keeping those people [the General never referred to them as Yankees] back."

—REV. J. WILLIAM JONES

*

The Trees of Chatham

*

ASCENDING THE HEIGHTS [at Fredericksburg, December 11, 1862], I soon reached what was called the headquarters battery of General Lee. Afar across the valley and river in the gray light of the early morning could be seen the white porches of my home, Chatham, made historic by Federal army correspondents, as the "Lacy House." The porches were filled with officers and gayly dressed women, and from half a score of brass bands rang out across the valley "Yankee Doodle" and "Hail, Columbia!" The commanding officer of the battery asked me if I would permit him to scatter the unbidden guests at my home. At his request I asked General Lee to authorize the fire of the heavy guns, which would have laid Chatham in the dust. With a smile he refused, and asking me to walk with him, we withdrew a short distance. He then motioned me to sit by him on the trunk of a large tree.

Looking across at Chatham through his field-glass he said, "Major, I never permit the unnecessary effusion of blood. War is terrible enough, at its best, to a Christian man; I hope yet to see you and your dear family happy in your old home. Do you know I love Chatham better than any place in the world except Arlington! I courted and won my dear wife under the shade of those trees. By the way, not long since I was riding out with my staff, and observing how your grand old trees had been cut down by those people, I saw that a magnificent tulip poplar at the head of the ravine, north of the house, was still standing, and, with somewhat of your rhetoric, I said to Venable and Taylor: 'There is nothing in vegetable nature so grand as a tree. Grappling with its roots the granite foundations of the everlasting hills, it reaches its sturdy and gnarled trunk on high, spreads its branches to the heavens, casts its shadow on the sward, and the birds build their nests and sing amid its umbrageous foliage. Behold, the monarch stripped of attendants and guards awes the vandal, by the simple majesty of his sublime isolation.' Pocketing my field-glass, and riding on, I heard mingled with laughter a request from the young gentlemen that I would bring my glass to bear once more on the monarch of the forest. I looked, and even while I had been talking the axe of the vandal was laid to the root, and the monarch had fallen."

Then, moved by emotion unusual to his calm and equable nature, he continued, "I had three hundred acres of woodland at Arlington. Serving the United States Government for many years on the frontier, I marked with my own hand each tree that was to be used for timber or fuel. They tell me all my trees are gone—yours are all gone"; then rising from the log, with a fire and a passion rarely witnessed in him, and with all the majesty of his sublime presence, he said: "Major, they have our *trees;* they shall never have the *land!*"

—J. Horace Lacy

*

What Lee Said at Fredericksburg

---

*

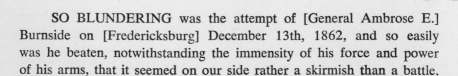

SO BLUNDERING was the attempt of [General Ambrose E.] Burnside on [Fredericksburg] December 13th, 1862, and so easily was he beaten, notwithstanding the immensity of his force and power of his arms, that it seemed on our side rather a skirmish than a battle,

202

though of the enemy the slaughter was terrific. Under the flag of truce sent by Burnside for permission to bury his dead, we rode over the field, and the sight of his dead and dying, in such amazing numbers, was absolutely sickening. From prominent points in our line almost the entire scene could be taken in by the eye. And at one of these, the most commanding, where we had a few powerful guns, General Lee remained much of the day, observing the field; only too indifferent, as was his wont, to danger from the large, numerous, and well-aimed missiles hurled especially thither from the enemy's heavy batteries across the Rappahannock. Seldom, in all the wars of the world, has a spectacle been presented like that which, from this central elevation, we looked upon. More than one hundred thousand blue-coated men in the open plain, with every military appliance, in battle order, and moving in their respective subdivisions to attack our line. Although our numbers were certainly not half those of the enemy, there was misgiving, probably, in no officer or man as to the result. Events in one quarter of the field, as it lay before us, attracted peculiar interest, and gave occasion to one of those characteristic remarks of General Lee which told at once of his capacity for enjoying the excitements of action, and of the good feeling and strong principle that kept it under control. A large force advanced rapidly to charge our right. Stonewall Jackson was there, and that he would promptly hurl them back little doubt was entertained. Still no such assault can be witnessed without earnest interest, if not concern. Nor was the shock received on our side without loss. There fell the heroic General Gregg, of the gallant and now vengeance-suffering state of South Carolina. Presently, however, as was anticipated, the spirited charge was reversed, and blue figures by thousands were seen recrossing, "double-quick," with faces to the rear, the space they had traversed, and hundreds of gray pursuers hastening their speed. While younger spectators near us gave expression to their feelings by shouts, clapping of hands, &c., the gratified yet considerate and amiable commander turned to myself, and with beaming countenance said, *"It is well war is so terrible, or we should get too fond of it."*

—W. N. PENDLETON

203

15. STONEWALL WAS "A POWERFUL FIGHTIN' AND PRAYIN' MAN"

"I Wish the Yankees Were in Hell"

*

[THE NIGHT OF JANUARY 1, 1862] was the most dismal and trying night of this terrible expedition [of Jackson's to Bath and Romney]. It had been and was still snowing lightly, and the small army was in uncomfortable bivouac. A squad of soldiers in the Stonewall Brigade had built a large fire and some of them were standing and some lying about it wrapped up in their thin and inadequate blankets. The sharp wind was blowing over the hills and through the trees with a

204

mocking whistle, whirling the sparks and smoke in eyes and over prostrate bodies.

A doleful defender, who had been lying down by the fire, with one side to it just long enough to get warm and comfortable, while the other got equally cold and uncomfortable, rose up and, having gathered his flapping blanket around him as well as possible, stood nodding and staggering over the flames. When the sparks set his blanket on fire it exhausted his patience and in the extremity of his disgust he exclaimed, "I wish the Yankees were in Hell!"

As he yawned this with a sleepy drawl, around the fire there went a drowsy growl of approbation. One individual, William Wintermeyer, however, lying behind a fallen tree, shivering with cold but determined not to get up, muttered, "I don't. Old Jack would follow them there, with our brigade in front!"

There seemed to be some force in the objection, but the gloomy individual continued, "Well, that's so, Bill,—but I wish the Yankees were in Heaven. They're too good for this earth!"

"I don't!" again replied the soldier behind the log, "because Old Jack would follow them there, too, and as it's our turn to go on picket, we wouldn't enjoy ourselves a bit!"

The discomfited soldier threw himself to the ground with a grunt, and all was quiet but the keen wind and crackling flames.

—MAJOR HENRY KYD DOUGLAS

*

Why Stonewall Jackson Did Not Drink

---

*

HAVING LINGERED to the last allowable moment with the members of my family . . . it was after ten o'clock at night [May 30, 1862], when I returned to headquarters for final instruction, and before going to the General's room [at the hotel in Winchester] I ordered two whiskey toddies to be brought up after me. When they appeared I offered one of the glasses to Jackson, but he drew back, saying: "No, Colonel, you must excuse me; I never drink intoxicating liquors."

"I know that, General," said I, "but though you habitually abstain, as I do myself, from everything of the sort, there are occasions, and this is one of them, when a stimulant will do us both good; otherwise, I would neither take it myself nor offer it to you. So you must make an exception to your general rule, and join me in a toddy to-night."

He again shook his head, but, nevertheless, took the tumbler and began to sip its contents. Presently putting it on the table, after having but partially emptied it, he said: "Colonel, do you know why I habitually abstain from intoxicating drinks?" And on my replying in the negative, he continued: "Why, sir, because I like the taste of them, and when I discovered that to be the case I made up my mind at once to do without them altogether."

—COLONEL A. R. BOTELER

*

"Kill the Brave Ones"

*

AT THE BATTLE of Port Republic [June 9, 1862] an officer commanding a regiment of Federal soldiers and riding a snow-white horse was very conspicuous for his gallantry. He frequently exposed himself to the fire of our men in the most reckless way. So splendid was this man's courage that General [Richard S.] Ewell, one of the most chivalrous gentlemen I ever knew, at some risk to his own life, rode down the line and called to his men not to shoot the man on the white horse. After a while, however, the officer and the white horse went down. A day or two after, when General Jackson learned of the incident, he sent for General Ewell and told him not to do such a thing again; that this was no ordinary war, and the brave and gallant Federal officers were the very kind that must be killed. "Shoot the brave officers and the cowards will run away and take the men with them!"

—As told by DR. HUNTER MCGUIRE to MAJOR ROBERT STILES

Jackson on Dodging

AT THE BATTLE of Port Republic, in the Valley of Virginia, Stonewall Jackson occupied a position at one time which exposed him to great personal peril. An artillery duel was in progress, and the missiles of the enemy fell thick around him.

A cannon-ball had just killed a soldier at his side, and the soldier's companion, who had escaped injury, dodged and retreated several yards, fearing that a shot might put an end to him also if he stood so near the fatal spot. Scarcely was he in his new position, ere another ball whistled past him, and he fell, stunned by atmospheric concussion. Had he remained at his former post the ball would have been harmless.

Stonewall who did not dodge, seeing all this, said in his plain, blunt way to the soldier when again on his feet: "What did you make by dodging? Dodgers often dodge into the danger they would avert. Don't dodge anything except sin, sir, and you will be all right."

—Southern Punch

Why Jackson Cleaned up the Battlefield

[AFTER THE BATTLE of Malvern Hill, July 1, 1862], it took several hours to collect all our slain, and I was more and more surprised that General Jackson should give so much of his personal attention to such a matter at such a time. He had the bodies laid side by side in rows, numbering from a dozen to forty or fifty, according to convenience to the places they occupied, and he then had their blankets and oil-cloths spread over the rows, concealing their faces and figures completely. After this was done he had their muskets and accoutrements collected and laid in piles in gullies so as to be out of sight; then, not satisfied with this, he made the men pick up every scrap of clothing and caps, and every piece of human flesh scattered around, such as legs, arms, etc., etc.

I had heard that "Old Stonewall" was eccentric, and indeed at that time some who disliked him said he was unsound in his mind; and I thought this, to me absurd, attention to cleaning up the battle-field was an evidence of it. Still he evidently had a motive and to him an urgent one. There was nothing idle or objectless in the way he acted, but on the contrary the intense vigor and sharpness of his commands, as he trotted incessantly about in every direction among the working parties, so hurried them that the men omitted even to rifle the pockets of the slain, venting their feelings at this loss of opportunity in suppressed curses, "not loud but deep," when their General's back was turned.

My curiosity was aroused, and I determined to watch for an opportunity and ask him his reasons. Stonewall Jackson was very pleasant and agreeable when he chose to be so and when his mind was at ease, but he was not the man to talk to when he was busy, by any manner of means. I exerted myself to the utmost in assisting him, for which he thanked me very graciously, and after a while even he could find nothing more to pick up, and the field certainly did look very differently; the dark bloodstains, soaking the ground, alone marked the numbers who had fallen. The number of the dead now appeared very much less. There did not appear to be one in ten since they were collected together. Jackson had swept his dust into piles, like a good housewife, and the floor looked clean though the piles were still there.

When at last he became quiet and disposed to talk, I asked him why he was having the field cleaned in that way. "Why," said he, "I am going to attack here presently, as soon as the fog rises, and it won't do to march the troops over their own dead, you know; that's what I am doing it for." Then, I thought to myself, if you are crazy there is surely "method in your madness," for it would have been a most demoralizing preparation for battle for men to have marched over the field as I first saw it that morning.

—LIEUTENANT COLONEL W. W. BLACKFORD

Jackson Takes a Nap

*

ON THE 8th of July the Army of Northern Virginia began to move back [from Harrison's Landing] to the vicinity of Richmond. When Jackson's command started he and his staff remained behind until some time after the rest of the army had gone. It was after dark when he started and about midnight when he reached his headquarters. He was riding along at ten or eleven o'clock with his drowsy staff, nodding on "Little Sorrel," as was his custom, and trusting to that intelligent beast not to give him a fall. More than once did we see his head nod and drop on his breast and his body sway a little to one side or the other, expecting to see him get a tumble; but he never got it. On this occasion our sleepy cavalcade at different times passed small squads of soldiers in fence corners before blazing fires, roasting green corn and eating it. Passing one of these, our staggering leader was observed by one of those thirsty stragglers, who was evidently delighted at the sight of a drunken cavalryman. Perhaps encouraged with the hope of a drink ahead, the ragged Reb jumped up from his fire and, brandishing a roasting-ear in his hand, sprang into the road and to the head of the General's horse, with, "Hello! I say, old fellow, where the devil did you get your licker?"

The General suddenly woke up and said, "Dr. McGuire, did you speak to me? Captain Pendleton, did you? Somebody did," and reined up his horse.

The soldier got a look at him and took in the situation; he saw whom he had thus spoken to. "Good God! it's Old Jack!" he cried, and with several bounds and a flying leap he had cleared the road, was over the fence, and disappeared in the dark.

As soon as the staff could recover from their laughter, McGuire explained the situation to the General, who was much amused. He immediately rode up to the fence, dismounted, and took half an hour's nap. Then he roused himself, said he felt better, and we went on to Headquarters.

—Major Henry Kyd Douglas

*

Jackson Disobeys His Own Orders

*

In camp, three miles from Richmond
Sunday, July 13, 1862

[JACKSON] got on his old sorrel horse, which his courier was holding for him, and without saying a word to anyone, in a deep brown and abstracted study started in a gallop towards the Mechanicsville Pike, which we soon reached. His orders, published to his corps, very strictly enjoined the preservation of the crops along which the army and its trains moved and forbade all officers and men from riding out into the fields on each side of the road. This day Jackson was especially anxious to get back to his quarters. Unfortunately for his speed, the pike was filled with long wagon trains, one set coming in, the other going out. It was impossible to make time under these circumstances and still obey orders. He had not spoken a word since we had gotten underway. He first dodged in and out among the wagons, but his progress was slow, much slower than his needs demanded. He obviously remembered his orders, but determined to violate them.

He told his adjutant to have the cavalcade fall into single file and thereupon dashed into an extensive field of oats, overripe for the harvest, on the left of the pike. Several hundred yards ahead of the place [where] he violated the sacred oat field, there was a very nice brick house sitting back some distance, in a grove of oaks with a lane leading down to the pike. On a porch a round and fat little gentleman was sitting smoking his pipe, with bald head and red face, in his shirtsleeves, with an eye on his morning *Examiner* and the other on his field of oats. When he saw the cavalcade ride out of the road, he threw down his paper, rushed down the steps and flew down the lane and before we reached the place where the lane and pike united he was standing like a lion in the path-

210

way. He was puffing and blowing, wiping the perspiration off his forehead and so bursting with rage that all power of articulation seemed for a moment suspended.

The General saw him and for the first time in his career seemed inclined to retreat, but our irate friend had regained his speech and made his attack as Jackson drew rein before him.

"What in hell are you riding over my oats for?" the little man shouted. "Don't you know it's against orders?"

The General looked confused, fumbled with his bridle rein and was as much abashed as any schoolboy ever caught in a watermelon patch. Before, with his slow speech, he could ever get out a word of explanation, our volcanic friend had another eruption: "Damnit! Don't you know it's against orders? I intend to have every damned one of you arrested! What's your name anyhow?"

"My name is Jackson," said the General, half as if, for the occasion, he wished it was something else.

"Jackson! Jackson!" in a voice of great contempt. "Jackson, I intend to report every one of you and have you every one arrested. Yes, I'd report you if you were old Stonewall himself instead of a set of damned quartermasters and commissaries riding through my oats! Yes, I'll report you to Stonewall Jackson myself, that's what I'll do!"

"They call me that name sometimes," said the General in the same subdued, half-alarmed tone.

"What name?"

"Stonewall."

"You don't mean to say you are Stonewall Jackson, do you?"

"Yes, sir, I am."

I can give no adequate description of the sudden change. His anger was gone in an instant and in its place came an admiring look that was adoring. His color vanished, his lips parted and tears stood in his eyes. His emotions stilled his tongue an instant, then his speech returned with all the vigor of his vernacular and he shouted as he waved his big bandana around his head: "Hurrah for Stonewall Jackson! By God, General, please do me the honor to ride all over my damned old oats!"

—Captain Charles Minor Blackford

"Nothing Else Will Suit a Mule"

Battlefield of Major's Gate, Slaughter Mountain, Va.
August 11, 1862

AS THE CANNON, caissons, and ammunition wagons and the other wagons were crossing Crooked Run there was a delay owing to the mud on the side of the ford where the wagons came out. Major John Harmon was superintending the transit in person, but there was much delay owing to the bad landing place. Harmon has a powerful and sharp-sounding voice and is very profane. It is said he can swear at a mule team and make it jerk a wagon out of a mud-hole as nothing else will. He was using his utmost endeavors in this line at the ford that day, but with no great success.

Jackson got impatient, especially for the ordnance wagons, and rode back a little with me as his only companion to hurry them along. Harmon was in full feather and the air was blue with his oaths. As Jackson came up he rather increased his energy. Jackson stood a moment and said very mildly: "Major, don't you think you would accomplish just as much without swearing so hard?"

Harmon turned with a smile that was almost contemptuous and said, "If you think anybody can make a set of damned mules pull without swearing at them, you just try it, General! Just try it! I'll stand by and see how damned quick you get tired of it!" With that he stood back and commenced impatiently to walk backwards and forwards and back again while Jackson watched the ford.

The first wagon was light and had a good team and pulled out. Jackson turned with some triumph to Harmon and said, "You see, Major, how easy it is?"

"Just wait," Harmon said, "till one of those damned ordnance wagons comes along! You haven't had anything but a bunch of empties yet; don't holler until you're out of the woods, General!"

As he said it a monster came to the exit of the ford and stalled.

212

The driver jerked the reins and whipped and did everything but swear, having recognized the General on the bank, and after some moments got it out while Harmon stood by obviously enjoying Jackson's impatience.

"Better let me damn 'em, General, nothing else will do!"

Jackson made no reply and another ordnance wagon came along. It was obviously heavily loaded and stuck at the edge of the ford despite every effort of the driver, some suggestions on the part of the General and some pushing by other drivers. Harmon was delighted and laughed a most triumphant laugh.

"What do you say now, General? Try swearing at them yourself, General, since nothing else will suit a mule!"

The General stood impatiently a moment longer, then gathered up the reins of his horse and moved off, saying in a crestfallen tone, "Well, Major, I suppose you will have to have your way!"

Before he had moved fifty yards all the pent-up energy of Harmon's nature found vent in a fluent damnation which so startled the mules and their Negro driver that the wagon was jerked out of the stream and was alongside the retreating General in half a minute.

—Captain Charles Minor Blackford

*

A Yankee's Trophies

---

*

Along the Rappahannock, August 17, 1862

AT MITCHELL'S STATION we captured a small picket under a very intelligent sergeant. After getting all the information in my reach I came back with our prisoners. The sergeant was communicative and I took him up to [General Jackson's] tent, thinking he might give some valuable information. When we got there the staff was standing around the tent, holding their horses and the General's sorrel was just in front, ready for him to mount. My prisoner took his stand at the sorrel's rump to await with the rest of us the General's advent. He at once commenced, I supposed in nervous agitation, to stroke the sorrel's rump with his right hand and to pass his left hand through the tail, pulling out each time a number of hairs. This he did so often that his hand was quite full of them and one of the staff, with some asperity, just as the General came up to the horse's head, ordered him to stop, which he did and at once commenced cramming the hair into his pocket. General Jackson saw what he was doing and, to my infinite relief, said in a mild voice, "My friend, why are you tearing the hair out of my horse's tail?" The prisoner took off his hat most respectfully and with a bright smile said, "Ah, General, each one of these hairs is worth a dollar in New York." Was there ever a more delicate compliment to a man's reputation? The General was both amused and pleased at the tribute, by an enemy, to his fame. He was confused by our presence and actually blushed. He merely directed me to send the prisoner to the rear and did not question him further. I did so, but he carried his trophies with him.

—CAPTAIN CHARLES MINOR BLACKFORD

*

Jubal Early Replies to Jackson

*

JACKSON'S WING of the army was left about Winchester after the battle of Sharpsburg [September 17, 1862], to remove the sick and wounded and army supplies, while Longstreet's wing was thrown in front of McClellan to Culpeper Court-house. When the object was effected, Jackson began one of his rapid marches to rejoin Longstreet before McClellan would attack him alone. Now General [Jubal A.] Early had the famous Louisiana brigade in his division, and a good many other troops, who would not have voted for the Maine liquor law. The Massanutten mountains were full of old peach and honey, and the men thought it would be a pity, almost a sin, to leave so much spoil to the enemy. Besides, they needed, or they thought they needed, something to support their strength on the forced march. General Jackson happened to ride in rear of this division that day, and he found the men scattered for miles along the road in every possible attitude, from dancing the polka to sprawling on the ground; in every possible mood,

214

from "grave to gay, from lively to severe"; some fighting over their battles again, others of a more sentimental turn, weeping about the wives and children far away. General Jubal had expended his eloquence and his emphatic Saxon in vain. He had even spread the report that the mountain huts were full of smallpox, but this had only stimulated the curiosity of his prying followers. Conquered at last, he had gone to camp and was toasting his shins that frosty night by a bright fire, when an orderly rode up with a note. "Dispatch from General Jackson, General." He rose from his seat and fumbled for his spectacles. But let the correspondence tell its own tale:

HEADQUARTERS LEFT WING

GENERAL: *General Jackson desires to know why he saw so many of your stragglers in rear of your division to-day?*

(*Signed*) A. S. PENDLETON,

To Major General Early   A.A.G.

HEADQUARTERS EARLY'S DIVISION

CAPTAIN: *In answer to your note I would state that I think it probable that the reason why General Jackson saw so many of my stragglers on the march to-day is that he rode in rear of my division.*

Respectfully,

J. A. EARLY,

To Captain A. S. Pendleton,   *Major General*

A.A.G.

—*The Land We Love*

*

A New Coat for Stonewall

---

*

FROM A LONG REST, after the dissipations of the past night [at the Grand Ball at "The Bower" on the Opequon, October 7, 1862], I was roused about noon by General Stuart, with orders to ride, upon some little matters of duty, to the camp of General Jackson. I was also honoured with the pleasing mission of presenting to old Stonewall, as a slight token of Stuart's high regard, a new and very "stunning" uniform coat, which had just arrived from the hands of a Richmond tailor. The garment, neatly wrapped up, was borne on the pommel of his saddle by one of our couriers who accompanied me; and starting at once I reached the simple tent of our great General just in time for dinner. I found him in his old weather-stained coat, from which all the buttons had been clipped long since by the fair hands of patriotic ladies, and which, from exposure to sun and rain and powder-smoke, and by reason of many rents and patches, was in a very unseemly condition. When I had despatched more important matters, I produced General Stuart's present, in all its magnificence of gilt buttons and sheeny facings and gold lace, and I was heartily amused at the modest confusion with which the hero of many battles regarded the fine uniform from many points of view, scarcely daring to touch it, and at the quiet way in which, at last, he folded it up carefully, and deposited it in his portmanteau, saying to me, "Give Stuart my best thanks, my dear Major—the coat is much too handsome for me, but I shall take the best care of it, and shall prize it highly as a souvenir. And now let us have some dinner."

But I protested energetically against this summary disposition of the matter of the coat, deeming my mission, indeed, but half executed, and remarked that Stuart would certainly ask me how the uniform fitted its owner, and that I should, therefore, take it as a personal favour if he would put it on. To this he readily assented with a smile, and, having donned the garment, he escorted me outside the tent to the table where dinner had been served in the open air. The whole of the staff were in a perfect ecstasy at their chief's brilliant appearance, and the old Negro servant, who was bearing the roast-turkey from the fire to the board, stopped in mid-career with a most bewildered expression, and gazed in wonderment at his master as if he had been transfigured before him. Meanwhile, the rumour of the change ran like electricity through the neighboring camps, and the soldiers came running by hundreds to the spot, desirous of seeing their beloved Stonewall in his new attire; and the first wearing of a fresh robe by Louis XIV, at whose morning toilet all the world was accustomed to assemble, never created half the sensation at Versailles that was made in the woods of Virginia by the investment of Jackson in this new regulation uniform.

—MAJOR HEROS VON BORCKE

If you want a good time,
Jine the cavalry; jine the cavalry!
—JEB STUART'S SONG

16. JEB STUART "JINES"
THE CAVALRY

A Fair Exchange

*

[DURING THE SECOND BULL RUN campaign, August, 1862, Stuart swept,] like the flight of eagles, around the flank of [John] Pope and came down with a rush upon his rear at Catlett's Station. This bold stroke was directed at the very center of the Federal Army on the night of the 22nd while a heavy rain storm was at its height. General Pope's headquarters wagon was captured and plundered with others of a large train. Stuart burned what wagons he could in the storm, and while the Federal army was looking at the flames of this destruction in their midst, he disappeared with his horsemen in the darkness and returned to his own people, with such plunder as he could carry off.

Stuart came galloping up next morning to where Jackson was

217

sitting on a fence and to everybody's amusement unrolled from behind his saddle and displayed a beautiful blue uniform coat, inside of which was a tag with the name of its owner "John Pope, Major General." Our cavalryman was in one of his jolly humors. He dismounted, and repeating to us what we knew, that a week or two before he was surprised in a house he was visiting by some Federal cavalry, and in his hasty flight left his hat and plume to the enemy, he said he had a proposition to make to General Pope. Taking a piece of paper, he wrote a communication about as follows:

HEADQUARTERS, CAVALRY, *etc.* . . .

Major General John Pope
Commanding, etc.

GENERAL: *You have my hat and plume. I have your best coat. I have the honor to propose a cartel for a fair exchange of the prisoners.*
Very respectfully,
(Signed) J. E. B. STUART
Major Gen. C.S.A.

—MAJOR HENRY KYD DOUGLAS

*

Jeb Stuart's Ball

---

*

IT WAS THE 11th of September before we were disturbed in our enjoyment of these scenes and pleasant associations at Urbana [Maryland]. One bright event occurred of which I must say something as illustrative of the life we led with the dashing and brilliant leader of our cavalry. A rosy light hovers around it still, illuminating the vista of dark and lowering clouds of war overhanging the past. General Stuart was fond of dancing, and in return for the hospitality we had received [from the Dandridges at "The Bower" on the Opequon] he determined to give a ball. On the edge of the village stood a large, vacant building which had been in peace-times used as a female academy, and the staff was soon busied in having a large room prepared there. The walls were decorated with regimental Confederate flags collected from the regiments around, an army band furnished the music, and lovely moonlight lit the beauty and fashion of the country on their way as they assembled in response to our invitation. The officers came prepared for any emergency, fully armed and equipped, picketing their horses in the yard and hanging their sabres against the walls of the dance hall. As the delightful strains of music floated through the vacant old house, and the dancing began, the strange accompaniments of war added zest to the occasion, and our lovely partners declared that it was perfectly charming. But they were destined to have more of the war accompaniment than was intended by the managers, for just as everything had become well started and the enjoyment of the evening was at its height, there came shivering through the still night air the boom of artillery, followed by the angry rattle of musketry. The lily chased the rose from the cheek of beauty, and every pretty foot was rooted to the floor where music had left it. Then came hasty and tender partings from tearful partners, buckling on of sabres, mounting of impatient steeds, and clattering of hoofs as the gay cavaliers dashed off to the front.

The ladies could not be persuaded to believe that they were not taking a last farewell of those who would sleep that night in bloody graves, but being assured that it was probably only a night attack on the outposts to feel our position, and that we might all return to finish the evening, and being influenced possibly by that curiosity which the dear creatures are said to possess, they at last agreed to await our return.

McClellan's advance guard had struck our outposts, but after a sharp skirmish they withdrew for the night and we hastened back "covered with glory," at least in the ladies' eyes. Dancing was resumed and was at its height again, when, alas, it was doomed to a final interruption. Heavy tramping of feet in the passage attracted the attention of the lady who was my partner, standing at the time next the door of the ballroom. Looking out, she clasped her hands and uttered a piercing scream. The scream brought all the dancers trooping out to see what was the matter now, and there on stretchers the wounded were being carried by to the vacant rooms upstairs.

It was no use talking to them of any more dancing that night. There, like a flock of angels in their white dresses assembled around the stretchers, they bent over the wounded men, dressing their wounds and ministering to their wants, with their pretty fingers all stained with blood. One handsome young fellow, as he looked up in their faces with a grateful smile, declared that he would get hit any day to have such surgeons to dress his wounds. All that was left for us now was to escort the "lovely angels" home by the light of the moon and to bid a last, tender farewell to them and to the happy days we had spent among them, for we knew that the morrow would bring again war's stirring scenes around us.

—Lieutenant Colonel W. W. Blackford

*

Boots and Spurs in Bed

*

ONE NIGHT, after the middle of it, General Stuart came riding into our Headquarters [at Bunker Hill, October, 1862], accompanied by his artillery pet, Captain John Pelham, the "boy Major," as he was afterwards called, or "the gallant Pelham," as General Lee named him at Fredericksburg. . . . Everyone had gone to rest. Stuart went directly to General Jackson's tent; Pelham came into mine. The General was asleep and the cavalry chief threw himself down by his side, taking off nothing but his sabre. As the night became chilly, so did he, and unconsciously he began to take possession of blankets and got between the sheets. There he discovered himself in the early morn in the full panoply of war, and he got out of it. After a while, when a lot of us were standing by a blazing log-fire before the General's tent, he came out for his ablutions.

"Good morning, General Jackson," said Stuart, "how are you?"

Old Jack passed his hands through his thin uncombed hair and then in tones as nearly comic as he could muster he said, "General Stuart, I'm always glad to see you here. You might select better hours sometimes, but I'm always glad to have you. But, General"—as he stooped and rubbed himself along the legs—"you must not get into my bed with your boots and spurs on and ride me around like a cavalry horse all night!"

—Major Henry Kyd Douglas

Jeb Stuart to Old Abe

*

[ON DECEMBER 28, 1862, we] crossed the Occoquan River, and proceeded to Burke Station, on the Orange and Alexandria Railroad, capturing the telegraph and operator, and some supplies. Here General Stuart opened communication with old Abe, and elicited several respectful responses; when he concluded by remonstrating with him respecting the inferior qualities of his mules, in the following despatch:

PRESIDENT LINCOLN:
The last draw of wagons I've just made are very good, but the mules are inferior stock, scarcely able to haul off the empty wagons; and if you expect me to give your lines any further attention in this quarter, you should furnish better stock, as I've had to burn several valuable wagons before getting them in my lines.
(Signed) J. E. B. STUART

A. Lincoln.
—U. R. BROOKS

One night an elderly gentleman from Buffalo said: "Up our way, we believe in God and Abraham Lincoln," to which the President replied, shoving him along the line, "My friend, you are more than half right."

—JOHN HAY

17. FATHER ABRAHAM

Stoddard Tells of His Target Practice with the President

✶

[FROM THE BEGINNING OF THE WAR] one universal idea seemed to be that if any given gun, cannon, ship, armor or all-killing or all-saving apparatus chanced to take the eye of the President, it must thereupon speedily be adopted for army use and forced into a grand success by Executive authority. It was in vain that Mr. Lincoln systematically discouraged this notion, and never went further, even with inventions that pleased him most, than to order an examination and trial by proper professional authorities. Every inventor posted straight to the White House with his "working model." Mr. Lincoln had very

222

good mechanical ability, and quick appreciation of what was practical in any proposed improvement. Here, as elsewhere, his strong common sense came into play, to the great discomfiture of many a shallow quack and mechanical enthusiast. It was a common thing for the makers of the new rifles, shells, armor-vests, gun-boats, breech-loading cannon, and the multitudinous nameless contrivances which came into being in the heat and excitement of the times by a species of spontaneous generation, either to invite him to witness a trial or to send him a specimen—the latter being frequently intended as a "presentation copy."

On the grounds near the Potomac, south of the White House, [early in 1862], was a huge pile of old lumber, not to be damaged by balls, and a good many mornings I . . . have been out there with the President, by previous appointment, to try such rifles as were sent in. There was no danger of hitting any one, and the President, who was a very good shot, enjoyed the relaxation very much. One morning early we were having a good time—he with his favorite "Spencer" and I with a villainous kicking nondescript, with a sort of patent back-action breech, that left my shoulder black and blue—when a squad from some regiment which had just been put on guard in that locality pounced on us for what seemed to them a manifest disobedience of all "regulations." I heard the shout of the officer in command and saw them coming, but as the President was busy drawing a very particular bead— for I had been beating him a little—I said nothing until down they came. In response to a decidedly unceremonious hail, the President, in some astonishment, drew back from his stooping posture, and turned upon them the full length six feet four of their beloved "Commander-in-Chief." They stood and looked one moment, and then fairly ran away, leaving his Excellency laughing heartily at their needless discomfiture. He only remarked: "Well, they might have stayed and seen the shooting."

—WILLIAM O. STODDARD

Anecdotes as Antidotes

✳

I · *"This Occasional Vent"*

DURING THE DARK DAYS of '62, the Honorable Mr. [James Mitchell] Ashley, of Ohio, had occasion to call at the White House early one morning, just after news of a disaster. Mr. Lincoln commenced some trifling narration, to which the impulsive congressman was in no mood to listen. He rose to his feet and said: "Mr. President, I did not come here this morning to hear stories; it is too serious a time." Instantly the smile faded from Mr. Lincoln's face. "Ashley," said he, "sit down! I respect you as an earnest, sincere man. You cannot be more anxious than I have been constantly since the beginning of the war; and I say to you now, that were it not for this occasional *vent,* I should die."

—HENRY J. RAYMOND

II · *Advice to a Sad Senator*

AFTER THE BATTLE of Malvern Hill [July 1, 1862] Lincoln was approached by a prominent Senator with a very dejected bearing, and the President said, "Why, Senator, you have a very sad face to-day. It reminds me of a little incident." The distinguished caller took it upon himself to rebuke Lincoln, saying, "Mr. President, this situation is too grave for the telling of anecdotes. I do not care to listen to one." Mr. Lincoln was aroused by this remark and replied, "Senator, do you think that this situation weighs more heavily upon you than it does upon me? If the cause goes against us, not only will the country be lost, but I shall be disgraced to all time. But what would happen if I appeared upon the streets of Washington to-day with such a countenance as yours? The news would be spread throughout the country that the President's very demeanor is an admission that defeat is inevitable. And I say to you, sir, that it would be better for you to infuse some cheerfulness into that countenance of yours as you go about upon the streets of Washington."

—THEODORE BURTON

*

Lincoln Prays with a Dying Confederate Soldier

*

It WAS ON the last Saturday of September, 1862, after the second battle of Bull Run. The forty-odd hospitals in Washington were filled with the sick and wounded soldier boys of both contending armies, the wounded Union and Confederate soldiers lying side by side on adjoining cots.

Early that morning President Lincoln left the White House, determined if possible to visit every hospital in the city before the day was done, in order that he might bring to the sick, the wounded, and the dying the comfort and consolation of his own presence. And so, early in the morning, beginning at Georgetown University Hospital, in the far western end of the city of Washington, he continued all day on his tour of mercy and love. Late in the afternoon, when the sun was fading over the western hills, he knelt beside the cot of a Confederate soldier boy in the Navy-yard Hospital, in the eastern end of the city, and there he prayed for the badly wounded lad, little more than a child, who lay dying.

Then, weary and worn, the tired President stepped into a waiting carriage. There came a nurse calling to him to say that the dying Confederate lad was pleading to see him again. Then, perhaps, that radiance lighted up the face of the weary Lincoln, that radiance which some have described as having seen on his face on some occasions, that light which never was on land or sea. Weary and worn though he was, he returned at once to the dying lad's bedside, and asked, "What can I do for you?"

"I am so lonely and friendless, Mr. Lincoln," whispered the lad, "and I am hoping that you can tell me what my mother would want me to say and do now."

225

"Yes, my boy," said Lincoln, as he again knelt beside the dying lad, "I know exactly what your mother would want you to say and do. And I am glad that you sent for me to come back to you. Now, as I kneel here, please repeat the words after me."

Then, while the lad, facing eternity with recollections of a good mother, rested his head upon the arm of Abraham Lincoln, he repeated after his only present friend the words that his mother, then praying at home for her boy, had taught him to say at her knees before bedtime:

Now I lay me down to sleep;
I pray the Lord my soul to keep.
If I should die before I wake,
I pray the Lord my soul to take.
And this I ask for Jesus' sake.

—ALBERT H. GRIFFITH

*

McClellan's Bodyguard

*

HONORABLE O. M. HATCH, a former Secretary of State of Illinois and an old friend of Lincoln's . . . relates that a short time before McClellan's removal from command [November 5, 1862] he went with President Lincoln to visit the army, still near Antietam. They reached Antietam late in the afternoon of a very hot day, and were assigned a special tent for their occupancy during the night.

"Early next morning," says Mr. Hatch, "I was awakened by Mr. Lincoln. It was very early—daylight was just lighting the east—the soldiers were all asleep in their tents. Scarce a sound could be heard except the notes of early birds, and the farm-yard voices from distant farms. Lincoln said to me, 'Come, Hatch, I want you to take a walk with me.' His tone was serious and impressive. I arose without a word, and as soon as we were dressed we left the tent together.

"He led me about the camp, and then we walked upon the sur-

226

rounding hills overlooking the great city of white tents and sleeping soldiers. Very little was spoken between us, beyond a few words as to the pleasantness of the morning or similar casual observations. Lincoln seemed to be peculiarily serious, and his quiet, abstract way affected me also. It did not seem a time to speak. We walked slowly and quietly, meeting here and there a guard, our thoughts leading us to reflect on that wonderful situation. A nation in peril—the whole world looking at America—a million men in arms—the whole machinery of war engaged throughout the country, while I stood by that kind-hearted, simple-minded man who might be regarded as the Director-General, looking at the beautiful sunrise and the magnificent scene before us. Nothing was to be said, nothing needed to be said.

"Finally, reaching a commanding point where almost that entire camp could be seen—the men were just beginning their morning duties, and evidences of life and activity were becoming apparent—we involuntarily stopped. The President, waving his hand towards the scene before us, and leaning towards me, said in almost whispering voice: 'Hatch—Hatch, what is all this?'

" 'Why, Mr. Lincoln,' said I, 'this is the Army of the Potomac.'

"He hesitated a moment, and then, straightening up, said in a louder tone: 'No, Hatch, no. This is *General McClellan's bodyguard.*'

"Nothing more was said. We walked to our tent, and the subject was not alluded to again."

—O. M. HATCH

*

Lincoln Visits the Contraband Camp

*

WHEN THE WAR broke out [Aunt Mary Dines, who had escaped from her master in Charles County, Maryland] went to live in an old contraband camp off 7th Street, near where Howard University now stands. The contrabands often lived in the old wooden barracks constructed for the soldiers. When the soldiers would change from these places, or the army would move away, the colored people would move in.

Contraband camps were all around the city limits, but efforts were made to gather them into schools by the American Tract Society of New York as early as March, 1862. Duff Green's Row on Capitol Hill was then crowded with this class of people, as contraband material of war. They were taught with printed cards, having on them verses of Scripture in large letters, and by using the *word method* which was very successful, they were able, to their great delight, to read whole verses in a very short time. Mary followed this system and became a teacher for older folks. Because of her training and her wonderful voice and knowledge of hymns, she became the leading soprano singer of the camp, and also the principal letter writer for the ignorant old folks.

These camps were crowded with visitors nearly every evening and especially on Sundays. Many white and colored folks came to teach reading, the Bible, sewing, and various branches of knowledge so necessary for them to know in order to adjust themselves to the new methods of living. But most came to listen to these people sing and pray and thank God for their deliverance from bondage. Mrs. Lincoln contributed money and sent gifts to the older people.

Not only citizens of Washington but members of the Cabinet and their families often came to help, and according to Aunt Mary Dines, President Lincoln stopped many times to visit and talk to them on his way to the Soldiers' Home. He was very fond of the hymns of the slaves and loved to hear them and even knew most of them by heart. Aunt Mary told me many stories, but the following was her prized one.

One Saturday morning, the sergeant in charge of the contrabands sounded the bugle for all to assemble. He told them that President Lincoln was coming out with some friends to visit them and wanted to hear them sing, and that everything should be in apple-pie order and gave them time to practice their pieces. Aunt Mary said the thought of singing before the President nearly killed her. All of the people dressed in their best clothes, some of which were gathered from the battlefield. Some men and boys had on soldiers' cast-off blue uniforms and some had on old rebel uniforms they had picked up after the rebels had been driven away by the Yankees.

The old folks always sat together on one side of the meeting place. When all was ready, a picture man drove out with his buggy and little tent and took pictures of everybody. Presently Aunt Mary saw soldiers coming on horseback, the bugle sounded "Halt" and President Lincoln

228

and his wife, and some more white folks, got out of their carriages, and while some sat on a little platform on the right, which the colored men had just finished decorating with flags, President Lincoln came over where the old folks were sitting and stood and watched everybody. She said Uncle Ben was a "spirit preacher," because he couldn't read a line but he just preached the gospel as God had taught him to do. He could certainly preach and pray and make everybody near him wake up when he began to moan and groan.

Uncle Ben, the oldest slave in the camp, was called on to open the meeting with prayer, and he called upon every saint in the Bible that he had heard about to bless President Lincoln and his good lady.

After he was through, all stood up and sang "My Country, 'Tis of Thee" and President Lincoln took off his hat and sang too. Aunt Mary was standing near him and heard him; she said he had a good voice. Then the commander of the camp called her aside and asked her what pieces she was going to have the people sing and to begin right away, for the President didn't intend to stay long.

Aunt Mary said she never forgot how her knees shook, as she stumbled in front of the people and opened the singing with "Nobody Knows What Trouble I See, but Jesus," always keeping one eye on the President. After the first verse, which she sang all by herself, all the colored people joined in the chorus and really sang as they never did before. To her great surprise, as she came out to call the next song, "Every Time I Feel the Spirit," she saw President Lincoln wiping the tears off his face with his bare hands. They sang for nearly an hour, and while the colored folks were singing, "I Thank God that I'm Free at Last," many of the real old folks forgot about the President being present and began to shout and yell, but he didn't laugh at them, but stood like a stone and bowed his head. She said she really believed that the Holy Ghost was working on him.

The last piece was "John Brown's Body." By this time President Lincoln must have been warmed up himself for he joined in the chorus and sang as loud as anyone there. She said he certainly had a sweet voice, and it sounded so sad, when he tried to follow her with the first tune. He really choked up once or twice.

President Lincoln returned to the camp with only a couple of orderlies on a damp, dreary evening and sent for her and said, "Well, Mary, what can the people sing for me today? I've been thinking about you all since I left here and am not feeling so well. I just want them to sing some more good old hymns for me again. Tell Uncle Ben to pray a good old-fashioned prayer." Well, if Uncle Ben prayed the first time, he certainly did more this time, for then he was scared to death. Now he knew President Lincoln had been emotionally moved and wanted the help of God to carry on. Aunt Mary said she never heard such a prayer before. Uncle Ben just talked with God—and cried, as he begged Him to send down His loving kindness and blessings on the colored people's friend. He wanted Him to give strength to carry the troubles of this world—and to throw around him the mantle of protection when he had finished working for the poor old folks below. He wanted the Golden Chariot, with its pale white horses, to swing low, and with companies of angels carry him to his Father above. Uncle Ben was always a praying man, but this day God must have been helping him out.

They all sang "Swing Low, Sweet Chariot," "Didn't My God Deliver Daniel?" "Go Down, Moses," "I Ain't Got Weary Yet," "I've Been in the Storm So Long," "Steal Away," and they closed with "Praise God from Whom All Blessings Flow." Then Uncle Ben gave the Benediction which was as long as his sermons. Aunt Mary said that President Lincoln actually joined in singing every piece and he was so tender-hearted that he filled up when he went over to bid the real old folks good-by.

Aunt Mary said when she gave out some words of a piece for the old folks to repeat after her, and the old people bowed in prayer, Lincoln did just like everybody else. She said he was no President when he came to camp. He just stood and sang and prayed just like all the rest of the people.

—JOHN E. WASHINGTON

January

S	M	T	W	T	F	S
.	.	.	.	1	2	3
4	5	6	7	8	9	10
11	12	13	14	15	16	17
18	19	20	21	22	23	24
25	26	27	28	29	30	31

February

S	M	T	W	T	F	S
1	2	3	4	5	6	7
8	9	10	11	12	13	14
15	16	17	18	19	20	21
22	23	24	25	26	27	28

March

S	M	T	W	T	F	S
1	2	3	4	5	6	7
8	9	10	11	12	13	14
15	16	17	18	19	20	21
22	23	24	25	26	27	28
29	30	31	.	.	.	.

THREE

In EIGHTEEN HUNDRED AND SIXTY-THREE
Abe Lincoln set the Negroes free.
We'll all drink stone blind;
Johnny, come fill up the bowl.

April

S	M	T	W	T	F	S
.	.	.	.	1	2	3	4
5	6	7	8	9	10	11
12	13	14	15	16	17	18
19	20	21	22	23	24	25
26	27	28	29	30	.	.
.	.	.	.	.	.	.

May

S	M	T	W	T	F	S
.	.	.	.	.	1	2
3	4	5	6	7	8	9
10	11	12	13	14	15	16
17	18	19	20	21	22	23
24	25	26	27	28	29	30
31						

June

S	M	T	W	T	F	S
.	.	1	2	3	4	5	6
7	8	9	10	11	12	13
14	15	16	17	18	19	20
21	22	23	24	25	26	27
28	29	30	.	.	.	.

July

S	M	T	W	T	F	S
.	.	.	.	1	2	3	4
5	6	7	8	9	10	11
12	13	14	15	16	17	18
19	20	21	22	23	24	25
26	27	28	29	30	31	.
.	.	.	.	.	.	.

August

S	M	T	W	T	F	S
.	.	.	.	.	.	1
2	3	4	5	6	7	8
9	10	11	12	13	14	15
16	17	18	19	20	21	22
23	24	25	26	27	28	29
30	31					

September

S	M	T	W	T	F	S
.	.	1	2	3	4	5
6	7	8	9	10	11	12
13	14	15	16	17	18	19
20	21	22	23	24	25	26
27	28	29	30	.	.	.

October

S	M	T	W	T	F	S
.	.	.	.	1	2	3
4	5	6	7	8	9	10
11	12	13	14	15	16	17
18	19	20	21	22	23	24
25	26	27	28	29	30	31

November

S	M	T	W	T	F	S
1	2	3	4	5	6	7
8	9	10	11	12	13	14
15	16	17	18	19	20	21
22	23	24	25	26	27	28
29	30	.	.	.	.	.

December

S	M	T	W	T	F	S
.	.	1	2	3	4	5
6	7	8	9	10	11	12
13	14	15	16	17	18	19
20	21	22	23	24	25	26
27	28	29	30	31	.	.

I's free, I's free, I's free at las'!
Thank God A'mighty, I's free at las'!

Once was a moaner, jus' like you;
Thank God A'mighty, I's free at las'!

I fasted an' I prayed tell I came thew;
Thank God A'mighty, I's free at las'!
—A FREEDOM SONG

18. "FREE AT LAST"

How Lincoln Signed
the Emancipation Proclamation

✱

THE ROLL CONTAINING the Emancipation Proclamation was taken to Mr. Lincoln at noon on the first day of January, 1863, by Secretary Seward and his son Frederick. As it lay unrolled before him, Mr. Lincoln took a pen, dipped it in ink, moved his hand to the place for the signature, held it a moment, and then removed his hand and dropped the pen. After a little hesitation he again took up the pen and went through the same movement as before. Mr. Lincoln then turned to Mr. Seward, and said:—

"I have been shaking hands since nine o'clock this morning, and my right arm is almost paralyzed. If my name ever goes into history it will be for this act, and my whole soul is in it. If my hand trembles when I sign the Proclamation, all who examine the document hereafter will say, 'He hesitated.' "

He then turned to the table, took up the pen again, and slowly, firmly wrote that "Abraham Lincoln" with which the whole world is now familiar. He looked up, smiled, and said: "That will do."

—*Rochester* (New York) *Express*

*

When the Angels Struck the Banjo Strings

---

*

THE NIGHT WAS DARK, the rain descended in torrents from the black and overhanging clouds, and the thunder, accompanied with vivid flashes of lightning, resounded fearfully, as I entered a Negro cabin in South Carolina. The room was filled with blacks, a group of whom surrounded a rough board table, and at it sat an old man holding in his hand a watch, at which all were intently gazing. A stout Negro boy held a torch which lighted up the cabin, and near him stood a Yankee soldier, in the Union blue, reading the President's Proclamation of Freedom.

As it neared the hour of twelve, a dead silence prevailed, and the holder of the time-piece said, "By de time I counts ten, it will be midnight an' de lan' will be free. One, two, three, four, five, six, seven, eight, nine,—" Just then a loud strain of music came from the banjo, hanging upon the wall, and at its sound the whole company, as if by previous arrangement, threw themselves upon their knees, and the old man exclaimed, "O God, de watch was a minit' too slow, but dy promises an' dy mercy is allers in time; dou did promise dat one of dy angels should come an' give us de sign, an' shore 'nuff de sign did come. We's grateful, oh, we's grateful, O Lord, send dy angel once moe to give dat sweet sound."

234

At this point another strain from the banjo was heard, and a sharp flash of lightning was followed by a clap of thunder, such as is only heard in the tropics. The Negroes simultaneously rose to their feet and began singing; finishing only one verse, they all fell on their knees, and Uncle Ben, the old white-haired man, again led in prayer, and such a prayer as but few outside of this injured race could have given. Rising to their feet, the leader commenced singing:—

Oh! breth-er-en, my way, my way's cloudy, my way,
  Go send dem angels down.
Oh! breth-er-en, my way, my way's cloudy, my way,
  Go send dem angels down.

There's fire in de east an' fire in de west,
  Send dem angels down.
An' fire among de Methodist,
  O, send dem angels down.

Ole Sa-tan's mad, an' I am glad,
  Send dem angels down.
He missed the soul he thought he had,
  O, send dem angels down.

I'll tell you now as I tole afore,
  Send dem angels down.
To de promised lan' I'm bound to go,
  O, send dem angels down.

Dis is de year of Jubilee,
  Send dem angels down.
De Lord has come to set us free,
  O, send dem angels down.

One more short prayer from Uncle Ben, and they arose, clasped each other around the neck, kissed, and commenced shouting, "Glory, to God, we's free."

Another sweet strain from the musical instrument was followed by breathless silence, and then Uncle Ben said, "De angels of de Lord is wid us still, an' dey is watching ober us, fer ole Sandy tole us moe dan a mont ago dat dey would."

I was satisfied when the first musical strain came, that it was merely a vibration of the strings, caused by the rushing wind through the aperture between the logs behind the banjo. Fearing that the blacks would ascribe the music to some mysterious Providence, I plainly told them of the cause.

"Oh, no ser," said Uncle Ben, quickly, his eyes brightening as he spoke, "dat come fum de angels. We been specken it all de time. We know the angels struck de strings of de banjo."

The news of the music from the instrument without the touch of human hands soon spread through the entire neighborhood, and in a short time the cabin was jammed with visitors, who at once turned their attention to the banjo upon the wall.

All sorts of stories were soon introduced to prove that angelic visits were common, especially to those who were fortunate enough to carry "de witness."

"De speret of de Lord come to me lass night in my sleep an' tole me dat I were gwine to be free, an' sed dat de Lord would sen' one of His angels down to give me de warnin'. An' when de banjo sounded, I knowed dat my bressed Marster were a' keepin' His word," said Uncle Ben.

An elderly woman amongst the visitors drew a long breath, and declared that she had been lifted out of her bed three times, on the previous night; "I knowed," she continued, "dat de angelic hos' was hoverin' round about us."

"I dropped a fork to-day," said another, "an' it stuck up in de floo', right afore my face, an' dat is allers good luck fer me."

"De mule kicked at me three times dis mornin' an' he never did dat afore in his life," said another, "an' I knowed good luck would come fum dat."

"A rabbit run across my path twice as I come fum de branch lass Saturday, an' I felt shor' dat somethin' mighty was gwine to happen," remarked Uncle Ben's wife.

"I had a sign that showed me plainly that all of you would be free," said the Yankee soldier, who had been silent since reading the proclamation. All eyes were instantly turned to the white man from the North, and half a dozen voices cried out simultaneously, "O Mr. Solger, what was it? what was it? what was it?"

"Well," said the man in blue, "I saw something on a large white sheet—"

"Was it a ghos'?" cried Uncle Ben, before the sentence was finished by the soldier. Uncle Ben's question about a ghost started quite a number to their feet, and many trembled as they looked each other in the face, and upon the soldier, who appeared to feel the importance of his position.

Ned, the boy who was holding the torch, began to tell a ghost story, but he was at once stopped by Uncle Ben, who said, "Shet your mouf, don't you see de gentmun ain't told us what he see in de 'white sheet?' "

"Well," commenced the soldier, again, "I saw on a large sheet of paper, a printed Proclamation from President Lincoln, like the one I've just read, and that satisfied me that you'd all be free to-day."

Every one was disappointed at this, for all were prepared for a ghost story, from the first remark about the "white sheet" of paper. Uncle Ben smiled, looked a little wise, and said, "I speck dat's a Yankee trick you's given us, Mr. Solger."

—William Wells Brown

*

"Linkum Comin' wid His Chariot"

---

*

FRIDAY [June 19, 1863] we marched five miles to near Guilford Station, went into bivouac, and sent out a picket-line towards Leesburg.

As we neared the end of our march to Guilford we passed an old plantation, shabby and serene, the house and ground undisturbed except by time. A tottery board fence fronted the road, and perched on the fence were darkies of all shades and sizes. The crazy contortions of their bodies and the grimaces of astonishment that spread over their faces as they saw regiment after regiment massed in a field and batteries parked beyond, would have driven a circus crowd wild. I drew rein to watch them.

One old Sambo bared his woolly poll, stretched forth a long and bony hand as if to cover us with a blessing, and sang out in a cracked voice: "Praise de Lawd fo' de glory ob dis yer 'casion! Heabenly Massa bress de Linkum sojers, an' show dese yer eyes de golden chariot b'fo' Ah die!"

Old hats, jackets, and shoes went high in air, and shouts of

"Glory! Hallelujah!" burst from along the fence. An excited patriarch got down and hobbled to the roadside and right up to the marching men, exclaiming: "Great King! How many mo' you-uns comin'? 'Spec's fo'ty milyuns toted by hyer since mo'nin'."

"Well, uncle," said one of our boys, "you can stand here three weeks and see the Yanks go by."

"B'fo' God, Ah reckon so! Massa Linkum mighty sojer, Ah reckon. He gwine by hyer, too?"

"Oh yes, uncle, he's at the rear of our corps, miles back; he'll be along in his chariot tomorrow."

Limping back to the fence, now alive with squirming legs and shining faces, the patriarch yelled:

"Chilluns, cotch off yer hats an' jine in de chorus!"

And swaying from side to side in grotesque attitudes, the old man leading, they sang in their peculiar way:

> *Don' yer see 'em comin', comin', comin'—*
> *Milyuns from de oder sho'?*
> *Glory! Glory! Hallelujah!*
> *Bress de Lawd fo' ebermo'!*
>
> *Don' yer see 'em goin', goin', goin'—*
> *Pas' ol' massa's mansion do'?*
> *Glory! Glory! Hallelujah!*
> *Bress de Lawd fo' ebermo'!*
>
> *Jordan's stream is runnin', runnin', runnin'—*
> *Milyuns sojers passin' o';*
> *Linkum comin' wid his chariot.*
> *Bress de Lawd fo' ebermo'!*
>
> *Don' yer hear him comin', [comin',] comin'?*
> *Yes, Ah do!*
> *Wid his robe an' mighty army?*
> *Yes, Ah do!*
> *Want ter march wid him to glory?*
> *Yes, Ah do!*

Long into the night I seemed to hear their chorus:

> *Glory! Glory! Hallelujah!*
> *Bress de Lawd fo' ebermo'!*

—MAJOR ABNER R. SMALL

238

"Massa Linkum"

*

IN 1863, Colonel McKaye, of New York, with Robert Dale Owen and one or two other gentlemen, were associated as a committee to investigate the condition of the freedmen on the coast of North Carolina. Upon their return from Hilton Head they reported to the President; and in the course of the interview Colonel McKaye related the following incident.

He had been speaking of the ideas of power entertained by these people. He said they had an idea of God, as the Almighty, and they had realized in their former condition the power of their masters. Up to the time of the arrival among them of the Union forces, they had no knowledge of any other power. Their masters fled upon the approach of our soldiers, and this gave the slaves a conception of a power greater than that exercised by them. This power they called "Massa Linkum."

Colonel McKaye said that their place of worship was a large building which they called "the praise house"; and the leader of the meeting, a venerable black man, was known as "the praise man." On a certain day, when there was quite a large gathering of the people, considerable confusion was created by different persons attempting to tell who and what "Massa Linkum" was. In the midst of the excitement the white-headed leader commanded silence. "Brederin," said he, "you don't know nosen' what you'se talkin' 'bout. Now, you just listen to me. Massa Linkum, he eberywhar. He know eberyting." Then, solemnly looking up, he added, *"He walk de earf like de Lord!"*

—F. B. CARPENTER

A Dilemma

*

[AT VICKSBURG in the summer of 1863] Sister Seraphena, one of the heroic Catholic nuns who labored among the sick and wounded soldiers [was] returning from an errand of mercy . . . guided by a small Negro boy. Sister Seraphena paused on a narrow footpath to talk with a convalescent corporal. Suddenly a shell of the smaller kind landed in the pathway almost at their feet, its fuse still burning. For a moment the corporal stood still, a statue of horrified surprise; then, leaping backward, he rolled down an embankment to ignominious safety.

Hardly had the man disappeared than the Negro boy stooped, seized the smoldering shell and threw it as far as he could in the opposite direction. He acted just in time as the deadly missile exploded in mid-air harmlessly.

"Why didn't you do that at once?" asked the trembling sister. "The moment you hesitated might have cost all of us our lives."

"Laws! Miss Sister Seraphena," replied the small black hero, "I's got too much respect fur white folks fur to do a thing like that while dar was a white gemman standin' dar."

—ROBERT TALLEY

*

The Town Clock of Vicksburg

*

THE COURT-HOUSE of Vicksburg stood on high ground in the centre of the city. It was surmounted by a tall tower, and near the top of the tower was placed a large white-faced clock, the four white faces

240

looking toward the four points of the compass. The black figures indicating the hour of the day and the hands could be seen miles away with the aid of field-glasses.

During the long weary months of the siege of Vicksburg when the heavy guns of the Union Army poured in hot shot and shell night and day, many a skilled gunner trained his gun at one of the white faces of that clock. Shot and shell came from every quarter, but the clock kept time for both armies unscathed. The Confederate flag-staff was cut to pieces above it; the tower above and below was riddled with flying missiles, but the clock remained untouched, and ticked off moment by moment, hour by hour the exact time, until the last gun was fired, and the last wail of agony was hushed in the solemn ceremonies of the historic surrender [July 4, 1863]. Even then the old clock went on unmoved, and told time with resonant tongue as though nothing had happened.

It was a matter of surprise to artillery men that they had not been able to send a ball through one or the other of the four great white faces of the clock at Vicksburg. After the surrender an old colored Methodist preacher explained it to the satisfaction of many. He said, speaking of the fall of their great brick church:

"You see, we ust to go dar to pray, an' we allers prayed for liberty an' dat de Yanks would git de victory, an' so to stop de prayin' dey jus' tore down de church."

"And that stopped your praying?"

"Oh, no, missus, dat couldn't stop our prayin'. We jus' 'greed to pray whenever de clock struck twelve, night or day. An' oh, missus, how we did pray!"

"The Union men tried very hard to hit that clock but somehow they didn't happen to strike it."

The old man's face was radiant. The joy of his heart was shining through the black skin, as he swayed and slapped his hands. "Oh, honey, dar's no happen about dat. De good Lor' He jus' put His han' over it, an' kep' it goin' an' goin', for us poor color folks to pray by!"

—*True Stories of the War for the Union*

241

The President last night had a dream. He was in a party of plain people and as it became known who he was they began to comment on his appearance. One of them said, "He is a very common-looking man." The President replied, "Common-looking people are the best in the world: that is the reason the Lord makes so many of them."

—JOHN HAY

19. MAN OF THE PEOPLE

The Sweat-Box

*

ON ONE OF LINCOLN'S excursions on the steamer *Hartford,* in 1863, his attention was directed to a narrow door, bound with iron.

"What is this?" he asked.

"Oh, that is the 'sweat-box,'" was the reply. "It is used for refractory and insubordinate seamen. A man in there is subjected to steam heat, and has very little ventilation. It generally brings him to terms very quickly."

As thousands of American seamen were subjected to this treatment every year, he decided to try it and see what it really was. Taking

242

off his hat, he entered the inclosure, which he found to be little more than three feet in length or width. He gave orders that at a signal from himself the door should be immediately opened. It was then closed, and the steam turned on.

He had been inside hardly three minutes before the signal was given. President Lincoln had experienced enough of what was then regarded as necessary punishment for American seamen. There was very little ventilation, and the short exposure to the hot and humid air had almost suffocated him.

Turning to Secretary Welles, the President ordered that no such inclosure as the sweat-box should ever after be allowed on any vessel flying the American flag.

It was not an hour after this order had been given before every sailor on every ship in Hampton Roads had heard of it. The effect was most remarkable on the older sailors, many of whom had themselves experienced the punishment of the sweat-box.

As soon as Great Britain, France, Germany and other European countries heard that the sweat-box had been abolished in America as inhuman, . . . one and all of these nations fell into line, and after that day the sweat-box was not to be found on any vessel flying the flag of a civilized nation through the world.

—Emanuel Hertz Scrapbooks

*

The Grant Whiskey Story

*

T. LYLE DICKEY, [later] a judge of the Illinois Supreme Court . . . , at the time of Grant's famous Vicksburg campaign [May-July, 1863], was on the General's staff as chief of cavalry. Judge (then Colonel) Dickey had been sent to Washington with private despatches for the President and the Secretary of War. Lincoln and Dickey had been intimate friends for years, and during the latter's visit to the former on that occasion, Dickey remarked, "I hear that some one has been trying to poison you against Grant by reporting that he gets drunk.

I wish to assure you, Mr. President, that there is not a scintilla of truth in the report."

"Oh, Colonel," replied the President, "we get all sorts of reports here, but I'll say this to you: that if those accusing General Grant of getting drunk will tell me *where he gets his whiskey,* I will get a lot of it and send it around to some of the other generals, who are badly in need of something of the kind."

—FRANCIS FISHER BROWNE

*

Mr. Lincoln's Stick

---

*

[ONE NIGHT in the early summer of 1863, just after the failure of the naval attack on Fort Sumter], as we walked back to the White House through the grounds between the War Department buildings and the house, I fancied that I saw in the misty moonlight a man dodging behind one of the trees. My heart for a moment stood still, but, as we passed in safety, I came to the conclusion that the dodging figure was a creature of the imagination. Nevertheless, as I parted from the President at the door of the White House, I could not help saying that I thought his going to and fro in the darkness of the night, as it was usually his custom, often alone and unattended, was dangerous recklessness. That night, in deference to his wife's anxious appeal, he had provided himself with a thick oaken stick. He laughed as he showed me this slight weapon, and said, but with some seriousness: "I long ago made up my mind that if anybody wants to kill me, he will do it. If I wore a shirt of mail, and kept myself surrounded by a body-guard, it would be all the same. There are a thousand ways of getting at a man if it is desired that he should be killed. Besides, in this case, it seems to me the man who would come after me would be just as objectionable to my enemies—if I have any."

The oaken stick to which I have just referred was fashioned from a bit of timber from one of the men-of-war sunk in the fight at Hampton Roads; the ferule was an iron bolt from the rebel ram *Merrimac,* and another bolt from the *Monitor* furnished the head of the cane. After Mr. Lincoln's death, Mrs. Lincoln gave me the stick, which had been presented to the President by an officer of the navy.

—NOAH BROOKS

*

News of Burnside

---

*

WHEN COLONEL HAY was private secretary at the White House he had instructions not to wake the President unless something of extreme importance was to be communicated. One night a dispatch came from General [Ambrose E.] Burnside from Knoxville, Tennessee, to the effect that defeat and surrender were practically upon him, and deeming this sufficiently urgent, Mr. Hay went upstairs and roused Mr. Lincoln with the information.

After yawning a little, Lincoln said, "I am glad of it; I am glad to hear it."

"But, Mr. President, that does not seem an item of news to be glad of."

"Well," said Lincoln, "it reminds me of a poor woman I used to know out in Menard County." (His illustrations usually came from Menard or Sangamon or Logan or other counties in that vicinity.) "She had a large brood of children. They wandered through the woods, and it was impossible for her to clothe them properly—she could hardly feed them. The woman always used to say that it did her heart good whenever any of those young ones came around squalling, because then she knew he was still alive.

—THEODORE BURTON

245

*

Lincoln and the "Cold-Water" Men and Women

*

September 29, 1863

TODAY came to the Executive Mansion an assembly of cold-water men & cold-water women to make a temperance speech at the Tycoon & receive a response. They filed into the East Room looking blue & thin in the keen autumnal air; Cooper, my coachman, who was about half tight, gazing at them with an air of complacent contempt and mild wonder. Three blue-skinned damsels did Love, Purity, & Fidelity in Red, White & Blue gowns. A few invalid soldiers stumped along in the dismal procession. They made a long speech at the Tycoon in which they called Intemperance the cause of our defeats. He could not see it, as the rebels drink more & worse whisky than we do. They filed off drearily to a collation of cold water & green apples, & then home to mulligrubs.

—JOHN HAY

*

Sister Emilie Visits the White House

*

November, 1863

SEEING SOME CARDS being handed to Sister Mary and hearing the callers were to be received in the room where we were sitting, I excused myself and slipped out. In a few minutes Sister Mary sent for me to come and see some friend who wished especially to see me that he might inquire about some mutual friend in the South. I went most reluctantly. It is painful to see friends and I do not feel like meeting strangers. I cannot bear their inquiring look at my deep crêpe. It was General [Daniel E.] Sickles again, calling with Senator Harris. General Sickles said, "I told Senator Harris that you were at the White House, just from the South, and could probably give him some news of his old friend, General John C. Breckinridge." I told Senator Harris that as I had not seen General Breckinridge for some time I could give him no news of the General's health. He then asked me several pointed questions about the South and as politely as I could I gave him non-committal answers.

Senator Harris said to me in a voice of triumph, "Well, we have whipped the rebels at Chattanooga and I hear, madam, that the scoundrels ran like scared rabbits."

"It was the example, Senator Harris, that you set them at Bull Run . . . ," I answered with a choking throat.

I was very nervous and I could see that Sister Mary was annoyed. She tactfully tried to change the subject, whereupon Senator Harris turned to her abruptly and with an unsmiling face asked sternly: "Why isn't Robert in the Army? He is old enough and strong enough to serve his country. He should have gone to the front some time ago."

Sister Mary's face turned white as death and I saw that she was making a desperate effort at self-control. She bit her lip, but answered quietly, "Robert is making his preparations now to enter the Army, Senator Harris; he is not a shirker as you seem to imply for he has been anxious to go for a long time. If fault there be, it is mine, I have insisted that he should stay in college a little longer as I think an educated man can serve his country with more intelligent purpose than an ignoramus."

General Harris rose and said harshly and pointedly to Sister, "I have only one son and he is fighting for his country." Turning to me and making a low bow, "And, madam, if I had twenty sons they should all be fighting the rebels."

"And if I had twenty sons, General Harris," I replied, "they should all be opposing yours."

I forgot where I was, I forgot that I was a guest of the President and Mrs. Lincoln at the White House. I was cold and trembling. I stumbled out of the room somehow, for I was blinded by tears and my heart was beating to suffocation. Before I reached the privacy of my room, where unobserved I could give way to my grief, Sister Mary overtook me and put her arms around me. I felt somehow comforted to weep on her shoulder—her own tears were falling but she said no word of the occurrence and I understood that she was powerless to protect a guest in the White House from cruel rudeness.

Cousin John Stuart told me that after I left the room and General Sickles and Senator Harris, on their way out, had reached the portico of the White House, that General Sickles had painfully stumped up the stairs again and declared he must see the President, who had not been feeling well and was in his own room lying down. When the President came in, General Sickles solemnly related the conversation between General Harris and myself, the President's eyes twinkled and he looked at Cousin John and chuckled, "The child has a tongue like the rest of the Todds."

This seemed to anger General Sickles and he said in a loud, dictatorial voice, slapping the table with his hand, "You should not have that rebel in your house."

Mr. Lincoln instantly drew himself up and said in a quiet, dignified voice, "Excuse me, General Sickles, my wife and I are in the habit of choosing our own guests. We do not need from our friends either advice or assistance in the matter. Besides," he added, "the little 'rebel' came because I ordered her to come, it was not of her own volition."

This is the only time a word of the war has been spoken—in my presence or to me—since I have been in the White House; it is most considerate. Although Brother Lincoln and Sister Mary have urged me to stay longer, I feel that my being here is more or less an embarrassment to all of us and I am longing for Kentucky and Mother. They have both (Mary and Mr. Lincoln) invited me to make them a long visit next summer at the Soldiers' Home. It is kind of them—but it will not be possible.

I had my little daughter with me. Tad, who was five or six years older, was playing host and entertaining her with photographs, both seated on the rug before the fire. He showed her a photograph of himself with great pride and then picking up one of his father, said, "This is the President." My little daughter looked at it, shook her head and said very emphatically, "No, that is not the President; Mr. Davis is President." Tad, to make his statement more emphatic, shouted, "Hurrah for Abe Lincoln." My little daughter defiantly replied, "Hurrah for Jeff Davis." Mr. Lincoln listened with an amused smile to the heated argument and when finally appealed to by Tad, he said, "Well,

Tad, you know who is your President, and I am your little cousin's Uncle Lincoln." So, taking one on each knee, he pacified the tense and glaring little belligerents.

I was at the White House nearly a week. As Mr. Lincoln handed me the safeguard, the paper protecting me from molestation except as to slaves, he looked at me earnestly and said gravely, "Little Sister, I never knew you to do a mean thing in your life. I know you will not embarrass me in any way on your return to Kentucky." Nothing was said to me then or afterwards about taking the oath of allegiance. Brother Lincoln knew, that, while under the circumstances this for me would be impossible, he could trust my honor to do nothing to make him regret his loving kindness and consideration for me. They were, both Sister Mary and Mr. Lincoln, careful not to allude to politics or to the South, or in any way to hurt me or make it difficult for me.

Mr. Lincoln in the intimate talks we had was very much affected over the misfortunes of our family; and of my husband he said, "You know, Little Sister, I tried to have Ben come with me. I hope you do not feel any bitterness or that I am in any way to blame for all this sorrow." I answered it was "the fortune of war" and that while my husband loved him and had been deeply grateful to him for his generous offer to make him an officer in the Federal Army, he had to follow his conscience and that for weal or woe he felt he must side with his own people. Mr. Lincoln put his arms around me and we both wept.

—Mrs. Ben Hardin Helm

Our women forever, God bless them, huzza!
With their smiles and favors, they aid us in the war;
In the tent and on the battle-field the boys remember them,
And cheer for the daughters of freedom.
—"THE BATTLE-CRY OF FREEDOM"

20. THE WOMEN AT HOME

The New Orleans "Pocket Handkerchief War"

*

[IN NEW ORLEANS] there was a great stir and intense excitement at one time during General Bank's administration. [On February 20, 1863,] a number of "Rebels" were to leave for the "Confederacy." Their friends, amounting to some 20,000 persons, women and children principally, wended their way down to the levee to see them off, and to take their last farewell.

Such a quantity of women frightened the officials; they were exasperated at their waving of handkerchiefs; their loud calling to their friends, and their going onto vessels in the vicinity!

Orders were given to "stand back," but no heed was given; the

250

bayonets were pointed at the ladies, but they were not to be scared. A lady ran across to get a nearer view—an officer seized her by the arm! but she escaped, leaving a scarf in his possession. At last the military received orders to do its duty.

A vessel lying beside the steamer, having a number of ladies on board, was started off! It was impossible to return. The ladies were on board all night and the greater part of the next day without food or extra clothing!

The affair was called the "Pocket Handkerchief War," and has been put in verse [by "Eugenie"].

THE GREATEST VICTORY OF THE WAR!

LA BATAILLE DES MOUCHOIRS

Fought Friday, February Twentieth, 1863.

* * * * *

Charge! *rang the cry, and on we dashed*
  Upon our female foes,
As seas in stormy fury lashed,
  Whene'er the tempest blows.

Like chaff their parasols went down,
  As our gallants rushed;
And many a bonnet, robe, and gown
  Was torn to shreds or crushed.

Though well we plied the bayonet,
  Still some our efforts braved.
Defiant both of blow and threat,
  Their handkerchiefs still waved.

Thick grew the fight, loud rolled the din,
  When charge! *rang out again,*
And then the cannon thundered in,
  And scoured o'er the plain.

Down, neath th' unpitying iron heels
  Of horses children sank,
While through the crowd the cannon wheels
  Mowed roads on either flank,

251

One startled shriek, one hollow groan,
  One headlong rush, and then
Huzza! the field was all our own,
  For we were BANKS'S *men.*

That night, released from all our toils,
  Our dangers past and gone;
We gladly gathered up the spoils
  Our chivalry had won!

Five hundred 'kerchiefs we had snatched
  From Rebel ladies' hands,
Ten parasols, two shoes (not matched)
  Some ribbons, belts, and bands,

And other things that I forgot;
  But then you'll find them all
As trophies in that hallowed spot—
  The cradle—Faneuil Hall!

And long on Massachusetts' shore,
  And on Green Mountains' side,
Or where Long Island's breakers roar,
  And by the Hudson's tide,

In times to come, when lamps are lit,
  And fires brightly blaze,
While round the knees of heroes sit
  The young of happier days,

Who listen to their storied deeds,
  To them sublimely grand—
Then glory shall award its meed
  Of praise to Banks's band,

And fame proclaim that they alone
  (In triumph's loudest note)
May wear henceforth, for valor shown,
  A woman's petticoat!

—MARION SOUTHWOOD

252

The Richmond Bread Riot

*

Richmond, Va.
April 4, 1863

MY DEAR:

I hope you appreciate the fact that you are herewith honored with a letter written in royal-red ink upon sumptuous gilt-edged paper. There is not, at the present writing, one inch of paper for sale in the capital of the Confederacy, at all within the humble means of the wife of a Confederate officer. Well is it for her—and I hope for you—that her youthful admirers were few, and so her gorgeous cream-and-gold album was only half filled with tender effusions. Out come the blank leaves, to be divided between her friend and her Colonel. Don't be alarmed at the color of the writing, I have not yet dipped my goose-quill (there are no steel pens) in the "ruddy drops that visit my sad heart," nor yet into good orthodox red ink. There are fine oaks in the country, and that noble tree bears a gall-nut filled with crimson sap. One lies on my table, and into its sanguinary heart I plunge my pen.

Something very sad has just happened in Richmond—something that makes me ashamed of all my jeremiads over the loss of the petty comforts and conveniences of life—hats, bonnets, gowns, stationery, books, magazines, dainty food. Since the weather has been so pleasant, I have been in the habit of walking in the Capitol Square before breakfast every morning. Somehow nothing so sets me up after a restless night as a glimpse of the dandelions waking up from their dewy bed and the songs of the birds in the Park. Yesterday, upon arriving, I found within the gates a crowd of women and boys—several hundreds of them, standing quietly together. I sat on a bench near, and one of the number left the rest and took the seat beside me. She was a pale, emaciated girl, not more than eighteen, with a sunbonnet on her head, and dressed in a clean calico gown. "I could stand no longer," she explained. As I made room for her, I observed that she had delicate features and large eyes. Her hair and dress were neat. As she raised her hand to remove her sunbonnet and use it for a fan, her loose calico sleeve slipped up, and revealed the mere skeleton of an arm. She perceived my expression as I looked at it, and hastily pulled down her sleeve with a short laugh. "This is all that's left of me!" she said. "It seems real funny, don't it?" Evidently she had been a pretty girl—a dressmaker's apprentice, I judged from her chafed forefinger and a certain skill in the lines of her gown. I was encouraged to ask: "What is it? Is there some celebration?"

"There *is*," said the girl, solemnly; "we celebrate our right to live. We are starving. As soon as enough of us get together we are going to the bakeries and each of us will take a loaf of bread. That is little enough for the government to give us after it has taken all our men."

Just then a fat old black Mammy waddled up the walk to overtake a beautiful child who was running before her. "Come dis a way, honey," she called, "don't go nigh dem people," adding, in a lower tone, "I's feared you'll ketch somethin' fum dem po' white folks. I *wonder* dey lets 'em into de Park."

The girl turned to me with a wan smile, and as she rose to join the long line that had now formed and was moving, she said simply, "Good-by! I'm going to get something to eat!"

"And I devoutly hope you'll get it—and plenty of it," I told her. The crowd now rapidly increased, and numbered, I am sure, more than a thousand women and children. It grew and grew until it reached the dignity of a mob—a bread riot. They impressed all the light carts they met, and marched along silently and in order. They marched through Cary Street and Main, visiting the stores of the speculators and emptying them of their contents. Governor [John] Letcher sent the mayor to read the Riot Act, and as this had no effect he threatened to fire on the crowd. The city battalion then came up. The women fell back with frightened eyes, but did not obey the order to disperse. The President then appeared, ascended a dray, and addressed them. It is said he was received at first with hisses from the boys, but after he had spoken some little time with great kindness and sympathy, the women quietly moved on, taking their food with them. General [Arnold] Elzey and General [John H.] Winder wished to call troops from the camps to "suppress the women," but Mr. [Secretary of War James A.] Seddon, wise man, declined to issue the order. While I write women and children are still standing in the streets, demanding food, and the government is issuing to them rations of rice.

This is a frightful state of things. I am telling you of it because *not one word* has been said in the newspapers about it. All will be changed, Judge Campbell tells me, if we can win a battle or two (but, oh, at what a price!), and regain the control of our railroads. Your General has been magnificent. He has fed Lee's army all winter—I wish he could feed our starving women and children.

Dearly,
AGNES

—MRS. ROGER A. PRYOR

∗

Emma Sansom's Ride with Forrest

∗

WHEN THE WAR came on, there were three children—a brother and sister older than I. In August, 1861, my brother enlisted in the second company that left Gadsden and joined the Nineteenth Alabama Infantry. My sister and I lived with our mother on the farm.

We were at home on the morning of May 2, 1863, when about eight or nine o'clock a company of men wearing blue uniforms and riding mules and horses galloped past the house and went on towards the bridge [over Black Creek, some two hundred yards away]. Pretty soon a great crowd of them came along, and some of them stopped at the gate and asked us to bring them some water. Sister and I each took a bucket of water, and gave it to them at the gate. One of them asked me where my father was. I told him he was dead. He asked me if I had any brothers. I told him I had *six*. He asked where they were, and I said they were in the Confederate Army.

"Do they think the South will whip?"

"They do."

"What do you think about it?"

"I think God is on our side and we will win."

"You do? Well, if you had seen us whip Colonel Roddey the other

255

day and run him across the Tennessee River, you would have thought God was on the side of the best artillery."

By this time some of them began to dismount, and we went into the house. They came in and began to search for firearms and men's saddles. They did not find anything but a side-saddle, and one of them cut the skirts off that. Just then some one from the road said in a loud tone: "You men bring a chunk of fire with you, and get out of that house." The men got the fire in the kitchen and started out and an officer put a guard around the house, saying: "This guard is for your protection." They all soon hurried down to the bridge, and in a few minutes we saw the smoke rising and knew they were burning the bridge. As our fence extended up to the railing of the bridge, mother said: "Come with me and we will pull our rails away, so they will not be destroyed." As we got to the top of the hill we saw the rails were already piled on the bridge and were on fire, and the Yankees were in line on the other side guarding it.

We turned back towards the house, and had not gone but a few steps before we saw a Yankee coming at full speed, and behind were some more men on horses. I heard them shout, "Halt! and surrender!" The man stopped, threw up his hands, and handed over his gun. The officer to whom the soldier surrendered said: "Ladies, do not be alarmed, I am General Forrest; I and my men will protect you from harm." He inquired: "Where are the Yankees?"

Mother said: "They have set the bridge on fire and are standing in line on the other side, and if you go down that hill they will kill the last one of you."

By this time our men had come up, and some went out in the field, and both sides commenced shooting. We ran to the house, and I got there ahead of all. General Forrest dashed up to the gate and said to me: "Can you tell me where I can get across that creek?"

I told him there was an unsafe bridge two miles farther down the stream, but that I knew of a trail about two hundred yards above the bridge on our farm, where our cows used to cross in low water, and I believed he could get his men over there, and that if he would have my saddle put on a horse I would show him the way.

He said: "There is no time to saddle a horse; get up here behind me." As he said this he rode close to the bank on the side of the road, and I jumped up behind him.

Just as we started off Mother came up about out of breath and gasped out: "Emma, what do you mean?"

General Forrest said: "She is going to show me a ford where I can get my men over in time to catch those Yankees before they get to Rome. Don't be uneasy; I will bring her back safe."

We rode out into a field through which ran a branch or small ravine and along which there was a thick undergrowth that protected us for a while from being seen by the Yankees at the bridge or on the other side of the creek. This branch emptied into the creek just above the ford. When we got close to the creek, I said: "General Forrest, I think we had better get off the horse, as we are now where we may be seen."

We both got down and crept through the bushes and when we were right at the ford I happened to be in front. He stepped quickly between me and the Yankees saying: "I am glad to have you for a pilot, but I am not going to make breastworks of you."

The cannon and the other guns were firing fast by this time, as I pointed out to him where to go into the water and out on the other bank, and then we went back towards the house. He asked me my name, and asked me to give him a lock of my hair. The cannon-balls were screaming over us so loud that we were told to leave and hide in some place out of danger, which we did. Soon all the firing stopped, and I started back home. On the way I met General Forrest again, and he told me that he had written a note for me and left it on the bureau. He asked me again for a lock of my hair, and as we went into the house he said: "One of my bravest men has been killed, and he is laid out in the house. His name is Robert Turner. I want you to see that he is buried in some graveyard near here." He then told me good-by and got on his horse, and he and his men rode away and left us all alone.

My sister and I sat up all night watching over the dead soldier, who had lost his life fighting for our rights, in which we were overpowered but never conquered. General Forrest and his men endeared themselves to us forever.

—EMMA SANSOM

257

*

_____

A Jaybird at Vicksburg

_____

*

WE WERE NOW swiftly nearing the end of our [Vicksburg] siege life [May 19-July 4, 1863]: the rations had nearly all been given out. For the last few days I had been sick; still I tried to overcome the languid feeling of utter prostration. My little one had swung in her hammock, reduced in strength, with a low fever flushing in her face. M—— was all anxiety, I could plainly see. A soldier brought up, one morning, a little jaybird, as a plaything for the child. After playing with it for a short time, she turned wearily away. "Miss Mary," said the servant, "she's hungry; let me make her some soup from the bird." At first I refused; the poor little plaything should not die; then, as I thought of the child, I half consented. With the utmost haste, Cinth disappeared; and the next time she appeared, it was with a cup of soup, and a little plate, on which lay the white meat of the poor little bird.

—MARY WEBSTER LOUGHBOROUGH

21. "EVEN IF HE BE AN ENEMY"

The Gallant Hood

*

I WAS ORDERED while at Culpeper [in May, 1863] to make a reconnaissance of the Rappahannock River from Chancellorsville up towards Warrenton and to make a topographical map showing the strategical strength of positions along the banks with reference to forcing a crossing. General Lee was slowly moving his forces up the river, to draw [General Joseph] Hooker out of his hole behind the deep part of the river, by threatening Washington. [John B.] Hood's division was in the advance, and I was to report to him all I found out. I took Frank Robertson and an escort of twenty-five cavalry, picked men, with me. The banks on the other side were occupied by the enemy. As we ascended the stream it became smaller and smaller and the fords became more and more frequent. Usually the enemy occupied the hills back from the river, but at one place, where there was an important road crossing, they had built a fort right on the river-bank at the toe of a horseshoe bend, with the concave of the bend on their side, and bold hills encircling it on ours, a most absurd location for a redoubt.

* * * * *

Not expecting anything of this kind so close to the river, which was there a small stream not twenty yards wide, I was riding unconcernedly at the head of my little party, along a path on the bank, when on emerging into an open field I saw the opposite side swarming with blue-jackets. They were mostly outside of the fort strolling about at their ease, unconscious of the approach of an enemy. To get a good idea of their position it was necessary to pass along the path, and seeing how much off their guard they were I concluded to try it, counting upon their mistaking us for a party of their own men. Passing the order for my men not to fire nor to appear on their guard but to go on talking and laughing as usual, I moved on. It turned out as I expected it would, for seeing a squad of cavalry walking their horses along fifty yards from the fort they never suspected for a moment who we were, but exchanged good-humored jokes with the men of my party. There was a full regiment of them, eight or ten hundred strong, and if they had only known it a volley would have settled us pretty effectually. I was enabled to make an accurate sketch of the position, and seeing what a blunder had been made in building the fort where it was and seeing that this point gave the best possible place to force a crossing, I at once reported to General Hood, whose command was moving up the turnpike parallel with the river a mile or two back. It was sundown when General Hood, at my representation, came down to look at the place and at once saw its advantages. His chief of artillery was with him and he gave him directions to select positions for the batteries, as he would make the attack in the morning. Seeing how much off their guard they were, scattered outside the fort, he laughed and said, "Major, send a shell first over their heads and let them get in their holes before you open with all your guns." This was a piece of chivalry characteristic of the gallant Hood.

During the night General Lee ordered Hood to move on up the river and the attack was not made.

—Lieutenant Colonel W. W. Blackford

*

Mrs. McLellan Asks Lee
for Bread and an Autograph

---

*

THE MILLS, provisions, and stores throughout the town [of Chambersburg, Pennsylvania,] and surrounding country were all in the hands of the enemy, and in many families supplies were running short. On [June 28, 1863] the Sunday before the battle of Gettysburg . . . matters had become so serious that it became necessary for some one to seek an interview with the enemy and obtain flour. I sent for one of the body-guards, and a captain came in response. From him I learned that I could see General Lee by going to his headquarters in Messer-smith's woods. The captain offered me an escort, but assured me that I could go alone with perfect safety, showing me a copy of General Lee's order that any one who would insult a woman by word, look, or act, would be instantly shot. I then decided to decline an escort, and taking my young daughter I set out for the camp. I found the rules were stringently enforced, but had no difficulty in passing through the ranks. Everything was in most perfect order; even the horses were picketed so as to do no injury to the trees in the grove where their tents were pitched. Reaching headquarters I found the General seated with his officers at the table. A subordinate met me, and learning my errand, placed two camp-stools, and in a short time I found myself seated by General Lee himself.

I stated to him our need, and told him starvation would soon be at hand upon many families unless he gave aid. He seemed startled by this announcement, and said that such destitution seemed impossible in such a rich and beautiful grain-growing country, pointing to the rich fields of grain all around his camp. I reminded him that this growing grain was useless to us now, and that many of our people had no means to lay in supplies ahead. He then assured me that he had turned over the supplies of food he found to his men, to keep them from ravaging

261

our homes. He said, "God help you if I permitted them to enter your houses. Your supplies depend upon the amount that is sent in to my men." He then told me to send one or two of our prominent men to him. I replied that they had nearly all gone away, fearing that they would be seized and taken off. (I feared to give him the names of any of our gentlemen.) He then asked me to send a miller who could give him an idea of the quantity required.

On leaving I asked him for his autograph. He replied: "Do you want the autograph of a rebel?" I said, "General Lee, I am a true Union woman, and yet I ask for bread and your autograph." The General replied: "It is to your interest to be for the Union, and I hope you may be as firm in your principles as I am in mine." He assured me that his autograph would be a dangerous thing to possess, but at length he gave it to me.

Changing the topic of conversation, he assured me that the war was a cruel thing, and that he only desired that they would let him go home and eat his bread there in peace. All this time I was impressed with the strength and sadness of the man.

—ELLEN MCLELLAN

*

General Pickett and
the Pennsylvania-Dutch Girl

---

*

AS [GEORGE E.] PICKETT'S DIVISION [of Longstreet's corps], weary, foot-sore and heart-sore, wended their toilsome way through Pennsylvania, on the march which ended on the field of Gettysburg, they passed a small Dutch house nestling away in the greenery of a pleasant village. As they came near, a little maid rushed out upon the porch, waving the stars and stripes in a wild burst of patriotic enthusiasm.

For a moment the leader of that way-worn band felt apprehensive that not all its members could be depended upon to maintain their chivalry in the presence of that banner which to them represented so much of wrong done upon their native soil. Many of them had come from the war-ravaged district of Suffolk, and Southerners will know what that flag meant to them. Instantly the General wheeled from the line and, taking off his cap, bowed to the little maid with all that grace for which he was noted in camp as well as drawing-room, and respectfully saluted the flag of his foes. Then turning he lifted his hand, and when the long line had passed every man in it had doffed his cap to the youthful patriot and had saluted the banner which she had made her gage of battle.

The delighted little maiden, who had never before received the homage of a whole division, cried out in a glow of gratitude: "I wish I had a Confederate flag; I would wave that, too!"

The General was asked afterward how he could bring himself to salute the enemy's flag.

"I did not salute the enemy's flag," he replied. "I saluted the heroic womanhood in the heart of that brave little girl, and the glorious old banner under which I won my first laurels."

—LaSalle Corbell Pickett

*

"I Am the Man, Sir"

---

*

RETURNING from the banks of the Susquehanna, and meeting at Gettysburg, July 1, 1863, the advance of Lee's forces, my command was thrown quickly and squarely on the right flank of the Union army. A more timely arrival never occurred. The battle had been raging for four or five hours. The Confederate General [James J.] Archer, with a large portion of his brigade, had been captured. [Henry] Heth and [Alfred M.] Scales, Confederate generals, had been wounded. The ranking Union commander on the field, General [John F.] Reynolds, had been killed, and [Winfield Scott] Hancock was assigned to command. The battle, upon the issue of which hung, perhaps, the fate of the Confederacy, was in full blast. The Union forces, at first driven back, now re-enforced, were again advancing and pressing back Lee's left and threatening to envelop it. The Confederates were stubbornly contesting every foot of ground, but the Southern left was slowly yielding. A few moments more and the day's battle might have been ended by the complete turning of Lee's flank. I was ordered to move at once to the aid of the heavily pressed Confederates. With a ringing yell, my command rushed upon the line posted to protect the Union right. Here occurred a hand-to-hand struggle. That protecting Union line once broken left my command not only on the right flank, but obliquely in rear of it. Any troops that were ever marshalled would, under like conditions, have been as surely and swiftly shattered. There was no alternative for Howard's men except to break and fly, or to throw down their arms and surrender. Under the concentrated fire from front and flank, the marvel is that any escaped.

In the midst of the wild disorder in his ranks, and through a storm of bullets, a Union officer was seeking to rally his men for a final stand. He, too, went down, pierced by a Minie ball. Riding forward with my rapidly advancing lines, I discovered that brave officer lying upon his back, with the July sun pouring its rays into his pale face. He was surrounded by the Union dead, and his own life seemed to be rapidly ebbing out. Quickly dismounting and lifting his head, I gave him water from my canteen, asked his name and the character of his wounds. He was Major General Francis C. Barlow, of New York, and of [Oliver O.] Howard's corps. The ball had entered his body in front and passed out near the spinal cord, paralyzing him in legs and arms. Neither of us had the remotest thought that he could possibly survive many hours. I summoned several soldiers who were looking after the wounded, and directed them to place him upon a litter and carry him to the shade in the rear. Before parting, he asked me to take from his pocket a package of letters and destroy them. They were from his wife. He had but one request to make of me. That request was that if I should live to the end of the war and should ever meet Mrs. Barlow, I would tell her of our meeting on the field of Gettysburg and of his thoughts of her in his last moments. He wished me to assure her that he died doing his duty at the front, that he was willing to give his life for his country, and that his deepest regret was that he must die without looking upon her face again. I learned that Mrs. Barlow was with the Union army, and near the battle-field. When it is remembered how closely Mrs. Gordon followed me, it will not be difficult to realize that my sympathies were especially stirred by the announcement that his wife was so near him.

Passing through the day's battle unhurt, I despatched at its close, under flag of truce, the promised message to Mrs. Barlow. I assured her that if she wished to come through the lines she should have safe escort to her husband's side.

In the desperate encounters of the two succeeding days, and the retreat of Lee's army, I thought no more of Barlow, except to number him among the noble dead of the two armies who had so gloriously met their fate. The ball, however, had struck no vital point, and Barlow slowly recovered, though this fact was wholly unknown to me. The following summer, in battle near Richmond, my kinsman with the same initials, General J. B. Gordon of North Carolina, was killed. Barlow, who had recovered, saw the announcement of his death, and entertained no doubt that he was the Gordon whom he had met on the field of Gettysburg. To me, therefore, Barlow was dead; to Barlow, I was dead. Nearly fifteen years passed before either of us was undeceived. During my second term in the United States Senate, the Honorable Clarkson Potter, of New York, was a member of the House of Representatives. He invited me to dinner in Washington to meet a General Barlow who had served in the Union army. Potter knew nothing of the Gettysburg incident. I had heard that there was another Barlow in the Union army, and supposed, of course, that it was this Barlow with whom I was to dine. Barlow had a similar reflection as to the Gordon he was to meet.

Seated at Clarkson Potter's table, I asked Barlow: "General, are you related to the Barlow who was killed at Gettysburg?"

He replied: "Why, I am the man, sir. Are you related to the Gordon who killed me?"

"I am the man, sir," I responded.

No words of mine can convey any conception of the emotions awakened by those startling announcements. Nothing short of an actual resurrection from the dead could have amazed either of us more. Thenceforward, until his untimely death in 1896, the friendship between us which was born amidst the thunders of Gettysburg was greatly cherished by both.

—GENERAL JOHN B. GORDON

Lee and the Wounded Union Soldier

*

I WAS AT THE BATTLE of Gettysburg myself, and an incident occurred there which largely changed my views of the Southern people. I had been a most bitter anti-Southman, and fought and cursed the Confederates desperately. I could see nothing good in any of them. The last day of the fight I was badly wounded. A ball shattered my left leg. I lay on the ground not far from Cemetery Ridge, and as General Lee ordered his retreat, he and his officers rode near me. As they came along I recognized him, and, though faint from exposure and loss of blood, I raised up my hands, looked Lee in the face, and shouted as loud as I could, "Hurrah for the Union!"

The General heard me, looked, stopped his horse, dismounted, and came toward me. I confess that I at first thought he meant to kill me. But as he came up he looked down at me with such a sad expression upon his face that all fear left me, and I wondered what he was about. He extended his hand to me, and grasping mine firmly and looking right into my eyes, said, "My son, I hope you will soon be well."

If I live a thousand years I shall never forget the expression on General Lee's face. There he was, defeated, retiring from a field that had cost him and his cause almost their last hope, and yet he stopped to say words like those to a wounded soldier of the opposition who had taunted him as he passed by! As soon as the General had left me I cried myself to sleep there upon the bloody ground!

—A. L. LONG AND MARCUS J. WRIGHT

266

General Grant Fixes Things for the Dockerys

*

ON THE 5th of July, 1863, a Southern planter and Mrs. Dockery, of Arkansas, slowly made their way to General Grant's headquarters, in the rear of Vicksburg. The day before, the long, tedious siege ended in the surrender of the Confederate forces to General Grant. All was, therefore, in confusion and bustle, but the Union soldiers were in excellent humor, and offered no opposition to the progress of the two visitors to see the "old man," as they loved to call their commander. Mrs. Dockery was the wife of a Confederate brigadier general [Thomas P. Dockery] who took part in the defense of the city. During the siege she had remained eleven miles in the rear of Vicksburg with the planter and his family. She could hear the fearful cannonading all during the long combat, and at times the reports of the cannon were as rapid as the notes of a quick tune on a violin. As soon as the city surrendered, she determined to hear the fate of her husband, so she persuaded the planter to get an old dilapidated buggy left on the place by some of the straggling soldiers, and with harness improvised with old straps, ropes, and strings, and a mule caught on the highway, to attempt the trip to General Grant's headquarters.

The mule pulled the buggy and its two occupants along the hot, dusty road at a lively pace, and by eleven o'clock Grant's shady retreat, about three miles to the rear of Vicksburg, was reached. His headquarter tents were pitched just a little to the north of the old Jackson road, on a ridge thickly covered with dense shade trees. As soon as the guards were reached, a sergeant informed the two they could proceed no further, as he knew General Grant would not see them. Mrs. Dockery, with tears in her eyes, begged the soldiers to go to Grant and tell him that a lady in great distress wished only to see him just "one little minute." The officer went into the General's tent, remained only one instant, returned, and invited Mrs. Dockery and the planter to walk in. They left the buggy with the guards, and tremblingly approached Grant's tent.

What was their agreeable surprise but to be cordially invited by Grant himself to be seated. Before hardly a word was spoken Grant instructed an orderly to serve his guests with cool water, and insisted on Mrs. Dockery taking an easy-chair, which he vacated for her. As soon as Mrs. Dockery could command language, she poured into the General's ears her fears that her husband was wounded or dead, and asked for a pass to go to Vicksburg and learn what was his fate. Grant replied, almost word for word, as follows: "Madam, General Grant has issued an order that there shall be no passing to and from Vicksburg, and he cannot set the example of violating his own orders."

Mrs. Dockery was in tears when she said: "Oh, my God! What shall I do?"

A smile almost passed over Grant's face as he replied: "Oh, don't distress yourself; I will take it upon myself to get news from your husband. He must be a gallant fellow to have won such a devoted wife."

"But when will you find out for me? Can you not see this suspense is almost killing me?" replied the lady.

"Right now," said Grant; "and you shall be my guest until my orderly can fly to General Pemberton's headquarters and get the news."

Grant instantly instructed one of his aides to write a note to General [John C.] Pemberton, and inquire of him whether or not General Dockery, of [John S.] Bowen's division, had escaped unharmed, and all the news about him, as Mrs. Dockery was at his headquarters exceedingly anxious to know. While the orderly was gone General Grant's dinner was served, and Mrs. Dockery and the planter dined with him and his friends. There were perhaps twenty generals, colonels, majors, aides, and others at the table, but not one of them spoke a word that could wound the feelings of the General's guests. The General himself was exceedingly agreeable, and instead of talking about war, or anything pertaining to it, devoted himself to getting all the information he could about the South and its productions. No cotton planter ever evinced more interest in cotton than did the great soldier to whom a strong city had surrendered the day before.

Soon after dinner the orderly returned with a note from General Pemberton, stating that General Dockery was in excellent health and would visit his wife as soon as General Grant would permit it. General Grant smiled and said: "You shall see him in a day or two; just as soon as we can fix things a little. I'll not forget your name, and of course will have to remember him."

When the General's visitors arose to depart, he assured them he appreciated their call, and taking a scrap of paper wrote on it for the guards to pass Mr. and Mrs. Dockery to their home, and signed his name. Only one picket had to be passed, but the pass looked so much more common than those regularly issued that the guard scanned it closely. When he read Grant's own signature, he said: "Humph, the 'old man' got to writing passes? Let them by."

—Vicksburg Commercial

*

They *Would* Mix on the Picket-Line

---

*

[IN LATE SUMMER, 1863] we were on the Rapidan River, where it was a little stream hardly one hundred feet wide. General Lee sent me word I must go out and break up the communication between our pickets and the enemy's.

They had got to trading with each other in newspapers, tobacco, lies, and whatever would vary the monotony of picket life. They would not shoot at each other, and so it was not military-like. So I started out one morning on my horse and rode the whole length of the picket-line, and just as I came to a certain point I saw that there was confusion and surprise, as if I had not been expected.

"What is the matter, men, here?" I asked.

"Nothing, General, nothing is here."

"You must tell me the truth," said I; "I am not welcome, I see, and there must be some reason for it. Now, what is the matter?"

"There has been nobody here, General. We were not expecting you; that is all."

I turned to two or three of the soldiers and said: "Beat down these bushes here." They had to obey, and there suddenly rose up out of the weeds a man as stark naked as he had come into the world. "Who are you?" asked I.

"I am from over yonder, General."

"Over yonder—where?"

He pointed to the other side of the river.

"What regiment do you belong to?"

"The One Hundred-fourth Pennsylvania, General."

"What are you doing in my camp?"

"Why, I thought I would just come over and see the boys."

"See the boys—what boys? Do you mean to say you have entered my camp except as a prisoner? Now, I am going to do this with you. I am going to have you marched to Libby Prison just as you are, without a rag of clothes on you!"

"Why, General, you wouldn't do that just because I came over to see the boys! I didn't mean any harm! I felt lonesome over there and wanted to talk to the boys a little. That is all."

"Never mind, sir; you march from this spot clothed as you are, to Libby Prison!"

"General," said the man, "I had rather you would order me to be shot right here."

"No sir, you go to Libby!"

Then several of my soldiers spoke up: "General, don't be too hard on him, he's a pretty good fellow! He didn't mean any harm; he just wanted to talk with us."

"This business must be broken up," said I, "—mixing on the picket-line."

It had not been in my heart, however, to arrest the man from the beginning. I only wanted to scare him, and he did beg hard. "I'll tell you what I will do with you this time," for I saw that he was a brave, good-humored fellow. "If you will promise me that neither you nor any of your men shall ever come into my lines again except as prisoners, I'll let you go."

"God bless you, General!" said the man, and without any more adieu he just leaped into that stream and came up on the other side, and took to the woods.

—General John B. Gordon

*

Reunion

---

*

THE THIRD OHIO REGIMENT were among the prisoners after a certain engagement, and when they entered a Tennessee town, on their way to the prisons in Richmond, they were visited, through curiosity, by a number of the Fifty-fourth Virginia, who wanted to see how the Yankees liked it to be hungry and tired and hopeless. The melancholy picture that met their gaze was enough to touch their hearts, and it did so. They ran back to their camp, and soon returned reinforced by others of their regiment, all bringing coffee (and kettles to boil it in), cornbread, and bacon; and with these refreshments, which were all they had themselves, they regaled the hungry prisoners, mingling with them and doing all they could to relieve their distress, and the next morning the prisoners departed on their weary way, deeply grateful for the kindness of their enemies, and vowing never to forget it.

It was not long before the opportunity came to them to show that they remembered it. In due time they were exchanged, and, returning to service, they found themselves encamped near Kelley's Ferry, on the Tennessee River. When Missionary Ridge was stormed [November 25, 1863], a lot of prisoners were taken from the Confederates, and among the number was the Fifty-fourth Virginia, and they were marched nine miles to Kelly's Ferry. It happened that at the landing there were some of the Third Ohio, and they asked what regiment this was. The answer, "The Fifty-fourth Virginia," had a most surprising effect on them. They left the spot on the run, and rushing up to their camp they shouted out to the boys, "The Fifty-fourth Virginia is at the ferry!" If they had announced the appearance of a hostile army in force, they could not have started up a greater or a quicker activity in the camp. The men ran about like mad, loaded themselves up with every eatable thing they could lay their hands on—coffee, bacon, sugar, beef, preserved fruits, everything—and started with a yell for the ferry, where they surrounded and hugged the Virginians like so many reunited college-mates, and spread before them the biggest feast they had seen since the Old Dominion seceded from the Union.

—ROSSITER JOHNSON

Says I, "John Morgan, where you been?"
"Down on the Ohio a-tryin' to swim."
Says I, "John Morgan, where's your hoss?"
Says he, "I lost it swimmin' across."
—"JOHN MORGAN"

22. 'SCAPES AND SCRAPES

A Good Day's Work and a Fine Turkey Dinner

*

GEORGE TODD had ten men under his command, and Cole Younger sixteen in his command. We continued to sleep in the woods at night and eat with our friends, and William Hopkins invited us all to meet at his house on February 14, 1863, and to enjoy a big turkey dinner. On the morning of the thirteenth of February, Captain Wagner came out of Independence with sixty-four men from the Fifth Missouri State Militia, looking for us, and went into camp in Mr. Hines's yard, whose son Jim was with us. That night twelve of us went to Hines's with the intention of firing on the militia, but before reaching there I suggested to Cole Younger that if we did, they would probably kill Mr. Hines and burn his house. We abandoned the trip and went back into

272

the woods. On that morning, Captain John Barrett and John Roth had returned from the South and joined us.

When the morning of the 14th of February came, Cole Younger suggested that if we expected to enjoy our turkey dinner we had better first get rid of Captain Wagner and his militia. The house of William Hopkins was on a high bluff and his father, Dick Hopkins, lived on the opposite side of the bottom on a high bluff. We agreed that Cole Younger should go with his men on the bluff near Will Hopkins' house at a point where the roads made a sharp turn around the bluff and John Roth should ride out where the militia could see them and when the militia attempted to capture them, make a rush to this place of ambush. When we reached the point near Will Hopkins' house, we met Captain Todd and his ten men and he took command and ordered us to form a line back from the road on the top of the hill. In a short time, we saw Barrett and Roth coming at full speed with the militia in full pursuit. When they had gotten into the cut, Barrett and Roth rushed around the turn and joined us.

Captain Wagner ordered his company in the cut between the bluff and the high rail fence and he and his first lieutenant rode around in sight of us. Captain Todd, who was standing in front of our lines, fired at him.

Wagner raised his hand with his revolver in it and shouted, "Don't fire, men, we are Federal soldiers and belong to the artillery; don't you see the brass on my saddle?"

Todd replied, "To hell with your artillery; kill them boys, kill them."

I was standing near Captain Todd at the time with a double-barrelled shot-gun, with each barrel loaded with fifteen pistol balls. I fired at Captain Wagner. Several of the balls struck his horse and one cut his little finger off, causing him to drop his revolver. Todd then yelled, "Charge." They became bunched up between the fence and the bluff and we were right on them before they could get their horses to running, and emptying saddles at every jump the horses made, they soon left the road and ran into the woods into a V-shaped place, where a drainage ditch entered the Little Blue.

Some of them forced their horses into the Little Blue and into the ditch. The water in the Blue was very deep and their horses were soon swimming. I rode up to the bank of the Blue and, emptying the other barrel of my shot-gun at them, dropped the gun and emptied my revolvers. In this company of militia, there was a man by the name of

273

Jim Lane, who before leaving Independence had said, "Before I return I will either kill a damned bushwhacker or one of their Southern sympathizers." When he reached the Blue, he turned and forced his horse into the ditch and was trying to force him up the opposite bank. Boone Shull saw him and yelled, "Boys, there goes the fellow that was going to kill 'a damned bushwhacker,' " and fired. Lane fell dead and Shull jumped off his own horse remarking, "That's too fine a horse to let get away," and ran into the ditch and captured the horse. Captain Todd then gave command to reload quick and tried to head them at Blue Springs.

While we were reloading, an old hypocrite, who under the guise of a Northern Methodist minister had been going over that country, robbing Southern people with the Redlegs and militia, rode up on a mule. He would go to the home of Southern people and hold family prayers with them and then charge them for divine service and, if they had no money, he would by force take their bedding, silverware or anything else of value, and at the time, he had a roll of blankets and comforts and two silk dresses and some silverware that he had forced Mrs. Stanley, the wife of Judge Stanley, to give him that morning. A short time before this, this old hypocrite, with a gang of militia, had gone to the house of Judge Stanley and demanded money from him. Upon failure of the Judge to comply with their demands, they had burned his feet, pulled his fingernails out and struck him over the head with their revolvers until he had lost his mind, and when this sanctimonious old hypocrite came riding up to us, Jim Little, who knew him too well, rode up to him and asked him what he wanted.

The preacher, thinking we were Federal soldiers, told Jim that he had been up and stayed all night at Judge Stanley's, and, hearing the firing, had ridden down to see about it.

Jim said to him, "You are the old devil we have been looking for. You have been going around this country praying with Southern people and in every one of your pretended prayers you would offer an insult to the South, and demanding pay, and when you were refused, you would rob defenceless women and children by taking what little property they had and you now have blankets and dresses belonging to Judge Stanley's wife, and now we've got you."

The preacher said, "I have a right to have pay for my divine services and ought to be paid for praying for sinners."

Jim remarked, "Well, you'd better be praying for yourself, and get at it damned quick."

The preacher asked him if he would kill a minister of the gospel.

274

Jim said, "No, but I am going to kill a damned thief and old hypocrite," and shot him and his mule. We afterwards came back and got what he had and took them back and delivered them to Mrs. Stanley.

We then wheeled our horses and tried to intercept the remaining militia at Blue Springs. When we reached the road leading into Blue Springs, they had just passed and [we] would have succeeded in slipping up on them if it had not been for Jim Little, who began to yell. The militia looked back and began to whip their horses with their rifles and, in a few minutes we were close enough to open fire on them, following them through the town of Blue Springs. About three-quarters of a mile from the town of Blue Springs, there was a very bad mud-hole in the road and there had been a number of poles laid across it, and, when the militia reached this place, their horses going in a run, quite a number of their horses stumbled and fell, piling men and horses in one promiscuous heap and ten of the militia ceased to bother us from that time on. We continued to follow them until they had reached the bridge across the Little Blue when Captain Wagner rode on to the bridge ahead of them and, drawing his revolver, commanded them to halt and face us, saying that he would shoot the first man who attempted to ride by him, to which command one of his men replied, "There's a damned sight more danger behind us than in front of us." We fired at them again and wheeled our horses, riding back.

We afterwards learned that out of the sixty-four men that had left Independence with Captain Wagner, only seven ever returned, and two of that number were badly wounded. Just before we reached the mud-hole, one of the militiamen fell off his horse in a fence corner. Mart Belt, who had been following him and shooting at him, rode up to him, took his pistols away from him and, leading the militiaman's horse, came galloping up to the rest of us and said, "Boys, I got that fellow all right." Some of the boys, who knew that Mart was a poor pistol shot, laughed at him and told him he couldn't hit a barn. Mart said, "Wait until we go back, and I'll show you where I shot him in the side of the head." When we got back to the place where the man had fallen, there was no man there, and an old gentleman, who lived nearby, came out into his yard and Mart asked him what had become of that dead man. The old man replied, "Dead man, Hell! If you'd have seen him running through that field after you boys rode off, you wouldn't have taken him for a corpse." We rode back to Will Hopkins' and arrived there at two o'clock in the afternoon, and did ample justice to a fine turkey dinner.

This had been a good day's work; twenty-seven of us had routed a company of sixty-four, killed fifty-seven of them and none of our men were wounded, and at this time, there were seven thousand Federal soldiers in Jackson county and a large Federal force in Lexington, Harrisonville and Pleasant Hill, and our little bunch of twenty-seven men, who were the only armed Confederates in that part of the country, caused all these soldiers to stay there and kept them from following General Price.

—JOHN MCCORKLE

*

Absalom Grimes, Confederate Mail Runner

*

BEFORE I LEFT St. Louis on May 12 [1863] I gave all our mail to Miss Bowen to carry on the *Graham* to Memphis, from which place she and Miss Perdue took it to Colonel Selby's home. Miss Selby had returned home about ten days before I arrived in Paducah on the thirteenth. Bob came in next night with Miss Sudie Kendall. On the fifteenth we left for Dixie, stopping at Colonel Selby's for the Missouri mail. Before arriving at Grenada we learned through the Northern papers that Pemberton's whole army was penned up in Vicksburg by General Grant's troops and we were undecided what to do with the mail we had for them. There were two or three small steamboats running on the Yallabusha and Yazoo rivers to Haines's Bluff, so we went to Yazoo City on the *Dew Drop,* a stern-wheel boat. We learned that our troops were hemmed in at the rear by Grant's troops and by Porter and Foote's fleets of gunboats on the Mississippi River front. For once we felt that we were checkmated. The night of the twenty-fifth, while Bob and I lay in bed together in a hotel in Yazoo City, we discussed the situation and determined that the two thousand letters we had brought should go into Vicksburg before forty-eight hours or we would die in the attempt. Neither of us had a wink of sleep that night as we lay there planning to run the blockade of the Federal fleet.

After breakfast we went to a tin shop and had four large square boxes made and had the tinner bring his soldering outfit to our room.

276

We packed all our mail in the boxes and soldered them up water-tight. We procured from a fisherman a good, doubled-ended skiff, pointed at each end like a canoe. We bought an extra pair of new oars and painted them and the boat a light lead color. We then procured two saucepans with long handles, two light dog-chains, some wire and staples, a hammer, and a pair of pliers to cut wire with. Last but by no means least, some ladies prepared a basket of lunch for us. We boarded a steamboat with our outfit that evening and soon arrived at Haines's Bluff, where a large raft of logs had been so arranged as to block the passage of boats either up or down the Yazoo.

On May 25 we wired our mail boxes and stapled them down in the bottom of the boat, two boxes at each end. Near each end, on opposite sides of the boat, we fastened a saucepan by means of a chain and staples. Then we arranged wire loops to stick the oars in so they would not float off or out of the locks. After we had everything in readiness we concluded to make a trial trip in the boat. We stripped off our clothing, fastened the oars inside the boat, and bore down on one side of the boat until it was filled with water to within three inches of the top. Each of us took a position at one end of the boat and with the saucepans (the handles of which passed through the loops of wire) we could paddle it anywhere we wanted to go, using one hand under water on the saucepan, and holding to the edge of the boat with the other hand. After paddling around awhile we used the saucepans to bail the water out of the boat, then we climbed in and rowed back to where we had left our clothing on the bank. We were delighted with the way our scheme worked.

At six o'clock we bade adieu to Captain Henry and the company of Confederates stationed at Haines's Bluff. "God bless you and see you safe through!" were the captain's parting words to us. It was dark when we reached the Mississippi River to make our start for Vicksburg. That morning I had procured a pair of field-glasses and gone on top of the high bluff where I could get a good view of the location of many of the boats of the Federal fleet. Most of the transports were two or three miles above the gun-boats and lay along the shore of the left bank. The gun-boats lay in about the middle of the stream, slightly nearer to the Vicksburg side. I planned our trip through the fleet accordingly. We kept our boat to the east bank until well past the transports, then we secured our oars inside the skiff and got out into the water with our clothes on.

After we had gone nearly across to the west side, using our saucepans under water as oars, we tipped and sank the boat to within three inches of the top edge and then went on west. The current carried us

277

forward and by the time we were within twenty yards of the west bank we were below the transports and all other non-combatant craft and immediately abreast of and opposite the gun-boats. We found these pretty well spread out across the river, and had to pass within three or four hundred yards of the extreme western gun-boat. We were afraid to get in too close to shore as we might attract the attention of the camp guards there. Three of the boats kept their lights moving all the time, and we did not dare use the saucepans too vigorously for fear our speed might attract attention to us. Our boat, sunk low in the water, presented little to arrest the eye of a lookout, but every little flash of light from those eight or ten gun-boats made us expect an unfriendly bullet. Although it seemed a long time to us, I think it was really not more than an hour from the time we reached the danger line until we were beyond reach of the searchlights of the gun-boats. We now employed the saucepans to bail out the skiff and soon were riding in it. Later we lighted our small, water-proof dark-lantern and headed across the river for the Vicksburg wharf. It was more than a mile across, and every few moments we waved our lantern to let the guards know that we intended to land in Vicksburg, and were not trying to run their blockade. Although it was midnight when we landed, at least fifty soldiers were waiting on the wharf to receive us.

The two guards said they would take good care of our boat and its precious contents until morning. We were then conducted to a rooming-house, where we were provided with night clothes while the folks in the house took our wet clothing and had it dry for us by six o'clock next morning. The news of our arrival in Vicksburg spread rapidly over the town, and when we stepped out of the house we found more than two hundred soldiers around the place. The crowd was composed mostly of Missouri and Kentucky soldiers whom we knew. We were simply crushed in their excited joy to see us once more and under such unfavorable circumstances and surroundings. They carried us about on their shoulders and cheered lustily. Many of them went with us to our boat and got the mail boxes. We had a tinner unsolder them carefully in order that we might use them to carry mail out of Vicksburg. I shall not attempt to describe the reception we had when we reached the Missouri and Kentucky sections of the camp. It would be impossible. However, all our vain ambitions, the glory of our perilous trip through the fleet, and the pleasure we had in the meeting were soon reversed when we were shown a list of the dear, heroic comrades who had been sacrificed at Port Gibson, Grand Gulf, Baker's Creek, and in the vicinity of Vicks-

278

burg since we had bade them such a happy farewell at the camp at Grand Gulf a little more than a month since. Oh, how dreadful the memory of that trip into Vicksburg, though now more than forty years ago! Over two hundred of those happy faces and eager hands that had been extended to receive loving messages from home were to be seen no more. How the joys of the mail-carrier in camp can so quickly be turned into grief and sorrow can scarcely be realized. I felt as if I never wanted to make another trip in the mail-carrying business.

Bob and myself were so grieved that we had about decided to notify the troops that they need not expect us in with any more mail, but when we mentioned the subject to generals Gates, Cockrell, and Breckinridge and the men in the ranks they cried out in dismay at such a proposition. The result was we assured them that we would continue to serve as long as life was in our possession and that thereafter our ghosts would wait upon them in their dreams of home unless the Yanks detained us involuntarily. Shame on us to think of deserting them! But the sad faces and down-hearted expressions of those noble men, coupled with the absence of hundreds whom we were accustomed to meet and render happy with letters, made our existence miserable and we felt as if we must get out of that horrid place as soon as possible.

We had been so interested in getting into Vicksburg that we had laid no plans for getting out. However, we were not long planning a way north. We borrowed General Cockrell's field-glasses and spent two or three hours on the bluff at the north end of the fortification. We decided that instead of floating south we would row north, whence we had come. We discovered that for a long way below where the transports lay and as far down as the gun-boats there were skiffs, launches, and other small craft rowing and moving freely about between points where camps were established along the canal some distance back from the river. I knew that with two good sets of oars we could make fair time upstream.

The boys in Vicksburg soon made ready a large return mail for our care and distribution. It filled our four boxes as full as they could be packed and we had them soldered as before, water-tight. Instead of wiring the boxes inside the skiff, as we had brought them down, we turned the boat bottom up on the bank and wired the boxes in a row, end to end, to the bottom of the boat. The boxes were a foot wide, eighteen inches long, and eight inches deep. We put them underneath the boat so that in the event we passed any boat or persons on the bank they would find nothing inside the boat. Before starting we ex-

279

changed our clothing for Federal uniforms, which were plentiful in our camp. One of the saddest good-bys I ever expect to undergo in all my life took place in the trenches, in the camps, and on the wharf at Vicksburg the night previous to our departure.

After our parting with the men, whom we never expected to see again, we slept, or rather we retired, in a house on the levee. At two o'clock in the morning we pulled across the river to the west bank, and keeping in its shadow, as it was a fine starlight night, rowed upstream. By daylight we were directly across from the gun-boats, without having received a single challenge from anyone. We were wearing Federal uniforms and our act was such a barefaced exhibition of lunacy and nerve that no one on the fleet suspected our character as we rowed up past the transports in full view and not more than a hundred yards from the boats of the fleet.

We rowed on up the western shore until we passed around a point three or four miles above the fleet. Here we landed and pulling our boat out of the water removed the mail boxes from the bottom, as they made it so much harder to row. Oh, what a relief to our overtaxed muscles, as well as our nerves and minds! We rested a short time and then launched our boat and made fine time rowing upstream. By one o'clock we were in the mouth of the Yazoo River, having been absent just six days. We received a hearty welcome from Captain Henry and our men at Haines's Bluff.

—ABSALOM GRIMES

*

Pauline Cushman Borrows a
Young Man's Suit

---

*

[IN JUNE, 1863] shortly after she left Shelbyville on her way to Nashville; and, during a short halt, at a place called Wartrace, [Pauline Cushman] undertook a scouting enterprise with the view of communicating valuable information to some of the roving bands of Union cavalry, who were almost daily engaged in skirmishing with the rebel cavalry. In carrying out this plan, her first requisite was, of course, a man's suit of clothes, and to get these she now set her wits to work. At the same hotel where she was stopping was a young man of about seventeen years of age, whose clothes she thought would just fit her, but how to get them was the question. With only the knowledge that he slept in the upper story of the house, but provokingly ignorant of which room he occupied, she resolved to "scout" around in the dark, and, "hit or miss," make a desperate attempt to secure the clothes.

So after a series of adventures in the dark, which succeeded only in arousing nearly all the inmates of the several rooms on the corridor, our discomfited heroine, beating a hasty retreat from the discovery which now seemed inevitable, desperately tried the handle of a small door near at hand. To her great joy it yielded, and slipping hastily in, she found herself in a low, poorly furnished chamber—in which lay sleeping the very man whose clothes she had been seeking. Luckily, the uproar in the hall had not awakened him, and waiting till all was quiet again, she grabbed the clothes and sped silently to her own room. Hastily dressing herself in the stolen suit, she crept softly down-stairs, past the sleeping Negro boy in the hall, out to the stables, and there she speedily saddled one of the best horses which she could find, and pushed her way out of the town.

Into the woods she rode, and finally, when some three miles out of Wartrace, came suddenly upon a guerrilla encampment, and was busily engaged in playing the eavesdropper to their camp-fire conversation when she unluckily stepped upon a brittle branch which snapped under her feet. Instantly they took the alarm, and she scarcely had time to mount her horse before they were in full chase after her. Gradually they gained upon her, when suddenly she found herself approaching, at full speed, a precipitous rock, at the foot of which meandered a small stream. It was impossible to check the headlong speed of her horse, and her pursuers were close upon her; so, shutting her eyes, and striking the spurs deep into the animal's flanks, she plunged down the mountain side. Her pursuers did not dare to follow, but standing at the top of the bluff, contented themselves with winging their pistol bullets after her. Suddenly, just as she hoped that she was fairly escaped, one of her pursuers discovered a bridle path, and the chase recommenced.

Pushing hastily into the woods which lined the creek, she endeavored to regain the road to Wartrace, for she was now threatened with two dilemmas; if daylight overtook her before she could get back to the hotel, her theft of the clothes and horse would be discovered; and if taken by her pursuers she would inevitably be taken to Wartrace, it being the nearest town. On she rode, at full speed, until she found herself gaining upon the rebel riders, and suddenly came upon a wounded Union cavalryman, scarce able to sit upon his horse, from the effects of a wound received while scouting, a few hours before. She at first mistook him for a "reb," but ascertaining the truth, a plan of escape flashed through her brain, and she quickly revealed to him her sex and name, and asked his aid. The brave fellow had heard of the "Woman scout of the Cumberland," and, faint and wounded as he was, gladly and bravely offered to carry out her plan at the risk of his life.

Firing her pistol into the air, she instructed the soldier to say to the pursuing party, who would inevitably be drawn thither by the report, that he had been met and shot by a "reb." She told him that he could not expect, from his wounds, to escape capture, and advised him to stir himself around so as to make his wound bleed afresh. He obeyed, and let himself fall off his horse, while Miss Cushman gave the animal a sharp blow which sent him flying down the road. When the rebel horsemen galloped up to the spot, they found the soldier lying at the foot of a tree, bleeding freely, and in a state of unconsciousness from his sudden fall, while over him bent our heroine, pistol in hand. To their surprised and hurried query who she was, she promptly replied: "I am a farmer's son, over near Wartrace, and I surrender to you; but I have shot your best fellow, here, and only wish I had shot more of ye."

To their astonished looks and questions as to what he meant, she replied in the same bitter vein, "I mean just what I say. I am only sorry that I didn't kill more of you darned Yankees, that comes down yhere and runs all our niggers off!"

Completely misled by her skilful acting, the rebels now saw that the boy had mistaken them for Yankees; and on questioning the Yankee soldier, who was gradually recovering from his faintness, the brave fellow, true to instructions, designated the "farmer's boy," as the one who had shot him, "because he was a Yankee." It now became evident to the "rebs" that each party had mistaken the other for "Yanks"; but for further precaution, Pauline was ordered to accompany them, and the wounded soldier was placed on a horse, and the party took up their march to Wartrace. This was a programme not at all agreeable to her, and as they rode along through the darkness of the forest, she conceived the idea of creating a "scare," hoping to avail herself of the confusion to get off and make her escape to Wartrace before daylight should make it too late to escape detection as a thief.

So as they were passing through a narrow gorge of the road, thickly overshadowed by tall forest trees—a nice place for an ambush— she managed to fall behind the party and become hidden by a bend in the road. Then taking out her revolver, she fired five shots in rapid succession. As she expected, her rebel companions were startled. Supposing themselves ambushed by Federal cavalry, fear lent a thousand terrors to their minds, and their imaginations gave new echoes to the reports of the pistol. Away they went, pell-mell, and laughing heartily at the success of her "scare," Miss Cushman rapidly galloped to Wartrace, where she luckily succeeded in comfortably housing her steed and in returning the borrowed clothes, without detection—and in due time, answered the summons of the breakfast bell, as rosy and fresh-faced, and as innocent in look and manner, as if the night had been spent comfortably in her bed.

—Dr. L. P. Brockett

*

How Frank Stringfellow
Overheard His Death Warrant

*

AMONG THE FEDERAL FORCES, S—— [Frank Stringfellow] had achieved a high reputation as a scout and a partisan; and had also aroused in his enemies a profound hatred. His daring reconnaissances, secret scouts, and audacious attacks on foraging parties had made them pass a lively time—and great was the joy of a Federal Colonel commanding pickets [in Fauquier County, Virginia] on the upper Rappahannock when he received intelligence one day in this summer of 1863 that the well known S—— was alone at a house not far from camp, where his capture would be easy.

S—— was, in fact, at the house indicated, without the least suspicion that his presence had been discovered. He had been sent upon a scout in that region, and finding himself in the neighbourhood of the family with whom he had long been on terms of intimacy, embraced the occasion to visit them and rest for a few hours before proceeding upon his way. On the evening when the events about to be related occurred, he was seated in the parlour, conversing with one of the young ladies of the family, and perfectly at his ease both in body and mind. His horse—an excellent one, captured a few days before from the enemy— was in the stable, enjoying a plentiful supply of corn; he had himself partaken of a most inviting supper, to which bright eyes and smiles had communicated an additional attraction; and he was now sitting on the sofa, engaged in conversation, not dreaming of the existence of an enemy within a thousand miles. . . . His eye wandered unconsciously, from pure habit, every few moments toward the door, and around his waist was still buckled the well-worn belt containing his pistols. These never left his person day or night as long as he was in the vicinity of his enemies.

. . . S—— was tranquilly enjoying himself in the society of his kind hostess, and laughing with the light-hearted carelessness of a boy who finds a "spirit of mirth" in everything, when suddenly his quick ear caught the clatter of hoofs upon the road without, and rising, he went to the window to reconnoitre. A glance told him that the new-comers were the enemy; and the crack through which he looked was sufficiently large to enable him to see that they consisted of a detach-ment of Federal cavalry, who now rapidly approached the house. With such rapidity did they advance, that before S—— could move they had reached the very door; and no sooner had they done so, than at a brief order from the officer commanding, several men detached themselves from the troop, hurried to the rear of the house, and in an instant every avenue of escape was effectually cut off.

S—— was now fairly entrapped. . . . To meet this sudden and dangerous advance of his foes, S—— saw that he must act with rapidity. Skill and decision would alone save him, if anything could; and in a few rapid words he explained the state of affairs. He informed his enter-tainers that he was the game for whom they were hunting; he had heard that a price was set upon his head; if there was no means of leaving the house or concealing himself, he did not mean to surrender; he would not be taken alive, but would fight his way through the whole party and make his escape, or die defending himself.

They informed him in quick words . . . that he need not despair, they would conceal him; and then the brave hearts set to work. One ran to the window and demanded who was without; another closed the door in rear, the front door being already shut; and while these movements were in progress S—— was hurried up the staircase by one of the young ladies, who was to show him his hiding-place. Before he had reached the head of the staircase a novel proof was given by the Federal cavalry of the terror which they attached to his name. A sudden explosion from without shook the windows; six or eight carbine-balls pierced the front door, passed through and whistled around the ladies; and a loud shout was heard, followed by heavy shoulders thrust against the door. It was afterwards discovered that the rattle of the door-latch in the wind had occasioned the volley; the noise was supposed to be that made by S—— as he was about to rush out upon them!

The scout had, meanwhile, been conducted by his fair guide to his hiding-place, which was in a garret entirely destitute of furniture, with bare walls, and apparently without any imaginable facility for enabling a man to escape the prying eyes of the "party of observation." Here, nevertheless, S—— was concealed; and his hiding-place was excellent, from its very simplicity. The garret had no ceiling, and the joists were even unboarded; but upon them were stretched two or three loose planks. The young lady hurriedly pointed to these. S—— understood, in an instant; and, swinging himself up, he reached the joist, lay down at full length upon one of the planks next to the eaves, and found himself completely protected from observation, unless the search for him was so minute as to leave no corner unexplored.

Having assisted the scout to ensconce himself in his hiding-place, the young lady hastened down from the garret, and descended the main staircase, just as the Federal soldiers burst open the front door and swarmed into the passage. From the plank beneath the eaves, as the door of the garret had been left open, S—— informed me he heard every word of the following colloquy:

"Where is the guerrilla we are after?" exclaimed the officer in command, sternly addressing the lady of the house.

"What guerrilla?" she asked.

"S——."

"He was here, but is gone."

"That is untrue, and I am not to be trifled with!" was the irate reply. "I shall search this house—but first read the orders to the men!" he added, addressing a non-commissioned officer of the troop.

This command was obeyed by a sergeant, holding an official paper in his hand; and S—— had the satisfaction of hearing read aloud a

285

paper which recited his various exploits, commented upon his character in terms far from flattering, declared him a bushwhacker and guerrilla, and ordered him to be put to death wherever he was found—the men being expressly forbidden to take him prisoner. This order was from Colonel ——, commanding the neighbouring force, and S—— heard every word of it. He was to be pistoled or sabred. No hope of mercy—no surrender taken. Death to him!

Peril unnerves the coward, but arouses a fierce pride and courage in the breast of the brave, to dare all, and fight to the death. S—— was made of the stuff which does not cower before danger, but enables a man to look the King of Terrors in the face without the shudder of a nerve. He was armed as usual with two pistols carefully loaded and capped—for he never neglected his arms—and before he was taken, or rather killed, he hoped to lay low more than one of his assailants. This was his calculation; but the scout was still a long way from regarding his fate as sealed, his death as certain. He had an obstinate faculty of hoping, and took the brightest view of his critical situation. He might not be discovered; or if discovered, he was in a position to fight to an advantage which would make the issue of the struggle exceedingly doubtful. He intended to spring to the floor, shoot the one or two men who would probably penetrate to the garret, and hurl them down the staircase—and then placing himself at the head of the stairs, sheltered from bullets by a projection of the wood-work, defy them to ascend.

"They never *could* have got me out of there," said S—— with a laugh, "unless they had burned the house, or brought *a piece of artillery to shell me out*. I had two pistols, and could have held my ground against the whole of them all day."

. . . The search for S—— speedily commenced. First the parlour and dining-room were subjected to a rigid examination, and finding there no traces of the scout, the men scattered themselves over the house, ransacking every apartment, and compelling the young ladies to throw open the most private recesses of their chambers. They looked under beds, into closets, and behind dresses hanging up in the wardrobes, in vain search for the game. Sabres were thrust into beds, . . . and the points of the weapons did not spare the female clothing depending from pegs in the closets. The scout might be straightened up against the wall, behind those white garments in closet or wardrobe; but an assiduous search failed to discover him, and soon no portion of the whole establishment remained unexplored but the garret. To this the party now directed their attention.

"What room is that up there?" was the curt question of one of the men to the young lady who stood near him.

"A garret," was the reply.

"He may be up there—show me the way!"

"You see the way—I do not wish to go up there; the dust will soil my dress."

A growl greeted these quiet words, and the trooper turned to a black servant-girl who had been made to go around with the party in their search, holding a lighted candle.

"You go before, and show us the way," said the trooper. The girl laughed, declared that nobody was up there; but on hearing the order repeated, ascended the stairs, followed by the man.

S—— had listened attentively and lost nothing; the architecture of the house enabling him to catch the least sound without difficulty. After the protracted search in the rooms beneath, during which his hiding-place had not been approached, he began to hope that the danger was over. This hope, however, was found to be illusory, and he prepared for the crisis.

The steps of the servant-girl were heard ascending, followed by the tramp of the trooper, whose heavy sabre rattled against the stairs as he moved. Then a long streak of light ran over the garret floor; and cautiously thrusting out his head from his hiding-place, S—— saw the head of the girl and her companion, as step by step they mounted to the apartment. The girl held up her dress with affected horror of the dust; and when she had reached a position from which a full stream of light could be directed into the room, she paused, and with a low laugh called her companion's attention to the fact that there was nothing whatever in the garret.

This, however, did not satisfy him, and he insisted upon making a thorough search. The girl was obliged to obey his order, and in a moment they were both standing in the room.

S—— measured the man before, or rather beneath him, through a crevice in the plank, and calculated where he could shoot him to the best advantage. This resource seemed all that was left. Discovery appeared inevitable. The scout was lying upon a single plank, directly over the head of his enemy, and it was only necessary, apparently, for the latter to possess ordinary eyesight to discover him. This was the scout's conviction, as he now cautiously moved his finger to the trigger of the pistol, which he had drawn and cocked, in expectation of the coming struggle. He would certainly be discovered in ten seconds, and then for an exhibition of his prowess as a Confederate soldier and scout, which should either extricate him from his peril, or force his very enemies to respect the courage of the man they overwhelmed and put to death! His plan, as I have said, was simple. He would throw himself upon this man, shoot him throught the heart, hurl the body upon the heads of those below, and then hold his position against the whole party at the pistol's muzzle. It was improbable that the Federal troopers could be induced to mount the narrow stairway, at the head of which stood at bay a desperate and determined man, armed with a revolver in each hand. It would be certain death to them; he must either be burned out or shelled out with artillery! That either of these courses, however, would be resorted to, appeared improbable; they would place a guard around the house, and either starve or attempt to dislodge him in some other manner. But then he would gain time; now if time were only gained, the scout had so much confidence in his own resources that he believed himself safe.

. . . The Federal trooper gazed around the garret for some hidden nook or cranny wherein a rebel could be stowed away. Some empty boxes attracted his attention, but an examination of them resulted in nothing. Then, all at once, the eyes of the man were directed toward the spot where the scout was concealed.

S—— gave himself up for lost; his finger was on the trigger, and he was about to forestall his enemy by sending a ball through his brain, when suddenly he drew a long breath, removed his finger from the trigger, and flattened himself almost to nonentity on his plank. The girl had adopted an excellent *ruse,* and as simple as it was excellent. Whilst conversing carelessly with the man, she had moved *directly beneath* S——, in consequence of which movement the candle threw the shadow of the plank on which he lay *directly upward.* Thus the person of the scout, prone on the plank, was wholly hidden from view. In vain did the man move from side to side, evidently suspecting something, and order the girl to hold the light in such a manner as to illuminate the dusky recess beneath the rafters. She readily did so, but so adroitly that at every movement the shadow was made still to conceal the scout; and ere long this comedy, in the issue of which the life of a man was involved, came to an end. Satisfied that the garret contained no one, the man retired, and the clank of his sabre on the staircase as he descended gradually receded from the hearing of S——. He was saved.

The Federal troopers remained at the house some time longer, their officer exhibiting the utmost anger and disappointment at the result of the expedition; but they finally departed, warning the lady of the mansion that if she harboured "guerrillas" thereafter, her house would be burned. Leaving videttes behind, the officer then departed with his detachment.

This was the signal for S—— to descend, which he did at once. A brief reconnaissance through the window revealed the dark figures posted at stated intervals around the house—but these only made him laugh. He did not fear them, and had only one regret—the impossibility of getting his horse off. The attempt would reveal his presence, involve the family in danger, and might fail. He accordingly resolved to retire on foot. This was at once and successfully accomplished. S—— bade his kind friends farewell, stole out of the back door, glided along the garden fence, beneath the shadow of the trees, and gained the wood near by without being challenged.

In an hour he was safe from all pursuit, at a friend's on one of the spurs of the Blue Ridge. Soon afterwards he was relating this narrative to the present writer, near Orange.

—JOHN ESTEN COOKE

*

Raider Morgan

*

1 · How Morgan Got Three Hundred Horses

JOHN MORGAN, during his celebrated raid through Indiana [in July, 1863], took occasion to visit a little town, hard by, with 350 of his guerrillas, while the main body was marching on.

Dashing suddenly into the little "burgh," he found about 300 home-guards, each having a good horse tied to the fences; the men standing about in groups, awaiting orders from their aged captain, who appeared to be on the shady side of sixty.

The Hoosier boys looked at the men with astonishment, while the captain went up to one of the party and said: "Whose company is this?"

289

"Wolford's cavalry," said the Reb.

"What? Kentucky boys? We're glad to see you, boys. Where's Wolford?"

"There he sits," said a ragged, rough Reb, pointing to Morgan, who was sitting sideways on his horse.

The captain walked up to Wolford (as he and all thought), and saluted him: "Captain, how are you?"

"Bully; how are you? What are you going to do with all these men and horses?" said Morgan, looking about.

"Well, you see that the d———d horse-thieving John Morgan is in this part of the country, with a passel of cut-throats and thieves; and between you and I, if he comes up this way, Captain, we'll give him the best we've got in the shop."

"He's hard to catch; we've been after him for fourteen days, and can't see him at all," said Morgan, good-humoredly.

"Ef our hosses would stand fire, we'd be all right."

"Won't they stand?"

"No, Captain Wolford, 'spose while you're restin' here, you and your company put your saddles on our hosses, and go through a little evolution or two, by way of a lesson to our boys? I'm told you're a hoss on the drill."

And the only man Morgan is afraid of, Wolford (as it were), alighted, and ordered his "boys" to dismount, as he wanted to show the Hoosier boys how to give Morgan a warm reception, should he chance to pay them a visit.

This delighted the Hoosier boys, so that they went to work, and assisted the men to tie their old, weary, worn-out bones to the fences, and place their saddles upon the backs of their fresh horses, which was soon done, and the men were in their saddles, drawn up in line, and ready for the word.

The boys were highly elated at the idea of having their "pet horses" trained for them by Wolford and his men, and more so, to think that they would stand fire, ever afterward.

The old captain advanced, and walking up to Wolford (as he thought), said, "Captain, are you all right now?" Wolford rode up one side of the column, and down the other, then he moved to the front, took off his hat, paused, and said, "Now, Captain, I'm ready. If you and your gallant men wish to witness an evolution, which you, perhaps, have never seen, form a line on each side of the road, and watch us closely, as we pass."

The captain did as he was directed. A lot of ladies were present on the occasion, and all was silent as a maiden's sigh.

"Are you ready?"

"All right, Wolford," shouted the captain.

"*Forward!*" shouted Morgan, as the whole column rushed through the crowd, with lightning speed, amid the shouts and huzzas of all present—some leading a horse or two, as they went, leaving their frail tenements of horseflesh tied to the fences, to be provided for by the citizens.

It soon became whispered about, that it was John Morgan and his gang; and there was not a man in the town who would "own up" that he was gulled out of his horse. The company disbanded that night, though the captain, at last advices, still held the horses as prisoners of war, awaiting an exchange.

—E. S. S. ROUSE

II · The Escape of Morgan

[AT THE OHIO PENITENTIARY, the prisoners' bedsteads] were small iron stools, fastened to the wall with hinges. They could be hooked up, or allowed to stand on the floor; and, to prevent any suspicion, for several days before any work was attempted, they made it a habit to let them down, and sit at their doors and read. Captain [Thomas H.] Hines superintended the work, while General Morgan kept watch to divert the attention of the sentinel, whose duty it was to come round during the day, and observe if anything was going on. One day this fellow came in while Hokersmith was down under the floor, boring away, and, missing him, said, "Where is Hokersmith?"

The General replied, "He is in my room sick"; and immediately pulled a document out of his pocket, and said to him, "Here is a memorial I have drawn up to forward to the Government at Washington. What do you think of it?"

The fellow, who, perhaps, could not read, being highly flattered at the General's condescension, took it, and very gravely looked at it for several moments before he vouchsafed any reply; then, handing it back, he expressed himself highly pleased with it. In the meantime, Hokersmith had been signalled, and came up, professing to feel "very unwell." This sentinel was the most difficult and dangerous obstacle in their progress because there was no telling at what time he would enter

291

during the day, and at night he came regularly every two hours to each cell, and inserted a light through the bars of their door, to see that they were quietly sleeping; and frequently, after he had completed his rounds, he would slip back in the dark, with a pair of India-rubber shoes on, to listen at their cells if anything was going on. The General says that he would almost invariably know of his presence by a certain magnetic shudder which it would produce; but, for fear that this acute sensibility might sometimes fail him, he broke up small particles of coal every morning, and sprinkled them before the cell-door, which would always announce his coming.

Everything was now ready to begin the work; so, about the latter part of October [1863] they began to bore. All were busy—one making a rope-ladder, by tearing and twisting up strips of bed-ticking, another making bowie knives, and another twisting up towels. They labored perseveringly for several days, and, after boring through nine inches of cement, and nine thicknesses of brick placed edgewise, they began to wonder when they should reach the soft earth. Suddenly a brick fell through. What could this mean? What infernal chamber had they reached? It was immediately entered; and, to their great astonishment and joy, it proved to be an air-chamber extending the whole length of the row of cells. Here was an unexpected interposition in their favor. Hitherto they had been obliged to conceal their rubbish in their bed-tickings, each day burning a proportionate quantity of straw. Now they had room enough for all they could dig. They at once commenced to tunnel at right angles with this air-chamber, to get through the foundation; and day after day they bored—day after day the blocks of granite were removed—and still the work before them seemed interminable.

After twenty-three days of unremitting labor, and getting through a granite wall of six feet in thickness, they reached the soil. They tunnelled up for some distance, and light began to shine. How glorious was that light! It announced the fulfillment of their labors; and if Providence would only continue its favor, they would soon be free. This was the morning of the 26th day of November, 1863. The subsequent night, at twelve o'clock, was determined on as the hour at which they would attempt their liberty. Each moment that intervened was filled with dreadful anxiety and suspense, and each time the guard entered increased their apprehensions. The General says that he had prayed for rain; but the morning of the 27th dawned bright and beautiful. The evening came, and clouds began to gather. How they prayed for them to increase! If rain should only begin, their chances of detection would be greatly lessened. While these thoughts were passing through their minds, the keeper entered with a letter for General Morgan. He opened it, and what was his surprise—and I may say, wonder—to find it from a poor Irish woman of his acquaintance, in Kentucky, commencing: "My dear Ginral—I feel certain you are going to try to git out of prison; but, for your sake, don't you try it, my dear Ginral. You will only be taken prisoner again, and made to suffer more than you do now."

The letter then went on to speak of his kindness to the poor when he lived at Lexington, and concluded by again exhorting him to trust in God, and wait his time. What could this mean? No human being on the outside had been informed of his intention to escape; and yet, just as all things were ready for him to make the attempt, here comes a letter from Winchester, Kentucky, advising him not to "try it." This letter had passed through the examining office of General Mason, and then through the hands of the lower officials. What if it should excite their suspicion, and cause them to exercise an increased vigilance? The situation, however, was desperate. Their fate could not be much worse, and they resolved to go. Nothing now remained to be done but for the General and Colonel Dick Morgan to change cells. The hour approached for them to be locked up. They changed coats, and each stood at the other's cell door with his back exposed, and pretended to be engaged in making up their beds. As the turnkey entered, they "turned in," and pulled their doors shut.

Six, eight, ten o'clock came. How each pulse throbbed as they quietly awaited the approach of twelve! It came—the sentinel passed his round—all well. After waiting a few moments to see if he intended to slip back, the signal was given. All quietly slipped down into the air-chamber, first stuffing their flannel-shirts, and placing them in bed as they were accustomed to lie. As they moved quietly along through the dark recess to the terminus where they were to emerge from the earth, the General prepared to light a match. As the lurid glare fell upon their countenances, a scene was presented which can never be forgotten. There were crouched seven brave men who had resolved to be free. They were armed with bowie knives made out of case-knives. Life, in their condition, was scarcely to be desired, and the moment for the desperate chance had arrived. Suppose, as they emerged from the ground, that the dog should give the alarm—they could but die.

But few moments were spent in this kind of apprehension. The hour had arrived. . . . Fortunately—yes, providentially—the night had suddenly grown dark and rainy, the dogs had retired to their kennels, and the sentinels had taken refuge under shelter. The inner wall, by the aid of the rope-ladder, was soon scaled, and now the outer one had to be attempted. Captain Taylor (who, by the way, is a nephew of Old Zach), being a very active man, by the assistance of his comrades reached the top of the gate, and was enabled to get the rope over the wall. When the top was gained, they found a rope extending all around, which the General immediately cut, as he suspected that it might lead into the Warden's room. This turned out to be correct. They then entered the sentry-box on the wall and changed their clothes, and let themselves down the wall. In sliding down, the General skinned his hand very badly, and all were more or less bruised. Once down, they separated—Taylor and Shelton going one way, Hokersmith, Bennett, and McGee another, and General Morgan and Captain Hines proceeding immediately towards the depot.

The General had, by paying fifteen dollars in gold, succeeded in obtaining a paper which informed him of the schedule time of the different roads. The clock struck one, and he knew, by hurrying, he could reach the down-train for Cincinnati. He got there just as the train was moving off. He at once looked around to see if there were any soldiers on board, and espying a Union officer, he boldly walked up and took a seat beside him. He remarked to him, that "as the night was damp and chilly, perhaps he would join him in a drink." He did so, and the party soon became very agreeable to each other. The cars, in crossing the Scioto, have to pass within a short distance of the Penitentiary. As they passed, the officer remarked: "There's the hotel at which Morgan and his officers are spending their leisure." "Yes," replied the General, "and I sincerely hope he will make up his mind to board there during the balance of the war, for he is a great nuisance." When the train reached Xenia, it was detained by some accident more than an hour. Imagine his anxiety, as soldier after soldier would pass through the train, for fear that when the sentinel passed his round at two o'clock their absence might be discovered.

The train was due in Cincinnati at six o'clock. This was the hour at which they were turned out of their cells, and, of course, their escape would be then discovered. In a few moments after it would be known all over the country. The train, having been detained at Xenia, was running very rapidly to make up the time. It was already past six o'clock. The General said to Captain Hines: "It's after six o'clock; if we go to the depot, we are dead men. Now or never." They went to the rear, and put on the brakes. "Jump, Hines!" Off he went, and fell heels over head in the mud. Another severe turn of the brakes, and the General jumped. He was more successful, and lighted on his feet. There were some soldiers near, who remarked, "What in h—l do you mean by jumping off the cars here?" The General replied: "What in the d—l is the use of my going into town when I live here? And, besides, what business is it of yours?"

They went immediately to the river. They found a skiff, but no oars. Soon a little boy came over, and appeared to be waiting.

"What are you waiting for?" said the General.

"I am waiting for my load."

"What is the price of a load?"

"Two dollars."

"Well, as we are tired and hungry, we will give you the two dollars, and you can put us over."

So over he took them.

"Where does Miss —— live?"

"Just a short distance from here."

"Will you show me her house?"

"Yes, sir."

The house was reached, a fine breakfast was soon obtained, money and a horse furnished, a good woman's prayer bestowed, and off he went. From there, forward through Kentucky, everybody vied with each other as to who should show him the most attention—even to the Negroes; and young ladies of refinement begged the honor to cook his meals.

He remained in Kentucky some days, feeling perfectly safe, and sending into Louisville for many little things he wanted. Went to Bardstown, and found a Federal regiment had just arrived there, looking for him. Remained here and about for three or four days, and then struck out for Dixie; sometimes disguising himself as a Government cattle-contractor, and buying a large lot of cattle; at other times a quartermaster, until he got to the Tennessee River. Here he found all means of transportation destroyed, and the bank strongly guarded; but with the assistance of about thirty others, who had recognized him, and joined him in spite of his remonstrances, he succeeded in making a raft, and he and Captain Hines crossed over. His escort, with heroic self-sacrifice, refused to cross until he was safely over. He then hired a Negro to get his horse over, paying him twenty dollars for it. The river was so high that the horse came near drowning, and after more than

295

one hour's struggling with the stream, was pulled out so exhausted as scarcely to be able to stand.

The General threw a blanket on him and commenced to walk him, when suddenly, he says, he was seized with a presentiment that he would be attacked, and remarking to Captain Hines, "We shall be attacked in twenty minutes," commenced saddling his horse. He had hardly tied his girth when "Bang! Bang!" went the Minie balls. He bounced his horse, and the noble animal, appearing to be inspired with new vigor, bounded off like a deer up the mountain. The last he saw of his poor fellows on the opposite side, they were disappearing up the river bank, fired upon by a whole regiment of Yankees. By this time it was dark, and also raining. He knew that a perfect cordon of pickets would surround the foot of the mountain, and if he remained there until morning he would be lost. So he determined to run the gantlet at once, and commenced to descend. As he neared the foot, leading his horse, he came almost in personal contact with a picket. His first impulse was to kill him, but finding him asleep, he determined to let him sleep on. He made his way to the house of a Union man that he knew lived near there, and went up and passed himself off as Captain Quartermaster of Hunt's regiment, who was on his way to Athens, Tennessee, to procure supplies of sugar and coffee for the Union people of the country. The lady, who appeared to be asleep while this interview was taking place with her husband, at the mention of sugar and coffee, jumped out of bed in her night-clothes, and said: "Thank God for that; for we ain't seen any rale coffee up here for God knows how long!" She was so delighted at the prospect, that she made up a fire and cooked them a good supper. Supper being over, the General remarked that he understood that some rebels had "tried to cross the river this afternoon."

"Yes," said the woman "but our men killed some on um, and driv the rest back."

"Now," said the General, "I know that; but didn't some of them get over?"

"Yes," was her reply, "but they are on the mountain, and cannot get down without being killed, as every road is stopped up."

He then said to her: "It is very important for me to get to Athens by to-morrow night, or I may lose that sugar and coffee; and I am afraid to go down any of these roads for fear my own men will kill me."

The fear of losing that sugar and coffee brought her again to an accommodating mood, and she replied: "Why, Paul, can't you show the Captain through our farm, that road down by the field?" The General says: "Of course, Paul, you can do it; and as the night is very cold, I will give you ten dollars in gold to help you along." The gold, and the prospect of sugar and coffee, were too much for any poor man's nerves, and he yielded, and getting on a horse, he took them seven miles to the big road.

From this time forward he had a series of adventures and escapes, all very wonderful, until he got near another river in Tennessee, when he resolved to go up to a house and find the way. Hines went to the house, while the General stood in the road. Hearing a body of cavalry come dashing up behind him, he quietly slipped to one side of the road, and it passed by without observing him. They went travelling after Hines, and, poor fellow! he has not been heard of since. How sad to think that he should be either captured or killed after so many brave efforts, not only in his own behalf, but also in that of the General; for the General says that it is owing chiefly to Hines's enterprise and skill that they made their escape.

When he arrived at the river referred to above, he tried to get over, intending to stop that night with a good Southern man on the other side. He could not get over, and had to stop at the house of a Union man. The next morning he went to the house that he had sought the night previous, and found the track of the Yankees scarcely cold. They had been there all night, expecting that he would come there, and had murdered everybody who had attempted to reach the house, without hailing them. In pursuing this brutal course, they had killed three young men, neighbors of this gentleman, and went away, leaving their dead bodies on the ground.

After he had crossed Okey's River, and got down into middle Tennessee, he found it almost impossible to avoid recognition. At one time he passed some poor women, and one of them commenced clapping her hands, and said, "O! I know who that is! I know who that is!" but, catching herself, she stopped short, and passed on with her companions.

The General says that his escape was made entirely without assistance from any one on the outside, and, so far as he knows, also without their knowledge of his intention; that the announcement of his arrival in Toronto was one of those fortuitous coincidences that cannot be accounted for; that it assisted him materially, no doubt. In fact, he says that his "wife's prayers" saved him, and, as this is the most agreeable way of explaining it, he is determined to believe it.

—FRANK MOORE, ed.
Anecdotes, Poetry and Incidents of the War:
North and South, 1860-1865

*

The Tailor's Joke

*

AMONG [Captain Willard Worcester] Glazier's fellow-prisoners [at the Libby Prison Hospital in November, 1863] was a certain Major Halsted. He was . . . prior to entering the army . . . a tailor. . . . Some of the little wits of the prison . . . were in the habit of jokingly asking him to repair their old and dilapidated clothes.

*   *   *   *   *

It happened . . . that one day the rebel surgeon accidentally tore his coat across the breast, and turning to Major H. said, he would give him a bottle of wine if he would repair it. "Yes, sir," said the Major, "if you will furnish me with a needle, thread, and a few other indispensables, I will take the whole suit and make it look very different." He added, "The fact is, I would rather do anything than rust in idleness in this d——d prison." Finding that he spoke seriously, and as if it were an ordinary business, the Confederate sawbones, who had a lively appreciation of Yankee handicraft, accepted the proposition, and all next day the Major was hard at work clipping and scouring and pressing the surgeon's uniform, every now and then the owner thereof passing by and smiling approval; and it was remarked that his face wore that complacent expression common to all good men when they have furnished employment for idle hands—and it is not going to cost them anything.

The same evening, however, when the work, so neatly done, was finished, the Major very quietly slipped it upon his own dignified person, and taking with him a fellow-prisoner as "hospital steward," coolly walked past the guard, remarking, to the great consternation of that personage, "My friend, there are unmistakable indications of *cerebro-spinal meningitis* in your eyes. Come over to the hospital as soon as you are relieved, and I will see what can be done for you," walked out into the street, and neither he nor the "hospital steward" was heard of again until they reached the Federal lines.

—JOHN ALGERNON OWENS

*

Quantrell Gets Even

---

*

A FEW MONTHS following the Lawrence [Kansas] "atrocity" [of Quantrell and his band on August 21, 1863] we were in the vicinity of Fort Webster [Missouri] when Quantrell got news that Adjutant General Curtis would pass that way the next day with a band of musicians, troubadours, cooks, flunkeys and other "Northern army accessories" on his way to Independence, and he forthwith made ready to take possession of the caravan. We came upon them about six miles from Fort Webster, and after a little skirmish, overpowered and captured them.

Curtis was literally scared out of his wits and piteously begged Quantrell to spare his life.

"Would you dare ask mercy of me?" asked Quantrell, as he took from his pocket a paper and, unfolding it, showed Curtis his own order to kill Quantrell's men wherever and whenever they could be found. "Is not that your order?" shrieked Quantrell.

"I was forced to issue the order," whined the craven-hearted wretch. "It was an order from headquarters."

"It is no such thing," said Quantrell. "Had it been from the Federal government, it would have been so worded. This is your infamous work, Curtis, and you've got to answer to me for it right here and now. I am going to kill you, sir, and I advise you not to appear before your maker with a lie on your lips. Now, sir; is not this your original order?"

Curtis hung his head for a moment, as if in prayer, and seeing death was inevitable, he said, with a sigh: "Yes, it is my work."

"And you wanted it obeyed, of course?"

"Yes."

"Would you have practiced the doctrine you preached, had the opportunity offered?"

299

"Yes, such are the fortunes of war."

"And you expect mercy at my hands?"

"No, nothing but death."

He was not disappointed.

With Curtis and his band of merrymakers was a Mr. O'Neill, an artist on *Leslie's Magazine.* He had in his possession an unfinished picture of some hypothetical battle, in which were portrayed Rebels in full flight before the gallant boys in blue, who were mowing them down in merciless abundance with rifles, pistols, swords and bayonets. Oh, our boys in gray were certainly having a tough time in that "Battle Scene." Poor O'Neill. It was his own Waterloo he had so graphically portrayed for the edification of the foulest periodical of that day and generation.

But *Leslie's* was not cheated out of the picture. Quantrell sent it in with these memorable words written in his own bold hand:

"O'Neill's last contribution to *Leslie's,* sent in by Quantrell, with regrets that the artist's physical condition was such that he could not attend to the matter in person."

I have no doubt that the picture is now somewhere in the old junk heaps of this illustrious periodical, and I sincerely trust that *Leslie's* has, by this time, come to look on the South as a considerable part of the Federal government.

Poor troubadours, they had twanged the last chord for the merriment of Northern audiences. Poor cooks, they had baked their last pone of bread for camp or festal board. Poor soldiers, they had for the last time tented on the old camp ground. Poor Curtis, he had lost his head—one of his most valuable possessions—also a magnificent silk banner, presented him by the worthy ladies of Leavenworth, Kansas.

—Captain Kit Dalton

*

A Ghost of a Chance

---

*

IN 1863, the Federal Cavalry were retiring from Culpeper Courthouse, marching in column. General [Thomas L.] Rosser was following them, and General "Fitz" Lee was expected to strike their flank by moving from the direction of Stevensburg. Rosser's advance regiment was the Twelfth Virginia Cavalry, and Company B was in front. . . . The dust raised by both parties was so great that the Federals did not recognize the enemy before the order to charge was given, and Company B had dashed right into the midst of them. . . .

The Federals soon perceived that Company B was far ahead of its support. Accordingly, they formed squadrons, charged and drove the company back by their overwhelming numbers.

All the men succeeded in getting back safely to the main column except Private B. C. Washington. The account of his capture is so graphic that it had better be told in his own words:

Ditches form a large part of the native products of Culpeper County. I thought, on this occasion, the crop seemed the largest I had ever seen—at least ten per acre. Most of our fellows cleared the ditches in true fox-hunter style, leaving the hounds behind them. But my horse was a Yankee horse, captured by me a few days before at the "Jack's Shop" fight from one Major McEwing, of [Hugh J.] Kilpatrick's staff, and this horse of Northern extraction "put up a job" on me by refusing the ditch, and, veering to the right, started on a tour of discovery for the end of the ditch. By this time some half-dozen Yankees were after me at full speed, yelling and firing. A bullet struck my gallant steed, which, aided by a tremendous effort on my part, accelerated a leap at the ditch. He cleared it but landed in a bog with his head under his knees and over I went into the mud. A similar performance was enacted by several of the pursuers, most of them being unhorsed, and all demanding a complete and unconditional surrender to each individually.

I don't like to boast, but I must say that this surrender of mine is a thing over which I have had moments of great inward pride. It is an easy thing to shine out in the supreme hour of victory, and ride with ten fellows after one retreating Yankee, yelling out, "Give him the [devil]," but when the supreme hour is reversed, and ten Yanks are after you, in the situation just described, yelling "Surren-dar!" at the top of their voices, requiring you to hand your pistol to each of them individually, each one with pistols pointed so straight at one's head that if he had ten eyes he could have seen down the barrels of each of them—I say, a situation like this develops a man; it is a crucial test of what is in him, and it developed my military talents in the twinkling of an eye. And I now make the following claim: I am the champion surrenderer in America, if not in the world, for

*I surrendered, under the afore-described circumstances, to not less than
five armed Yankees.*

He was taken to the North, back of the Rappahannock, which river
[General George G.] Meade had made his line of defense. Private Washington was placed with a number of other prisoners, and a strong guard
surrounded them. He had been a captive in a Yankee prison in the
early part of the war, having been captured at Kernstown while attempting to carry off his wounded brother. The recollection of a six-
months' sojourn in a Yankee prison naturally made him rather depressed
on this occasion. He consequently determined to make his escape if there
was a ghost of a chance shown him. The chance came. The guard was
ordered to remove the prisoners farther back from the river. The
prisoners were formed in column and marched off.

A large body of Yankee troops were encamped on the plain, and
they gathered in crowds to get a sight of the rebels as they were marched
off. It was about an hour after sunset, and as the column of prisoners
marched along between the two walls of spectators, Washington quietly
stepped out of the column of prisoners and joined the *spectators*. The
darkness and the crowd helped him, his change of base was unobserved,
and after watching the line pass by, he concluded that it would probably
be conducive to his health to take a little stroll down to the banks of
the lovely Rappahannock. Accordingly he took off his *gray* jacket (possibly being rather warmed up by the proximity of so many men), rolled
it up in a bundle, tucked it under his arm, and having on a pair of blue
pantaloons, he was not molested in his quiet stroll to the river. The river
was not "wadeable," as he found by trial, and the only way to reach his
Southern friends was by way of the railroad bridge.

Naturally Major General Meade had placed a guard at the bridge,
for at sunset this astute general had removed his "head (?) quarters
from the saddle," and desired rest with *security*. Private Washington
observed the sentinel, and examined the surroundings for a long time before a plan—a daring plan—occurred to him. He walked down the
bank to the front of the abutment, climbed up it, and when he reached
the wooden streets, climbed out on them, and up on to the bridge to
the south of the sentinel. Gayly he walked the bridge, almost ready to
whistle, he felt so joyous. But alas! As he neared the southern end,
out against the sky he saw the form of *another sentinel!* He watched that
sentinel a long time, saw no chance of surprising him, and knew that

when *daylight* came, he would be discovered and ingloriously led back to prison.

After gazing at that sentinel as long, as intently, and as *silently* as a lover gazes at his sweetheart, he heard a tramp, tramp, tramp *behind* him. The guard was coming to relieve the sentinel. Quick as lightning an idea strikes him. He gets behind an upright beam, waits till the last man passes, falls in, in the rear, and, for the time being, becomes a Yankee soldier. The real rear man looked around, seemed to study awhile how there could be *two last* men in a column, gave it up as an insoluble problem, and marched on without saying a word. When the south end of the bridge was reached, the officer ordered his men in line to be counted. It occurred to Private Washington that the term of his enlistment in the Yankee army had better cease. So, taking advantage of the darkness, he gradually sidled off, made his way off the bridge, took a bee-line south as gay as any lark *you* ever saw. Alas! alas! He had not proceeded far before his heart sank into his boots again, and he felt that some Yankee prison must have marked him for its own, for right in front he saw a line of sentinels.

He got down on the ground and crawled up as near as he dared, to a point where two adjacent sentinels joined each other in their beat backward and forward. The only chance was to get through the line before daybreak, for then he certainly would be discovered; and yet he lay on the ground watching these walking sentinels for fully an hour, afraid to try to cross the path lest he lose all he had so far gained. At last, growing desperate, he waited till the two sentinels met each other, turned back to back, and walked apart. Then he rose, stepped quickly and lightly across the path, and when the sentinels turned again, Washington was twenty yards *south* of their line, and flat on the ground. He soon crawled out of all danger from the sentinels, arose and walked off rapidly to find some Confederate camp.

After walking a mile or two he came in sight of a campfire, around which some soldiers were reclining, but look as hard as he could, for the life of him he could not make out whether the soldiers were Yankees or Confederates. For a long, long time he stood near, waiting for something to indicate to what side the soldiers belonged. At last one fellow arose, threw some wood on the fire, and said, "When the sun rises I hope there won't be a —— Yankee this side of the Rappahannock!" The word "Yankee" was enough for Washington. With a joyous shout he rushed up, and was prepared to hug everybody around the fire.

He told his story, and it seemed so wonderful that a detachment

303

was sent with him to General J. E. B. Stuart's headquarters. Washington related the mode of his escape to General Stuart, and the latter was so much struck with the boldness displayed, that he renewed a recommendation sent to army headquarters, just after the "Jack's Shop" fight, that Private Washington be made a lieutenant in the Provisional army of the Confederate States, for "gallant and meritorious conduct on the field." This was done, and Washington served the rest of the war as an officer in the company in which he had been private.

—J. S. B.

"A Yankee cheese box on a raft" they named our little boat,
I'm sure no better box of cheese was ever set afloat;
For catching rats we bait with cheese, for rebels do the same,
And if they'll only take the bait we'll surely catch our game.
—"THE MERRIMAC AND MONITOR"

23. RUSES AND STRATAGEMS

Porter's "Black Terror"

*

THE CONFEDERATE RAM *Webb* joined the *Queen of the West* from Alexandria, and the two vessels, well manned and armed, proceeded in search of the *Indianola,* came up with her at Davis' plantation, rammed her, and she ran into shoal water and sank, February 24, 1863.

We heard of the disaster a few hours after, and all my calculations for stopping the enemy's supplies were for the time frustrated; but I took a philosophical view of the matter as one of the episodes of the war. However, it was necessary to try and prevent the rebels from raising the *Indianola,* and, as I was not ready to go down the river myself, as it would interfere with an important military movement, I hit upon a cheap expedient, which worked very well.

I set the whole squadron at work and made a raft of logs, three hundred feet long, with sides to it, two huge wheel-houses and a formidable log casemate, from the port-holes of which appeared sundry wooden guns. Two old boats hung from davits fitted to the "ironclad," and two smoke-stacks made of hogsheads completed the illusion; and on her wheel-houses was painted the following: "Deluded Rebels, Cave In!" An American flag was hoisted aft, and a banner emblazoned with skull and cross-bones ornamented the bow.

When this craft was completed, she resembled at a little distance the ram *Lafayette,* which had just arrived from St. Louis.

The mock ram was furnished with a big iron pot inside each smoke-stack, in which was tar and oakum to raise a black smoke, and at midnight she was towed down close to the water-batteries of Vicksburg and sent adrift.

It did not take the Vicksburg sentinels long to discover the formidable monster that was making its way down the river. The batteries opened on her with vigor, and continued the fire until she had passed beyond the range of their guns.

The Vicksburgers had greatly exulted over the capture of the *Queen of the West,* and the *Indianola*; the local press teemed with accounts of the daring of the captors, and flattered themselves that, with the *Indianola* and *Queen of the West* in their possession, they would be able to drive the Union navy out of the Mississippi. What was their astonishment to see this huge ironclad pass the batteries, apparently unharmed, and not even taking the trouble to fire a gun!

Some of our soldiers had gone down to the point below Vicksburg to see the fun, and just before reaching Warrenton the mock monitor caught the eddy and turned toward the bank where these men were gathered.

The soldiers spent several hours in trying to shove the dummy off into the stream, when daylight overtook them in the midst of their work, and the *Queen of the West,* with the Confederate flag flying, was seen coming up the river and stopping at Warrenton.

As we afterward learned, she came up for pumps, etc., to raise the *Indianola.*

In the meanwhile the military authorities in Vicksburg had sent couriers down to Joe Davis' plantation to inform the people on board the *Webb* that a monster ironclad had passed the batteries and would soon be upon them. The crew of the *Webb* were busy in trying to remove the guns from their prize, and, when they heard the news, determined to blow her up.

Just after the *Queen of the West* made the Warrenton landing the soldiers succeeded in towing the mock ironclad into the stream, and she drifted rapidly down upon the rebel prize, whose crew never stopped to deliberate, but cut their fasts and proceeded down the river. Their steam was low, and for a time the mock ironclad drifted almost as fast as the *Queen of the West;* but at length the latter left her formidable pursuer far behind.

The *Queen of the West* arrived at the point where the *Indianola* was sunk just as the people on board the *Webb* were preparing to blow her up, bringing the news that the "great ironclad" was close behind. So the *Webb* cast off and, with her consort, made all speed down the river.

The *Webb* had been so greatly injured in ramming the *Indianola* that she had to go to Shreveport for repairs, and the *Queen of the West* was shortly after recaptured and destroyed.

* * * * *

The Vicksburg people were furious at the trick we played them, and the newspapers reviled their military authorities for not being able to distinguish an old raft from a monster ironclad! They were consoled, however, in a day or two when the news of the destruction of the *Mississippi* reached Vicksburg.

—ADMIRAL DAVID D. PORTER

*

All's Fair with Forrest

---

*

WHEN [General Nathan Bedford] Forrest, with about twelve hundred men, set out in pursuit of [Colonel Abel D.] Streight [in the spring of 1863], he was more than a day behind him. Streight had several hundred more men in the saddle than Forrest, and being far in advance could replace a broken-down horse by a fresh one from the farms through which his route lay, while Forrest, when he lost a horse, lost a soldier, too; for no good horses were left for him. After a hot pursuit of five days and nights, during which he had lost two-thirds of his forces from broken-down horses, he overhauled his enemy and brought him to a parley. This conference took place in sight of a cut-off in the mountain road, Captain Morton and his horse artillery, which had been so long with Forrest, passing in sight along the road till they came to the cut-off, into which they would turn, re-entering the road out of view, so that it seemed that a continuous stream of artillery was passing by. Forrest had so arranged that he stood with his back to the guns while Streight was facing them.

Forrest, in his characteristic way, described the scene to me. He said, "I seen him all the time he was talking, looking over my shoulder and counting the guns. Presently he said: 'Name of God! How many guns have you got? There's fifteen I've counted already!' Turning my head that way, I said, 'I reckon that's all that has kept up.' Then he said, 'I won't surrender till you tell me how many men you've got.' I said, 'I've got enough to whip you out of your boots.' To which he said, 'I won't surrender.' I turned to my bugler and said, 'Sound to mount!' Then he cried out 'I'll surrender!' I told him, 'Stack your arms right along there, Colonel, and march your men away down that hollow.'

"When this was done," continued Forrest, "I ordered my men to come forward and take possession of the arms. When Streight saw they were barely four hundred, he did rear! demanded to have his arms back and that we should fight it out. I just laughed at him and patted him on the shoulder, and said, 'Ah, Colonel, all is fair in love and war, you know.' "

—GENERAL DABNEY HERNDON MAURY

*

Fitzhugh Lee and Averell Exchange Notes

*

IT WAS WHILE LEADING a raiding party, that Fitzhugh Lee, nephew of the great general and one of Stuart's division commanders, fell upon a Pennsylvania regiment near Leedstown and killed, wounded or captured about a hundred men. Learning that the troops belonged to the brigade of an old West Point classmate, General [William W.] Averell, the successful trooper left this note behind him:

DEAR AVERELL:

I wish you would put up your sword, leave my State, and go home. You ride a good horse. I ride a better. Yours can beat mine running. Send me over a bag of coffee.

FITZ

General Averell disliked the reference to the speed of his horse and determined to pay his old classmate a visit. On March 17 [1863], he led a cavalry column of five regiments to the Rappahannock at Kelly's ford, and crossed in the teeth of a vicious fire from the enemy's sharp-shooters, of whom twenty-five were captured. The remnant of the Confederate skirmishers fled, to warn Fitzhugh Lee of his impending danger. Averell's men followed in hot pursuit. Lee, in no wise daunted, comes out to meet them. The adversaries meet a little more than a mile from the ford, and Lee, little knowing that he is greatly outnumbered, leads a squadron against the Federals, a large number of whom have dismounted and aligned themselves behind a stone wall. This assault is easily repulsed, but is followed up by a second; the Third Virginia, a famous cavalry command, sweeps across the field and down upon the stone wall which checks its progress. Over that wall the horses cannot leap, and as the squadron halts in momentary confusion, the First Rhode Island cavalry plunges fiercely in upon its flank, throwing it into a rout. Its commander, cut off from his men and surrounded, is captured. Scarce a hundred troopers of the Virginia command return to place themselves under Lee's orders; the rest have been killed, wounded or hopelessly dispersed.

The situation now becomes desperate for the Confederates. Retreating by a narrow road they are exposed to the murderous artillery fire of their assailants, who thus have added to their advantage in numbers the advantage of position. Lee determines to make one fierce effort to avert the disaster which threatens him. He has but three or four hundred men left. Of these he dismounts about two hundred and posts them behind an adjacent wall; his artillery he stations in a commanding position, and placing himself at the head of a hundred mounted men—the shattered remnant of the Third Virginia—he charges furiously upon his enemy's line. But once more failure only attends his efforts. A high wooden fence, behind which a Union regiment lies in ambush, breaks the fury of the charge, and a flank attack by a Pennsylvania regiment sends the assailants back pell-mell upon their supports. The Federals follow close, but so hot a fire is poured upon them from the Confederate artillery and foot-soldiers, that their advance is checked.

Now is Averell's opportunity. Nothing would be easier for him with his overpowering numbers than to ride over and sweep from his path the slender body of men which disputes his further progress. But so gallant has been Lee's attitude, so fearless and dashing the repeated assaults of the Confederates, that Averell never for a moment suspects how weak, numerically, is the enemy with whom he has to do. Night is fast coming on. He is far away from Hooker's army and in a country thick with Confederates. Accordingly he begins to withdraw his forces, greatly to the delight of Lee's troopers, who had begun to see annihilation staring them in the face. Some of the Federal soldiers are too severely wounded to be moved, so these are left behind in charge of a surgeon, to whom General Averell entrusted a sack of coffee and this note for General Lee:

DEAR FITZ:

Here's your coffee. Here's your call. How do you like it? How's that horse?

AVERELL

—WILLIS J. ABBOT

＊

General Wheeler's Leap

＊

THE CAVALRY FIGHT at Shelbyville [Tennessee] was the liveliest engagement which marked the retreat of Bragg's army from Tullahoma to Chattanooga in the summer of 1863. Inasmuch as the Confederates were finally driven from the field, the honors of the day rested with the Union troopers, although they stopped short of reaping the full success which was in their grasp as the result of the brilliant fighting they had done. The Southern troops, who for more than three hours, in the outskirts of Shelbyville, stood up before and held at bay a largely superior force of Federals were a forlorn hope numbering 1200 men, placed there and commanded by Major General Joseph Wheeler, in the desperate effort to protect from capture or destruction an immense wagon-train loaded with supplies invaluable to Bragg's army. While the fighting was going on, this immense train was filing across the narrow bridge which two miles from the battle-field spans Duck River, and was making its snail-like progress over the muddy and almost impassable road to Tullahoma.

*   *   *   *   *

. . . Wheeler, in command of all the cavalry operating in the department of which General Bragg was commander-in-chief, was directed to withdraw his troops south of Duck River by way of Shelbyville, holding off the Federal advance until the wagon-trains were across, when, by destroying the bridge, they would be safe from pursuit.

*   *   *   *   *

. . . At last, about five o'clock [June 27], taking advantage of a momentary lull in the attack, General Wheeler, with the exception of Russell's Fourth Alabama Regiment, withdrew the troops and ordered them to retire as rapidly as possible to the bridge and cross the river; 200 of us were left under command of Colonel A. A. Russell, with orders to stay until they rode us down, in the hope that this catastrophe would be delayed long enough to permit General Wheeler to clear the bridge in our rear.

I did not understand this movement at the time, but have learned since from General Wheeler that it was only then that the last wagon had passed over Duck River, and he felt now that he could save, at least, a portion of his troops on the field by a rapid retreat. We were told, when we were beaten, to make our way, every man for himself as best he could. Before the Federal cavalry realized what had been done, he was gone at full speed, and, reaching the bridge, had the troops and artillery which accompanied him safe on the southern bank. . . .

. . . General Wheeler . . . was in the act of firing this structure when a member of General Forrest's staff, Major Rambaut, reported to him that Forrest, with two brigades, was within two miles of Shelbyville, and advancing rapidly to cross. Realizing the danger which threatened

311

Forrest, Wheeler, notwithstanding the Federals were in strong force in the suburbs of Shelbyville and advancing into town, taking with him two pieces of artillery and 500 men of Martin's division, with this officer, hastily recrossed to the north side in order to hold the bridge and save Forrest from disaster.

The guns were hastily thrown into position, but the charges had scarcely been rammed home when the Union troops came in full sweep down the main street. When within a few paces of the muzzle of the guns they were discharged, inflicting, however, insignificant loss. With their small force of 500 men Generals Wheeler and Martin stood up as best they could under the pressure of this charge. They held their ground manfully as the cavalry rode through and over them, sabring the cannoneers from the guns, of which they took possession, and then passed on and secured the bridge, leaving the two Confederate generals and their troops well in the rear. The bridge had become blocked by one of the caissons, which had been overturned, and now, thinking they had them in a trap, the Union forces formed a line of battle parallel with the bank of Duck River and across the entrance to the bridge.

The idea of surrendering himself and his command had not entered the mind of General Wheeler. . . . He now shouted to his men that they must cut their way through and attempt to escape by swimming the river. With General Martin by his side, sabres in hand, they led the charge, which, made in such desperate mood, parted the Federals in their front as they rode through. Without a moment's hesitation, and without considering the distance from the top of the river-bank, which was here precipitous, to the water-level, these gallant soldiers followed their invincible leader and plunged at full speed sheer fifteen feet down into the sweeping current.

They struck the water with such velocity that horses and riders disappeared, some of them to rise no more. The Union troopers rushed to the water's edge and fired at the men and animals struggling in the river, killing or wounding and drowning a number. Holding to his horse's mane, General Wheeler took the precaution to shield himself as much as possible behind the body of the animal, and, although fired at repeatedly, he escaped injury and safely reached the opposite shore. Some forty or fifty were said to have perished in this desperate attempt. "Fighting Joe Wheeler" never did a more heroic and generous deed than when he risked all to save Forrest from disaster.

—JOHN A. WYETH

312

The explosion of a shell was frequently followed by the crack of a joke, and a bullet or a bayonet produced more fun than fear; yet neither were ever so close that they left no time for a prayer.

—WASHINGTON DAVIS

24. STRANGE THINGS HAPPEN IN THE ARMY

Sheridan and the Two Women Soldiers

*

IN JANUARY, 1863, when my division had settled quietly down in its camp south of Murfreesboro [Tennessee], Colonel [Joseph] Conrad, of the Fifteenth Missouri, informed me that . . . he had been mortified greatly by the conduct of *the two females belonging to the detachment and division train at my headquarters.* These women, he said, had given much annoyance by getting drunk, and to some extent demoralizing his men. To say that I was astonished at his statement would be a mild way of putting it, and had I not known him to be a most upright man and of sound sense, I should have doubted not only his veracity, but his sanity. Inquiring who they were and for further details, I was informed that there certainly were in the command two females, that in some mysterious manner had attached themselves to the service as soldiers; that one, an East Tennessee woman, was a teamster in the division wagon-train and the other a private soldier in a cavalry company temporarily attached to my headquarters for escort duty. While out on the foraging expedition these Amazons had secured a supply of "apple-jack" by some means, got very drunk, and on the return had fallen into Stones River and been nearly drowned. After they ad been fished from the water, in the process of resuscitation their sex was disclosed, though up to this time it appeared to be known only to each other.

The story was straight and the circumstance clear, so, convinced of Conrad's continued sanity, I directed the provost-marshal to bring in arrest to my headquarters the two disturbers of Conrad's peace of mind. After some little search the East Tennessee woman was found in camp, somewhat the worse for the experiences of the day before, but awaiting her fate contentedly smoking a cob-pipe. She was brought to me, and put in duress under charge of the division surgeon until her companion could be secured. To the doctor she related that the year before she had "refugeed" from East Tennessee, and on arriving in Louisville assumed men's apparel and sought and obtained employment as a teamster in the quartermaster's department. Her features were very large, and so coarse and masculine was her general appearance that she would readily have passed as a man, and in her case the deception was no doubt easily practiced. Next day the "she dragoon" was caught, and proved to be a rather prepossessing young woman, and though necessarily bronzed and hardened by exposure, I doubt if, even with these marks of campaigning, she could have deceived as readily as did her companion. How the two got acquainted I never learned, and though they had joined the army independently of each other, yet an intimacy had sprung up between them long before the mishaps of the foraging expedition. They both were forwarded to army headquarters, and, when provided with clothing suited to their sex, sent back to Nashville, and thence beyond our lines to Louisville.

—General Philip H. Sheridan

*

A Poetic "Special Order"

*

ONE DAY [in March, 1863, at Beaufort, South Carolina,] came in the *Arago,* and in her, certain pleasant-voiced ladies, on a tour of pleasure. Now the sweet smile of woman is a rarity in the Department of the South. The Secretary of War has forbidden her presence here, except as teacher to the colored children. Only a very few of the officers have their families here. Therefore a strange face, and what is more a young face, and what is more a pretty face, such a phenomenon was sure to create some stir among the staff. Straightway plots were laid against this celestial visitor—or rather *for* her; and the Adjutant General of the Department conceived the happy idea of conferring upon her a staff appointment, with what views you will perceive if you read the following "special order," couched in proper military phrase:

HEADQUARTERS, DEPT. OF THE SOUTH,
Hilton Head, S.C., March 25, 1863

SPECIAL ORDERS, }
  A. No. 1. }

    ¶I. With her charming looks
        And all her graces,
     Miss Mary Brooks,
       Whose lovely face is
 The sweetest thing we have seen down here
On these desolate Islands for more than a year,
    Is hereby appointed an extra Aide
       On the Staff of the General Commanding,
   With a Captain of Cavalry's strap and grade,
    And with this most definite understanding:

    ¶II. That Captain Mary,
      Gay and airy,

At nine each day, until further orders,
 To Colonel Halpine shall report
For special duty at these Headquarters:
  And Captain Mary,
  (Bless the fairy!)
Shall hold herself, upon all occasions,
  Prepared to ride
  At the Adjutant's side
And give him of flirting his regular rations;
  And she shan't vamoose
  With the younglings loose
Of the junior Staff, such as Hay and Skinner;
  But galloping onward, she shall sing,
  Like an everlasting lark on the wing—
And she shan't keep the Adjutant late for dinner.

¶III. The Chief Quartermaster of Department
 Will give Captain Mary a riding garment—
 A long, rich skirt of a comely hue,
 Shot silk, with just a suspicion of blue,
 A gipsy hat, with an ostrich feather,
 A veil to protect her against the weather,
 And delicate gauntlets of pale buff leather;
 Her saddle with silver shall all be studded,
 And her pony—a sorrel—it shall be blooded:
 Its shoes shall be silver, its bridle all ringing
 With bells that shall harmonize well with her singing,
  And thus Captain Mary,
  Gay, festive, and airy,
  Each morning shall ride
  At the Adjutant's side
 And hold herself ready, on all fit occasions,
 To give him of flirting his full army rations.
    BY COMMAND OF, ETC.

I am sorry to have to add that the Captain proved insubordinate, and retired from the service after some days because she did not receive at once the promotion which she felt herself to deserve.

       —CHARLES NORDHOFF

*

The Scriptural Sentinel

*

[IN MARCH, 1863] one of our captains was a quaint, impulsive, energetic officer, and good disciplinarian. A private named Hackett, in Company E [Eleventh Vermont Volunteers], was the most ungainly soldier in the regiment; he could not keep step with one marching by his side, or in front of him, and never learned the manual of arms. He should have remained at home and become a minister of the gospel. He was eccentric and had formerly been a Biblical student. He could recite Scripture from Genesis to Exodus.

The guard-house was located just inside the Fort [Lincoln, Washington, D.C.] entrance and a bridge spanned the moat to the entrance. Once, when Captain R. was Officer of the Day, it was his duty to inspect the guard at least once after midnight. Hackett was at Post Number One, near the gate-way of the Fort. It was a dark, rainy night, when Hackett heard Captain R. approach, and called out, "Who comes there?"

Captain R., being on one side of the bridge, stumbled and fell headlong into the moat; as he fell he exclaimed in a loud voice, "J——s C——t."

Hackett faced about and called out promptly, "Turn out the Apostles. J——s C——t is coming." Then the guard helped the Captain out of the moat.

—BREVET MAJOR CHARLES H. ANSON

317

The Origin of the Cartridge Box Badge

*

IT WAS . . . on [the] return march from Knoxville, that the incident occurred which gave the badge to the 15th army corps. . . .

On the march, the Loomis Brigade passed through a bivouac of the 11th army corps. It will be remembered that this corps with the 12th had come out from the Potomac army with General Hooker. It will also be remembered that the record of the 11th army corps in the Chancellorsville fight [May 1–5, 1863] had been an unfortunate one. Perhaps no stronger contrast could have been found in the army, than that presented by the Potomac boys, and the ragged, dirty, hungry 90th.

A soldier of the 90th—McGuffy, of Co. G—came straggling along by the headquarters of General [Daniel] Butterfield. He was thinly and poorly clad; one foot was partly covered by an old army shoe, and the other with an old blanket, tied on with strings, both feet cut and bleeding. He was plodding on, intent only upon overtaking his regiment, when he was halted by a sentinel in a clean uniform, paper collar and trim rig, who said: "Halt! what regiment is that?"

McG.—"The 90th Illinois—Irish Legion."

Sentinel—"What corps do you belong to?"

McG.—"Fifteenth."

Sentinel—"What's the badge of your corps?"

McG.—"Badge! What the blazes is that?"

Sentinel—"What do you wear to distinguish you from other troops? Our corps, the 11th, wears a crescent—a half moon—the 12th corps wears a star! What do you wear?"

McG. had halted, rested his chin upon the muzzle of his gun, and was taking a leisurely and contemptuous survey of the sleek and well-dressed soldiers that were gathering around. Looking up at his interlocutor he says:

"Yes, I know what ye mane now. Moon and stars! Be jabbers, ye needed them both to show ye the way back from Chancellorsville. Badge is it!" And then executing a "round about" and giving his cartridge box a slap, "That's the badge of the 15th corps, forty rounds of cartridge!"

The story reached the ears of General [John A.] Logan, the corps commander, who thinking it too good to be lost, adopted the "cartridge box with forty rounds," as the badge of the corps.

—GEORGE H. WOODRUFF

*

The Clothes-Line Telegraph

*

IN THE EARLY PART of 1863, when the Union army was encamped at Falmouth, and picketing the banks of the Rappahannock, the utmost tact and ingenuity were displayed, by the scouts and videttes, in gaining a knowledge of contemplated movements on either side; and here, as at various other times, the shrewdness of the African camp attendants was very remarkable.

One circumstance in particular shows how quick the race are in learning the art of communicating by signals.

There came into the Union lines a Negro from a farm on the other side of the river, known by the name of Dabney, who was found to possess a remarkably clear knowledge of the topography of the whole region; and he was employed as cook and body servant at headquarters. When he first saw our system of army telegraphs, the idea interested him intensely, and he begged the operators to explain the signs to him. They did so, and found that he could understand and remember the meaning of the various movements as well as any of his brethren of paler hue.

Not long after, his wife, who had come with him, expressed a great anxiety to be allowed to go over to the other side as servant to a "secesh woman," whom General Hooker was about sending over to her friends. The request was granted. Dabney's wife went across the Rappahannock, and in a few days was duly installed as laundress at the headquarters of a prominent rebel general. Dabney, her husband, on the north bank, was soon found to be wonderfully well informed as to all the rebel plans. Within an hour of the time that a movement of any kind was projected, or even discussed, among the rebel generals, Hooker knew all about it. He knew which corps was moving, or about to move, in what direction, how long they had been on the march, and in what force; and all this knowledge came through Dabney, and his reports always turned out to be true.

Yet Dabney was never absent, and never talked with the scouts, and seemed to be always taken up with his duties as cook and groom about headquarters.

How he obtained his information remained for some time a puzzle to the Union officers. At length, upon much solicitation, he unfolded his marvellous secret to one of our officers.

Taking him to a point where a clear view could be obtained of Fredericksburg, he pointed out a little cabin in the suburbs near the river bank, and asked him if he saw that clothes-line with clothes hanging on it to dry. "Well," said he, "that clothes-line tells me in half an hour just what goes on at Lee's headquarters. You see my wife over there; she washes for the officers, and cooks, and waits around, and as soon as she hears about any movement or anything going on, she comes down and moves the clothes on that line so I can understand it in a minute. That there gray shirt is Longstreet; and when she takes it off, it means he's gone down about Richmond. That white shirt means Hill; and when she moves it up to the west end of the line, Hill's corps has moved up stream. That red one is Stonewall. He's down on the right now, and if he moves, she will move that red shirt."

One morning Dabney came in and reported a movement over there. "But," says he, "it don't amount to any thing. They're just making believe."

An officer went out to look at the clothes-line telegraph through his field-glass. There had been quite a shifting over there among the army flannels. "But how do you know but there is something in it?"

"Do you see those two blankets pinned together at the bottom?" said Dabney. "Yes, but what of it?" said the officer. "Why, that's her way of making a fish-trap; and when she pins the clothes together that way, it means that Lee is only trying to draw us into his fish-trap."

As long as the two armies lay watching each other on opposite banks of the stream, Dabney, with his clothes-line telegraph, continued to be one of the promptest and most reliable of General Hooker's scouts.

—Frank Moore, ed.
Anecdotes, Poetry and Incidents of the War:
North and South, 1860-1865

The Warning Bullet

[THE SECOND ATTACK on Port Hudson, Louisiana, June 14, 1863] was the only fight that I ever went into with an expectation of being hit; and perhaps the cause of the presentiment may be philosophically worthy of notice. Two days before the assault, as I was crossing a dangerous hillock just in rear of our bivouac, a Minie buzzed through the trees on my right, glanced downward from a branch to a prostrate log, and then glanced across my right leg.

The human intellect is capable of running several trains of thought at once. I heard the bullet singing hoarsely on its way and consciously sent an instantaneous malediction after it, while I hastened to pull up the leg of my trousers and see if the bone were broken, remembering what a bad thing it was to have an amputation in such hot weather. Great was my satisfaction when I found that no important harm had been done. A hole in my dirty pantaloons, a slight abrasion on the shin, and a large bruise, which soon bloomed into blue and saffron, were the only results. My main feeling so far was exultation at the escape. The cause of the presentiment of evil was yet to come.

When the accident and its harmless nature became known in my company, my veteran sergeant, Weber, muttered, "It is a warning."

"What is that, Weber?" I asked.

"Oh, it is a foolish saying, Captain. But we used to say, when a bullet merely drew blood, that it was a forerunner of another that would kill."

I am as little superstitious as a human being can well be, but Weber's speech made me very uncomfortable till the 14th of June was over. I went to the assault with a gloomy expectation of "the bullet that would kill," and hardly forgot it for a quarter of an hour together during the whole day. Even at night, while moving stealthily into the covered way, I still had a fear of the coming of that fated bullet; and when I emerged from the trenches, practically beyond the reach of hostile musketry, I experienced a distinct sense of elation at having baffled Destiny. Moreover, this one victory knocked out the presentiment, and I never had a second.

—CAPTAIN JOHN WILLIAM DE FOREST

*

Hood's Boys and the Chambersburg Ladies

---

*

June 27, 1863

I ENTERED CHAMBERSBURG at 6 P. M. This is a town of some size and importance. All its houses were shut up; but the natives were in the streets, or at the upper windows, looking in a scowling and bewildered manner at the Confederate troops, who were marching gayly past to the tune of "Dixie's Land." The women (many of whom were pretty and well dressed) were particularly sour and disagreeable in their remarks. I heard one of them say, "Look at Pharaoh's army going to the Red Sea."

Others were pointing and laughing at Hood's ragged Jacks, who were passing at the time. This division, well known for its fighting qualities, is composed of Texans, Alabamians, and Arkansians, and they certainly are a queer lot to look at. They carry less than any other troops; many of them have only got an old piece of carpet or rug as baggage; many have discarded their shoes in the mud; all are ragged and dirty, but full of good humor and confidence in themselves and in their general, Hood. They answered the numerous taunts of the Chambersburg ladies with cheers and laughter.

One female had seen fit to adorn her ample bosom with a huge Yankee flag, and she stood at the door of her house, her countenance expressing the greatest contempt for the bare-footed Rebs; several companies passed her without taking any notice, but at length a Texan gravely remarked, "Take care, madam, for Hood's boys are great at storming breastworks when the Yankee colors is on them." After this speech the patriotic lady beat a precipitate retreat.

—LIEUTENANT COLONEL ARTHUR JAMES LYON FREMANTLE

322

General Lee and the Flapjacks

---

*

GENERAL LEE was very fond of old Virginia flapjacks. . . .
Thin as a wafer and big nearly as a cart wheel; and when made of new
flour and served hot with fresh butter and maple molasses and folded
and folded, layers thick, they are a feast for the gods. But General Lee,
the best and tenderest of men, as well as the greatest, hadn't it in his
heart to fare well—much as his ample means would have allowed, when
his men were suffering for food; and if one wanted a poor dinner he had
only to drop in on General Lee at that hour. He lived but little better
than his men.

This greatly disturbed his cook; and when the army advanced into
Pennsylvania, flowing with milk and honey and other good things edible,
he said: "Well, I'se gwine to git something good for Marse Robert for
once, if he never eats none no mo'." So, skirmishing around, he got up
the necessary ingredients for the General's favorite cake. The cook, in
his pride as chef and zealous love for his master, outdid himself on
that 30th of June. The cakes were too tempting; the General ate too
plentifully, was sick accordingly, and Gettysburg was lost.

—*New Orleans Times-Democrat*

*

Fighting for Their Rights

---

*

"WHAT ARE YOU FIGHTING FOR?" says an officer of Meade's
staff to a hairy Mississippian, captured in Pennsylvania in 1863.

"Fightin' for ouah rights," the Mississippian told him.

323

"But friend, what earthly right of yours have I ever interfered with?" the major asked him.

"I don't know," the soldier answered honestly, after some thought. "None that I know of, seh. But maybe I've got rights I haven't heard tell about, an' if so, I'm fightin' for them, too."

—JOHN W. THOMASON, JR.

*

Swamped

---

*

[IN JULY, 1863] we remained some time in this vicinity [of Fort Wagner] and suffered the discomforts of camp life on Bird Island and Folly Island, as well as Morris Island. The extremely hot weather, fleas, sand, and disagreeable swamps, all conspired to disgust our men.

The celebrated "Swamp-Angel" gun was mounted on a platform resting upon oozy, almost bottomless mud.

A rich thing was reported in camp, about the time this gun was first mounted. Colonel Serrell, the very embodiment of energy, who was in charge of the enterprise, ordered one of his lieutenants to take twenty men, and commence work in that swamp.

The Lieutenant reported that he could not do it, the mud was too deep.

"Try," was the Colonel's reply.

The Lieutenant did so, but soon returned, with his men covered with mud, and reported: "Colonel, the mud is over my men's heads; I can't do it."

The Colonel insisted and ordered the Lieutenant to make a requisition for anything he needed.

He did so, putting it in writing on the spot: "I want twenty men, eighteen feet long, to cross a swamp fifteen feet deep."

The Lieutenant was arrested for disrespect, and some one else built the battery.

—ONLY A PRIVATE

*

Uncle Sam

---

*

Dechard, Tenn.
July 14, 1863

MY DEAREST MARY,

. . . We have very little to amuse us except the talk of our contrabands of whom we have quite a team with us, every officer has one if not more besides laborers, teamsters, road makers, &c., &c. I was most amused yesterday at my tent companion's man "Sam"; he has been with the Doctor for a year and of course had seen a great deal of the army. He said to the Doctor with a look of wonder: Doctor, who is dis Uncle Sam, dat you all talk about so much, de soldiers say dey are working for Uncle Sam, dat he pays um all, dat he sends all dese hard bread and bacon &c. here, dat he owns all dese mules and wagons, &c. What kind of man is he? The Doctor replied gravely, that Uncle Sam was a great man north that owned the whole country and governed it &c. &c. Sam listened with wonder, and said Gor-a-mighty, Doctor, how de secesh would like to get a hold of him, wouldnt dey bushwack him! then soliloquized as he walked off—"De norf must be a heep richer dan de souf, a white man here, if he hab two or three hundred niggers ragged and half-starved, tinks he a rich man, but just tink of Uncle Sam!"

—ALFRED LACEY HOUGH

*

Letter to the Chaplain of Posey's Brigade

---

*

DURING THE WAR was published in one of the Richmond papers a humorous letter from Reverend T. D. Gwin, chaplain of the First South Carolina Regiment, calling upon the man who stole his buffalo robe and sundry other baggage, to return the same if he valued at all the blessings of a clear conscience and an improved prospect of future salvation. The response to the reverend gentleman will show that the appeal was not altogether unproductive:

> *Sixteenth Mississippi Regiment, Posey's Brigade,*
> *Camp near Bunker Hill, Va.,*
> *July 16, 1863*

MY DEAR GWIN:

I was inexpressibly shocked to learn from your letter in the *Inquirer,* of the 14th inst., that the temporary loss of your "buffalo robe," blankets, pillow, and shawl, should have given you such inconvenience, and even suspended your arduous duties in the field for a week.

But supposing from the mark "Captain," that it belonged to some poor officer of the line, and knowing that it was more baggage than he was entitled to carry, I relieved him of it from motives that will be appreciated by any officer of the line in the field.

On my arrival in camp I divided the blankets among my mess, and in a sudden fit of generosity I retained the buffalo robe, shawl, and pillow, for my own use.

The other members now join me in returning thanks, and feel that, to your warm and gushing heart, these thanks will be the richest recompense.

I am now patiently waiting for your coat and boots, which I presume you will send me, in accordance with the following injunctions:

"If any man take away thy coat, let him have thy cloak also."— Matt: chap. 5, verse 40.

For the regulation of the amount of baggage which a chaplain in the army should carry, we refer you to the following.

"Provide neither gold, nor silver, nor brass in your purses. Nor scrip for your journey, neither two coats, neither shoes, nor yet staves, for the workman is worthy of his meat."—Matt: chap. 10, verses 9 and 10.

Anything you may have in excess of the above allowance will be most respectfully received by me.

I remain, dear Gwinny, with sentiments of eternal gratitude,

PRESENT OWNER OF BUFFALO ROBE
—*The New Eclectic Magazine*

✳

"The Parson Isn't Hungry"

✳

ON OUR WAY to Lafayette from Lee & Gordon's mill [after the First Tennessee Regiment evacuated Chattanooga, September 8, 1843], I remember a ludicrous scene, almost bordering on sacrilege. Rosecrans' army was very near us, and we expected before three days elapsed to be engaged in battle. In fact, we knew there must be a fight or a foot race, one or the other. We could smell, as it were, "the battle afar off."

One Sabbath morning it was announced that an eloquent and able LL.D., from Nashville, was going to preach, and as the occasion was an exceedingly solemn one, we were anxious to hear this divine preach from God's Holy Word; and as he was one of the "big ones," the whole army was formed in close column and stacked their arms. The cannon were parked, all pointing back toward Chattanooga. The scene looked weird and picturesque. It was in a dark wilderness of woods and vines and overhanging limbs. In fact, it seemed but the home of the owl and the bat, and other varmints that turn night into day. Everything looked solemn. The trees looked solemn, the scene looked solemn, the men looked solemn, even the horses looked solemn. You may be sure, reader, that we felt solemn.

The reverend LL.D. had prepared a regular war sermon before

he left home, and of course had to preach it, appropriate or not appropriate; it was in him and had to come out. He opened the service with a song. I did remember the piece that was sung, but right now I cannot recall it to memory; but as near as I can now recollect here is his prayer, *verbatim et literatim:*

"O, Thou immaculate, invisible, eternal and holy Being, the exudations of whose effulgence illuminate this terrestrial sphere, we approach Thy presence, being covered all over with wounds and bruises and putrifying sores, from the crowns of our heads to the soles of our feet. And Thou, O Lord, art our dernier resort. The whole world is one great machine, managed by Thy puissance. The beatific splendors of Thy face irradiate the celestial region and felicitate the saints. There are the most exuberant profusions of Thy grace, and the sempiternal efflux of Thy glory. God is an abyss of light, a circle whose center is everywhere and His circumference nowhere. Hell is the dark world made up of spiritual sulphur and other ignited ingredients, disunited and unharmonized, and without that pure balsamic oil that flows from the heart of God."

When the old fellow got this far, I lost the further run of his prayer, but regret very much that I did so, because it was so grand and fine that I would have liked very much to have kept such an appropriate prayer for posterity. In fact, it lays it on heavy over any prayer I ever heard, and I think the new translators ought to get it and have it put in their book as a sample prayer. But they will have to get the balance of it from the eminent LL.D. In fact, he was so "high larnt" that I don't think anyone understood him but the generals. The colonels might every now and then have understood a word, and maybe a few of the captains and lieutenants, because Lieutenant Lansdown told me he understood every word the preacher said, and further informed me that it was none of your one-horse, old-fashioned country prayers that privates knew anything about, but was bang-up, first-rate, orthodox.

Well, after singing and praying, he took his text. I quote entirely from memory. "Blessed be the Lord God, who teaches my hands to war and my fingers to fight." Now, reader, that was the very subject we boys did not want to hear preached on—on that occasion at least. We felt like some other subject would have suited us better. I forget how he commenced his sermon, but I remember that after he got warmed up a little, he began to pitch in on the Yankee nation, and gave them particular fits as to their genealogy. He said that we of the South had descended from the royal and aristocratic blood of Huguenots of

France, and of the cavaliers of England, etc.; but that the Yankees were descendants of the crop-eared Puritans and witch burners, who came over in the Mayflower, and settled at Plymouth Rock. He was warm on this subject, and waked up the echoes of the forest. He said that he and his brethren would fight the Yankees in this world, and if God permit, chase their frightened ghosts in the next, through fire and brimstone.

About this time we heard the awfullest racket produced by some wild animal tearing through the woods toward us, and the cry, "Look out! look out! hooie! hooie! hooie! look out!" and there came running right through our midst a wild bull, mad with terror and fright, running right over and knocking down the divine, and scattering Bibles and hymn books in every direction. The services were brought to a close without the doxology.

This same brave chaplain rode along with our brigade, on an old string-haltered horse, as we advanced to the attack at Chickamauga, exhorting the boys to be brave, to aim low, and to kill the Yankees as if they were wild beasts. He was eloquent and patriotic. He stated that if he only had a gun he too would go along as a private soldier. You could hear his voice echo and re-echo over the hills. He had worked up his patriotism to a pitch of genuine bravery and daring that I had never seen exhibited, when fliff, fluff, fluff, *fluff,* FLUFF, FLUFF—a whir, a BOOM! and a shell screams through the air. The reverend LL.D. stops to listen, like an old sow when she hears the wind, and says, "Remember, boys, that he who is killed will sup tonight in Paradise." Some soldier hallooed at the top of his voice, "Well, parson, you come along and take supper with us." *Boom! whir!* a bomb burst, and the parson at that moment put spurs to his horse and was seen to limber to the rear, and almost every soldier yelled out, "The parson isn't hungry, and never eats supper."

—SAM R. WATKINS

Operating on Himself

Chickamauga, September 19-20, 1863

IT WAS NOW a month since I had been wounded. The surgeon in charge told me the bullet could not be taken out and that he would not attempt it.

I had been in the practice four years with my preceptor, who was a fine surgeon. I had assisted the surgeons often when crowded with work. From day to day I called my case to the notice of the surgeon. He still flatly refused to do the work for me. I now made up my mind to do it myself, with the assistance of a young widow nurse, who was in the hospital. She had lost her husband in the first battle of Bull Run and thereupon had become a nurse for wounded and sick soldiers. I told her of my plans and told her, too, that I was dying by inches every day. I asked her if she would bring me the necessary instruments, while the surgeon was gone to his dinner. She said, "Yes, and I will help you, too." I told her to get some hot water, some carbolic acid, two pairs of scissors, one curved pair, a sharp knife, a blunt, curved hook. She had all these ready when the doctor started to dinner. I asked her to bring me a bullet, a Minie ball. I got very busy at once. The nurse also brought me six surgeon's needles threaded with cat-gut sutures. I placed the bullet between my teeth to bite on while doing this work, for I knew it would hurt badly.

I took up the blunt, curved hook and slowly introduced it into the wound by a slight rotary, oscillating movement from side to side. I rested a short time, for it was very painful. I pressed it further in until I felt that I had gotten the hook over the bowel. I slowly drew the bowel toward the opening, which had sloughed considerably, and left a large hole in my side. The cut in the bowel could be plainly seen. I now placed a roll of bandages in the loop of the bowel between it and my side, to keep the bowel from slipping back into the cavity. Then I took

330

the curved scissors, snipped off the sloughing, ragged edges to freshen them. I was gritting my teeth upon the bullet. Cold perspiration was pouring off my face and body. I must not and could not stop now.

There was a horrid fascination about it. I was suffering torture. I held my breath. [When the bullet was out] the widow handed me the curved, threaded needles; I dreaded these more than the cutting, but with a renewed determination, I placed six stitches in my bowel; I then tightened these alternately, so as to have the fresh edges fit closely without puckering. Having drawn all up tightly, I took sponges and moistened them in hot water and bathed the bowel, removing all the blood clots. I took a large syringe and washed out the cavity thoroughly. After cleansing the gut wound I placed eight stitches in the outside wound.

The operation was finished. The cold perspiration was standing in great beads upon my face and body. I was frozen almost to death. The work finished, I looked up into the face of this heroic, beautiful woman. Both of us fell in a dead faint across the cot. The doctor stood in the doorway and saw this last scene. He came forward, swearing like a madman, picked up the beautiful widow and carried her to her own room. Unconscious, I lay oblivious to passing events.

I learned, after my return to life, that the doctor said: "Let the fool die, if he will"; he was also heard to say some very tender and endearing words while bending over this dear young widow.

After a while the surgeon came to my cot and said in a very gruff tone, "You have played hell, haven't you. I hope you are satisfied." I replied, "Doctor, I am not entirely satisfied, but will be as soon as I am well and strong enough to slap your jaws for your insults. I would do so now if I were able, you vulgar puppy."

About suppertime, the nurse came and brought me supper. She looked very beautiful to me. She had saved my life and I—well, I was very grateful.

I was healthy and vigorous at the time I received these wounds, and my recovery was uninterrupted. I am sure that mine was one of the few recoveries from such a bowel wound. Most patients would have given up without an effort, and died. At this period surgeons regarded wounds of the bowels as necessarily fatal. When I was wounded, I had not drawn my rations, nor eaten anything, save some parched corn, for five days. I feel certain that if I had been well fed my wound would have killed me.

I received the most diligent and kind attention. On the 15th of November, following, I began to hobble about on crutches. My leg was also healing rapidly. My friend, Captain Fulton, took me out riding. The warm sunshine, fresh air and exercise were very beneficial to both of us. I was, from this time on, a welcome guest in any home in this fine little settlement.

—COLONEL THOMAS F. BERRY

*

Eugenics in the Confederacy

*

Near Raymond, Miss., October 23, 1863

A SOLDIER in W. H. T. Walker's division applied for a furlough. Gen'l Walker disapproved but respectfully forwarded to the HdQrtrs of Gen'l [D. H.] Hill where it was endorsed as follows: "Approved for the reason that a brave soldier ought to be allowed to go home whenever practicable, else all the children born during the war or within the usual period afterwards will be the offspring of the cowards who remain at home by reason of substitutes or other exemption." The soldier went home. I have a notion to apply for a furlough and attach that scrap to it which I have clipped from a newspaper and send it up and I believe Gen'l Johnston will approve it.

—SERGEANT EDWIN H. FAY

*

The Mule Heroes

*

THE SUCCESS of the movement [under General W. F. Smith, to open the Tennessee River route to our base of supplies at Bridgeport] had been prompt and complete . . . within five days after General Grant's arrival at the [Chattanooga] front. As soon as the enemy recovered from his surprise, he woke up to the importance of the achievement; Longstreet was despatched to retrieve, if possible, the lost ground. His troops reached Wauhatchie in the night of the 28th [of October], and made an attack upon Geary's division of Hooker's forces. The fight raged for about three hours, but Geary succeeded in holding his ground against greatly superior numbers.

During the fight Geary's teamsters had become scared, and had deserted their teams, and the mules, stampeded by the sound of battle raging about them, had broken loose from their wagons and run away. Fortunately for their reputation and the safety of the command, they started toward the enemy, and with heads down and tails up, with trace-chains rattling and whiffletrees snapping over the stumps of trees they rushed pell-mell upon Longstreet's bewildered men. Believing it to be an impetuous charge of cavalry, his line broke and fled.

The quartermaster in charge of the animals, not willing to see such distinguished services go unrewarded, sent in the following communication: "I respectfully request that the mules, for their gallantry in this action, may have conferred upon them the brevet rank of horses." Brevets in the army were being bestowed pretty freely at the time, and when this recommendation was reported to General Grant, he laughed heartily at the humor of the suggestion.

—GENERAL HORACE PORTER

＊

Where States' Rights End

＊

ON THE 25th of November [1863], during the action on Missionary Ridge, General [George H.] Thomas thought of the burial of the officers and men who were then falling as well as those who had yielded their lives on other fields. Previous to the advance which resulted in the rout of the Confederate army, a line of troops in reserve coursed over a hill to the right and rear of Sheridan's position, revealing a suitable configuration for a national cemetery. Subsequently, by his order, this hill was taken for this use. During the preparation of the ground he manifested great interest in the work, and frequently rode out from the town to note the progress and to make suggestions. He provided amply for the work, by detaching troops, at times whole regiments, for this duty. He directed not only that his soldiers should be carefully buried, but that the grounds should be beautified. And through his action in its establishment, and his support of those in charge, he made it the type of national cemeteries in the West, and caused a change for the better in those in the East. It was meet that the first national cemetery, founded by military orders, should give the ideal of the last resting-places of the nation's heroes.

In conferring with General Thomas in regard to the plan of burial, the chaplain in charge asked if the dead should be buried according to their several states. The general was silent for a moment and then said very positively, "No, no. Mix them up; mix them up. I am tired of state-rights."

—THOMAS B. VAN HORNE

My mother said to me, "You can do your part, my boy, for the land. For if you will beat the drum, you will take the place of a man."

—"THE DRUMMER BOY"

25. BRAVE LADS

The Death of Wilkeson

*

LIEUTENANT BAYARD WILKESON . . . was but a lad in years. When but seventeen years old he had received his commission. Two years he had spent in active service on the field. At Fredericksburg and at Chancellorsville he had smelt gunpowder and learned to look with calmness on wounds and death. He had long been the ranking officer in his battery, and had brought the soldiers under his command to so high a degree of proficiency and discipline that men forgot his youth in admiration of his soldierly ability.

So it happened that on this first day of the great battle [of Gettysburg, July 1, 1863] which was to prove the turning point in the war for the Union, the task of holding one of the most critical and decisive positions was left to this nineteen-year-old soldier. Four guns he had—light twelve-pound field-pieces. With these he plunged gallantly into the conflict and for a time held in check the advancing troops of General [John B.] Gordon. But the Confederate commander, soon discovering that his infantry was making no headway against Wilkeson's telling fire, brought up two batteries, and posting them on a commanding hill, ordered the cannoneers to silence or to drive away the spiteful little Union battery that was working such havoc in his ranks. Twelve guns were turned on Wilkeson's four cannon, and as the Confederate battery was posted on a hill which towered above the knoll on which his guns were posted the advantage of position, as well as in weight of metal, rested with the enemy. But though the solid shot and shell fell thick and fast among his guns and artillerymen, Wilkeson never faltered. Bestriding his well-trained horse, he rode about among the guns, speaking a word of encouragement here, giving an order there, never once losing his complete self-possession, and everywhere cheering his men up by his display of calm courage. Finally, seeing that the situation was becoming desperate, he spurred his horse to the front and sat there immovable and statuesque, seeking by this means to inspire his men with confidence. Animated by their commander's daring example, the men of the battery worked their guns with such rapidity and precision that the utmost efforts of the Confederate infantry failed to force the battery from its position.

Through their field-glasses the officers of the Confederate artillery could clearly see that it was Wilkeson who was thus doggedly holding the Union cannoneers to their work. General Gordon himself pressed forward to discover what it was that thus delayed the advance of his lines. It needed but a glance to convince him that if the officer who so defiantly rode about among the Union guns could be disabled, the battery would soon be silenced.

"Turn your guns on that fellow on horseback," he said to the Confederate artillerymen. "When he is out of the way we can silence his cannon."

With twelve guns turned upon him Wilkeson could not long go unscathed. A rifle-shot struck his leg, cutting and tearing the flesh and shattering the bone. His horse fell to the ground with him. His comrades picked him up and started to bear him to the rear, but he ordered them to lay him on the ground where he could watch the progress of the conflict. No surgeon was on the field, and with his own hand the wounded youth twisted a handkerchief about his mangled limb to serve for a tourniquet, and with a jack-knife cut away the lacerated flesh and shattered bones of the leg. Fever came upon him and parching thirst took possession of him. An artilleryman went back to the well at the Almshouse, a few rods to the rear, and brought thence a canteen of cool water. Wilkeson's eyes brightened as he saw the messenger return with the water, but just as he took the canteen and was raising it eagerly to his lips, a wounded soldier lying near cried: "For God's sake give me some." Unmindful of his own suffering the young officer handed the canteen to his wounded neighbor, who drank greedily every drop it contained. Wilkeson smiled on the man, turned slightly, and was dead in a few minutes.

—WILLIS J. ABBOT

*

Johnny Clem

*

LITTLE JOHNNY CLEM [was] the atom of a drummer-boy, "aged ten," who strayed away from Newark, Ohio, and the first we know of him, though small enough to live in a drum, was beating the long roll for the 22d Michigan. At Chickamauga, he filled the office of a "marker," carrying the guidon whereby they form the lines, a duty having its counterpart in the surveyor's more peaceful calling in the flagman who flutters the red signal along the metes and bounds. On the Sunday of the battle [September 20, 1863] the little fellow's occupation gone, he picked up a gun that had slipped from some dying hand, provided himself with ammunition, and began putting in the periods quite on his own account, blazing away close to the ground, like a fire-fly in the grass. Late in the waning day, the waif left almost alone in the whirl of the battle, one of Longstreet's colonels dashed up, and, looking down at him, ordered him to surrender: "Surrender!" he shouted, "you little d——d son of a ——!" The words were hardly out of the officer's mouth, when Johnny brought his piece to "order arms," and as his hand slipped down to the hammer he pressed it back, swung up the gun to the position of "charge bayonet," and as the officer raised his sabre to strike the piece aside, the glancing barrel lifted into range, and the proud Colonel tumbled dead from his horse, his lips fresh stained with the syllable of reproach he had hurled at the child.

—BENJAMIN F. TAYLOR

*

Where He Was Shot

*

BEFORE THE BATTLE of Chickamauga [September 19-20] "Billy" Bethune, a little red-haired boy from Columbus, Georgia, came to the regiment and requested me to muster him into the service; but I declined upon the ground that he was too young and too small. He was barely fifteen years old, and not well grown at that. After we went over in the valley he came to me again and said that if I would not give him a gun and let him perform service as a soldier he would go off and join some other command. I compromised with him by giving him a gun and agreeing that he might go into the next fight, but would not put him on other duty. On the morning of the 28th of October he went through the engagement unhurt. During the next night, when the enemy routed the regiment, little "Billy" got shot in the back. Down near Lookout Creek one of the Irishmen of Company K came along with the wounded boy on his back.

Major Lowther called out, "Who is that?"

The answer was, "Jimmie Rutledge, sir."

"Who is that you have there?"

"Billy Bethune, sir," was the response.

"Is he wounded?"

"He is, sir," said Jimmie.

"How is he wounded?"

The reply was, "He is shot in the back, sir."

That moment Billy's childish voice rang out in a sharp tone of indignation, "Major, he is a d——d liar; I am shot *across* the back."

—COLONEL WILLIAM C. OATES

*

Sam Davis

*

IN [NOVEMBER] 1863, General [Braxton] Bragg was in command at Missionary Ridge. Before he could dispose of his army to advantage in any direction it was necessary for him to have a plan of the Federal army in Tennessee. Three scouts were selected who had before done valuable service, and they were informed by General Bragg of the extreme danger of the duty, and were asked if they were willing to undertake it, if need be, to the tragic end. They replied they were. He noticed a young, handsome, eager lad, listening with great attention to his orders. When he had finished speaking, the boy, Sam Davis, came up to him and said, "General Bragg, I should very much like to be your fourth scout."

"Don't you think you are rather young for such a dangerous mission?" General Bragg asked.

The boy smiled cheerfully and said, "Well, try me."

The next day the four scouts started off together, and Sam Davis, with almost miraculous quickness, obtained all the information required. He found out that the Federal army in middle Tennessee was likely to move from Nashville to Corinth, and reinforce the army at Chattanooga. He got an exact account of the number of regiments and the whole of the artillery in the 16th Corps, and, what was even more remarkable, he got complete maps of the fortifications at all the principal points, including Nashville, and an accurate report of the entire Federal army in the whole of Tennessee.

Sam Davis was so pleased with his rapid success that he wanted the praise and sympathy of the person he loved best in the world, his young sweetheart, to whom he was engaged to be married; and he recklessly stopped to visit her. A small company of Federal cavalry saw a grey uniform enter a little rose-covered house, and they followed him as he came out. But their horses were jaded by a long march, while Sam Davis was mounted on a thoroughbred Kentucky mare, and he

339

rushed past them on the roads he knew so well, making a detour, and they lost him in the sheltering darkness.

The Seventh Kansas Cavalry, however, were scattered over his entire course, and while he was resting the next day in a scrub thicket at Pulaski, trying to conceal himself, a squad of soldiers belonging to the Seventh Cavalry discovered his hiding-place and captured him and his horse. They proceeded to take him to General [Grenville M.] Dodge, who was in command at Pulaski, only a mile and a half distant. When the frank, handsome, fearless, gay-spirited lad, in his shabby grey uniform, stood before the General, he was immediately prepossessed in his [the boy's] favour. At that moment there was no evidence against him, but when they unbuckled Davis' saddle a fat budget of papers was discovered under the seat, and upon examination, General Dodge found that all the information given, the number of regiments, the movements of the artillery in the 16th Corps, the reinforcements from Nashville to Corinth, and to Chattanooga, the fortifications at Nashville, the fine maps, and the perfectly accurate report of the whole Federal army in Tennessee, had been furnished Davis by a member of his own staff, and that probably the man who stood at his right hand was a traitor of the deepest dye. A captured map was a copy of the very one he carried in his pocket.

He said, "Davis, you evidently have a good friend at court?" Davis made no reply. "I could have sworn to trust my life to every officer at my table, but the information which you have, could only have been given you by a friend. Young man, I must have the name of your informer." Davis was still silent, with, as General Dodge could see, a steadfast gleam of danger in his eye. There was no weakening there. And, at all costs, it was necessary to have the name of the traitor. "You will," he said, "without any court-martial have your freedom the moment you speak or write down the name of the man who has betrayed me." And he handed Davis a pencil and a sheet of paper. "Write it," he said, "if you cannot speak it."

Davis gave back a clean sheet of paper and the pencil to General Dodge, and for the first time spoke, in a quiet, even voice. "General Dodge," he replied, "when I undertook this duty from my commanding officer, General Bragg, I did it with a full knowledge of what the consequences might be. I cannot give you the information you want."

The General said, "You are very young. Life must hold a good deal for you. Think over the situation for five minutes and speak again. I positively must have the information I am asking from you."

Davis answered without hesitation, "Honour requires no thought; it comes from"—he lifted his hand and pointed upward—"God. I can only repeat that I cannot give the information."

General Dodge said, "If you persist in this silence you know, of course, that, as a soldier, I must call a court-martial, and then the matter passes out of my hands."

"I know that," Davis replied. "I am a soldier myself; I don't criticise military methods. Call your court-martial."

General Dodge said, "It is with extreme regret that I am forced to such a measure. I am giving you your chance now; it won't be repeated later."

"A court-martial will give me a death sentence," said Davis, "but not even death will make me betray my word. We are both soldiers doing our duty. When the last moment of my life comes, I shall have acted fair to God and to myself."

By this time the young soldier's spotless honour and unassailable loyalty had deeply moved General Dodge, and he began to plead with genuine emotion to the boy to be saved. But Davis, his young face set in noble lines, said, "General Dodge, I have never lied or broken my word in my life; I will willingly die now rather than do it. My mind is firmly made up. A court-martial may condemn me, but do not expect me to betray my trust. I will never do it, never."

A court-martial was then called. General Dodge was filled with regret, thinking that the very man who furnished Davis with the information was probably at that moment giving him his death sentence. It seemed too horrible. The execution was delayed while enquiries were made about Davis and his family. It was found that an old friend of his mother was living in Pulaski. General Dodge sent for her and said to her, "Talk to the boy about his home and about his mother. He looks to me, with all his courage and his steadfastness, a sort of mother's boy. Surely at twenty he is not going to sacrifice his life to save a traitor. I don't know who the man is who gave him the information, but he isn't worth the death of Sam Davis."

The lady used all her eloquence; she repeated what General Dodge had said; she spoke of his mother's devotion to him, of her love, and of the close bond that existed between them, and she asked if he realised that he was never to see her again and of the great grief he was to give her.

"Why," said the young man, crying like a little child, "my mother is the person who taught me never to lie and to keep my word. She will grieve, I know, not to see me again, but I will never betray the man who gave me the information, and he knows it. It isn't only the *other* man I am saving. How could I live through all the years and despise the man I have to live with, myself? How could I wake through the nights and remember the man I lied to and condemned? No, I will die with honour; I will never live dishonoured. God knows I will not."

The lady returned to General Dodge and repeated her conversation, and they both wrung their hands with helplessness.

On Friday, Davis was handcuffed, and he walked steadily and sat down on his coffin with the fresh-faced look of a boy who has slept well and is the possessor of a glorious conscience.

General Dodge had passed a sleepless night and was awake long before the condemned man. He called his staff together and ordered them to the place of execution, hoping that even at the last moment Davis would speak, or the man who had furnished Davis with his information would be touched by the boy's great valour, and that he might still be saved.

A rope was placed around his neck by hesitating hands; the lines of quiet determination in the exalted face deepened. There stood the martyr of all ages.

"Wait!" The voice of General Dodge rang out like a pistol shot. "Davis, in the name of God, give me the name of your informant! Your horse is waiting for you. Look, she is there in the thicket, and here is your escort to carry you back to your own lines in safety. One word, and you are a free man."

Davis turned his young head, and looked longingly at the horse. "Queenie, old girl," he called; the mare whinnied, the boy's eyes filled with tears. Then he smiled and with his handcuffed hands gently touched the rope around his neck and said: "General Dodge, this is my badge of freedom. I have only one life, and I give it for honour. Take it."

There he stood, tall, brave, healthy, strong, handsome, intelligent, unflinching, ready to die rather than betray his word. Officers and men were by this time quietly and unashamedly weeping. The only calm and steadfast soul was his. The boy gave some little keepsakes to the Provost Marshal for his mother and his sweetheart. Then he turned his young face squarely towards the sun, looked at it like a young eagle, and waited.

There was a dead silence. No man could speak. Presently a quiet, steady voice said, "Do your duty, men." Davis had himself bravely given the order.

—Mrs. T. P. O'Connor

342

*The day after his death two angels came down from heaven
to carry General Jackson back with them. They searched all
through the camp. They went to the prayer-meeting, to the hospital, and to every other place where they thought themselves
likely to find him, but in vain. What was their surprise [on their
return] to find that he had just executed a splendid flank movement, and got into heaven before them!*

                                —A CIVIL WAR ANECDOTE

26. JACKSON PASSES OVER THE RIVER

Ill Omen

*

[AT CHANCELLORSVILLE] on the morning of May 2d [1863],
Jackson was the first to rise from the bivouac . . . , and observing a staff
officer (General W. N. Pendleton) without cover, he spread over him
his own overcoat. The morning being chilly, he drew near a small fire
that had been kindled by a courier, and the writer, who soon after sought
the same place, found him seated on a cracker-box. He complained of
the cold, and as the cooks were preparing breakfast, I managed to procure him a cup of hot coffee, which by good fortune our cook was able
to provide.

While we were still talking, the general's sword, which was leaning against a tree, without *apparent* cause fell with a clank to the ground. I picked it up and handed it to him. He thanked me and buckled it on. It was now about dawn; the troops were on the march and our bivouac was all astir. After a few words with General Lee he mounted his horse and rode off. This was the last meeting of Lee and Jackson.

I have spoken of the falling of Jackson's sword, because it strongly impressed me at the time as an omen of evil—an indefinable superstition such as sometimes affects persons on the falling of a picture or mirror. This feeling haunted me the whole day, and when the tidings of Jackson's wound reached my ears it was without surprise that I heard this unfortunate confirmation of the superstitious fears with which I had been so oppressed.

—A. L. LONG

*

Death of Jackson

*

THE WRITER of this narrative, an aide-de-camp of Jackson's, was ordered to remain at the point where the [Chancellorsville] advance began, to be a center of communication between the General and the cavalry on the flanks, and to deliver orders to detachments of artillery still moving up from the rear. A fine black charger, with elegant trappings, deserted by his owner and found tied to a tree, became mine only for that short and eventful night-fall; and about 8 P. M., in the twilight, thus comfortably mounted, I gathered my couriers about me and went forward to find General Jackson [who with Brigadier General Robert E. Rodes and Major Eugene Blackford had opened the attack on Major General Oliver O. Howard]. The storm of battle had swept far on to the east and become more and more faint to the ear, until silence came with night over the fields and woods.

As I rode along that old turnpike, passing scattered fragments of Confederates looking for their regiments, parties of prisoners concentrating under guards, wounded men by the roadside and under the trees at Talley's and Chancellor's, I had reached an open field on the right, a mile west of Chancellorsville, when, in the dusky twilight, I saw horsemen near an old cabin in the field. Turning toward them, I found Rodes and his staff engaged in gathering the broken and scattered troops that had swept the two miles of battle-field. "General Jackson is just ahead on the road, Captain," said Rodes; "tell him I will be here at this cabin if I am wanted."

I had not gone a hundred yards before I heard firing, a shot or two, and then a company volley upon the right of the road, and another upon the left. A few moments farther on I met Captain Murray Taylor, an aide of A. P. Hill's, with tidings that Jackson and Hill were wounded, and some around them killed, by the fire of their own men. Spurring my horse into a sweeping gallop, I soon passed the Confederate line of battle, and, some three or four rods on its front, found the General's horse beside a pine sapling on the left, and a rod beyond a little party of men caring for a wounded officer. The story of the sad event is briefly told, and, in essentials, very much as it came to me from the lips of the wounded General himself, and in everything confirmed and completed by those who were eye-witnesses and near companions.

When Jackson had reached the point where his line now crossed the turnpike, scarcely a mile west of Chancellorsville, and not half a mile from a line of Federal troops, he had found his front line unfit for the farther and vigorous advance he desired, by reason of the irregular character of the fighting, now right, now left, and because of the dense thickets, through which it was impossible to preserve alignment. Division commanders found it more and more difficult as the twilight deepened to hold their broken brigades in hand. Regretting the necessity of relieving the troops in front, General Jackson had ordered A. P. Hill's division, his third and reserve line, to be placed in front. While this change was being effected, impatient and anxious, the General rode forward on the turnpike, followed by two or three of his staff and a number of couriers and signal sergeants. He passed the swampy depression and began the ascent of the hill toward Chancellorsville, when he came upon a line of the Federal infantry lying on their arms. Fired at by one or two muskets (two musket-balls from the enemy whistled over my head as I came to the front), he turned and came back toward his line, upon the side of the road to his left.

As he rode near to the Confederate troops, just placed in position and ignorant that he was in the front, the left company began firing to the front, and two of his party fell from their saddles dead—Captain

345

Boswell, of the Engineers, and Sergeant Cunliffe, of the Signal Corps. Spurring his horse across the road to his right, he was met by a second volley from the right company of Pender's North Carolina Brigade. Under this volley, when not two rods from the troops, the General received three balls at the same instant. One penetrated the palm of his right hand and was cut out that night from the back of his hand. A second passed around the wrist of the left arm and out through the left hand. A third ball passed through the left arm half-way from shoulder to elbow. The large bone of the upper arm was splintered to the elbow-joint, and the wound bled freely. His horse turned quickly from the fire, through the thick bushes which swept the cap from the General's head and scratched his forehead, leaving drops of blood to stain his face. As he lost his hold upon the bridle-rein, he reeled from the saddle, and was caught by the arms of Captain Wilbourn, of the Signal Corps.

Laid upon the ground, there came at once to his succor General A. P. Hill and members of his staff. The writer reached his side a minute after, to find General Hill holding the head and shoulders of the wounded chief. Cutting open the coat-sleeve from wrist to shoulder, I found the wound in the upper arm, and with my handkerchief I bound the arm above the wound to stem the flow of blood. Couriers were sent for Dr. Hunter McGuire, the surgeon of the corps and the General's trusted friend, and for an ambulance.

Being outside of our lines, it was urgent that he should be moved at once. With difficulty litter-bearers were brought from the line near by, and the General was placed upon the litter and carefully raised to the shoulder, I myself bearing one corner. A moment after, artillery from the Federal side was opened upon us; great broadsides thundered over the woods; hissing shells searched the dark thickets through, and shrapnels swept the road along which we moved. Two or three steps farther, and the litter-bearer at my side was struck and fell, but, as the litter turned, Major Watkins Leigh, of Hill's staff, happily caught it. But the fright of the men was so great that we were obliged to lay the litter and its burden down upon the road.

As the litter-bearers ran to the cover of the trees, I threw myself by the General's side and held him firmly to the ground as he attempted to rise. Over us swept the rapid fire of shot and shell—grape-shot striking fire upon the flinty rock of the road all around us, and sweeping from their feet horses and men of the artillery just moved to the front. Soon the firing veered to the other side of the road, and I sprang to my feet, assisted the General to rise, passed my arm around him, and with the wounded man's weight thrown heavily upon me, we forsook the road.

Entering the woods, he sank to the ground from exhaustion, but the litter was soon brought, and again rallying a few men, we essayed to carry him farther, when a second bearer fell at my side. This time, with none to assist, the litter careened, and the General fell to the ground, with a groan of deep pain. Greatly alarmed, I sprang to his head, and, lifting his head as a stray beam of moonlight came through clouds and leaves, he opened his eyes and wearily said: "Never mind me, Captain, never mind me." Raising him again to his feet, he was accosted by Brigadier General Pender: "Oh, General, I hope you are not seriously wounded. I will have to retire my troops to re-form them, they are so much broken by this fire." But Jackson, rallying his strength, with firm voice said: "You must hold your ground, General Pender; you must hold your ground, sir!" and so uttered his last command on the field.

Again we resorted to the litter, and with difficulty bore it through the bush, and then under a hot fire along the road. Soon an ambulance was reached, and stopping to seek some stimulant at Chancellor's (Dowdall's Tavern), we were found by Dr. McGuire, who at once took charge of the wounded man. Passing back over the battle-field of the afternoon, we reached the Wilderness store, and then, in a field on the north, the field-hospital of our corps under Dr. Harvey Black. Here we found a tent prepared, and after midnight the left arm was amputated near the shoulder, and a ball taken from the right hand.

All night long it was mine to watch by the sufferer, and keep him warmly wrapped and undisturbed in his sleep. At 9 A. M., on the next day, when he aroused, cannon firing again filled the air, and all the Sunday through the fierce battle raged, General J. E. B. Stuart commanding the Confederates in Jackson's place. A dispatch was sent to the Commanding General to announce formally his disability—tidings General Lee had received during the night with profound grief. There came back the following note:

GENERAL:

I have just received your note, informing me that you were wounded. I cannot express my regret at the occurrence. Could I have directed events, I should have chosen, for the good of the country, to have been disabled in your stead. I congratulate you upon the victory which is due to your skill and energy.

Most truly yours,
R. E. LEE, GENERAL

347

When this dispatch was handed to me at the tent, and I read it aloud, General Jackson turned his face away and said, "General Lee is very kind, but he should give the praise to God."

The long day was passed with bright hopes for the wounded General, with tidings of success on the battle-field, with sad news of losses, and messages to and from other wounded officers brought to the same infirmary.

On Monday the General was carried in an ambulance, by way of Spotsylvania Court-house, to most comfortable lodging at Chandler's, near Guinea's Station, on the Richmond, Fredericksburg and Potomac railroad. And here, against our hopes, notwithstanding the skill and care of wise and watchful surgeons, attended day and night by wife and friends, amid the prayers and tears of all the Southern land, thinking not of himself, but of the cause he loved, and for the troops who had followed him so well and given him so great a name, our chief sank, day by day, with symptoms of pneumonia and some pains of pleurisy, until, at 3:15 P. M., on the quiet of the Sabbath afternoon, May 10th, 1863, he raised himself from his bed, saying, "No, no, let us pass over the river, and rest under the shade of the trees"; and, falling again to his pillow, he passed away, "over the river, where, in a land where warfare is not known or feared, he rests forever 'under the trees.' "

His shattered arm was buried in the family burying-ground of the Ellwood place—Major J. H. Lacy's—near his last battle-field.

His body rests, as he himself asked, "in Lexington, in the Valley of Virginia." The spot where he was so fatally wounded in the shades of the Wilderness is marked by a large quartz rock, placed there by the care of his chaplain and friend, the Reverend Doctor B. F. Lacy, and the latter's brother, Major Lacy.

Others must tell the story of Confederate victory at Chancellorsville. It has been mine only, as in the movement of that time, so with my pen now, to follow my General himself. Great, the world believes him to have been in many elements of generalship; he was greatest and noblest in that he was good, and, without a selfish thought, gave his talent and his life to a cause that, as before the God he so devoutly served, he deemed right and just.

—REV. JAMES POWER SMITH

Tender Memory

*

THE ARMY OF LEE was on its march to Gettysburg [June, 1863] and the commanding general had given strict orders for its discipline in Pennsylvania. An officer riding to camp from Chambersburg, late at night, was halted by the outposts. Having neither pass nor countersign, in his dilemma he bethought him of an old pass in his pocketbook, signed by General Jackson, whose recent death hung like a cloud over the army. He found it, handed it with confidence to the sentinel. The trusty fellow managed to read it by the light of a match, and as he did so he seemed to linger and hesitate over the signature. And then, as the light went out, he handed it back, and looking up toward the stars beyond, he said, sadly and firmly: "Captain, you can go to heaven on that paper, but you can't pass this post."

—MAJOR HENRY KYD DOUGLAS

*

Restless Spirit

*

Richmond, Va., December 5, 1863

GENERAL [ALEXANDER R.] LAWTON was here last night. . . . He was one of Stonewall's generals, so I listened with all my ears. "Stonewall could not sleep, so every two or three nights you were waked up by orders to have your brigade in marching order before daylight, and to report in person to the Commander. Then you were marched a few miles out and then a few miles in again."

349

"A little different from the western stories [I said], and some generals nearer Richmond asleep several hours after they have been expected to attack."

General Lawton said: "The restless, discontented spirits move the world. All this of Stonewall's was to make us always ready, ever on the alert; and the end of it was this. Jackson's men had gone half a day's march before Pete Longstreet waked and breakfasted." He added: "I think there is a popular delusion about the amount of praying Jackson did. He certainly preferred a fight on Sunday to a sermon. Failing to manage a fight, he loved next best a long Presbyterian sermon, Calvinistic to the core.

"He had no sympathy with human infirmity. He was a one-idea man. He looked upon broken-down men and stragglers as the same thing. He classed all who were weak and weary, who fainted by the way-side, as men wanting in patriotism. If a man's face was white as cotton and his pulse so low that you could not feel it, he merely looked upon him impatiently as an inefficient soldier, and rode off out of patience. He was the true type of all great soldiers. He did not value human life where he had an object to accomplish. He could order men to their death as a matter of course. Napoleon's French conscription could not have kept him supplied with men, he used up his command so rapidly. Hence, while he was alive there was more pride than truth in the talk of his soldiers' love for him. They feared him, and obeyed him to the death; faith they had in him, a faith stronger than death. But I doubt if he had their love, though their respect he did command. And now that they begin to see that a few years more of Stonewall Jackson would have freed them from the yoke of the hateful Yankee, they deify him. They are proud to have been one of the famous Stonewall Brigade, to have been a brick in that wall.

"But be ye sure, it was bitter hard work to keep up with Stonewall Jackson, as all know who ever served with him. He gave his orders rapidly and distinctly, and rode away without allowing answer or remonstrance. When you failed, you were apt to be put under arrest. When you succeeded, he only said 'good.' "

—Mary Boykin Chesnut

	January					
S	M	T	W	T	F	S
.	.	.	.	.	1	2
3	4	5	6	7	8	9
10	11	12	13	14	15	16
17	18	19	20	21	22	23
24	25	26	27	28	29	30
31	.	.	.	.	.	.

	February					
S	M	T	W	T	F	S
.	1	2	3	4	5	6
7	8	9	10	11	12	13
14	15	16	17	18	19	20
21	22	23	24	25	26	27
28	29	.	.	.	.	.

	March					
S	M	T	W	T	F	S
.	.	1	2	3	4	5
6	7	8	9	10	11	12
13	14	15	16	17	18	19
20	21	22	23	24	25	26
27	28	29	30	31	.	.

FOUR

In EIGHTEEN HUNDRED AND SIXTY-FOUR
We'll all go home and fight no more.
We'll all drink stone blind;
Johnny, come fill up the bowl.

	April					
S	M	T	W	T	F	S
.	.	.	.	.	1	2
3	4	5	6	7	8	9
10	11	12	13	14	15	16
17	18	19	20	21	22	23
24	25	26	27	28	29	30

	May					
S	M	T	W	T	F	S
1	2	3	4	5	6	7
8	9	10	11	12	13	14
15	16	17	18	19	20	21
22	23	24	25	26	27	28
29	30	31	.	.	.	.

	June					
S	M	T	W	T	F	S
.	.	.	1	2	3	4
5	6	7	8	9	10	11
12	13	14	15	16	17	18
19	20	21	22	23	24	25
26	27	28	29	30	.	.

	July					
S	M	T	W	T	F	S
.	.	.	.	.	1	2
3	4	5	6	7	8	9
10	11	12	13	14	15	16
17	18	19	20	21	22	23
24	25	26	27	28	29	30
31	.	.	.	.	.	.

	August					
S	M	T	W	T	F	S
.	1	2	3	4	5	6
7	8	9	10	11	12	13
14	15	16	17	18	19	20
21	22	23	24	25	26	27
28	29	30	31	.	.	.

	September					
S	M	T	W	T	F	S
.	.	.	.	1	2	3
4	5	6	7	8	9	10
11	12	13	14	15	16	17
18	19	20	21	22	23	24
25	26	27	28	29	30	.

	October					
S	M	T	W	T	F	S
.	.	.	.	.	.	1
2	3	4	5	6	7	8
9	10	11	12	13	14	15
16	17	18	19	20	21	22
23	24	25	26	27	28	29
30	31	.	.	.	.	.

	November					
S	M	T	W	T	F	S
.	.	1	2	3	4	5
6	7	8	9	10	11	12
13	14	15	16	17	18	19
20	21	22	23	24	25	26
27	28	29	30	.	.	.

	December					
S	M	T	W	T	F	S
.	.	.	.	1	2	3
4	5	6	7	8	9	10
11	12	13	14	15	16	17
18	19	20	21	22	23	24
25	26	27	28	29	30	31

Election day comes soon again;
  Hurra! Hurra!
And we will put old Abe in then. . . .
  Hurra! Hurra!

Get ready, then, for the jubilee, etc.
And give honest Abe a three times three, etc.
        —"WHEN ABE GOES IN AGAIN"

27. LINCOLN GIVES SATISFACTION

A Fair Rebel's Interview with Lincoln

✱

DURING BUCHANAN'S ADMINISTRATION, Francis P. Blair, Sr., had a country place in Maryland, called "Silver Spring." George Beale and his family, who were intimate friends of ours, also had a place in Maryland called "Indian Spring," which adjoined or nearly adjoined the Blair Place. I often visited the Beales as a girl, and it was through this association I knew Mr. Blair, who subsequently introduced me to Mr. Lincoln.

My only brother, Thomas H. Neilson, was at school preparing for the University of Virginia when the War broke out in 1861. As soon as Virginia seceded, he joined the Confederate Army in Staunton, Virginia, under John D. Imboden. Communication between the North and South was cut off by blockade and picket guard. Occasionally the blockade was evaded by Confederates and thus intelligence of Southern friends was received.

We learned that General Imboden's command had been sent to join "Stonewall" Jackson's Brigade. I had not heard from my brother for eighteen months when "Stonewall" Jackson was defeated and report said his army was cut to pieces. [My mother] was heartbroken lest her only son had been killed. I implored her to keep up her courage as there were Confederate prisoners taken, and Tom might be among them. I suggested that I ask Mr. Blair to introduce me to the President with the view of obtaining a pass to go through the forts containing rebel prisoners. Mr. Blair willingly consented, provided I could get two Army officers to indorse me. This, fortunately, I was able to do. Colonel Samuel Bowman, a lifelong friend of the family, and Colonel Roger Jones, were then stationed in Washington, and both agreed to do this.

I then wrote to Mr. Blair telling him that Colonel Bowman and Colonel Roger Jones would go with me, and asked him to arrange an interview with the President. This he readily did, and wrote me that such an interview had been granted. Soon after, I met Colonel Bowman in Philadelphia, and we went to Washington, where we were joined by Roger Jones, and all four proceeded to the White House. After a long wait we were ushered into the President's room. I well remember how small I felt before the tall, lank, angular figure of the President as he arose to receive us, but was immediately put at my ease by his most kindly manner.

He shook hands with all; then placing one hand behind him with the other in his trousers' pocket, he listened attentively to what Mr. Blair said.—I omitted to state that while waiting, Mr. Blair had said to me, "Mary, be very guarded in all you say"; and to Colonel Roger Jones, "You cannot be too careful as this is a serious undertaking."

Then Colonel Bowman said, "Birdie, do not get excited and make a fool of yourself."

When Mr. Blair had finished, the President turned to me with a searching look from his deep-set eyes and said, "You are loyal, of course?"

I replied, "Yes, loyal to the heart's core—to Virginia."

The President just seemed as if he was trying to look me through, withdrawing his hand from his pocket and stroking his chin—we both gazed steadily at each other a moment. Then turning to his desk, he wrote a few lines, handed the paper to me, and bowed us out.

All three—Mr. Blair, Colonel Bowman, and Colonel Roger Jones —were infuriated with me. Colonel Roger Jones was so indignant that he rushed down Pennsylvania Avenue without speaking.

Colonel Bowman said, "Birdie, I told you not to make a fool of yourself."

I replied, "I did not, for as Mr. Lincoln had asked me a straight-forward question I answered him truly."

Mr. Blair replied, "You have no one to thank for this but yourself."

I said, "Let us see what the President has written," and opening the paper, read:

To COMMANDERS OF FORTS CONTAINING REBEL PRISONERS:
Permit the bearer, Miss Neilson, to pass in and make inquiries about her brother; she is an honest girl and can be trusted.
(*Signed*) A. LINCOLN

I then bid them good morning, but could not resist saying to Mr. Blair, "I have nobody to thank but myself."

As I remember, this was in March, or early April, 1864.
—MARY NEILSON JACKSON

*

A Visit from Uncle Dennis

---

*

"MR. HANKS, I believe you had the honor of visiting Mr. Lincoln at the Executive Mansion in Washington, did you not?"

He looked at me a moment, and laughing heartily, said: "So that's the yarn ye're after, is it?" Chuckling to himself for a moment, he winked his eye at Mr. Hall and then his tongue became nimble as a school girl's. "Ye've heerd how some fellers down at Charleston got into trouble and wus sent to the Dry Tortugas, ain't ye?" said Mr. Hanks. I informed him that I knew all about that, and begged him to proceed with his own part in the drama. He proceeded, saying: "Wal, some of 'em smart lawyers down in Charleston tried to get Abe to let the boys come home, but they didn't fetch 'em worth a cent. So I ses to myself, Dennis y'ur the boy to du it, and I jest told the citizens of Charleston so, and they said, 'Hanks, we will give you twelve hundred dollars if you will get the prisoners released.' Ye better believe that I took that offer up and waded right in, got my ticket, rode down to Washington and [May 15, 1864] went right up to Uncle Abe's house and asked to see President Lincoln. The feller what stood at the door told me there wus jest a certain way to get in, but anyhow, the President wus crowded now. Says he, 'There's lots of fellers in talking with him and more that want to get in that come before you did.' Then I said to him, ses I, 'If you'll jest show me the hole where the President goes in and out I'll get to see him.' The feller at the door then said to me, 'Who are you?' I ses my name is Hanks, I'm an American citizen, and I want to see Abe Lincoln. Then another feller says, 'Where are you from?' I ses, ses I, 'Wal, I am from Charleston, Coles County, Illinois.' Then some other feller said, 'That man talks like the President, his voice sounds like his, and maybe he is a relation.'

"I waited a minute and nobody done nothing, so I jest speaks up ag'in and ses I, 'Ef you'll take me up to his bedroom I'll have no trouble in gettin' in.' A feller took me up to a door to where Seward wus a settin', and I looked through a bunch of men and saw Uncle Abe by a stove playin' with his little boy, and handin' him some lemonade or somethin' like that and laughin' and talkin' with him. I looked at him a little bit and spoke out in a loud voice, 'Abe, what you doin' thur?' Abe knowed my voice, straightened up, and said, 'Dennis, is that you?' He then invited me in and asked Mr. Seward and the other fellers to jest step out a few minutes, 'fur,' said he, 'I want to see this man privately.' So they all went out but me and Uncle Abe. He then askt me, 'How is Mother gettin' along and all the balance of the family?'

"I jest open'd up and told Abe my business, and let him know what I hed come fur. Abe then told me that Colonel Ficklin hed ben thar twice on the same business, but he hed not then thought the men hed ben punished long enough, so he ses, ses he, 'Now I guess they can go home and take care of their families and try to be good men.' He wrote out a piece of writin' and told me to hand that to Stanton. Wal, I took it to him, but he flew into a passion and ses he, 'They did too bad a deed to be pardoned.' He talked a little bit with me and then said, 'I will go and see Mr. Lincoln,' and took me with him. Abe talked with me a little and then he turned around and spoke to Mr. Stanton and said, 'These men all have families and they want to go back and take care of them and behave themselves, and now whose business is it?' Stanton jest shet up and never said no more, nohow.

"Abe told me to look around the city and enjoy myself. 'Twould be all right,' he said, so I did, and shore nuff when I got back to Charleston I found the fellers hed got thar afore me and everybody was rejoicing."

—As told by DENNIS HANKS to ELEANOR GRIDLEY

*

Lieutenant Tad

*

THE HOUSE was thrown into an uproar by a performance of little "Tad's." I was sitting in Mr. Nicolay's room, about ten o'clock, when Robert Lincoln came in with a flushed face. "Well," said he, "I have just had a great row with the President of the United States!"

"What?" said I.

"Yes," he replied, "and very good cause there is for it, too. Do you know," he continued, " 'Tad' went over to the War Department to-day, and Stanton, for the fun of the thing—putting him a peg above the 'little corporal' of the French Government—commissioned him 'lieutenant.' On the strength of this, what does 'Tad' do but go off and order a quantity of muskets sent to the house! To-night he had the audacity to discharge the guard, and he then mustered all the gardeners and servants, gave them the guns, drilled them, and put them on duty in their place. I found it out an hour ago," continued Robert, "and thinking it a great shame, as the men had been hard at work all day, I went to father with it; but instead of punishing 'Tad,' as I think he ought, he evidently looks upon it as a good joke, and won't do anything about it!"

"Tad," however, presently went to bed, and then the men were quietly discharged. And so it happened that the presidential mansion was unguarded one night, at least, during the war!

—F. B. CARPENTER

＊

"Why the Lord Put a Curl in a Pig's Tail"

＊

AT THE SOLDIERS' HOME . . . our duties, of course, were
principally guard duties, and if there is any one thing that becomes more
irksome than another to the average soldier, it is continuous guard
duty. Under it soldiers are liable to become restless and sometimes
fractious, especially when there are stirring times at the front.

There came a time during the early summer of 1864 when the
men of our Company became very restless. There were reports of great
activity at the front, and we longed to be in it. So one evening, when
the President was strolling near the men's tents, emboldened by his
kindly manner, one of the men took it upon himself to approach him
in regard to the matter of a change of service, stating in substance that
the men felt that they were not needed where they were, and that there
was greater need of their services at the front.

The President listened patiently to all the man had to say, and then
with a twinkle in his eye said, "Well, my boy, that reminds me of an
old farmer friend of mine in Illinois, who used to say he never could
understand why the Lord put a curl in a pig's tail; it did not seem to him
to be either useful or ornamental, but he guessed the Lord knew what
he was doing when he put it there. I do not myself," he said, "see the
necessity of having soldiers traipsing around after me wherever I go,
but Stanton"—referring to Secretary of War Stanton—"who knows a
great deal more about such things than I do, seems to think it is necessary, and he may be right; and if it is necessary to have soldiers here,
it might as well be you as some one else. If you were sent to the front,
some one would have to come from the front to take your place." Then,
in a tone of mild rebuke, he added, "It is a soldier's duty to obey orders
without question, and in doing that you can serve your country as faithfully here as at the front, and," said he, with another smile, "I reckon
it is not quite as dangerous here as it is there." And with a gentle wave
of his hand, he passed on.

The other boys had the laugh on the good fellow's brave effort to get to the front, but you can rest assured that no other member of that Company ever ventured to carry any further complaints to the President about their service.

—SMITH STIMMEL

*

Lincoln under Fire

*

[ON JULY 12, 1864] leaving the ditch, my pass carried me into . . . Fort [Stevens] where, to my surprise, I found the President, Secretary Stanton, and other civilians. A young colonel of artillery, who appeared to be the officer of the day, was in great distress because the President would expose himself, and paid little attention to his warnings. He was satisfied the Confederates had recognized him, for they were firing at him very hotly, and a soldier near him had just fallen with a broken thigh. He asked my advice, for he said the President was in great danger.

"What would you do with me under like circumstances?" I asked.

"I would civilly ask you to take a position where you were not exposed."

"And if I refused to obey?"

"I would send a sergeant and a file of men, and make you obey."

"Then treat the President just as you would me or any civilian."

"I dare not. He is my superior officer; I have taken an oath to obey his orders."

"He has given you no orders. Follow my advice, and you will not regret it."

"I will," he said. "I may as well die for one thing as another. If he were shot, I should hold myself responsible."

He walked to where the President was looking over the parapet. "Mr. President," he said, "you are standing within range of five hundred rebel rifles. Please come down to a safer place. If you do not, it will be my duty to call a file of men, and make you."

359

"And you would do right, my boy!" said the President, coming down at once. "You are in command of this fort. I should be the last man to set an example of disobedience."

He was shown to a place where the view was less extended, but where there was almost no exposure.

—L. E. CHITTENDEN

*

"Re-enlist" Lincoln!

*

JUST AFTER the presidential nominations had been made in 1864, a discussion arose in a certain regiment in the Army of the Potomac as to the merits of the two candidates. Various opinions had been warmly expressed, when at length a German spoke. "I goes," said he, "for Fader Abraham. Fader Abraham, he likes the soldier-boy. Ven he serves tree years he gives him four hundred tollar, and re-enlists him von veteran. Now Fader Abraham, he serves four years. We re-enlist him four years more, and make *von veteran of him*."

—HENRY J. RAYMOND

*

Voting for Lincoln in Andersonville

*

THE DAY of the Presidential election of 1864 approached. The Rebels were naturally very much interested in the result, as they believed that the election of McClellan meant compromise and cessation of hostilities, while the election of Lincoln meant prosecution of the war to the bitter end. The toadying Raiders [at Andersonville] who were perpetually hanging around the gate to get a chance to insinuate themselves into the favor of the Rebel officers, persuaded them that we were all so bitterly hostile to our Government for not exchanging us that if we were allowed to vote we would cast an overwhelming majority in favor of McClellan.

The Rebels thought that this might perhaps be used to advantage as political capital for their friends in the North. They gave orders that we might, if we chose, hold an election on the same day of the Presidential election. They sent in some ballot boxes, and we elected Judges of the Election.

About noon of that day Captain Bowes, and a crowd of tight-booted, broad-hatted Rebel officers, strutted in with the peculiar "Ef-yer-don't-believe-I'm-a-butcher-jest-smell-o'-me-boots" swagger characteristic of the class. They had come in to see us all voting for McClellan. Instead, they found the polls surrounded with ticket pedlars shouting:

"Walk right up here now, and get your Unconditional-Union-Abraham Lincoln tickets!"

"Here's your straight-haired prosecution-of-the-war ticket."

"Vote the Lincoln ticket; vote to whip the Rebels, and make peace with them when they've laid down their arms."

"Don't vote a McClellan ticket and gratify —— Rebels, everywhere," etc.

The Rebel officers did not find the scene what their fancy painted it, and turning around they strutted out.

When the votes came to be counted out, there were over seven thousand for Lincoln, and not half that many hundred for McClellan. The latter got very few votes outside the Raider crowd. The same day a similar election was held in Florence, with like result. Of course this did not indicate that there was any such preponderance of Republicans among us. It meant simply that the Democratic boys, little as they might have liked Lincoln, would have voted for him a hundred times rather than do anything to please the Rebels.

I never heard that the Rebels sent the result to the North.

—JOHN McELROY

"Too Many Pigs"

*

IN THE WINTER OF 1864, after serving three years in the Union Army, and being honorably discharged, I made application for the post sutlership at Point Lookout. My father being interested, we made application to Mr. Stanton, then Secretary of War.

We obtained an audience, and were ushered into the presence of the most pompous man I ever met. As I entered he waved his hand for me to stop at a given distance from him, and then put these questions, viz.:

"Did you serve three years in the army?"

"I did, sir."

"Were you honorably discharged?"

"I was, sir."

"Let me see your discharge."

I gave it to him. He looked it over, then said: "Were you ever wounded?"

I told him yes, at the battle of Williamsburg, May 5, 1862.

He then said: "I think we can give this position to a soldier who has lost an arm or leg, he being more deserving"; and he then said I looked hearty and healthy enough to serve three years more. He would not give me a chance to argue my case.

The audience was at an end. He waved his hand to me. I was then dismissed from the august presence of the Honorable Secretary of War.

My father was waiting for me in the hallway, who saw by my countenance that I was not successful. I said to my father: "Let us go over to Mr. Lincoln; he may give us more satisfaction."

He said it would do me no good, but we went over. Mr. Lincoln's reception room was full of ladies and gentlemen when we entered, and the scene was one I shall never forget.

On her knees was a woman in the agonies of despair, with tears rolling down her cheeks, imploring for the life of her son, who had deserted and had been condemned to be shot. I heard Mr. Lincoln say: "Madam, do not act in this way, it is agony to me; I would pardon your son if it was in my power, but there must be an example made or I will have no army."

At this speech the woman fainted. Lincoln motioned to his attendant, who picked the woman up and carried her out. All in the room were in tears.

But now, changing the scene from the sublime to the ridiculous, the next applicant for favor was a big, buxom Irish woman, who stood before the President, with arms akimbo, saying: "Mr. Lincoln, can't I sell apples on the railroad?"

Lincoln said: "Certainly, madam, you can sell all you wish."

But she said: "You must give me a pass, or the soldiers will not let me."

Lincoln then wrote a few lines and gave it to her, who said: "Thank you, sir; God bless you."

This shows how quick and clear were all this man's decisions.

I stood and watched him for two hours, and he dismissed each case as quickly as the above, with satisfaction to all.

My turn soon came. Lincoln turned to my father and said: "Now, gentlemen, be pleased to be as quick as possible with your business, as it is growing late."

My father then stepped up to Lincoln and introduced me to him. Lincoln then said: "Take a seat, gentlemen, and state your business as quickly as possible."

There was but one chair by Lincoln, so he motioned my father to sit, while I stood. My father stated the business to him as stated above. He then said: "Have you seen Mr. Stanton?"

We told him yes, that he had refused. He (Mr. Lincoln) then said: "Gentlemen, this is Mr. Stanton's business; I cannot interfere with him; he attends to all these matters and I am sorry I cannot help you."

He saw that we were disappointed, and did his best to revive our spirits. He succeeded well with my father, who was a Lincoln man, and who was a staunch Republican.

Mr. Lincoln then said: "Now, gentlemen, I will tell you what it is; I have thousands of applications like this every day, but we cannot satisfy all for this reason, that these positions are like office seekers— there are too many pigs for the tits."

The ladies who were listening to the conversation placed their handkerchiefs to their faces and turned away. But the joke of Old Abe put us all in a good humor. We then left the presence of the greatest and most just man who ever lived to fill the Presidential chair.

—PAUL SELBY, *Lincoln's Life, Stories and Speeches*

363

*He doesn't ask me to do impossibilities for him, and he's
the first general I've had that didn't!*

—A. LINCOLN

28. GRANT FIGHTS IT OUT
ON HIS LINE

How Lincoln Defended Grant

*

[LINCOLN AND GRANT] did not meet till March [8], 1864,
and previous to that time had had but little personal correspondence.
Most of the communications which the General received from the President had been in the form of executive orders sent through the War
Department. Lincoln had early formed a high opinion of the Western
General, in consequence of his victories at Donelson and Shiloh, and
because he did not spend his time in calling for troops, but made the
best use of those that were sent him. In other words, he was a man
who asked for nothing, and gave the executive no trouble.

Grant's successes brought with them the usual number of jeal-
ousies and rivalries. Political generals had their advocates in Washington

to plead their cause, while Grant stood without friends at court. His detractors gathered at times a great deal of strength in their efforts to supplant him with a general of their own choosing, and Lincoln was beset by many a delegation who insisted that nothing would harmonize matters in the West but Grant's removal. This nagging continued even after his great triumph at Vicksburg.

Lincoln always enjoyed telling the General, after the two had become personally intimate, how the cross-roads wiseacres had criticised his campaigns.

One day, after dwelling for some time on this subject, he said to Grant: "After Vicksburg I thought it was about time to shut down on this sort of thing. So one day, when a delegation came to see me and had spent half an hour in trying to show me the fatal mistake you had made in paroling Pemberton's army, and insisting that the rebels would violate their paroles and in less than a month confront you again in the ranks, and have to be whipped all over again, I thought I should get rid of them best by telling them a story about Sykes's dog.

" 'Have you ever heard about Sykes's yellow dog?' said I to the spokesman of the delegation. He said he hadn't. 'Well, I must tell you about him,' said I. 'Sykes had a yellow dog he set great store by, but there were a lot of small boys around the village, and that's always a bad thing for dogs, you know. These boys didn't share Sykes's views, and they were not disposed to let the dog have a fair show. Even Sykes had to admit that the dog was getting unpopular; in fact it was soon seen that a prejudice was growing up against that dog that threatened to wreck all his future prospects in life. The boys, after meditating how they could get the best of him, finally fixed up a cartridge with a long fuse, put the cartridge in a piece of meat, dropped the meat in the road in front of Sykes's door, and then perched themselves on a fence a good distance off with the end of the fuse in their hands. Then they whistled for the dog. When he came out he scented the bait, and bolted the meat, cartridge and all. The boys touched off the fuse with a cigar and in about a second a report came from that dog that sounded like a small clap of thunder. Sykes came bouncing out of the house, and yelled: "What's up! Anything busted?"

" 'There was no reply except a snicker from the small boys roosting on the fence, but as Sykes looked up he saw the whole air filled with pieces of yellow dog. He picked up the biggest piece he could find, a portion of the back with a part of the tail still hanging to it, and after turning it around and looking it all over he said, "Well, I guess he'll never be much account again—as a dog." And I guess Pemberton's forces will never be much account again—as an army.'

"The delegation began looking around for their hats before I had quite got to the end of the story, and I was never bothered any more after that about superseding the commander of the Army of the Tennessee."

—GENERAL HORACE PORTER

*

"—if It Takes All Summer"

*

THE 11th of May [1864] gave promise of a little rest for everybody, as the commander expressed his intention to spend the day simply in reconnoitering for the purpose of learning more about the character and strength of the enemy's intrenchments, and discovering the weakest points in his line, with a view to breaking through. He sat down at the mess-table that morning, and made his entire breakfast off a cup of coffee and a small piece of beef cooked almost to a crisp; for the cook had by this time learned that the nearer he came to burning up the beef the better the General liked it. During the short time he was at the table he conversed with Mr. Elihu B. Washburne, who had accompanied headquarters up to this time, and who was now about to return to Washington. After breakfast the General lighted a cigar, seated himself on a camp-chair in front of his tent, and was joined there by Mr. Washburne and several members of his staff.

At half-past eight the cavalry escort which was to accompany the congressman was drawn up in the road near by, and all present rose to bid him good-by. Turning to the chief, he said: "General, I shall go to see the President and the Secretary of War as soon as I reach Washington. I can imagine their anxiety to know what you think of the prospects of the campaign, and I know they would be greatly gratified if I could carry a message from you giving what encouragement you can as to the situation."

The General hesitated a moment, and then replied: "We are certainly making fair progress, and all the fighting has been in our favor; but the campaign promises to be a long one, and I am particularly anxious not to say anything just now that might hold out false hopes to the people"; and then, after a pause, added, "However, I will write a letter to Halleck, as I generally communicate through him, giving the general situation, and you can take it with you." He stepped into his tent, sat down at his field-table, and, keeping his cigar in his mouth, wrote a despatch of about two hundred words. In the middle of the communication occurred the famous words, *"I propose to fight it out on this line if it takes all summer."*

When the letter had been copied, he folded it and handed it to Mr. Washburne, who thanked him warmly, wished him a continuation of success, shook hands with him and each of the members of the staff, and at once mounted his horse and rode off. The staff officers read the retained copy of the despatch, but neither the General himself nor any one at headquarters realized the epigrammatic character of the striking sentence it contained until the New York papers reached camp a few days afterward with the words displayed in large headlines, and with conspicuous comments upon the force of the expression.

—GENERAL HORACE PORTER

∗

"Ulysses Don't Scare Worth a Damn"

∗

WHILE THE GENERAL-IN-CHIEF was out on the lines supervising the afternoon attack [in the battle of the Bloody Angle, May 12, 1864], he dismounted and sat down on a fallen tree to write a despatch. While thus engaged a shell exploded directly in front of him. He looked up from his paper an instant, and then, without the slightest change of countenance, went on writing the message. Some of the Fifth Wisconsin wounded were being carried past him at the time, and Major E. R. Jones of that regiment said . . . that one of his men made the remark: "Ulysses don't scare worth a d———n."

—GENERAL HORACE PORTER

*

Grant Loses His Temper

*

RAWLINS rode with the General at the head of the staff. As the party turned a bend in the road near the crossing of the Totopotomoy [May, 1864], the General came in sight of a teamster whose wagon was stalled in a place where it was somewhat swampy, and who was standing beside his team beating his horses brutally in the face with the butt-end of his whip, and swearing with a volubility calculated to give a sulphurous odor to all the surrounding atmosphere. Grant's aversion to profanity and his love of horses caused all the ire in his nature to be aroused by the sight presented. Putting both spurs into "Egypt's" flanks, he dashed toward the teamster, and raising his clenched fist, called out to him: "What does this conduct mean, you scoundrel? Stop beating those horses!" The teamster looked at him, and said coolly, as he delivered another blow aimed at the face of the wheel-horse: "Well, who's drivin' this team anyhow—you or me?"

The General was now thoroughly angered, and his manner was by no means as angelic as that of the celestial being who called a halt when Balaam was disciplining the ass. "I'll show you, you infernal villain!" he cried, shaking his fist in the man's face. Then calling to an officer of the escort, he said: "Take this man in charge, and have him tied to a tree for six hours as a punishment for his brutality." The man slunk off sullenly in charge of the escort to receive his punishment, without showing any penitence for his conduct. He was evidently a hardened case. Of course he was not aware that the officer addressing him was the General-in-Chief, but he evidently knew that he was an officer of high rank, as he was accompanied by a staff and an escort, so that there was no excuse for the insubordinate and insolent remark. . . .

During the stirring scenes of that day's battle the General twice referred to the incident in vehement language, showing that the recollection of it was still rankling in his mind. This was the one exhibition of temper manifested by him during the entire campaign, and the only one I ever witnessed during my many years of service with him.

I remarked that night to Colonel Bowers, who had served with his chief ever since the Fort Donelson campaign: "The General to-day gave us his first exhibition of anger. Did you ever see him fire up in that way in his earlier campaigns?"

"Never but once," said Bowers; "and that was in the Iuka campaign. One day on the march he came across a straggler who had stopped at a house and assaulted a woman. The General sprang from his horse, seized a musket from the hands of a soldier, and struck the culprit over the head with it, sending him sprawling to the ground."

He always had a peculiar horror of such crimes. They were very rare in our war, but when brought to his attention the General showed no mercy to the culprit.

—GENERAL HORACE PORTER

✳

Why Grant Never Swore

✳

WHILE SITTING with [Grant] at the camp-fire late one night, after every one else had gone to bed, I said to him: "General, it seems singular that you have gone through all the rough and tumble of army service and frontier life, and have never been provoked into swearing. I have never heard you utter an oath or use an imprecation."

"Well, somehow or other, I never learned to swear," he replied. "When a boy I seemed to have an aversion to it, and when I became a man I saw the folly of it. I have always noticed, too, that swearing helps to rouse a man's anger; and when a man flies into a passion his adversary who keeps cool always gets the better of him. In fact, I could never see the use of swearing. I think it is the case with many people who swear excessively that it is a mere habit, and that they do not mean to be profane; but, to say the least, it is a great waste of time."

His example in this respect was once quoted in my hearing by a member of the Christian Commission to a teamster in the Army of the

Potomac, in the hope of lessening the volume of rare oaths with which he was italicizing his language, and upon which he seemed to be placing his main reliance in moving his mule-team out of a mud-hole. The only reply evoked from him was: "Then thar's one thing sart'in: the old man never druv mules."

—GENERAL HORACE PORTER

*

When Grant Was Stumped

*

AT CITY POINT, in 1864, I was General Grant's guest, by special invitation, and witnessed a scene of rare interest.

It was announced at supper that the General would receive a delegation of citizens from Philadelphia, coming with an unknown purpose.

"We must be there," said Bowers, the Assistant Adjutant General; "and you must watch Grant when it comes time for him to reply. You see, if he's a little stumped, and wants a moment to think, he always gets it by striking matches, pretending he can't get one to burn. Sometimes he'll spoil a bowlful; but when he has his idea clear, the trouble is over. The match goes off all right, and, his cigar lit, he turns and speaks."

The meeting took place in the little box the General called his office. We were all there; so was the delegation. The spokesman took the floor and delivered a speech the substance of which may be given.

"General Grant, we represent the business men of Philadelphia, and have been charged to tell you frankly that the country is suffering, and that you must do something decisive immediately. In the South, and along the Mississippi, operations are going on by land and water, and everybody is active. Sherman is absorbing all the attention. He is thundering away in the heart of the rebellion. You alone are doing nothing. We have come to implore you to wake up."

Grant, at the end, turned to the mantel above the fireplace, on which there was a bowlful of matches and a box of cigars. Taking a fresh cigar, he struck match after match without avail; it looked as if the supply would all go. Minutes passed; at last he struck fire.

Then Bowers nudged me, and whispered:

"Listen—he's ready."

I give the reply substantially.

"Gentlemen," the General said, "I am glad to hear from you that the country has not lost its interest in the war. You urge me to move, and have been at pains to come and tell me that Sherman will shortly shut me out of public attention if I don't hurry and head him off. Well" —he stopped and whiffed a moment—"I will take you into my confidence, provided you do not take the newspapers into your confidence. Sherman is acting by order, and I am waiting on him. Just as soon as I hear that he is at some of the points designated on the sea-coast, then, the Mississippi River being secured for our boats, I will take Richmond. Were I to move now without advices from Sherman, Lee would evacuate Richmond, taking his army somewhere South, and I would have to follow him to keep him from jumping on Sherman. That would be very inconvenient to me, as it would compel me to haul supplies in wagons over unknown dirt roads to an unknown distance. I hope, gentlemen, you will report to your constituents how much obliged I am to General Lee for staying where he is; and be careful, please, to tell them that jealousy between General Sherman and me is impossible. Please smoke with me."

—LEW WALLACE

371

And yet they call me barbarian, vandal, a monster. . . . All I pretend to say, on earth as in heaven, man must submit to some arbiter. . . . I would not subjugate the South . . . but I would make every citizen of the land obey the common law, submit to the same that we do—no more, no less—our equals and not our superiors.

—WILLIAM TECUMSEH SHERMAN

29. SHERMAN WAS "A KIND OF CARELESS MAN ABOUT FIRE"

Sherman and "Miss Cecilia"

*

ON SHELLMAN HEIGHTS, on the Etowah, near Cartersville, Georgia, there stood an old ante-bellum mansion, among the few which escaped Sherman's torch in his resistless "march to the sea." The lady who became mistress of this mansion and queened it there in the old days, was Miss Cecilia Stovall, a noted Southern belle. At West Point, where she spent many of her summers, she was surrounded by a train of admirers, among whom were William T. Sherman and Joseph Hooker. In the spring of 1864, Sherman and Joseph Hooker both paused on the heights of Etowah. As his soldiers were ransacking the mansion, Sherman's attention was attracted by the wails of an old Negress: "O Lawd, what's Miss Cecilia gwine ter do now?" Sherman made inquiries and learned that the "Miss Cecilia" was his old sweetheart. Thereupon, orders were issued to the soldiers to replace what they had taken. A guard was thrown around the house, and the man who had said "war is hell" left the following note for its mistress:

DEAR MADAM:

You once said that you would pity the man who would ever become my enemy. My answer was that I would ever protect and shield you. That I have done. Forgive me all else. I am but a soldier.

Respectfully,
W. T. SHERMAN

—HELEN DORTCH LONGSTREET

*

Smoke Signals

---

*

THE ONLY TIME I saw General Sherman was after we had failed to break Joe Johnston's front at Kenesaw Mountain [Georgia, June 27, 1864]. It was plain that more flanking must be done, so the "Great Flanker" ordered General [Jacob D.] Cox's division of the 23rd Corps to make a detour and threaten the enemy's left.

This involved a long march, and General Sherman made his way to the top of a high hill, where we were lying, to enable him to overlook the country and see operations better. He sat on a stump with a map spread out on his knees, and was giving General Cox directions as to his line of march. After doing this, he mounted his horse and started away, but after having gone away a little distance he shouted back, "See here, Cox, burn a few barns occasionally, as you go along. I can't understand those signal flags, but I know what smoke means."

—WASHINGTON DAVIS

373

*

Sherman and the Northern Citizen of Atlanta

---

*

[IN 1864] an order was promulgated directing all civilians to leave Atlanta (North or South) within twelve days. On the day of its issue a gentleman entered Sherman's office and enquired for the General. The latter answered, very promptly, "I am General Sherman." The colloquy was very nearly as follows:

Citizen—General, I am a Northern man from the State of Connecticut; I have been living at Atlanta for nearly seven years; have accumulated property here, and as I see that you have ordered all citizens to leave within twelve days, I came to see if you would make an exception in my case. I fear, if I leave, my property will be destroyed.

General Sherman—What kind of property do you own, sir: Perhaps I will make an exception in your case, sir.

Citizen—I own a block of stores, three buildings, a plantation two miles out of town, and a foundry.

General Sherman—Foundry, eh! What have you been doing with your foundry?

Citizen—Have been making castings.

General Sherman—What kind of castings? Shot and shell, and all that kind of thing?

Citizen—Yes, I have made some shot and shell.

General Sherman—You have been making shot and shell to destroy your country, have you? And you still claim favor on account of being a Northern man! Yes, sir, I will make an exception in your case; you shall go South to-morrow morning at sunrise. Adjutant, see that this order is carried out. Orderly, show this man the door.

Citizen—But, General, can't I go North?

General Sherman—No, sir. Too many of your class there already, sir.

—REV. G. S. BRADLEY

Advice to a Southern Minister
Whose Horse Had Been Stolen

*

Atlanta, Ga.
September 16, 1864

Rev. ——, Confederate Army:
DEAR SIR:

Your letter of September 14 is received. I approach a question involving a title to a "horse" with deference for the laws of war. That mysterious code, of which we talk so much but know so little, is remarkably silent on the "horse." He is a beast so tempting to the soldier, to him of the wild cavalry, the fancy artillery, or the patient infantry, that I find more difficulty in recovering a worthless, spavined beast, than in paying a million of "Greenbacks"; so that I fear I must reduce your claim to one of finance, and refer you to the great board of claims in Washington, that may reach your case by the time your grandchild becomes a great grandfather.

Privately, I think it was a shabby thing in that scamp of the Thirty-first Missouri who took your horse, and the colonel or his brigadier should have restored him. But I cannot undertake to make good the sins of omission of my own colonels and brigadiers, much less of those of a former generation. "When this cruel war is over," and peace once more gives you a parish, I will promise, if near you, to procure out of Uncle Sam's corrals a beast that will replace the one taken from you, so wrongfully; but now it is impossible. We have a big journey before us and need all we have, and, I fear, more too; so look out when the Yanks are about and hide your beasts, for my experience is that all soldiers are very careless in a search for title. I know that General [William J.] Hardee will confirm this, my advice.

With great respect, yours truly,
W. T. SHERMAN,
Major General

—REV. G. S. BRADLEY

*

Sherman's "Duplicates"

---

*

[IN OCTOBER, 1864] the rebels had struck our railroad a heavy blow, burning every tie, bending the rails for eight miles, from Big Shanty to above Acworth, so that the estimate for repairs called for thirty-five thousand new ties, and six miles of iron. Ten thousand men were distributed along the break to replace the ties, and to prepare the road-bed, while the regular repair-party, under Colonel W. W. Wright, came down from Chattanooga with iron, spikes, etc., and in about seven days the road was all right again. It was by such acts of extraordinary energy that we discouraged our adversaries, for the rebel soldiers felt that it was a waste of labor for them to march hurriedly, on wide circuits, day and night, to burn a bridge and tear up a mile or so of track, when they knew that we could lay it back so quickly. They supposed that we had men and money without limit, and that we always kept on hand, distributed along the road, duplicates of every bridge and culvert of any importance.

[According to] one who was on Kenesaw Mountain during our advance in the previous June or July, a group of rebels lay in the shade of a tree, one hot day, overlooking our camps about Big Shanty.

One soldier remarked to his fellows:

"Well, the Yanks will have to git up and git now, for I heard General Johnston himself say that General Wheeler had blown up *the tunnel* near Dalton, and that the Yanks would have to retreat, because they could get no more rations."

"Oh, hell!" said a listener, "don't you know that old Sherman carries a *duplicate* tunnel along?"

—GENERAL WILLIAM T. SHERMAN

The Sleeping General

I · Why Sherman Slept in the Daytime

Camp in Pine Grove, near "Rocky Creek,"
Fourteenth Day out of Gilkeson Co., Ga.
November 29/64

HE IS PROVERBIALLY the most restless man in the army at night—never sleeps a night straight through, and frequently comes out and pokes round in this style, disregarding all remonstrance as to taking cold. His staff think that just such a freak at Rome brought on the neuralgia attack in the right arm and shoulder which has been troubling him for a month. Joined him and chatted a while about weather, climate, late hours, etc., etc. Says he always wakes up at 3 or 4 A. M. and can't sleep again till after daylight: and always likes at that hour to be up and about camp—"best time to hear any movement at a distance." He makes up by snatches of sleep in daytime. I asked him today if any truth in story of newspapers about two or three soldiers seeing him (unrecognized) lying asleep in fence corner one day on Atlanta campaign. . . .

—MAJOR HENRY HITCHCOCK

II · How He Was Caught Napping

SHERMAN was anxiously engaged maturing his plans [the night of May 13, 1864, before the battle of Resaca]. Next day, wearied and sleepy, he sat on a log, beside a shady tree, to rest himself, and soon fell asleep. He had but a single orderly with him; and few of the men, as they marched by, knew that he was Sherman.

"Is that a general?" asked one of the men.

"Yes," said the orderly.

377

"A pretty way we are commanded when our generals are lying drunk beside the road!" exclaimed the soldier, walking off in disgust.

"Stop, my man," said Sherman, jumping up; for Sherman sleeps with one eye and one ear, too, open, and heard him. "Stop, my man. I am not drunk. While you were sleeping last night, I was planning for you, sir; and now I was taking a nap. General Sherman never gets drunk, sir."

The soldier slunk away, and never minded a sleeping general again.

—CAPTAIN D. P. CONYNGHAM

30. MISSION ACCOMPLISHED

Mother Bickerdyke's Unauthorized Exploit

*

THE LAST DAY of the year 1863 was one of memorable coldness, as were the first few days of the year 1864. The rigor of the weather in Chicago at that time actually suspended all outdoor business, and laid an embargo on travel in the streets. It was even severer weather in Mother Bickerdyke's location; for the icy winds swept down Lookout Mountain, where they were re-enforced by currents of air that tore through the valleys of Mission Ridge, creating a furious arctic hurricane that overturned the hospital tents in which the most badly wounded men were located. It hurled the partially recovered patients out into the pouring rain, that became glare-ice as it touched the earth, breaking

379

anew their healing bones, and chilling their attenuated frames with the piercing mountain gales.

The rain fell in torrents in the mountains, and poured down their sides so furiously and suddenly that it made a great flood in the valleys at their base. Before the intense cold could stiffen the headlong current into ice, it swept out into the swollen creeks several of the feeblest of the men under single hospital tents; and they were drowned. Night set in intensely cold, for which the badly fitted up hospitals were wholly unprepared.

All that night Mother Bickerdyke worked like a Titan to save her bloodless, feeble patients from being frozen to death.

There were several hundred in hospital tents—all wounded men —all bad cases. The fires were piled higher and higher with logs, new fires were kindled which came nearly to the tents, until they were surrounded by a cordon of immense pyres, that roared and crackled in the stinging atmosphere. But before midnight the fuel gave out. To send men out into the forests to cut more, in the darkness and awful coldness, seemed barbarous. The surgeon in charge dared not order them out, and it is doubtful if the order could have been obeyed had it been given. "We must try and pull through until morning," he said, "for nothing can be done to-night." And he retired to his own quarters, in a helpless mood of mind.

Mother Bickerdyke was equal to the emergency. With her usual disdain of red tape, she appealed to the Pioneer Corps to take their mules, axes, hooks, and chains, and tear down the breastworks near them, made of logs with earth thrown up against them. They were of no value, having served their purpose during the campaign. Nevertheless, an order for their demolition was necessary if they were to be destroyed. There was no officer of sufficiently high rank present to dare give this order; but, after she had refreshed the shivering men with a cup or two of panado, composed of hot water, sugar, crackers, and whiskey, they went to work at her suggestion, without orders from officers. They knew, as did she, that on the continuance of the huge fires through the night, depended the lives of hundreds of their wounded comrades; for there was no bedding for the tents, only a blanket or two for each wounded suffering man.

The men of the corps set to work tearing down the breastworks, and hauling the logs to the fierce fires, while Mother Bickerdyke ordered half a dozen barrels of meal to be broken open, and mixed with warm water, for their mules. Immense caldrons of hot drinks were renewedly made under her direction—hot coffee, panado, and other nourishing potables; and layers of hot bricks were put around every wounded and sick man of the entire fifteen hundred as he lay in his cot. From tent to tent she ran all the night in the icy gale, hot bricks in one hand, and hot drinks in the other, cheering, warming, and encouraging the poor shivering fellows.

Suddenly there was a great cry of horror; and looking in the direction whence it proceeded, she saw thirteen ambulances filled with wounded men, who had been started for her hospital from Ringgold, in the morning, by order of the authorities. It had become necessary to break up the small outlying post hospitals, and concentrate at Chattanooga. These had been delayed by the rain and the gale, and for hours had been travelling in the darkness and unparalleled coldness, both mules and drivers being nearly exhausted and frozen. On opening the ambulances, what a spectacle met Mother Bickerdyke's eyes! They were filled with wounded men nearly chilled to death. The hands of one were frozen like marble. The feet of another, the face of another, the bowels of a fourth, who afterwards died. Every bandage had stiffened into ice. The kegs of water had become solid crystal; and the men, who were past complaining, almost past suffering, were dropping into the sleep that ends in death. The surgeons of the hospital were all at work through the night with Mrs. Bickerdyke, and came promptly to the relief of these poor men, hardly one of whom escaped amputation of frozen limbs from that night's fearful ride.

As the night was breaking into the cold gray day, the officer in command of the post was informed of Mother Bickerdyke's unauthorized exploits. He hastened down where the demolished breastworks were being rapidly devoured by the fierce flames. He took in the situation immediately, and evidently saw the necessity and wisdom of the course she had pursued. But it was his business to preserve order and maintain discipline; and so he made a show of arresting the irregular proceeding. By no mere order of his could this be done. Not until day-dawn, when they could go safely into the woods to cut fuel, were the men disposed to abate their raid on the breastworks, which had served their purpose of defence against the enemy weeks before.

"Madam, consider yourself under arrest!" was the Major's address to ubiquitous Mother Bickerdyke.

To which she replied, as she flew past him with hot bricks and hot drinks, "All right, Major! I'm arrested! Only don't meddle with me till the weather moderates; for my men will freeze to death, if you do!"

A story got in circulation that she was put in the guardhouse by the Major; but this was not true. There was some little official hubbub over her night's exploits, but she defended herself to the officers who reproved her, with this indisputable statement, "It's lucky for you, old fellows, that I did what I did. For if I hadn't, hundreds of men in the hospital tents would have frozen to death. No one at the North would have blamed *me,* but there would have been such a hullabaloo about your heads for allowing it to happen, that you would have lost them, whether or no." Some of the officers stood boldly by her, openly declaring that she had done right, and advised her to pursue the same course again, under the same circumstances. This was needless advice, as she would assuredly have done so.

The men for whom she labored so indefatigably could mention her name only with tears and benedictions. And those in camp manifested their approval of her by hailing her with three times three deafening hurrahs whenever she appeared among them, until, annoyed, she begged them "for Heaven's sake to stop their nonsense, and shut up!"

—MARY A. LIVERMORE

*

The Water-Carriers

---

*

[AT THE BATTLE of Cold Harbor, Virginia, June 3, 1864] the Seventh New York Heavy Artillery, armed as infantry, were intrenched about eighty yards in front of us. We were on the crest of a ridge; they were below us. Behind us, for supports, were two Delaware regiments, their combined strength being about one hundred and twenty men. Back of us was the alder swamp, where springs of cool water gushed forth. The men in front of us had to go to these springs for water. They would draw lots to see who should run across the dangerous, bullet-swept ground that intervened between our earthworks and theirs. This settled, the victim would hang fifteen or twenty canteens around him; then, crouching low in the rifle-pits, he would give a great jump, and when he struck the ground he was running at the top of his speed for our earthwork. Every Confederate sharpshooter within range fired at him. Some of these thirsty men were shot dead; but generally they ran into the earthwork with a laugh. After filling their canteens, they would sit by our guns and smoke and talk, nerving themselves for the dangerous return. Adjusting their burden of canteens, they would go around the end of our works on a run and rush back over the bullet-swept course, and again every Confederate sharpshooter who saw them would fire at them.

Sometimes these water-carriers would come to us in pairs. One day two Albany men leaped into our battery. After filling their canteens, they sat with us and talked of the beautiful city on the Hudson, and finally started together for their rifle-pits. I watched through an embrasure, and saw one fall. Instantly he began to dig a little hollow with his hands in the sandy soil, and instantly the Confederate sharpshooters went to work at him. The dust flew up on one side of him, and then on the other. The wounded soldier kept scraping his little protective trench in the sand. We called to him. He answered that his leg was broken below the knee by a rifle-ball. From the rifle-pits we heard his comrades call to him to take off his burden of canteens, to tie their strings together, and to set them to one side. He did so, and then the thirsty men in the pits drew lots to see who should risk his life for the water. I got keenly interested in this dicing with death, and watched intently.

A soldier sprang out of the rifle-pits. Running obliquely, he stooped as he passed the canteens, grasped the strings, turned, and in a flash was safe. Looking through the embrasure, I saw the dust rise in many little puffs around the wounded man, who was still digging his little trench, and, with quickening breath, felt that his minutes were numbered. I noted a conspicuous man, who was marked with a goitre, in the rifle-pits, and recognised him as the comrade of the stricken soldier. He called to his disabled friend, saying that he was coming for him, and that he must rise when he came near and cling to him when he stopped. The hero left the rifle-pits on the run; the wounded man rose up and stood on one foot; the runner clasped him in his arms; the arms of the wounded man twined around his neck, and he was carried into our battery at full speed, and was hurried to the rear and to a hospital. To the honour of the Confederate sharpshooters be it said, that when they understood what was being done they ceased to shoot.

—FRANK WILKESON

383

Sharpshooters' Duel

Hospital near Petersburg, Va., June 20, 1864

LIEUTENANT G—— was in command of the sharpshooters attached to the [Twentieth Virginia] regiment, but who are not under its
absolute control. They form an independent organization, going where
they can most injure the enemy. We had been fighting for several days
in the most advanced trenches amidst persistent firing from both sides,
which, however, did little damage, except to prevent all rest and sleep.
Finally both armies saw the folly of such warfare and desisted. Towards
noon yesterday, weary, I suppose, of the inaction, a Confederate sharpshooter mounted his earthwork and challenged any one of our sharpshooters to single combat. Lieutenant G——, a fine fellow, standing at
least six feet two in his stockings, accepted the challenge, and they commenced what to them was sport. Life is cheap in this campaign! Both
fired, and the Confederate dropped. G——'s great size was so unusual
that his opponent had the advantage, and our men tried to make him
give way to a smaller man. But, no! He would not listen, became very
excited as his successes multiplied, and when darkness stopped the
duelling he remained unscathed, while every opponent had fallen victim
to his unerring aim.

The Lieutenant was so exhilarated that he claimed with much
bluster a charmed life; said nothing would kill him; that he could stand
any amount of duelling, and this he would prove in the morning. When
he was in his tent for the night, we officers used every argument and
entreaty to convince him of the foolhardiness and criminality of such
a course, and also assured him of the certainty of his death. But the man
seemed crazed with the faith in his charmed life. He would not yield
his determination, and when we left him he was simply waiting, as best
he could, for daylight, to begin the duelling again.

As we all foretold, he was finally killed, but his death was due to

384

treachery. In the morning, true to his mistaken conviction, he stood upon the works again and challenged an opponent. Instantly one appeared, and as both were taking aim, a man from another part of the Confederate line fired and shot G—— through the mouth, the ball lodging in the spinal vertebrae, completely paralyzing him below the head. We dragged the poor, deluded fellow to his tent, where, after uttering inarticulately, "I hit him anyway, Doctor," he died.

We then heard a tremendous uproar outside, and found that our men were claiming the murderer of their lieutenant; but the Confederates shouted that they had already shot him for a cowardly villain, and then came praises across the line for Lieutenant G——'s pluck and skill.

—John Gardner Perry

*

The Hero of the Petersburg Mine

*

IN THE RANKS of the Forty-eighth Pennsylvania, the regiment which placed the powder magazine of Burnside's mine, at Petersburg, underneath the doomed Confederate fort [July 30, 1864], was a sergeant known as Harry Reese.

He had been the first to propose the mine seriously. Permission to construct it having been granted at headquarters, he, with a score of his fellows, all experienced coal miners, set to work with their ordinary camp tools, and, under cover of night, in one month excavated, concealed from the enemy's eyes, eighteen thousand cubic feet of earth, creating a tunnel nearly six hundred feet long. On two occasions, Reese, by personal effort, saved the enterprise from failure; once when the shaft opened into a bed of quicksand, and again when the army engineers through faulty measurements located the powder-chamber outside the limits of the fort to be destroyed, instead of directly under it.

Finally came the hour for the explosion. The troops stood ready to charge into the breach, and the long fuse was ignited by Reese, who, with a group of his mining companions, stayed at the mouth of the shaft, awaiting the result. Generals and aides anxiously studied their watch-dials, that would show the flight of moments beyond the appointed time. Grant telegraphed from army headquarters over his special field-wire: "Is there any difficulty in exploding the mine?" and again: "The commanding general directs, if your mine has failed, that your troops assault at once."

The mine had failed. Daylight was spreading over the trenches, and the enemy were alert even to the point of expecting an assault.

Reese drew his soldier's clasp dirk and, turning to a comrade, said: "I am going into the mine. If it don't blow up, give me time to reach the splice in the fuse, and then come to me with fresh fuse and twine." He creeps into the shaft with resolute caution, following up the tell-tale streak of black ashes, which shows that the fuse has surely burned its way toward the powder-cells in the chamber beyond. It may reach there any second, and then! At last, just ahead of him, the brave miner sees a stretch of fuse outwardly uncharred. A fine thread of flame may be eating through its core, nevertheless, one spark of which is enough to set the terrible train ablaze. Reese knows this, for a man accustomed to handling powder cannot for an instant lose consciousness of its quick and awful violence when the connecting flash is struck. He knows his peril, yet presses on, and with his blade severs the fuse beyond the charred streak. Danger for that moment is over.

The delay had been caused by a splice wound so tightly that the fire could not eat through freely. He made a new short fuse, relit the flashing string, and escaped to the mouth of the tunnel, just as the magazine chambers exploded, spreading a mass of ruin where the armament of Lee had stood grim and threatening in the morning light but a moment before.

—ROSSITER JOHNSON

*

The "Big Fill" at Kenesaw

---

*

OUR INSTRUCTIONS when in Sherman's rear were to avoid, if possible, a conflict with the enemy. We were not sent to do battle. Orders read: "Use every endeavor to destroy and interrupt all railroads, wire and bridge communication between General Sherman's army at Atlanta and the North."

Colonel [Benjamin J.] Hill tried to obey orders. Again and again, he would shout, "Run, I tell you, run. Never fight unless cornered." Had his command been composed of a regular detail of one hundred men it would have been possible to have controlled them, but not so with his dare-devil lot. Each one seemingly vied with the other to do the most reckless thing.

We were only a few in number. With more Federal cavalry continually on our trail, we were on the move. From mountain peaks, our pickets kept us informed of the enemy's movements. Our advantage was the smallness of our command. They moved against us only in large bodies. The heavy force that protected their wooden bridges (steel bridges were almost unknown in those days) made them almost free from our attack. I only remember two bridges that we destroyed, and on one occasion we had quite a fight. We caught them unawares with our surprise charge and drove them back before they could rally.

Our detail had placed the gunpowder (dynamite was unknown) under the bridge, lighted the fuse and then scampered away. We saw the bridge crumble and fall. General Sherman's organization was so perfect that to our great surprise trains were passing over the bridge next day. Almost every night, details were sent to different parts of the railroad to place derailing switches. I do not think we ever failed to throw one or more trains into the ditch at each attempt.

We had all met at our appointed rendezvous, and just before sundown, Colonel Hill ordered the men in line, saying, "Tonight I am going to send ten men to the railroad to derail trains. I have selected the location for the placing of the ten switches some fifteen miles apart. As some of these places are so much more hazardous than others, I cannot force myself to select the men, so I have decided to have you draw lots. In this hat on slips are written the ten locations. As I pass down the line I wish every man with closed eyes to draw a slip from the hat. Those drawing a slip on which a location is written will prepare immediately to go alone to the designated place, and if possible derail a train."

Lieutenant Sloan had just drawn a blank. I was next. Now although I was ever ready at all times for any escapade, I felt my pulse quicken when I read on the slip I drew, "The Big Fill at Kenesaw."

Lieutenant Sloan tried to force his blank into my hand, and to take mine. One who has passed over the Georgia road could not help having noticed that mighty embankment or fill between two mountain ranges. At that time it was known as the longest and highest earthen fill in the entire South. For twenty years after the war, as the train passed slowly over it, one could see, at the bottom, parts of an engine and hundreds of wheels and twisted iron which the fire could not destroy.

When Brother Jim saw what I had drawn, he said, "Johnnie, give it to me."

"Not on your life," I replied.

Had I permitted Brother Jim to take my place, and had it become known, I do not believe a man would ever have recognized or spoken to me again. It would have meant disgrace forever.

We ten, who had drawn the fated slips, got busy preparing for our long night ride. I changed my clothing and to my back was tied the derailing switch. Jim tied his much prized heavy riding gloves to my belt. They were my salvation, as my gloves were worthless before I was half way up the fill. Only one who is familiar with the tropical growth of the South can appreciate the difficulty of that undertaking. This fill or embankment was fifteen years old. Its sides were a mass of tangled shrubs and vines more impenetrable than a cane brake. The blackberry, like an octopus, had pushed its long tentacles around and through every shrub and vine, and made a barrier which no man had ever attempted to pass.

General Sherman knew there was a body of men trying to destroy his communications. Hence nothing seemed to him impossible for us to attempt. For every hundred yards of track across this fill, and on his entire line of communications, for that matter, one of his pickets walked their beat. In my opinion they walked it very unwisely, as each picket would march a hundred yards, and meet another, then about face and march back. In this way they left exposed to our attack a portion of the track when they turned to march in opposite directions.

At sundown I bid all good-by. They seemed more impressed than I. I was only a boy and did not have the realization of danger that was given to men. Charles Augustus Ebenezer carried me many miles to the base of the fill. I selected the tallest pine tree near to which I might tie him, so that he would be more easily found. I started with a large corn knife to cut my way to the top of the fill. Fortunately I never learned to swear, or I most surely would have given vent to my feelings. To me the climb was never monotonous. My mind was continually saying, over and over, "What will I find at the top of the fill?"

Three o'clock was the time set for the placing of all the derailing switches. I arrived where I could see the picket walking his beat. It was an hour before the time. The briers had torn my heavy clothes in shreds. I was bleeding from many scratches. How long that hour seemed! I took my watch, time and again, from my pocket. When the picket's back was turned I crawled closer and closer through the tangled mass. Now I was so close I scarcely breathed. The picket was twenty yards away; now I was lying on the track. Before he turned, my derailing switch was made fast, and I fell over the bank and lay motionless, the thorns sticking seemingly into my every pore. When he again turned I scrambled to my feet and started downward. I had lost the trail I had cut when I heard a train coming around the bend. In my excitement I had not noticed it. Horror upon horror flashed through my brain. On what side of the track did I set the switch to throw the train? For the life of me, I could not remember but felt sure it was on my side. The thought made me fall twenty feet. I lost my knife, canteen, and all. Twice I hung suspended by the few clothes that were still left on my body. Down, down, regardless of bruises or briers, was my only thought. The train was almost to the switch. I knew it would not lodge but go the three hundred feet to the bottom. I felt there was no chance of escape, yet I actually leaped at every chance I had to get away. A crash came like a peal of loudest thunder. Again and again it continued. I felt the great iron wheels crushing me and I fainted.

It was daylight when my mind grew normal and my senses returned. I lay for some time where I fell, thinking it all over. I was in tatters and bleeding, but felt no pain. From this I knew that the train had gone over the other side of the fill. Finally I found Charles Augustus Ebenezer. After many efforts I pulled myself into the saddle. My hands refused to hold the reins, but the trusty fellow carried me safely to the camp. They took my bruised and bleeding body from his back and laid me on a blanket. It was like the homecoming of the prodigal.

—JOHN T. WICKERSHAM

*

Corporal Peck Builds a Corduroy Bridge

---

*

IT WAS IN 1864 that I joined a cavalry regiment in the department of the Gulf, a raw recruit in a veteran regiment. . . . The Colonel sent for me to come to his tent. . . . I went to the Colonel's tent and

389

there was quite a crowd of officers, some with artillery uniforms, several colonels, and one general with a star on his shoulder straps, and a crooked sword with a silver scabbard, covered with gold trimmings. I felt quite small with those big officers, but I tried to look brave, and as though I was accustomed to attending councils of war. The Colonel smiled at me as I came in, which braced me up a good deal.

"General, this is the sergeant I spoke to you about," said the Colonel, as he turned from a map they had been looking at. I felt pale when the Colonel addressed me as Sergeant, and was going to call his attention to the mistake, when the General said:

"Sergeant, the Colonel tells me that you can turn your hand to almost anything. What line of business have you worked at previous to your enlistment?"

"Well, I guess there is nothing that is usually done in a country village that I have not done. I have clerked in a grocery, tended bar, drove team on a threshing machine, worked in a slaughter house, drove omnibus, worked in a saw-mill, learned the printing trade, rode saw-logs, worked in a pinery, been brakeman on a freight train, acted as assistant chambermaid in a livery stable, clerked in a hotel, worked on a farm, been an auctioneer, edited a newspaper, took up the collection in church, canvassed for books, been life-insurance agent, worked at bridge-building, took tin-types, sat on a jury, been constable, been deck-hand on a steamboat, chopped cord-wood, run a cider-mill, and drove a stallion in a four-minute race at a county fair."

"That will do," said the General. "You will be placed in charge of a pioneer corps, and you will go four miles south, on the road, where a bridge has been destroyed across a small bayou, build a new bridge strong enough to cross artillery, then move on two miles to a river you will find, and look out a good place to throw a pontoon bridge across. The first bridge you will build under an artillery fire from the rebels, and when it is done let a squad of cavalry cross, then the pontoon train, and a regiment of infantry. Then light out for the river ahead of the pontoon train, with the cavalry. The pioneer corps will be ready in fifteen minutes."

The Colonel told me to hurry up, but I called him out of his tent and asked him if I was really a sergeant, or if it was a "mirage." He said if I made a success of that bridge, and the command got across, and I was not killed, I would be appointed a sergeant. He said the General would try me as a bridge-builder, and if I was a success he would try me, no doubt, in other capacities, such as driving team on a threshing machine, and editing a newspaper.

Well, I went off after my horse, feeling pretty proud. The idea of being picked out of so many non-commissioned officers, and placed in charge of a pioneer corps, and sent ahead of the army to rebuild a bridge that had been destroyed, with a prospect of being promoted or killed, was glory enough for one day, and I rode back to headquarters feeling that the success of the whole expedition rested on me. If I built a corduroy bridge that would pass that whole army safely over, artillery and all, would anybody enquire who built the bridge. Of course, if I built a bridge that would break down, and drown somebody, everybody would know who built it.

The twenty men were mounted, and ready, and the General told me to go to the quartermaster and get all the tools I wanted, and I took twenty axes, ten shovels, two log chains, and was riding away, when the General said: "When you get there, and look the ground over, make up your mind exactly at what hour and minute you can have the bridge completed, and send a courier back to inform me, and at that hour the head of the column will be there, and the bridge must be ready to cross on."

I said that would be all right, and we started out. In about forty minutes we had arrived at the bayou, and I called a private soldier who used to do logging in the woods, and we looked the thing over. The timber necessary was right on the bank of the stream.

"Jim," I said to the private, "I have got to build a bridge across this stream strong enough to cross artillery. I shall report to the General that he can send along his artillery at seventeen minutes after eight o'clock this evening. Am I right?"

"Well," said Jim, as he looked at the standing timber, at the stream, and spit some black tobacco juice down on the red ground, "I should make it thirty-seven minutes after eight. You see, a shell may drop in here and kill a mule, or something, and delay us. Make it thirty-seven and I will go you."

We finally compromised by splitting the difference, and I sent a courier back to the General, with my compliments, and with the information that at precisely eight o'clock and twenty-seven minutes he could start across. Then we fell to work. Large, long trees were cut for stringers, and hewn square, posts were made to prop up the stringers, though the stringers would have held any weight. Then small trees were cut and flattened on two sides, for the road-bed, holes bored in them

391

and pegs made to drive through them into the stringers. A lot of cavalry soldiers never worked as those men did. Though there was only twenty of them, it seemed as though the woods were full of men. Trees were falling, and axes resounding, and men yelling at mules that were hauling logs, and the scene reminded me of logging in the Wisconsin pineries, only these were men in uniform doing the work.

About the middle of the afternoon we had the stringers across, when there was a half-dozen shots heard down the stream, and bullets began "zipping" all around the bridge, and we knew the rebels were onto the scheme, and wanted it stopped. I got behind a tree when the bullets began to come, to think it over. My first impulse was to leave the bridge and go back and tell the General that I couldn't build no bridge unless everything was quiet. That I had never built bridges where people objected to it. I asked the private what we had better do. He said his idea was to knock off work on the bridge for just fifteen minutes, cross the stream on the stringers, and go down there in the woods and scare the life out of those rebels, drive them away, and make them think the whole army was after them, and cross back and finish the bridge. That seemed feasible enough, so about a dozen of us squirreled across the stringers with our carbines, and the rest went down the stream on our side, and all of us fired a dozen rounds from our Spencer repeaters, right into the woods where the rebels seemed to be. When we did so, the rebels must have thought there was a million of us, for they scattered too quick, and we had a quiet life for two hours.

We had got the bridge nearly completed, when there was a hissing sound in the air, a streak of smoke, and a powder magazine seemed to explode right over us. I suppose I turned pale, for I had never heard anything like it. Says I, "Jim, excuse me, but what kind of a thing is that?" Jim kept on at work, remarking, "Oh, nothin', only they are a-shellin' on us." And so that was a shell. I had read of shells and seen pictures of them in *Harper's Weekly*, but I never supposed I would hear one. Presently another came, and I wanted to pack up and go away. I looked at my pioneers, they did not pay any more attention to the shells than they would to the braying of mules.

I asked Jim if there wasn't more or less danger attached to the building of bridges, in the South, and he, the old veteran, said: "Corp, don't worry as long as they hain't got our range. Them 'ere shell are going half a mile beyond us, and we don't need to worry. Just let 'em think they are killing us off by the dozen, and they will keep on sending shells right over us. If we had a battery here to shell back, they would get our range, and make it pretty warm for us. But now it is all guess work with them, and we are safe as we would be in Oshkosh. Let's keep right on with the bridge."

I never can explain what a comfort Jim's remarks were to me. After listening to him, I could work right along, driving pegs in the bridge, and pay no attention to the shells that were going over us. In fact, I lit my pipe and smoked, and began to figure how much it was going to cost the Confederacy to "celebrate" that way. It was costing them at the rate of fourteen dollars a minute, and I actually found myself laughing at the good joke on the rebels. Pretty soon a courier rode up, from the General, asking if the shelling was delaying the bridge. I sent word back that it was not delaying us in the least; in fact, it was hurrying us a little, if anything, and he could send along his command twenty-seven minutes sooner than I had calculated, as the bridge would be ready to cross on at eight o'clock sharp. At a quarter to eight, just as the daylight was fading, and we had lighted pine torches to see to eat our supper, an orderly rode up and said the General and staff had been looking for me for an hour, and were down at the forks of the road. I told the orderly to bring the General and staff right up to the headquarters, and we would entertain them to the best of our ability, and he rode off. Then we sat down under a tree and smoked and played seven up by the light of pine torches, and waited.

I was never so proud of anything in my life as I was of that bridge, and it did not seem to me as though a promotion to the position of sergeant was going to be sufficient recompense for that great feat of engineering. It was as smooth as though sawed plank had covered it, and logs were laid on each side to keep wagons from running off. I could see, in my mind, hundreds of wagons, and thousands of soldiers, crossing safely, and I would be a hero. My breast swelled so my coat was too tight. Presently I heard some one swearing down the road, the clanking of sabres, and in a few moments the General rode into the glare of the torch-light. I had struck an attitude at the approach of the bridge, and thought that I would give a good deal if an artist could take a picture of my bridge, with me, the great engineer, standing upon it, and the head of the column just ready to cross.

I was just getting ready to make a little speech to the General, presenting the bridge to him, as trustee of the nation, for the use of the army, when I got a sight of his face, as a torch flared up and lit the surroundings. It was pale, and if he was not a madman, I never saw one. He fairly frothed at the mouth, as he said—addressing a soldier who had fallen in the stream, during the afternoon, and who was putting on his shirt, which he had dried by a fire—"Where is the corporal, the star idiot, who built that bridge?"

I couldn't have been more surprised if he had killed me. This was a nice way to inquire for a gentleman who had done as much for the country as I had, in so short a time. I felt hurt, but, summoning to my aid all the gall I possessed, I stepped forward, and, in as sarcastic a manner as I could, I said: "I am the *sergeant,* sir, who has wrought this work, made a highway in twelve hours, across a torrent, and made it possible for your army to cross."

"Well, what do you suppose my army wants to cross this confounded ditch for? What business has the army got in that swamp over there? You have gone off the main road, where I wanted a bridge built, and built one on a private road to a plantation, where nobody wants to cross. This bridge is of no more use to me than a bridge across the Mississippi River at its source. You, sir, have just simply raised hell, that's what you have done."

Talk about being crushed! I was pulverized. I felt like jumping into the stream and drowning myself. For a moment I could not speak, because I hadn't anything to say. Then I thought that it would be pretty tough to go off and leave that bridge without the General's seeing what a good job it was, so I said: "Well, General, I am sorry you did not give me more explicit instructions, but I wish you would get down and examine this bridge. It is a daisy, and if it is not in the right place we can move it anywhere you want it."

That seemed to give the General an idea, and he dismounted and examined it. He said it was as good a job as he ever saw, and if it was a mile down the road, across another bayou, where he wanted to cross, he would give a fortune. I told him if he would give me men enough and wagons enough, I would move it to where he wanted it, and have it ready by daylight the next morning. He agreed, and that was the hardest night's work I ever did. Every stick of timber in my pet bridge had to be taken off separately, and moved over a mile, but it was done, and at daylight the next morning I had the pleasure of calling the General and telling him that the bridge was ready. I thought he was a little mean when he woke up and rubbed his eyes, and said: "Now, you are sure you have got it in the right place this time, for if that bridge has strayed away onto anybody's plantation this time, you die."

The army crossed all right, and I had the proud pleasure of standing by the bridge until the last man was across, when I rode up to my regiment and reported to the Colonel, pretty tired. He was superintending the laying of a pontoon bridge across a large river, a few miles from my bridge, and he said: "George, the General was pretty hot last night, but he was to blame about the mistake in the location, and he says he is going to try and get you a commission as lieutenant."

I felt faint, but I said, "How can he recommend a star idiot for a commissioned officer?"

"Oh, that is all right," said the Colonel, "some of the greatest idiots in the army have received commissions."

* * * * *

[In 1887] I met a member of my old regiment, who [was] travelling through the South as agent for a beer bottling establishment in the North. He was with me when we built the corduroy bridge twenty-two years ago. As we were talking over old times he asked me if I remembered that bridge we built one day in Alabama, in the wrong place, and moved it during the night. I told him I wished I had as many dollars as I remembered that bridge. "Well," said my comrade, "on my last trip through Alabama I crossed that bridge, and paid two bits for the privilege of crossing. A man has established a toll-gate at the bridge, and they say he has made a fortune. I asked him how much his bridge cost him, and he said it didn't cost him a cent, as the Yankees built it during the war. He said they cut the timber on his land, and when he got out of the Confederate army he was busted, and he claimed the bridge and got a charter to keep a toll-gate."

My comrade added that the bridge was as sound as it was when it was built. He said he asked the toll-gate keeper if he knew the bridge was first built a mile away, and he said he knew the timber was cut up there, and he wondered what the confounded Yankees went away off there to cut the timber for, when they could get it right on the bank. Then my comrade told the toll-gate keeper that he helped build the bridge, the rebel thanked him, and wanted to pay back the two bits. Some day I am going down to Alabama and cross on that bridge again, the bridge that almost caused me to commit suicide, and if that old rebel —for he must be an old rebel now—charges me two bits toll, I shall very likely pull off my coat and let him whip me, and then as likely as not there will be another war.

—GEORGE W. PECK

395

---

31. RAID, RUSE, RESCUE, REVENGE

The Scout, the Lady Major, and
the Rebel Benefactress

---

*

A DARK VOLUME of smoke shot up from the city [of Atlanta] in one vast spiral column; and then came a dead, heavy, rumbling report. One of the arsenals was blown up by a shell. This was followed by a fierce fire, which shot up, almost simultaneously, in different points. A cheer came from our batteries, and was taken up along the whole line.

"War is a cruelty," said the General beside me; "we know not how many innocents are now suffering in this miserable city."

"I'm dog-gone if I like it," said a soldier, slapping his brawny hand upon his thigh; "I can fight my weight of rattlesnakes, scaramouches, or sneaking rebels; but this thing of smoking out women and children, darn me if it's fair."

"Psha!" exclaimed an orderly near us, on whom the General placed great reliance as a scout, and who went through some hairbreadth escapes; "the women are the worst of them; one of them put the rope on my neck to hang me."

"Indeed! how was that, Bentley?"

"At the battle of Peach Tree Creek [July 20, 1864], I got captured, and was brought before General Hood to be pumped; and as he could not get anything out of me, he had ordered me back to the other prisoners, when an officer, attended by an escort, rode up and saluted the General.

" 'Ha! Mademoiselle Major, how do you do?' replied the General, doffing his hat.

" 'Well, General'; and she jumped off her horse, throwing the bridle to her orderly, and politely returned the salute.

"The She-Major was strangely dressed; she wore a cap decked with feathers and gold lace, flowing pants, with a full kind of velvet coat coming just below her hips, and fastened with a rich crimson sash, and partly open at the bosom.

"In her belt she carried a revolver, and by her side a regulation sword. I looked at her; her features were rather sunburned, giving her a manly appearance. Only for her voluptuous bust, little hands, and peculiar airs, I might have taken her to be a very handsome little officer of the masculine gender.

"As I gazed at her, she looked full into my face; and turning to the General, she pointed her whip at me, and asked, 'Who is that fellow, General?'

" 'A prisoner that has just come in—a dunce; I couldn't get a word out of him.'

" 'Indeed, General, that is a spy'; and she again pointed her whip at me.

" 'Oh, no; he is only just brought in captured.'

" 'That may be; but he is a spy. I saw him at General Johnston's,

397

one day, and he was full of lying information, which cost the General many a life.'

" 'Is that so?' said the General.

" 'On my honor; come here, Hartly'; and she called over her orderly. 'Did you ever see that man before?'

" 'Yes, Mademoiselle Major.'

" 'Where?'

" 'At General Johnston's, where he was giving information as a scout.'

" 'What have you to say to all this, my man?' said the General.

"I had nothing to say, for it was true.

" 'What shall I do with him; shall I hang him?' said the General.

" 'Give him to me,' said she, with a sweet smile; 'I am going to General Johnston's; it might be well to take him there.'

" 'I make you a present of him,' said the General.

"After spending some time with the General in the tent, she came out, and placing me between herself and her orderly, rode off. When she came into the wood, she and her orderly alighted, and she pulled out from under her dress a strong, but fine, rope.

" 'Sneaking dog of a Yankee!' she exclaimed, looking at me with a vengeful eye, 'you hung the only man I ever loved; I swore I'd have vengeance. I have had it; but I have it doubly now, by giving you a similar death.'

"My hands, all this time, were firmly tied, so I was powerless. While the orderly stood with a pistol before me, she tied the rope firmly around my neck, giving it several good pulls, to make sure it was all right. They then helped me to get up on the saddle of one of the horses, so as to have a fall, while the orderly proceeded up the tree to tie the rope to a limb.

"Now was my time. While the orderly was climbing, I flung my two hands across the rope and snatched it from him, and drove my heels furiously into the horse's side, which made him plunge and rear. She held him bravely with one hand, while pulling out her pistol with the other. Before she could fire, I got a chance, and struck her with my heavy boot right in the face, spoiling her beauty, and giving the dentist a job. She fell. The horse bounded off with me, and I escaped.

"After that, I believe I would swear against women in general, had not a woman saved my life in return.

"I could not get off the mule-chain with which she fastened my hands, though I tugged until the blood was oozing out of them, and my teeth filed almost to the gums. The cord, too, was so firmly tied to my neck that I could not get rid of it. There I was, like a half-strangled whelp, with all my credentials about me. I had no control over my horse; so, fearing that he would take me back to the rebel lines, I slipped from him, and skulked away as well as I could. I got into a little by-road, and thought I would venture up to a shanty where I saw some nigger children playing around the door. They ran in, frightened, when they saw my hands tied, and I trailing my rope.

"I followed them in, when—heavens, how I shook!—there were two rebel soldiers, drinking some whiskey.

" 'Hilloo!' said one, 'here is a d——d Yank, that cheated the gallows; well, I hain't against a man settling his accounts; so we'll take care of him until he gets another swing.'

"They questioned me, and taunted me with brutal jeers and laughs.

"At length they took me away; and not having enough of whiskey to get there, they called to another house for more. To make the more sure of me, they locked me into a dark room without any window, so that I could not possibly escape, while they were enjoying their debauch.

"For a time I heard the drunken soldiers, noisy, and singing; and then they evidently had fallen asleep, for I heard their loud snores.

"It was now a bit into the night. I presumed they had made up their minds to remain where they were; so I threw myself down, and tried to sleep. Though death stared me in the face, I had fallen into a sound slumber, when I felt myself gently shook by the shoulder. I looked up, saying, 'I'm ready'; but instead of the two drunken soldiers, a gentle young woman stood over me, with a shaded light in her hands.

" 'Make no noise,' she whispered, 'but get up.' I looked at her as I sat up. She took a knife and cut the cord from my neck, and then tried to open the chain.

" 'Your poor hands are all torn,' said she, compassionately, as she unloosed the bloody chain.

" 'Alas! yes,' said I; 'but why do you try to save me?'

" 'Because I am a woman, and true to the instincts of a woman, which is to save and not to kill. Poor boy! some sister or mother would fret for you. If you should ever meet one in such a situation, do as much for him. Now go, but very quietly.'

" 'But you! Will they hurt you?'

" 'No, no. I know them; it would not do for them to quarrel with me; follow me.'

399

"I glided through the kitchen; the two rebels were sleeping beside the fire. I passed out, then imprinted a grateful kiss upon my deliverer's cheek, fled, and got into camp next day."

—Captain D. P. Conyngham

*

Ranger Mosby's Berryville Raid

*

ON THE 7th of August, 1864, Major General Philip H. Sheridan assumed command of the Middle Military Division of the Federal Army, with headquarters at Harper's Ferry, Virginia. Colonel [John S.] Mosby set to work on a large scale to "annoy" Sheridan. On the 13th, Mosby took three hundred of his Command, the largest number he had ever had in any single engagement up to that time, and marched from Upperville in Fauquier County over into the valley. We went into camp about midnight not far from Berryville in Clark County, a maneuver which consisted of unsaddling our horses and lying down on the landscape to sleep. Scouts sent out to look the situation over presently returned with the information that a wagon train was moving up the pike a few miles distant. While John Russell, our most prominent valley scout, was reporting to the Colonel, I was engaged just at that moment in trying to spread my saddle blanket among the rocks and tree roots, so it would resemble a curled hair mattress as nearly as possible. I stopped for a moment to listen to John's report, hoping secretly that it did not mean any change in the camping program, but my hopes faded away when the Colonel said: "Saddle up, Munson, and come along with me."

Taking a few more of us, we started off for the valley turnpike, leaving the rest of the Command to get some much needed sleep. We struck out in the direction whence, in the stillness of the night, came the rumbling echoes of the heavily laden wagons. In olden times, when the stages were run up and down the valley turnpike, it was said that the rumbling of the coach on the hard, rocky road could be heard for miles on a still night and, on this quiet August night of which I am writing, we heard the wagon train long before we came in sight of it, which we did in an hour after Russell reported to the Colonel. We found a long line of wagons winding along the road and stretching away into the darkness as far as the eye could reach. We rode among the drivers and the guards, looking the stock over and chatting with the men in a friendly way. I asked one of the cavalrymen for a match to light my pipe and he gave it to me, and when I struck it, revealing his face and mine by its light, he did not know I was pretty soon going to begin chasing him. It was too dark to distinguish us from their own men and we mingled with them so freely that our presence created no suspicion.

Colonel Mosby asked them whatever questions he chose to, and learned that there were one hundred and fifty wagons in the train, with more than a thousand head of horses, mules, and cattle guarded by about two thousand men, consisting of two Ohio regiments and one Maryland regiment, besides cavalry distributed along the line; all under orders of Brigadier General [John R.] Kenly, commanding. Having pumped the men dry of all the information he needed, the Colonel withdrew us from their line into the field, one by one, and sent me back to our sleeping comrades to arouse them and bring the full force up in a hurry. Just as day was beginning to dawn Chapman and Richards, with the whole Command of about three hundred men and two pieces of light artillery, twelve-pounders, came out of the woods on a run and met the Colonel, who was impatiently awaiting them in full view of the wagon train. . . .

In the hurried rush through the woods to get to the Colonel, or immediately after it was fired, I don't remember which, one of these guns commanded by Lieutenant Frank Rahm of Richmond, was disabled and drawn out of the way. The other was posted on a little eminence looking down on the turnpike along which the wagon train was moving. A streak of light broke in the east, and our force was hustled into position, Mosby giving his instructions to the Command. His trouble seemed to be to keep the men from charging before he was ready. Three hundred against over two thousand meant carefulness. The flush of the morning began to blow over that beautiful valley landscape—there are few lovelier spots than the Valley of Virginia around Berryville—and down on the pike we saw a cloud of dust rising as though a giant serpent was creeping along towards Berryville from Harper's Ferry. The entire train was soon in sight, all unmindful of our presence. From our position on the low hill, while we watched them in breathless suspense, Frank Rahm sent a twelve-pound shell over the train. It exploded like a clap of thunder out of a clear sky, and was followed by another which burst in the midst of the enemy. The whole train stopped and writhed in its centre as if a wound had been opened in its vitals. Apparently its guards did not see us and we got another charge into the little twelve-pounder and let it fly, and then; oh then! What on earth ever possessed them I am unable even at this date to say. Two thousand infantry and a force of cavalry all at sea, but, as with one mind, and without making the least concerted resistance, the train began to retreat. Then we rushed them, the whole Command charging from the slope, not in columns, but spread out all over creation, each man doing his best to outyell his comrade and emptying revolvers, when we got among them, right and left.

The whole wagon train was thrown into panic. Teamsters wheeled their horses and mules into the road and, plying their black-snake whips, sent the animals galloping madly down the pike, crashing into other teams which, in turn, ran away. Infantry stampeded in every direction. Cavalry, uncertain from which point the attack came, bolted backward and forward without any definite plan. Wounded animals all along the train were neighing and braying, adding to the confusion. Pistols and rifles were cracking singly and in volleys.

Colonel Mosby was dashing up and down the line of battle on his horse, urging the men by voice and gesture. I never saw him quite so busy or so interested in the total demolition of things.

Before the attack he expressed the hope and the belief that his men would give Kenly the worst whipping any of Sheridan's men ever got, and it delighted him to see the work progressing so satisfactorily. At several points along the line Kenly's men made stands behind the stone fences, and poured volleys into us but, when charged, they invariably retreated from their positions. The conflict was strung out over a mile and a half, which was the length of the wagon train when the fight was at its best. Our men were yelling, galloping, charging, firing, stampeding mules and horses and creating pandemonium everywhere. It was not long before we had the enemy thoroughly demoralized and were able to turn our attention to the prisoners and the spoils.

Mosby gave orders to unhitch all the teams that had not run away and to set fire to the wagons, and very soon smoke and flames filled the air and made a grand picture. Among the wagons burned was one containing a safe in which an army pay-master had his greenbacks, said to be over one hundred thousand dollars. We overlooked it, unfortunately, and it was recovered the next day by the enemy, as we always supposed; but there is a story afloat in the town of Berryville that a shoemaker who lived there at the time of the fight got hold of something very valuable among the wreckage of our raid and suddenly blossomed out into a man of means, marrying later into one of the best families of the Valley. He never would tell what his new-found treasure was. Maybe he got the safe and greenbacks.

By eight o'clock in the morning the fight was over, the enemy ours, and the wagons burning. Then a serious problem arose: how were we to get three hundred prisoners, nearly nine hundred head of captured stock, and the other spoils of war out of Sheridan's country into our own? News of the raid had gone in every direction and we were threatened with an overwhelming assault at any moment. I should have said the problem was serious to the men only. Mosby solved it very promptly by saying: "We will go directly to Rectortown and take all the prisoners and animals and booty with us." There was not anything more to be said on the subject. Rectortown lay twenty-five miles to the south, back in Fauquier County. Stonewall Jackson's forced marches were not in it with this one of ours. Our disabled cannon had to be taken care of. When Mosby asked Frank Rahm what he proposed to do with his broken-down gun, Frank promptly replied; "I'm going to take it back home on the other gun, if I have to hold it there," and he did.

We fastened the loose harness as best we could and, herding the animals into one drove, started at a trot down the pike towards the Shenandoah River several miles away. It was the most extraordinary procession that ever headed for that historic stream; our captives were on foot while we were mounted, the victors and vanquished chatting freely together and speculating on the trip before them. A number of the Rangers, in a spirit of gayety, had decked themselves out in the fine uniforms found in the baggage of the Northern officers. Some of the coats were turned inside out so as to display the fine linings. From one of the wagons we had resurrected a lot of musical instruments and the leaders of the mounted vanguard made the morning hideous with attempts to play plantation melodies on tuneless fiddles.

No more motley throng ever came back from a successful raid. There was a song on every man's lips and those who had yelled or sung themselves hoarse waved captured flags. In the midst of the nondescript legion the nine hundred head of stock, bellowing, neighing, and braying, wallowed along in the hot dust of that August morning, the steam rising from their bodies and the saliva dripping from the mouths of the fat steers, of which we had nearly two hundred and fifty head. Down the turnpike into the rushing Shenandoah, regardless of ford or pass, dashed the whole cavalcade; some swimming, some wading, others finding ferriage at the tail of a horse or steer. The orchestra in the lead scraped away bravely at their fiddles. Only the unhorsing of some of the worst of the performers saved them from bodily violence at the hands of their justly indignant comrades. In a short time, dripping but refreshed, we emerged from the stream, struggled on up the road and began the ascent of the Blue Ridge Mountains.

Strange to say, not a man nor an animal was lost in the passage. We crossed the mountain at a breakneck pace, made a rapid descent into the Piedmont Valley, and at four o'clock that afternoon, with all hands present, the captured property was divided at Rectortown, twenty-five miles from the scene of the action fought on the morning of the same day!

Our loss in the affair was two killed and two wounded. . . .

* * * * *

We brought out more than six hundred horses and mules, more than two hundred and fifty head of fat cattle, and about three hundred prisoners, destroying more than one hundred wagons with their valuable contents.

—JOHN W. MUNSON

*

Avenging Morgan's Betrayal

*

MY GREATEST ACTIVITY was when I belonged to Morgan's Raiders. There was a $1,000 reward offered for me, dead or alive. So I was glad when the war was over and I could go home. There was $1,000 reward offered for my buddy, Frank Fletcher, and also for General Morgan.

General Morgan was killed near Greenville, Tennessee, while resting up at the Williams' home. Mrs. Thompson betrayed him and got the $1,000 reward. I was with General Morgan at four o'clock on the morning he was killed [September 4, 1864]. My camp was located two miles southeast of Greenville, and I had gone to receive orders as to what we should do. General Morgan told me to tell the troops to dry their guns and clothes and not to move before seven o'clock. That morning at six o'clock the Yankees came with eighty men from Bull Gap and surrounded the Williams' home. When General Morgan realized what had happened he grabbed his pants and boots and ran, still in his night clothes, out into the garden. The Williams woman shouted, "There he goes." He hid behind some lumber in the shrubbery and the Yankees ran in and shot him through the chest. It was a mistake that the General hadn't placed a picket line on the north side of the house. While Mrs. Thompson was the one that disappeared the night before and notified the Yankees, those Williamses were in the plot.

I and Frank Fletcher were captured twenty miles south of Greenville. We were sent to an Ohio prison and tried as spies. They didn't get any papers off me, but I was convicted and sentenced to die. In pleading my case, I asked for thirty days grace to prove my innocence, but November 30, 1864, was set as the date for my execution. I told Fletcher I would gain out. He said, "You are in for it this time; there ain't no chance."

Ten days before the date set for my execution I made a trade with the guards to eat cake and coffee with me on my last morning. I had them bring me one-half gallon of coffee. Into this I slipped some cayenne pepper. At the proper moment, I took the cakes in my left hand and a pint cup of boiling coffee in my right. Just as they reached for some cake, I dashed the coffee in their eyes, blinding them. I grabbed my gun, knocked them in the head, snatched their pistols, and went for the back derrick. I jumped over and made for the Ohio River. I found a small boat and rowed across. I walked two miles before I could find a barn, then I stole a horse and saddle and rode for dear life, all that night and next day. Then I hid in a creek bayou and rested one whole day; stole a fresh horse and left for Tennessee. In three days I was back safe to the scene of my capture and General Morgan's death.

On December 25th, early in the morning, I went to visit the lady who betrayed General Morgan. I met her coming from the cowpen. I spoke to her and she exclaimed, "Oh, Captain Dowdy!" I said, "Correct, Ma'm." We engaged in a little heated argument. She told me that she thought I was in prison and admitted getting the thousand dollars. She said, "Captain, don't kill me, I'll give you the thousand dollars." But I told her, "No, no, not me. If you have anything to say, you have five minutes to talk." She knelt down and prayed. When the five minutes were up, my gun went off—she was dead. I laid her on the porch, crossed her hands, rode off, and I ain't been back there since.

—CAPTAIN JOHN DOWDY

∗

The "Sudden Death" of James Hancock

∗

ONE OF THE OCCUPANTS of [Castle Thunder in Richmond] in the winter of 1864-5 was a Federal named James Hancock, claiming to be a scout attached to Grant's army. He was captured under circumstances which seemed to prove him a spy, and while waiting for his case to be investigated he was sent to Castle Thunder. Hancock was a jolly, rollicking fellow, having wonderful facial expression, and great powers of mimicry. One evening, while singing a song for the amusement of his fellow prisoners, he suddenly stopped, threw up his hands, staggered, and then fell like a bag of sand to the floor. There was great confusion at once, and as some of the men inspected the body and pronounced it without life, the guards were notified of what had occurred. The post surgeon was called in to say whether it was a faint or a case of sudden death. He had just come in from a long, cold ride, and his examination was a hasty one.

"Dead as a door-nail!" he said as he rose up, and in the course of twenty minutes the body was deposited in a wagon and started for the hospital, to be there laid in a cheap coffin and forwarded to the burying-place. When the driver reached the end of his journey the corpse was gone! There was no tail-board to his vehicle, and thinking he might have jolted the body out on the way, he drove back and made inquiry of several persons if they had seen a lost corpse anywhere.

Hancock's "sudden death" was a part of his plan to escape. While he had great nerve and an iron will, he could not have passed the surgeon under favorable circumstances. On the way to the hospital he dropped out of the wagon and joined the pedestrians on the walk. When the driver returned to the Castle and told his story, a detail of men was at once sent out to capture the tricky prisoner, and the alarm was given all over Richmond. To leave the city was to be picked up by a patrol; to remain was to be hunted down.

Hancock had money sewed in the lining of his vest, and he walked straight to the best hotel, registered himself as from Georgia, and put in a good night's sleep. In the morning he procured a change of clothing and sauntered around with the greatest unconcern, carrying the idea to some that he was in Richmond on a government contract, and to others that he was in the secret service of the Confederacy. Shortly after dinner he was arrested on Main Street by a squad of provost troops who had his perfect description. But lo! no sooner had they put their hands on him than the prisoner was seen to be cross-eyed and to have his mouth drawn to one side. The men were bewildered, and Hancock was feeling "for letters to prove his identity" when the hotel clerk happened to pass and at once secured his liberty.

Four days after his escape from the Castle, the scout found himself out of funds, and while in the corridor of the post-office he was again arrested. This time he drew his mouth to the right, brought a squint to his left eye, and pretended to be very deaf. He was, however, taken to the Castle, and there a wonderful thing occurred. Guards who knew Hancock's face perfectly well were so confused by the squint that no man dared to give a certain answer. Prisoners who had been with him for four months were equally at fault, and it was finally decided to lock him up and investigate his references. For seven long days the scout kept his mouth skewed around and his eye on the squint, and then he became tired of it and resumed his natural appearance. The minute he did he was recognized by everybody, and the Confederates admired his nerve and perseverance fully as much as did his fellow prisoners. The close of the war gave him his liberty with the rest, but ten days longer would have seen him shot as a spy.

—M. QUAD [CHARLES BERTRAND LEWIS]

The privates eat the middlin,
The officers eat the ham.
They put me in the guardhouse,
But I don't care a damn.
—"GET ALONG HOME, CINDY"

32. OFFICERS AND MEN

The "Red Tapeism" of Furloughs

*

WHILE HERE [in winter quarters at Dalton, Georgia, in 1863-64] I applied for a furlough. Now, reader, here commenced a series of red tapeism that always had characterized the officers under Braggism. It had to go through every officer's hands, from corporal up, before it was forwarded to the next officer of higher grade, and so it passed through every officer's hands. He felt it his sworn and bound duty to find some informality in it, and it was brought back for correction according to his notions, you see. Well, after getting the corporal's consent and approval, it goes up to the sergeant. It ain't right! Some informality, perhaps, in the wording and spelling. Then the lieutenants had to have a say in it, and when it got to the captain, it had to be read and re-read, to see that every "i" was dotted and "t" crossed, but returned because there was one word that he couldn't make out. Then it was forwarded to the colonel. He would snatch it out of your hand, grit his teeth, and say, "D——n it"; feel in his vest pocket and take out a lead pencil, and simply write "app." for approved. This would also be returned, with instructions that the colonel must write "approved" in a plain hand, and with pen and ink. Then it went to the brigadier-general. He would be engaged in a game of poker, and would tell you to call again, as he didn't have time to bother with those small affairs at present. "I'll see your five and raise you ten." —"I have a straight flush."—"Take the pot." After setting him out, and when it wasn't his deal, I get up and walk around, always keeping the furlough in sight. After reading carefully the furlough, he says, "Well, sir, you have failed to get the adjutant's name to it. You ought to have the colonel and adjutant, and you must go back and get their signatures."

After this, you go to the major-general. He is an old aristocratic fellow, who never smiles, and tries to look as sour as vinegar. He looks at the furlough, and looks down at the ground, holding the furlough in his hand in a kind of dreamy way, and then says, "Well, sir, this is all informal." You say, "Well, General, what is the matter with it?" He looks at you as if he hadn't heard you, and repeats very slowly, "Well, sir, this is informal," and hands it back to you. You take it, feeling all the while that you wished you had not applied for a furlough, and by summoning all the fortitude that you possess, you say in a husky and choking voice, "Well, General (you say the "general" in a sort of gulp and dry swallow), what's the matter with the furlough?" You look askance, and he very languidly re-takes the furlough and glances over it, orders his Negro boy to go and feed his horse, asks his cook how long it will be before dinner, halloos at some fellow away down the hill that he would like for him to call at 4 o'clock this evening, and tells his adjutant to sign the furlough.

The adjutant tries to be smart and polite, smiles a smile both child-like and bland, rolls up his shirt-sleeves, and winks one eye at you, gets astraddle of a camp-stool, whistles a little stanza of schottische, and with a big flourish of his pen, writes the major-general's name in small letters, and his own—the adjutant's—in very large letters, bringing the pen under it with tremendous flourishes, and writes approved and forwarded. You feel relieved, you feel that the anaconda's coil has been suddenly relaxed. Then you start out to the lieutenant-general; you find him. He is in a very learned and dignified conversation about the war in Chile. Well, you get very anxious for the war in Chile to get to an end. The general pulls his side-whiskers, looks wise, and tells his adjutant to look over it, and, if correct, sign it. The adjutant does not deign to condescend to notice you. He seems to be full of gumbo or calf-tail soup, and does not wish his equanimity disturbed. He takes hold of the document, and writes the lieutenant-general's name, and finishes his own name while looking in another direction—approved and forwarded. Then you take it up to the general; the guard stops you in a very formal way, and asks, "What do you want?" You tell him. He calls for the orderly; the orderly gives it to the adjutant, and you are informed that it will be sent to your colonel tonight, and given to you at roll-call in the morning. Now, reader, the above is a pretty true picture of how I got my furlough.

—SAM R. WATKINS

＊

"Re-enlisting"

＊

Near Cedar Mt., Va., January 1, 1864

DURING THIS TIME we were asked to re-enlist. The commanding officer of each regiment was instructed to make an effort to this end. We were drawn up in line, and had explained to us that the country needed men; that it was a critical period; the old soldiers were worth so much more than new ones, etc.; to all of which we listened with respectful attention. It was very sweet to hear all this, but the Thirteenth was not easily moved by this kind of talk. The boys knew too well what sacrifices they had made, and longed to get home again, and, if possible, resume the places they had left. Four times we were addressed as to our duty about re-enlisting. On two or three of these occasions there was an unusual amount of grog floating about. Who the mysterious benefactor was, we are unable to recall, but it was evident to us that some one was interested in putting a halo of attractiveness on the service that didn't seem to fit. On one of these occasions, eleven men yielded to the influence of oratory or rum, though some of them afterwards said it was the rum, and were given thirty days' furlough. Seven of this number succeeded in obtaining commissions in other regiments, so that only four returned.

About this time one of the boys in another regiment, whose wife had died, requested leave of absence to attend her funeral, and the application was returned from headquarters with the indorsement,

This man can have thirty-five days' furlough by re-enlisting.
(*Signed*) GENERAL S. WILLIAMS, A.A.G.

When this came to our ears a good deal of feeling was expressed in terms not very complimentary to the government.

—CHARLES E. DAVIS, JR.

*

Trouble with the Colonel

*

WE CAMPED THAT NIGHT [in February, 1864] at a little place called Vernon [Mississippi]. In an abandoned house I found a trunk addressed to Captain —— of a rebel regiment; broke it open, and among other things that were evidently intended for a soldier at camp, there was a pair of fine woolen blankets and a little bag of silver. These I took. I presented the blankets to our Colonel, Stevens, and kept the silver, four or five dollars.

A few days after that, Uncle Tommy, as the boys called the Colonel, got on his ear because so many of us left the ranks to forage. Had he kept us where there was fighting to do, he would have had no trouble, but fighting wasn't in his line, and we all knew it. I had been scouting on my own hook one day, and on coming to camp, found a camp-guard out. Not expecting anything of the kind, I was captured and taken before Colonel Stevens. He was in a great rage. Had my forage, of which I had a load, taken from me, and ordered me to get off my horse and be searched. I told him I had not taken anything but forage, and was not in the habit of taking anything else. Adjutant Scott asked to see what I had in my pockets. As the Colonel, who was a rank Englishman, saw the silver, he fairly frothed at the mouth.

411

"Where di' 'e get that?"

"In a house at Vernon," I replied.

"Been a burnin' 'ouses, 'ave 'e, been a robbin' of people and burnin' 'ouses, 'ave 'e? I'll teach 'e to break horders and burn 'ouses, so I will. Hadjutant, send this man to his company under harrest."

I tried to explain but he ordered me off. Lieutenant Riley saw Adjutant Scott next morning, and together they pacified the Colonel. Nothing further would have been said or done had I been content to let the matter rest. The Colonel called me hard names, had taken money from me that he had no better right to than I had, and, as I did not have much respect for him anyway, the more I thought of it the more I thought I had been misused.

Examining the army regulations, I found that valuables taken from the enemy should be turned over to the hospital department. From Adjutant Scott I learned that the Colonel had kept my silver and made no report of it. After talking the matter over with Captain Woods, who was then acting as major, I concluded to ask the Colonel for the silver. So one day when we had halted for a noon-day rest, I walked up to the Colonel, who was lying in the shade, surrounded by other officers, and asked him to return the silver that he had taken from me. He reached for his sabre, jumped up and made for me as though he meant to run me through on the spot. Captain Woods and the other officers stopped him and reminded him that he had no right to use his sabre on a soldier for asking a question.

A few weeks after this, we were in camp near Vicksburg and orders came from Washington to grant furloughs for meritorious conduct to two soldiers in each company. My conduct had not been in all respects meritorious, but I had, on several occasions, volunteered for hazardous service, and had never been known to shirk when there was dangerous work to do. I was one of the two recommended by the officers of my company for furlough. Had never had or asked for a furlough, and now to get one for meritorious conduct, and visit my home in the North during the hot, sickly weather when the army would be idle, nothing could have pleased me more.

Imagine my feelings when the recommendation came back disapproved by Colonel Stevens. I went with Captain Woods to see him. We had a stormy interview. The Colonel said I deserved a court-martial rather than a furlough. The Captain then demanded a court-martial.

I was subsequently tried before a court-martial on charges preferred by Colonel Stevens. The trial was in the Colonel's tent. I did not hear the evidence submitted against me, but I was called in and asked to explain how and where I obtained the silver, and why I asked the Colonel to return it to me. I sat on a cot in the Colonel's tent, and turning up the blankets, noticed the very same white blankets that I took from the trunk in which I found the silver. When I had told where I got the silver, I said: "Gentlemen, I took a pair of white wool blankets from the same trunk and presented them to Colonel Stevens. He thanked me with great kindness and made no inquiries as to where I got them. I think these are the same blankets."

I uncovered a pair of white blankets on the cot. The officers of the court smiled; the Colonel got red in the face and tried to explain, but all that he could say was that he did not know that I was the boy that gave him the blankets. As I never heard anything more from the court-martial, I suppose that the charges were not sustained.

I liked my companions in the company and never had any trouble with my company officers, but, knowing that the Colonel was watching for a chance to get me into trouble, and fearing that he might, I obtained through Captain Woods an order from the division commander, placing me on detached service, and assigning me for duty at the division head-quarters in Vicksburg. There I was an orderly for two or three months and was then made chief of orderlies.

—COLONEL MELVIN GRIGSBY

*

Forrest Breaks in a Conscript

---

*

I HAD CONSIDERABLE curiosity to observe General [Nathan B.] Forrest, but up to nine o'clock that morning [February 21, 1864], he had not appeared upon the scene. Suddenly, out of a cloud of dust, accompanied by an orderly, he came dashing up the road towards [Ellis' bridge across the Sakatonchee]. As he approached me and reined up his horse I noticed that his face was greatly flushed, and that he seemed very much more excited than I thought was necessary under the circumstances. In rather a harsh, quick tone he asked me what the condition of affairs was at the front. As I had not been on the firing-line, and did not know anything definite excepting that the firing indicated quite a severe skirmish, I replied that Colonel [Jeffrey] Forrest had reported nothing to me beyond the fact that there was some skirmishing going on at the front, and added that I thought it was not a very severe affair. Forrest said quickly, and with evident impatience: "Is that all you know? Then I'll go there and find out for myself."

It was about four hundred yards from the bridge to where Jeffrey Forrest was in line, and a portion of the Federal advance had now reached a position where their shots were falling pretty thick in the road, and where they could readily fire at any one crossing on the bridge. Even as we were conversing the bullets were falling about us, and I thought, even there, we were unnecessarily exposed; but as General Forrest and his orderly dashed across the bridge (it seemed to me then in a spirit of bravado), I followed him, more out of curiosity to observe him than for any definite purpose. As we galloped over the bridge and up the road the enemy's skirmishers singled us out and commenced firing directly at us.

We had proceeded not more than a hundred yards in the direction of the skirmishers when I noticed, coming at full tilt towards us from that direction a Confederate soldier, who, dismounted and hatless, had thrown away his gun and everything else that could impede his rapid flight to the rear. He was badly demoralized and evidently panic-stricken. As he approached General Forrest, the latter checked up his horse, dismounted quickly, threw the bridle-reins to the orderly who accompanied him, and rushing at the demoralized soldier, seized him by the collar, threw him down, dragged him to the side of the road, and, picking up a piece of brush that was convenient, proceeded to give him one of the worst thrashings I have ever seen a human being get. The terror and surprise of the frightened Confederate at this unexpected turn in affairs, at a point where he thought he had reached safety, were as great as to me they were laughable. He offered no resistance, and was wise in this discretion, for the General was one of the most powerful men I ever saw, and could easily have whipped him in a free-for-all encounter.

At last he turned him loose, faced him again in the direction of his comrades, and thundered at him: "Now,—damn you, go back to the front and fight; you might as well be killed there as here, for if you ever run away again you will not get off so easy." It is unnecessary to say that the poor fellow marched back and took his place in line, a wiser if not a braver man. The news of this incident spread rapidly through the command and even through the Southern army, and, almost as soon, it appeared in one of the Northern periodicals of this time, which came out in illustrated form, and was entitled, "Forrest breaking in a conscript."

—BRIGADIER GENERAL JAMES R. CHALMERS

*

"Sit Up or You'll Be Killed"

*

WHEN THE DARING CHARGE of the North Carolina brigade had temporarily checked that portion of the Federal forces struck by it [at Spotsylvania, May 12, 1864], and while my brigades in the rear were being placed in position, I rode with Thomas G. Jones, the youngest member of my staff, into the intervening woods, in order, if possible, to locate [General Winfield Scott] Hancock more definitely. Sitting on my horse near the line of the North Carolina brigade, I was endeavoring to get a view of the Union lines, through the woods and through the gradually lifting mists. It was impossible, however, to see those lines; but . . . the direction from which they sent their bullets soon informed us that they were still moving and had already gone beyond our right. One of those bullets passed through my coat from side to side, just grazing my back. Jones, who was close to me, and sitting on his horse in a not very erect posture, anxiously inquired: "General, didn't that ball hit you?"

"No," I said; "but suppose my back had been in a bow like yours? Don't you see that the bullet would have gone straight through my spine? Sit up or you'll be killed."

The sudden jerk with which he straightened himself, and the duration of the impression made, showed that this ocular demonstration of the necessity for a soldier to sit upright on his horse had been more effective than all the ordinary lessons that could have been given.

—GENERAL JOHN B. GORDON

415

The Colonel Puts On His War Paint

*

[ON THE NINTH DAY'S fighting around Spotsylvania, May 15, 1864, I] volunteered to go to a spring a quarter of a mile to the rear, the first portion of the path to which was commanded by Confederate rifles. The crew of the gun I belonged to loaded me down with their empty canteens, and I ran, to avoid the sharpshooters' fire, to the protection of the forest behind us. There I saw many soldiers. Hollow-eyed, tired-looking men they were too, but not "coffee-boilers," lying on the ground, sleeping soundly. They had sought the comparative safety of the forest to sleep. Near the spring, which rose in a dense thicket through which a spring run flowed, the shade was thick and the forest gloomy. The water in the spring had been roiled, so I reached for another higher up the run. While searching for it I saw a colonel of infantry put on his war paint. It was a howling farce in one act—one brief act of not more than twenty seconds' duration, but the fun of the world was crowded into it. This blonde, bewhiskered brave sat safely behind a large oak tree. He looked around quickly; his face hardened with reso-lution. He took a cartridge out of his vest pocket, tore the paper with his strong white teeth, spilled the powder into his right palm, spat on it, and then, first casting a quick glance around to see if he was observed, he rubbed the moistened powder on his face and hands, and then dust-coated the war paint. Instantly he was transformed from a trembling coward who lurked behind a tree into an exhausted brave taking a little well-earned repose. I laughed silently at the spectacle, and filled my canteens at a spring I found, and then rejoined my comrades, and together we laughed at and then drank to the health of the blonde warrior. That night I slept and dreamed of comic plays and extrava-gant burlesques; but in the wildest of dream vagaries there was no picture that at all compared with the actual one I had seen in the forest. That colonel is yet alive. I saw him two years ago.

—FRANK WILKESON

*

The Quartermasters Make
Themselves Comfortable

*

THE DISLIKE of the private soldiers for quartermasters and commissaries was well-nigh universal, and frequently did great injustice to worthy officers and gentlemen. The ragged jokers of our army never neglected an opportunity of making a hit at these officers, and many were their practical jokes at their expense.

When Lee's weary boys were hurrying on to reinforce Beauregard, at Petersburg, in [June] '64, they passed a spot near the city in striking contrast with the dusty roads. A beautiful grove shaded the green yard of a stately mansion, a cool spring gushed forth from the hillside, and it seemed indeed an oasis inviting to repose. The attention of the men was called to a large placard, bearing the inscription: "This yard has been selected as Headquarters of Maj. ——, Q.M. of —— division." Many jests were passed about the Q.M.'s always contriving "to make themselves comfortable," when a ragged Confed stepped from the ranks and wrote in large characters under the inscription, "Maj. —— will *hold his position at all hazards.*"

The men used to call shot or shell that passed overhead and went far to the rear, "Quartermaster hunters." Upon one occasion, at Petersburg, during a severe artillery fire, a gallant fellow with more humor than prudence—jumped upon the parapet, and pointing to a shell then passing over, exclaimed: "A little more to the right, a little more to the right, the quartermasters are *down behind that hill.*

—*The Land We Love*

417

Wormy Hardtack

---

*

WHILE BEFORE PETERSBURG, doing siege work in the summer of 1864, our men had wormy "hardtack," or ship's biscuit, served out to them for a time. It was a severe trial, and it taxed the temper of the men. Breaking open the biscuit, and finding live worms in them, they would throw the pieces in the trenches where they were doing duty day by day, although the orders were to keep the trenches clean, for sanitary reasons.

A brigade officer of the day, seeing some of these scraps along our front, called out sharply to our men: "Throw that hardtack out of the trenches." Then, as the men promptly gathered it up as directed, he added: "Don't you know that you've no business to throw hardtack in the trenches? Haven't you been told that often enough?" Out from the injured soldier heart there came the reasonable explanation: "We've thrown it out two or three times, sir, but it crawls back."

—H. CLAY TRUMBULL

*

Deburgh, the Overseer

---

*

IN THE SUMMER OF 1864, when I was in my fourteenth year, another call was made for Negro laborers for the Confederate government, and fifteen from our plantation, including myself, with thousands from other plantations, were sent down to Charleston again.

. . . The name of the overseer in charge of the Negroes in the fort

418

[Sumter] was Deburgh—whether that was his right name I cannot say.

Deburgh was a foreigner by birth. He was one of the most cruel men I ever knew. . . .

Fort Sumter had been so badly damaged by the Union forces in 1863 that unless something had been done upon the top, the continued bombardment which it suffered up to the close of the war would have rendered it uninhabitable.

The fort was being fired upon every five minutes with mortar and Parrott shells by the Yankees from Morris Island. The principal work of the Negroes was to secure the top and other parts against the damage from the Union guns.

Large timbers were put on the ramparts of the fort and boards laid on them, then baskets, without bottoms, about two feet wide and four feet high, were put close together on the rampart, and filled with sand by the Negroes.

The work could only be done at night, because, besides the bombardment from Fort Wagner, which was about a mile or a little less from us, there were also sharpshooters there who picked men off whenever they showed their heads on the rampart.

* * * * *

If my readers could have been in Fort Sumter in July, 1864, they would have seen Deburgh with a small bar of iron or a piece of shell in his hand forcing the surviving portion of the Negroes back into line and adding to these other Negroes kept in the Rat-hole [Negro quarters] as reserves to fill the places of those who were killed or wounded.

They would also have heard him swearing at the top of his voice, while forcing the Negroes to rearrange themselves into line from the base of the fort to the top.

This arrangement of the Negroes enabled them to sling to each other the bags of sand which was put in the baskets on the top of the fort. My readers ask, What was the sand put on the fort for? It was to smother the fuses of such shells as reached the ramparts before bursting.

* * * * *

But while destruction of life was lessened by the sand, it was fully made up by the hand of that brute, the overseer. God only knows how many Negroes he killed in Fort Sumter under the shadow of night. Every one he reached while forcing the slaves back into working position after they had been scattered by the shells, he would strike on the head with the piece of iron he carried in his hand, and, as his victim fell, would cry out to some other Negro, "Put that fellow in his box," meaning his coffin.

Whether the superior officers in Fort Sumter knew that Deburgh was killing the Negroes off almost as fast as the shells from Fort Wagner or whether they did not know and did not care, I never have learned. But I have every reason to believe that one of them at least, namely, Major John Johnson, would not have allowed such a wholesale slaughter had he known. On the other hand I believe that Captain J. C. Mitchell was not only mean enough to have allowed it, but that he was fully as heartless himself.

Whatever became of Deburgh, whether he was killed in Fort Sumter or not, I never knew.

—JACOB STROYER

*

The Quartermaster Corners
the Mule Market

---

*

PRIOR TO THE BATTLE of Nashville [December 15-16, 1864] . . . Major General James L. Donaldson . . . was quartermaster under General Thomas. . . .

Having occasion to purchase mules for the army, he ordered a person in whom he had confidence to visit the contiguous Northern States, inadvertently saying to him, "Buy as many as you can"—not supposing he would be able to secure more than a few thousand at the most. Some weeks afterward, just before the attack upon Hood's army, General Donaldson, on meeting his agent, inquired how many mules he had been able to secure. To the amazement of the General, he was informed that *twenty thousand* or more had been obtained. Upon which the astonished General exclaimed. "I am a ruined man! I shall be court-martialed and driven from the army for not limiting you in the purchase. You have procured many times more than I had any idea or intention of purchasing; but the fault is mine, not yours. I ought to have been particular in my orders." In an extremely disheartened state he went to his home, believing that such a thoughtless act on his part could not be overlooked by the Commanding General.

He had scarcely reached his home before a messenger came from General [George H.] Thomas with an order for General Donaldson to come immediately to headquarters. This seemed to be the sealing of his fate, and in a state of trepidation bordering on frenzy he appeared before General Thomas, whom he found in a mood, apparently, of great depression. Soon after Donaldson had entered his presence General Thomas said, "Donaldson, how many mules have you?" With some perturbation he replied, "Upwards of twenty-five thousand." "*Twenty-five thousand,* did you say?" repeated the General. "Is it possible that you have this number? Donaldson, accept my most heartfelt thanks; *you have saved this army!* I can now have transportation, and can fight Hood, and will do so at once."

—R. H. EDDY

*

A Thousand Shirts

---

*

UPON HOOD'S RETREAT [from Nashville, in December, 1864] many of his soldiers lost all of their clothing, and for many weeks quite a number were scarcely able to cover their nakedness, anything available being appropriated, and used as a substitute for the regular uniform. One day, while Hood and his staff were on the march, they overtook a regiment, and among the soldiers was one whose uniform consisted of only a long coffee sack, in lieu of a shirt, and with nothing else on. A hole had been cut for his head as also for his bare arms, and over this garment was suspended his canteen, and around him his cartridge belt, while he carried his musket as is usual.

421

Observing this novel sight, Hood reined up his horse, and demanded his name and regiment. "Martin Brown, Company I, Texas," was the prompt response of the soldier. "Well, have you no better uniform than that?" The soldier laid down his gun, looked the General straight in the face, and as the blood rushed indignantly to his cheeks, he said: "Look here, General Hood, do you expect a man to have a thousand shirts?"

—Rev. Theodore Gerrish and Rev. John S. Hutchinson

"Well you may order us to 'move on, move on,'" one [of the stragglers] retorted, "when you are mounted on a horse and have all the rations that the country can afford!" Lee made no answer and needed to make none, for some of the men nearest to him peered into his face, half-suspecting who he was. "Marse Robert!" they exclaimed. The effect was instantaneous. The soldiers got up as if they had never known weariness, and gave him a shout. "Yes, Marse Robert," they said, "we'll move on and go anywhere you say, even to hell!"

—DOUGLAS SOUTHALL FREEMAN

33. "MARSE ROBERT" AND HIS MEN

Lee and the Courier

*

IN JANUARY . . . 1864, Colonel Chapman went to Petersburg to see General Lee about moving a part of Mosby's command for the remainder of the winter down near Kinsale, on the Potomac River. While the Colonel was talking to General Lee they were interrupted by the arrival of a special courier.

The day was very cold. There had been rain for several days, but

423

on this day the rain had fallen in torrents, evening was coming on and rations and clothing were very scarce.

The courier was wretchedly clad. His suit was very much worn and was soaking wet, for he had ridden many miles that day in the drenching rain. General Lee drew a chair to a small wood fire and bade the man take a seat. When he had concluded his errand and was thoroughly warmed, he rose to go. General Lee glanced at him almost furtively, as if he felt that the soldier was ashamed to have his poor attire observed.

"Are you returning at once to your General?" inquired General Lee.

"Yes, sir," was the response, "if my horse has finished feeding."

"It is still raining very hard," said General Lee; "have you no rubber coat?"

"Oh, that don't matter, General," was the evasive but brave answer.

"Then," said Colonel Chapman, "General Lee remained silent a moment, walked to the wall where his rubber coat hung, took it down and gave it to the soldier, who protested in vain against General Lee's depriving himself."

—ALEXANDER HUNTER

*

How to Tame a High-Strung Horse

---

*

IT WAS ON the fighting line in front of Petersburg one day that General Lee rode up to General Heth's headquarters, and as the latter emerged from his tent and saluted, said, "Harry, I should like to ride down your line."

Heth expressed pleasure at the proposal, mounted his horse, and as they rode along side by side he called the attention of his superior officer to what he considered the positions of vantage and the points of danger, when suddenly they came upon a space where for several hundred yards no breastworks had been thrown up. Surprised, General Lee turned to Heth, and asked why the defenses were not completed.

The latter replied that he had given instructions to the engineers, and until now was under the impression that his orders had been obeyed. "See that the works are completed at once, Harry," said General Lee, and turning his horse, he rode back to his own headquarters.

Two or three days passed, and again he appeared at General Heth's tent, with the same expression of his desire. Delighted, Heth once more accompanied his chief; but when they arrived at the ill-fated spot where General Lee had previously noticed the unfinished fortifications, they found, to Heth's dismay, that nothing had been done since their last inspection. The position was one of great strategic importance, and General Grant was a most vigilant, active, and pugnacious commander, always on the lookout for just such weak spots in his antagonist's lines. General Lee was evidently much annoyed; without uttering a word, however, he rode back to Heth's quarters, and, much to that discomfited officer's astonishment, he dismounted, entered the tent, and sat down. Heth remained standing, silently wondering what his fate would be. At last General Lee said, in the kindest tone of voice:

"Harry, that chestnut horse your wife rides worries me more than I can tell. The other day she passed by my quarters on that plunging brute, and he was as much of the time in the air as he was on the ground. He kicked and at the same time fought the bit until I thought he would either break her delicate wrists or pull her arms out of their sockets. I do wish that you would not let her ride that horse again until he is somewhat toned down."

"But, General," said Heth, feeling much relieved at the turn the conversation had taken, "my wife is a splendid horsewoman, and she is not a bit afraid of the animal."

"Yes," replied General Lee, "but it worries me to see her on the brute, and keeps me anxiously fearing that some dreadful accident is going to happen. Now, Harry, I was once the colonel of a dragoon regiment, and some of the smartest and most knowing horsemen in the command held the opinion that the best way to take the wiry edge off an excitable or nervous horse is to give him plenty of exercise—regular exercise, morning, noon, and night, until he quiets down. For the sake of your wife, as well as for your own, I beg of you to try the experiment; and I know of no better place for you to ride the horse while taming him than just up and down in front of that gap I ordered you to have closed, until a good breastwork has been completed. Good afternoon, sir."

—JAMES MORRIS MORGAN

425

Lee's Prophecy

---

*

ON THE SECOND DAY [in the Wilderness, May 6, 1864], while riding over the field covered with the dead, General Lee indicated by the peculiar orders he gave me, his high estimate of General Grant's genius for war. He ordered me to move that night to Spotsylvania Court-house. I asked if scouts had not reported that General Grant had suffered heavy losses and was preparing to retreat. Lee's laconic answer revealed his appreciation, I repeat, of the character and ability of his great antagonist. "Yes," he replied, "my scouts have brought me such reports; but General Grant will not retreat, sir; he will move to Spotsylvania Court-house." I asked if he had information to that effect. "No," he replied, "but General Grant ought to move to Spotsylvania. That is his best manoeuvre and he will do what is best." General Lee then added, "I am so sure of it that I have had a short road cut to that point, and you will move by that route." This was Lee's prophecy. Its notable fulfillment was the arrival of Grant's troops at Spotsylvania almost simultaneously with the head of the Confederate column and the beginning of the great battle of Spotsylvania.

—GENERAL JOHN B. GORDON

*

"General Lee to the Rear!"

---

*

DURING THE NIGHT preceding May 12, 1864, the report brought by scouts of some unusual movements in General Grant's army left little doubt that a heavy blow was soon to fall on some portion of the Confederate lines; but it was impossible to obtain reliable information as to whether it was to descend upon some part of that wide and long crescent or upon one of the wings. It came at last where it was perhaps least expected—at a point on the salient from which a large portion of the artillery had been withdrawn for use elsewhere.

* * * * *

. . . [General Lee's army] had been cut in twain by [General Winfield Scott] Hancock's brilliant *coup de main*. Through that wide breach in the Confederate lines, which was becoming wider with every step, the Union forces were rushing like a swollen torrent through a broken mill-dam. General Lee knew, as did every one else who realized the momentous import of the situation, that the bulk of the Confederate army was in such imminent peril that nothing could rescue it except a countermovement, quick, impetuous, and decisive. Lee resolved to save it, and, if need be, to save it at the sacrifice of his own life. With perfect self-poise, he rode to the margin of that breach, and appeared upon the scene just as I had completed the alignment of my troops and was in the act of moving in that crucial countercharge upon which so much depended. As he rode majestically in front of my line of battle, with uncovered head and mounted on Old Traveller, Lee looked a very god of war. Calmly and grandly, he rode to a point near the centre of my line and turned his horse's head to the front, evidently resolved to lead in person the desperate charge and drive Hancock back or perish in the effort.

I knew what he meant; and although the passing moments were of priceless value, I resolved to arrest him in his effort, and thus save to the Confederacy the life of its great leader. I was at the centre of that line when General Lee rode to it. With uncovered head, he turned his face toward Hancock's advancing column. Instantly I spurred my horse across Old Traveller's front, and grasping his bridle in my hand, I checked him. Then, in a voice which I hoped might reach the ears of my men and command their attention, I called out, "General Lee, you shall not lead my men in a charge. No man can do that, sir. Another is here for that purpose. These men behind you are Georgians, Virginians, and Carolinians. They have never failed you on any field. They will not fail you here. Will you, boys?" The response came like a mighty anthem that must have stirred his emotions as no other music could have done. Although the answer to those three words, "Will you, boys?" came in

the monosyllables, "No, no, no; we'll not fail him," yet they were doubtless to him more eloquent because of their simplicity and momentous
meaning.

But his great heart was destined to be quickly cheered by a still
sublimer testimony of their deathless devotion. As this first thrilling
response died away, I uttered the words for which they were now fully
prepared. I shouted to General Lee, "You must go to the rear." The
echo, "General Lee to the rear, General Lee to the rear!" rolled back
with tremendous emphasis from the throats of my men; and they
gathered around him, turned his horse in the opposite direction, some
clutching his bridle, some his stirrups, while others pressed close to
Old Traveller's hips, ready to shove him by main force to the rear. I
verily believe that, had it been necessary or possible, they would have
carried on their shoulders both horse and rider to a place of safety.

This entire scene, with all its details of wonderful pathos and deep
meaning, had lasted but a few minutes, and yet it was a powerful factor
in the rescue of Lee's army. It had lifted these soldiers to the very
highest plane of martial enthusiasm. The presence of their idolized
Commander-in-Chief, his purpose to lead them in person, his magnetic
and majestic presence, and the spontaneous pledges which they had
just made to him, all conspired to fill them with an ardor and intensity
of emotion such as have rarely possessed a body of troops in any war.
The most commonplace soldier was uplifted and transformed into a
veritable Ajax. To say that every man in those brigades was prepared
for the most heroic work or to meet heroic death would be but a lame
description of the impulse which seemed to bear them forward in
wildest transport. Fully realizing the value of such inspiration for the
accomplishment of the bloody task assigned them, I turned to my men
as Lee was forced to the rear, and reminding them of their pledges to
him, and of the fact that the eyes of their great leader were still upon
them, I ordered, "Forward!" With the fury of a cyclone, and almost
with its resistless power, they rushed upon Hancock's advancing column.
With their first terrific onset, the impetuosity of which was indescribable,
his leading lines were shivered and hurled back upon their stalwart supports. In the inextricable confusion that followed, and before Hancock's
lines could be re-formed, every officer on horseback in my division, the
brigade and regimental commanders, and my own superb staff, were
riding among the troops, shouting in unison: "Forward, men, forward!"
. . . Hancock was repulsed and driven out. Every foot of the lost salient

and earthworks was retaken, except that small stretch which the Confederate line was too short to cover.

—GENERAL JOHN B. GORDON

*

Lee and Gracie

---

*

A FEW DAYS BEFORE [General Archibald Gracie, Jr.'s death on December 2, 1864] General Lee went to the trenches, as was his habit, to inspect them in person. He always went alone. When he came to Gracie's line he stepped upon the "banquette" of the work, and taking out his field-glasses began quietly to examine the position of the enemy. He was in danger, and General Gracie placed himself in front of him and obstructed his view, pretending to be pointing out objects to General Lee. Lee said, "General, you should not expose yourself so much." Gracie replied, "If *I* should not, General Lee, why should you, the Commander-in-Chief?" The General smiled, and understood then that Gracie had so placed himself to cover him with his own body in case the enemy had fired. Lee stepped down from the "banquette" and continued his walk down the line.

—LIEUTENANT COLONEL WILLIAM MILLER OWEN

*The pickets were there to watch, and not to kill. Quietly
they sat at the little "gopher pits," chaffing and sending back
and forth boisterous jokes, while perhaps shrieking messengers
of death, unheeded and unnoticed, flew over our heads.*
—J. S. FULLERTON

34. ON PICKET

A Tarheel Picket Yarn

*

THE WINTER [of 1863-64 at Morton's Ford] had now worn
away and the spring had come. Vegetation began to show signs of life.
Its coming bore us one comfort in one way—among others. It was not
so cold, and we did not have to tote so many logs of wood to keep up
our fires. Down on the river flats, where vegetation showed sooner than
it did on the hills, green things began to shoot up. Dandelions, sheep
sorrel, poke leaves and such, though not used in civil life, were welcome
to us, for they were much better than no salad at all. The men craved
something green. The unbroken diet of just bread and meat, generally
salt meat at that—gave some of the men scurvy. The only remedy for

that was something acid, or vegetable food. The men needed this and craved it—so when the green shoots of any kind appeared we would go down on the flats, and gather up all the green stuff we could find, and boil it with the little piece of bacon we might have. It improved the health of the men very much.

At this time, there was a North Carolina Brigade of Infantry at the front furnishing pickets for the river-bank. They were camped just back of our winter quarters. Those fellows seemed to be very specially strong in their yearning for vegetable diet, so much so that they attracted our attention. Every day we would see long lines of those men passing through our camp. They would walk along, one behind another, in almost unending procession, silent and lonesome, never saying a word and never two walking together—and all of them meandered along intent on one thing—getting down to the flats below "to get some sprouts" as they would say when asked where they were going.

Later on, we would see them in the same solemn procession coming back to camp—every man with a bunch of something green in his fist.

This daily spectacle of Tarheels swarming through our camp interested us; we watched them mooning along. We tried to talk with them, but all we got from them was, "We'uns is going to git some sprouts. Don't you'uns love sprouts?"

We did, but we didn't go after them in such a solemn manner. Our "sprout" hunts were not so funereal a function; rather more jovial, and much more sociable. Also this devotion to the search for the herb of the field excited our curiosity. They were all the time craving green stuff, and going after it so constantly. We had a story going around which was supposed to explain the craving of a Tarheel's insides for greens.

This was the story:

One of these men got into the hospital. He had something the matter with his liver. The doctor tried his best to find out what was the matter, and tried all sorts of remedies—no results. At last, in desperation, the doctor decided to try heroic treatment. He cut the fellow open, took out his liver, fixed it up all right (whatever that consisted in), washed it off and hung it on a bush to dry, preparatory to putting it back in place. A dog stole the liver, and carried it off. Here was a bad state of things—the soldier's liver gone, the doctor was responsible. The doctor was up against it. He thought much, and anxiously. At last a bright idea struck him. He sent off, got a sheep, killed it, took out

431

its liver, got it ready, and sewed it up in that soldier in place of his own. The man got well, and about his duties again. One day, soon after, the doctor met him and said with much friendly interest, "Well, Jim, how are you?"

"Oh, Doctor," he replied in a very cheerful tone, "I'm well and strong again."

The doctor looked at him, and asked him significantly, "Jim, do you feel *all right?*"

Falling into that characteristic whine, Jim said, "Yes, sir, I am well and strong, but, Doctor, all the time, now, I feel the strangest hankering after grass."

That was the sheep's liver telling. Our theory was that all of those fellows had sheep's livers, and that accounted for the insatiable "hankering after grass."

—PRIVATE WILLIAM MEADE DAME

*

Turning the Tables on Old Jube

---

*

IT WAS a frightfully stormy night [during the campaign of 1864 in the Shenandoah Valley], and, after standing on picket duty for an unaccountably long time, I learned that the army had departed without warning. As I trudged after it, wet, forlorn, and very angry, I ran into a stone wall in the dark. Before I could fairly pick myself up and feel of my new bruises, I was accosted by a lonely horseman who came plodding along through the mud, his nag's hoofs splashing it over me as he rode by. He wanted to know who I was and what I was doing there, and in the same breath cursed me for a straggler and fired at me a volley of abuse. With the first word I knew it was Old Jube. That shrill voice and that style of interrogative scolding could not be counterfeited. But I knew just as well that I had the call on the old man. I could not see the stars on his coat or distinguish his features, and I was not bound to know his voice or to recognize him as an officer when outside his own lines and unattended.

So I gave the lock of my gun a significant click and called a halt on him. He knew the sound and slowed up his tongue a little until I could ask him who he was. He replied that he was General Early. He could easily tell from my speech that I was not a Federal. I told him he lied; that I believed he was a Yankee spy; and that I intended to take him into camp. Then the old fellow started his swearing again, and as I had a good deal of grist on hand, I started an opposition that fairly took his breath away. I asked him where General Gordon's command was. This started him again to cursing me as a straggler, and he refused to tell me. I told him that satisfied me that he was not General Early, but a spy, and that he had to go with me to camp. He saw he was in a bad box, and screeched at me to go on through Winchester and I would find Gordon camped out on the Front Royal pike about four miles from town. With this he hurled a final shot or two at me, and, putting spurs to his horse, went flapping and flopping off into the deeper darkness like an ill-omened old raven with an impediment in his croak. What upon earth he was doing out there by himself I could never understand.

—*The Century Magazine*

∗

"Now Hunt Your Hole!"

∗

COLD HARBOR [Virginia, June 3, 1864] was a fearful trap to have gotten men into, for the lines were almost in half circles, and ours, being the inner one, was exposed to an incessant, murderous firing from every direction. The picket lines were holes, banked on all sides, into which the men crawled after dark, there to remain until relieved the following night under the cover of darkness—a period of twenty-four straight hours.

About six one evening a Yank called to his opposite, "Hello, Johnny, got anything for supper?"

"Yes—hoecake, Yank; what you got?"

"Coffee and hardtack. Say, Johnny, if you will let me boil my coffee, I'll let you cook your hoecake."

"All right, Yank, stand up."

"Stand up you, Johnny."

"Here goes then."

Both stood erect—a mark for three hundred guns; yet so clearly had their challenge been heard, or surmised, that not a shot was fired in their direction. Taking a last look to make sure that the other was in earnest, they stepped from behind their works, started their little fires, cooked and ate their meals with all the leisure of a Delmonico spread, and then, having finished, the Yank called, "Are you through, Johnny?"

"Yes, Yank. Now hunt your hole!"

—Brevet Lieutenant Colonel Seward Fobes Gould

*

Tillotson Counts the Pickets

---

*

CAPTAIN THOMAS E. TILLOTSON, of the Sixty-fourth [Ohio]—his comrades usually addressed him by his middle name, Eugene—was at this time serving on the staff of General John Newton commanding the division, his position being that of acting assistant inspector general. While the army was lying in the trenches before Atlanta [in 1864], Tillotson had an experience that was enough to bleach the hair of the average man. One of his functions was to have supervision of the picket-line. Whenever the troops halted in a new position, it was his duty to post the pickets. One day General Newton, who was sometimes a little querulous, asked the captain how many men he had on the picket-line covering the front of the division.

"I cannot say exactly, sir," answered Tillotson, saluting, "but we have the usual force out there."

"You don't know!" exclaimed the general, fiercely. "A fine inspector you are, not to know how many men you have on post. It's your business to know, and I want you to find out, and be quick about it, too!"

Now everyone who remembers Tillotson as a soldier, knows that he never flinched in the face of danger, and that he was conspicuously faithful and conscientious in the performance of duty. So marked were his courage and efficiency that at the close of the war he was brevetted major, for "gallant and meritorious services."

Stung by the sharp and ungracious words of his chief, his face flushed as he touched his hat and replied: "All right, General, I'll find out at once and let you know." Then he put spurs to his horse and dashed away.

Tillotson decided that the way to obtain the desired information was to go and see. He determined not to go on foot, either, although that would have been far less dangerous. So he picked his way on horseback through the opening in the abattis and brush in front of the breastworks, and rode out so near to the picket-line that he could see the piles of fresh earth which indicated the location of the picket posts; for all the videttes were protected by small intrenchments. So close were the hostile lines that the change of pickets could only be made at night. He began at the left and counted the dirt piles, multiplying the total by three, that being the number of men on each post. They were stationed in this way so that if one or two should be killed or wounded, the post would not be left unguarded.

Soon after the captain started on his perilous ride, he was discovered by the sharp eyes of the rebel pickets, who promptly opened fire upon him. The firing rapidly increased until it seemed that an attack upon the Union line was about to be made. The bullets flew thickly above and around him, but Tillotson heeded them not until his task was fully accomplished. Then he galloped back within the works as fast as his horse could carry him. That he was not struck by the flying missiles was to him as strange as it was gratifying.

Meanwhile, the rebel fusillade had been attended with the usual result. The entire division was formed in line of battle at the works, to await the onslaught of the foe. But our pickets did not come in, as they would have done had the enemy advanced, and the scare soon wore itself out. After Tillotson disappeared, the firing ceased.

Captain Tillotson rode directly to the spot where he had left General Newton, whom he supposed to be impatiently awaiting the report for which he had made such a peppery demand. But the General had returned to his headquarters as soon as he discovered that the noise on the picket-line did not mean business. Tillotson found him and reported the exact number of men on the line of outposts. The General had evidently forgotten the errand upon which he had sent him, for as he looked at man and horse, both dripping with perspiration, he asked: "How do you know?"

"I counted them, sir!" said Tillotson.

"Was that you out there in front drawing the fire of the rebels, which alarmed the army and caused that rush to the works?"

"Yes, General, it was!"

"Well, sir," replied Newton, "all I have to say is that you were a fool!" prefacing the last word with the usual Sheolic adjective.

"Yes, General Newton, I believe I was!" said Tillotson, dumbfounded to find that his dangerous ride had been worse than useless.

—LIEUTENANT COLONEL WILBUR F. HINMAN

*

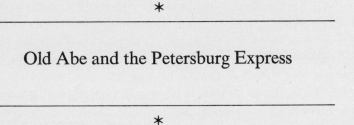

Old Abe and the Petersburg Express

*

THERE WAS A CORN-FIELD between the Union and Confederate lines at a certain point before Petersburg, a little to the left of Cemetery Hill. The opposing pickets of the two great confronting armies would in spite of all occasionally creep into that field for a friendly chat or for a game of cards, or would swap papers for papers, tobacco for coffee, or jack knives, hard tack or sugar for corn-cake. Two of them were playing a game of cards one day [in 1864] with Abe Lincoln and Jeff Davis as imaginary stakes; the Lincolnite lost. "There," says the winner, "Old Abe belongs to me." "Well, I'll send him over by the Petersburg Express." The express was a very large mortar on a car built expressly for it, and every morning and evening it would run up around the bluff near the fort line on the City Point R.R., and throw a monstrous shell into Petersburg.

—WILLIAM H. SALLADA

436

An Emetic for a Picket

. . . IT WAS WELL ON in August [1864] when I joined the regiment [the One Hundred and Eighty-seventh Pennsylvania Volunteer Infantry] in front of Petersburg. . . .

We were camped in a pleasant little grove of pines and lived very well. An occasional shell from the Confederates would trouble us and one man was killed by a shell. It was soon after I joined the regiment that we were moved out to the Weldon Railroad, which we captured, and the Confederates were driven back. We hastily scooped up dirt with our hands and tin plates and threw it on to logs and rails in front, making a rude rifle-pit. We piled the ties up and set them on fire and threw the rails on the fire, which bent them out of shape under the heat.

That night I was put on picket duty for the first time. We expected the Confederates, who were on the other side of a piece of woods in our front, to attempt to recapture the road, and were given specific instructions by the officer of the guard. We were told that if any man went to sleep on his post he would be court-martialed and shot. We were marched out to the edge of the woods, and I, being a sergeant, was placed in charge of three picket posts, my own and two on the left of me. I was expected to visit them at intervals during the night. There were five men in each post. I suppose the posts were one hundred and fifty yards apart.

A nasty, drizzling rain had set in and it was very disagreeable. We were all tired, hungry and exhausted from our march through the day. And as our supplies had not come up we had only what our haversacks contained. We were told by the officer of the guard that a week before, a picket post had been found with their throats cut from ear to ear. In front of each post was a man called the vedette, who was a lookout. He was supposed to watch and report to his post any advance of the enemy. The vedette in front of our post was Nelse Starkweather, a man that I knew very well. In the post was Jud Hall, Palmer Wilcox, Wesley Saxbury, George B. McGonigal and myself.

I started to visit the two posts on my left. It was pitch-dark. I found one, I do not know whether it was the nearest or the farthest one away. They seemed all right and I started to return. The edge of the woods was angular and I could see nothing. I walked slowly and pushed through the low brushwood and over the logs. Because of the darkness I could not tell whether I was in the woods or the underbrush. I knew that Nelse Starkweather was the vedette in front of my post. I knew that he had orders to shoot at anyone moving in front of him. I knew that he was the most advanced man of our army. I lost all calculation of distance or direction. I was a non-commissioned officer. I was in a dilemma. I was more afraid of Starkweather than the Confederates.

I stood behind a big tree and the rain dripped and there was a chilly wind. I did not know my position, but I called in a whisper "Nelse." He answered only a few feet away. He knew me and said, "I had a rest on you; if you had moved again I would have fired. Here, let me take you back to the post." Knowing that he was a deer slayer and one of the best shots in the northern tier of counties of Pennsylvania, I appreciated the fact that had he fired at me I surely would have been hit in a vital spot.

He led me back to the picket post and there they were, all sound asleep and snoring. Expecting the grand rounds every minute, and knowing that if they came and found the men asleep they would be court-martialed and shot, I was in a terrible predicament. There they lay, snoring loud enough to be heard very plainly quite a distance. Nelse Starkweather crawled back to his vedette post and I undertook to waken the sleepers. I pulled them, rolled them about, but they would not get up. They were asleep or pretended to be. They were very tired, having marched a long distance, and I could not rouse them.

I also was very tired and sleepy, and I sat down with my back against a tree. I saw that in spite of my efforts I might go to sleep. I had never used tobacco and I knew that it would make me sick. Palmer Wilcox always carried fine-cut chewing tobacco loose in his blouse pocket, so I crawled to him and got some of it and put it in my mouth, swallowing some of the juice. It made me so sick that I vomited at intervals, which kept me awake. I knew that the officers of the guard would come around and, finding us asleep, we would be court-martialed and shot and, being an officer, they would probably shoot me twice.

It still rained and was cold and I was watching and listening for the officers of the guard, wondering why they did not come and "have it over with." I was so sick and miserable that I doubted that I could prove I was awake if they did come. There was no sound but the loud and regular snores of my sleeping comrades. I knew that some one should crawl out and relieve the vedette. I tried to rouse the sleepers again, but could not, so I got a fresh supply of tobacco and crawled out to relieve Starkweather. When I got to him he was also sound asleep. I could not rouse him, so I kept watch. Everything was quiet in front, so I crawled back to the men. I could easily find them by their snores. When I got there I could hear Starkweather snore in front.

I passed the night watching both posts, and never in my life have I passed such a horrible night. The fate of the army might hang on me, for I was there to give the alarm by shooting my gun if there was an advance. We were in an old lane bordered on each side by persimmon trees, and the Confederates would naturally come up this lane. I could still shoot my gun, but I could not retreat. I was too sick to stand up, but I took a little tobacco emetic occasionally and hung on.

Along toward morning it stopped raining and the moon came out. Then I again thought of the men in the post whose throats were cut. I tried not to think about them, but I could not help it. I sat with my back against a tree about half-way between the post and the vedette. I could see by the light of the moon, and suddenly I saw three or four men crawling stealthily toward the post. I sat frozen with fear. I dare not shoot and alarm the whole army. I was only to shoot in case a force advanced. I was concealed by a bush in front of me. I thought I would wait until they got near enough to make sure of hitting one of them and then shoot. Perhaps they would go back. I was in great trouble. I could see them crawling slowly but surely towards the post. I had often been frightened in my life, but never like that, for it was torture. No one on the rack ever suffered more than I did. I was so frightened that I could then keep awake, but I dared not move for fear of discovery. I knew they would not expect to find any one awake. The snorers did not keep time and it sounded as if the whole army lay about that post asleep.

How long this lasted I do not know. It finally occurred to me that they were a long time crawling up to the post. I shifted my position slightly and then could not see them. It was growing lighter, and I knew that day was breaking. It was some time before I could convince myself that there had been no one there. It was my imagination helped by the tobacco and the story of the men in the other post with their throats cut, but while it lasted it was just as real to me as if there were men crawling up to the post.

With daylight the men got awake, stretched themselves and talked. I was too sick to berate them. I slept a while, but soon got up and when the officers of the guard came around—all was well. The men were all awake and looked refreshed. I was awake, but did not look refreshed. I made up my mind to say nothing about the previous night to any one, not even to the men, for I knew that they could not keep it. They might deny being asleep, and I could not prove that they were. I had learned that it is just as hard for the average man to keep a thing like that as it is for a woman, and perhaps harder. Gossiping is not confined to either sex.

We had nothing to eat all day. There was no fruit except the persimmons, but they were not ripe, for there had been no frost to ripen them. A green persimmon is much worse than a green apple, for they have a griping, puckering effect like choke cherries. Fortunately, we had nothing to do but sit around, as the Confederates did not attack us that day. At six o'clock we were relieved by another detail and we marched slowly into camp. My tent-mate, Sergeant Bricker, had supper waiting, and after drinking some coffee and eating some hardtack I felt better. He then brought out a watermelon which he had purchased. That was my undoing. I was very sick that night, and I have never eaten watermelon since.

—William A. Stone

*

Pat and Johnny

---

*

Before Petersburg, Va., June 19, 1864

ONE MOONLIGHT EVENING, when both sides were top of the trenches, the other side was particularly noisy. That day, or the day before, the enemy had captured a large herd of our beef cattle which were corralled in our rear near Fort Powhatan, and there was hilarity over it. We were loudly and boastingly invited to roast beef and beefsteak feasts. They were vociferously noisy, when an Irishman shouted with a distinct "old sod" accent: "Say, you Johnnies, stop yer hollerin' so soldiers can slape!" Back came, "Hello, Pat! How long you been over? Suppose you are soldiering for the Yankees'—beautiful greenbacks."

"Well," said the Irishman, "yees is fightin' for money that has nayther beauty nor value."

Laughter followed from both sides with cheers on our side for the Irishman's rejoinder.

Then from the other side: "Come over with us, Pat; we are fighting for honor and you are fighting for money."

"Thin we is both fightin' for what we most nade."

—MAJOR JOHN L. CUNNINGHAM

Then I'll tell those conscript soldiers
How they use us here;
Giving us an old corn-dodger,
They call it prisoner's fare.

Weeping, sad and lonely—
Oh! how bad I feel;
Down in Charleston, South Car'lina,
Praying for a good square meal.
                            —"IN CHARLESTON JAIL"

---

35. "PRISONER'S FARE"

Talkative Tarheel

---

*

ON THE MORNING of the 29th [of May, 1864] Wright, Hancock, and Warren were directed to move forward and make a reconnaissance in force, which brought about some spirited fighting. The movement disclosed the fact that all of Lee's troops were in position on the north side of the Chickahominy, and were well intrenched.

General Grant was particularly anxious, that evening, to obtain information of the enemy from some inside source. Several prisoners had been taken, and one of them who was disposed to be particularly talkative was brought into headquarters, it being thought that the General might like to examine him in person. He was a tall, slim, shock-headed, comical-looking creature, and proved to be so full of native humor that I give the portion of his conversation which afforded us the most amusement. He, of course, did not know in whose presence he was as he rattled off his quick-witted remarks.

"What command do you belong to?" asked the General.

"I'm in Early's corps, and I belong to No'th Ca'lina reegiment, suh," was the reply.

"Oh, you're from North Carolina," remarked the General.

"Yes," said the prisoner, "and a good deal fa'thah from it jes' now than I'd like to be, God knows."

"Well, where were you taken, and how did you get here?" was next asked.

"How did I get h'yah! Well, when a man has half a dozen o' them thah reckless and desp'rit dragoons o' yourn lammin' him along the road on a tight run, and wallopin' him with the flats o' thah sabahs, he don't have no trouble gittin' h'yah."

"Is your whole corps in our front, and when did it arrive?" inquired the General.

"Well, now, jes' let me tell you about that," said the prisoner; "and let me begin right from the sta't. I'm not goin' to fool you, 'cause I'm fast losin' interest in this fight. I was a peaceful man, and I didn't want to hurt nobody, when a conscript officah down thah in the ole Tar State come around, and told me I would have to get into the ranks, and go to fightin' fo' my rights. I tried to have him p'int 'em out for me. I told him I'd as lief have 'em all, but I wasn't strenuous about it. Then he begun to put on more airs than a buckin' hoss at a county fair, and told me to come right along—that the country wanted me. Well, I had noticed that our folks was losin' a good many battles; that you-all was too much for 'em; and I got to flatterin' myself that perhaps it was only right for me to go and jine our army, jes' to kind o' even things up. But matters has been goin' pretty rough with us ever since, and I'm gettin' to feel peacefuller and peacefuller every day. They're feedin' us half the time on crumbs, and thah's one boy in my company that's got so thin you have to throw a tent-fly over him to get up a respectable shadow. Then they have a way of campin' us alongside o' creeks not much biggah than a slate-pencil; and you have to be powerful quick about gettin' what watah you want, or some thirsty cow'll come along and drink up the

443

whole stream. I thought, from all the fuss she had made at the sta't, that South Ca'lina was goin' to fight the whole wah through herself, and make it a picnic for the rest of us; but when thah's real trouble she has to get the ole Tar State to do the solid work."

"Are there any men from South Carolina in your brigade?" was the next question.

The answer came with a serio-comic expression of countenance: "Yas; a few—in the band."

The General suppressed the laugh with which he was now struggling, and feeling that an effort to get any useful information from the North Carolinian would be a slow process, disappeared into his tent to attend to some correspondence, and left the prisoner to be further interviewed by the staff.

"I tell you, gentlemen," went on the Confederate, "thah's lots o' cobwebs in my throat, and I could talk to you-all a good deal bettah if I only had a dish o' liquor. Thah's nothin' braces a man up like takin' a little o' the tanglefoot."

Thereupon a canteen and cup were brought, and after the man had poured out about four fingers of commissary whisky and tossed it off as if it were water, he looked considerably invigorated. "Nothin' as soothin' as co'n-juice, aftah all," he continued. "I'd like to live in Kaintucky; them Kaintucky fellers say they can walk right into a co'n-field, strip off an eah, and jes' squeeze a drink of whisky right out'n it."

"How did you happen to be picked up?" was now asked.

"Well, you see, suh," he replied, "our cap'n, Jimmy Skipwo'th, marched me out on the picket-line. Cap'n Jimmy's one o' them thah slack-twisted, loose-belted, toggle-j'inted kind o' fellers that sends you straight out to the front; and if you don't get killed right off, why, he gets all out o' patience, an' thinks you want to live fo'evah. You can't get away, because he's always keepin' tab on you. When he marched us out to-day I says to him: 'Cap'n Jimmy, thah don't 'pear to be enough of the boys a-comin' along with us. Now I tell you, when we go to monkeyin' with them Yankees we ought to have plenty o' company; we don't want to feel lonesome.' Well, we got thah, and went to diggin' a ditch so we could flop down in it and protect our heads, and could use it afterward fo' buryin' you-all in it, ef we could get hold o' you. Well, jes' then you opened lively, and come at us a-whoopin' and a-careerin' like sin; and ez fo' me, I took a header for the ditch. The boys saw somethin' drop, and I didn't make any effo't to pick it up ag'in till the misunderstandin' was ovah. The fust thing I knowed aftah that, you lighted onto me,

444

yanked me out o' the hole, and then turned me ovah to some of you' dragoons; and Lo'd! how they did run me into you' lines! And so h'yah I am."

After the provost-marshal's people had been told to take the prisoner to the rear and treat him well, the man, before moving on, said: "Gentlemen, I would like mighty well to see that thah new-fangled weepon o' yourn that shoots like it was a whole platoon. They tell me, you can load it up on Sunday and fiah it off all the rest o' the week." He had derived this notion from the Spencer carbine, the new magazine-gun which fired seven shots in rapid succession. After this exhibition of his talent for dialogue, he was marched off to join the other prisoners.

—GENERAL HORACE PORTER

*

Chinch Harbor

---

*

I WAS TRANSFERRED to the old Capitol Prison in Washington City. I do not know why it was called the "Old Capitol." It was a large old building on one of the main avenues and not far from the capitol of the city and I imagine it had once been a hotel. It was about the first day of July [1864] when I was taken there and not another prisoner was there. I learned that about one week before, some three hundred prisoners had been taken out and sent to some other prison. At dinner-time I was called to the mess-hall for dinner. I had a very good dinner and made the acquaintance of a spritely young Negro, who served in that department. Being the only boarder, I was permitted to remain in the mess-hall as long as I wished. John was quite friendly and told me many things connected with the prison and prison rules. I told him that I appreciated his kindness and the good dinner he had given me and asked if it would be possible for him to get a blanket or two for me, as I had nothing but an oil-cloth and there was nothing in my room.

He scratched his head and thought a while and said, "It is against the rules, Boss, but I likes you and I am going to see what I can do for you. After I cleans up I will be up in your room." I thanked him and told him I had a little bit of money and would divide with him. I returned to my room, hoping John would see his way clear to keep me from having to sleep on the floor with only an oil-cloth covering. In an hour or so my friend came in with a small iron bedstead or cot, and returned soon again with a straw tick, two blankets and a clean sheet. He said there being no prisoners there was less help about the kitchen and dining room, so he had borrowed this outfit from that department. To say I appreciated this kindness would be putting it mildly. He made up the bed and did all he could for me. I had three dollars left of the five I had been given and gave John one of them. He hesitated about taking it but I insisted, so I had a good bed and had made a good friend who was to favor me more than once while I remained there.

That nice clean bed induced me to retire early. I was soon asleep, but, oh, what an awakening awaited me! I seemed to have hardly gotten to sleep when I awoke itching and burning with something crawling all over me with thousands of hot feet. Did you ever smell a mashed bed-bug? I rolled out of my little bed scratching and slapping.

There was a gas jet kept burning in my room all night and I could see them by the hundreds, chinches, all over me, all over my bed. The sentinel posted in the hall, hearing the racket, opened the door and inquired what was the matter. I told and showed him; he gave a very broad grin and retired. I brushed them off my clothes, stripped and threw my clothing as far from me as I could, knocked them off my body and shook out my sheet, replaced it, rubbed off what climbed back on my legs and jumped in bed. I slept but little that night and in the morning I gathered up my clothing and disposed of what bugs I could find. At breakfast, I told John of my night's experience. He sympathized with me but could do nothing but suggest that we scald the bedstead, which we did. We examined the bedding and thought the trouble would at least be very much lessened, but alas, the next night was no better. I thought of the three hundred prisoners who had recently been removed. I was up the greater part of the second night and in walking the floor noticed the walls of the room over which the bugs were running in streams and gangs. I called the guard in to see them and he actually looked sorry for me and said the damn bugs must expect me to do the feeding of the three hundred men who had been taken away.

It is said necessity is the mother of invention, so in trying to think of some way to better my apparently helpless condition, I knew they could only get on my bed by climbing up the legs of the bed, which were small. All at once the thought occurred to me to get some pint cups filled with water and place the legs in the center of the cups and maybe they could not swim. I called my friend, John, gave him my idea and asked if he could furnish the cups. He said he certainly would and did. I cleaned my bed and bedding thoroughly, filled my cups with water, and placed each leg of the bed in a brimming cup of water, and it was a complete success. Oh, the good, undisturbed sleeping I had. I found but very few that even attempted to swim and they were drowned.

I had been here about a week when a batch of ten prisoners was brought in. They came to my room early next morning and the first question was, "How have you lived so long in this damned chinch harbor? We did not sleep a minute last night." I showed them my bed and my defense.

—CAPTAIN JAMES N. BOSANG

*

How Abner Small Was Taken Prisoner

---

*

ALL THROUGH JULY and halfway through August [1864] the chief occupation of our corps was the strengthening of its works in front of Petersburg. We almost came to suspect that the war was degenerating into a digging match. We were pleased when early in the morning of Monday, August 15th, the corps was relieved and moved quietly to the rear. After two days of rest and a day of rain, we were put in motion early Thursday morning [the 18th] and marched, out of sight of the enemy, towards the left. The heat was terrific. Our progress was pardonably slow. It was about noon when our brigade was halted near the Yellow House, on the Weldon Railroad, about four miles south of Petersburg.

We were sent there to seize and hold the railroad; the rebels used it to get supplies to their army. We proceeded to take possession. [Romeyn B.] Ayres's division was started up the west side of the track and [Samuel W.] Crawford's division up the east side, our brigade forming Crawford's left and my regiment forming the left of the brigade and moving nearest to the railroad. We were supposed to connect with the right of Ayres's division; but we didn't, whatever the official records may say to the contrary. A most unaccountable posting of our brigade, by a bewildered commander who moved it in all directions but the right one, left us pulling away at a slant, more than a hundred yards from the track and over ground thickly covered with trees and underbrush.

We were slowed up and somewhat disordered by the tangle of bushes, and proceeded cautiously. Regimental commanders were informed that a strong line of skirmishers was posted close in front, awaiting orders to advance; meanwhile, there must be no firing of muskets. Then suddenly we heard the rebel yell and the crash of a volley; and the skirmishers came running in, apparently without having fired a shot. Some officer ordered our men to lie down and blaze away, and we opened fire to our front; but the rebels, taking advantage of the gap between the divisions, filed through on our left and closed in upon us from both front and rear, and many of us were captured. I found myself looking into the muzzle of a gun with a determined face behind it.

Cursing the blundering stupidity of whoever had let us into that fix, we were started with a most willing escort towards the rebel rear. As we climbed the fence of a cornfield beyond the woods, we heard our batteries begin to fire. I was both angry and mortified at being a prisoner, and when a shell burst near me and drove a rebel through the fence into Kingdom Come, I was more than glad. I was double-quicked out of range into open ground, and there I was astonished to see that the enemy had no infantry support whatever. For obvious reasons I used all my persuasive powers on my captor to allow me to escape. I sincerely believe that he thought twice about it, for he halted and looked me full in the face and said:

"Yank, I'm damned sorry you didn't capture me."

Naturally, I was in full accord with that sentiment and argued to effect the exchange; but the Johnnie didn't quite feel that he could swap places with me. My acute disappointment was tempered with admiration for his loyalty to honor; he was too conscientious to gain release from his starving service at such a price. He didn't scruple, however, to relieve me of my new hat and rubber coat. He offered me a grey cap to wear until we should reach the rebel quartermaster, when I would have to give it up. I didn't wish to wear any part of a rebel uniform, but just then it came on to rain, and the drenching downpour drove me to cover my head.

I was led like a lamb to an officer mounted on a sorrel horse and wearing stars on the collar of his badly fitting coat. He was a cadaverous, dyspeptic-looking man, with nerves all over him and an eye as cold as a glacier. This, I was told, was "Billy" Mahone. General Mahone was possibly in command, as he was exceedingly anxious to know what he was facing.

"What corps do you belong to? What batteries have you got? Any cavalry? Is Grant there? Who commands?"

He fired his questions at me in a breath. My only reply was: "General, you are too good an officer to expect me to give you correct answers."

Smiling with the lower muscles of his face, he motioned me to the rear. Under the guidance of my captor, who clung to me like a brother, I started away. We were hardly out of earshot of General Mahone when an incident occurred that suggested a relapse of discipline in the rebel army. An officer spoke sharply to my guide.

"Go back to the front," said the officer.

"Go to hell," said the private.

"Keep nearer to the front," I felt like saying, "and you'uns will all go to hell soon."

We went toward Petersburg, all of us that were prisoners now being herded together. Remembering what my captor had said about a visit to the quartermaster, I dropped my watch through the armscye of my vest. As it left my hand and made its way down, with a short prayer from me at every stop, I had troubled thoughts of the suffering in store for me if I should land in prison penniless. Near the town, sure enough, we were halted and stripped of our outward valuables. I had the dubious satisfaction of seeing my captor despoiled of his plunder; the quartermaster was enriched by my hat, rubber coat, and an elegant silver corps badge presented to me a few days before by Colonel Farham. I gave up the grey cap to its proper owner, with thanks which he didn't seem to appreciate.

Under a strong guard with loaded muskets and bayonets fixed, we were marched through the principal streets of Petersburg. The sidewalks were lined with old men, boys, and decrepit women, who vied with one another in flinging insults and venom. The women were the worst of the lot; they spat upon us, laughed at us, and called us vile and filthy names.

Our first night in rebeldom was passed in an old outbuilding, a sort of shed, strongly flavored with Africa. In the black darkness of the night I felt a hand light on my shoulder and glide toward my watch pocket. Thoroughly awakened, I grabbed something tangible and held on. I heard a whispered warning: "Keep quiet! There are friends around."

This particular friend seemed anxious to supply me with greenbacks and directions how to escape. He said that he was a Northern man there to aid us. When next he asked me if I had a gold watch, negotiations were suspended. I requested him to move on, and he was kept moving until the hole called a door allowed him to crawl out with a kick in the rear. I later sold my watch to a more reputable tradesman, and put the money where I thought it would be safest hid, in odd corners of my clothes.

Towards noon of the next day we were moved to an island in the Appomattox River; and from there, the day following we were sent to Manchester, and across the James into Richmond. Arriving in the rebel capital, Saturday evening, we were received at Libby Prison as if at a palatial hotel. Most courteously we were requested to announce our names for register. The commandant, Major Turner, asked us sweetly if we desired to deposit in the office safe our watches, jewels, or other valuables, and assured us that he would give us receipts which would redeem our property on our release. He was not at all anxious to receive our treasures. We soon learned why.

Ordered into line in a room adjoining the reception room, we were called by name, one by one, to the rear of the prison; and there, out of sight, a little puppy named Ross went through the clothes of every prisoner who denied the possession of money or valuables. Not a garment escaped inspection; yet the money that I had hidden stayed hidden for my use. One by one we went to that room, and none went back. We were shown up the stairs to the second floor of the prison. Only after the last of us had come up, and seen the stairs pulled up after him, did we know of the indignity inflicted upon our comrades. We cursed our keepers from that hour.

—MAJOR ABNER R. SMALL

*

Hucksters, Smugglers, and Dead Yankees

*

A BRIGADE, several regiments and a battery, in all about 3,000 men, taken at Plymouth, North Carolina, had received their veteran bounty and new clothes, with which to go home on veteran furlough, but a few days before their capture. They were taken on conditional surrender, and one of the conditions was that private property was to be respected. They came in [to Andersonville] about the middle of May [1864] with their entire camp outfit, tents and all, and must have had an average of hundreds of dollars in money to the man. Previous to their arrival hucksters handled but small stocks of tobacco, meal, beans, rice, potatoes, wood, etc., and the peddler's cry usually was, "Who wants to trade rice for beans!" or, "a pone of bread for a dish of soup!" or, "a ration of meat for a ration of meal!" and the gambling was all on a small scale. Soon after the arrival of the Plymouth prisoners bedlam was indeed let loose. Peddlers and hucksters multiplied, gamblers and tricksters increased, and new kinds of business sprang up.

The hucksters obtained supplies, in part from the prison sutler, who had a store in the prison under the protection of the rebels in command, and in part from those of the prisoners who went outside to carry out the sick to the hospital, or the dead to the dead-house, and who managed to carry on trade with the rebels on the outside and smuggle in goods. The officers, too, who came in once a day, one or two to each division, to call the roll of the prisoners, were nearly all smugglers and brought in tobacco, eggs, and other articles that they could conceal about their persons to trade and sell to the prisoners.

The profits in smuggled goods were so much greater than those bought at wholesale from the prison sutler, that a separate branch of trade sprang up, which was selling chances to go outside. For instance, a sick man would go, or get his friends to carry him out to sick-call. If, on being examined by the rebel physician, he was ticketed for the hospital, and, if he could not walk, as was usually the case, there would be a chance for two other prisoners to go under guard and carry the sick man on a stretcher to the hospital. This chance to go out belonged to the companions who had assisted him to sick-call. They would often sell it to others engaged in the smuggling business, and the smuggler buying such a chance would often realize a handsome profit on goods that he could buy, on the outside, of the guards and other traders, and bring in concealed in his clothes, or in the pine boughs, or a hollow log, which he would be allowed to carry in.

In this way the dead soon became articles of merchandise and were bought and sold. The number that died in camp daily, especially in July and August, was from 50 to 120, according to the state of the weather. After a stormy day and night there would be many more dead than during the same number of hours of fair weather. The dead were carried to the gate every morning and laid in a line commencing at the dead-line and reaching back into the prison. Each corpse was carried to the dead-house on a stretcher by two prisoners guarded by a rebel soldier. The corpse of a prisoner belonged to his bed-fellow, if he had one, if not, to his mess-mates who had the disposal of the chances (two of them) to go with the stretcher to the dead-house. Smugglers bought these chances, also.

The first man brought to the dead-line in the morning would be taken out first, and they [the corpses] would be taken two or three at a time, according to the number of guards detailed. The first smugglers out in the morning would have the best chance to trade and so the chance to carry out the first corpse was worth more, and sold for more, than the chance to go out with one that would not be reached until later. It soon became the custom for the price of a corpse to be written on a piece of paper and pinned to the rags of the corpse. The first dozen or so would be marked as high, sometimes, as three dollars each, and if there were 80 or 100 in the row of corpses, as low as fifty cents would buy some of the last. If you paid three dollars for a corpse you would get out early while trade was brisk, and before the best bargains were gone. If you paid fifty cents for a corpse you had to sit by it perhaps until afternoon, and watch it to keep it from being stolen, and when it did come your turn to go the stench of your corpse would make you sick and chances for trade would be slim.

I saw many fights over the disputed ownership of dead bodies. I remember one in particular. A poor starved creature who seemed to have no friend had for a long time been in the habit of coming at night and lying down just outside of my shanty close up to the side where I slept. When he thus lay down there would be nothing between us but a thin thatching of pine leaves. He was literally alive with vermin and would no sooner lie down than I would be awakened by the lice crawling over my face, and would get up and drag the poor fellow away, sometimes twice in one night. One morning after I had thus dragged him away I saw a bloody fight going on between two men, and going to the spot found that they were fighting because each claimed to be the next friend, and, therefore, the owner of the body of the man who had died where I had left him. I often heard it said that death was sometimes assisted by the would-be mourners that the corpse might reach the dead-line among the first in the morning.

Great God! Think of it. Men brought so low by the thousand, systematically and purposely too, and by their own countrymen, civilized,

Christianized, chivalrous countrymen, that to save life, to get food and wood, where food and wood were plenty, they will barter and sell, and fight over the dead bodies of their friends. What are Heathen?

I bought a chance once to go out with a dead body. I had to carry the end of a stretcher on which the head lay because the man at the other end had been hungry so much that he was thin and weak. The stretcher was an old gunny-sack nailed to poles. The sack part was too short. The feet hung over it at one end and the head at the other. There had been no tender loving hand to close those eyes when the last breath had gone. They were open wide and glaring. The head hung over my end of the stretcher and the eyes glared up at me. They haunted me for weeks. I never bought another corpse.

—COLONEL MELVIN GRIGSBY

When Federal troops were passing through Baltimore [Miss Hetty Cary] stood at an open window of her home and waved a Confederate flag. One of the officers . . . noticed the demonstration and calling it to the attention of the Colonel asked: "Shall I have her arrested?" The Colonel, glancing up and catching a glimpse of the vision of defiant loveliness, answered emphatically: "No, she is beautiful enough to do as she damn pleases."

—MRS. D. GIRAUD [LOUISE WIGFALL] WRIGHT

36. FAIR REBELS

"Charcoal!"

*

Richmond, Va., February 20, 1864

ANNIE HAD HEARD so much of the wounded in Richmond hospitals that a few days ago she said to Mrs. Preston: "Auntie, I must go home. I can't stay here, their cries break my heart!"

"What cries? Whose cries?"

"The poor wounded soldiers! I cannot sleep!"

"Nonsense, you cannot hear any such thing. The wounded soldiers are nowhere near us, and they never cry out. When you hear one, call me."

Annie came flying in ten minutes. "There! There!" and she clapped her hands to her ears to keep out the cruel sound.

"Charcoal! Charcoal!" was being shrieked in tones of agony, like a soul in torment, by a vendor in the street, a sound so familiar to us all in Richmond that we never hear it.

—MARY BOYKIN CHESNUT

*

Aunt Abby, the Irrepressible, Rallies Lee's Men

---

*

WHEN GENERAL LEE had his army entrenched at the Wilderness [May, 1864] Aunt Abby made one of her usual trips to it, and was present at a sharp attack, in which the Confederate troops were driven by sharp-shooters from a portion of the entrenchments, which it was important to defend. While the officers were attempting to rally the men, Aunt Abby, with a hop, skip and jump, mounted the works and went dancing along in full view of the enemy, calling out, "Hand me up a broom, boys; and the ole woman will sweep the bullets out'n your way if it's them you are a-fear'd on." Those who have heard a Confederate battle-yell can imagine the shout with which those works were remanned, but I cannot describe it.

—*The Land We Love*

Lee's Miserables

DURING THE . . . days of battle [in the Wilderness, at Spotsylvania, and at the "Bloody" Angle, May 6-12, 1864], through which we had just passed, very little relief, physical or mental, had been obtained; but there was one staff officer, a Colonel B——, who often came as bearer of messages to our headquarters, who always managed to console himself with novel-reading, and his peculiarity in this respect became a standing joke among those who knew him. He went about with his saddle-bags stuffed full of thrilling romances, and was seen several times sitting on his horse under a brisk fire, poring over the last pages of an absorbing volume to reach the dénouement of the plot, and evincing a greater curiosity to find how the hero and the heroine were going to be extricated from the entangled dilemma into which they had been plunged by the unsympathetic author than to learn the result of the surrounding battle. One of his peculiarities was that he took it for granted that all the people he met were perfectly familiar with his line of literature, and he talked about nothing but the merits of the latest novel.

For the last week he had been devouring Victor Hugo's *Les Misérables*. It was an English translation, for the officer had no knowledge of French. As he was passing a house in rear of the "angle" he saw a young lady seated on the porch, and, stopping his horse, bowed to her with all the grace of a Chesterfield, and endeavored to engage her in conversation. Before he had gone far he took occasion to remark: "By the way, have you seen 'Lees Miserables?' " anglicizing the pronunciation.

Her black eyes snapped with indignation as she tartly replied: "Don't you talk to me that way; they're a good deal better than Grant's miserables anyhow!"

—GENERAL HORACE PORTER

Mrs. Davis Intercedes

Camden, S.C., May 27, 1864

I WAS TELLING THEM today of a woman who came to Mrs. Davis in Richmond, hoping to get her help. She wanted her husband's pardon. He was a deserter. The woman was shabbily dressed, chalk-white and with a pinched face. She spoke very good English, and there was an attempt to be dressed up apparent in her forlorn clothes; knots of ribbon, rusty artificial flowers, and draggled feathers in her old hat. Her hands hung down at her side. She was strong, and her way of telling her story was hard and cold enough. She told it simply, but over and over again, with slight variations as to words and never as to facts. She seemed afraid we would forget. The army had to pass so near her. Her poor little Susie had just died, and the boy was ailing; food was so scarce and so bad. They all had chills, and she was so miserable. The Negroes had all gone to the Yankees. There was nobody to cut wood, and it was so cold. "The army was coming so near. I wrote, and I wrote: 'If you want to see the baby alive, come! If they won't let you, come anyhow!' So you see, if he is a deserter, I did it. For they would not let him come. Only colonels and generals can get furloughs now. He only intended to stay one day, but we coaxed and begged him, and then he stayed and stayed; and he was afraid to go back afterwards. He did not mean to be a coward, nor to desert, so instead of going back to his regiment, he went on the gun-boats on the river, to serve there; and then some of his old officers saw him, and they would not believe his story. I do not know if he told them anything. He does not talk much any time. They are going to shoot him. But it was I who did it. I would not let him alone. Don't you see?"

Mrs. Davis went to the President. She was gone ever so long, and the stiff, cold woman, as white as a wall, sat there and told it over to me so many times. I wanted to go home, but she clutched me. "You stay! You are sorry for me!" Then Mrs. Davis came in, smiling. "Here it is,

457

all that you want." The creature stood straight up; then she fell down on the sofa, sobbing as if soul and body would come asunder. So I fled, blind with tears.

—MARY BOYKIN CHESNUT

*

A Tryst with a Twist

*

[WHILE THE FOURTH New York Heavy Artillery was besieging Petersburg in June, 1864] a number of raids were made near Natchez Run. Three times was it my misfortune to be ordered there.

The tedium, however, was relieved by a chance stumbling upon an attractive girl, who lived near by with her parents and an elder sister, who made a very obliging chaperone. In consideration of coffee, sugar, and some extras, I was invited to join them at mealtime.

The second trip down to the Run, we, the attractive girl and I, dined alone. The third time we were dear old friends. She imparted a scheme to me: there was to be a ball that night in Petersburg, to which she was dying to go, but our soldiers, you see, had shut her in. Now, if I liked her a little bit, I would help her to her heart's desire. Of course I promised—who would not when looking into the eyes of a Southern girl? So she said that if I would pass her through our lines, she would see that I got through theirs and—we were to have a beautiful time, returning before daylight.

It was all very jolly—in anticipation. Unfortunately, I was unable to keep the tryst until nearly midnight. I expected to have to throw pebbles at her window to tell her how sorry I was, but she was waiting for me, impatient to start. I suggested that the hour was late—she asked me if I were afraid. I smiled. Losing her temper, she exclaimed, "It is downright mean of you. I wanted to capture one Yankee officer all by myself!"

—BREVET LIEUTENANT COLONEL SEWARD FOBES GOULD

The Lord Takes the Shells in His Hands

---

*

IT WAS A SAD TIME indeed, for the inmates of old Chelsea House at Petersburg, Virginia, June 9, 1864, for the dear father had been brought home shot through the head while bravely defending the town against Kautz's Raiders. . . . All the citizens who could left, but we were unable to leave due to the fact that my brother, fifteen years of age, was ill unto death, from exposure in camp while fighting in the defense of Petersburg. Chelsea, our home, was opposite the South Carolina Hospital and so we were in exact range of shells from the Yankees' Fort Stedman and Battery Number Five. For safety we were compelled to live in two large rooms in our basement. . . .

At last one morning about daybreak, after my brother had spent a night of most intense agony and had just fallen asleep, it seemed as if the very earth would open and swallow us up. Window panes were shattered and the whole air was filled with rumbling noises which terrified and deafened one. We could not hear each other when we spoke, the din was so great. What was it? Could it be the end of all things? Then through a lull one could hear a battle had begun.

My mother seemed as one turned to stone and spoke as though in a horrible dream: "My husband killed, one boy dying here, and two in the midst of battle, and the rest of us in the midst of shells and balls! Oh, God, what will become of us?"

Aunty Silvy, an old colored servant standing by, said in a confident tone, "The shells *is* falling all around us, but, Miss Caroline, you is sech a good woman dat it peers to me dat de Lord jes takes all dese here shells in his hands, and eases 'em right over dis here house, into South Ca'lina Hospital, even if de garden do look like 'tis ploughed up, but he ain't even let one o' 'em shells hit this house, even if de shells has taken off the end o' Mr. Cooper's house cross the street and cut the piano in half."

—ANNE A. BANISTER

*

Aunt Abby Under Fire

*

[AUNT ABBY] was as fearless under fire as she was in the use of her tongue, and more than one officer has testified to the coolness with which she would walk through the trenches during the fearful bombardment of Petersburg; and she has frequently been known to go under a heavy fire to carry water to our wounded. On one occasion an officer met her coolly walking down the road leading two horses by their bridles, with the bullets whistling round her like hail.

"My God! old lady," he exclaimed, "what are you doing here?"

"I'm a taking Colonel McRae's and Captain Young's horses to 'em. They jumped off 'em and turned 'em into the yard, while they run through the bushes down yonder to whar the Yankees begun a firing on our boys; and when they opened on 'em with the cannon, and the shells begun to 'bust round headquarters, these here foolish horses got sorter cantankerous, so I cotch 'em by the bridles, and as they'd 'er bin killed maybe if I left 'em up yonder, I'm gwine to take 'em down to whar the boys is under cover."

The officer, who told the story said she was as cool as though she was leading the horses to water on a summer's day at home; and only got excited and used expressions more forcible than elegant when they, snorting and jerking back at the whiz of every shell, came near stepping on her. She said the woman at the house had run into the cellar when the bombardment began, and called to her to come in too, ". . . but I told her I was a-gwine to carry them thar horses to ther owners,—for maybe they'd need 'em yet afore the day was over."

—MARY BAYARD CLARKE

*

The Old Lady from Atlanta

*

Hascosea, N. C., August, 1864

WE GET SOME GOOD STORIES of our common people from Yankee correspondents. One old lady near Atlanta said to a Yankee officer who rode up to her house immediately after the attempted flanking of Joe Johnston by Sherman, "You'uns don't fight we'uns fair. Mr. Hooker now, *he* went round." Good soul, her notions of military strategy were comprised in a fair stand-up and give-and-take fight.

Another was accosted by a party of Yankees.

"Well, how goes it, old lady, you are Secesh too I suppose?"

"No, I ain't, honey."

"Why, how's that, you're Union then?"

"No, thank the Lord I ain't that either."

"Well, what in the name of wonder are you then?"

"I'm a Baptist, honey, a Baptist, for forty years I'se been a hardshell Baptist, and please the Lord I'll die one."

—CATHERINE DEVEREUX EDMONDSTON

January						
S	M	T	W	T	F	S
1	2	3	4	5	6	7
8	9	10	11	12	13	14
15	16	17	18	19	20	21
22	23	24	25	26	27	28
29	30	31	..	..	..	..

February						
S	M	T	W	T	F	S
..	..	..	1	2	3	4
5	6	7	8	9	10	11
12	13	14	15	16	17	18
19	20	21	22	23	24	25
26	27	28	..	..	..	..

March						
S	M	T	W	T	F	S
..	..	..	1	2	3	4
5	6	7	8	9	10	11
12	13	14	15	16	17	18
19	20	21	22	23	24	25
26	27	28	29	30	31	..

FIVE

In EIGHTEEN HUNDRED AND SIXTY-FIVE
The soldiers at home with their wives.
We'll all drink stone blind;
Johnny, come fill up the bowl.

April						
S	M	T	W	T	F	S
..	..	..	..	..	..	1
2	3	4	5	6	7	8
9	10	11	12	13	14	15
16	17	18	19	20	21	22
23	24	25	26	27	28	29
30	..	..	..	..	..	..

May						
S	M	T	W	T	F	S
..	1	2	3	4	5	6
7	8	9	10	11	12	13
14	15	16	17	18	19	20
21	22	23	24	25	26	27
28	29	30	31	..	..	..

June						
S	M	T	W	T	F	S
..	..	..	..	1	2	3
4	5	6	7	8	9	10
11	12	13	14	15	16	17
18	19	20	21	22	23	24
25	26	27	28	29	30	..
..	..	..	..	..	..	..

July						
S	M	T	W	T	F	S
..	..	..	..	..	..	1
2	3	4	5	6	7	8
9	10	11	12	13	14	15
16	17	18	19	20	21	22
23	24	25	26	27	28	29
30	31	..	..	..	..	..

August						
S	M	T	W	T	F	S
..	..	1	2	3	4	5
6	7	8	9	10	11	12
13	14	15	16	17	18	19
20	21	22	23	24	25	26
27	28	29	30	31	..	..

September						
S	M	T	W	T	F	S
..	..	..	..	..	1	2
3	4	5	6	7	8	9
10	11	12	13	14	15	16
17	18	19	20	21	22	23
24	25	26	27	28	29	30

October						
S	M	T	W	T	F	S
1	2	3	4	5	6	7
8	9	10	11	12	13	14
15	16	17	18	19	20	21
22	23	24	25	26	27	28
29	30	31	..	..	..	..
..	..	..	..	..	..	..

November						
S	M	T	W	T	F	S
..	..	..	1	2	3	4
5	6	7	8	9	10	11
12	13	14	15	16	17	18
19	20	21	22	23	24	25
26	27	28	29	30	..	..

December						
S	M	T	W	T	F	S
..	..	..	..	..	1	2
3	4	5	6	7	8	9
10	11	12	13	14	15	16
17	18	19	20	21	22	23
24	25	26	27	28	29	30
31	..	..	..	..	..	..

37. "AND I HAVE SUFFERED ALL THIS FOR MY COUNTRY"

"Coming In"

*

"WHAT IS YOUR GOVERNMENT going to do with us when we surrender?" inquired a reb of a blue-jacket as they stood together on the "neutral ground" between the lines at Petersburg.

"You must be pretty certain that you are nearly played out, or you wouldn't ask that."

"We are nearly played out; our confederacy is going to tumble right soon, and I am going to 'git from under.' I've stuck, now, since

465

1861; enlisted for a year then; been over four years here, and now that they've brought my old father, and my little brother, who wasn't quite ten years old when I left home, I think the jig is nearly up, and I'm going to leave. What are you going to do with us?"

"Send you home," said the Yankee soldier, "send you home in good shape; we don't believe that the rank and file of the Confederate army have any heart in this rebellion; our government blames the leaders only, they'll have to suffer for all this."

"That's what I always said," quoth the rebel. "This is the rich man's war and the poor man's fight, with us; in your army every one turned in and took a hand, but they didn't in our country. I believe I'll get taken prisoner in the first brush we have with you; I've been too long here to desert."

The two men looked into one another's eyes, and understood each other in a moment.

"I'll take you now," said Yank, sliding his hand into his breast as though for a pistol (the soldiers never carried their muskets "between the lines"); "I'll take you now. You are my prisoner—come in."

"All right, my boy; I'll come," said the not unwilling gray-jacket, and in toward our lines they trudged, while half a dozen harmless shots from the enemy whistled around their heads.

"But say, Yank," said Johnnie, after they got safely in, "do all you fellows carry pistols?"

"Pistols? No—what makes you ask that?"

"Why, when you took me prisoner out there," said Reb, with a sly wink, "you put your hand into your breast for your shooting iron, didn't you?"

"No—I only carry my pipe there—have a smoke?" said he, presenting the article mentioned.

They smoked, of course, and not long after our soldier received a letter telling him that his prisoner had been "galvanized," and was wearing the army blue.

—*The Soldiers' and Sailors' Half-Dime Tales of the Late Rebellion*

The Soldier and the Naval Officer

AFFAIRS WERE LOOKING very badly for us about this time—the winter of [1864-]1865. Men were deserting in large numbers from General Lee's army and from the James River squadron. The cause of the large desertion in the army was the march of General Sherman through Georgia and South Carolina. The letters received by the soldiers from their wives and families describing their sufferings maddened these poor fellows, and they could not resist their appeals to return for their protection. In the squadron, where very few of the men were "to the manner born," the scanty ration was the principal cause of their leaving. A man shut up in an ironclad with nothing to do after the morning drill broods over his hunger—it is not like being on shore, where a man can move about and forage a little. Still the sailors, with all their sufferings, were better off than General Lee's soldiers, inasmuch as they were well-clothed and had always a dry hammock at night.

One of my officers, who was remarkably neat in his dress, told me that coming on from Charleston he had a seat alongside a soldier who was returning to his regiment in the field. The soldier was very badly clad and looked haggard and care-worn. Eyeing my friend critically and earnestly, he asked him a number of questions: If he was a general (we wore silver stars on our straps, as the brigadier generals did); if he was returning to his regiment; where it was stationed; etc., etc. My friend finally told him that he belonged to the navy. After some reflection, the soldier said, confidentially: "I tell you what it is, if things don't soon look better, I'll be dogged if I don't try to navy it a little too."

—CAPTAIN WILLIAM HARWAR PARKER

467

*

A Peace Petition to President Davis

*

THIS LETTER or petition was found in General Early's headquarters wagon, when captured by General Custer at Waynesboro, Virginia, March 2, 1865, by me.

(Signed) E. W. WHITAKER,
General Custer's Chief of Staff

Army of the Valley
February 5, 1865

TO PRESIDENT DAVIS:

The [peace] mission of Vice-President Stephens is the most momentous of any that has been undertaken by any person or persons on this continent.

The soldiers of this army, the people of this section, all pray for their success.

We have fought, we think, well, against heavy odds, for near four years, and still, so far as fighting is concerned, peace seems afar off. The lives of many good and wise men have been taken. Science and the arts have been crippled—but still the war goes on.

Suppose Fulton had conceived his idea of steam power, and before communicating his scheme had been thrown in the ranks and slain in battle; the same supposition with regard to Morse, how great the loss would have been to the present age. And yet we know not but that as great discoveries have been lost to us by this cruel war. We deplore, and know that you deplore, the loss and suffering entailed upon us by this war.

Therefore, we pray you to strive every way in your power to settle our troubles by arbitration. Let the sword have no more bloody work to do. If nothing but reunion can be had, let it come, lest a worse fate befall us. It is clear that England and France from the first till now have held a hand upon the fates of the contending parties and stimulated the weaker by turns. They now wonder why we should hesitate to make soldiers of our slaves. This is to strengthen us for another year or two of resistance. They hope by this means to weaken both sections, and then they will divide the spoil.

Is this a better fate than reunion? Perhaps we can get better terms, but, if not, let us accept them; build up our own factories, have our own shipping and thus secure the only independence we can ever have. Most of us have fought our last battle. Our property has all been lost to us, our wives and children are bound to suffer, if not starve, in the next six or eight months, and we beg you to enable us to quit this war with honor.

The odds to us is too great—the world; we can't resist with any show of success in another campaign. 'Tis folly to try.

Then strive, honored sir, through Commissioners, to settle speedy this horrid war. God Almighty aid you in the good work.

MANY SOLDIERS

———

This letter was sent to Jeff Davis and returned by him to General Early endorsed in his own handwriting, as follows:

It is to be hoped that this is not a fair sample of the feeling of the "Army of the Valley."
To General Early

(Signed) J. D.

—Virginia State Library, Archives

*

———

"You Can Keep Your Stick"

———

*

ABOUT 10 A.M., Friday, February 17, 1865, the main army [of Sherman] entered the city [of Columbia, South Carolina]. Officers established headquarters at the market and court-house. Here the troops were disbanded and freed from all restraint. Cotton fires on Main Street, looting and general destruction of property commenced. These cotton fires during the morning were extinguished and had no connection with the fires at night. About 3 P.M. General [Wade] Hampton's and two other residences were burned two or three miles from the city. At 8 o'clock three signal rockets went up, this meant that the fires should be started.

Our soldiers meantime had left the city, feeling resistance against such odds was useless. Never shall I forget the dejected looks of our cavalry as they rode past my door, on Laurel Street near Sumter, quite a number halting to say "good-by" and "God help you." As the last of the little band disappeared I felt for the first time my courage fail and realized that we were an unprotected community of women and children in the hands of a merciless foe. It was a moment to try the souls of the most courageous, but the best must be made of the emergency.

By this time, and in fewer moments than it takes to write it, the "blue-coats" were swarming on every side. In hurried consultation with one of my neighbors, we decided to go immediately to headquarters and request a guard. Never shall I forget my feelings when walking from my residence, through Main Street to the market, where General Stone had established his headquarters. Every store that we passed, the length of this business street, had been broken open and the contents scattered. Our servants were completely demoralized. They were made welcome to whatever they could lay their hands on. The scenes, although trying, were some of them truly laughable. Some had washtubs filled with treasures. Molasses poured loosely in, bottles of medicine, toys, confectionery, cloth of various kinds, in fact a little of everything they could grasp, without regard to quality or utility. It was only to get the most that could be carried off. In many instances our servants brought their treasures home and placed them at our disposal.

The friend who had accompanied me to headquarters soon found an audience with General Stone, who very readily gave us each two soldiers to guard our homes, with the assurance that we, together with everything contained in our houses, would be perfectly safe while the guard remained on duty. So with our soldier protectors we felt, after all, it might not be as bad as we had feared. We fed them well, and gave them, alternately, the rest they seemed so much to need.

In this way the day flew by, and such a day! Cold, cloudy, and with a storm of wind, such as I have never seen away from the sea coast.

Meantime, the soldiers had been busy foraging and appropriating whatever in the way of provision they could find. Many had found amusement in tearing open the cotton bales with their bayonets and scattering the fleecy contents, which light material, blown by the high wind, was readily lodged in the leafless branches of the trees and rolled into immense bundles, gathering the dried leaves with which the avenues were strewn, and making on the streets and overhead the most combustible material. Altogether the city presented the most peculiar appearance, and the elements seemed to combine with the enemy to make the impression appalling. The women who were in the doomed city that day will ever remember their experiences.

Towards twilight two officers stopped at my balcony and ordered supper. I told them it would be ready in a half hour, and promptly they returned at the time appointed. We served them a comfortable meal. One was a captain, James G. Crosier, of 21st Illinois regiment, the other his lieutenant. I do not know his name. They questioned us very closely and seemed anxious to find out what they could of our surroundings, etc. I had but one spoon visible, and told them they would have to stir their coffee by turns. They seemed to doubt my assertion, and on urging me, I told them *truthfully* I had sent such articles of value as could be conveniently removed to a place of safety before the army entered the city. One looked significantly at the other, saying, "She acted wisely." After supper they drew around the fire, lit their pipes and prepared for a talk. We treated them with civility, and after a while they disgorged their pockets, which consisted of articles from a drug store, and among other things gave me a bottle of glycerine and licorice, which they remarked I would have use for before morning. Soon after this they left.

About this time my mother and grandmother, who shared our home, suggested that it would be well to take an out-look and see how matters stood. It was then about 9 P.M., and if the city was quiet we would rest alternately.

We had not feared the destruction of private property, although we felt assured that all public stores, warehouses and factories would be destroyed. Imagine, then, our dismay, on looking out, to see *fires* in every part of the city; they had all been started within a half hour and no alarm sounded. The work was being systematically carried on. We *knew,* we *felt,* what was our doom.

At that moment an old gentleman living near by, who had an invalid daughter, came in to consult me as to what could be done. We had no time for planning, what was to be done must be done quickly. A stretcher was procured, upon which the sufferer was placed and borne by two men into the streets. Never shall I forget the lovely face of that pale maiden as she lay in the firelight, homeless, on that inclement night, with no shelter save the clouds that now and then let fall their drops, as though weeping with us in our desolation. When it became inevitable that we must abandon our house, I called my boys, lads of seven and nine, and equipped them with everything I felt they could carry—filled their pockets, belted their waists and adorned them with coffee pot and small cooking utensils. Brushes, combs, and such articles of apparel as could be stowed in pockets were tucked away, and it is wonderful under such circumstances, how many things can be collected, and we remembered that our worldly possessions would be only what we could save in this way. As I was leaving the house I saw standing in my room a gold-headed palmetto walking cane; this had been presented by my husband and myself to my brother on his twenty-first birthday. This brother was killed in the battle of Secessionville, and the cane had been returned to us, to keep until our oldest son, who had his name, should become of age, and presented to him. I stuck this cane in my belt like a sword, the gold head showing just above the belt. After leaving the house a soldier came up to me, and with an insulting remark, jerked the cane out of my belt. I snatched the end of the cane and jerked it from him, at the same time saying, "That cane belonged to a dead Confederate soldier who would never have harmed or insulted a woman, and if you will have this cane, I will break it over your head and you can take it in two pieces," and suiting the action to the words, I lifted the cane, the man dodged and said, "Woman, you can keep your stick" (and that stick today is in the possession of my oldest son). The man immediately disappeared. It was useless to try to remove bedding or furniture, they would be destroyed or stolen.

My house was fired from a back room, which, being of wood, rapidly communicated to other parts of the building, and the flames soon swept over the entire house. I did not leave it until the smoke became so dense it was impossible to remain longer, and had the satisfaction of knowing that the house, with all its contents, was burned without being first rifled. In a half hour from the time I stepped from my balcony into the streets all that remained of my home was the smouldering ruins.

—MARY S. WHILDEN

*

A Deserter's Farewell

---

*

March the 3rd, 1865

MY DEAR WIFE:

I have to state to you the sad news that tomorrow at 12 o'clock I have to die. I have to be shot to death for starting home to see my wife and dear children and [w]as arrested and brought back and court-martialed and am to be shot at 12 o'clock. Me and D. M. Furr have to die, but thanks be to God, I am not afraid to die. I think when I leave this world I shall be where Mary and Martha are. Dear wife, don't grieve for me. Try and not. I drempt last night of seeing you, but I shall never. You shall see your hubby no more. I want you to raise my children in the way that they should go. My dear son, Julius, this is my last order to you. I want you to be a good boy and try to serve God and be a good man. Farewell, Julius, I must leave this world. And my son, Ephraim, try and be a good man and serve God. My dear daughter, Haseltine, I bid farewell to you. Be a good girl and go to preaching. Farewell, my dear son, Joel. You have no daddy now. Be a smart boy and mind your mother. My dear Nancy, I bid farewell to you. I want you to keep what things I have and pay my debts. And I want Julius and Ephraim to have my tools and I want them to take good care of them and remember me. I have a little looking glass that I want to send to Rebecca. I want her to remember. I have a good blanket I will get and send home. Will send my things with —— Lefler and try and get him to send them home if he will and I have 25 or 30 dollars and I shall spend $5 of that in the morning before I suffer. Dear wife, that is four months' service. I can't write like if I was not in trouble. I don't mind death like I do to leave my family for I have to suffer so much here that I don't fear. I don't want you to grieve for me, for I feel like I am going home to die no more. I hope I shall be with shining angels and be out of trouble. I have got a little book I want Joel to have and remember me. It has some pretty lines. I want you to send the children to school, and son Julius, I can't hear from you any more. I sent him a letter, but got no answer. I pity poor Julius, for he has had no chance. I have got no chance to write for I have to close my letter.

March the 4th, 1865

A few lines to Daniel Lefler and Jane Lefler. I bid farewell to you and my dear mother; I bid farewell to you and fathers and brothers and sisters. I must leave the world. Farewell, Julius, my dear son; farewell, Joel, my dear son. I want you all to meet me in heaven.

JOSEPH HONEYCUTT

To Nancy Honeycutt, farewell, farewell.

P.S.—I want you to have my funeral preached at Pleasant Grove. I want Columbus Foreman to preach it and sing "I am Going Home to Die no More." This is the 4th day of March at nine o'clock. I must soon be in eternity. I don't desire this, but I am not afraid to die. I want you to get all of the children's funerals preached that are dead. Nancy, I want to see you one more time if I could, but we can't meet any more. I want you all and the children to meet me in heaven.

—*Catawba County* (North Carolina) *News*

*

"I Have Seen the 'Yankies'"

*

Glen Burnie, N.C.
March 21, 1865

MY DEAR COUSIN,

Well Pattie I have seen the Yankies at last, and I earnestly will pray heaven that I may never see them again. The 9th of March will ever be remembered by me. The vagabonds appeared here early on that morning, we had no idea they were within fifty miles of here, it seemed that day that heaven had forever turned from us. There was a hundred and fifty men in the first squad that came here, and such a yell as they gave when they rode in the gate mortal never heard. I was not frightened one bit, it seemed as though my very soul had turned to stone and I knew, felt nor cared for anything.

Papa ran to the swamp as soon as he saw them coming, and they were almost frantic with rage when they found he had left and started in the woods to find him and swore by all the saints in heaven that they would kill him if they found him. You can imagine what agony we suffered on his and Willie's account who was with him. The rascals all came in, and in less than ten minutes the house was stripped of almost every thing. Pa had the night before fortunately concealed his two watches and your jewelry in a very nice place, somewhere about the house, I did not know where, and the Yankies of course concluded as there was so much in the house there must be some watches too. One of them came to me to know where they were, I of course refused to tell, he then immediately presented a pistol to my head and swore he would take my life if I did not tell him, but I was as firm as a rock and though I was completely in his power, I defied him to touch me, finding at last that twas utterly useless to try to get anything out of me, he went off swearing, "I was the d——st rebel he had ever seen," which I considered was very much of a compliment.

There was no officer with the first men that came, and our drooping spirits were revived about one o'clock by the sight of a Yankie officer. He came in the house and introduced himself as Lt. Bracht (queer name isn't it?). Mamma and I immediately appealed to him for protection and he soon had order restored in the house, and gave us a guard. I think he was very much of a gentleman. He was very kind to me, that was something I did not expect, I did not think there was a gentleman in the whole Yankie Army, but now I know there is one if no more. He came too late to save any of our property that the Yankies wanted. They carried off every earthly thing we had to eat, did not leave a grain of corn or coffee, or anything that would sustain life one day, they found all our silver and took every knife, fork and spoon we had in the world.

Twenty-five thousand men passed here and I assure you I could not see across the road for three whole days for the men. They set the Pine Woods on fire all around us. Tell Aunt Jennie they set on fire all the rosin she saw, and turned day into night. I hope to gracious Pat, that you may never go through all the agony I did in that one week. They carried off a great many of our clothes, have not left me a cloak or shawl of any kind, tore the silk you gave Jennie all to flinders and carried off my best dresses and two of Mamma's silks. Have not one blanket in the house, have only a half dozen quilts. Every one of our darkies went and Ma and I have had to do all of the washing and ironing and scouring. I have done all the cooking. The house is so dirty I don't think we will get it clean in ten months. The Yankies burned our barn and swore they would burn the house over our heads, but Providence saved it, I can't tell you now how.

We have not heard from Archie in more than a month, have an idea he is with the Boys Army. The 14th Yankie Army Corps, one that was here, has been cut all to pieces so I hear, I hope they will not spare one of them.

The "Yanks" were just about to find the watches, and Mamma took them to Lt. Bracht and he took care of them for us as long as he stayed, he was here all Thursday and that night and guarded the house for us. I sat up in the parlor and played on the piano and sang for the Yankies till twelve o'clock Thursday night. The first that came compelled me to play for them, but I vowed I would play nothing but Southern songs and I know you would have been surprised if you could have looked in and seen how coolly I was sitting there surrounded by my deadly enemies singing the "Bonnie Blue, Flag" and "Dixie" with all my might. I am confident that I never in my life sang so well. I breathed all the fire in my soul into those two songs.

Well, Pat, I must close by telling you that the Yankies never caught Papa and that we are not quite starved to death, though we came very near it, we went five days without a mouthful of bread. You will excuse the paper I know as it is all the Yankies left in the house, and tis a wonder they left this. Oh how I do hate the very name of Yankie! They can never prosper. May the chilling blight of heaven fall on their dark and damned souls. May all the powers of earth and heaven combine to destroy them, may their land be one vast scene of ruin and desolation as ours is. This is the blessing of the innocent and injured one. I forgive them? May heaven never.

Tell Mary not to be uneasy about us, we will try to keep from starving. I heard from Uncle Archie's folks and they are well. Write soon, and don't for mercy's sake let any one see this horribly written letter.

NELLIE

—MRS. GEORGE FRENCH

"Men Are Going the Wrong Way"

Chester, S.C., March 30, 1865

I SAID to General [John S.] Preston: "I pass my days—and my nights, partly—at this window. I am sure our army is silently dispersing. Men are going the wrong way all the time. They slip by now with no songs or shouts. They have given the thing up. See for yourself! Look!" For a while the streets were thronged with soldiers, and then they were empty again; but the marching now is without tap of drum. I told him of the woman in the cracker bonnet at the depot at Charlotte who squalled to her husband as they dragged him off: "Take it easy, Jake. You desert again, quick as you kin. Come back to your wife and children." And she continued to yell: "Desert, Jake! Desert again, Jake!"

—MARY BOYKIN CHESNUT

Constance Cary's Skirt

Grace Street, Richmond, April 4, 1865

MY PRECIOUS MOTHER AND BROTHER:

I ought to tell you the important news that your tin box of securities is safe and in my keeping. How do you think this happened? On Sunday, after Clarence left, and we were wandering around the streets like forlorn ghosts, I chanced to meet our friend, Mr. ——, the president of the —— Bank, in which I knew you kept them. He was very pale and wretched-looking, said he could not vouch for the safe-keeping of anybody's property, asked after you and wondered if I would feel like taking your papers in charge. I walked with him to the bank, where he put the box in my hands, and then I hurried back with it to my uncle's house. I slept with the papers under my head Sunday night, and spent Monday afternoon in ripping apart the trimming of my gray beige skirt. You know that trimming, like a wide battlement of brown silk all around the hem? Well, into this wall of Troy I sewed with the tightest stitches I could make (you would say those were nothing to boast of, remembering the sleeve that came apart) every one of your precious documents. And here I am with the family fortune stitched into my frock, which I have determined to wear every day with a change of white bodices, till I see you or can get to some place where it is safe to take it off. . . .

I will say in concluding the episode of the hidden papers, that the next day after I had received them, the bank went down in the track of the awful Main Street fire, its contents destroyed utterly. I continued to wear the skirt, heartily sick of it before I dared lay the thing aside, until the day late in April when I went by flag of truce to Baltimore, and there, at the home of my uncle, Mr. Cary, extracted the papers, put them in a new tin box, and consigned them to proper safe-keeping. I have certainly never since worn a gown of the value of that one, ungratefully cast aside at the first opportunity!

—CONSTANCE CARY HARRISON

*

The Evacuation of Richmond

*

Richmond, April 5, 1865

MY DEAR:

I am not at all sure you will ever receive this letter, but I shall risk it. *First,* I join you in humble thanks to God for the great mercy accorded both of us. Your General lives. My Colonel lives. What words can express our gratitude? What is the loss of home and goods compared with the loss of our own flesh and blood? Alas! Alas! for those who have lost all!

I am sure you have heard the grewsome story of Richmond's evacuation. I was at St. Paul's Sunday, April 1, when a note was handed to President Davis. He rose instantly, and walked down the aisle—his face set, so we could read nothing. Dr. Minnegerode gave notice that General Ewell desired the force to assemble at 3 P. M., and also that there would be no further service that day. I had seen no one speak to the doctor, and I wonder at the acuteness of his perception of the state of affairs. As soon as I reached the hotel I wrote a note to the proprietor, asking for news. He answered that grave tidings had come from Petersburg, and for himself he was by no means sure we could hold Richmond. He requested me to keep quiet and not encourage a tendency to excitement or panic. At first I thought I would read my services in the quiet of my little sky parlor at the Spotswood, but I was literally in a fever of anxiety. I descended to the parlor. Nobody was there except two or three children with their nurses. Later in the afternoon I walked out and met Mr. James Lyons. He said there was no use in further evading the truth. The lines were broken at Petersburg and that town and Richmond would be surrendered late at night—he was going out himself with the mayor and Judge Meredith with a flag of truce and surrender the city. Trains were already fired to carry the archives and bank officials. The President and his Cabinet would probably leave at the same time.

"And you, Judge?"

"I shall stand my ground. I have a sick family, and we must take our chances together."

"Then seriously—really and truly—Richmond is to be given up, after all, to the enemy?"

"Nothing less! And we are going to have a rough time, I imagine."

I could not be satisfied until I had seen Judge Campbell, upon whom we so much relied for good, calm sense. I found him with his hands full of papers, which he waved deprecatingly as I entered.

"Just a minute, Judge! I am alone at the Spotswood and—"

"Stay there, my dear lady! You will be perfectly safe. I advise all families to remain in their own houses. Keep quiet. I am glad to know the Colonel is safe. He may be with you soon now."

With this advice I returned and mightily reassured and comforted the proprietor of the Spotswood. He immediately caused notice to be issued to his guests. I resolved to convey my news to the families I knew best. The Pegrams were in such deep affliction there was no room there for anxious fears about such small matters as the evacuation of cities, but I could see my dear Mrs. Paul, and Mrs. Maben, and say a comforting word at the Allan home,—closed to all the world since poor John fell at Gettysburg. Mrs. Davis was gone and out of harm's way. The Lees were sacred from intrusion. Four members of that household—the General, "Rooney," Custis, and Robert—were all at the post of danger. Late in the afternoon three hundred or more prisoners were marched down the street; the Negroes began to stand about, quietly observant, but courteous, making no demonstration whatever.

The day, you remember, was one of those glorious days we have in April, and millions on millions of stars watched at night, looking down on the watchers below. I expected to sit by my window all night as you always do in a troubled time, but sleep overtook me. I had slept, but not undressed, when a loud explosion shook the house—then another. There were crashing sounds of falling glass from the concussion. I found the sun had risen. All was commotion in the streets, and agitation in the hotel. The city government had dragged hogsheads of liquor from the shops, knocked in the heads, and poured the spirits into the gutters. They ran with brandy, whiskey, and rum; and men, women, and boys rushed out with buckets, pails, pitchers and in the lower streets hats and boots, to be filled. Before eight o'clock many public buildings were in flames, and a great conflagration was evidently imminent. The flames swept up Main Street, where the stores were quickly burned, and then roared down the side streets almost to Franklin.

The doors of all the government bakeries were thrown open and food was given to all who asked it. Women and children walked in and helped themselves. At ten o'clock the enemy arrived,—ten thousand Negro troops, going on and on, cheered by the Negroes on the streets.

So the morning passed—a morning of horror, of terror! Drunken men shouted and reeled through the streets, a black cloud from the burning city hung like a pall over us, a black sea of faces filled the street below, shells burst continuously in the ashes of the burning armory. At four in the afternoon a salute of thirty-four guns was fired. A company of mounted dragoons advanced up the street, escorting an open carriage drawn by four horses in which sat Mr. Lincoln and a naval officer, followed by an escort of cavalry. They drove straight to Mr. Davis' house, and returned the way they came. I had a good look at

480

Mr. Lincoln. He seemed tired and old—and I must say, with due re-spect to the President of the United States, I thought him the ugliest man I had ever seen. He was fairly elected the first time, I acknowledge, —but was he the last? A good many of the "free and equal" were not allowed a vote then.

The next day I persuaded one of the lads in the hotel to take a walk with me early in the morning, and I passed Lee's house. A Yankee guard was pacing to and fro before it—at which I felt an impulse of indignation,—but presently the door opened, the guard took his seat on the steps and proceeded to investigate the contents of a very neatly furnished tray, which Mrs. Lee in the kindness of her heart had sent out to him.

I am obliged to acknowledge that there is really no hope now for our ultimate success. Everybody says so. My heart is too full for words. General Johnston says we may comfort ourselves by the fact that war may decide a *policy,* but never a *principle.* I imagine our *principle* is all that remains to us of hope or comfort.

> Devotedly,
> AGNES
>
> —Letter to MRS. ROGER A. PRYOR

✳

Gambling with the Confederate Treasury

✳

WITH THE FALL of Richmond and Petersburg, the enemy, closely pursued by the Union army, retreated to Chesterfield Court-house, Amelia Court-house, Jetersville, Deatonsville, and Sailors' Creek. Whenever they made a halt or stand they were attacked, routed, and pursued by the Union army.

✳ ✳ ✳ ✳ ✳

. . . At Sailor's Creek [April 6, 1865], the enemy made a final stand. Without a moment's hesitation the division charged the enemy's line, capturing the entire train of two hundred and fifty wagons, two pieces of artillery, twelve battle-flags, and upward of one thousand prisoners.

Then, as night mantled the field of slaughter, a scene of comedy was enacted about the bivouac fires. After the troops were in position for the night, and the soldiers had partaken of their spare meal of coffee and crackers, they gratified their curiosity by a rigid inspection of the day's trophies. Several of the wagons were found loaded with the assets of the Confederate treasury, which had been brought out from Richmond. Then followed a most extraordinary spectacle of jollity and good humor. A Monte Carlo was suddenly improvised in the midst of the bivouac of war.

"Here's the Confederate treasury, as sure as you are a soldier!" shouted one.

"Let's all be rich!" said another.

"Boys, fill your pockets, your hats, your haversacks, your handkerchiefs, your arms, if you please," was the word, and the Confederate notes and bonds were rapidly disbursed.

If they were at a discount, they were crisp and new and in enormous denominations. Spreading their blankets on the ground by the bivouac fires, the veterans proceeded with the comedy, and such preposterous gambling was probably never before witnessed. Ten thousand dollars was the usual "ante." Often twenty thousand to "come in"; a raise of fifty thousand to one hundred thousand was not unusual, and frequently from one million to two millions of dollars were in the "pool."

"Be prudent, stranger,"—"Don't go beyond your means, my friends," were some of the remarks frequently heard amid roars of laughter, together with an occasional shout of, "Freedom forever"—"Rally 'round the flag, boys"—"Ain't I glad I'm in *this* army"—"We are coming, Father Abraham"—"Boys, what do you say—let's pay off the Confederate debts," etc., etc. They were seemingly as light-hearted and oblivious as it is possible for soldiers to be to what might follow. They kept up the revelry during most of the night, though some were to make the soldiers' sacrifice on the morrow, while others were to witness the scene of final triumph.

—NELSON A. MILES

*

The Yankee's Prize

*

IT WAS TOWARD the end of the terrible struggle between the States. A weary and dusty Confederate sat cooling his tired feet in a stream, while, with a rusty needle and coarse thread he was endeavoring to mend his ragged coat. Suddenly a mounted Federal dashed into view, and riding rapidly toward the Confederate, he shouted: "Hi, there, Johnny Reb. I've got you this time."

Without looking up from his mending the half-starved, ragged and dirty fellow replied: "Yes, and a h—l of a git you got."

—*Confederate Women of Arkansas in the Civil War, 1861-'65,*
Memorial Reminiscences

38. APPOMATTOX

Flags of Truce

*

I · The Towel

THE FLAG was a new and clean white crash towel, one of a lot for which I had paid $20 or $40 apiece in Richmond a few days before we left there. I rode alone up a lane (I believe there was only a fence on my right intact), passing by the pickets or sharpshooters of Gary's (Confederate) Cavalry Brigade stationed along the fence, enclosing the lane on my right as I passed. A wood was in front of me occupied by

Federals, unmounted cavalry, I think. I did not exhibit the flag until near your line, consequently was fired upon until I got to or very near your people. I went at a full gallop. I met a party of soldiers . . . and near them, two or three officers. One was Lieutenant Colonel Whitaker, now in Washington, and the other a major.

I said to them: "Where is your commanding officer, General Sheridan? I have a message for him."

They replied: "He is not near here, but General Custer is, and you had better see him."

"Can you take me to him?"

"Yes."

They mounted and we rode up the road that I came but a short distance, when we struck Custer's division of cavalry, passing at full gallop along a road crossing our road and going to my left. We galloped down this road to the head of the column, where we met General Custer.

He asked: "Who are you, and what do you wish?"

I replied: "I am of General Longstreet's staff, but am the bearer of a message from General Gordon to General Sheridan, asking for a suspension of hostilities until General Lee can be heard from, who has gone down the road to meet General Grant to have a conference."

General Custer replied: "We will listen to no terms but that of unconditional surrender. We are behind your army now and it is at our mercy."

I replied: "You will allow me to carry this message back?"

He said: "Yes."

"Do you wish to send an officer with me?"

Hesitating a little, he said: "Yes," and directed the two officers who came with me, Lieutenant Colonel Whitaker and the major, whose name I don't know, to go with me.

We rode back to Gordon in almost a straight line. Somewhere on the route a Major Brown, of General Gordon's (Confederate) staff, joined me, I think after I had left Custer.

On our way back to Gordon two incidents occurred. Colonel Whitaker asked me if I would give him the towel to preserve that I had used as a flag. I replied: "I will see you in hell first; it is sufficiently humiliating to have had to carry it and exhibit it, and I shall not let you preserve it as a monument of our defeat." I was naturally irritated and provoked at our prospective defeat, and Colonel Whitaker at once apologized, saying he appreciated my feelings and did not intend to offend. Passing some artillery crossing a small stream, he asked me to stop this artillery, saying: "If we are to have a suspension of hostilities, everything should remain in *statu quo*."

I replied: "In the first place, I have no authority to stop this artillery; and, secondly, if I had, I should not do so, because General Custer distinctly stated that we were to have no suspension of hostilities until an unconditional surrender was asked for. I presume this means continuing the fight. I am sure General Longstreet will construe it so."

When I reached General Gordon he asked me to go in another direction, almost opposite to the one I had been, and take the flag to stop the firing. I replied that I could not so go, as I must go to General Longstreet; besides some of his (Gordon's) staff were now with him. He directed Major Brown to go. Major Brown came to me and asked me to loan him the towel. I took him off to a private place and told him I would let him have the towel on condition that he would not let the Federal officer get possession of it and that I would call in the afternoon for it. He took the towel, and in going into your lines (so he reported to me that afternoon) Colonel Whitaker asked for the towel to display to keep his own people from firing on him, and, as soon as he got into the lines, he mixed up with the others and disappeared with the towel.

I learned a few years ago that Mrs. General Custer has the towel. When I reached General Longstreet, after leaving General Gordon, I found General Custer and he talking together at a short distance from the position occupied by the staff. Custer said he would proceed to attack at once and Longstreet replied: "As soon as you please," but he did not attack. Just after I left Custer he came in sight of our lines. He halted his troops and, taking a handkerchief from his orderly, displayed it as a flag and rode into our lines. He was surrounded by some of our people and was being handled a little roughly when an old classmate of his recognized him and rescued him.

Upon frequent applications from General Gordon to General Longstreet for reinforcements, he (Longstreet) sent me to say to General Gordon that General Lee had ridden down the road to meet General Grant and that if he thought proper he could send a message to General Sheridan, who was in command in his front, asking him for a suspension of hostilities until General Lee could be heard from. I found General Gordon without a staff officer near him, and he begged me to take the flag, which I did. Major Brown, of his staff, joined me somewhere on the route, I think as I was returning from General Custer.

—R. M. Sims

II · *The Shirt*

MY MEN were drawn up in the little town of Appomattox that night. I still had about four thousand men under me, as the army had been divided into two commands and given to General Longstreet and myself. Early on the morning of the 9th [of April, 1865] I prepared for the assault upon the enemy's line, and began the last fighting done in Virginia. My men rushed forward gamely and broke the line of the enemy and captured two pieces of artillery. I was still unable to tell what I was fighting; I did not know whether I was striking infantry or dismounted cavalry. I only knew that my men were driving them back, and were getting further and further through. Just then I had a message from General Lee, telling me a flag of truce was in existence, leaving it to my discretion as to what course to pursue. My men were still pushing their way on. I sent at once to hear from General Longstreet, feeling that, if he was marching toward me, we might still cut through and carry the army forward. I learned that he was about two miles off, with his face just opposite from mine, fighting for his life. I thus saw that the case was hopeless. The further each of us drove the enemy the further we drifted apart, and the more exposed we left our wagon trains and artillery, which were parked between us. Every line either of us broke only opened the gap wider. I saw plainly that the Federals would soon rush in between us, and then there would have been no army. I, therefore, determined to send a flag of truce. I called Colonel Peyton of my staff to me, and told him that I wanted him to carry a flag of truce forward.

He replied: "General, I have no flag of truce."

I told him to get one. He replied:

"General, we have no flag of truce in our command."

Then said I, "Get your handkerchief, put it on a stick, and go forward."

"I have no handkerchief, General."

"Then borrow one and go forward with it."

He tried, and reported to me that there was no handkerchief in my staff.

"Then, Colonel, use your shirt!"

"You see, General, that we all have on flannel shirts."

At last, I believe, we found a man who had a white shirt. He gave it to us, and I tore off the back and tail, and, tying this to a stick, Colonel Peyton went out toward the enemy's lines. I instructed him to simply say to General Sheridan that General Lee had written me that a flag of truce had been sent from his and Grant's headquarters, and that he could act as he thought best on this information. In a few moments he came back with some one representing General Sheridan.

This officer said: "General Sheridan requested me to present his compliments to you, and to demand the unconditional surrender of your army."

"Major, you will please return my compliments to General Sheridan, and say that I will not surrender."

"But, General, he will annihilate you."

"I am perfectly well aware of my situation. I simply gave General Sheridan some information on which he may or may not desire to act."

He went back to his lines, and in a short time General Sheridan came forward on an immense horse, and attended by a very large staff. Just here an incident occurred that came near having a serious ending. As General Sheridan was approaching I noticed one of my sharpshooters drawing his rifle down upon him. I at once called to him: "Put down your gun, sir: this is a flag of truce." But he simply settled it to his shoulder and was drawing a bead on Sheridan, when I leaned forward and jerked his gun. He struggled with me, but I finally raised it. I then loosed it, and he started to aim again. I caught it again, when he turned his stern white face, all broken with grief and streaming with tears, up to me, and said: "Well, General, then let him keep on his own side."

The fighting had continued up to this point. Indeed, after the flag of truce, a regiment of my men, who had been fighting their way through toward where we were, and who did not know of a flag of truce, fired into some of Sheridan's cavalry. This was speedily stopped, however. I showed General Sheridan General Lee's note, and he determined to await events. He dismounted, and I did the same. Then, for the first time, the men seemed to understand what it all meant, and then the poor fellows broke down. The men cried like children. Worn, starved, and bleeding as they were, they had rather have died than have surrendered. At one word from me they would have hurled themselves on the enemy, and have cut their way through or have fallen to a man with their guns in their hands. But I could not permit it. The great drama had been played to its end. But men are seldom permitted to look upon such a scene as the one presented here. That these men should have wept at surrendering so unequal a fight, at being taken out of this constant carnage and storm, at being sent back to their families; that they should

have wept at having their starved and wasted forms lifted out of the
jaws of death and placed once more before their hearthstones, was an
exhibition of fortitude and patriotism that might set an example.

—GENERAL JOHN B. GORDON

＊

Tales That Virginia Negroes
Tell of the Surrender

＊

NINETY-TWO-YEAR-OLD Cornelius Garner of the Thirty-
eighth Regiment of United States Infantry says:

"Sho', I was at de surrender. We chased Lee from Petersburg
over to Appomattox and dat's where we catched up wid him. Lee
charged us seven times tryin' to break our lines an' git out. But we had
him bottled up. He couldn't go back, he couldn't go forward, an' he
couldn't go sideways. Wasn't nothin' fo' him to do but surrender. When
Lee saw our colored regiment come marchin' up, he sent word to General Grant dat he would 'gree to his terms. So General Grant come
ridin' up in a blue uniform an' General Lee waited for him under a
apple tree. Den dey walked on into de McLean House dere at Appomattox, an' Lee signed de surrender papers."

To most of the Union soldiers the real surrender came the next
day when Grant met Lee in full sight of both armies under the famous
apple tree. There are many versions of that meeting, told by those who
saw, as well as by those who "only heard." One story has Lee fleeing
afoot across the field with Grant chasing him on a huge black charger.
Another has Lee climbing the apple tree, while Grant circled beneath
it with levelled pistols, calling out: "Does you surrender?" Still another
has it that the blue-clad and the gray-clad generals "met under de tree,
took offen dey hats an' embraced an' kissed to make up de diff'rences
'tween North an' South."

And Jimmy Green of Lawrenceville, who says he is "goin' on a
hundred," although neighbors say he is in his eighties, declares "de
history books is wrong."

489

" 'Twas Abe Lincoln an' Jeff Davis dat met under de ole apple tree. Lincoln stuck a shot-gun in Jeff Davis' face an' yelled, 'Better surrender, else I shoot you an' hang you.' Davis tole him, 'Yessir, Marse Lincoln, I surrender.' An' de soldiers heard it, an' made up a song 'bout it. Ain't you never heard dat song? 'Hang Jeff Davis to a sour apple tree.' Dat's de song an' dat's what de soldiers yelled at Lincoln to do, but he was too kind."

Ninety-four-year-old Tom Hester of Suffolk, who had begun at Manassas in the Confederate Army and ended at Appomattox with the Union forces, saw it "jus' as it happened." Tom Hester had served the Southern troops as mule-tender until a wild bullet at the first battle of Manassas "passed clean through both cheeks an' carried three teeth wid it." Picked up by a Union ambulance-crew, he had stayed on in the Army of the Potomac as ambulance-tender under Captain Bob Durham, supply-master. Tom Hester knows that Grant and Lee met under the apple tree because he was "right dere lookin' at dem."

"Gen'ral Lee tipped his hat fust, an' den Gen'ral Grant tipped hissen. Gen'ral Lee got offen his horse, an' Gen'ral Grant got offen hissen. Gen'ral Lee got on a new uniform wid gold braid an' lots of buttons, but Gen'ral Grant got on an old blue coat dat's so dirty it look black. Dey stood dere talkin' 'bout half an hour, an' den dey shake hands an' us what was watchin' know dat Lee done give up. Den Gen'ral Lee got on his horse an' Gen'ral Grant got on hissen, an' Gen'ral Lee tipped his hat, an' Gen'ral Grant tipped hissen, an' Gen'ral Lee rode over to de rebel side, an' Gen'ral Grant rode over to our side, an' de war was over.

"De nex' day I went out dere to cut a branch off dat tree, but dere wasn't no sign of it—jus' a hole in de groun'. De soldiers done cut dat apple tree down an' taken it fo' souvenees. Yessir, ev'y las' little piece of it, even de roots."

In the little village of Pamplin, near Appomattox, Fannie Berry, house-maid for Miss Sara Anne, stood in the yard watching the flagpole of the village square while her near-sighted mistress paced nervously back and forth.

"What's it say, Fannie? Cain't you see it?" the old mistress demanded. "Don't say nothin', Miss Sara Anne," replied the young slave girl. "Watch it close, Fannie, an' tell me what it say."

"Dey's gettin' ready to hist a flag now, Miss Sara Anne."

"See what color it is, Fannie. Is it raid?"

"Cain't see yit, Miss Sara Anne."

490

"Well, hurry up an' tell me what color it is."

"It's a white flag, Miss Sara Anne."

"Oh, Lordy, Lee done surrendered."

—The Negro in Virginia

＊
_____

The Double Jeopardy of Wilmer McLean

_____
＊

WHEN I FIRST JOINED the Army of Northern Virginia in 1861, I found a connection of my family, Wilmer McLean, living on a fine farm through which ran Bull Run, with a nice farm-house about opposite the center of our line of battle along that stream. General Beauregard made his headquarters at this house during the first affair between the armies—the so-called battle of Blackburn's Ford, on July 18. The first hostile shot which I ever saw fired was aimed at this house, and about the third or fourth went through its kitchen, where our servants were cooking dinner for the headquarters staff.

I had not seen or heard of McLean for years, when [April 10], the day after the surrender, I met him at Appomattox Court-house, and asked with some surprise what he was doing there. He replied, with much indignation: "What are you doing here? These armies tore my place on Bull Run all to pieces, and kept running over it backward and forward till no man could live there, so I just sold out and came here, two hundred miles away, hoping I should never see a soldier again. And now, just look around you! Not a fence-rail is left on the place, the last guns trampled down all my crops, and Lee surrenders to Grant in my house." McLean was so indignant that I felt bound to apologize for our coming back, and to throw all the blame for it upon the gentlemen on the other side.

—BRIGADIER GENERAL E. P. ALEXANDER

How Captain Ricks Carried
the News of the Surrender

*

ON A BRIGHT DAY in April, 1865, Major General J. D. Cox, commanding the Twenty-third Army Corps, with his staff and escort, was riding leisurely at the head of the marching column on the road to Raleigh. The latest news we had from Grant was of the fierce struggle about Richmond, its evacuation, and Lee's flight toward Central Virginia. We were passing on toward Raleigh to prevent a consolidation of Johnston's and Lee's armies, and though hourly expecting news of important movements, we had no expectation of any decided victory. As I was riding by the General's side speculating as to Johnston's probable movements, an orderly from General Sherman's headquarters rode slowly toward us, bearing a message. General Cox opened it in the usual manner and read it over as he would have done an ordinary official communication. There was nothing in the manner of the messenger to indicate that he was the bearer of any unusual or important news, and he sat listlessly on his horse while a receipt was being written for the message. Happening then to cast my eyes toward the General, I noticed his face to suddenly brighten, and in great excitement he turned and directed that the escort and staff be drawn up in line that he might read to them a message from General Sherman. It was done in a hurry, and with his head uncovered he read a brief dispatch that said that General Lee, with his entire army, had surrendered to Grant at Appomattox.

It was a message long looked for, long fought for, and though it came to us on the roadside so unexpectedly, its full significance was at once appreciated. It meant home and wife and children and happy meetings throughout the land. Such cheers as rang through that North Carolina pine thicket from the headquarters' staff and escort of a battalion of cavalry were never heard before nor since. Before the message was read, General Cox ordered all hats off, and throats cleared for three rousing cheers. Our horses' reins were loosened and thrown on their necks, and hats were off as quickly as ready hands could catch them. As the cheers rang out quick and sharp, my horse became frightened, and quick as a flash he whirled around, and before I could gather up my reins to check him, he was at full speed, headed toward the approaching column.

I had hardly checked his rapid strides when the thought flashed upon me that it would be a glorious thing to carry the news to the twenty thousand men of the Twenty-fifth Army corps who were marching on the broad road before me, all unconscious of the glad tidings that awaited them. It needed no second thought. Spurring up, and giving free rein to the excited horse, he flew over the ground like a bird, seeming to know that a ride of unusual significance was before him. Soon I came in sight of the first column, Major General Couch and staff heading the Second division. They heard our cheers, and as they saw me coming down the road at full speed, with hat off, waving for a clear road by which to pass to the rear, they opened ranks to the right and left, and opened a clear passage in the center of the road. As soon as I was within shouting distance I cried out, "Lee, with his whole army, has surrendered to Grant; make way for the bearer of the glorious news." Then their wild cheers rang out to swell those of the headquarters, which could still be heard at my rear.

But a few rods back of General Couch and his staff was the head of the infantry column, the One Hundred and Eleventh Ohio regiment. The men saw how the right of way had been quickly given to the horse and rider by the General and his escort in front of them, and as I waved to them to open ranks and give me the roadway, they responded with a will, and spreading to the right and left gave me a straight, open road to the rear. At the head of the column, and as often and as fast as I could repeat it to the anxious listeners, with horse at full speed, I cried out, with the waving of my hat, "Lee has surrendered with his whole army to Grant."

Onward I pressed my way through the surging ranks—before me an open road, lined on each side with anxious men, leaning forward to catch the first sound of the good news they were all so impatient to hear; behind me a wild, exultant, indescribable set of men suddenly transformed into lunatics, if they were to be judged by their actions, pounding each other with knapsacks, waving blankets on the points of their bayonets, pounding canteens with belt buckles, and making a pandemonium of sounds and a circus of tumbling and vaulting. It was news that needed no explanation. . . .

493

. . . And for eight miles, through ranks of infantry regiments, through batteries of artillery, by the ambulances and hospital trains, rode the one man to whom every ear was turned, the one bearer of tidings, whose voice filled every heart with joy and gratitude.

. . . Some were too much overcome to speak; some shouted themselves hoarse, while others cried; some were wild with their demonstration, while some were calm and thoughtful, and secretly breathing a prayer for their safe deliverance from the long series of dangers to which they had been exposed. . . .

* * * * *

. . . In one of the regiments, as I was sweeping through the ranks, I caught the bright face of a soldier leaning out from the lines as far as possible into the road, to catch the message that fell from my lips. "What is it? What is it?" he anxiously shouted. "Lee has surrendered with his whole army to Grant," was the reply. Clear and loud, above all the voices, and quick as the message fell upon his ears, was his answer: "Great God! You're the man I've been looking for for the last four years." . . .

—CAPTAIN A. J. RICKS

*

How General Henry A. Wise Saved His Mare

---

*

EARLY IN THE MORNING [of April 10] it became noised abroad that General Grant was to have another interview with General Lee, and a number of our generals and staff officers assembled in the village to witness it. . . .

* * * * *

. . . After talking a little while General Grant beckoned me forward, and . . . said: "General Lee is desirous that his officers and men should have on their persons some evidence that they are paroled prisoners, so that they will not be disturbed"; and General Lee remarked that he desired simply to do whatever was in his power to protect his

494

men from anything disagreeable. I said I thought that could be arranged, as I had a small printing-press, and could have blank forms struck off, which could be filled up, and one given to each officer and man of the army, signed by their own officers, and distributed as required. To this he assented. . . .

* * * * *

Some months after the surrender I heard General Henry A. Wise give an amusing account of his experience with the printed parole he carried with him. He was on his way to his home near Norfolk, mounted on a fine blooded mare, when he stopped one day at a roadside tavern in Mecklenburg County to get something to eat. Our cavalry was then in that part of Virginia on its way to Danville, and good horses were very rapidly picked up by straggling and foraging parties. On coming out of the tavern to where he had hitched his mare, General Wise found a cavalry soldier mounted on her back and about to ride off, while a sergeant stood looking on. Wise demanded in a sharp tone what the man was doing, at the same time ordering him to get off the mare. The sergeant turned to him and asked: "Who the devil are you?"

"I am General Wise of the Confederate army, and you can't have my mare," was the reply.

Neither the sergeant nor the man appeared to attach much importance to this piece of information, and the latter was about to ride off, when Wise exclaimed in a loud tone:

"I have got General Grant's *safeguard,* and am under its protection!"

The sergeant demanded to see this "safeguard," and Wise produced his printed parole, duly filled out with his name and signed.

The sergeant's countenance fell, for he had evidently heard of the penalty (death) attached to the violation of a safeguard. But suddenly his face brightened with hope, as he said, with considerable contempt in his voice:

"How do I know but what this a forgery?"

Wise, however, was equal to the occasion, and exclaimed:

"A forgery! You know perfectly well it's no forgery, sir, and that no enterprising Yankee would go up to a d—— little country village like Appomattox Court-house and set up a printing-press to print off a *forgery!* Now get off that mare"—to the soldier—"and give her up, or I will follow you to your commanding officer, if it's to h—— or Halifax!" (the next county).

Wise said the man quietly got down off the mare and gave her up to him without another word. This he thought an evidence of the power of his parole. I considered, however, that he was fortunate in striking a rather mild specimen of a cavalry "bummer."

—MAJOR GENERAL JOHN GIBBON

*

The Wrong Lee

---

*

AFTER GENERAL ROBERT E. LEE had surrendered, General Fitzhugh Lee rode away from Appomattox. While riding through a lane he met an old North Carolina soldier.

"Ho, there," cried General Lee, "where are you going?"

"I've been off on a furlough, and am now going back to join General Bob Lee," replied the soldier.

"You needn't go back, but can throw your gun away and return home for Lee's surrendered."

"Lee surrendered?"

"That's what I said," said General Lee.

"It must have been that damned Fitz Lee, then. Bob Lee would never surrender," and the old soldier put on a look of contempt and walked on.

—*Louisville Courier-Journal*

*

Singing Yankees

---

*

A DAY OR TWO AFTER Lee's surrender in April, 1865, I left our ship at "Dutch Gap," in the James River, for a run up to Richmond, where I was joined by the ship's surgeon, the paymaster, and one of the junior officers. After "doing" Richmond pretty thoroughly we went in the evening to my rooms for dinner. Dinner being over and the events of the day recounted, the doctor, who was a fine player, opened the piano, saying: "Boys, we've got our old quartette here; let's have a sing." As the house opposite was occupied by paroled Confederate officers, no patriotic songs were sung. Soon the lady of the house handed me this note: "Compliments of General —— and Staff. Will the gentlemen kindly allow us to come over and hear them sing?" Of course we consented, and they came.

As the General entered the room, I recognized instantly the face and figure of one who stood second only to Lee or Jackson, in the whole Confederacy. After introductions and the usual interchange of civilities, we sang for them glees and college songs, until at last the General said: "Excuse me, gentlemen, you sing delightfully, but what *we* want to hear is your army songs." Then we gave them the army songs with unction, the "Battle Hymn of the Republic," "John Brown's Body," "We're Coming, Father Abraham," "Tramp, Tramp, Tramp, the Boys Are Marching," through the whole catalogue, to the "Star-Spangled Banner" —to which many a foot beat time as if it had never stepped to any but the "music of the Union,"—and closed our concert with "Rally Round the Flag, Boys."

When the applause had subsided, a tall, fine-looking fellow in a major's uniform exclaimed, "Gentlemen, if we'd had your songs we'd have licked you out of your boots! Who couldn't have marched or fought with such songs? While we had nothing, absolutely nothing, except a bastard 'Marseillaise,' the 'Bonnie Blue Flag,' and 'Dixie,' which were nothing but jigs. 'Maryland, My Maryland' was a splendid song, but the true, old 'Lauriger Horatius' was about as inspiring as the 'Dead March in Saul,' while every one of these Yankee songs is full of marching and fighting spirit." Then turning to the General, he said: "I shall never forget the first time I heard 'Rally Round the Flag.' 'Twas a nasty night during the 'Seven Days' Fight,' and if I remember rightly it was raining. I was on picket, when, just before taps, some fellow on the other side struck up that song and others joined in the chorus until it seemed to me the whole Yankee army was singing. Tom B——, who was with me, sung out, 'Good heavens, Cap, what are those fellows made of, anyway? Here we've licked 'em six days running and now, on the eve of the seventh, they're singing "Rally Round the Flag."' I am not naturally superstitious, but I tell you that song sounded to me like the 'knell of doom,' and my heart went down into my boots; and though

I've tried to do my duty, it has been an up-hill fight with me ever since that night."

The little company of Union singers and Confederate auditors, after a pleasant and interesting interchange of stories of army experiences, then separated, and as the General shook hands at parting, he said to me: "Well, the time *may* come when we can *all* sing the 'Star-Spangled Banner' again." I have not seen him since.

—RICHARD WENTWORTH BROWNE

*

Aunt Abby's "Crap Critter"

*

AUNT ABBY arrived in Raleigh by the first train that came from Greensboro after Sherman had possession of the town [April 13, 1865]. When she got out at the depot a Yankee soldier, standing on the platform seeing an old woman stumbling along loaded down with bags and bundles, said to her good-naturedly: "Hand up your traps, my grandmother, and give us your hand, and I'll help you up these steps."

"No you won't," was her abrupt reply. "I raised my right hand once to a whole army of ye, but I'll never give it willingly to any *one* on you."

She did not escape the fate of most dwellers in the track of the "great destroyer," and lost her "crap critter" which was "picked up" by Sherman's bummers. As fearlessly as she had heretofore sought General Lee and President Davis, she now marched into the office of the Provost Marshal and demanded the surrender of her property.

"I've come here to git back my crap critter that some 'er your men has stole from me," was her abrupt address to the official who sat in state in the room so lately vacated by Governor Vance.

"And pray, madam, what is a crap critter?" said he, politely offering her a chair.

"No, I'm not gwine to set down in this here office till them as oughter be here is back whar they belongs," said she, contemptuously pushing the chair aside. "I've sot here many a time with Governor

498

Vance and your betters, and had many a talk with 'em, but I wants nothing from you but my crap critter that was stole Thursday a week ago by your thievish soldiers."

"Well, madam, if you will tell me what a crap critter is, and where I am to look for it, I will do my best to have it restored to you whatever it may be."

"Where are you to look for it? Why look in your own cattle pens where you won't find much that hain't been stole."

"Ah, I understand now, it's a cow that you've lost; can you identify it?"

"Lord sakes, who but a Yankee ever heard tell o' tending of a crap with a cow; it's a mule, man, that I'm arter, not a cow."

The Provost Marshal, who was quite equal to Aunt Abby, and told of his interview with her afterward (asking if there were "many more sich" in the state), directed her to the proper officer, and told her if she could not find her own "crap critter" she might take her choice of any of those in the yard where the stolen animals were kept.

"I expected," he said afterward, "that she would be at least a little mollified by my polite deportment, and I even ventured to hope— when I added that if she liked to do so, she could take two mules in the place of her 'crap critter'—that she'd think I was not, in spite of my blue coat, unworthy to sit in the seat of the departed Zebulon. Instead of which, she turned on me with, 'Ah! easy comes and easy goes; but you needn't think to make up for stealing from one by giving to another; I'll have nothing from ye but my own crap critter.' "

Her own crap critter, however, could not be found among the stolen mules, and after much persuasion she was induced, on the representation of the Provost Marshal, that she could return it when it was called for, to pick out another mule. He pointed out one that he thought the best in the lot, but she rejected it, and finally selected one of the worst, and replied, when asked, why she did not take a better one: "I'm not gwine to be beholden to no hatchet-faced Yankee among ye for nothing. Some 'on ye tuck my crap critter, and if ye can't give hit back to me, I'll take one as nigh hit's vally as I can git, and that's this here one."

"All right, old lady, take the one that suits you best. Jeff Davis himself couldn't say more if he was President of the United States."

"And that he'll never be-mean hisself to be," she replied indignantly, "for he never had an *on*gentlemanly thought, or did an *on*gen-

tlemanly act in his life, and being President of the United States ain't no
gentlemanly calling now, since rail-splitters and tailors is tuck it up."

—MARY BAYARD CLARKE

---

*

"Who Is Doing This Surrendering, Anyhow?"

---

*

[GENERAL JOSEPH E.] JOHNSTON had known Sherman well
in the United States Army. Their first interview near Greensboro [April
17, 1865] resulted in an engagement to meet for further discussion the
following day. As they were parting, Johnston remarked: "By the way,
Cumps, Breckinridge, our Secretary of War, is with me. He is a very
able fellow, and a better lawyer than any of us. If there is no objection,
I will fetch him along to-morrow."

Bristling up, General Sherman exclaimed, "Secretary of War! No,
no; we don't recognize any civil government among you fellows, Joe.
No, I don't want any Secretary of War."

"Well," said General Johnston, "he is also a major general in the
Confederate army. Is there any objection to his presence in the capacity
of major general?"

"Oh!" quoth Sherman, in his characteristic way, "major general!
Well, any major general you may bring, I shall be glad to meet. But
recollect, Johnston, no Secretary of War. Do you understand?"

The next day, General Johnston, accompanied by Major General
[John C.] Breckinridge and others, was at the rendezvous before Sherman.

"You know how fond of his liquor Breckinridge was?" added
General Johnston, as he went on with his story. "Well, nearly everything
to drink had been absorbed. For several days, Breckinridge had found
it difficult, if not impossible, to procure liquor. He showed the effect of
his enforced abstinence. He was rather dull and heavy that morning.
Somebody in Danville had given him a plug of very fine chewing tobacco,
and he chewed vigorously while we were awaiting Sherman's coming.
After a while, the latter arrived. He bustled in with a pair of saddle-bags

500

over his arm, and apologized for being late. He placed the saddle-bags carefully upon a chair. Introductions followed, and for a while General Sherman made himself exceedingly agreeable. Finally, some one suggested that we had better take up the matter in hand.

" 'Yes,' said Sherman; 'but, gentlemen, it occurred to me that perhaps you were not overstocked with liquor, and I procured some medical stores on my way over. Will you join me before we begin work?' "

General Johnston said he watched the expression of Breckinridge at this announcement, and it was beatific. Tossing his quid into the fire, he rinsed his mouth, and when the bottle and the glass were passed to him, he poured out a tremendous drink, which he swallowed with great satisfaction. With an air of content, he stroked his mustache and took a fresh chew of tobacco.

Then they settled down to business and Breckinridge never shone more brilliantly than he did in the discussions which followed. He seemed to have at his tongue's aid every rule and maxim of international and constitutional law, and of the laws of war—international wars, civil wars, and wars of rebellion. In fact, he was so resourceful, cogent, persuasive, learned, that, at one stage of the proceedings, General Sherman, when confronted by the authority, but not convinced by the eloquence or learning of Breckinridge, pushed back his chair and exclaimed: "See here, gentlemen, who is doing this surrendering anyhow? If this thing goes on, you'll have me sending a letter of apology to Jeff Davis."

Afterward, when they were nearing the close of the conference, Sherman sat for some time absorbed in deep thought. Then he arose, went to the saddle-bags, and fumbled for the bottle. Breckinridge saw the movement. Again he took his quid from his mouth and tossed it into the fireplace. His eye brightened, and he gave every evidence of intense interest in what Sherman seemed about to do.

The latter, preoccupied, perhaps unconscious of his action, poured out some liquor, shoved the bottle back into the saddle-pocket, walked to the window, and stood there, looking out abstractedly, while he sipped his grog.

From pleasant hope and expectation the expression on Breckinridge's face changed successively to uncertainty, disgust, and deep depression. At last his hand sought the plug of tobacco, and, with an injured, sorrowful look, he cut off another chew. Upon this he ruminated during the remainder of the interview, taking little part in what was said.

501

After silent reflections at the window, General Sherman bustled back, gathered up his papers, and said: "These terms are too generous, but I must hurry away before you make me sign a capitulation. I will submit them to the authorities at Washington, and let you hear how they are received." With that he bade the assembled officers adieu, took his saddle-bags upon his arm, and went off as he had come.

General Johnston took occasion, as they left the house and were drawing on their gloves, to ask General Breckinridge how he had been impressed by Sherman.

"Sherman is a bright man, and a man of great force," replied Breckinridge, speaking with deliberation, "but," raising his voice and with a look of great intensity, "General Johnston, General Sherman is a hog. Yes, sir, *hog*. Did you see him take that drink by himself?"

General Johnston tried to assure General Breckinridge that General Sherman was a royal good fellow, but the most absent-minded man in the world. He told him that the failure to offer him a drink was the highest compliment that could have been paid to the masterly arguments with which he had pressed the Union commander to that state of abstraction.

"Ah!" protested the big Kentuckian, half sighing, half grieving, "no Kentucky gentleman would ever have taken away that bottle. He knew we needed it, and needed it badly."

—JOHN S. WISE

*

The Unforgiving

*

211 Camp Street, New Orleans
April 22, 1865

COMING BACK in the cars, I had a *rencontre* that makes me gnash my teeth yet. It was after dark, and I was the only lady in a car crowded with gentlemen. I placed little Miriam on my lap to make room for some of them, when a great, dark man, all in black, entered, and took the seat and my left hand at the same instant saying, "Good-evening, Miss Sarah." Frightened beyond measure to recognize Captain Todd [a cousin of Mrs. Lincoln] of the Yankee army in my interlocutor, I, however, preserved a quiet exterior, and without the slightest demonstration answered, as though replying to an internal question, "Mr. Todd."

"It is a long while since we met," he ventured.

"Four years," I returned mechanically.

"You have been well?"

"My health has been bad."

"I have been ill myself"; and determined to break the ice, he diverged with "Baton Rouge has changed sadly."

"I hope I shall never see it again. We have suffered too much to recall home with any pleasure."

"I understand you have suffered severely," he said, glancing at my black dress.

"We have yet one left in the army, though," I could not help saying.

He, too, had a brother there, he said.

He pulled the check-string as we reached the house, adding, "This is it," and absurdly correcting himself with "Where do you live?"

"Two hundred eleven. I thank you. Good-evening"; the last with emphasis as he prepared to follow.

He returned the salutation, and I hurriedly regained the house. Monsieur stood over the way. A look through the blinds showed him returning to his domicile, several doors below.

I returned to my own painful reflections. The Mr. Todd who was my "sweetheart" when I was twelve and he twenty-four, who was my brother's friend, and daily at our home, was put away from among our acquaintance at the beginning of the war. This one, I should not know. Cords of candy and mountains of bouquets bestowed in childish days will not make my country's enemy my friend now that I am a woman.

—SARAH MORGAN DAWSON

39. LAST DAYS OF LINCOLN

The Case of Betsy Ann

*

THE DOORS of the White House were always open. Mr. Lincoln was always ready to greet visitors, no matter what their rank or calling—to hear their complaints, their petitions, or their suggestions touching the conduct of public affairs. The ease with which he could be approached vastly increased his labor. It also led to many scenes at the White House that were strangely amusing and sometimes dramatic.

Early in the year 1865, certain influential citizens of Missouri, then in Washington, held a meeting to consider the disturbed state of the border counties, and to formulate a plan for securing Executive inter-ference in behalf of their oppressed fellow-citizens. They "where-ased" and "resolved" at great length, and finally appointed a committee charged with the duty of visiting Mr. Lincoln, of stating their grievances, and of demanding the removal of General [Clinton B.] Fisk and the appointment of General John B. McPherson in his place. The com-mittee consisted of an ex-governor and several able and earnest gentle-men deeply impressed with the importance of their mission.

They entered the White House with some trepidation. It was at a critical period of the war, and they supposed it would be difficult to get the ear of the President. Grant was on the march to Richmond, and Sherman's army was sweeping down to the sea. The committee knew that Mr. Lincoln would be engaged in considering the momentous events then developing, and they were therefore greatly surprised to find the doors thrown open to them. They were cordially invited to enter Mr. Lincoln's office.

The ex-governor took the floor in behalf of the oppressed Mis-sourians. . . .

. . . With the most solemn deliberation he began: "Mr. President, I want to call your attention to the case of Betsy Ann Dougherty,—a good woman. She lived in ——— County, and did my washing for a long time. Her husband went off and joined the rebel army, and I wish you would give her a protection paper." The solemnity of this appeal struck Mr. Lincoln as uncommonly ridiculous.

The two men looked at each other,—the governor desperately in earnest, and the President masking his humor behind the gravest ex-terior. At last Mr. Lincoln asked with inimitable gravity, "Was Betsy Ann a good washerwoman?"

"Oh, yes, sir; she was indeed."

"Was your Betsy Ann an obliging woman?"

"Yes, she was certainly very kind," responded the governor, soberly.

"Could she do other things than wash?" continued Mr. Lincoln, with the same portentous gravity.

"Oh, yes; she was very kind—very."

"Where is Betsy Ann?"

"She is now in New York, and wants to come back to Missouri; but she is afraid of banishment."

"Is anybody meddling with her?"

505

"No; but she is afraid to come back unless you will give her a protection paper."

Thereupon Mr. Lincoln wrote on a visiting card the following:—

Let Betsy Ann Dougherty alone as long as she behaves herself.
                                                            A. LINCOLN

He handed this card to her advocate, saying, "Give this to Betsy Ann."

"But, Mr. President, couldn't you write a few words to the officers that would insure her protection?"

"No," said Mr. Lincoln, "officers have no time now to read letters. Tell Betsy Ann to put a string in this card and hang it round her neck. When the officers see this, they will keep their hands off your Betsy Ann."

*   *   *   *   *

After patiently hearing all the Missouri committee had to say, and giving them the best assurances circumstances would allow, he dismissed them from his presence, enjoyed a hearty laugh, and then relapsed into his accustomed melancholy, contemplative mood, as if looking for something else,—looking for the end. He sat for a time at his desk thinking, then turning to me he said: "This case of our old friend, the governor, and his Betsy Ann, is a fair sample of the trifles I am constantly asked to give my attention to. I wish I had no more serious questions to deal with. If there were more Betsy Anns and fewer fellows like her husband, we should be better off. She seems to have laundered the governor to his full satisfaction, but I am sorry she didn't keep her husband washed cleaner."

—WARD HILL LAMON

"Mama Says You Must Come Instantly"

*

DURING the last six months of the war, Mr. Lincoln and family made several short visits to City Point on a small steamboat, the *River Queen,* which he was in the habit of taking for such purposes. On one of these visits, their youngest son, familiarly called "Tad," came with them. The boat always anchored out in the river, and Mrs. Lincoln rarely came ashore. But the President, and "Tad," landed in a tug regularly every morning, soon after breakfast.

Mr. Lincoln would go directly to the Adjutant's Office to hear all the news from the front which had been received during the night; and would often have long conferences with General Grant and others concerning prospective operations. When these subjects had been exhausted the chat would take another turn, and Mr. Lincoln's propensity for story telling would be given free-play, and be encouraged to the utmost. His faculty in this way was absolutely marvelous. It has never been exaggerated, and never can be. He abounded in apt illustrations, and his stories were side-splitting. He would occasionally join as heartily as any one else in the laughter his stories provoked; and enjoyed these seasons of relaxations in a way that was charming to all who were present.

Mrs. Lincoln seemed insanely jealous of every person, and everything, which drew him away from her and monopolized his attention for an hour. She would send "Tad" with a message to come to the boat, nearly every day. At one time "Tad" found his father enjoying himself in animated conversation, and a little oblivious it may have been to his wife's message. "Tad" went back to the boat but soon returned with a more urgent command, which he kept repeating loud enough for all to hear. He finally burst out: "Come, come, come now, mama says you must come instantly." Mr. Lincoln's countenance fell from unconstrained good-humor and gayety to the sober, careworn, lugubrious expression so common to him in those days. After a moment's silence

507

he rose, saying: "My God, will that woman never understand me"; and
departed meekly, and sadly, convoyed by "Tad."

—SYLVANUS CADWALLADER

*

"On the Side of Mercy"

*

FROM 1862 TO 1865 the conditions were such in Missouri that
every man was obliged to espouse actively either the Union or the
Confederate cause. No man really was safe out of one army or another.
Property was insecure, and if a person attempted to remain neutral he
was suspected by both Confederates and Federals, and was liable to be
arrested by either side, and his property destroyed. During the progress
of the war a large number of Missourians had been arrested by the
Federals and were confined in the military prisons, many of them at
St. Louis where the McDowell Medical College had been taken and
used for the purpose, and some at Alton, Illinois, about twenty-five miles
above St. Louis on the river. The friends and relations of many of
these military prisoners appealed to me to secure their release, or to
save them from whatever sentence had been pronounced. These sentences, of course, varied. In flagrant cases where they were convicted of
acting as spies, or of prosecuting guerrilla warfare, the death sentence
was sometimes ordered but not often inflicted. Others were condemned
to prison for life or during the war. Few of the death sentences were ever
inflicted. There was a tacit understanding among the military authorities
that while a show of severity be kept up, it was only under extreme
circumstances that a prisoner should be executed. Towards the close of
the winter of 1864-65, I found that I had a large number of these
applications for clemency and pardon on hand.

Congress adjourned on March 4, 1865, and Mr. Lincoln on that
day was inaugurated for a second term. An extra session, of the Senate
only, was called immediately to act on presidential nominations, but it
continued in session until about the 18th of March. I was anxious to
clear up as many as possible of these imprisonment cases before leaving

508

for home. I accordingly had my clerk classify them, according to the evidence in each case, giving the name of the prisoner, the character of his offense, together with a statement of the proofs or evidence against him. I caused them to be divided into three classes. Into the first class I put those of whose innocence I had but little doubt; into the second class those whose innocence was more doubtful, but whom I believed it would be safe and proper, under the circumstances, to release; the third class consisted of those who ought still to be retained in confinement. As I had very little time before leaving for the West, I took the first and second classes to the President and asked their pardon and release.

Mr. Lincoln looked over the list and then said: "Do you mean to tell me, Henderson, that you wish me to let loose all these people at once?"

"Yes," I said, "I believe it can be easily done."

"But," said Mr. Lincoln, "I have no time to examine the evidence. I am constantly reproached for my too abundant charity, and what would be said if I should turn loose so many sinners at once. And again, what would be the influence in Missouri?"

"I believe, Mr. President," I said, "that the influence would be most beneficial. The war is nearly over. The day for generosity and kindness has come."

"Do you really think so?" said the President.

"Yes, the rebellion is broken; the rebels will soon be returning to their homes if permitted to do so. What I especially wish is to prevent in my state a prolonged guerrilla warfare. The rebels are already conquered in war. Let us try charity and kindness rather than repression and severity. The policy of mercy will prove to be a wise reconstruction measure."

"I hope you are right," said the President; "but I have no time to examine this evidence. If I sign this list as a whole, will you be responsible for the future good behavior of the men?"

"Yes," I said.

"Then I will take the risk and sign it," said the President. And after inserting, in his own hand-writing, the word "pardoned" after the name of each person who had been convicted of offenses by military commission, he signed the general order of release, and returned the paper to me.

"Thank you, Mr. President; but that is not all; I have another list here."

"I hope you not going to make me let loose another lot?"

509

"Yes. I am not quite so sure of the merits of this list but I believe the men are not dangerous, and it will be good policy to let them go. I think it safer and better to err on the side of mercy."

"Yes," said Mr. Lincoln; "but you know I am charged with making too many mistakes on the side of mercy."

"Mr. President, my argument for this is the same as in the other case. The war is substantially over. The guilt of these men is at least doubtful. And mercy is and must be after all the policy of peace."

"I guess you are right," said Mr. Lincoln.

"Yes," I said, "I am sure I am, and I think that you ought to sign it."

"Well, I'll be durned if I don't," said the President, and he signed his name after inserting the word "pardoned" over the name of those laboring under conviction.

This was the only time that I ever heard Mr. Lincoln use a word which approached profanity.

"Now, Henderson," he said, as he handed the list back to me, "remember you are responsible to me for these men. If they do not behave, I shall have to put you in prison for their sins."

—JOHN B. HENDERSON

*

Should Jeff Davis Be Allowed to Escape?

---

*

DURING [my] interview [with President Lincoln aboard the *River Queen,* March 28, 1865] I inquired of the President if he was all ready for the end of the war. What was to be done with the rebel armies when defeated? And what should be done with the political leaders, such as Jeff Davis, etc.? Should we allow them to escape, etc.? He said he was all ready; all he wanted of us was to defeat the opposing armies, and to get the men composing the Confederate armies back to their homes, at work on their farms and in their shops. As to Jeff Davis, he was hardly at liberty to speak his mind fully, but intimated that he ought to clear out, "escape the country," only it would not do for him to say so openly. As usual, he illustrated his meaning by a story: "A man once had taken the total-abstinence pledge. When visiting a friend, he was invited to take a drink, but declined, on the score of his pledge; when his friend suggested lemonade, which was accepted. In preparing the lemonade, the friend pointed to the brandy-bottle, and said the lemonade would be more palatable if he were to pour in a little brandy; when his guest said, if he could do so 'unbeknown' to him, he would not object."

—GENERAL WILLIAM T. SHERMAN

*

Lincoln Visits General Pickett's Wife

*

I WAS IN RICHMOND when my Soldier fought the awful battle of Five Forks [April 1, 1865]. Richmond surrendered, and the surging sea of fire swept the city. News of the fate of Five Forks had reached us, and the city was full of rumors that General Pickett was killed. I did not believe them. I knew he would come back; he had told me so. But they were very anxious hours. The day after the fire, there was a sharp rap at the door. The servants had all run away. The city was full of Yankees, and my environment had not taught me to love them. The fate of other cities had awakened my fears for Richmond. With my baby on my arm I opened the door and looked up at a tall, gaunt sad-faced man in ill-fitting clothes. He asked: "Is this George Pickett's home?"

With all the courage and dignity I could muster, I replied: "Yes, and I am his wife, and this is his baby."

"I am Abraham Lincoln."

"The President!" I gasped. I had never seen him, but I knew the intense love and reverence with which my Soldier always spoke of him. The stranger shook his head and replied: "No; Abraham Lincoln, George's old friend."

The baby pushed away from me and reached out his hands to Mr. Lincoln, who took him in his arms. As he did so an expression of rapt, almost divine tenderness and love lighted up the sad face. It was a look

511

that I have never seen on any other face. The baby opened his mouth wide and insisted upon giving his father's friend a dewy infantile kiss. As Mr. Lincoln gave the little one back to me, he said: "Tell your father, the rascal, that I forgive him for the sake of your bright eyes."

It was through Mr. Lincoln that my Soldier, as a lad of seventeen, received his appointment to West Point. Mr. Lincoln was at that time associated in his law practice with George Pickett's uncle, Mr. Andrew Johnson, a distinguished lawyer and scholar, who was very anxious that his nephew follow in his footsteps and study for the law—an ambition which, it is needless to say, my Soldier did not share. He confided his perplexities to Mr. Lincoln, who was very fond of the lad; and the great statesman went at once to work to secure his appointment.

—LaSalle Corbell Pickett

∗

Strong Man

∗

ON MONDAY before the assassination, when the President was on his return from Richmond, he stopped at City Point. Calling upon the head surgeon at that place, Mr. Lincoln told him that he wished to visit all the hospitals under his charge, and shake hands with every soldier. The surgeon asked if he knew what he was undertaking, there being five or six thousand soldiers at that place, and it would be quite a tax upon his strength to visit all the wards and shake hands with every soldier. Mr. Lincoln answered with a smile, he "guessed he was equal to the task; at any rate he would try, and go as far as he could; he should never, probably, see the boys again, and he wanted them to know that he appreciated what they had done for their country."

Finding it useless to try to dissuade him, the surgeon began his rounds with the President, who walked from bed to bed, extending his hand to all, saying a few words of sympathy to some, making kind inquiries of others, and welcomed by all with the heartiest cordiality.

As they passed along, they came to a ward in which lay a Rebel who had been wounded and was a prisoner. As the tall figure of the kindly visitor appeared in sight he was recognized by the Rebel soldier, who, raising himself on his elbow in bed, watched Mr. Lincoln as he approached, and extending his hand exclaimed, while tears ran down his cheeks: "Mr. Lincoln, I have wanted to see you, to ask you forgiveness for ever raising my hand against the old flag." Mr. Lincoln was moved to tears. He heartily shook the hand of the repentant Rebel, and assured him of his good-will, and with a few words of kind advice passed on.

After some hours the tour of the various hospitals was made, and Mr. Lincoln returned with the surgeon to his office. They had scarcely entered, however, when a messenger came saying that one ward had been omitted, and "the boys" wanted to see the President. The surgeon, who was thoroughly tired, and knew Mr. Lincoln must be, tried to dissuade him from going; but the good man said he must go back; he would not knowingly omit one, "the boys" would be so disappointed. So he went with the messenger, accompanied by the surgeon, and shook hands with the gratified soldiers, and then returned again to the office.

The surgeon expressed the fear that the President's arm would be lamed with so much handshaking, saying that it certainly must ache. Mr. Lincoln smiled, and saying something about his "strong muscles," stepped out at the open door, took up a very large, heavy axe which lay there by a log of wood, and chopped vigorously for a few moments, sending the chips flying in all directions; and then, pausing, he extended his right arm to its full length, holding the axe out horizontally, without its even quivering as he held it. Strong men who looked on—men accustomed to manual labor—could not hold the same axe in that position for a moment. Returning to the office, he took a glass of lemonade, for he would take no stronger beverage; and while he was within, the chips he had chopped were gathered up and safely cared for by a hospital steward, because they were "the chips that Father Abraham chopped." In a few hours more the beloved President was at home in Washington; in a few days more he had passed away, and a bereaved nation was in mourning.

—*New York Independent*

*

Lincoln Captures "Dixie"

*

GENERAL LEE'S SURRENDER had been announced; Washington was ablaze with excitement. [On April 10, 1864] delirious multitudes surged to the White House, calling the President out for a speech. It was a moment for easy betrayal into words that might widen the breach between sections. He said in his quaint way that he had no speech ready, and concluded humorously: "I have always thought 'Dixie' one of the best tunes I ever heard. I insisted yesterday that we had fairly captured it. I presented the question to the Attorney-General and he gave his opinion that it is our lawful prize. I ask the band to give us a good turn upon it." In that little speech, he claimed of the South by right of conquest a song—and nothing more.

—MYRTA LOCKETT AVARY

*It reminded him . . . of an ominous incident of mysterious
character which occurred just after his election in 1860. It was
the double image of himself in a looking-glass, which he saw
while lying on a lounge in his own chamber at Springfield. There
was Abraham Lincoln's face reflecting the full glow of health
and hopeful life; and in the same mirror, at the same moment of
time, was the face of Abraham Lincoln showing a ghostly pale-
ness.*

—WARD HILL LAMON

40. DEATH OF LINCOLN

The Shadow of Coming Events

*

[IN THE WINTER of 1864-65] our Uncle Brutus J. Clay invited
my sister and myself to visit him in Washington, he being Congressman
at that time. Mrs. Ninian Edwards (born Elizabeth Todd) and Mrs.
Lincoln (born Mary Todd) were intimate childhood friends of my
mother, Mary Jane Warfield Clay, Elizabeth Todd being one of her
bridesmaids, so that when we arrived in Washington we sent our cards
to Mrs. Lincoln who soon sent her carriage for us to come to see her.
The Lady of the White House at that time made no calls upon anyone,

but took her friends driving, invited them to see her or to go with her to the theatre, concerts, etc. Mrs. Lincoln invited us to go with her to Ford's Theatre one night, sending the carriage to take us to the White House, thence to the theatre. President and Mrs. Lincoln, my sister and myself occupied one carriage. Mr. Nicolay and John Hay went in another with a guard of eight men, I believe on horseback, which had been voted by Congress to escort and guard Mr. Lincoln.

As we drove along, the carriage being swung very low, an iron hoop was caught under it and pierced through the seat, coming through between Mr. and Mrs. Lincoln who occupied the back seat. Mrs. Lincoln was very much alarmed and feared an attack was being made. The hoop was removed and we proceeded on our way. I said to Mr. Lincoln, "What do you think of this guard as a protection?"

"Not much," he said, "for I believe when my time comes there is nothing that can prevent my going, but the people will have it." When we stopped at the theatre the pavement about the door was packed with people. The guard made a way for us into the theatre and I thought as we passed that an assassin might easily kill the President in that crowd and escape detection.

In the theatre President and Mrs. Lincoln, Miss Sallie Clay and I, Mr. Nicolay and Mr. Hay, occupied the same box which the year after saw Mr. Lincoln slain by Booth. I do not recall the play, but Wilkes Booth played the part of the villain. The box was right on the stage, with a railing around it. Mr. Lincoln sat next to the rail, I next to Mrs. Lincoln, Miss Sallie Clay and the other gentlemen farther around. Twice Booth in uttering disagreeable threats in the play came very near and put his finger close to Mr. Lincoln's face; when he came a third time I was impressed by it, and said, "Mr. Lincoln, he looks as if he meant that for you."

"Well," he said, "he does look pretty sharp at me, doesn't he?"

At the same theatre, the next April, Wilkes Booth shot our dear **President.**

—MARY B. CLAY

The Prophetic Dreams

THE MOST STARTLING INCIDENT in the life of Mr. Lincoln was a dream he had only a few days before his assassination. To him it was a thing of deadly import, and certainly no vision was ever fashioned more exactly like a dread reality. . . . After worrying over it for some days, Mr. Lincoln seemed no longer able to keep the secret. I give it as nearly in his own words as I can, from notes which I made immediately after its recital. There were only two or three persons present. The President was in a melancholy, meditative mood, and had been silent for some time. Mrs. Lincoln, who was present, rallied him on his solemn visage and want of spirit. This seemed to arouse him, and without seeming to notice her sally he said, in slow and measured tones:

"About ten days ago," said he, "I retired very late. I had been up waiting for important dispatches from the front. I could not have been long in bed when I fell into a slumber, for I was weary. I soon began to dream. There seemed to be a death-like stillness about me. Then I heard subdued sobs, as if a number of people were weeping. I thought I left my bed and wandered downstairs. There the silence was broken by the same pitiful sobbing, but the mourners were invisible. I went from room to room; no living person was in sight, but the same mournful sounds of distress met me as I passed along. It was light in all the rooms; every object was familiar to me; but where were all the people who were grieving as if their hearts would break? I was puzzled and alarmed. What could be the meaning of all this? Determined to find the cause of a state of things so mysterious and so shocking, I kept on until I arrived at the East Room, which I entered. There I met with a sickening surprise. Before me was a catafalque, on which rested a corpse wrapped in funeral vestments. Around it were stationed soldiers who were acting as guards; and there was a throng of people, some gazing mournfully upon the corpse, whose face was covered, others weeping pitifully. 'Who is dead in the White House?' I demanded of one of the

517

soldiers. 'The President,' was his answer; 'he was killed by an assassin!' Then came a loud burst of grief from the crowd, which awoke me from my dream. I slept no more that night; and although it was only a dream, I have been strangely annoyed by it ever since."

"That is horrid!" said Mrs. Lincoln. "I wish you had not told it. I am glad I don't believe in dreams, or I should be in terror from this time forth."

"Well," responded Mr. Lincoln, thoughtfully, "it is only a dream, Mary. Let us say no more about it, and try to forget it."

* * * * *

Mr. Lincoln had another remarkable dream, which was repeated so frequently during his occupancy of the White House that he came to regard it as a welcome visitor. It was of a pleasing and promising character, having nothing in it of the horrible. It was always an omen of a Union victory, and came with unerring certainty just before every military or naval engagement where our arms were crowned with success. In this dream he saw a ship sailing away rapidly, badly damaged, and our victorious vessels in close pursuit. He saw, also, the close of a battle on land, the enemy routed, and our forces in possession of vantage ground of incalculable importance. Mr. Lincoln stated it as a fact that he had this dream just before the battles of Antietam, Gettysburg, and other signal engagements throughout the war.

The last time Mr. Lincoln had this dream was the night before his assassination. On the morning of that lamentable day there was a Cabinet meeting at which General Grant was present. During an interval of general discussion, the President asked General Grant if he had any news from General Sherman, who was then confronting Johnston. The reply was in the negative, but the general added that he was in hourly expectation of a dispatch announcing Johnston's surrender. Mr. Lincoln then with great impressiveness said: "We shall hear very soon, and the news will be important." General Grant asked him why he thought so. "Because," said Mr. Lincoln, "I had a dream last night; and ever since this war began I have had the same dream just before every event of great national importance. It portends some important event that will happen very soon."

After this Mr. Lincoln became unusually cheerful. In the afternoon he ordered a carriage for a drive. Mrs. Lincoln asked him if he wished any one to accompany them. "No, Mary," said he, "I prefer that we ride by ourselves to-day."

Mrs. Lincoln said afterwards that she never saw him look happier than he did during that drive. In reply to a remark of hers to that effect, Mr. Lincoln said: "And well may I feel so, Mary; for I consider that this day the war has come to a close. Now, we must try to be more cheerful in the future; for between this terrible war and the loss of our darling son we have suffered much misery. Let us both try to be happy."

On the night of the fatal 14th of April, 1865, when the President was assassinated, Mrs. Lincoln's first exclamation was, "His dream was prophetic."

—WARD HILL LAMON

*

The Last Laugh

*

[ON FRIDAY, APRIL 14, 1865, just four years to the day after the American flag was hauled down from Fort Sumter] Mr. Lincoln, accompanied by his wife, Miss Harris and Major Rathbone, of Albany, New York, was occupying a box at Ford's Theatre, in the city of Washington. The play was *Our American Cousin,* with the elder Sothern in the principal role. Mr. Lincoln was enjoying it greatly. Lee had surrendered on the 9th; on the 13th the war was everywhere regarded as ended, and upon that day Secretary Stanton had telegraphed to General Dix, Governor of New York, requesting him to stop the draft. Sothern as Lord Dundreary was at his best. Lincoln was delighted. The lines which care and responsibility had so deeply graven on his brow were now scarcely visible. His people had just passed through the greatest civil war known in the history of nations and he had become well convinced that now, the cause of strife being destroyed, the government over which he was ruling would be made stronger, greater, and better by the crucial test through which it had passed. Before leaving for the theatre he had pronounced it the happiest day of his life. He looked, indeed, as if he now fully realized the consummation of the long cherished and fondest aspiration of his heart. He was at length the undisputed Chief Magistrate of a confederation of States, constituting the freest and most powerful commonwealth of modern times.

At some part of the performance Sothern appeared on the stage with Miss Meridith, the heroine, on one arm and a wrap or shawl carelessly thrown over the other. The latter seats herself upon a garden lounge placed on the stage near the box occupied by the President on this occasion. Lord Dundreary retires a few paces distant from the rustic seat when Miss Meridith, glancing languidly at his lordship, exclaims: "Me lord, will you kindly throw my shawl over my shoulders—there appears to be a draught here." Sothern, at once complying with her request, advanced with a mincing step that immortalized him; and with a merry twinkle of the eye, and a significant glance directed at Mr. Lincoln, responded in the happy impromptu: "You are mistaken, Miss Mary, the draft has already been stopped by order of the President!" This sally caused Mr. Lincoln to laugh, as few except himself could laugh, and an outburst of merriment resounded from all parts of the house. It was Mr. Lincoln's last laugh!

—WARD HILL LAMON

*

Walt Whitman on the Death of Lincoln

*

THE DAY, April 14, 1865, seems to have been a pleasant one throughout the whole land—the moral atmosphere pleasant too—the long storm, so dark, so fratricidal, full of blood and doubt and gloom, over and ended at last by the sun-rise of such an absolute National victory, and utter break-down of Secessionism—we almost doubted our own senses! Lee had capitulated beneath the apple-tree of Appomattox. The other armies, the flanges of the revolt, swiftly follow'd. And could it really be, then? Out of all the affairs of this world of woe and failure and disorder, was there really come the confirm'd, unerring sign of plan, like a shaft of pure light—of rightful rule—of God? So the day, as I say, was propitious. Early herbage, early flowers, were out. (I remember where I was stopping at the time, the season being advanced, there were many lilacs in full bloom. By one of those caprices that enter and give tinge to events without being at all a part of them, I find myself always reminded of the great tragedy of that day by the sight and odor of these blossoms. It never fails.)

But I must not dwell on accessories. The deed hastens. The popular afternoon paper of Washington, the little *Evening Star,* had spatter'd all over its third page, divided among the advertisements in a sensational manner, in a hundred different places, *The President and his Lady will be at the Theatre this evening. . . .* (Lincoln was fond of the theatre. I have myself seen him there several times. I remember thinking how funny it was that he, in some respects the leading actor in the stormiest drama known to real history's stage through centuries, should sit there and be so completely interested and absorb'd in those human jack-straws, moving about with their silly little gestures, foreign spirit, and flatulent text.)

On this occasion the theatre was crowded, many ladies in rich and gay costumes, officers in their uniforms, many well-known citizens, young folks, the usual clusters of gas-lights, the usual magnetism of so many people, cheerful, with perfumes, music of violins and flutes—(and over all, and saturating all, that vast, vague wonder, *Victory,* the nation's victory, the triumph of the Union, filling the air, the thought, the sense, with exhilaration more than all music and perfumes).

The President came betimes, and, with his wife, witness'd the play from the large stage-boxes of the second tier, two thrown into one, and profusely draped with the National flag. The acts and scenes of the piece —one of those singularly written compositions which have at least the merit of giving entire relief to an audience engaged in mental action or business excitements and cares during the day, as it makes not the slightest call on either the moral, emotional, esthetic, or spiritual nature —a piece *(Our American Cousin)* in which, among other characters, so call'd, a Yankee, certainly such a one as was never seen, or the least like it ever seen, in North America, is introduced in England, with a varied fol-de-rol of talk, plot, scenery, and such phantasmagoria as goes to make up a modern popular drama—had progress'd through perhaps a couple of its acts, when in the midst of this comedy, or nonsuch, or whatever it is to be call'd, and to offset it, or finish it out, as if in Nature's and the great Muse's mockery of those poor mimes, came interpolated that scene, not really or exactly to be described at all (for on the many hundreds who were there it seems to this hour to have left a passing blur, a dream, a blotch)—and yet partially to be described as I now proceed to give it.

There is a scene in the play representing a modern parlor, in which two unprecedented English ladies are inform'd by the impossible Yankee that he is not a man of fortune, and therefore undesirable for marriage-catching purposes; after which, the comments being finish'd, the dramatic trio make exit, leaving the stage clear for a moment. . . . Through the general hum following the stage pause, with the change of positions, came the muffled sound of a pistol-shot, which not one-hundredth part of the audience heard at the time—and yet a moment's hush—somehow, surely, a vague startled thrill—and then, through the ornamented, draperied, starr'd and striped space-way of the President's box, a sudden figure, a man, raises himself with hands and feet, stands a moment on the railing, leaps below to the stage (a distance of perhaps fourteen or fifteen feet), falls out of position, catching his boot-heel in the copious drapery (the American flag), falls on one knee, quickly recovers himself, rises as if nothing had happen'd (he really sprains his ankle, but unfelt then)—and so the figure, Booth, the murderer, dress'd in plain black broadcloth, bareheaded, with full, glossy, raven hair, and his eyes like some mad animal's flashing with light and resolution, yet with a certain strange calmness, holds aloft in one hand a large knife—walks along not much back from the footlights—turns fully toward the audience his face of statuesque beauty, lit by those basilisk eyes, flashing with desperation perhaps insanity—launches out in a firm and steady voice the words *Sic semper tyrannis*—and then walks with neither slow nor very rapid pace diagonally across to the back of the stage, and disappears. (Had not all this terrible scene—making the mimic ones preposterous—had it not all been rehears'd, in blank, by Booth, beforehand?)

A moment's hush—a scream—the cry of *murder*—Mrs. Lincoln leaning out of the box, with ashy cheeks and lips, with involuntary cry, pointing to the retreating figure, *He has kill'd the President*. And still a moment's strange, incredulous suspense—and then the deluge—then that mixture of horror, noises, uncertainty—(the sound, somewhere back, of a horse's hoofs clattering with speed)—the people burst through chairs and railings, and break them up—there is inextricable confusion and terror—women faint—quite feeble persons fall, and are trampled on—many cries of agony are heard—the broad stage suddenly fills to suffocation with a dense and motley crowd, like some horrible carnival —the audience rush generally upon it, at least the strong men do—the actors and actresses are all there in their play-costumes and painted faces, with mortal fright showing through the rouge—the screams and calls, confused talk—redoubled, trebled—two or three manage to pass up water from the stage to the President's box—others try to clamber up—&c., &c.

In the midst of all this, the soldiers of the President's guard, with others, suddenly drawn to the scene, burst in—(some two hundred altogether)—they storm the house, through all the tiers, especially the upper ones, inflamed with fury, literally charging the audience with fix'd bayonets, muskets and pistols, shouting *Clear out! clear out! you sons of* ——. . . . Such the wild scene, or a suggestion of it rather, inside the play-house that night.

Outside, too, in the atmosphere of shock and craze, crowds of people, fill'd with frenzy, ready to seize any outlet for it, come near committing murder several times on innocent individuals. One such case was especially exciting. The infuriated crowd, through some chance, got started against one man, either for words he utter'd, or perhaps without any cause at all, and were proceeding at once to actually hang him on a neighboring lamp-post, when he was rescued by a few heroic policemen, who placed him in their midst, and fought their way slowly and amid great peril toward the station house. It was a fitting episode of the whole affair. The crowd rushing and eddying to and fro—the night, the yells, the pale faces, many frighten'd people trying in vain to extricate themselves—the attack'd man, not yet freed from the jaws of death, looking like a corpse—the silent, resolute, half-dozen policemen, with no weapons but their little clubs, yet stern and steady through all those eddying swarms—made a fitting side-scene to the grand tragedy of the murder. They gain'd the station house with the protected man, whom they placed in security for the night, and discharged him in the morning.

And in the midst of that pandemonium, infuriated soldiers, the audience and the crowd, the stage, and all its actors and actresses, its paint-pots, spangles, and gas-lights—the life blood from those veins, the best and sweetest of the land, drips slowly down, and death's ooze already begins its little bubbles on the lips.

—WALT WHITMAN

Elizabeth Keckley Shares Mrs. Lincoln's Grief

*

[THE MORNING OF APRIL 15] came at last, and a sad morning was it. The flags that floated so gayly yesterday now were draped in black, and hung in silent folds at half-mast. The President was dead, and a nation was mourning for him. Every house was draped in black, and every face wore a solemn look. People spoke in subdued tones, and glided whisperingly, wonderingly, silently about the streets.

About eleven o'clock on Saturday morning a carriage drove up to the door, and a messenger asked for "Elizabeth Keckley."

"Who wants her?" I asked.

"I come from Mrs. Lincoln. If you are Mrs. Keckley, come with me immediately to the White House."

I hastily put on my shawl and bonnet, and was driven at a rapid rate to the White House. Everything about the building was sad and solemn. I was quickly shown to Mrs. Lincoln's room, and on entering saw Mrs. L. tossing uneasily about upon a bed. The room was darkened, and the only person in it besides the widow of the President was Mrs. Secretary Welles, who had spent the night with her. Bowing to Mrs. Welles, I went to the bedside.

"Why did you not come to me last night, Elizabeth—I sent for you?" Mrs. Lincoln asked in a low whisper.

"I did try to come to you, but I could not find you," I answered, as I laid my hand upon her hot brow.

I afterwards learned that when she had partially recovered from the first shock of the terrible tragedy in the theatre, Mrs. Welles asked:

"Is there no one, Mrs. Lincoln, that you desire to have with you in this terrible affliction?"

"Yes, send for Elizabeth Keckley. I want her just as soon as she can be brought here."

Three messengers, it appears, were successively despatched for me, but all of them mistook the number and failed to find me.

Shortly after [my] entering the room on Saturday morning, Mrs. Welles excused herself, as she said she must go to her own family, and I was left alone with Mrs. Lincoln.

She was nearly exhausted with grief, and when she became a little quiet, I asked and received permission to go into the guests' room, where the body of the President lay in state. When I crossed the threshold of the room, I could not help recalling the day on which I had seen little Willie lying in his coffin where the body of his father now lay. I remembered how the President had wept over the pale beautiful face of his gifted boy, and now the President himself was dead. The last time I saw him he spoke kindly to me, but alas! the lips would never move again. The light had faded from his eyes, when the light went out the soul went with it. What a noble soul was his—noble in all the noble attributes of God! Never did I enter the solemn chamber of death with such palpitating heart and trembling footsteps as I entered it that day. No common mortal had died. The Moses of my people had fallen in the hour of his triumph. Fame had woven her choicest chaplet for his brow. Though the brow was cold and pale in death, the chaplet should not fade, for God had studded it with the glory of the eternal stars.

When I entered the room, the members of the Cabinet and many distinguished officers of the army were grouped around the body of their fallen chief. They made room for me, and approaching the body, I lifted the white cloth from the white face of the man that I had worshipped as an idol—looked upon as a demi-god. Notwithstanding the violence of the death of the President, there was something beautiful as well as grandly solemn in the expression of the placid face. There lurked the sweetness and gentleness of childhood, and the stately grandeur of god-like intellect. I gazed long at the face, and turned away with tears in my eyes and a choking sensation in my throat. Ah! never was man so widely mourned before. The whole world bowed their heads in grief when Abraham Lincoln died.

Returning to Mrs. Lincoln's room, I found her in a new paroxysm of grief. Robert was bending over his mother with tender affection, and little Tad was crouched at the foot of the bed with a world of agony in his young face. I shall never forget the scene—the wails of a broken heart, the unearthly shrieks, the terrible convulsions, the wild, tempestuous outbursts of grief from the soul. I bathed Mrs. Lincoln's head with cold water, and soothed the terrible tornado as best I could. Tad's grief at his father's death was as great as the grief of his mother, but her terrible outbursts awed the boy into silence. Sometimes he would throw

525

his arms around her neck, and exclaim, between his broken sobs, "Don't cry so, Mamma! don't cry, or you will make me cry, too! You will break my heart."

Mrs. Lincoln could not bear to hear Tad cry, and when he would plead to her not to break his heart, she would calm herself with a great effort, and clasp her child in her arms.

Every room in the White House was darkened, and every one spoke in subdued tones, and moved about with muffled tread. The very atmosphere breathed of the great sorrow which weighed heavily upon each heart. Mrs. Lincoln never left her room, and while the body of her husband was being borne in solemn state from the Atlantic to the broad prairies of the West, she was weeping with her fatherless children in her private chamber. She denied admittance to almost every one, and I was her only companion, except her children, in the days of her great sorrow.

—ELIZABETH KECKLEY

*

"Half News" of Lincoln's Death

*

ON THE DAY when there came to our boys at the front the news of Lincoln's death, I was, with my division, in the little village of Durham. We had no telegraphic communication with the North, but were accustomed to receive dispatches about noon each day, carried across the swamps from a station through which connection was made with Wilmington and the North. In the course of the morning I had gone to the shanty of an old darky, whom I had come to know during the days of our sojourn, for the purpose of getting a shave. The old fellow took up his razor, put it down again, and then lifted it up; but his arm was shaking, and I saw he was so agitated that he was not fitted for the task.

Finally, he said, "Massa, I can't shave yer this mornin'."

"What is the matter?" I asked.

"Well," he replied, "somethin's happened to Massa Linkum."

"Why," I rejoined, "nothing can have happened to Lincoln that we do not know. What are you talking about?"

"Well," the old man replied with a half-sob, "we colored folks— we get news, or we get half news, sooner than you-uns. I don't know jes' what it is, but somethin' has gone wrong with Massa Linkum."

I could get nothing more out of the old man, but I was sufficiently anxious to make my way to headquarters to see if there was any news in advance of the arrival of the regular courier. The colored folks were standing in little groups along the village street, murmuring to each other, or waiting with anxious faces for the bad news that they were sure was coming. I found the division Adjutant and those with him were puzzled like myself at the troubled minds of the darkies. While still sceptical as to the possibility of any information having come to them, they realized, as I had realized, that in some mysterious manner it had before happened that news (often more or less inaccurate, but still news) had got into the heads of the darkies before we white folks knew anything about it.

At noon the courier made his appearance riding across the fields; and the instant he was seen we realized that there was bad news. The man was hurrying his mule, and yet seemed to be unwilling to reach the house at which his report was to be made. In this instance (as was of course not usually the case) the courier knew what was in his dispatches. The big mail was carried in the saddle-bags, but he had in his hands a separate envelope which was handed to the Adjutant. The Adjutant stepped out on to the porch and opened the envelope, but he broke down before he could begin to give the word to us. The lieutenant took the paper from his hand but blinded with tears was able simply to pronounce: "Lincoln is dead."

—George Haven Putnam

✳

Chittenden and the Angry Mob

✳

AT AN EARLY hour, long before daylight [April 15], as I lay awake in bed [in the Hoffman House on Madison Square], I heard voices in the hall. "Revolution in Washington—the President murdered.

They are killing everybody!" I bounded to my feet, hastily dressed, and, clearing three or four steps at a time, reached the office, which was already filled with an anxious and excited crowd. There was a bulletin board on which was written: "Murder of the President! Secretaries Seward and Stanton assassinated! Terrible excitement at Washington! The President dying!" too soon followed by the words, "The President is dead!"

The mind acts quickly under great pressure; mine leaped to the conclusion that we might have a day of bloody revolution. Counseling my family on no account to leave their rooms until I returned, I called a carriage and told the driver to take the back streets and drive to Pine Street as rapidly as possible. It was not yet daylight, and yet the open space on the west side of Madison Square was filled with excited people. We drove rapidly to the Assistant Treasury in Pine Street, which was not yet open. Here I dismissed my carriage and made my way on foot down William and across Wall Street to the Custom House. As I ascended the stone steps, forcing my way through the crowd, some one exclaimed: "He can tell us about Lincoln!" It was Prosper M. Wetmore. "Speech! Speech!" roared the crowd as I sought to make my way into the building. Then the thought flashed over me that I might say something which would allay the excitement. I turned and, standing on a narrow ledge of stone that formed the ledge or sill of a window, faced such a crowd as I have never since seen in Wall Street. Up to Broadway, down toward the ferry, filling William Street in front and Broad Street as far on my left as I could see, was a crowd of excited men, shouting, groaning, and demanding "Speech! Speech! Tell us about Lincoln! Lincoln!" . . .

There was no introduction. I was unknown to most of the audience. "Who are you?" they shouted. "You may read his name on your greenbacks," exclaimed Wetmore, and in a moment busy Wall Street, with its twenty thousand spectators, was so silent that I sincerely believe my voice could have been heard at Broadway.

. . . The thought which I endeavored to enforce was that the Confederates had no hand in the murder of their best friend—of the friend of a great people about to be reunited in a great Republic. "You will soon know that he fell by the hand of a madman," I exclaimed, just as some one at a window below me read out a dispatch that *Wilkes Booth* was the assassin.

Then a change swept over that multitude of men. They had been furiously, dangerously angry. They had charged their loss upon an enemy already crushed in the field. They were ready to fall upon the disloyal and tear them limb from limb. The knowledge that the public calamity was the act of a madman relieved them. A wave of grief swept over the crowd, beneath which the very stones seemed to tremble with emotion. As rapidly as it had collected, the crowd melted away, and silence fell upon the theatre of speculation.

—L. E. Chittenden

*

The Capture of John Wilkes Booth

*

ABOUT THE HOUR of 4 P. M., April 24, 1865, when Booth and Herold were taken by their newly made Confederate friends to the Garrett farm . . . I was seated, with another officer of the 16th New York Cavalry, on a bench in the park opposite the White House. There I received the following orders from a messenger:

Headquarters, Department of Washington *April 24, 1865. Commanding Officer 16th New York Cavalry. Sir: You will at once detail a reliable and discreet commission officer with twenty-five men, well mounted, with three days' rations and forage, to report at once to Colonel L. C. Baker, Agent of the War Department, at 211 Pennsylvania Ave. Command of General C. C. Augur.—J. C. Sewell, A.A.A. Gen'l.*

In accordance with the foregoing order First Lieutenant E. P. Doherty is hereby detailed for the duty, and will report at once to Colonel Baker, 211 Pennsylvania Ave.

N. B. Switzer
*Colonel 16th New York Cavalry
Bvt. Brig. Gen'l, U.S.A.*

I proceeded to the barracks, had "boots and saddles" sounded, and in less than half an hour had reported to Colonel Baker. I took the first twenty-five men in the saddle, Sergeant Boston Corbett being the only member of my own company. Colonel Baker handed me photographs of the assassins of President Lincoln. He told me no troops had yet been in Fredericksburg, but that I must reach that vicinity with all dispatch. He introduced me to E. J. Conger and L. B. Baker, of the detective force, and said they would accompany me. I proceeded down to the Sixth Street wharf, where I found the steamer *John S. Ide,* and directed Captain Wilson to move down to Aquia Creek and to Belle Plain. After the detachment had landed I directed the captain of the boat to move off to a place of safe anchorage and await my return. Should I not return before 6 P. M. on the 26th he was to go back to Washington and report to Captain Allen, assistant quartermaster. I proceeded directly south until I struck the main road to Fredericksburg. Here I halted at 4 A. M. A Negro informed me that a regiment of cavalry had passed to Fredericksburg the previous evening, going along on the north side of the Rappahannock River. I then determined to push down and go up on the south side, where no troops had been.

The detectives asked for a detail of four men and a sergeant to scour the country, while I with the rest of the men continued on towards the Rappahannock. The detectives returned about 3 P. M. without any clue to the whereabouts of the assassins. I went to the ferry at Port Conway and saw Mrs. Rollins, the ferryman's wife, and another woman sitting on the steps of the ferry-house. Drawing Booth's picture from my pocket I showed it to them, and inferred from their looks that Booth was not far distant. One of them said that Booth and Herold had been brought there in a wagon the evening before by a Negro named Lucas, who would carry them no farther. While they were bargaining with her husband to take them to Orange Court-house, three Confederate soldiers, Ruggles, Bainbridge, and Jett, rode up and they entered into conversation. By and by they were all taken over the ferry. Booth was put on Ruggles' horse and they proceeded towards Bowling Green.

I at once sent the bugler to Sergeant Corbett, telling him to mount the detachment, which I had left a mile behind, feeding, and move down as quickly as possible. Mrs. Rollins went for her husband, who was fishing, and I sent him for the scow, which was on the other side of the river. During his absence the command arrived at the ferry and we were soon over the river. I arrested Rollins the ferryman, and took him as guide to Bowling Green. At dark we passed the Garrett farm, not then dreaming that the assassins were concealed there. Arriving at Bowling Green, I surrounded Goldman's Hotel. After some hesitation the door was opened by Mrs. Goldman. I inquired of her who were the male inmates of the house. She replied that there was only her wounded son, and I directed her to show me his room, telling her that if my men were fired on I should burn the building and take the inmates prisoners to Washington. She took me up one flight of stairs to her son's room, and as I entered Captain Jett sprang from his bed, half-dressed. Her son lay on another bed, wounded. Jett admitted his identity, and drawing Mr. Stanton's proclamation from my pocket I read it to him, and then said, "I have known your movements for the past two or three days, and if you do not tell me the truth I will hang you; but if you give me the information I want, I will protect you." He was greatly excited, and told me that he had left Booth at Garrett's house, three miles from Port Conway, the evening before, and that Herold had come to Bowling Green with him, and returned that morning. I had Jett's horse taken from the stable, and, placing a guard over him, we retraced our steps towards Garrett's.

It was now about midnight, and my men, having been out since the 24th without sleep and with very little food, were exhausted; those who had been left on the edge of the town had fallen asleep. I had some difficulty in arousing them, but when they learned that we were on Booth's track new life seemed to be infused into them. I placed Corbett in the rear with orders to allow no man to fall out of line. Upon reaching Garrett's orchard fence I halted, and in company with Rollins and the detectives took a survey of the premises. I had the fence taken down. I told off six men, gave out the countersign of "Boston," and sent the six men as a patrol in rear of the outbuildings, with instructions to allow no one to pass through the field or to approach them without the countersign. The gates in front of Garrett's house were quietly opened, and in a minute the whole premises were surrounded.

I dismounted, and knocked loudly at the front door. Old Mr. Garrett came out. I seized him, and asked him where the men were who had gone to the woods when the cavalry passed the previous afternoon. While I was speaking with him some of the men had entered the house to search it. Soon one of the soldiers sang out, "O Lieutenant! I have a man here I found in the corn-crib." It was young Garrett, and I demanded the whereabouts of the fugitives. He replied, "In the barn." Leaving a few men around the house, we proceeded in the direction of the barn, which we surrounded. I kicked on the door of the barn several times without receiving a reply. Meantime another son of Garrett's had been captured. The barn was secured with a padlock, and young Garrett carried the key. I unlocked the door, and again summoned the inmates of the building to surrender.

After some delay Booth said, "For whom do you take me?"

I replied, "It doesn't make any difference. Come out."

He said, "I am a cripple and alone."

I said, "I know who is with you, and you had better surrender."

He replied, "I may be taken by my friends, but not by my foes."

I said, "If you don't come out, I'll burn the building." I directed a corporal to pile up some hay in a crack in the wall of the barn and set the building on fire.

As the corporal was picking up the hay and brush Booth said, "If you come back here I will put a bullet through you."

I then motioned to the corporal to desist, and decided to wait for daylight and then to enter the barn by both doors and overpower the assassins.

Booth then said, in a drawling voice, "Oh Captain! There is a man in here who wants to surrender awful bad."

I replied, "You had better follow his example and come out."

His answer was, "No, I have not made up my mind; but draw your men up fifty paces off and give me a chance for my life."

I told him I had not come to fight; that I had fifty men, and could take him.

Then he said, "Well, my brave boys, prepare me a stretcher, and place another stain on our glorious banner."

At this moment Herold reached the door. I asked him to hand out his arms; he replied that he had none. I told him I knew exactly what weapons he had. Booth replied, "I own all the arms, and may have to use them on you, gentlemen." I then said to Herold, "Let me see your hands." He put them through the partly opened door and I seized him by the wrists. I handed him over to a non-commissioned officer. Just at this moment I heard a shot, and thought Booth had shot himself. Throwing open the door, I saw that the straw and hay behind Booth were on fire. He was half-turning towards it.

He had a crutch, and he held a carbine in his hand. I rushed into the burning barn, followed by my men, and as he was falling caught him under the arms and pulled him out of the barn. The burning building becoming too hot, I had him carried to the veranda of Garrett's house.

Booth received his death-shot in this manner. While I was taking Herold out of the barn one of the detectives went to the rear, and pulling out some protruding straw set fire to it. I had placed Sergeant Boston

Corbett at a large crack in the side of the barn, and he, seeing by the igniting hay that Booth was leveling his carbine at either Herold or myself, fired, to disable him in the arm; but Booth making a sudden move, the aim erred, and the bullet struck Booth in the back of the head, about an inch below the spot where his shot had entered the head of Mr. Lincoln. Booth asked me by signs to raise his hands. I lifted them up and he gasped, "Useless, useless!" We gave him brandy and water, but he could not swallow it. I sent to Port Royal for a physician, who could do nothing when he came, and at seven o'clock Booth breathed his last. He had on his person a diary, a large bowie knife, two pistols, a compass, and a draft on Canada for £60.

I took a saddle blanket off my horse, and, borrowing a darning needle from Miss Garrett, sewed his body in it. The men found an old wagon, and impressed it, with the Negro driver. The body was placed upon it, and two hours after Booth's death I was on the way back to Belle Plain, where I had left the steamboat.

I had released Rollins and sent him ahead to have his ferryboat ready to take us across the river. About 6 P. M. I reached the boat, and found the captain preparing to return to Washington. We reached Washington at 2 A. M, April 27. I placed the body of Booth and the prisoner Herold on board the monitor *Montauk,* after which I marched my worn-out command up through the navy yard to their quarters.

The next morning an autopsy was held, and measures were taken to identify the body of Booth. The portion of the neck and head through which the bullet had passed was cut out, and is to-day preserved in the National Museum of Anatomy at Washington. The body was buried in a cell in the Penitentiary, where it remained nearly four years, with the bodies of the other assassins. It was then given to his friends, and now lies in a cemetery in Baltimore.

—EDWARD P. DOHERTY

41. THE FLIGHT OF JEFFERSON DAVIS

Aunt Abby Says Good-by
to Mr. Davis

*

[AUNT ABBY] was on her way to General Lee's army when she heard of the evacuation of Richmond [April 2-3, 1865], and Mr. Davis' arrival at Greensboro [April 9]. "I couldn't work my way through to Gin'ral Lee afore he give up under that thar apple-tree, so I said to the boys: 'Boys, I'm a-gwine to jine Pres*ident* Davis since I can't git to Gin'ral Lee; do you all take to the bushes so as not to git cotched by the Yankees, and I'll foot it down the railroad track.' One on 'em told me to be sure when I got in sight of the inemy to raise my right hand, 'and now, Aunt Abby,' says he, 'don't you sass 'em none 'cause they ain't like us, and would as lieve shoot an old woman as not.'

"When I seed 'em, honey, I did raise my right hand, but Lord bless your soul, it was the heaviest lift ever I tried, it seemed like 't was made o' lead and had a hundered pound weight hung on the eend o' my fingers. But I knowed it wasn't my hand, but my heart that was so heavy, and I said to myself, 'Now, Abby House,' says I, 'there ain't a grain o' use in telling of you to keep a civil tongue in your head if you's got to talk to Yankees; I knows it ain't your natur, so I tells you insted to keep a dumb one thar.'

"And I did. I walked through ten mile o' 'em, honey, and never said nar'er a word. I thought I should er choked, for when they 'cussed Jeff Davis, the words kep' er rising up in my throat, and I thought they would come out anyhow; but I kep' er wiping of my hand over my mouth and a doing like I was a taking of 'em out and a flinging of 'em behind me at 'em, and that sorter eased my mind like."

She got to Greensboro in time to see Mr. Davis before he left there; and staid by the train in which he was until it left. "I cooked the last mouthful o' vittils he eat in North Car'lina, and he shuck hands with me when he started, and said, 'Good-by, Aunt Abby, you are true grit and stick to your friends to the last, but's no more than I thought you'd do.'"

—Mary Bayard Clarke

*

A Raglan and a Shawl

---

*

I · Mr. Davis' Account of His Capture

I STEPPED out of my wife's tent and saw some horsemen, whom I immediately recognized as cavalry, deploying around the encampment. I turned back and told my wife these were not the expected marauders, but regular troopers. She implored me to leave her at once. I hesitated, from unwillingness to do so, and lost a few precious moments before yielding to her importunity. My horse and arms were near the road on which I expected to leave, and down which the cavalry approached; it was, therefore impracticable to reach them. I was compelled to start in the opposite direction. As it was quite dark in the tent, I picked up what was supposed to be my "raglan," a waterproof light overcoat, without sleeves; it was subsequently found to be my wife's, so very like my own as to be mistaken for it; as I started, my wife thoughtfully threw over my head and shoulders a shawl. I had gone perhaps fifteen or twenty yards when a trooper galloped up and ordered me to halt and surrender, to which I gave a defiant answer, and dropping the shawl and raglan from my shoulders advanced toward him; he leveled his carbine at me, but I expected, if he fired, he would miss me, and my intention was in that event to put my hand under his foot, tumble him off on the other side, spring into his saddle and attempt to escape. My wife, who had been watching, when she saw the soldier aim his carbine at me, ran forward and threw her arms around me. Success depended on instantaneous action, and recognizing that the opportunity had been lost I turned back, and the morning being damp and chilly, passed on to a fire beyond the tent.

—JEFFERSON DAVIS

II · *James H. Jones's Narrative*

I BECAME Mr. Davis' servant in 1862, and when his family came to Raleigh the next year I accompanied them here. I aided in packing the property when the family left Richmond in 1865, and accompanied Mrs. Davis and the children southward.

We got a wagon and an ambulance at Newberry, South Carolina. Mr. Davis joined us down in Georgia one Sunday morning. We camped when we stopped at night. Mr. Davis rode his favorite saddle-horse, a splendid bay named Kentucky. I always looked after the comfort of the party. In one tent were Mr. and Mrs. Davis and in another their four children—Maggie, Jeff, Willie, and Varina—and Miss Maggie Howell, Mrs. Davis' sister; also, two maids—one white and one colored.

The night of the capture was foggy. I was up all night, washing and drying clothes at a fire which burned near the tents. A creek ran close by, in a sort of ravine, and there was a road passing by the camp. I heard noises about midnight, but they were not alarming, and I saw gleams which I now know were the glitter of sabres. About 4 o'clock in the morning, and before daylight, I heard the sound of horses' hoofs on the soft pine straw which covered the ground. The tents were closed. All the people were asleep. I was the only one awake. There was a very heavy dew.

As soon as I heard the noise I went to Mr. Davis' tent and aroused him. I also remember that I waked Mr. Reagan, Colonel Joseph Johnston, Colonel Wood, Colonel Burton Harrison, Colonel Lovett, of Texas, and Mr. William Howell, Mrs. Davis' brother; also some other gentlemen who were asleep here and there, some under tent flies. Colonel Harrison was nearest the creek and directly he was awake, he halted a Federal soldier who was the first to cross the creek. I told Colonel Harrison it must be the enemy I had seen moving about in the pines all night. By the time Mr. Davis had dressed himself the enemy were in the camp. I had meanwhile saddled Mr. Davis' horse, which was tied between the camp and the creek. It was Mr. Davis' purpose to get on his horse, make a dash into the ravine, and so escape. As Mr. Davis stepped from his tent he saw before him a man mounted on horseback, armed with a carbine, which was pointed at him. Mr. Davis had on Mrs. Davis' waterproof raglan, which by mistake he had taken for his own, and as he was a great sufferer from neuralgia he had put a light hood over his head and shoulders which he frequently wore. Mrs. Davis, solicitous of his health as she always was, as he stepped out of the tent threw her shawl upon him. Mr. Davis seeing the cavalryman at once advanced fearlessly towards him and called upon him to fire. The cavalryman did not fire, and Mr. Davis again called to him to do so. At this moment, Mrs. Davis, in her night dress, sprang from the tent, threw her arms around her husband's neck and addressing the cavalryman, said: "For God's sake don't shoot."

Mr. Davis' plan had been to let the cavalryman fire at him and taking the chances of a miss, rush upon him, unseat him, and mount his horse and escape. But at Mrs. Davis' words he went back to the tent with her. There he was given a bucket, I think, by her and started towards the creek as if for water, intending to get into the ravine and escape on his horse, but he was again halted by the same trooper. He then returned to the fire. Just about this time lively firing was heard fifty yards off and across the creek. Colonel Pritchard next made his appearance, and walking up to the fire looked at Mr. Davis and said to me: "Is that Jefferson Davis?" I said "Yes," and Colonel Pritchard then said to Mr. Davis: "You are my prisoner." Colonel Pritchard was very courteous and gentlemanly. He permitted no insult to be given then or at any time while he was in command, and gave particular instructions to that effect.

Mr. Davis had very little to say at the time of his capture and exhibited no fear whatever. He and his party had breakfast before they left and then the camp was struck and the wagon loaded. The party started off under a cavalry guard, the maids and children in the wagon in charge of myself and Robert Brown (colored), who had been Mr. Davis' butler, Mr. and Mrs. Davis and others traveling in the ambulance. I pitched camp for them at night. I was kept under arrest all the while and was not permitted even to go after milk for the children unless a guard accompanied me. I was taken to Fortress Monroe with Mr. Davis. There I was released and came to Raleigh.

—JAMES H. JONES

*

The Shackling of Jefferson Davis

---

*

ON THE MORNING of the 23d of May . . . at Fort Monroe, Captain Jerome E. Titlow, of the 3d Pennsylvania Artillery, entered the prisoner's cell, followed by the blacksmith of the fort and his assistant, the latter carrying in his hands some heavy and harshly-rattling shackles. As they entered, Mr. Davis was reclining on his bed, feverish and weary after a sleepless night, the food placed near to him the preceding day still lying untouched on its tin plate near his bedside.

"Well?" said Mr. Davis as they entered, slightly raising his head.

"I have an unpleasant duty to perform, Sir," said Captain Titlow; and as he spoke, the senior blacksmith took the shackles from his assistant.

Davis leaped instantly from his recumbent attitude, a flush passing over his face for a moment, and then his countenance growing livid and rigid as death.

He gasped for breath, clutching his throat with the thin fingers of his right hand, and then recovering himself slowly, while his wasted figure towered up to its full height—now appearing to swell with indignation and then to shrink with terror, as he glanced from the captain's

538

face to the shackles—he said slowly and with a laboring chest: "My God! You cannot have been sent to iron me?"

"Such are my orders, Sir," replied the officer, beckoning the blacksmith to approach, who stepped forward, unlocking the padlock and preparing the fetters to do their office. These fetters were of heavy iron, probably five-eighths of an inch in thickness, and connected together by a chain of like weight. I believe they are now in the possession of Major General Miles, and will form an interesting relic.

"This is too monstrous," groaned the prisoner, glaring hurriedly round the room, as if for some weapon, or means of self-destruction. "I demand, Captain, that you let me see the commanding officer. Can he pretend that such shackles are required to secure the safe custody of a weak old man, so guarded and in such a fort as this?"

"It could serve no purpose," replied Titlow; "his orders are from Washington, as mine are from him."

"But he can telegraph," interposed Mr. Davis, eagerly; "there must be some mistake. No such outrage as you threaten me with is on record in the history of nations. Beg him to telegraph, and delay until he answers."

"My orders are peremptory," said the officer, "and admit of no delay. For your own sake, let me advise you to submit with patience. As a soldier, Mr. Davis, you know I must execute orders."

"These are not orders for a soldier," shouted the prisoner, losing all control of himself. "They are orders for a jailor—for a hangman, which no soldier wearing a sword should accept! I tell you the world will ring with this disgrace. The war is over; the South is conquered; I have no longer any country but America, and it is for the honor of America, as for my own honor and life, that I plead against this degradation. Kill me! kill me!" he cried, passionately, throwing his arms wide open and exposing his breast, "rather than inflict on me, and on my people through me, this insult worse than death."

"Do your duty, blacksmith," said the officer, walking towards the embrasure as if not caring to witness the performance. "It only gives increased pain on all sides to protract this interview."

At these words the blacksmith advanced with the shackles, and seeing that the prisoner had one foot upon the chair near his bedside, his right hand resting on the back of it, the brawny mechanic made an attempt to slip one of the shackles over the ankle so raised; but, as if with the vehemence and strength which frenzy can impart, even to the

539

weakest invalid, Mr. Davis suddenly seized his assailant and hurled him halfway across the room.

On this Captain Titlow turned, and seeing that Davis had backed against the wall for further resistance, began to remonstrate, pointing out in brief, clear language, that this course was madness, and that orders must be enforced at any cost. "Why compel me," he said, "to add the further indignity of personal violence to the necessity of your being ironed?"

"I am a prisoner of war," fiercely retorted Davis; "I have been a soldier in the armies of America, and know how to die. Only kill me, and my last breath shall be a blessing on your head. But while I have life and strength to resist, for myself and for my people, this thing shall not be done."

Hereupon Captain Titlow called in a sergeant and file of soldiers from the next room, and the sergeant advanced to seize the prisoner. Immediately Mr. Davis flew on him, seized his musket and attempted to wrench it from his grasp.

Of course such a scene could have but one issue. There was a short, passionate scuffle. In a moment Davis was flung upon his bed, and before his four powerful assailants removed their hands from him, the blacksmith and his assistant had done their work—on securing the rivet on the right ankle, while the other turned the key in the padlock on the left.

This done, Mr. Davis lay for a moment as if in stupor. Then slowly raising himself and turning around, he dropped his shackled feet to the floor. The harsh clank of the striking chain seems first to have recalled him to his situation, and dropping his face into his hands, he burst into a passionate flood of sobbing, rocking to and fro, and muttering at brief intervals: "Oh, the shame, the shame!"

It may here be stated, though out of its due order—that we may get rid in haste of an unpleasant subject—that Mr. Davis some two months later, when frequent visits had made him more free of converse, gave me a curious explanation of the last feature in this incident.

He had been speaking of suicide, and denouncing it as the worst form of cowardice and folly. "Life is not like a commission that we can resign when disgusted with the service. Taking it by your own hand is a confession of judgment to all that your worst enemies can allege. It has often flashed across me as a tempting remedy for neuralgic torture; but thank God! I never sought my own death but once, and then when completely frenzied and not master of my actions. When they came to

540

iron me that day, as a last resource of desperation, I seized a soldier's musket and attempted to wrench it from his grasp, hoping that in the scuffle and surprise, some one of his comrades would shoot or bayonet me."

—Brevet Lieutenant Colonel John J. Craven

42. "I WON'T BE RECONSTRUCTED"

John S. Wise's Will

*

Richmond, April 27, 1865

I, J. REB, being of unsound mind and bitter memory, and aware that I am dead, do make, publish, and declare the following to be my political last will and testament.

1. I give, devise, and bequeath all my slaves to Harriet Beecher Stowe.

2. My rights in the territories I direct shall be assigned and set

over, together with the bric-a-brac known as State Sovereignty, to the Honorable J—— R—— T——, to play with for the remainder of his life, and remainder to his son after his death.

3. I direct that all my shares in the venture of secession shall be canceled, provided I am released from my unpaid subscription to the stock of said enterprise.

4. My interest in the civil government of the Confederacy I bequeath to any freak museum that may hereafter be established.

5. My sword, my veneration for General Robert E. Lee, his subordinate commanders and his peerless soldiers, and my undying love for my old comrades, living and dead, I set apart as the best I have, or shall ever have, to bequeath to my heirs forever.

6. And now, being dead, having experienced a death to Confederate ideas and a new birth unto allegiance to the Union, I depart, with a vague but not definite hope of a joyful resurrection, and of a new life, upon lines somewhat different from those of the last eighteen years. I see what has been pulled down very clearly. What is to be built up in its place I know not. It is a mystery; but death is always mysterious. AMEN.

—JOHN S. WISE

*

Hell at Chickamauga

*

A NUMBER OF MEN were before [General Butler] to take the oath of allegiance. One of them, a wag in his way, looked at the General, and with a peculiar Southern drawl, said: "We gave you hell at Chickamauga, General!"

The General was furious at the man's familiar impudence and threatened him with all sorts of punishment, but again came that drawling voice, repeating the first part of the statement, but he was stopped by the General, who ordered him to take the oath of allegiance to the United States at once or he would have him shot. After some hesitation, looking into General Butler's fierce eye, he reluctantly consented to take the oath. After taking the oath, he looked calmly into General Butler's face, and drew himself up as if proud to become a citizen of the United States and a member of the Yankee Army, and said: "General, I suppose I am a good Yankee and citizen of the United States now?"

The General replied in a very fatherly tone, "I hope so."

"Well, General, the rebels did give *us hell* at Chickamauga, didn't they?"

—HERBERT W. BEECHER

＊

"Whatever General Lee Says"

＊

FRICTION RESULTED from efforts to ram the oath down everybody's throat at once. I recite this instance because of the part General Lee took and duplicated in multitudes of cases. Captain George Wise was called before the Provost to take the oath. "Why must I take it?" asked he. "My parole covers the ground. I will not."

"You fought under General Lee, did you not?"

"Yes. And surrendered with him, and gave my parole. To require this oath of me is to put an indignity upon me and my general."

"I will make a bargain with you, Captain. Consult General Lee and abide by his decision."

The Captain went to the Lee residence, where he was received by Mrs. Lee, who informed him that her husband was ill, but would see him. The General was lying on a lounge, pale, weary-looking, but fully dressed, in his gray uniform, the three stars on his collar; the three stars —to which any Confederate colonel was entitled—was the only insignia of rank he ever wore. "They want me to take this thing, General," said the Captain, extending a copy of the oath. "My parole covers it, and I do not think it should be required of me. What would you advise?"

"I would advise you to take it," he said quietly. "It is absurd that it should be required of my soldiers, for, as you say, the parole practically covers it. Nevertheless, take it, I should say."

"General, I feel that this is submission to an indignity. If I must

544

continue to swear the same thing over at every street corner, I will seek another country where I can at least preserve my self-respect."

General Lee was silent for a few minutes. Then he said, quietly as before, a deep touch of sadness in his voice: "Do not leave Virginia. Our country needs her young men now."

When the Captain told Henry A. Wise that he had taken the oath, the ex-Governor said: "You have disgraced the family!"

"General Lee advised me to do it."

"Oh, that alters the case. Whatever General Lee says is all right, I don't care what it is."

—MYRTA LOCKETT AVARY

∗

The "Button Trouble"

∗

SOME MILITARY ORDERS were very irritating.

The "Button Order" prohibited our men from wearing Confederate buttons. Many possessed no others and had not money wherewith to buy. Buttons were scarce as hens' teeth. The Confederacy had been reduced to all sorts of makeshifts for buttons. Thorns from thornbushes had furnished country folks with such fastenings as pins usually supply, and served convenience on milady's toilette-table when she went to do up her hair.

One clause in that monstrous order delighted feminine hearts! It provided as thoughtful concession to all too glaring poverty that: "When plain buttons cannot be procured, those formerly used can be covered with cloth." Richmond ladies looked up all the bits of crepe and bombazine they had, and next morning their men appeared on the streets with buttons in mourning! "I would never have gotten Uncle out of the front door if he had realized what I was up to," Matoaca relates. "Not that he was not mournful enough, but he did not want to mourn that way."

Somehow, nobody thought about Sam's button; he was a boy, only fifteen. He happened to go out near Camp Grant in his old gray jacket,

545

the only coat he had; one of his brothers had given it to him months before. It was held together over his breast by a single button, his only button. A Yankee sergeant cut it off with his sword. The jacket fell apart, exposing bepatched and thread-bare underwear. His mother and sisters could not help crying when the boy came in, holding his jacket together with his hand, his face suffused, his eyes full of tears of rage and mortification.

The "Button Trouble" pervaded the entire South. The Tennessee Legislature, Brownlow's machine, discussed a bill imposing a fine of $5 to $25 upon privates, and $25 to $50 upon officers for wearing the "rebel uniform." The gaunt, destitute creatures who were trudging, stumping, limping, through that State on their way from distant battlefields and Northern prisons to their homes, had rarely so much as fifty cents in their pockets. Had that bill become a law enforced, Tennessee prisons must have overflowed with recaptured Confederates, or roads and woods with men in undress.

Many a distinguished soldier, home-returning, ignorant that such an order existed, has been held up at the entrance to his native town by a saucy Negro sergeant who would shear him of his buttons with a sabre, or march him through the streets to the Provost's office to answer for the crime of having buttons on his clothes.

The provision about covering buttons has always struck me as the unkindest cut of all. How was a man who had no feminine relatives to obey the law? Granted that as a soldier, he had acquired the art of being his own seamstress, how, when he was in the woods or the roads, could he get scraps of cloth and cover buttons?

—MYRTA LOCKETT AVARY

*

Lovers and War Lords: The "Marriage Oath"

*

MY MARRIAGE was appointed for May 2d, which would have been on Tuesday. Early Saturday morning, April 29, 1865, I was aroused by my maid, who handed me the morning paper [Richmond *Dispatch*], saying, "Mr. Carrington is here, and told me to give you this." Mr. Carrington was a widower, and quite an old gentleman, who was very fond of a joke and also of saying airy nothings to young girls. He and I had been quite friendly for a long time, and he had frequently threatened to give Captain Sloan a dose of arsenic, if the Yankees did not put a bullet through his head and save him the trouble, &c. The paper was open at official news, and great black lines enclosed a small printed space, which proved to be an order from General Halleck, forbidding the courts of Virginia to issue any marriage licenses, unless both parties took the oath of allegiance to the United States. On the margin of the paper Mr. Carrington had written: "If the Captain is not willing to take that oath, I am." Of course I was much dismayed at this news, and at once sent the paper to my father. By the time I had made a hasty toilet Captain Sloan had arrived at the house; and very soon my own family and several of our neighbors, dear old Mr. Carrington included, had assembled in the parlor and were discussing the matter with great indignation and disgust. Up to that time my father had not been a very enthusiastic promoter of our marriage. He thought, and very wisely, that as everything was in such an unsettled condition, and as we were both quite young, it would be wiser for us to wait, at least until the fall.

A report that eleven Confederate officers were to be exiled at once frightened us into a haste, which the memory of the terrible suspense and anxiety of the past two weeks only accelerated; and, as my dear, good father always yielded his will to my pleasure, he had given a reluctant consent. But, after reading General Halleck's order, his indignation knew no bounds, and now he was as much determined we should be married as before he had been opposed. Many were the expedients suggested, discussed, and rejected to circumvent this petty tyranny of conquering foe. Everyone whom we could think of, whose legal knowledge was worth anything, was sought and consulted, but all to no purpose; no one had any plan to suggest which was at all feasible.

At last, after much weary tramping the streets and much useless talking, Captain Sloan suddenly remembered that General Halleck and General Jerry Gilmer, of South Carolina, were classmates at West Point, and such dear and intimate friends that General Gilmer had named a son Henry Halleck. General Gilmer was related to Captain Sloan by marriage, and he and his sisters always called him Uncle Jerry. As drowning men catch at straws, Captain Sloan and my father at once proceeded to act on this inspiration. My father was well and intimately acquainted with Judge Ould, the Confederate Commissioner of Exchange; and, as a member of the Ambulance Committee, also knew Colonel Mulford, the United States Commissioner of Exchange, quite well. Through the influence of these gentlemen, though after much delay and a great deal of red tape, they succeeded in gaining an audience with General Halleck.

The General was very courteous, and seemed much amused at the consternation created by his order. Captain Sloan had no difficulty in convincing him of his relationship to his friend, General Gilmer, and, in consideration of that fact, General Halleck good-naturedly declared that the order under discussion should not go into effect until Monday morning. Writing a few words on a slip of official paper, he handed it to Captain Sloan with a smile, saying as he did so: "Let every one know of this countermand, and I suppose there will be many weddings between this time and Monday morning." As *this* time was six o'clock Saturday afternoon, and as there were no Sunday papers in those days, not many people out of our immediate circle of friends were informed of it. We were married on Sunday night at nine o'clock, April 30, 1865.

The order countermanding the first order was for a long time in our possession in a scrap-book, but was not returned by R. O. Polkinhour, a Washington publisher, who reprinted the scrap-book in the form of a history for Captain Sloan, although every effort was made to have him do so. It ran thus, and I may be mistaken as to the number of the order:

HEADQUARTERS ARMY POTOMAC
Order No. 46 will not go into effect until Monday, May 1st, 1865.
(Signed) H. W. HALLECK
Commandant

City of Richmond, Virginia

The gown I wore the day after my marriage was a buff calico with tiny brown spots in it, and as it was prettily and becomingly made, I looked as well, and I know I was as happy, as if it had been one of Worth's or Redfern's most bewildering conceits, and I am sure it was as expensive, as it cost $30 per yard.

—MRS. MORTON WORTHAM SLOAN

43. RETURN OF THE SOLDIER

Going Home to Stay

*

AS THE CONFEDERATES were taking leave of Appomattox, and about to begin their long and dreary tramp homeward, many of the Union men bade them cordial farewell.

One of Grant's men said good-naturedly to one of Lee's veterans: "Well, Johnny, I guess you fellows will go home now to stay."

The tired and tried Confederate, who did not clearly understand the spirit in which the playful words were spoken, and who was not at the moment in the best mood for badinage, replied:

"Look here, Yank; you *guess,* do you, that we fellows are going

549

home to stay? Maybe we are. But don't be giving us any of your impudence. If you do, we'll come back and lick you again."

—GENERAL JOHN B. GORDON

*

Johnny Wickersham Comes Marching Home

*

NOW, here is a picture which can be erased only by death. The exact location I do not know, but on a hill to our right the enemy had planted a battery and the next morning began to pour grape-shot into our thin ranks while solid lines advanced in our front. We repulsed them, at nine o'clock the battery on the hill ceased firing and there ensued a calm. The men looked into each other's faces with wonder and amazement. One man said, "Boys, Kirby Smith has gotten in their rear, and they are in full retreat." All that afternoon not a shot was fired, and how long that night seemed to those men watchful and sleepless. The only sound to be heard was the steady tramp of the sentinel. We could sleep under the roar of artillery and rattle of musketry, but what meant this deathly stillness? Unconsciously the men spoke in whispers, and the question that passed from lip to lip was, "What does it mean?"

The stillness was yet unexplained when the next morning some one mentioned he had not seen "Big Officer" lately. Just then we saw our gallant Colonel riding toward us on his emaciated horse, and a moment later the bugle rang out the command to fall in.

It seems to me too pitiful to write that on that day those of our regiment answering for duty numbered much less than a company. "Color-bearers ten paces to the front. About face." These were the Colonel's orders, and his next "Present arms." Stopping a moment he looked at us and then slowly turned and rode down the hill. "Look at the Colonel, he's drunk. See, he can't keep his saddle," said the men. The Colonel checked his horse at some distance and beckoned the bugler to approach. A moment later the boy came running back, and with tears streaming down his face, said, "Boys, the Colonel says it's all over. You will have to ground arms."

No tongue or pen can ever describe this scene. Our eyes involuntarily turned in the direction of that beloved battle flag which had never known dishonor or disgrace, and we thought of the many, many heroes who had died under it, and with one accord we struggled to obtain a scrap of it. I cannot write more.

The war was over, and we had lost. God only knows the price we paid.

We were paroled and sent to the Mississippi River and promised transportation to St. Louis. The war at a close, and the necessity that had kept us blind to our own condition removed, our neglected bodies suffered an almost total collapse. Physically, we were in a worse condition than when we surrendered at Vicksburg, and much more exhausted from the strenuous marching, to which was added the disease that was rife among us. Our clothing would scarcely cover our bodies, and we were, almost without exception, shoeless.

Without regard to commands we were loaded on every passing steamboat in much the same manner that cattle are loaded in a box car, and on the little steamboat on which I was packed there was not room for the men to lie down, while at almost every stop some poor, sick fellow was shoved from the gang plank. The crew was composed of men too cowardly to fight with the army, but brave enough now that the war was over, to curse and abuse us. My exhaustion became so great that I could stand upright no longer. The boat was landing at Helena, Arkansas, when the mate spied me lying on the deck—he ordered two brutal Negro deck hands to carry me off, and the boat pulled off, leaving me lying there on the levee bank. A Negro woman found me and took me to her cabin. Poor woman, she had nothing but corn-cake and dried pumpkin, but she gave me freely of it, and would go with me when I became able to walk, to the landing place, and as boats landed would plead with them to take me aboard, only to be refused. I had no money, and no hope.

After weeks of her motherly nursing I felt much better, and one day told her I was going to walk to Missouri. "No, honey, don't try it. You sure will die if you do," was her advice. However, with a big hoe-cake, the only provision which she had made for me, I started on that long, weary tramp over a country that had been ravished by both armies, and in which not a building or so much as a fence, or head of stock remained. During the ninety miles I covered I did not see a white person. It seemed as if some terrible scourge had destroyed every living thing. I met several parties of Negroes, some hunting their former master or mistress, and others going North for that "mule and forty acres." Without exception they shared their scanty provisions with me, and one very kindly tied up my sore feet, as only a darkie knows how. I must have been a pitiful sight, for I won the sympathy of all I met. At last I came to a wide, seemingly endless prairie. How hot the sun was, and how hard it was to drag my poor, sore feet and weary legs over that rough and overgrown road. It was more than twenty-four hours since the last bit of my hoe-cake had been eaten, and sick, discouraged, and exhausted, I dropped on the grass, and feeling myself now thoroughly beaten, I prayed that I might die. Nothing seemed to matter to me now but to be at peace.

I must have lain there hours, for when I partly aroused myself it was dark, then I saw to my great amazement and surprise, in the timber to my left, a light. It was the first indication of life or habitation that had crossed my vision in that long and weary struggle I had made against exhaustion and death. I lay there pondering—somehow it seemed the light said, "Come on," but my poor weakened body refused to obey my mind's command. The dew had fallen, and the chill of the night air had so encompassed me that I was only able to get on my hands and feet—to in a moment fall. It seemed someone said—"What's the use, by morning you will be at peace"—but more persistent came a pleading voice, "Come on, come on." The light seemed to haunt me, and I resolved to make one more effort. I got on my feet, and with the aid of my stick took a few steps. The light seemed to keep saying, "Come on."

I reached the clearing, and saw two log cabins with a passageway between. There was no fence or out-buildings. The passageway was raised. I was just about to knock when the sound of voices reached my ears, and I realized that family prayer was being held within. I heard the voice of an old man praying for Dick, Jim, and Little Johnnie, and then I recognized my father's voice. It seemed the most natural thing in the world to me, as I rested against the side of the wall, fascinated by the latch on the door, and wondering in a vague sort of way why they put it on the outside of the door. It never occurred to me to interrupt the prayer, but I mentally wondered if he would ever cease. My sensibilities were numbed and nothing seemed unusual. I never questioned as to why he was here in this log cabin in such a God-forsaken country. At last came the "Amen," and I knocked. A woman's voice said, "Come in," and I opened the door.

552

There was a fire on the hearth where they had cooked their evening meal. On a shelf on the wall a candle was burning. And there, all three standing, were my old father, sisters Sarah and Mary, brother Dick's wife. Instinctively I had known who would be there before I opened the door. They stared at me with wondering eyes. Something held us all speechless. I was groping blindly in my mind for words. Finally they came—"I've come home," I said and collapsed. Sister Sarah caught my tottering body and helped me to a bench. "Something to eat," I managed to say. Sister Mary ran to start the fire and put the bacon in the skillet and the rye in the coffee pot. My old father supported me while Sarah brought me a drink. They knew I had been a Confederate soldier, although none recognized me. It was no wonder, for since leaving Memphis nearly a year ago, I had scarcely seen a piece of soap. I was now almost nineteen years of age with only sufficient flesh to cover my bones.

"To what command did you belong?" asked my father, but to all his questions I could only shake my head. The frying pan had all my attention. Thank God, Mary was placing it on the table, and Father and Sarah were taking me to the bench in front of it. . . . When they placed me at the table I seized the bacon in both my hands and devoured it like an animal. Mary was at the other side of the table with her chin resting on her hands watching me, when suddenly she gave a scream and cried, "It is Jim." (Jim was my next oldest brother.) They gathered around me embracing me between their tears, and when I could sufficiently control my voice, I told that I was Johnnie. My father brought the water and they all helped to bathe me. My sisters that night made me underclothes from their skirts.

Weeks after I learned that Father and my sisters, knowing that the war was over, and unable to wait longer for news of us, had started South with a pair of horses and carry-all, or light spring wagon, loaded with provisions and supplies. On reaching that lonely place robbers had captured the horses, wagon and all they had brought, and had left them stranded in that little cabin.

—JOHN T. WICKERSHAM

553

＊

Veteran's First Lie

＊

[STOPPING OVERNIGHT in Manhattan, on my way to Fitchburg, Massachusetts] I went into French's Hotel to have my hair cut and the barber observed a scar on the left side of my head, about where the part would usually be, caused in my infancy by my jumping from my mother's arms in a fit of anger and striking upon the edge of a hot stove.

"Get this in the army?" he queried.

The temptation was too great. "Yes," I replied indifferently, "at Chancellorsville. Our color-bearer fell, and just as I seized the flag a rebel cavalry officer cut my head open with his sword. Fortunately one of our boys shot him and we got away with our colors."

The barber was interested and wanted particulars. I could supply them, for I really had the correct background and soon there was a gathering about my chair. Who could fail to take advantage of a credulous and sympathetic audience? I turned my early dreams of valor into the past tense, and really felt to be the hero I had represented myself.

—CHARLES W. BARDEEN

＊

When the Privates Ranked the Generals

＊

SINCE THE WAR . . . privates have told with great relish of the old farmer near Appomattox who decided to give employment, after the surrender, to any of Lee's veterans who might wish to work a few days for food and small wages. He divided the Confederate employés into squads according to the respective ranks held by them in the army. He was uneducated, but entirely loyal to the Southern cause. A neighbor inquired of him as to the different squads:

"Who are those men working over there?"

"Them is privates, sir, of Lee's army. Very fine, sir; first-rate workers."

"Who are those in the second group?"

"Them is lieutenants and captains, and they works fairly well, but not as good workers as the privates."

"I see you have a third squad: who are they?"

"Them is colonels."

"Well, what about the colonels? How do they work?"

"Now, neighbor, you'll never hear me say one word ag'in any man who 'fit' in the Southern army; but I ain't a-gwine to hire no generals."

—GENERAL JOHN B. GORDON

*

Working His Passage

*

AT THE BREAK-UP of the great Rebellion I found myself at Selma, Alabama, still in the service of the United States, and although my duties were now purely civil my treatment was not uniformly so, and I am not surprised that it was not. I was a minor official in the Treasury Department, engaged in performance of duties exceedingly disagreeable not only to the people of the vicinity, but to myself as well. They consisted in the collection and custody of "captured and abandoned property." The Treasury had covered pretty nearly the entire area of "the States lately in rebellion" with a hierarchy of officials, consisting, as nearly as memory serves, of one supervising agent and a multitude of special agents. Each special agent held dominion over a collection district and was allowed an "agency aide" to assist him in his purposeful activity, besides such clerks, laborers and so forth as he could persuade himself to need. My humble position was that of agency aide. When the special agent was present for duty I was his chief executive officer; in his absence I represented him (with greater or less fidelity to the original and to my conscience) and was invested with his powers. In the Selma agency the property that we were expected to seize and defend as best we might was mostly plantations (whose owners had disappeared; some were dead, others in hiding) and cotton. The country was full of cotton which had been sold to the Confederate Government, but not removed from the plantations to take its chance of export through the blockade. It had been decided that it now belonged to the United States. It was worth about five hundred dollars a bale—say one dollar a pound. The world agreed that that was a pretty good price for cotton.

* * * * *

There were queer characters in Alabama in those days, as you shall see. Once upon a time the special agent and I started down the Tombigbee River with a steamboat load of government cotton—some six hundred bales. At one of the military stations we took on a guard of a dozen or fifteeen soldiers under command of a non-commissioned officer. One evening, just before dusk, as we were rounding a bend where the current set strongly against the left bank of the stream and the channel lay close to that shore, we were suddenly saluted with a volley of bullets and buckshot from that direction. The din of the firing, the rattle and crash of the missiles splintering the woodwork and the jingle of broken glass made a very rude arousing from the tranquil indolence of a warm afternoon on the sluggish Tombigbee. The left bank, which at this point was a trifle higher than the hurricane deck of a steamer, was now swarming with men who, almost near enough to jump aboard, looked unreasonably large and active as they sprang about from cover to cover, pouring in their fire. At the first volley the pilot had deserted his wheel, as well he might, and the boat, drifting in to the bank under the boughs of a tree, was helpless. Her jack-staff and yawl were carried away, her guards broken in, and her deck-load of cotton was tumbling into the stream a dozen bales at once. The captain was nowhere to be seen, the engineer had evidently abandoned his post and the special agent had gone to hunt up the soldiers. I happened to be on the hurricane deck, armed with a revolver, which I fired as rapidly as I could, listening all the time for the fire of the soldiers— and listening in vain. It transpired later that they had not a cartridge among them; and of all helpless mortals a soldier without a cartridge is the most imbecile. But all this time the continuous rattle of the enemy's

556

guns and the petulant pop of my own pocket firearm were punctuated, as it were, by pretty regularly recurring loud explosions, as of a small cannon. They came from somewhere forward—I supposed from the opposition, as I knew we had no artillery on board.

The failure of our military guard made the situation somewhat grave. For two of us, at least, capture meant hanging out of hand. I had never been hanged in all my life and was not enamored of the prospect. Fortunately for us the bandits had selected their point of attack without military foresight. Immediately below them a bayou, impassable to them, let into the river. The moment we had drifted below it we were safe from boarding and capture. The captain was found in hiding and an empty pistol at his ear persuaded him to resume command of his vessel; the engineer and pilot were encouraged to go back to their posts and after some remarkably long minutes, during which we were under an increasingly long-range fire, we got under way. A few bales piled about the pilot-house made us tolerably safe from that sort of thing in the future and then we took account of our damages. Nobody had been killed and only a few were wounded. This gratifying result was attributable to the fact that, being unarmed, nearly everybody had dived below at the first fire and taken cover among the cotton bales. While issuing a multitude of needless commands from the front of the hurricane-deck I looked below, and there, stretched out at full length on his stomach, lay a long, ungainly person, clad in faded butternut, bareheaded, his long, lank hair falling down each side of his neck, his coat-tails similarly parted, and his enormous feet spreading their soles to the blue sky. He had an old-fashioned horse-pistol, some two feet long, which he was in the act of sighting across his left palm for a parting shot at the now distant assailants. A more ludicrous figure I never saw; I laughed outright; but when his weapon went off it was matter for gratitude to be above it instead of before it. It was the "cannon" whose note I had marked all through the unequal fray.

The fellow was a returned Confederate whom we had taken on at one of the upper landings as our only passenger; we were dead-heading him to Mobile. He was undoubtedly in hearty sympathy with the enemy, and I at first suspected him of collusion, but circumstances not necessary to detail here rendered this impossible. Moreover, I had distinctly seen one of the "guerrillas" fall and remain down after my own weapon was empty, and no man else on board except the passenger had fired a shot or had a shot to fire. When everything had been made snug again, and we were gliding along under the stars, without apprehension; when I had counted fifty-odd bullet holes through the pilot-house (which had not received the attention that by its prominence and importance it was justly entitled to) and everybody was variously boasting his prowess, I approached my butternut comrade-in-arms and thanked him for his kindly aid. "But," said I, "how the devil does it happen that *you* fight *that* crowd?"

"Wal, Cap," he drawled, as he rubbed the powder grime from his antique artillery, "I allowed it was mouty clever in you-all to take me on, seein' I hadn't ary cent, so I thought I'd jist kinder work my passage."

—AMBROSE BIERCE

*

Salvage

---

*

IN APRIL, 1865, Lawrence Taliaferro, who for four years had been with Lee's army, returned to his home on the north side of the Rappahannock, perhaps twelve miles from Fredericksburg. He was twenty-five years of age. When he went into the war his father owned a farm of several hundred acres, with handsome buildings, fine stock, and 150 Negroes. Lawrence Taliaferro had always lived the life of a son of a country gentleman. . . .

The Army of the Potomac of over 100,000 men had occupied this place almost continuously from November, 1862, until May, 1863. They had cut every tree and sapling for miles in every direction, to get fuel to burn, logs for their huts, and corduroy for their roads. When Lawrence Taliaferro attempted to return to his old home, he was in a country of which he knew nothing. His way lost, he could only wander from one new road to another, until at last he came upon an unfamiliar hut. He rapped and an old darky came out. He was one of his father's former slaves, and the man conducted him to his old home. All outhouses and fences had disappeared, as well as the shade trees and shrubbery. There was only the shell of the house. He found his father and sister living there. Two of the old servants had remained, refusing to leave their master. Upon inquiry he found that all that was left of the farm property was one old mule and a much-patched harness. A few days after his return, an older brother came back from Lee's army and brought with him a worn-out horse. Then began the struggle for daily bread. The two young men patched up the harness for the mule and horse; borrowed an old plow, and began to prepare the ground for a garden.

They had not been at home many days when they learned that a couple of men were in Fredericksburg buying bones. Now for miles around Fredericksburg the fields were thick with the bones of worn-out mules and horses, which had died during that long period when the country was occupied by Northern and Southern troops. As soon as the Taliaferros discovered that these bones were salable, they borrowed from a friend the remnant of a wagon and started out to pick them up. As the result of two days' work, they found they had 2,000 pounds, which they sold for two cents a pound. "I thought my fortune was made, when I got that money," said Mr. Taliaferro. From that time on they put in every hour of daylight gathering up bones, while the two old darkies were putting in the garden and preparing the ground for corn. They carried on the bone business for a month, when they made a new discovery. Quantities of iron were lying on the fields. This they found was salable, and accordingly they went into the junk business. They were much crippled in their work by the fact that their team was so poor that not more than half a day's work could possibly be gotten out of it.

This had been going on about a month when a great piece of good fortune fell to them. A wing of the Federal army in marching north passed near their home, and one night the Taliaferros were visited by two Union officers. They had come, they said, to see if old Mr. Taliaferro was living and in good health. It seems that at the time the Union army had been encamped on and around his plantation the old gentleman had become a great favorite with the officers. The visitors were invited in, and the Taliaferros did their best to get them a good supper. The men were very much pleased with their entertainment, and when they went home, insisted that the boys should go over to the army with their wagon the next day and return their visit. This they did, and when they started to go home, they found that the wagon had been filled with coffee, sugar, bacon, etc.

"Enough," said Mr. Taliaferro, "to last six months."

And not only this: one of the officers went to the quartermaster and said, "See here, aren't you turning loose every day jaded mules which can't keep up with the army? Haven't you now three or four which you know you will soon have to drop out? If so, give them to these men."

"Well, sir," said Mr. Taliaferro, "do you know that that man actually brought out four mules and turned them over to us? They were pretty thin and tired, and he rather apologized for them and said, 'Do you think you can get them home?' Well, sir, the tears just ran down my face. I said, 'If they can't walk, I'll carry them.' We took them home and turned them out to grass, for grass was one thing we did have. The whole country was green with it, and in two months those mules were fat as butter and able to do a full day's work.

"The only thing outside of grass which the country afforded was rabbits and birds. They had been left alone for so long a time while the men were away that they were thick, but we did not have powder or bullets and for some time did not know exactly how to catch them; but we took up so much lead and so many shells in the battle-field, and were saving them all the time, that at last we got powder by unscrewing the caps off the shells and taking it out, and bullets by melting the lead and running it through holes punched in a piece of tin and letting it run into tubs of cold water. After we got this bullet factory started, we had plenty of birds and rabbits.

"We got on pretty well that summer. Our garden was good, and we laid up a good deal for winter, but when winter came it was mighty hard to get wood. There was not any left in the country. I don't know what we would have done if it hadn't been for the Yankees' corduroy roads. They were all through our plantation in every direction. We pulled up the pieces, which were, of course, water-soaked, and set them up on end in stacks so they would dry out, and for two winters this is how we got our wood. It took us five years to get our plantation into shape to keep us and the two old darkies, and after that we began to buy groceries and clothes, but it has been hard work."

—IDA M. TARBELL

*

"Dear Unknown"

*

Letter from Emma De Witt postmarked Weston, Ohio, November 13, 1865, to Mr. Abel Findley, Olivet, Armstrong County, Pennsylvania, Company B, Sixth Pennsylvania Regiment.

HIGHLY ESTEEMED UNKNOWN:

[Your] kind letter was read with a smiling countenance. How pleased I was to know who it was from. If you knew what a lonely life I lead, you (I know) would sympathize with me. By your writing I know you. You are a real kindhearted fellow, and I hope it may prove to be so.

You say that S. S. Nicodemus is discharged and for all that you know he was still writing to me yet—but in this case you are sadly mistaken for I know nothing of him any more. I had lost track of him a long time since. Indeed I had almost forgotten that I had known any one by that name. I like your letter much better than I did the former S. S. N. I do not wish to flatter you in the least but I must say that you write the best letter that I have ever got from an unknown, and I will drop all others for you. I don't care about writing to any one unless I get letters worth reading. As I said before I do not mean to flatter you in the least. I had but one when I got yours and I have not answered his last nor do I intend to. What do you think of that?

You said in your letter that you was looking for a wife. Well, I am doing the same, only searching among the opposite sex. But that is hard to find out here. I never was out here before. I am on a visit to my aunts and will perhaps stay all winter. Now as you are going to be discharged soon (if not already) I should be much pleased to have you come out this winter and see if you are as good looking as I imagine you are. I love black whiskers and black hair, and I imagine you are a real smart fellow and I hope it will prove to be as I think.

I beg your pardon for not giving you my age. It was through negligence only. I will be 19 the 13th of next April coming and in my life I have seen a great deal of sorrow. I was once blessed with a dear good mother and in my younger days knew naught but joy and happiness. But when five years of age an unwelcome visitor came. It was the hand of death came and snatched away my darling mother. Then soon after our quiet happy home was haunted with an unprincipled stepmother. Oh! the sorrow that woman brought into our family. I stayed at home and bore with her as long as I could. Then went and lived with an aunt of mine. That was two years ago. Father went after me so much and I finely concluded to go and try her again. I comensed going to school soon after I came home and that made her awful firey. I went the term out however and then went off to Oberlin to college and have been there ever since till of late. I went home and stayed a short time and then came here and I expect to stay all winter. In the last three years I have lost two darling brothers, all the brothers I had in the world. Oh! it was so hard. It seemed like almost taking the heart from me, and since their deaths my life seems very lonely. I can and do appear gay when out in company, but still all the while there is a burden on my mind. I have of late given myself the name of the lone star. [Here "and I hope" is crossed out.] Perhaps you do not like one that is as downhearted and to write as I do. If so I beg your pardon and will try to not give vent to my feelings so much and write more cheerful. But if you have seen trouble (as you doubtless have, being a Soldier) you know how I feel and can sympathize with me.

You say that you threw a note off of the train the same time that S. S. N. did. He said the same, but upon my word I did not get it. When he wrote that you threw one, I went out to find it but it was not to be found. So of course you cannot blame me for not writing.

And you have two twin brothers, have you? It is rather late and them most too young or there would be a good chance for them at our house, for my only sister and I are twins. I think it would be quite a miracle if twin sisters would marry twin brothers—but the reason I say it is too late is that my sister has allready a suiter and expects to step off soon.

But your brothers are (as I said before) rather young to think of such. You will please excuse nonsense. I am just trying to see what my pen will say. You know these young folks will say things often that they ought not to say and sometimes make trouble. I know I often say things I had better not said, but I say it all in fun and am afterwards ashamed of it for fear that those around would think me bold. I was once a regular quoquett. I would pretend that I thought a sight of the gay gents and when I would get to a good turning point, then snap them off. I kept at it till I got myself in trouble. Then I was glad to let quoquettish ways alone, and since the last one I have never trifled with a single young man's affections nor do I intend to. I am very plain out what I think of a young man. If I don't like him, he knows it, and if I do like him, he knows it. I suppose you see that by this letter. You already know that I think a great deal of you although I never seen you. Remember that if I love or like you, you will soon find it out, for I am plain spoken, too plain I sometimes think but I always liked that way best and of course I follow the example that I think the more of.

I think you are home by this time and I will close hoping to hear from you very soon. Write a good long letter.

Yours Respectfully,

EMMA DE WITT

[*A postscript in pencil*] I thank you for the stamp but still you need not have did it. Of course, they came very good and hurryed more about my answering your letter, for I am sure I would not have answered it very soon had you not did so for I was entirely out of money and I should have had to send to father for more and that would have been some time. If you are acquainted with S. S. N., please tell me what kind of a young gent he is. But you had be sure and report yourself regularly!

Yours truly

Weston, Ohio, December 24, 1865

UNKNOWN:

Your kind letter was received yesterday and I was indeed pleased with its contents. You wrote as any sensible young man would. If you had written a foolish sickening letter as I did I should have called you—well, I shant say what—I was telling you I used to flatter young men. I hardly think I have got over it yet. My Coz and myself adopted that plan to see what sort of a young man you was. In the first place my sister tried it so I thought I would try it—I will stop and tell what my sister did. She was writing to an Unknown so one Sunday morn she said she was going to write a real love letter to this young man and if he answered and wrote a loveing letter back, she would take it for granted that he was a fool and if not, a gentleman.

So in a very short time she got an answer, and the most loveing letter I ever read that one was, and asked her for her heart and hand to pop off on. My sister was engaged to be married at the time and I tell

563

you we had fun about it—and I was telling my Coz about it and she allowed it would be a good way to try you, and I did so and found it to accomplish well.

Indeed I enjoy your letters. She answered and told him that she had already given her heart away and expected soon to give her hand also and that someone else filled the place he wished for, that no one else could and that her affections—well, well, this don't interest you, I know, telling about my sister's affairs. I guess I will drop this subject entirely. I have said enough.

I was glad to know that you had got home again and was enjoying yourself among your old friends. It is very pleasant to sit among your old friends after being absent so long. I know how that goes for I have experienced it. I have enjoyed myself highly since I have been in Weston, so well that I have not really wanted to see my only sister till today and I have thought that I could not stand it without seeing her but I guess I will. But indeed I should love to spend Christmas or New Year's with her and I would if it took the last cent I had but I have other things to keep and other places to go.

I wish you a Merry Christmas and a happy New Year and many crowning blessings on its fleeting hours. I had thought all along that we would have sleighing by Christmas but today the Sun has come out warm and I am afraid that by tomorrow there will be no sleighing. As it is about Church time I will close—but first I must tell you the reason I did not receive your letter sooner was that I was away and staid about three weeks and did not get it till I came back. Hoping you will write soon, I will say no more.

Yours with respect
EMMA DE WITT

Just write as you please or think, the same privilege you gave me. I should be pleased to keep up correspondence with you if it is your desire. Yours and no more.

SIX: Aftermath

I never quite swallowed the story of the Connecticut lady of abolitionist stock who was alleged to have exclaimed, "Those damn Yankees!" as she read Miss Mitchell's description of Sherman's march to the sea; but I began to wonder if the children of the Confederates who lost the war in the field were, in the realm of letters, winning the peace.

—Douglas Southall Freeman

A real good hearty war like that dies hard. No country likes to part with a good earnest war. It likes to talk about the war, write its history, fight its battles over and over again, and build monument after monument to commemorate its glories.

—CARLTON MCCARTHY

44. A GOOD WAR DIES HARD

Letter from a Freedman to His Old Master
(Written Just as He Dictated It)

*

Dayton, Ohio, August 7, 1865

To my old Master, COLONEL P. H. ANDERSON, *Big Spring, Tenn.*

SIR: I got your letter, and was glad to find that you had not forgotten Jourdon, and that you wanted me to come back and live with you again, promising to do better for me than anybody else can. I have often felt uneasy about you. I thought the Yankees would have hung you long before this, for harboring Rebs they found at your house. I

567

suppose they never heard about your going to Colonel Martin's to kill the Union soldier that was left by his company in their stable. Although you shot at me twice before I left you, I did not want to hear of your being hurt, and am glad you are still living. It would do me good to go back to the dear old home again, and see Miss Mary and Miss Martha and Allen, Esther, Green, and Lee. Give my love to them all, and tell them I hope we will meet in the better world, if not in this. I would have gone back to see you all when I was working in the Nashville Hospital, but one of the neighbors told me that Henry intended to shoot me if he ever got a chance.

I want to know particularly what the good chance is you propose to give me. I am doing tolerably well here. I get twenty-five dollars a month, with victuals and clothing; have a comfortable home for Mandy —the folks call her Mrs. Anderson—and the children—Milly, Jane, and Grundy—go to school and are learning well. The teacher says Grundy has a head for a preacher. They go to Sunday school, and Mandy and me attend church regularly. We are kindly treated. Sometimes we over-hear others saying, "Them colored people were slaves" down in Tennessee. The children feel hurt when they hear such remarks; but I tell them it was no disgrace in Tennessee to belong to Colonel Anderson. Many darkeys would have been proud, as I used to be, to call you master. Now if you will write and say what wages you will give me, I will be better able to decide whether it would be to my advantage to move back again.

As to my freedom, which you say I can have, there is nothing to be gained on that score, as I got my free papers in 1864 from the Provost-Marshal-General of the Department of Nashville. Mandy says she would be afraid to go back without some proof that you were dis-posed to treat us justly and kindly; and we have concluded to test your sincerity by asking you to send us our wages for the time we served you. This will make us forget and forgive old scores, and rely on your justice and friendship in the future. I served you faithfully for thirty-two years, and Mandy twenty years. At twenty-five dollars a month for me, and two dollars a week for Mandy, our earnings would amount to eleven thousand six hundred and eighty dollars. Add to this the interest for the time our wages have been kept back, and deduct what you paid for our clothing, and three doctor's visits to me, and pulling a tooth for Mandy, and the balance will show what we are in justice entitled to. Please send the money by Adams' Express, in care of V. Winters, Esq., Dayton, Ohio. If you fail to pay us for faithful labors in the past, we can have little faith in your promises in the future. We trust the good Maker has opened your eyes to the wrongs which you and your fathers have done to me and my fathers, in making us toil for you for generations without recompense. Here I draw my wages every Saturday night; but in Tennessee there was never any pay-day for the Negroes any more than for the horses and cows. Surely there will be a day of reckoning for those who defraud the laborer of his hire.

In answering this letter, please state if there would be any safety for my Milly and Jane, who are now grown-up, and both good-looking girls. You know how it was with poor Matilda and Catherine. I would rather stay here and starve—and die, if it come to that—than have my girls brought to shame by the violence and wickedness of their young masters. You will also please state if there has been any schools opened for the colored children in your neighborhood. The great desire of my life now is to give my children an education, and have them form virtuous habits.

Say howdy to George Carter, and thank him for taking the pistol from you when you were shooting at me.

From your old servant,

—JOURDON ANDERSON

*

"Whip Them with Pop-Guns"

*

JUDGE JOHN RICE was a very violent secessionist, and in a speech urging secession, said, "Why —— the Yankees! If they show fight, we can whip them with pop-guns." A short time after the war, Judge Rice was making a speech at the same cross-roads where he had made his boasting speech before the war. One of the audience asked if he was not the same Judge Rice that spoke there in 1860.

"I am," he replied.

"Well, didn't you say we could whip the Yankees with pop-guns?"

"I did; and we could have done it; but, —— 'em, they wouldn't fight us that way!"

—*The Bivouac*

569

He Might Have Slept with God

*

AFTER THE WAR, on nice days Lee was in the habit of riding Traveller around Lexington. On one occasion he was caught in a terrible storm and flash flood and found that he was not going to be able to get back to Lexington. As a result he spent the night with one of his old soldiers up on the hillside. It was a poor house and they didn't have too much furniture, but finally Lee was persuaded to go to bed when the man agreed that they would sleep together and his wife would sleep with the children. And so they spent the night, Lee and his old soldier, in the same bed.

The next day the old soldier was telling his friends about Lee having spent the night in his home.

"Where did he sleep?" they wanted to know.

"Why, he slept with me," he replied.

"How did it feel?"

"I'll tell you, I never closed an eye. I didn't sleep a wink. I might have slept with God."

—As told by ROSANNA A. BLAKE to B. A. BOTKIN

*

The Vanquished Saluting the Victor

*

MY FATHER, you know, was well in his eighties, when he learned in some way that I was near the end of a rather long study of the army in which he had belonged. He was a gentleman who loved the old phrasing and the old beautiful language, and he said to me, "My son,

570

I understand that you are writing a history of the Army of Northern Virginia."

I answered, "Not directly, sir, I'm writing a biography of General Lee in which, of course, the life of the army appears rather conspicuously."

"Well, it is a very good approach, to study the army through its commanding General, because nothing that every happened to us was more inspiring than the fact that we had General Lee as our commander. But I have one admonition to give you."

I asked, "What is that, sir?"

He replied, "Never depreciate the adversary. What honor was there for a Confederate, if he was supposed to be fighting a coward? They were not cowards, those men of the North. Indeed"—and he drew himself up with all his Confederate discipline of spirit—"Indeed, there never was a greater army in the world than the Army of the Potomac, save one, which modesty forbids me to mention."

—DOUGLAS SOUTHALL FREEMAN

*

Sleeping with Jackson

---

*

THE MORNING AFTER the unveiling of the Lee Statue in Richmond as the sun rose over the city, its first rays fell upon a row of figures, wrapped in gray blankets and sleeping on the grass around the Statue of Jackson in Capitol Square. One by one these sleepers began to unroll themselves—here a gray head, there a gray beard—got up, yawned and stretched themselves in the morning air. Just then a passing citizen said to them in kindly anxiety, "Heavens, men, could you find no other beds in Richmond last night?"

"Oh, yes, there was plenty of places; all Richmond was open to us," said one, and turning his eyes toward the silent face of his immortal chief he added, "but we were his boys and we wanted to sleep with the old man just once more."

—MAJOR HENRY KYD DOUGLAS

The Widow from Maine

*

AFTER THE BATTLE of Williamsburg, when the Confederate army, though victorious, fell back, like a spent wave, in the tempest-tossed tide of war, it left wrecks upon the shore—human wrecks, men wounded and maimed and dying, victor and vanquished. Confederate and Federal intermingled in one common plight of suffering and anguish. The good women of the little town came forward to minister to the sufferers, and all, of course, wanted to nurse the Confederates. But as this would have left no one to care for the Yankees, it was decided that the younger women should have the privilege of tending their own men, while the older ones should take care of the wounded "enemy." To one of these ladies was assigned a man from Maine, whose condition was so desperate it was evident he must soon die. His nurse did all she could for him, and wrote for him a letter to his wife. He was conscious of his approaching end, and among his last requests was the one that his grave should be marked, and his wife told of it, for he said, "I know she will want to come for me, if she can find my grave, and move me back home." The man soon after died, and the lady, faithful to her trust, marked the grave and sent the widow her husband's dying message.

The war closed, and several years later the soldier's widow wrote to Williamsburg that she was coming to move her husband's remains back to Maine, and she accordingly arrived on the day appointed. Her friend, the Williamsburg lady, accompanied the woman to the grave yard and pointed out the spot where the soldier was buried. But she said, "It has been so long since your husband died, the coffin must have fallen to pieces, and there should be another provided."

"You never mind about that," was the response; "let them men there dig him up," pointing to some Negro workmen near at hand. And they began to dig—down, down went the spades, until finally they struck the broken and crumbling remains of a coffin in which lay the skeleton of the poor soldier. The Williamsburg lady had noticed that the Yankee woman had brought with her a large enameled cloth *carpet-bag* (it was the era of the "carpet-baggers") and at the point where the ghastly spectacle of the skeleton came to light, the carpet-bag was brought forward, and opened. "Now," said the widow, "you men just double him up and put him in here." And so the skeleton was doubled up, and without further ado stowed away in the carpet-bag and the key turned in the lock. The Virginia lady was struck dumb with horror. But, after all, it was no affair of hers, so she silently walked by the woman's side, as she made her way, carpet-bag in hand, to the railroad station, where, taking her seat in the train, she called out cheerfully, "Good-by!" as she dumped her spouse down on the floor beside her.

—KATE MASON ROWLAND

*

They Met at the Panorama
of the Battle of Shiloh

*

AT THE PANORAMA of the Battle of Shiloh in this city [of Chicago] a few days ago a small shriveled-up man made himself conspicuous by going around the place sniveling dolorously. He did not appear to be more than five feet high. He was dressed all in black and his attenuated form and gray whiskers gave him a peculiarly grotesque appearance. He seemed to be greatly interested in the panorama and as he moved from one point of view to another he groaned and wept copiously. A tall, raw-boned man approached him; he wore gray clothes and a military slouch hat and he had the general appearance of a Missourian away from home on a holiday.

"Reckon you were at Shiloh, eh, stranger?" asked the tall, raw-boned man.

"Yes," replied the small, shriveled-up man, "and I shall never forget it; it was the toughest battle of the war."

573

"I was thar," said the tall, raw-boned man, "and my regiment was drawn up right over yonder where you see that clump of trees."

"You were a rebel, then?"

"I was a Confederate," replied the tall, raw-boned man, "and I did some right smart fighting among that clump of trees that day."

"I remember it well," said the small, shriveled-up man, "for I was a Federal soldier, and the toughest scrimmage in all that battle was just among that clump of trees."

"Prentiss was the Yankee General," remarked the tall, raw-boned man, "and I'd have given a pretty to have seen him that day. But, doggone me, the little cuss kept out of sight, and we'uns came to the conclusion he was hidin' back in the rear somewhar."

"Our boys were after Marmaduke," said the small, shriveled-up man, "for he was the rebel General and had bothered us a great deal. But we could get no glimpse of him—he was too sharp to come to the front, and it was lucky for him, too."

"Oh; but what a scrimmage it was!" said the tall, raw-boned man.

"How the sabers clashed and how the Minies whistled!" cried the small, shriveled-up man.

The panorama brought back the old time with all the vividness of yesterday's occurrence. The two men were filled with a strange yet beautiful enthusiasm.

"Stranger," cried the tall, raw-boned man, "we fought each other like devils that day and we fought to kill. But the war's over now, and we ain't soldiers any longer—gimme your hand!"

"With pleasure," said the small, shriveled-up man, and the two clasped hands.

"What might be your name?" inquired the tall, raw-boned man.

"I am General B. M. Prentiss," said the small, shriveled-up man.

"The —— you say!" exclaimed the tall, raw-boned man.

"Yes," reaffirmed the small, shriveled-up man; "and who are you?"

"I," replied the tall, raw-boned man, "I am General John S. Marmaduke."

—Chicago News

Point of View

WE HAVE A FRIEND, a Miss Anderson who lives in Washington, D. C. One time another mutual friend, an army officer, invited her to go with him to the battlefield of Gettysburg. Arriving there they went to the scene of Pickett's Charge, which he was studying. He said to the young lady: "Now this is where the troops were and the enemy was over there," indicating the position.

Miss Anderson said: "No, the enemy was [where] the troops were and the troops were over there"—indicating the opposite situation.

He said: "No, you do not understand—the troops were here and the enemy were there."

To which she replied: "I understand you, but I still maintain that the troops were *here* and the enemy there," as she had previously indicated.

Her friend paused, looked quizzically at her for a few moments and then said: "Where were you born and reared?"

With a smile she replied: "In Tennessee."

—ANNIE C. MASSEY

"It Was Best"

[SHE] is in her eighties, the daughter of one of Stonewall Jackson's bodyguard, and indomitably Virginian. Not so many years ago, at an age when few of us would be interested in further pursuit of

575

learning, she enrolled in a university summer course in the history of the South. One day during the session, the lecturer made the usual comment, namely, that it was best that the war had ended with a Northern victory. Later on during his talk he made the same apologetic interjection. The smoldering little lady could stand his treason no longer. She rose from her chair and interrupted him.

"Professor," she challenged, "you keep saying that it was best that the North won the war. But how do you know? We didn't get a chance to even *try* it our way."

—Hodding Carter

*

"That Wasn't the Way It Happened"

*

I REMEMBER a Civil War story that I used to hear Irvin S. Cobb tell when he was a newspaper reporter and I was a struggling lawyer in Paducah. It seemed that two Confederate veterans were reminiscing about the days during the war when Paducah was being fought over by the Northern and Southern forces. "I remember," one veteran said, "when we pushed those damyankees all the way across the Ohio and up into Illinois!" The other old soldier regretfully corrected him. "I was there, old friend," he said, "and I'm afraid that wasn't the way it happened at all. Those Yankees drove *us* out of Paducah and almost to the Tennessee line." The first veteran reflected a bit, then sourly remarked, "Another good story ruined by an eyewitness!"

—Alben W. Barkley

Notes

FULL TITLES AND SUBTITLES, author and publication data are given only the first time a work is cited. Thereafter, if an author is represented by more than one work, the title of each work is repeated; otherwise, the author's name and *op. cit.* are used.

MOTTO

Sam R. Watkins, Columbia, Tenn., *1861 vs. 1862: "Co. Aytch," Maury Grays, First Tennessee Regiment: Or, A Side Show of the Big Show* (Nashville, Tenn.: Cumberland Presbyterian Publishing House, 1882), p. 11.

INTRODUCTION

MOTTO: Ambrose Bierce, "What I Saw of Shiloh," *The Collected Works of Ambrose Bierce* (New York: The Neale Publishing Co., 1909), I, 234.

[1] "Specimen Days and Collect" (copr. 1882 by Walt Whitman), *Complete Poems and Prose of Walt Whitman, 1855 . . . 1888: Authenticated & Personal Book (Handled by W. W.),* (Philadelphia: [The Author, 1888]), pp. 44-45 ("Soldiers and Talks"); pp. 80-81 ("The Real War Will Never Get in the Books").

[2] F. Y. Hedley, Adjt. 32d Ill. Inf., *Marching Through Georgia: Pen-Pictures of Every-Day Life in General Sherman's Army, from the Beginning of the Atlanta Campaign Until the Close of the War* (Chicago: Donohue, Henneberry & Co., 1890), pp. 293-294.

[3] "The Art of Story Telling," *The Southern Packet* (Asheville, N.C.: The Stephens Press), II (February, 1946), 4.

ONE: 1861

MOTTO: "In Eighteen Hundred and Sixty-one," informant Bertha Pendergraph, Durham, N.C., in *The Frank C. Brown Collection of North Carolina Folklore,* general ed. Newman Ivey White (Durham, N.C.: Duke University Press, 1952), *Vol. II: Folk Ballads from North Carolina,* eds. Henry M. Belden and Arthur Palmer Hudson, p. 528.

The stanza begins:

In eighteen hundred and sixty-one,
    hurrah, hurrah,
In eighteen hundred and sixty-one,
    hurrah, says I.

The song is sung to the tune of "When Johnny Comes Marching Home."

1. MR. LINCOLN COMES TO WASHINGTON

MOTTO: Lincoln Campaign Song of 1860 (tune, "The Old Gray Mare"), in Carl Sandburg, ed. *The American Songbag* (New York: Harcourt, Brace & Co., 1927), p. 168.

A SCOTCH CAP AND A MILITARY CLOAK: I. Joseph Howard's Dispatch. Joseph Howard, Jr., *New York Times,* February 25, 1861, p. 1. II. A Belated Explanation. Joseph Howard, Jr., *Philadelphia Press,* reprinted in the *Burlington* (Vt.) *Free Press,* November 21, 1884; as quoted in Louis A. Warren, "A Scotch Cap and Military Coat," *Lincoln Lore* (Fort Wayne, Ind.: The Lincoln National Life Foundation), No. 886, April 1, 1946.
I. The Scotch plaid cap may have been suggested by the plaid shawl which Lincoln carried, after the fashion of the time. Besides the Howard hoax, the mass hysteria occasioned by rumors and newspaper stories of the Baltimore plot inspired such crackpot schemes as the proposal of a former chemistry professor, A. H. Flanders, of Burlingon, Iowa, that the President be outfitted for the inaugural journey with a coat of steel mail, "plated with gold, so that the perspiration shall not affect it, and to be covered with silk and worn over an ordinary undershirt." (Letter to John G. Nicolay, January 12, 1861, quoted in *Lincoln Lore,* No. 1435, September, 1957, pp. 3-4.)
II. The "Wide Awakes" were an association of enthusiastic supporters of Lincoln in the 1860 campaign, originating in Hartford, Conn. They were known especially for their semi-military torchlight processions, in which they wore glazed caps and black cambric capes to protect them from the coal-oil torches, and displayed a banner with a wide-open eye below the word "Wide" and above the word "Awake."

A WAGER: C. B. Edwards, "An Incident of Lincoln's First White House Reception," *The Century Magazine,* LXXII (August, 1906), 636-637.

THE WAR COMET: Julia Taft Bayne, *Tad Lincoln's Father* (Boston: Little, Brown & Co., 1931), pp. 71-74.
Julia Taft was sixteen years old when Lincoln was inaugurated. With her two brothers, who were about the same age as Willie and Tad Lincoln, she was in and out of the White House during most of Lincoln's administration. Her girlhood memories, as she says, "cast a ray of human softness over the sad, stern face."

LINCOLN RAISES A NEW FLAG: *Ibid.,* pp. 114-117.

SHERMAN TELLS OF LINCOLN'S VISIT: William Tecumseh Sherman, *Memoirs of Gen. W. T. Sherman,* (4th ed.; New York: Charles L. Webster & Co., 1891), I, 215-219.

CHITTENDEN'S STORY OF LINCOLN AND THE SLEEPING SENTINEL: L. E. Chittenden, Lincoln's Register of the Treasury, *Recollections of President Lincoln and His Administration* (New York: Harper & Bros., 1891), pp. 266-280.
Waldo F. Glover defends the "general accuracy" of Chittenden's story of the "Sleeping Sentinel" in *Abraham Lincoln and the Sleeping Sentinel of Vermont* (Montpelier: The Vermont Historical Society, 1936). In *Abraham Lincoln: The War Years* (New York: Harcourt, Brace & Co., 1939), II, 528-533, Carl Sandburg debunks the story.

2. "SECESSION IS OUR WATCHWORD"

MOTTO: "The Southern Wagon" (tune, "Wait for the Wagon"), in Frank Moore, ed. *Anecdotes, Poetry and Incidents of the War: North and South, 1860-1865* (copr. 1865; New York: The Arundel Print, 1882), p. 397.

THE WAR COMES TO RICHMOND CHILDREN: Miss Sallie Hunt, Lynchburg, Va., in *"Our Women in the War": The Lives They Lived, the Deaths They Died; From The Weekly News and Courier, Charleston, S.C.*

578

(Charleston, S.C.: The News & Courier Book Presses, 1885), pp. 41-42.

THE *Pawnee* SUNDAY: A Richmond Lady [Mrs. Sallie A. Putnam], *Richmond During the War: Four Years of Personal Observation* (New York: G. W. Carleton & Co., 1867), pp. 24-26.

The celebration of April 19 marked the passage of the secession ordinance by the Virginia Convention in secret session on April 17. The Convention voted to submit the ordinance to popular vote, by which it was adopted on May 23.

EGGLESTON'S RIDE WITH STUART WITHIN THE UNION LINES: George Cary Eggleston, *A Rebel's Recollections* (2d ed.; New York: G. P. Putnam's Sons, 1878), pp. 117-120.

MAGRUDER AND SHARPE: PROMOTION BY POTION: In anecdote column, "Our Camp Chest," *Our Living and Our Dead, Devoted to North Carolina —Her Past, Her Present, and Her Future* (Raleigh, N.C.: Official Organ, N.C. Branch Southern Historical Society), I (November, 1874), 222-223.

CONGRESSIONAL "BULL RUNNERS": A CONFEDERATE VIEW: Mrs. Cornelia McDonald, Louisville, Ky., *A Diary with Reminiscences of the War and Refugee Life in the Shenandoah Valley, 1860-1865* (1875), annotated and supplemented by Hunter McDonald (Nashville, Tenn.: Cullom & Ghertner Co., 1935), pp. 29-31.

JACKSON STANDS LIKE A STONE WALL: *Charleston* (S.C.) *Mercury,* July 25, 1861.

In a letter to coeditor Gen. D. H. Hill (*New Eclectic Magazine,* IV [June, 1869], 746) Gen. W. P. Shingler writes: "The first appearance in print of these remarks will be found in a copy of the *Charleston Mercury* under the head of 'Telegraphs from Richmond,' two or three days after the battle [of Manassas]. This telegram was written by me, and forwarded by Capt. (afterwards Brig. Gen.) John Dunnovant. It is scarcely

necessary to say a word in vindication of the propriety or proper application of the figure of speech to General Jackson on that occasion. He was on a stationary line, resisting the current that had swept over General Bee; and then, too, it will be remembered that at the date of this occurrence, General Jackson had not electrified the country with the dash that better likened him to 'a thunderbolt of war than so pacific a thing as a stone wall.'"

In *Lee's Lieutenants* (New York, 1942), I, 733-734, Douglas Southall Freeman cites the testimony of Maj. Burnett Rhett in *The Reminiscences of Col. J. C. Haskell,* to the effect that "Bee said that his and Barstow's brigades were hard pressed and Jackson refused to move to their relief; and in a passionate expression of anger he denounced him for standing like a stone wall and allowing them to be sacrificed."

BEAUREGARD AND THE CONFEDERATE BATTLE-FLAG: Carlton McCarthy, Pvt. 2d. Co. Richmond Howitzers, Cutshaw's Bat. Art., 2d Corps A.N.V., *Detailed Minutiae of Soldier Life in the Army of Northern Virginia, 1861-1865* (Richmond: Carlton McCarthy & Co., 1882), pp. 219-223.

In *Recollections Grave and Gay* (New York: Charles Scribner's Sons, 1911), p. 61, Constance Cary (Mrs. Burton) Harrison gives her version of the making of the first battle flags. "It is generally stated by historians that these flags were constructed from our own dresses, but it is certain that we possessed no wearing apparel in the flamboyant hues of poppy red and vivid dark blue required. We had a great search for materials. I had to content myself with a poor quality of red silk for the field of mine, necessitating an interlining, which I regretted."

STUART AND GRIFFIN WERE CHUMS: Rev. Theodore Gerrish, Pvt. in the Army of the Potomac, and Rev. John S. Hutchinson, Pvt. in the Army of Northern Va., *The Blue and the Gray: A Graphic History of the Army of the Potomac and That of Northern Virginia, Including the Brilliant Engagements of These Forces from 1861 to 1865, the Campaigns of the Shenandoah Valley and the Army of the James, Together with Reminiscences of Tent and Field, Acts of Personal Daring, Deeds of Heroic Suffering and Thrilling Adventure, Coupled with Which Will Be Found Many Tales of Individual Achievements, Army Yarns, and Pen Pictures of Officers and Privates . . .* (Portland, Me.: Hoyt, Fogg & Donham, 1883), pp. 184-185.

The theme of "classmates divided" represents the officers' equivalent of rank and file fraternization between the opposing armies. Similar stories are told of other West Point classmates of Stuart, such as Capt. Perkinson and Orlando M. Poe. In a letter to me, Mrs. Lucy Rosser Herberick, of Darien, Conn., relates the following "classmates divided" story of her cousin, Maj. Gen. Thomas Lafayette Rosser, told to her by Rosser's daughter, Mrs. Elliott, of Charlottesville, Va.: "Once during the war, possibly in Custer's attack on Charlottesville, Rosser threw back over his shoulder his gray, red-lined cape. Custer, in the Yankee lines, noticed the glow of the bright red in the sunlight, and recognized his old friend. The next day, General Rosser received a note which, mysteriously, had come through the Yankee lines. It addressed him as 'Tam,' a nickname by which his West Point classmates had known him, and read as follows: 'Tam, do not expose yourself so. Yesterday I could have killed you. Custer.' "

See also "Fitzhugh Lee and Averell Exchange Notes," below.

CONFEDERATE OVERCOATS OF OIL-CLOTH TABLE-COVERS: "War Diary of a Union Woman in the South," ed. G. W. Cable, in *Famous Adventures and Prison Escapes of the Civil War* (New York: The Century Co., 1917), pp. 11-12.

JACKSON KEEPS THE SABBATH: Margaret J. Preston, "Personal Reminiscences of Stonewall Jackson," *The Century Magazine*, XXXII (October, 1886), 931-932.

THE MYSTERIOUS STRANGER: George Cary Eggleston, *op. cit.*, pp. 142-143.

A favorite theme of Civil War stories is that of the general who passes freely among his men and because of his unexpected, unfamiliar, or shabby appearance, or the ignorance or drunkenness of the soldier, is unrecognized and ridiculed or reviled by the latter. Sometimes the general is discovered asleep and is himself mistaken for drunk. In the end the general reprimands or disciplines the soldier but more often sees and laughs at the joke upon himself. From the point of view of the rank and file, these stories seemed to satisfy a desire for equality above etiquette—a desire that was especially strong among citizen soldiers, who saw something both admirable and amusing in getting back at or talking back to an officer and who at the same time liked to think that officers were "just folks."

3. "RALLY ROUND THE FLAG"

MOTTO: "I Want to Be a Soldier" (tune, "Wait for the Wagon") (Philadelphia: Johnson, Song Publisher, n.d.).

MRS. ANDERSON BRINGS REINFORCEMENT TO FORT SUMTER: Paul F. Mottelay, ed. *The Soldier in Our Civil War: A Pictorial History of the Conflict, 1861-1865, Illustrating the Valor of the Soldier as Displayed on the Battle-Field from Sketches Drawn by Forbes, Waud, Taylor, Hall, Becker, Lovie, Schell, Crane and Numerous Other Eye-Witnesses to the Strife* (New York: The J. H. Brown Publishing Co., 1884), I, 22-23.

FRANCIS BROWNELL AVENGES THE DEATH OF ELLSWORTH: Francis E. Brownell, 11th N. Y. Vol. Inf. (N. Y. Fire Zouaves), in *The Story of American Heroism: Thrilling Narratives of Personal Adventure During the Great Civil War, As Told by the Medal*

Winners and Roll of Honor Men (Chicago: The Werner Co., 1896), pp. 27-30.

In "Assassination of Ellsworth" (Philadelphia: Johnson, Song Publisher), one of several ballads on the subject, William Sutherland describes Brownell's revenge as follows:

Then the fearless private Brownell,
  when he saw his leader fall,
He rushed up to the traitor, and
  through his brain he sent a ball;
Then with his bayonet bright, he
  run him through and through.
And vowed that was the way he'd
  serve the whole Secession crew.

In her *Diary of a Southern Refugee During the War* (3d ed.; Richmond, 1889), Mrs. Judith W. McGuire gives Jackson's side of the story: "Fairfax Court House, May 25, 1861. Poor Jackson the proprietor [of the Marshall House] had always said that the Confederate flag which floated from the top of his house should never be taken down but over his dead body. It was known that he was a devoted patriot, but his friends had amused themselves at this rash speech. He was suddenly aroused by the noise of men rushing by his room-door, ran to the window, and seeing at once what was going on, he seized his gun, his wife trying in vain to stop him; as he reached the passage he saw Colonel Ellsworth coming from the third story, waving the flag. As he passed Jackson he said, 'I have a trophy.' Jackson immediately raised his gun, and in an instant Ellsworth fell dead. One of the party immediately killed poor Jackson. . . . Jackson leaves a wife and children. I know the country will take care of them. He is the first martyr. I shudder to think how many more there may be."

THE HAVELOCK AND THE "CAKE AND PIE BRIGADE": Mary A. Livermore, *My Story of the War: A Woman's Narrative of Four Years Personal Experience as Nurse in the Union Army, and in Relief Work at Home, in Hospitals, Camps, and at the Front, During the War of the Re-*bellion. *With Anecdotes, Pathetic Incidents, and Thrilling Reminiscences Portraying the Lights and Shadows of Hospital Life and the Sanitary Service of the War* (Hartford, Conn.: A. D. Worthington & Co., 1888), pp. 112-113.

"The decline of the Havelock fever," writes Mrs. Livermore (p. 121), "was followed by a 'lint and bandage' mania, which set in with great fury. . . . 'What is the best material for lint?' 'How is it best scraped and prepared?' 'By what means can it be best gathered, in the largest quantities?' These were the questions of the hour, discussed gravely by professional men. And the 'New York Medical Association for Furnishing Hospital Supplies' actually held meetings to discuss the lint question, and finally opened a 'lint and bandage depot.' Thus stimulated, every household gave its leisure time to scraping lint and rolling bandages, till the mighty accumulations compelled the ordering of a halt. A little later, the making of lint by machine relieved women of any further effort in this direction."

TOBY TESTS THE MAYNARD RIFLE: *The* (Oxford, Miss.) *Intelligencer,* as quoted in Frank Moore, ed. *The Rebellion Record: A Diary of American Events, with Documents, Narratives, Illustrative Incidents, Poetry, Etc.* (New York: G. P. Putnam, 1861), I, "Poetry and Incidents," 99.

FIGHTING PREACHER: Henry Howe, *The Times of the Rebellion in the West: A Collection of Miscellanies Showing the Part Taken in the War by Each Western State—Notices of Eminent Officers—Descriptions of Prominent Battles—Conspiracies in the West to Aid the Rebellion—Incidents of Guerrilla and Border Warfare — Individual Adventures — Anecdotes Illustrating the Heroism of Western Soldiers, Etc., Etc., Etc.* (Cincinnati: Howe's Subscription Book Concern, 1867), p. 38.

The "fighting preacher" is a familiar character in Civil War storytelling, folksy when he mixes religion with humor, and propagandist when he preaches hate. A comic variant is the battle-shy chaplain or theologian, to be seen in "The Parson Wasn't Hungry," below. For portraits of the Southern "fighting preacher," see Rev. H. A. Graves, *Andrew Jackson Potter: The Fighting Parson of the Texan Frontier* (Nashville, 1881), and John Thomason, Jr., *Lone Star Preacher: Being a Chronicle of the Acts of Praxiteles Swan, M. E. Church South, Captain, 5th Texas Regiment, Confederate States Provisional Army* (New York, 1945).

THE MUTINY OF THE HIGHLANDERS: Julia Taft Bayne, *op. cit.*, pp. 145-151.
Julia's "flat" was a broad-brimmed, low-crowned straw hat.

CORPORAL CASEY'S SCRIMMAGE: John Beatty, Lt. Col. 3d Ohio Vol. Inf., *The Citizen-Soldier: Or, Memoirs of a Volunteer* (Cincinnati: Wilstach Baldwin & Co., 1879), pp. 54-55.
"Who can really know what an army is," writes Beatty (p. vii), "unless he mingles with the individuals who compose it, and learns how they live, think, talk, and act?"

GRANT IS PAID IN HIS OWN COIN: As told by Capt. John R. Steere, Cincinnati Soldiers' Home, in the *Cincinnati Enquirer;* as quoted in *The* (N.Y.) *Sun,* July 26, 1885.

IT HAD HIS NAME ON IT: Ambrose Bierce, "On a Mountain," *op. cit.*, I, 229.

4. RUN, SLAVE, RUN

MOTTO: Elizabeth Hyde Botume, *First Days Amongst the Contrabands* (Boston: Lee & Shepard, 1893), p. 13.

BUTLER DECLARES RUNAWAY SLAVES "CONTRABAND OF WAR": Benjamin F. Butler, *Butler's Book: Autobiography and Personal Reminiscences of Major General Benj. F. Butler: A Review of His Legal, Political, and Military Career* (Boston: A. M.

Thayer & Co., 1892), pp. 256, 257-258.
Regarding the origin of the term "contraband of war," Nicolay and Hay note: "Whether the suggestion was struck out in Butler's interview with the flag-bearer, or at the general's mess-table in a confidential review of the day's work; or whether it originated with some imaginative member of his staff, or was contributed as a handy expedient by the busy brain of a newspaper reporter, will perhaps forever remain an historical riddle." (*Abraham Lincoln: A History,* New York, 1890, IV, 388.)

HOW WILLIAM TILLMAN RECAPTURED THE *S. J. Waring:* [Opening paragraph: William Wells Brown, *The Negro in the American Rebellion: His Heroism and His Fidelity* (new ed.; Boston: A. G. Brown & Co., 1880), p. 74.] Lt. Col. Charles S. Greene, late of the U.S.A., *Thrilling Stories of the Great Rebellion: Comprising Heroic Adventures and Hairbreadth Escapes of Soldiers, Scouts, Spies, and Refugees; Daring Exploits of Smugglers, Guerrillas, Desperadoes, and Others; Tales of Loyal and Disloyal Women; Stories of the Negro, Etc., Etc., With Incidents of Fun and Merriment in Camp and Field. Together with an Account of the Death of President Lincoln; Fate of the Assassins; Capture of Jefferson Davis, and End of the War* (Philadelphia: John E. Potter, 1866), pp. 22-25.

THESE TIMES JUST SUIT *Me!:* Albert D. Richardson, N. Y. *Tribune* Correspondent, *The Secret Service: The Field, the Dungeon, and the Escape* (Hartford, Conn.: American Publishing Co., 1865), pp. 175-176.
"Kingdom Coming" is by Henry C. Work (Chicago: Root & Cady, 1862).

REWARD FOR A RUNAWAY MASTER: *The Camp Kettle;* as quoted in Mary A. Hedrick, ed. *Incidents of the Civil War During the Four Years of Its Progress, 1861-1865* (Lowell, Mass.: Vox Populi Press; S. W. Huse & Co. 1888), p. 97.

"The *Camp Kettle* is a small sheet 'published every opportunity by the Field and Staff of the Roundhead Regiment, Colonel Leasure commanding, at Hilton Head.' "—M.A.H.

TWO: 1862

MOTTO: "Johnny, Come Fill Up the Bowl," as sung by Sally Neeley, Pine Bluff, Ark., to Mrs. Bernice Bowden, "Slave Narratives," compiled by workers of the Federal Writers' Project, Works Progress Administration, in seventeen states, 1936-38 (MSS in Rare Book Division, Library of Congress), II, Pt. V, "Arkansas Narratives," 186-187.

5. GONE TO LIVE IN A TENT

MOTTO: Henry Clay Work, "Grafted into the Army" (Chicago: Root & Cady, 1862).

THE INSANITY DODGE: As told by Col. Thomas B. Van Buren of the 102d N.Y., in Washington Davis, *Camp-Fire Chats of the Civil War: Being the Incident, Adventure and Wayside Exploit of the Bivouac and Battle Field, as Related by Veteran Soldiers Themselves. Embracing the Tragedy, Romance, Comedy, Humor and Pathos in the Varied Experiences of Army Life* . . . (Chicago: A. B. Gehman & Co., 1888), pp. 259-261.

THE COLONEL DID THE THINKING—AND WASHING: Warren Lee Goss, "Recollections of a Private—II: Campaigning to No Purpose," *The Century Magazine,* XXIX (December, 1884), 279.

THE BUGLER: Dan Owen Mason, Corp. Co. D, 6th Vt. Regt., "Letters to Miss Harriet B. Clark, West Glover, Orleans Co., Vt., Oct. 1861-Oct. 1865, from Dan Owen Mason." (MS in possession of Mrs. Maud Mason Botkin, his grandniece.) On May 1, 1862, Dan Mason was promoted to sergeant. On March 30, 1864, he was commissioned captain in the regular army, Co. H, 19th Regt. U. S. Colored Troops. On March 20, 1865, he returned to Glover on a furlough to marry Harriet. On November 20, 1865, while waiting to be mustered out, he died of yellow fever in camp near Brownsville, Tex.

For a discussion of bugle calls and their uses and accompanying words, see John D. Billings, *Hardtack and Coffee* (Boston, 1887), pp. 164-197, and O. W. Norton, *Army Letters, 1861-1865* (Chicago, 1903), pp. 323-326.

PASSOVER IN CAMP: Rabbi Bertram Wallace Korn, *American Jewry and the Civil War* (Philadelphia: The Jewish Publication Society of America, 1951), pp. 90-92.

Rabbi Korn quotes from J. A. Joel, 23d Regt. Ohio Vols., Fayette, W. Va., in *The Jewish Messenger,* New York, XIX (March 30, 1866), 2.

FORFEITS: Willoughby M. Babcock, Jr., ed. *Selections from the Letters and Diaries of Brevet Brigadier General Willoughby Babcock of the Seventy-fifth New York Volunteers: A Study of Camp Life in the Union Armies During the Civil War,* War of the Rebellion Series, Bull. No. 2 (n.p.: The University of the State of New York, Division of Archives and History, 1922), pp. 94-95.

ONE OF OUR CAMP SONGS: "THE GIRLS AT HOME": Corp. Dan Owen Mason, "Letters."

"THE BOYS HAD HOME-SICKNESS BAD": Leander Stillwell, Late of Co. D, 61st Ill. Inf., *The Story of a Common Soldier of Army Life in the Civil War 1861-1865* (Erie, Kan.: Franklin Hudson Publishing Co., 1920), pp. 69-71.

"FOOL LIEUTENANT": John William De Forest, *A Volunteer's Adventures: A Union Captain's Record of the Civil War,* ed. James H. Croushore (New

Haven: Yale University Press, 1946), pp. 23-24.

TWO KINDS OF "DAMNED FOOL": James Franklin Fitts, "Facetiae of the War," *The Bivouac, An Independent Military Magazine* (Boston: Edward F. Rollins), I (September, 1883), 259.

LOUSE RACE: Sam R. Watkins, *op. cit.,* p. 46.

THE JOINT-STOCK FRYING-PAN COMPANY: Charles E. Davis, Jr., *Three Years in the Army: The Story of the Thirteenth Massachusetts Volunteers from July 16, 1861, to August 1, 1864* (Boston: Estes & Lauriat, 1894), pp. 98-99.

COLONEL COULTER ORDERS A BAPTIZING: Maj. Abner R. Small, *The Road to Richmond: The Civil War Memoirs of Major Abner R. Small of the Sixteenth Maine Volunteers. Together with the Diary Which He Kept When He Was a Prisoner of War,* ed. Harold Adams Small (Berkeley: University of California Press, 1939), pp. 47-48. Reprinted by permission of the publishers.

COMRADES IN CONTROVERSY: George W. Darby, *Incidents and Adventures in Rebeldom, Libby, Belle-Isle, Salisbury* (Pittsburgh, Pa.: Press of Rawsthorne Engraving & Printing Co., n.d.), pp. 74-75.

CATO, THE SLAVE-COMEDIAN: Thomas Wentworth Higginson, late Col. 1st S. C. Vols., *Army Life in a Black Regiment* (Boston: Fields, Osgood & Co., 1870), pp. 11-13.

THE REVIVAL AT FREDERICKSBURG: Robert Stiles, Maj. of Art. A.N.V., *Four Years under Marse Robert* (New York: The Neale Publishing Co., 1910), pp. 139, 140-143.

6. BROTHERS' WAR

MOTTO: "The Battle of Antietam Creek," sung by Warde H. Ford at Central Valley, Calif., 1939, and recorded by Sydney Robertson, in

Duncan Emrich, ed. *Songs and Ballads of American History and the Assassination of Presidents,* Folk Music of the United States, Issued from the Collections of the Archive of American Folk Song, Long Playing Record L29 (Washington, D.C.: Library of Congress, Music Division, Recording Laboratory, n.d.).

MCCLELLAN PROTECTS A LANDMARK: Edward A. Pollard, *Lee and His Lieutenants: Comprising the Early Life, Public Services, and Campaigns of General Robert E. Lee and His Companions in Arms, With a Record of Their Campaigns and Heroic Deeds* (New York: E. B. Treat & Co., 1867), pp. 67-68.

FLOWERS FOR THE YANKEES: Mrs. Fannie Gaines Tinsley, "Mrs. Tinsley's War Recollections, 1862-1865," *The Virginia Magazine of History and Biography,* XXXV (October, 1927), 394-395.
Mrs. Seaton Garland Tinsley (1836-91) was the daughter of Dr. William Fleming Gaines, of "Powhite," Hanover Co., owner of Gaines's Mill, where the battle of June 27, 1862, was fought.

TWO BRAVE FELLOWS: Capt. D. P. Conyngham, A.D.C., *The Irish Brigade and Its Campaigns, With Some Account of the Corcoran Legion, and Sketches of the Principal Officers* (New York: William McSorley & Co., 1867), pp. 237-238.

FLIRTATIONS IN WARRENTON: George Alfred Townsend, *Campaigns of a Non-Combatant, And His Romaunt Abroad During the War* (New York: Blelock & Co., 1866), pp. 225, 227.

HOW COLONEL WILDER SOUGHT GENERAL BUCKNER'S ADVICE ON SURRENDER: John R. Procter, "A Blue and Gray Friendship," *The Century Magazine,* LIII (April, 1897), 944-945.

HENRY KYD DOUGLAS DROPS IN ON HIS FOLKS: Maj. Henry Kyd Douglas, as quoted in *History of the*

Corn Exchange Regiment, 118th Pennsylvania Volunteers, by The Survivors' Association, 118th (Corn Exchange) Regt. P.V. (Philadelphia, Pa.: J. L. Smith, 1888), pp. 91-94.

THE BARGAIN: John N. Edwards, Shelby and His Men: Or, The War in the West (Cincinnati: Miami Printing & Publishing Co., 1867), pp. 122-123.

BROTHERS DIVIDED: The Soldiers' and Sailors' Half-Dime Tales of the Late Rebellion (New York: Soldiers' and Sailors' Publishing Co., 1868), I, No. 13, 272.

7. THE BULLETS WHISTLE PRETTY

MOTTO: As told by Eli Billings to Clifton Johnson, Highways and Byways from the St. Lawrence to Virginia (New York: The Macmillan Co., 1913), p. 152.

The title of this section is taken from the sentence, "The bullets whistle pretty but we did not loose a man." It appears in a letter from Pvt. Alfred L. Hall, a distant kinsman of Abraham Lincoln, to his brother John J. Hall, Murfreesboro, Tenn., February 17, 1863, in Carl Sandburg's Lincoln Collector: The Story of Oliver R. Barrett's Great Private Collection (New York: Harcourt, Brace & Co., 1949), p. 102.

NEARLY BURIED ALIVE: Capt. D. P. Conyngham, op. cit., pp. 189-192.

HELPING A SURGEON TO HIS SENSES: Capt. Musgrove Davis, "Some Personal Experiences in the War," McClure's Magazine, IX (June, 1897), 663.

THE EMBALMER: George Alfred Townsend, op. cit., pp. 180-181.

"GO IT, MOLLY COTTONTAIL!": I. Rebel Refrain. Gen. John B. Gordon, of the Confederate Army, Reminiscences of the Civil War (New York: Charles Scribner's Sons, 1903),

p. 46. II. Vance's Version. Maj. Gen. A. W. Greeley, U.S.A., Ret., Reminiscences of Adventure and Service: A Record of Sixty-five Years (New York: Charles Scribner's Sons, 1927), p. 61.

At this time Col. Zebulon Baird Vance, of the 26th North Carolina, had been nominated for governor, but continued to serve until his election in August, 1862. His sally is said to have relieved the tension of his regiment, which suffered heavy losses in the battle.

A CRACK SHOT: Frank Moore, ed. Anecdotes, Poetry and Incidents of the War: North and South, 1860-1865, pp. 338-339.

CROCKER'S ERRAND OF MERCY: History of the Corn Exchange Regiment, 118th Pennsylvania Volunteers, pp. 76-78.

HE KEPT HIS PROMISE: John N. Edwards, op. cit., p. 123.

BUCK'S BABY: Maj. Robert Stiles, op. cit., pp. 130-131.

HOW BILL TUCKER GOT HURT: The Raleigh (N.C.) Register, n.d. (Clipping files in North Carolina Collection, University of North Carolina Library, Chapel Hill.)

LIEUTENANT BRADY INSISTED ON HIS RIGHTS: Maj. John Dwyer, "63d Regiment Infantry, Historical Sketch," in New York Monuments Commission for the Battlefields of Gettysburg and Chattanooga, Final Report on the Battlefield of Gettysburg (Albany, N.Y.: J. B. Lyon Co., Printers, 1902), II, 501-502.

8. HARD MARCHES, HARDTACK, SHORT FARE, AND SHORT WEAR

MOTTO: "Hard Crackers, Come Again No More" (tune, "Hard Times, Come Again No More," by Stephen Foster), in John D. Billings, formerly of Sickles' 3d and Hancock's 2d Corps, Army of the Potomac, *Hardtack and Coffee: Or, The Unwritten Story of Army Life, Including Chapters on Enlisting, Life in Tents and Log Huts, Jonahs and Beats, Offences and Punishments, Raw Recruits, Foraging, Corps and Corps Badges, the Wagon Trains, the Army Mule, the Engineer Corps, the Signal Corps, Etc.* (Boston: George M. Smith & Co., 1887), p. 119.

"For some weeks before the battle of Wilson's Creek, Mo. (August 10, 1861), where the lamented [Brig. Gen. Nathaniel] Lyon fell, the First Iowa Regiment had been supplied with a very poor quality of hard bread (they were not then [1861] called hard *tack*). During this period of hardship to the regiment, so history goes, one of its members was inspired to produce the following touching lamentation."—J.D.B., p. 118.

The title of this section is taken from the sentence, "But I will at once pass over the three years which followed—years of hard marches, 'hardtack,' short fare and short wear—victories and reverses—to the 9th of April at Appomattox." (A Private, "Reminiscences of Lee and Gordon at Appomattox Court-house," *Southern Historical Society Papers,* VIII, January, 1880, 37-38.)

THE HIGH PRICE OF CHICKENS: Lt. Col. Charles S. Greene, *op cit.,* p. 93.

"I MOURN YOUR UNTIMELY DEMISE": J. B. Polley, of Hood's Tex. Brig., *A Soldier's Letters to Charming Nellie* (New York: The Neale Publishing Co., 1908), pp. 108-110.

MAGRUDER AND THE HUNGRY SOLDIER: Frank Moore, ed. *Anecdotes, Poetry and Incidents of the War: North and South, 1860-1865,* p. 488.

CAPTAIN JACK AND THE SUTLER: As told by Captain Jack, in D. P. Conyngham, *The Irish Brigade and Its Campaigns,* pp. 232-235.
Conyngham's book exemplifies the fighting and comic spirit of the Irish-

man in the Civil War. For his qualities as a soldier and a joker see Ella Lonn, *Foreigners in the Confederacy* (Chapel Hill, 1940), pp. 228-234, and *Foreigners in the Union Army and Navy* (Baton Rouge, 1951), pp. 645-648.

"There was the Irish Brigade, in all the glory of a fair, free fight. Other men go into fights finely, sternly, or indifferently, but the only man that really loves it, after all, is the green, immortal Irishman. So there the brave lads from the old sod, with the chosen Meagher at their head, laughed and fought, and joked, as if it were the finest fun in the world. We saw one sitting on the edge of a ditch with his feet in the water, and the sun and the water, too, very hot, and he apparently wounded. As we rode by he called out to know if we had ever seen a boiled Irishman." (Thomas T. Ellis, *Leaves from the Diary of an Army Surgeon,* New York, 1863, p. 54.)

HOW JIM FERRIS GOT HIMSELF A PAIR OF LEGGIN'S: J. B. Polley, *op. cit.,* pp. 77-79.

UNPATRIOTIC FEET: Helen Dortch Longstreet, *In the Path of Lee's "Old War Horse"* (Atlanta, Ga.: A. B. Caldwell Publishing Co., 1917), p. 22.

THE MUD MARCH: Leverett D. Holden, *My First and Last Fights . . . , Fredericksburg to Gettysburg,* Delivered before the Malden Club, April 24, 1914; *Memories of the Civil War* (Malden, Mass.: S. Tilden, Printer), pp. 47-51.

THE SPOTTED COW'S HIDE: George H. Woodruff, *Fifteen Years Ago: Or, The Patriotism of Wills County* (Joliet, Ill.: Printed and Published for the Author by James Goodspeed, 1876), pp. 448-450.

9. HOME FRONT

MOTTO: A Comfort Note, as quoted in Lloyd Lewis, *Sherman, Fighting Prophet* (New York: Harcourt, Brace & Co., 1932), p. 240.

Mr. Davis Is Inaugurated: Constance Cary Harrison, "A Virginia Girl in the First Year of the War," *The Century Magazine*, xxx (August, 1885), 610.

A Heroine in Homespun: A Lady of Virginia [Mrs. Judith W. McGuire], *Diary of a Southern Refugee During the War* (3d ed.; Richmond, Va.: J. W. Randolph & English, 1889), pp. 98-100.

The Contraband's Prayer: Willoughby M. Babcock, Jr., *op. cit.*, p. 101.

"The Southerners Are a Noble Race": Kate Stone, *Brokenburn, The Journal of Kate Stone, 1861-1868*, ed. John Q. Anderson (Baton Rouge: Louisiana State University Press, 1955), pp. 109-110.

A Refugee Story for Young Confederates: [Edward M. Boykin,] *The Boys and Girls Stories of the War* (Richmond: West & Johnston [1863?]), pp. 1-8.

A Rebel Lady's Stratagem: [Mrs. Sallie A. Putnam,] *op. cit.*, pp. 165-166.

A Wartime Marriage: Mary Boykin Chesnut [wife of James Chesnut, Jr., U. S. Senator from South Carolina, 1859-61, and afterward an aide to Jefferson Davis and a brigadier general in the Confederate army], *A Diary from Dixie*, ed. Ben Ames Williams (Boston: Houghton Mifflin Co., 1949), pp. 248-249, 258-259, 260.
The story of Decca Singleton (Mrs. Alexander Cheves Haskell) was omitted by Isabella D. Martin and Myrta Lockett Avary in their edition of the Diary (New York: D. Appleton & Co., 1905). "Mrs. Chesnut of course does not say so, but her thoughts [on June 13, 1862] were certainly prompted by the fact that Decca . . . was about to have a baby. The baby was born a week later; and Decca . . . died on the 26th of June." —B.A.W., p. 248, n.

The Last Silk Dress: Gen. James Longstreet, "Our March against Pope," in *Battles and Leaders of the Civil War; Being for the Most Part Contributions by Union and Confederate Officers, Based upon "The Century War Series,"* eds. Robert Underwood Johnson and Clarence Clough Buel (New York: The Century Co., 1887-1888), II, 512-513.

A War Correspondent Among the Cotton-Brokers: Franc B. Wilkie (Poliuto), *Pen and Powder* (Boston: Ticknor & Co., 1888), pp. 224-227.

10. WOMEN AT THE FRONT

Motto: Clinton Scollard, "The Daughter of the Regiment (Fifth Rhode Island)," in Clinton Scollard and Wallace Rice, *Ballads of Valor and Victory: Being Stories in Song from the Annals of America* (New York: Fleming H. Revell Co., 1903), p. 87.

How Emma Edmonds Tamed a Rebel Vixen: S. Emma E. Edmonds, *The Female Spy of the Union Army: The Thrilling Adventures, Experiences, and Escapes of a Woman, as Nurse, Spy, and Scout, in Hospitals, Camps, and Battle-Fields* (Boston: DeWolfe, Fiske & Co. [1864]), pp. 90-97.

Kady Brownell Serves with the Fifth Rhode Island: Frank Moore, *Women of the War: Their Heroism and Self-Sacrifice* (Hartford: S. S. Scranton & Co., 1866), pp. 59-64.

Belle Boyd Aids Stonewall Jackson: I. Henry Kyd Douglas Tells How Belle Boyd Pinned a Rose on Him. Maj. Henry Kyd Douglas, *I Rode with Stonewall: Being Chiefly the War Experiences of the Youngest Member of Jackson's Staff from the John Brown Raid to the Hanging of Mrs. Surratt* (Chapel Hill: The University of North Carolina Press, 1940), pp. 51-52. II. Belle Boyd Recalls Her Wild Ride on Fleeta. As Told by Belle Boyd to reporter Charles F. W. Archer, in *Stories of Our Soldiers: War Reminiscences by "Carleton" and by Soldiers of New England, Collected from the Series Written Especially for The Boston Journal* (Boston: The Journal Newspaper Co., 1893), 2d Ser., pp. 47-48.

MOTHER BICKERDYKE CUTS RED TAPE: I. The "Tin Cup Brigade." Frank Moore, *Women of the War*, p. 468. II. The Delinquent Surgeon. Dr. L. P. Brockett, *Lights and Shadows of the Great Rebellion: Or, The Camp, the Battle Field and Hospital, Including Thrilling Adventures, Daring Deeds, Heroic Exploits, and Wonderful Escapes of Spies and Scouts, Together with the Songs, Ballads, Anecdotes, and Humorous Incidents of the War* (Philadelphia: William Flint, 1866), pp. 295-296. III. "Loyal Cows and Hens." Mary A. Livermore, *op. cit.*, pp. 511-514.

II. and III. The 1863 Gayoso Hospital exploits of Mrs. Bickerdyke have been placed here in order to keep the Bickerdyke material together. In addition to her defiance of army protocol and red tape, Mother Bickerdyke was noted for her devotion to the rank and file. "That homely figure, clad in calico, wrapped in a shawl, and surmounted with a 'Shaker' bonnet," Mary A. Livermore (p. 477) quotes an officer as saying, "is more to this army than the Madonna to the Catholics."

PHOEBE YATES PEMBER LENDS A HELPING HAND: I. "You Wait!" II. A Compliment. III. "You Can Let Go." IV. Rats. Phoebe Yates Pember, *A Southern Woman's Story* (New York: G. W. Carleton & Co., 1879), pp. 37-40, 40-42, 73-76, 102-104.

III. and IV. These two stories belong to 1863; they have been placed here in order to keep the Pember material together.

11. "A FIGHTING RACE"

MOTTO: Song written by a private in Co. A, 54th (colored) Regt., Mass.

Vols., in *The Boston Transcript;* as quoted in William Wells Brown, *op. cit.*, p. 158.

HARRIET TUBMAN ACCOMPANIES THE UNION GUN-BOATS: Sarah H. Bradford, *Scenes in the Life of Harriet Tubman* (Auburn: W. J. Moses, Printer, 1869), pp. 38-42.

Although Harriet Tubman's gunboat expedition with Col. James Montgomery took place in 1863, she has been placed here as the "Moses" of her "fighting race." A slave from the eastern shore of Maryland, she first became famous before the war as an Underground Railroad conductor who led her people out of bondage, from Maryland to Canada. During the war she served as nurse and scout.

THE CAPTAIN OF THE *Planter:* House Rept. No. 3505, 49th Cong., 2d Sess.; as quoted in House Rept. No. 120, 55th Cong., 2d Sess., subject, *Robert Smalls,* January 12, 1898 (Washington, D.C.: Government Printing Office, 1898), pp. 1-3.

The feat of this twenty-three-year-old South Carolina slave made him a hero overnight. Thereafter he took part in many fights as blockading pilot, visited the President, and became master of the *Planter* in the supply service of the Quartermaster's Department. After the war he was a leader in the "equalization war," as state representative and senator, delegate to the Republican convention which nominated Grant, brigadier general of the state militia, congressman, and Beaufort's leading citizen.

"WE ARE WILLING TO FIGHT": Benjamin F. Butler, *op. cit.*, pp. 491-493.

"One regiment was mustered within fourteen days of the call, the first regiment of colored troops ever mustered into the service of the United States during the War of the Rebellion; established and became soldiers of the United States on the 22d day of August, 1862."—B.F.B., p. 493.

According to Benjamin Quarles, in

The Negro in the Civil War (Boston, 1953), p. 113, it was "on September 27, 1862 [that] this group of free Negroes was mustered in as 'The First Regiment Louisiana Native Guards,' thus becoming the first Negro soldiers mustered as a unit into the United States Army during the Civil War. The Native Guards were proud of their regiment and were fond of calling themselves the 'Chasseurs d'Afrique.'" Quarles describes other attempts to jump the gun made in August, 1862, by Col. David Hunter, in South Carolina, and in June and October by Brig. Gen. Jim Lane in Kansas.

A VETERAN EXPLAINS WHY THE UNION ARMY LET NEGROES FIGHT: As told by Richard Slaughter, in *The Negro in Virginia,* compiled by workers of the Writers' Program of the Work Projects Administration in the State of Virginia, sponsored by The Hampton Institute (New York: Hastings House, 1940), pp. 194-195.

12. DANGER WAS THEIR
BUSINESS

MOTTO: "I'll Lay Ten Dollars Down," Basil W. Duke, *Reminiscences of General Basil W. Duke, C.S.A.* (Garden City, N.Y.: Doubleday, Page & Co., 1911), p. 295.

THE ANDREWS RAID: Rev. William Pittenger, 2d Ohio Vols., in *Battles and Leaders of the Civil War,* II, 709-716.

CHICKASAW THE SCOUT GOES AFTER SALT: L. H. Naron, in R. W. Surby, *Grierson Raids, and Hatch's Sixty-four Days March: With Biographical Sketches, Also the Life and Adventures of Chickasaw, the Scout* (Chicago: Rounds & James, Steam Book & Job Printers, 1865), pp. 314-316.

THE MAN IN BLUE: J. H. Clark, 1st Lt., Bvt. Capt., Co. H, 115th N. Y. Vols., Half Moon, N.Y., in *The Story of Our Mess and Other Stories of the War, Told by Soldiers and Sailors: Reprinted from the New York Weekly Tribune; The Tribune Prize War Stories* (Lovell's Library [New York: John W. Lovell Co.]), xx, May 7, 1887, No. 966, 157-164.

13. HIGH COMMAND

MOTTO: Eleanor Gridley, *The Story of Abraham Lincoln: Or, The Journey from the Log Cabin to the White House* (copr. 1902; Chicago and New York: M. A. Donohue & Co., 1927), p. 332.

GRANT READS THE SIGNS: "Anecdotes of General Grant," *The New York Daily Tribune,* August 5, 1885.

GENERAL FITZ-JOHN PORTER AND THE RUNAWAY BALLOON: C. B. Fairchild, of Co. "D," compiler, *History of the 27th Regt. N. Y. Vols.: Being a Record of Its More Than Two Years of Service in the War for the Union, from May 21st, 1861, to May 31st, 1863. With a Complete Roster, and Short Sketches of Commanding Officers. Also, a Record of Experience and Suffering of Some of the Comrades in Libby and Other Rebel Prisons* (Binghamton, N.Y.: Carl & Matthews, Printers, 1888), pp. 46-48.

JOHNSON PRAYS WITH MOODY: As told by Abraham Lincoln, in F. B. Carpenter, *Six Months at the White House with Abraham Lincoln: The Story of a Picture* (New York: Hurd & Houghton, 1866), pp. 102-103.

BEAUTY AND THE "BEAST": BUTLER'S "WOMAN ORDER": Benjamin F. Butler, *op. cit.,* pp. 414, 416-419.

HOW "FIGHTING JOE" HOOKER WON HIS SOBRIQUET: Sidney V. Lowell, proofreader of the New York *Courier and Enquirer,* as quoted in John Bigelow, Jr., Maj. U.S.A., Ret., *The Campaign of Chancellorsville: A Strategic and Tactical Study* (New Haven: Yale University Press, 1910), p. 6.

For a discussion of various derivations of Hooker's sobriquet, see Walter H. Hebert, *Fighting Joe*

Hooker (New York, 1944), pp. 91, 318-319.

According to Samuel P. Bates ("Chancellorsville Revisited by General Hooker," *The Century Magazine,* XXXIII, 779), "the general never heard [the epithet, 'Fighting Joe,'] without expressing his deep regret that it was ever applied to him. 'People will think I am a highwayman or a bandit,' he said; when in fact he was one of the most kindly and tender-hearted of men."

THE FIRST DUTY OF A SOLDIER: J.H.L., in *Battles and Leaders of the Civil War,* II, 276.

THE RIVALS: Maj. Henry Kyd Douglas, *op. cit.,* pp. 177-178; as heard from Col. Wright of McClellan's staff.

"FIRST WITH THE MOST" FORREST: Gen. Basil W. Duke, *op. cit.,* pp. 344-346.

HINDMAN'S LETTER-WRITING RUSE: John N. Edwards, *op. cit.,* pp. 188-191.

JEFFERSON DAVIS TAKES ORDERS FROM LEE: Constance Cary Harrison, "A Virginia Girl in the First Year of the War," pp. 613-614; as heard from the author's husband, Col. Burton Harrison, private secretary to Jefferson Davis.

JACKSON'S BRIDGE-BUILDER: J. William Jones, "Reminiscences of the Army of Northern Virginia," Paper No. 8, "Seven Days around Richmond," *Southern Historical Society Papers,* IX (October, November, December [combined] 1881), Nos. 10-11-12, 564.

A SPECIAL PROVIDENCE: J. William Jones, *op. cit.,* pp. 566-567.

SHERMAN AND THE MEMPHIS MINISTER: E. V. Smalley, "General Sherman," *The Century Magazine,* XXVII (February, 1884), 460-461.

KEARNY MISTAKES THE CONFEDERATES FOR HIS OWN MEN: Thomas

Kearny, *General Philip Kearny, Battle Soldier of Five Wars: Including the Conquest of the West by General Stephen Watts Kearny* (New York: G. P. Putnam's Sons, 1937), pp. 387-388.

MAGRUDER AND HIS OLD E COMPANY: Franc B. Wilkie, *op. cit.,* pp. 187-189.

THE "BISHOP" BRAZENS IT OUT: "Co. Aytch" [Sam R. Watkins], *The Southern Bivouac* (Louisville, Ky.: Tne Courier-Journal Job Printing Co.), II (May, 1884), 403-404.

SHERMAN AND THE COLDWATER BRIDGE: John J. Taylor, Capt. U. S. Vols., "Reminiscences of Services as an Aide-de-Camp with General William Tecumseh Sherman," in *War Talks in Kansas: A Series of Papers Read Before the Kansas Commandery of the Military Order of the Loyal Legion of the United States* (Kansas City, Mo.: Franklin Hudson Publishing Co., 1906), pp. 137-138.

14. "FIRST GENTLEMAN OF VIRGINIA"

MOTTO: R. E. Lee to Gen. Winfield Scott, Arlington, Va., April 20, 1861, tendering his resignation from the U. S. Army; as quoted in Capt. Robert E. Lee, *Recollections and Letters of General Robert E. Lee* (New York: Doubleday, Page & Co., 1904), p. 25.

THE ORIGIN OF THE LEE TOMATOES: Maj. W. Roy Mason, C.S.A., in *Battles and Leaders of the Civil War,* II, 277.

FATHER AND SON: Rev. J. William Jones, *Personal Reminiscences, Anecdotes and Letters of Gen. Robert E. Lee* (New York: D. Appleton & Co., 1874), p. 182.

THE TREES OF CHATHAM: J. Horace Lacy, "Lee at Fredericksburg," *The Century Magazine,* XXXII (August, 1886), 606.

WHAT LEE SAID AT FREDERICKS-BURG: W. N. Pendleton "Personal Recollections of General Lee: An Address delivered at Washington and Lee University, at the Request of the University Authorities, on General Lee's Birthday, Jan. 19, 1873," *The Southern Magazine,* Official Organ of the Southern Historical Society (Baltimore, Md.: Turnbull Bros.), VIII (December, 1874), 620.

Commenting on the deaths of Brig. Gens. Maxcy Gregg and Thomas R. R. Cobb at Fredericksburg, the editor of the *Southern Literary Messenger* said: "The annihilation of the entire Yankee nation . . . would hardly compensate for the death of the meanest Southern private, much less such heroic spirits as Gregg and Cobb." (Quoted in E. Merton Coulter, *The Confederate States of America, 1861-1865,* Baton Rouge, 1950, p. 74.)

15. STONEWALL WAS "A POWERFUL FIGHTIN' AND PRAYIN' MAN"

MOTTO: Jennings Cropper Wise, *The Long Arm of Lee: Or, The History of the Artillery of the Army of Northern Virginia* (Lynchburg, Va.: J. P. Bell Co., 1915), I, 106, n.

"I WISH THE YANKEES WERE IN HELL": Maj. Henry Kyd Douglas, *op. cit.,* pp. 20-21.

WHY STONEWALL JACKSON DID NOT DRINK: Col. A. R. Boteler, in the *Philadelphia Weekly Times;* as quoted in "Sparks from the Camp Fire," *Southern Historical Society Papers,* X (June, 1882), 287.

"KILL THE BRAVE ONES": As told by Dr. Hunter McGuire to Maj. Robert Stiles, *op. cit.,* pp. 245-246.

JACKSON ON DODGING: *Southern Punch* (Richmond: Overall, Campbell, Hughes & Co.), II (July 2, 1864), 5.

WHY JACKSON CLEANED UP THE BATTLEFIELD: Lt. Col. W. W. Black-ford, C.S.A., *War Years with Jeb Stuart* (New York: Charles Scribner's Sons, 1945), pp. 81-82.

JACKSON TAKES A NAP: Maj. Henry Kyd Douglas, *op. cit.,* pp. 115-116.

JACKSON DISOBEYS HIS OWN ORDERS: Charles Minor Blackford, Capt., Wise Troop, Co. B, 2d Va. Cav., in *Letters from Lee's Army: Or, Memoirs of Life in and out of the Army of Virginia During the War Between the States,* compiled by Susan Leigh Blackford, from original and contemporaneous memoirs, correspondence and diaries, annotated by her husband Charles Minor Blackford, edited and abridged for publication by Charles Minor Blackford, III (New York and London: Charles Scribner's Sons, 1947), pp. 87-88.

"NOTHING ELSE WILL SUIT A MULE": *Ibid.,* pp. 101-103.

A YANKEE'S TROPHIES: *Ibid.,* pp. 109-110.

JUBAL EARLY REPLIES TO JACKSON: Gen. D. H. Hill, late of the Southern Army, in "The Haversack," *The Land We Love* (Charlotte, N.C.), I (May, 1866), 71-72.

A NEW COAT FOR STONEWALL: Maj. Heros Von Borcke, Chief of Staff to Gen. J. B. Stuart, *Memoirs of the Confederate War for Independence* (London: 1866; reprinted New York: Peter Smith, 1938), I, 295-297.

16. JEB STUART "JINES" THE CAVALRY

MOTTO: Jeb Stuart's Song, in Capt. Thomas Nelson Conrad, A.N.V., *The Rebel Scout: A Thrilling History of Scouting Life in the Southern Army* (Washington: The National Publishing Co., 1904), p. 80.

A FAIR EXCHANGE: Maj. Henry Kyd Douglas, *op. cit.,* pp. 133-134.

JEB STUART'S BALL: Lt. Col. W. W. Blackford, *op. cit.*, pp. 140-142. Cf. the account by Maj. Heros von Borcke, *op. cit.*, I, 193-198.

BOOTS AND SPURS IN BED: Maj. Henry Kyd Douglas, *op. cit.*, pp. 196-197.

JEB STUART TO OLD ABE: U. R. Brooks, ed. *Stories of the Confederacy* (Columbia, S.C.: The State Co., 1912), p. 125.

17. FATHER ABRAHAM

MOTTO: John Hay, "Life in the White House in the Time of Lincoln," *The Century Magazine*, XLI (November, 1890), 35.

STODDARD TELLS OF HIS TARGET PRACTICE WITH THE PRESIDENT: William O. Stoddard, Lincoln's private secretary, 1861-64, quoted in *Lincoln's Anecdotes: A Complete Collection of the Anecdotes, Stories, and Pithy Sayings of the Late Abraham Lincoln, 16th President of the United States* (New York: The American News Co., 1867), pp. 40-41.

ANECDOTES AS ANTIDOTES: I. "This Occasional Vent." Hon. Henry J. Raymond, as quoted in F. B. Car-
penter, *op. cit.*, pp. 151-152. II. Advice to a Sad Senator. Address of Hon. Theodore Burton, at the Twenty-third Annual Lincoln Dinner of the Republican Club of the City of New York, February 12, 1909, *Addresses Delivered at the Lincoln Dinners of the Republican Club of New York in Response to the Toast Abraham Lincoln, 1887-1909* (New York: The Republican Club of the City of New York, 1909), pp. 307-308.

LINCOLN PRAYS WITH A DYING CONFEDERATE SOLDIER: Albert H. Griffith, *The Heart of Abraham Lincoln, Man of Kindness and Mercy*. Historical Bull. No. 6 (Madison: Lincoln Fellowship of Wisconsin, 1948), pp. 11-12.

MCCLELLAN'S BODYGUARD: O. M. Hatch, as quoted in Francis Fisher Browne, *The Every-Day Life of Abraham Lincoln: A Narrative and Descriptive Biography with Pen-Pictures and Personal Recollections by Those Who Knew Him* (New York and London: G. P. Putnam's Sons, 1915), pp. 417-418.

LINCOLN VISITS THE CONTRABAND CAMP: John E. Washington, *They Knew Lincoln* (New York: E. P. Dutton & Co., 1942), pp. 83-87.

THREE: 1863

MOTTO: "Johnny, Come Fill Up the Bowl," in *Louisiana, A Guide to the State,* compiled by workers of the Writers' Program of the Work Projects Administration in the State of Louisiana (New York: Hastings House, 1941), p. 472.

18. "FREE AT LAST"

MOTTO: As sung by Annie Harris, of Petersburg, Va., in Writers' Program, WPA, *The Negro in Virginia,* pp. 211-212.

HOW LINCOLN SIGNED THE EMANCIPATION PROCLAMATION: *The Rochester* (N.Y.) *Express;* as quoted in F. B. Carpenter, *op. cit.*, pp. 269-270.

WHEN THE ANGELS STRUCK THE BANJO STRINGS: William Wells Brown, *My Southern Home: Or, The South and Its People* (Boston: A. G. Brown & Co., 1880), pp. 154-159.

"LINKUM COMIN' WID HIS CHARIOT": Maj. Abner R. Small, *op. cit.,* pp. 95-96.

"MASSA LINKUM": F. B. Carpenter, *op. cit.*, pp. 208-209.

A DILEMMA: Robert Talley, *The Commercial Appeal*, Memphis, Tenn., Centennial Edition, January 1, 1940, Sect. K, p. 4.

THE TOWN CLOCK OF VICKSBURG: *True Stories of the War for the Union: Written by Union Soldiers and Sailors, Who Bore a Part in the Incidents Narrated; Library of Tribune Extras, The Tribune Monthly,* V (March, 1893), 32.

19. MAN OF THE PEOPLE

MOTTO: John Hay, Diary, Dec. 23, 1863, in Tyler Dennett, ed. *Lincoln and the Civil War in the Diaries and Letters of John Hay . . .* (New York: Dodd, Mead & Co., 1939), p. 143.

THE SWEAT-BOX: Emanuel Hertz, "Collection of Various Material Relating to Abraham Lincoln," I, 231-233. (Emanuel Hertz Scrapbooks in New York Public Library.)

THE GRANT WHISKEY STORY: Francis Fisher Browne, *op. cit.,* p. 524.
"[When Major Thomas T. Eckert] asked Mr. Lincoln if the story of his interview with complainants against General Grant was true . . . Mr. Lincoln said that he had heard the story before, and that it would have been very good if he had said it, but that he didn't. He supposed it was 'charged to him, to give it currency.' He then said the original of the story was in King George's time. Bitter complaints were made to the King against his General Wolfe, in which it was charged that he was mad. The King replied angrily: 'I wish he would bite some of my other generals then.' " (Albert B. Chandler, in *Abraham Lincoln: Tributes from His Associates,* New York, 1895, pp. 219-220.)

MR. LINCOLN'S STICK: Noah Brooks, *Washington in Lincoln's Time* (New York: The Century Co., 1894), pp. 37-38.

NEWS OF BURNSIDE: Address of Hon. Theodore Burton, *op. cit.,* p. 307.

LINCOLN AND THE "COLD WATER" MEN AND WOMEN: John Hay, in Tyler Dennett, *op. cit.,* p. 96.

SISTER EMILIE VISITS THE WHITE HOUSE: Mrs. Ben Hardin Helm, War Diary, as quoted in Katherine Helm (her niece), *The True Story of Mary, Wife of Lincoln: Containing the Recollections of Mary Lincoln's Sister Emilie (Mrs. Ben Hardin Helm), Extracts from Her War-Time Diary, Numerous Letters and Other Documents Now First Published* (New York: Harper & Bros., 1928), pp. 228-233.

20. THE WOMEN AT HOME

MOTTO: "The Battle Cry of Freedom": words by William H. Barnes, music by H. L. Schreiner (Macon & Savannah, Ga.: J. C. Schreiner & Son, 1864).

THE NEW ORLEANS "POCKET HAND-KERCHIEF WAR": Marion Southwood, *"Beauty and Booty": The Watchword of New Orleans* (New York: Published for the Author by M. Doolady, 1867), pp. 278-281.

THE RICHMOND BREAD RIOT: Letter from "Agnes" to Sara Agnes Pryor, in Mrs. Roger A. [Sara Agnes] Pryor, *Reminiscences of Peace and War* (New York: The Macmillan Co., 1904), pp. 237-239.

EMMA SANSOM'S RIDE WITH FORREST: From the MS of Emma Sansom [Johnson], Calloway, Tex.; as quoted in John Allan Wyeth, *Life of Nathan Bedford Forrest* (New York: Harper & Brothers, 1901), pp. 209-212.
Emma Sansom was sixteen years old at the time of her exploit, for which the Alabama Legislature signalized her in a special resolution in 1899, voting her a gift of 640 acres of land. Apart from its heroism, her ride with Forrest had the value of gaining him three hours of time, so that he could overtake and compel the surrender of Streight almost within sight of Rome.

A JAYBIRD AT VICKSBURG: A Lady [Mary Webster Loughborough], *My Cave Life in Vicksburg, with Letters of Trial and Travel* (New York: D. Appleton & Co., 1864), pp. 136-137.

21. "EVEN IF HE BE AN ENEMY"

MOTTO: An Impressed New Yorker [William G. Stevenson], *Thirteen Months in the Rebel Army: Being a Narrative of Personal Adventures in the Infantry, Ordnance, Cavalry, Courier, and Hospital Services; With an Exhibition of the Power, Purposes, Earnestness, Military Despotism, and Demoralization of the South* (New York: A. S. Barnes & Burr, 1862), p. 158.

THE GALLANT HOOD: Lt. Col. W. W. Blackford, *op. cit.,* pp. 210-211.

MRS. MCLELLAN ASKS FOR BREAD AND AN AUTOGRAPH: Letter from Mrs. Ellen McLellan to Jacob Hoke, *The Great Invasion of 1863: Or, General Lee in Pennsylvania* . . . (Dayton, Ohio: W. J. Shvey, 1887), pp. 197-198.
Mrs. Ellen McLellan was the widow of a former citizen of Chambersburg, William McLellan. On the same or following day, adds Hoke, an officer of General Lee's staff visited Judge Kimmell, bearing an order from General Lee on the guard at Stouffer's mill for a number of barrels of flour for the poor of the town. Before he could use the order General Lee had left and it was of no assistance.

GENERAL PICKETT AND THE PENN-SYLVANIA-DUTCH GIRL: LaSalle Corbell Pickett (Mrs. G. E. Pickett), *Pickett and His Men* (copr. 1899; Philadelphia: J. B. Lippincott Co., 1913), pp. 288-289.

"I AM THE MAN, SIR": Gen. John B. Gordon, *op. cit.,* pp. 150-153.

LEE AND THE WOUNDED UNION SOLDIER: As told by an old Grand Army man who has been viewing the panorama of the battle of Gettysburg, in an unidentified newspaper, and as quoted in A. L. Long, formerly Military Secretary to Gen. Lee, afterward Brig. Gen. and Chief of Artillery, 2d Corps, A.N.V., and Marcus J. Wright,

formerly Brig. Gen. Army of the Tennessee and Agent of the U.S. for the Collection of Confederate Records, *Memoirs of Robert E. Lee: His Military and Personal History, Embracing a Large Amount of Information Hitherto Unpublished, Together with Incidents Relating to His Private Life Subsequent to the War* (New York: J. M. Stoddart, 1887), p. 302.

GENERAL GRANT FIXES THINGS FOR THE DOCKERYS: The *Vicksburg Commercial,* n.d.; as quoted in *The Magazine of American History; With Notes and Queries* (New York: Historical Publications Co.) XIV (September, 1885), 313-314.

THEY *Would* MIX ON THE PICKET-LINE: Gen. John B. Gordon, *Southern Historical Society Papers,* X (August and September [combined], 1882), Nos. 8-9, 422-423.

REUNION: Rossiter Johnson, *Campfire and Battlefield: An Illustrated History of the Campaigns and Conflicts of the Great Civil War* (New York: Bryan, Taylor & Co., 1894), p. 468.

22. 'SCAPES AND SCRAPES

MOTTO: "John Morgan," in Jean Thomas, *Ballad Makin' in the Kentucky Mountains* (New York: Henry Holt & Co., 1939), p. 66.

A GOOD DAY'S WORK AND A FINE TURKEY DINNER: John McCorkle, *Three Years with Quantrell: A True Story,* told by his scout, John McCorkle, and written by O. S. Barton (Armstrong, Mo.: Armstrong Herald Print, n.d.), pp. 56-62.

ABSALOM GRIMES, CONFEDERATE MAIL RUNNER: Capt. Absalom Grimes, *Absalom Grimes, Confederate Mail Runner,* edited from Captain Grimes's own Story by M. M. Quaife, of the Burton Historical Collection (New Haven: Yale University Press, 1926), pp. 122-128.
In "The Private History of a Campaign That Failed" (*The Century*

Magazine, XXXI, December, 1885, p. 203), Mark Twain recalls meeting "Ab Grimes, an Upper Mississippi pilot, who afterwards became famous as a dare-devil rebel spy, whose career bristled with desperate adventures." Grimes's opening chapter tells of "Campaigning with Mark Twain."

PAULINE CUSHMAN BORROWS A YOUNG MAN'S SUIT: Dr. L. P. Brockett, *op. cit.,* pp. 114-118.

HOW FRANK STRINGFELLOW OVERHEARD HIS DEATH WARRANT: John Esten Cooke, formerly of General Stuart's Staff, *Wearing of the Gray: Being Personal Portraits, Scenes and Adventures of the War* (New York: E. B. Treat & Co., 1867), pp. 501-508.

RAIDER MORGAN: I. How Morgan Got Three Hundred Horses. E. S. S. Rouse, *The Bugle Blast: Or, Spirit of the Conflict* (Philadelphia: James Challen & Son, 1864), pp. 299-301. II. The Escape of Morgan. As quoted in Frank Moore, ed. *Anecdotes, Poetry and Incidents of the War: North and South, 1860-1865,* pp. 314-317.

THE TAILOR'S JOKE: John Algernon Owens, *Sword and Pen: Or, Ventures and Adventures of Willard Glazier (the Soldier-Author) in War and Literature; Comprising Incidents and Reminiscences of His Childhood; His Chequered Life as a Student and Teacher, and His Remarkable Career as a Soldier and Author; Embracing Also the Story of His Unprecedented Journey from Ocean to Ocean on Horseback* (Philadelphia: P. W. Ziegler & Co., 1882), pp. 171-173.

QUANTRELL GETS EVEN: Capt. Kit Dalton, a Confederate soldier, a guerrilla captain under the fearless leader Quantrell, and a border outlaw for seventeen years following the surrender of the Confederacy, associated with the most noted band of freebooters the world has ever known, *Under the Black Flag* (Memphis, Tenn.: Lockard Publishing Co., 1914), pp. 107-109.

A GHOST OF A CHANCE: As told by one of B. C. Washington's comrades, J.S.B., *The Southern Bivouac,* II (April, 1884), 356-360.

23. RUSES AND STRATAGEMS

MOTTO: A. Van Dyke, 1st Mich. Inf., "The Merrimac and Monitor" (tune, "The Taxation of North America") (Baltimore, Md.: James Young, n.d.).

PORTER'S "BLACK TERROR": Adm. [David D.] Porter, *Incidents and Anecdotes of the Civil War* (New York: D. Appleton & Co., 1886), pp. 133-135, 136.

ALL'S FAIR WITH FORREST: Gen. Dabney Herndon Maury, *Recollections of a Virginian in the Mexican, Indian, and Civil Wars;* as quoted in Francis Trevelyan Miller and Robert S. Lanier, ed. *The Photographic History of the Civil War* (New York: The Review of Reviews Co., 1911), IV, 280, 282.

FITZHUGH LEE AND AVERELL EXCHANGE NOTES: Willis J. Abbot, *Battle Fields and Camp Fires: A Narrative of the Principal Military Operations of the Civil War from the Removal of McClellan to the Accession of Grant (1862-1863)* (New York: Dodd, Mead & Co., 1890), pp. 165-167.

GENERAL WHEELER'S LEAP: John A. Wyeth, "General Wheeler's Leap," *Harper's Weekly,* XLII (June 18, 1898), 601-602.

24. STRANGE THINGS HAPPEN IN THE ARMY

MOTTO: Washington Davis, *op. cit.,* p. 15.

SHERIDAN AND THE TWO WOMEN SOLDIERS: Philip H. Sheridan, *Personal Memoirs of P. H. Sheridan, General United States Army* (New York: Charles L. Webster & Co., 1891), I, 253-255.

A POETIC "SPECIAL ORDER": Charles Nordhoff, "Two Weeks at Port Royal," *Harper's New Monthly Magazine*, XXVII (June, 1863), 116-117.

THE SCRIPTURAL SENTINEL: Charles H. Anson, Bvt. Maj. 1st Vt. Heavy Art., "Reminiscences of an Enlisted Man," in *War Papers, Read Before the Commandery of the State of Wisconsin, Military Order of the Loyal Legion of the United States* (Milwaukee: Burdick & Allen, 1914), IV, 288.

THE ORIGIN OF THE CARTRIDGE BOX BADGE: George H. Woodruff, *op. cit.*, pp. 393-394.

THE CLOTHES-LINE TELEGRAPH: Frank Moore, ed. *Anecdotes, Poetry and Incidents of the War: North and South, 1860-1865*, pp. 263-264.

THE WARNING BULLET: John William De Forest, *op. cit.*, pp. 142-143.

HOOD'S BOYS AND THE CHAMBERSBURG LADIES: Lt. Col. Arthur James Lyon Fremantle, Coldstream Guards, *Three Months in the Southern States, April–June, 1863* (Mobile, Ala.: S. H. Goetzel, 1864), p. 121.

GENERAL LEE AND THE FLAPJACKS: *New Orleans Times-Democrat,* as quoted in *The* (N. Y.) *Sun*, February 21, 1897.

FIGHTING FOR THEIR RIGHTS: Lt. Col. John W. Thomason, Jr., *Lone Star Preacher: Being a Chronicle of the Acts of Praxiteles Swan, M. E. Church South, Sometime Captain, 5th Texas Regiment Confederate States Provisional Army* (New York: Charles Scribner's Sons, 1945), pp. x-xi.

SWAMPED: *Only a Private: A Sketch of the Services of a Private Soldier Who Took Part in the Battles of Fort Pulaski, Fort Wagner, Olustee, and Coal* [*sic*] *Harbor, by Himself* (Boston: Pratt Bros., n.d.), pp. 9-10.

UNCLE SAM: Alfred Lacey Hough, *Soldier in the West; The Civil War Letters of Alfred Lacey Hough,* ed. Robert G. Athearn (Philadelphia: University of Pennsylvania Press, 1957), p. 113.

LETTER TO THE CHAPLAIN OF POSEY'S BRIGADE: "The Haversack," *The New Eclectic Magazine* [combined with *The Land We Love*] (Baltimore: Turnbull & Murdoch), IV (May, 1869), 617-618.

"THE PARSON ISN'T HUNGRY": Sam R. Watkins, *op. cit.*, pp. 88-91.

OPERATING ON HIMSELF: Col. Thomas F. Berry, *Four Years with Morgan and Forrest* (Oklahoma City: The Harlow-Ratliff Co., 1914), pp. 253-256.

EUGENICS IN THE CONFEDERACY: Edwin H. Fay, *"This Infernal War": The Confederate Letters of Sgt. Edwin H. Fay,* ed. Bell Irvin Wiley, with the assistance of Lucy E. Fay (Austin: University of Texas Press, 1958), p. 350.
"Another story that made the rounds of Confederate camps told of Hill's endorsing a bugler's request for a furlough with the comment: 'Disapproved—shooters before tooters.' "—B.I.W.

THE MULE HEROES: Gen. Horace Porter, "Campaigning with Grant," *The Century Magazine*, LIII (November, 1896), 23.

WHERE STATES' RIGHTS END: Thomas B. Van Horne, U.S.A., *The Life of Major General George H. Thomas* (New York: Charles Scribner's Sons, 1882), pp. 212-213.

25. BRAVE LADS

MOTTO: "The Drummer Boy," in William A. Campbell and William R. J. Dunn, *The Child's First Book* (Richmond: Ayres and Wade, 1864), p. 31.

THE DEATH OF WILKESON: Willis J. Abbot, *op. cit.*, pp. 212-216.

JOHNNY CLEM: Benj. F. Taylor, *Pictures of Life in Camp and Field* [written to the Chicago *Evening Jour-*

nal while serving as correspondent with the Army of the Cumberland] (Chicago: S. C. Griggs & Co., 1875), pp. 168-169.

WHERE HE WAS SHOT: Col. William C. Oates, *The War Between the Union and the Confederacy and Its Lost Opportunities: With a History of the 15th Alabama Regiment and the Forty-eight Battles in Which It Was Engaged; Being an Account of the Author's Experiences in the Greatest Conflict of Modern Times; A Justification of Secession, and Showing that the Confederacy Should Have Succeeded; A Criticism of President Davis, the Confederate Congress, and Some of the General Officers of the Confederate and Union Armies; Praise of Line Officers and Soldiers in the Ranks for Their Heroism and Patriotism* . . . (New York: The Neale Publishing Co., 1905), pp. 285-286.

SAM DAVIS: Mrs. T. P. O'Connor, *My Beloved South* (New York: G. P. Putnam's Sons, 1913), pp. 316-322.

26. STONEWALL JACKSON PASSES OVER THE RIVER

MOTTO: *Modern Eloquence*, eds. Thomas B. Reed, Justin McCarthy,

Rossiter Johnson, Albert Ellery Bergh (Philadelphia: John D. Morris & Co., 1900), x, 101.

ILL OMEN: A. L. Long, formerly military secretary to Gen. Lee, afterward Brig. Gen. and Chief of Art., 2d Corps, A.N.V., *Memoirs of Robert E. Lee: His Military and Personal History, Embracing a Large Amount of Information Hitherto Unpublished; Together with Incidents Related to His Private Life Subsequent to the War,* collected and edited with the assistance of Marcus J. Wright, formerly Brig. Gen., Army of Tenn., and Agent of the United States for the Collection of Confederate Records (New York: J. M. Stoddart, 1887), pp. 257-258.

DEATH OF JACKSON: Rev. James Power Smith, Capt. and Asst. Adjt. Gen., C.S.A., "Stonewall Jackson's Last Battle," in *Battles and Leaders of the Civil War,* III, 209-214.

TENDER MEMORY: Maj. Henry Kyd Douglas, "Stonewall Jackson and His Men," in *The Annals of the War,* p. 653.

RESTLESS SPIRIT: Mary Boykin Chesnut, *op. cit.,* pp. 330-331.

FOUR: 1864

MOTTO: "Johnny, Come Fill Up the Bowl," as sung by Sally Neeley, *loc. cit.*

27. LINCOLN GIVES
SATISFACTION

MOTTO: "When Abe Goes in Again" (tune, "When Johnny Comes Marching Home"), *The Tremaine Brothers' Lincoln and Johnson Campaign Song-Book: Containing 40 Pages of Soul-Stirring Pieces, Written Expressly for the Campaign* (New York: The American News Co., 1865), pp. 4-5.

A FAIR REBEL'S INTERVIEW WITH LINCOLN: [Mary Neilson Jackson,]

A Fair Rebel's Interviews with Abraham Lincoln (New York: S. W. Jackson of Montclair, N.J., son of the Fair Rebel, 1917), unpaged.

A VISIT FROM UNCLE DENNIS: As told by Dennis Hanks, in Eleanor Gridley, *The Story of Abraham Lincoln: Or, The Journey from the Log Cabin to the White House* (Chicago: M. A. Donohue & Co., 1900, 1927), pp. 157-158.

"The date of Hanks's May trip to Washington [not given by Gridley] is established by Lincoln's endorsement, dated May 15, 1864, on a letter presented to him by Hanks from W. F. Shriver, which informed Lincoln that it would 'be presented to you by

Father Hanks.' Furthermore on June 8, 1864, in a letter to John J. Hall, Hanks stated, 'I have bin to see Old Abe.'" (Charles H. Coleman, *Abraham Lincoln and Coles County, Illinois,* New Brunswick, 1955, pp. 230-231.)

LIEUTENANT TAD: F. B. Carpenter, *op. cit.,* p. 300.

"WHY THE LORD PUT A CURL IN A PIG'S TAIL": Smith Stimmel, a member of the Union Light Guard, personal escort of President Lincoln, *Personal Reminiscences of Abraham Lincoln* (Minneapolis: William H. M. Adams, 1928), pp. 25-27.

LINCOLN UNDER FIRE: L. E. Chittenden, *op. cit.,* pp. 415-416.

For other versions of the Fort Stevens episode see John Henry Cramer, *Lincoln under Enemy Fire: The Complete Account of His Experiences During Early's Attack on Washington* (Baton Rouge, 1948). In *"The Cannoneer"* (Washington, D.C., 1890, pp. 271-273), Augustus Buell relates the following camp story: "It was said that Mr. Lincoln remarked to Gen. Wright that 'as Constitutional Commander-in-Chief, he thought he had a right at least to watch a battle fought by his own troops,' and that the General retorted that 'there was nothing in the Constitution authorizing the Constitutional Commander-in-Chief to expose himself to the enemy's fire where he could do no good!'"

"RE-ENLIST" LINCOLN!: Hon. Henry J. Raymond, as quoted in F. B. Carpenter, *op. cit.,* p. 231.

VOTING FOR LINCOLN IN ANDERSONVILLE: John McElroy, late of Co. L 16th Ill. Cav., *Andersonville: A Story of Rebel Military Prisons, Fifteen Months a Guest of the So-Called Southern Confederacy; A Private Soldier's Experience in Richmond, Andersonville, Savannah, Millen, Blackshear and Florence* (Washington: The National Tribune, 1913), II, 154-155.

"TOO MANY PIGS": An unidentified Chicago journal, as quoted in Paul Selby, *Lincoln's Life, Stories and Speeches* (Chicago: John R. Stanton Co., 1902), pp. 207-210.

28. GRANT FIGHTS IT OUT ON HIS LINE

MOTTO: A. Lincoln, in William O. Stoddard, *Lincoln's Third Secretary: The Memoirs of William O. Stoddard,* ed. William O. Stoddard, Jr. (New York: Exposition Press, 1955), p. 199.

HOW LINCOLN DEFENDED GRANT: Gen. Horace Porter, "Lincoln and Grant," *The Century Magazine,* VIII (October, 1885), 940.

"—IF IT TAKES ALL SUMMER": Gen. Horace Porter, *Campaigning with Grant* (New York: The Century Co., 1897), pp. 97-98.

"ULYSSES DON'T SCARE WORTH A DAMN": *Ibid.,* pp. 96-97.

GRANT LOSES HIS TEMPER: *Ibid.,* pp. 164-165.

WHY GRANT NEVER SWORE: *Ibid.,* p. 251.

WHEN GRANT WAS STUMPED: Lew Wallace, *An Autobiography* (New York: Harper & Bros., 1906), I, 335, n.

29. SHERMAN WAS "A KIND OF CARELESS MAN ABOUT FIRE"

MOTTO: W. T. Sherman to Mrs. Annie Gilman Bower, Marietta, Ga., June 30, 1864; as quoted in Lloyd Lewis, *op. cit.,* p. 421.

The description of Sherman as "a kind of careless man about fire" appears in Henry W. Grady's address "The New South," delivered at the 81st anniversary celebration of the New England Society in New York City, December 22, 1886 (*Modern Eloquence,* VIII, 584).

SHERMAN AND "MISS CECILIA": Helen Dortch Longstreet, *op. cit.,* p. 21.

SMOKE SIGNALS: Washington Davis, *op. cit.,* p. 211.

SHERMAN AND THE NORTHERN CITIZEN OF ATLANTA: Rev. G. S. Bradley, Chaplain, 22d Wisconsin, *The Star Corps: Or, Notes of an Army Chaplain, During Sherman's Famous "March to the Sea"* (Milwaukee: Jermain & Brightman, Book & Job Printers, 1865), pp. 159-160.

ADVICE TO A SOUTHERN MINISTER WHOSE HORSE HAD BEEN STOLEN: Rev. G. S. Bradley, *op. cit.,* pp. 161-162.

SHERMAN'S "DUPLICATES": *Memoirs of Gen. W. T. Sherman,* II, 150-151.

THE SLEEPING GENERAL: I. Why Sherman Slept in the Daytime. Henry Hitchcock, Maj. and Asst. Adjt. Gen. of Vols., November, 1864–May, 1865, *Marching with Sherman: Passages from the Letters and Campaign Diaries of Henry Hitchcock,* ed. M. A. DeWolfe Howe (New Haven: Yale University Press, 1927), pp. 112-113. II. How He Was Caught Napping. David P. Conyngham, *Sherman's March Through the South, With Sketches and Incidents of the Campaign* (New York: Sheldon & Co., 1865), pp. 48-49.
The sleeping general, mistaken for drunk, is a variant of the unrecognized general. (See "The Mysterious Stranger," above.)

30. MISSION ACCOMPLISHED

MOTTO: Booker T. Washington, "Heroes in Black Skins," *The Century Magazine,* LXVI (September, 1903), 725.

MOTHER BICKERDYKE'S UNAUTHORIZED EXPLOIT: Mary A. Livermore, *op. cit.,* pp. 520-524.

THE WATER-CARRIERS: Frank Wilkeson, a survivor of Grant's last campaign, *The Soldier in Battle: Or, Life in the Ranks of the Army of the Potomac* (London: Bellairs & Co., 1896), pp. 110-112.

SHARPSHOOTERS' DUEL: [John Gardner Perry,] *Letters from a Surgeon of the Civil War,* compiled by Martha Derby Perry (Boston: Little, Brown & Co., 1906), pp. 190-193.

THE HERO OF THE PETERSBURG MINE: Rossiter Johnson, *Campfire and Battlefield,* pp. 469-470.

THE "BIG FILL" AT KENESAW: John T. Wickersham, *The Gray and the Blue* (Berkeley, Calif.: Mimeographed for private distribution, 1915), pp. 140-146.

CORPORAL PECK BUILDS A CORDUROY BRIDGE: [George W. Peck,] *How Private Geo. W. Peck Put Down the Rebellion: Or, The Funny Experiences of a Raw Recruit; By the Author of "Peck's Fun," "Peck's Sunshine," "Peck's Bad Boy and His Pa," "Peck's Boss Book," and Lots of Such Stuff* (Chicago: Belford, Clarke & Co., 1887), pp. 13, 141-150.

31. RAID, RUSE, RESCUE, AND REVENGE

MOTTO: Songs of Mosby's Rangers, in Virgil Carrington Jones, *Ranger Mosby* (Chapel Hill: The University of North Carolina Press, 1944), pp. 14, 39.

THE SCOUT, THE LADY MAJOR, AND THE REBEL BENEFACTRESS: Capt. David P. Conyngham, *Sherman's March Through the South,* pp. 194-197.

RANGER MOSBY'S BERRYVILLE RAID: John W. Munson, *Reminiscences of a Mosby Guerrilla* (New York: Moffat, Yard & Co., 1906), pp. 102-109.

AVENGING MORGAN'S BETRAYAL: Capt. John Dowdy (alias John Evans), Seagoville, Tex., Confederate veteran, in Martha Norris McLeod, *Brother Warriors: The Reminiscences of Union and Confederate Veterans* (Washington, D.C.: The Darling Printing Co., 1940), pp. 86-88.

THE "SUDDEN DEATH" OF JAMES HANCOCK: M. Quad [Charles Bertrand Lewis], *Field, Fort and Fleet: Being a Series of Brilliant and Authentic Sketches of the Most Notable Battles of the Late Civil War, Including Many Incidents and Circumstances Never Before Published in Any Form, 1861-1863* (Detroit: Detroit Free Press Publishing Co., 1885), pp. 210-211.

32. OFFICERS AND MEN

MOTTO: "Get Along Home, Cindy," collected from V. C. Royster, Wake Co., N.C., in Newman Ivey White, *op. cit., Vol. III. Folk Songs from North Carolina*, eds. Belden and Hudson, p. 462.

THE RED "TAPEISM" OF FURLOUGHS: Sam R. Watkins, *op. cit.*, pp. 141-143.

As an example of truly informal furloughs, Mark Twain, in "The Private History of a Campaign That Failed" (*The Century Magazine*, XXXI, December, 1885, 201) quotes James Redpath's story of the big private who appeared at the door of a colonel's tent in East Tennessee and "without salute or other circumlocution said to the colonel: 'Say, Jim, I'm a-goin' home for a few days.' 'What for?' 'Well, I hain't b'en there for a right smart while, and I'd like to see how things is comin' on.' 'How long are you going to be gone?' ' 'Bout two weeks.' 'Well, don't be gone longer than that; and get back sooner if you can.' "

RE-ENLISTING: Charles E. Davis, Jr., *op. cit.*, pp. 302-303.

TROUBLE WITH THE COLONEL: Melvin Grigsby, late Col. 3d U. S. Vol. Cav., known as Grigsby's Cowboys (Spanish-American War), *The Smoked Yank* (2d ed.; no place, no publisher, 1888), pp. 41-44.

FORREST BREAKS IN A CONSCRIPT: Brig. Gen. James R. Chalmers, as quoted in John Allan Wyeth, *op. cit.*, pp. 301-303.

"SIT UP OR YOU'LL BE KILLED": Gen. John B. Gordon, *op. cit.*, p. 277.

THE COLONEL PUTS ON HIS WAR PAINT: Frank Wilkeson, *op. cit.*, pp. 77-78.

THE QUARTERMASTERS MAKE THEMSELVES COMFORTABLE: An ex-Chaplain, Lexington, Va., "The Haversack," *The Land We Love*, V (September, 1868), 443.

WORMY HARDTACK: H. Clay Trumbull, formerly Chaplain of the 10th Regt. of Conn. Vols., later Chaplain of the Army of the James, *War Memories of an Army Chaplain* (New York: Charles Scribner's Sons, 1898), pp. 52-53.

DEBURGH, THE OVERSEER: Jacob Stroyer, *My Life in the South* (new and enlarged ed.; Salem, Mass.: Newcomb & Gauss, Printers, 1898), pp. 86-92.

THE QUARTERMASTER CORNERS THE MULE MARKET: R. H. Eddy, "General Donaldson's Fortunate Mistake," *The Century Magazine*, XXXIV (August, 1887), 617.

A THOUSAND SHIRTS: Rev. Theodore Gerrish and Rev. John S. Hutchinson, *op. cit.*, p. 61.

33. "MARSE ROBERT" AND
HIS MEN

MOTTO: Douglas Southall Freeman, *R. E. Lee: A Biography* (New York: Charles Scribner's Sons, 1935), III, 347.

LEE AND THE COURIER: Col. Chapman, of Mosby's bat., as quoted in Alexander Hunter, *Johnny Reb and Billy Yank* (New York: The Neale Publishing Co., 1905), p. 664.

HOW TO TAME A HIGH-STRUNG HORSE: James Morris Morgan, *The Century Magazine*, LX (May, 1900), 156.

LEE'S PROPHECY: Gen. John B. Gordon, "Last Days of the Confederacy," *Modern Eloquence*, V, 484-485.

"GENERAL LEE TO THE REAR!": Gen. John B. Gordon, *Reminiscences of the Civil War*, pp. 274, 278-280.

LEE AND GRACIE: William Miller Owen, *In Camp and Battle with the Washington Artillery of New Orleans* (Boston: Ticknor & Co., 1885), p. 356.

34. ON PICKET

MOTTO: J. S. Fullerton, "The Army of the Cumberland at Chattanooga," *The Century Magazine*, XXXIV (May, 1887), 137.

A TARHEEL PICKET YARN: William Meade Dame, Pvt. 1st Co. Richmond Howitzers, *From the Rapidan to Richmond and the Spotsylvania Campaign: A Sketch in Personal Narrative of the Scenes a Soldier Saw* (Baltimore: Green-Lucas Co., 1920), pp. 59-61.

As a nickname for North Carolinians, the term "Tarheel" goes back to the early days of wooden sailing ships when naval stores were among the state's leading exports and when workers in tar kilns and turpentine distilleries went barefooted, preferring to have the tar stick to their heels instead of their shoes. See Haywood Parker, quoted in B. A. Botkin, ed. *A Treasury of Southern Folklore* (New York, 1949), pp. 40-41. During the war the term was common in soldier repartee expressive of state rivalry.

TURNING THE TABLES ON OLD JUBE: "Recollections of Jubal Early," by One Who Followed Him, *The Century Magazine*, LXX (June, 1905), 312-313.

"NOW HUNT YOUR HOLE!": Seward Fobes Gould, Bvt. Lt. Col. and last commander of the 4th N. Y. Heavy Art., "Reminiscences of the Civil War," pp. 5-6. (MS in Special Collections, University of Rochester Library, Rochester, N.Y.)

TILLOTSON COUNTS THE PICKETS: Wilbur F. Hinman, late Lt. Col., 65th Ohio Regt., *The Story of the Sherman Brigade: The Camp, the March, the Bivouac, the Battle, and How "The Boys" Lived and Died During Four Years of Active Field Service. Sixty-fourth Ohio Veteran Volunteer Infantry. Sixty-fifth Ohio Veteran Volunteer Infantry. Sixth Battery, Ohio Veteran Volunteer Artillery. McLaughlin's Squadron, Ohio Veteran Volunteer Cavalry.* (Published by the Author, 1897), pp. 590-593.

OLD ABE AND THE PETERSBURG EXPRESS: William H. Sallada, *Silver Sheaves: Gathered Through Clouds and Sunshine* (Des Moines, 1879), pp. 101-102.

AN EMETIC FOR A PICKET: William A. Stone, *The Tale of a Plain Man* (Philadelphia: The John C. Winston Co., 1918), pp. 115-124.

PAT AND JOHNNY: John L. Cunningham, Maj. 118th N. Y. Vols. Inf., Bvt. Lt. Col. U. S. Vols., *Three Years with the Adirondack Regiment, 118th New York Volunteers Infantry: From the Diaries and Other Memoranda of John L. Cunningham* (Glens Falls, N.Y.: For Private Circulation, 1920), pp. 137-138.

35. "PRISONER'S FARE"

MOTTO: "In Charleston Jail" (tune, "Weeping, Sad and Lonely"), in Captain Willard Worcester Glazier, *The Capture, the Prison Pen, and the Escape: Giving a Complete History of Prison Life in the South . . .* (New York: R. H. Ferguson & Co., copr. 1865, 1870), p. 152.

TALKATIVE TARHEEL: Gen. Horace Porter, "Campaigning with Grant," *The Century Magazine*, LIII (March, 1897), 714-715.

CHINCH HARBOR: James N. Bosang, Capt. Co. C, 4th Va. Inf., Stonewall Brig., *Memoirs of a Pulaski Veteran* (Pulaski, Va., 1912), pp. 14-17.

How Abner Small Was Taken Prisoner: Maj. Abner R. Small, *op. cit.*, pp. 154-158.

Hucksters, Smugglers, and Dead Yankees: Col. Melvin Grigsby, *op. cit.*, pp. 107-111.

36. FAIR REBELS

Motto: Mrs. D. Giraud [Louise Wigfall] Wright, *A Southern Girl in '61: The War-Time Memories of a Confederate Senator's Daughter* (New York: Doubleday, Page & Co., 1905), pp. 119-120.

"Charcoal!": Mary Boykin Chesnut, *op. cit.*, p. 383.

Aunt Abby, the Irrepressible, Rallies Lee's Men: "The Haversack," *The Land We Love*, III (August, 1867), 339-340.

"We have been frequently asked whether, 'Aunt Abby [House], the Irrepressible' was a real character, and whether there were many more 'sich' in the Old North State. The indomitable fighting qualities of our North Carolina soldiers proved that they came from the right kind of mothers—women of energy, pluck and endurance. Aunt Abby's character has not been over-drawn. She lives in her own proper person, as we trust that she will live in the history of her State." (D. H. Hill, ed. *The Land We Love, ibid.*, p. 339.)

Lee's Miserables: Gen. Horace Porter, "Campaigning with Grant,"

The Century Magazine, LIII (February, 1897), 486.

Mrs. Davis Intercedes: Mary Boykin Chesnut, *op. cit.*, pp. 412-413.

A Tryst with a Twist: Col. Seward Fobes Gould, *op. cit.*, pp. 10-11.
Bvt. Lt. Col. Gould's experience recalls the saying of the Federal soldier that if the Southern girls could love as they hate, "it would be well worth one's trying to get one of them." (Kate Mason Rowland and Mrs. Morris L. Croxall, eds. *The Journal of Julia LeGrand, New Orleans, 1862-1863*, Richmond, 1911, p. 86; as quoted in E. Merton Coulter, *The Confederate States of America, 1861-1865*, p. 421.)

The Lord Takes the Shells in His Hands: Anne A. Banister (Mrs. A. Campbell Pryor), "Incidents in the Life of a Civil War Child," pp. 1, 2-3. (MS in Southern Historical Collection, University of North Carolina Library, Chapel Hill.)

Aunt Abby Under Fire: Mrs. Mary Bayard Clarke, *The Land We Love*, III (June, 1867), 124-125.

The Old Lady from Atlanta: *The Journal of Catherine Devereux Edmondston, 1860-66*, ed. Margaret Mackay Jones (Mrs. George Lyle Jones) (Mebane, N.C.: Privately published, Mrs. Stephen H. Millender), pp. 85-86.

FIVE: 1865

Motto: "In Eighteen Hundred and Sixty-one"; in Newman Ivey White, *op cit.*, II, 529.

37. "AND I HAVE SUFFERED ALL THIS FOR MY COUNTRY"

Motto: A. A. McCormick, in *Modern Eloquence*, X, 104.

"Coming In": *The Soldiers' and Sailors' Half-Dime Tales of the Late*

Rebellion (New York: Soldiers' and Sailors' Publishing Co., 1868), I, No. 12, 241-242.

"The poor Confederate soldier, who succumbed morally to the privations and sufferings of Northern prisons and penitentiaries, and in his dire need took the oath and enlisted in the United States Army, was contemptuously called a *galvanized Yankee*— probably by an indistinct association with the worthless galvanized imitations of gold and silver, now so popular with the masses." (M. Schele De Vere, *Americanisms: The English of the New World,* New York, 1872, p. 23.)

THE SOLDIER AND THE NAVAL OFFICER: Capt. William Harwar Parker, *Recollections of a Naval Officer, 1841-1865* (New York: Charles Scribner's Sons, 1885), pp. 346-347.

A PEACE PETITION TO PRESIDENT DAVIS: (MS in Archives Division, Virginia State Library, Richmond.)

"YOU CAN KEEP YOUR STICK": Mrs. Mary S. Whilden, *Recollections of the War, 1861-1865,* Charleston, S.C., April, 1887 (Columbia, S.C.: The State Co., Printers, 1911), pp. 9-13.

A DESERTER'S FAREWELL: Letter from Joseph Honeycutt, Stanley Co., N.C., to his family, written while under sentence of death for starting home to see his wife and children. He was shot a short time after the letter was written and before it reached its destination. (Undated clipping from *Catawba Co.* [N.C.] *News* in Clipping File, North Carolina Collection, University of North Carolina Library, Chapel Hill.)

"I HAVE SEEN THE 'YANKIES' ": Copy of letter by Nellie Worth (Mrs. George French, Wilmington, N.C.) written during Sherman's raid. (MS in North Carolina Collection, University of North Carolina Library, Chapel Hill.)

"MEN ARE GOING THE WRONG WAY": Mary Boykin Chesnut, *op. cit.,* p. 512.

CONSTANCE CARY'S SKIRT: Mrs. Burton Harrison, *Recollections Grave and Gay* (New York: Charles Scribner's Sons, 1911), pp. 212-213.

THE EVACUATION OF RICHMOND: "Agnes" to Sara Agnes (Mrs. Roger A.) Pryor, Richmond, April 5, 1865, Mrs. Roger A. Pryor, *op. cit.,* pp. 354-357.

GAMBLING WITH THE CONFEDERATE TREASURY: Nelson A. Miles, *Serving the Republic: Memoirs of the Civil and Military Life of Nelson A. Miles, Lieutenant General, United States Army* (New York: Harper & Bros., 1911), pp. 87, 88-89.

THE YANKEE'S PRIZE: *Confederate Women of Arkansas in the Civil War, 1861-'65, Memorial Reminiscences* (Little Rock, Ark.: Published by the United Confederate Veterans of Arkansas, H. G. Pugh Ptg. Co., 1907), p. 162.

38. APPOMATTOX

MOTTO: Allan M. Trout, *Greetings from Old Kentucky* (Louisville, Ky.: *The Courier-Journal,* 1947), p. 70.

FLAGS OF TRUCE: I. The Towel. R. M. Sims, late Capt. C.S.A., to J. L. Smith, Charleston, S.C., May 22, 1886, *History of the Corn Exchange Regiment, 118th Pennsylvania Volunteers,* p. 590, n. II. The Shirt. Gen. John B. Gordon, C.S.A., "Last Days of the Confederacy," as quoted in Rossiter Johnson, *Campfire and Battlefield,* pp. 493-494.

TALES THAT VIRGINIA NEGROES TELL OF THE SURRENDER: Writers' Program, WPA, *The Negro in Virginia,* pp. 203-205.

THE DOUBLE JEOPARDY OF WILMER MCLEAN: E. P. Alexander, Brig. Gen., C.S.A., "Lee at Appomattox: Personal Recollections of the Breakup of the Confederacy," *The Century Magazine,* LXIII (April, 1902), 931.

HOW CAPTAIN RICKS CARRIED THE NEWS OF THE SURRENDER: Capt. A. J. Ricks, Cleveland, O., as quoted in Rev. Theodore Gerrish and Rev. John S. Hutchinson, *op. cit.,* pp. 748-752.

HOW GENERAL HENRY A. WISE SAVED HIS MARE: John Gibbon, Maj. Gen. U.S.A., "Personal Recollections of Appomattox," *The Century Magazine,* LXIII (April, 1902), 940, 943.

THE WRONG LEE: *Louisville* (Ky.) *Courier-Journal;* as quoted in *Confederate Veteran* (Nashville, Tenn.), IV (January, 1896), 23.

SINGING YANKEES: Richard Wentworth Browne, in "Memoranda on the Civil War," *The Century Magazine,* XXXV (January, 1888), 478.

AUNT ABBY'S "CRAP CRITTER": Mary Bayard Clarke, "Aunt Abby, the Irrepressible," *The Land We Love,* III (June, 1867), 125-127.

"WHO IS DOING THIS SURRENDERING, ANYHOW?": John S. Wise, *The End of an Era* (Boston: Houghton Mifflin Co., 1902), pp. 450-453.

THE UNFORGIVING: Sarah Morgan Dawson, *A Confederate Girl's Diary* (Boston and New York: Houghton Mifflin Co., 1913), pp. 438-439.

39. LAST DAYS OF LINCOLN

MOTTO: Julia Taft Bayne, *op. cit.,* p. 165.

THE CASE OF BETSY ANN: Ward Hill Lamon, *Recollections of Abraham Lincoln, 1847-1865,* ed. Dorothy Lamon (Chicago: A. C. McClurg & Co., 1895), pp. 81-85.

"MAMA SAYS YOU MUST COME INSTANTLY": Sylvanus Cadwallader, *Three Years with Grant,* as recalled by war correspondent Sylvanus Cadwallader, ed. Benjamin P. Thomas (New York: Alfred A. Knopf, 1955), pp. 281-282.

"ON THE SIDE OF MERCY": Sen. John B. Henderson, as quoted in Ida M. Tarbell, *The Life of Abraham Lincoln: Drawn from Original Sources and Containing Many Speeches, Letters and Telegrams Hitherto Unpublished, and Illustrated with Many Reproductions from Original Paintings, Photographs, et cetera* (New York: McClure, Phillips & Co., 1902), II, 223-225.

SHOULD JEFF DAVIS BE ALLOWED TO ESCAPE?: W. T. Sherman, *op. cit.,* II, 326-327.

According to Charles A. Dana, Lincoln told a similar story when asked by a member of the Cabinet if it would be proper to permit Jacob M. Thompson, Confederate agent in Canada, to slip through Maine in disguise and embark from Portland. For this and other stories told by Lincoln regarding the problem of what to do about Davis, see Emanuel Hertz, *Lincoln Talks: A Biography in Anecdote* (New York, 1939), pp. 368-371.

LINCOLN VISITS GENERAL PICKETT'S WIFE: LaSalle Corbell Pickett "My Soldier," *McClure's Magazine,* XXX (March, 1908), 567-568.
When the Picketts' first baby was born, May 17, 1864, another friend of George Pickett since the Mexican War, General Grant, matched the celebration bonfires along the former's line with his own. A few days later he sent through the lines a gift of a baby's silver service, engraved with the names of U. S. Grant, Rufus Inglas, and George Suckley. (LaSalle Corbell Pickett, *ibid.,* p. 568.) This is another example of fraternization among the brass, already seen in "classmates divided."

STRONG MAN: Correspondence of the New York *Independent;* as quoted in F. B. Carpenter, *op. cit.,* pp. 287-289.
As shown by this and similar stories of Lincoln's chopping prowess, the pioneer symbol of the ax and the myth of the axman and strong man clung to Lincoln to the end, indicating that under the father image the backwoods hero image persisted.

LINCOLN CAPTURES "DIXIE": Myrta Lockett Avary, *Dixie After the War* (Boston: Houghton Mifflin Co., 1937), p. 43.

40. DEATH OF LINCOLN

MOTTO: Ward Hill Lamon, *op. cit.,* pp. 111-112.

THE SHADOW OF COMING EVENTS: Mary B. Clay [daughter of Cassius M. Clay, minister to Russia and major general of volunteers under Lincoln], in the *Lexington* (Ky.) *Herald;* as quoted in Katherine Helm, *op. cit.,* pp. 241-243.

John Hay noted in his diary that the Lincolns attended a performance of Wilkes Booth in *The Marble Heart* on November 9, 1863 (Tyler Dennett, *op. cit.,* p. 118).

THE PROPHETIC DREAMS: Ward Hill Lamon, *op. cit.,* pp. 113, 115-116, 117-119.

THE LAST LAUGH: Ward Hill Lamon, *Recollections of Abraham Lincoln, 1847-1865,* ed. Dorothy Lamon Teillard (Washington, D.C.: Published by the Editor, 1911), pp. 282-283.

WALT WHITMAN ON THE DEATH OF LINCOLN: Walt Whitman, "Death of Abraham Lincoln: Lecture Deliver'd in New York, April 4, 1879—in Philadelphia, '80—in Boston, '81," *Specimen Days & Collect., op. cit.,* pp. 310-313.

"Of the actual murder of President Lincoln, though so much has been written, probably the facts are yet very indefinite in most persons' minds. I read from my memoranda written at the time, and revised frequently and finally since."—W. W., *ibid.,* p. 310.

ELIZABETH KECKLEY SHARES MRS. LINCOLN'S GRIEF: Elizabeth Keckley, formerly a slave, but more recently modiste, and friend to Mrs. Abraham Lincoln, *Behind the Scenes: Or, Thirty Years a Slave, and Four Years in the White House* (New York: G. W. Carleton & Co., 1868), pp. 187-193.

The seamstress, Elizabeth Keckley, and her relations with Mrs. Lincoln and James Redpath, who "ghosted" her book, are discussed at length by John E. Washington in *They Knew Lincoln* (cited above), pp. 205-241. In spite of his promise to print nothing injurious to Mrs. Lincoln, Redpath included some of the latter's intimate letters in an appendix, resulting in the book's suppression by the publisher at the insistence of Robert Lincoln. For James Redpath and other Civil War publishers see Madeleine B. Stern, *Imprints on History* (Bloomington, Ind., 1956). D. Ottolengul satirized *Behind the Scenes* in a parody entitled *Behind the Seams* (New York, 1868).

"HALF NEWS" OF LINCOLN'S DEATH: George Haven Putnam, *Abraham Lincoln the Great Captain: Personal Reminiscences by a Veteran of the Civil War: A Lecture Delivered at Oxford, May the 7th, 1928* (Oxford: The Clarendon Press, 1928), pp. 28-30.

CHITTENDEN AND THE ANGRY MOB: L. E. Chittenden, *Personal Reminiscences, 1840-1890, Including Some Not Hitherto Published of Lincoln and the War* (New York: Richmond, Croscup & Co., 1893), pp. 241-243.

THE CAPTURE OF JOHN WILKES BOOTH: Edward P. Doherty, "Pursuit and Death of John Wilkes Booth," *The Century Magazine,* XXXIX (January, 1890), 446-449.

41. THE FLIGHT OF JEFFERSON DAVIS

MOTTO: *The Saint Paul Press,* April 16, 1865; as quoted in *Lincoln Lore* (Fort Wayne, Ind.: The Lincoln National Life Foundation), No. 1424 (October, 1956), p. 3.

AUNT ABBY SAYS GOOD-BY TO MR. DAVIS: Mary Bayard Clarke, "Aunt Abby, the Irrepressible," *The Land We Love,* III (June, 1867), 125.

A RAGLAN AND A SHAWL: I. Mr. Davis' Account of His Capture. John G. Nicolay and John Hay, *Abraham Lincoln: A History* (New York: The Century Co., 1890), X, 271, n. II. James H. Jones's Narrative. As told by Davis' body-servant, James J. Jones, Raleigh, N.C., to a correspondent of the *Richmond Dispatch.* (Undated clipping in Walter H. Lee Scrapbook, Vol. III, Southern Historical Collection, University of North Carolina Library, Chapel Hill.)

THE SHACKLING OF JEFFERSON DAVIS: Bvt. Lt. Col. John J. Craven, late surgeon U. S. Vols., and physician of the prisoner during his confinement in Fortress Monroe, from May 25, 1865, up to December 25, 1865, *Prison Life of Jefferson Davis: Embracing Details and Incidents in His Captivity, Particulars Concerning His Health and Habits, Together with Many Conversations on Topics of Great Public Interest* (New York: Geo. W. Carleton, 1867), pp. 33-40.

42. "I WON'T BE RECONSTRUCTED"

MOTTO: Maj. Innes Randolph, "Lay of the Last Rebel" (Broadside collection of the Boston Athenaeum).

JOHN S. WISE'S WILL: John S. Wise, *The End of an Era, op. cit.,* pp. 461-462.

HELL AT CHICKAMAUGA: Herbert W. Beecher, *History of the First Light Battery Connecticut Volunteers, 1861-1865: Personal Records and Reminiscences; The Story of the Battery from Its Organization to the Present Time, Compiled from Official Records, Personal Interviews, Private Diaries, War Histories and Individual Experiences* (New York: A. T. De La Mare Ptg. & Pub. Co., Ltd., n.d.), II, 552.

"WHATEVER GENERAL LEE SAYS": Myrta Lockett Avary, *op. cit.,* pp. 70-71.

THE "BUTTON TROUBLE": *Ibid.,* pp. 123-124.

LOVERS AND WAR LORDS: THE "MARRIAGE OATH": Mrs. Morton Wortham Sloan to Lizzie Cary Daniel, Baltimore, March 21, 1893, in Lizzie Cary Daniel, *Confederate Scrap-Book: Copied from a Scrap-book Kept by a Young Girl During and Immediately After the War; With Additions from War Copies of the "Southern Literary Messenger" and "Illus-* *trated News" Loaned by Friends, and Other Selections as Accredited.* Published for the benefit of the Memorial Bazaar, held in Richmond, April 11, 1893. (Richmond, Va.: J. L. Hill Printing Co., 1893), pp. 187-190.

43. RETURN OF THE SOLDIER

MOTTO: Leander Stillwell, late of Co. D, 61st Ill. Inf., *The Story of a Common Soldier of Army Life in the Civil War, 1861-1865* ([Erie, Kan.:] Franklin Hudson Publishing Co., 1920), p. 278.

GOING HOME TO STAY: Gen. John B. Gordon, *op. cit.,* 452-453.

JOHNNY WICKERSHAM COMES MARCHING HOME: John T. Wickersham, *op. cit.,* pp. 179-186.

VETERAN'S FIRST LIE: Charles W. Bardeen, formerly of Co. D, 1st Mass. Vol. Inf., *A Little Fifer's War Diary* (Syracuse, N.Y.: C. W. Bardeen, Publisher, 1910), pp. 313-314.

WHEN THE PRIVATES RANKED THE GENERALS: Gen. John B. Gordon, *op. cit.,* p. 453.

WORKING HIS PASSAGE: Ambrose Bierce, "Bits of Autobiography," *op. cit.,* I, 328-329, 344-348.

SALVAGE: Ida M. Tarbell, "Disbanding of the Confederate Army," *McClure's Magazine,* XVI (April, 1901), 534-536.

"Perhaps nothing could illustrate better the straits to which the planters were put than the following actual experience related to the writer [by Lawrence Taliaferro]."—I.M.T.

"DEAR UNKNOWN": Letters from Emma De Witt, of Ohio, to "Unknown," preserved in the family of Abel Findley, Olivet, Pa., and now in possession of Harry Henderson, Croton-on-Hudson, N.Y.

"No more letters have been found and apparently none were written. Abel Findley, who had been hospitalized following the Battle of the Wilderness, married Mary Elizabeth McLaughlin shortly after receiving this last letter but preserved these romantic letters from Emma De Witt. His daughters found them after his death.

"It was the practice of soldiers in the Union Army while in camp to write romantic notes to 'dream girls,' telling how lonely and hard their lives were and of their great plans for the future, intimating that they were looking for wives, begging the recipients to write, and giving their names and addresses. The note would be carried by the soldier until, from a passing troop train, he saw a pretty girl on a farm or at a village grade cross-ing, when he would hurl the note conspicuously from the train. Apparently sometime two soldiers would throw out their notes together in a contest to see whose letter would be responded to. Judging from their correspondence with 'Unknown,' the farm girls responded quite eagerly, and carried on flirtations by mail with several soldiers at once, for life on the farms was always isolated and lonely, and with all the able-bodied young men in the Army their opportunities to meet them and to marry were severely curtailed."—Harry Henderson.

SIX: AFTERMATH

MOTTO: Douglas Southall Freeman, *The South to Posterity: An Introduction to the Writing of Confederate History* (New York: Charles Scribner's Sons, 1939), pp. ix-x.

44. A GOOD WAR DIES HARD

MOTTO: Carlton McCarthy, *op. cit.*, p. 193.

LETTER FROM A FREEDMAN TO HIS OLD MASTER (WRITTEN JUST AS HE DICTATED IT): Jourdon Anderson, in *The Freedmen's Book,* ed. L. Maria Child (Boston: Ticknor & Fields, 1865), pp. 265-267.

"WHIP THEM WITH POP-GUNS": *The Bivouac: An Independent Military Monthly* (Boston: Edward F. Rollins), I (September, 1883), 287.

HE MIGHT HAVE SLEPT WITH GOD: As told by Rosanna A. Blake, Colesville, Md., to B. A. Botkin. Recorded October 23, 1958.

THE VANQUISHED SALUTING THE VICTOR: Douglas Southall Freeman, "An Address," given before the Civil War Round Tables in Richmond, May 7, 1953, from a tape recording, *Civil War History* (Iowa City, State University of Iowa), I (March, 1955), 14.

SLEEPING WITH JACKSON: Maj. Henry Kyd Douglas, *op. cit.,* p. 238.

THE WIDOW FROM MAINE: Kate Mason Rowland, *Confederate Relief Bazaar Journal* (Baltimore, Md.: Published Daily During the Continuance of the Bazaar, Press of Guggenheimer, Weil & Co.,), I (April 12, 1898), No. 2, 7.

THEY MET AT THE PANORAMA OF THE BATTLE OF SHILOH: *Chicago News;* as quoted in the *Philadelphia Weekly Times,* September 12, 1885.

POINT OF VIEW: Annie C. Massey to Henry Lee Kinnison, III, Fort Riley, Kan., May 16, 1935, "Some Incidents Which Occurred in South-East Missouri in Connection with the War Between the States" (Kinnison Papers, Civil War Articles, in Southern Historical Collection, University of North Carolina Library, Chapel Hill), p. 11.

"IT WAS BEST": Hodding Carter, *Southern Legacy* (Baton Rouge: Louisiana State University Press, 1950), p. 26.

"THAT WASN'T THE WAY IT HAPPENED"; Alben W. Barkley, *That Reminds Me*—(Garden City, N.Y.: Doubleday & Co., Inc., 1954), p. 35.

Acknowledgments

THIS BOOK GREW out of a Lincoln folklore book suggested by Ralph G. Newman, of the Abraham Lincoln Bookshop, Chicago. In connection with my Lincoln research in 1957-58, I want to thank him and the following (in the order of our meeting): Dr. Reinhard H. Luthin, New York City; Dr. R. Gerald Mc-Murtry, Director, and Dr. Louis A. Warren, founder and former Director, Lincoln National Life Foundation, Fort Wayne, Ind.; Dr. R. M. Potterf, Librarian, and Albert F. Diserens, Chief Reference Librarian, Fort Wayne and Allen County Public Library; Dr. Clyde C. Walton, State Historian, Margaret A. Flint, Reference Librarian, and S. A. Wetherbee, in charge of the Horner Lincoln Collection, Illinois State Historical Library, Springfield; King V. Hostick, Springfield; Philip Mohr Benjamin, Librarian, and Dr. Stanley S. Swartley, Curator, Ida M. Tarbell Lincoln Collection, Reis Library, Allegheny College, Meadville, Pa. I am also grateful to these Lincoln and Civil War experts at the Library of Congress: Dr. Roy P. Basler, David C. Mearns, Dr. C. Percy Powell, and Col. Willard Webb.

In planning my Southern field trip in the fall of 1958 the Library of Congress group and "Pete" Long were especially helpful. So were other Washington people, including Lee A. Wallace, of the National Park Service, and Rosanna A. Blake (Mrs. Fred Hulse), of Owings, Md. For putting me in touch with Miss Blake, I am grateful to Helen Lichtenberg.

In Richmond I want to thank the following for their hospitality and help: India W. Thomas, House Regent, and Eleanor S. Brockenbrough, Assistant House Regent, the Confederate Museum; John Melville Jennings, Director, Virginia Historical Society; Ray O. Hummel, Jr., Assistant Librarian, William J. Van Schreeven, Archivist, and John W. Dudley, Assistant Archivist, Virginia State Library; also Clifford Dowdey, Hubel Robins, and "visiting fireman" Bell Irvin Wiley.

In Petersburg I am indebted to Tom Harrison, Historian, Petersburg National Military Park; Mrs. Jane Bernard Nichols, daughter of George S. Bernard, author of *War Talks of Confederate Veterans* (1892), and the staff of the Centre Hill Museum; and in Fredericksburg, to the following Historians of the Fredericksburg and Spotsylvania National Military Park: Albert Dillahunty, Ralph Happel, and R. L. Hilldrup.

At the University of North Carolina Library, Chapel Hill, I should like to express my thanks to Dr. James W. Patton, Director, and Dr. Carolyn A. Wallace, Senior Curator of Manuscripts, Southern Historical Collection; Lawrence F. London, Curator of Rare Books; and William S. Powell, Librarian, the North Carolina Collection. For Civil War songs, stories, and bibliographical suggestions, I want to thank the following at and around the University of North Carolina: Porter Cowles, Paul and Elizabeth Lay Green, Mr. and Mrs. Isaac Greer, Dr. and Mrs. Arthur Palmer Hudson, Dr. Guy B. Johnson, George Scheer, Dr. and Mrs. Rupert B. Vance, Mr. and Mrs. Manly Wade Wellman, and graduate assistants Robert Rennick and Herbert Shellans.

Also in North Carolina thanks are due to Dr. Mattie Russell, Curator of Manuscripts, Duke University Library, Durham, and D. L. Corbitt and A. G.

Jones of the North Carolina State Department of Archives and History, Raleigh.

At the Library of Congress I want to thank, in addition to those already mentioned, Mrs. Rae Korson and Don Leavitt of the Archive of American Folk Song; Richard S. Hill and William Lichtenwanger of the Music Division; Milton Kaplan of the Prints and Photographs Division; and Frederick R. Goff and staff of the Rare Book Division.

In Washington I also received help from William Campbell, Curator of Painting, and Dr. Erwin O. Christensen, Curator of the Index of American Design, National Gallery of Art; Elizabeth O. Cullen, Bureau of Railway Economics Library; Sheila M. Parker, Art Collection, National Library of Medicine; Mrs. Dorothy Porter, Librarian, Moorland Room, Founders' Library, Howard University; and the Still Picture Collection and Leonard Rapport of the National Archives.

At home I have benefited from the collections of Columbia University Library, the Library of the General Society of Mechanics and Tradesmen of the City of New York, the New-York Historical Society Library (with the help of Geraldine Beard, Arthur B. Carlson, and Sylvester L. Vigilante), and the New York Public Library (with the help of Gerald D. McDonald and staff of the American and Local History Rooms, and Charles E. Dornbusch). To Mr. Dornbusch (now engaged in the monumental task of revising and bringing up to date the *Bibliography of State Participation in the Civil War*) I am particularly indebted for bibliographical and biographical data in military history. As a place to work while gathering and organizing my material I found the Frederick Lewis Allen Memorial Room at the New York Public Library of great aid and comfort.

In Westchester County I have made many demands on the Croton Free Library, the Field Library of Peekskill (whose Director, Nicholas N. Smith, was particularly helpful in digging out scarce material and otherwise supplementing the Library's fine Lincoln collection), the Ossining Public Library, the Westchester Historical Society, and the White Plains Public Library. At the United States Military Academy at West Point, I want to acknowledge with thanks the help of the Library (especially Egon Weiss, Assistant Librarian, and Thelma Bedell, Reference Librarian) and the Museum (especially Richard E. Kuehne). Thanks are also due to Margaret Butterfield, Assistant Librarian in charge of the Special Collections, Rush Rhees Library, University of Rochester.

In the Boston area I want to thank the staffs of the Boston Athenaeum, the Boston Public Library (Manuscript Division), the Massachusetts Historical Society, and the Widener Library at Harvard.

During the three years I worked on this book many more persons than can be named here contributed suggestions, ideas, and materials—many more than could possibly be used in a single volume. Among those who contributed or loaned material I want to thank first and foremost the aforementioned Rosanna A. Blake for her hospitality and generosity in making available to me her outstanding collection of 4,500 Confederate items. Mamie Meredith, of Lincoln, Nebraska, and Paul Flowers, of the Memphis *Commercial Appeal,* were, as always, invaluable in supplying me with leads and material. For other loans and contributions I want to thank Russell Ames, Mrs. Maude Mason Botkin, Prof. Sterling Brown, Mrs. Edith Fowke, Robert W. Fowler, Helen A. Fraser, Harry Henderson, Mrs. Lucy Rosser Herberick, R. A. Kishpaugh, W. F. Leonard, Francis A. Lord, Milton Meltzer, Dr. Chapman J. Milling, Ruth Ann Musick, Horace Reynolds, Hans Schoenfeld, and Dorothy Sterling.

For her collaboration in assembling and preparing the manuscript and her counsel in solving its many problems I am, as ever, grateful to my wife, Gertrude F. Botkin.

609

ACKNOWLEDGMENTS

Finally, I want to thank my publishers, my editors, Hiram Haydn and Robert Loomis, Bertha Krantz and the staff of the copy-editing and production departments of Random House for their assistance in shaping the book; also Warren Chappell, for his sensitive design and decorations.

B.A.B.

Index

CAPS AND SMALL CAPS indicate names of authors, editors, informants, and other sources quoted. The page number following the name indicates the page on which the story begins. Song titles are in italics; first lines of songs or stanzas, in quotes. U stands for Union, C for Confederate.

611

*

About the Author

*

B. A. BOTKIN became interested in folklore in 1921, when, fresh from Harvard and Columbia, he went out to Oklahoma to teach English to the sons and daughters of oil millionaires and dirt farmers. Out of his interest in people and places came four volumes of *Folk-Say: A Regional Miscellany* (1929-1932). In explaining the word *folk-say,* which he coined, he has written: "It sums up the two phases of my interest in folklore—collecting and compiling what people have to say about themselves, especially in their own words; and interpreting America through its basic oral culture, popular fantasy, symbols and myths."

In 1937 Mr. Botkin went to Washington on a Julius Rosenwald Fellowship for the study of Southern regional and folk literature. Subsequently he became National Folklore Editor of the Federal Writers' Project, Library of Congress Fellow in Folklore, and Chief of the Archive of American Folk Song. He is a former president of the American Folklore Society, honorary vice-president of the New York Folklore Society, and a former Guggenheim Fellow. Since 1944, when *A Treasury of American Folklore* appeared, he has edited or coedited a dozen folklore collections. In two of them, *Lay My Burden Down* and *A Treasury of Southern Folklore,* he has dealt with Civil War lore.

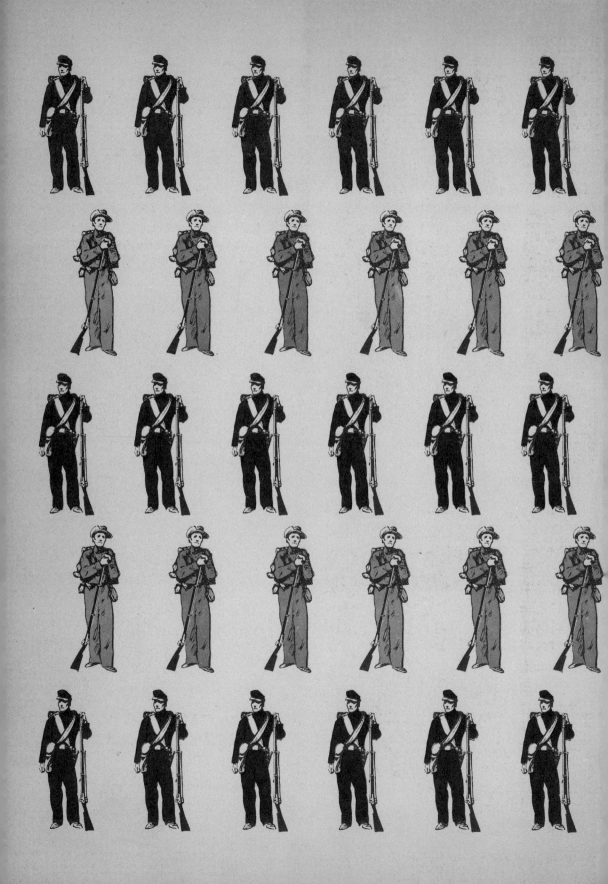